# Computers!

**5**TH EDITION

# Computers!

▲

## Timothy N. Trainor
## Diane Krasnewich

▼

*The McGraw-Hill Companies, Inc.*

New York  St. Louis  San Francisco  Auckland  Bogotá
Caracas  Lisbon  London  Madrid  Mexico City  Milan
Montreal  New Delhi  San Juan  Singapore  Tokyo  Toronto

# McGraw-Hill

*A Division of The **McGraw·Hill** Companies*

## Computers! Fifth Edition

*Sponsoring editor:* Frank Ruggirello
*Associate editor:* Rhonda Sands
*Editorial assistant:* Kyle Thomes
*Production supervisor:* Natalie Durbin
*Project manager:* Gary Palmatier
*Photo Researcher:* Laurel Anderson, Photosynthesis
*Copyeditor:* Elizabeth von Radics
*Illustrator:* Robaire Ream
*Interior designer:* Gary Palmatier
*Cover designer:* Gary Palmatier
*Cover photographers:* Chigmaross/Davison (Superstock)
*Compositor:* Ideas to Images
*Printer and binder:* Von Hoffman Press, Inc.

3 4 5 6 7 8 9 0   VNH   VNH   9 0 9 8 7

ISBN 0-07-065297-X

Library of Congress Card Catalog No. 95-79166

International Edition

Copyright © 1996

When ordering this title, use ISBN 0-07-114778-0

*We dedicate this book to*
*Denisa, Natalie Sue, Skylar, Delanie, and Gabriel*

*"In the hope that they make this world*
*a better place in which to live"*

# Photo Credits

**Chapter 1**

4 (left) Courtesy Autodesk
4 (right) William S. Helsel / Tony Stone Worldwide
5 Sepp Seitz / Woodfin Camp & Associates
6 Courtesy Ameritech
7 (top) Bettmann
7 (bottom) Corp Data
10 Bonnie Kamin
13 Alexander Teshin Associates
15 Courtesy Apple Computer, Inc.
17 Courtesy Apple Computer, Inc.
18 Lou Jones
19 Stephen Frisch
20 Bob Mason / Courtesy Ameritech
21 (top) Fredrik D. Bodin / Offhshoot Stock
21 (bottom) Courtesy Hewlett-Packard

**Chapter 2**

29 Fredrik D. Bodin / Offhshoot Stock
30 Wayne Aldridge / International Stock Photo
31 Courtesy Hewlett-Packard
35 J. Leland / Offhshoot Stock
37 Courtesy Tim Trainor
38 Courtesy GTE
39 Courtesy Hewlett-Packard
41 Courtesy Texas Instruments
43 Bonnie Kamin
46 Stephen Frisch
48 Stephen Frisch
49 (top) Stephen Frisch
49 (bottom) Bonnie Kamin

**Chapter 3**

56 Courtesy Hewlett-Packard
63 Lou Jones
69 Courtesy Microsoft
73 Sepp Seitz / Woodfin Camp & Associates

**Chapter 4**

90 Courtesy IBM
92 Charlyn Zlotnik / Woodfin Camp & Associates
94 Courtesy NEC Tech
95 Fredrik D. Bodin / Offshoot Stock
100 Courtesy Tandem Corporation
108 Courtesy AT&T

**Chapter 5**

124 Courtesy Sperry Corp.
125 (left) Dan McCoy / Rainbow
125 (top right) Courtesy Novasensor
125 (bottom right) Reg Watson / Tony Stone Worldwide
129 Courtesy AT&T
134 Greg Pease / Tony Stone Worldwide
135 Fredrik D. Bodin / Offshoot Stock
138 Courtesy Intel
139 (middle) Courtesy Intel
139 (portraits) Courtesy Texas Instruments
142 (a) Courtesy Cray Research
142 (b) Jim Brown / Offshoot Stock
142 (c) Frank Maresca / International Stock Photo
143 (d) Courtesy Hewlett-Packard
143 (e) Courtesy Unisys
143 (f) Courtesy Deskpro
143 (g) Frank Moscati
144 Bonnie Kamin

147 Stewart Cohen / Tony Stone Worldwide
148 (left) Chuck O'Rear / Woodfin Camp & Associates
148 (right) Russell Schleipman / Offshoot Stock
149 (top) Chuck O'Rear / Woodfin Camp & Associates
149 (middle) Charles D. Winters / Photo Researchers
149 (bottom) Lou Jones
150 (left) Courtesy AT&T
150 (right) Corp Data
150 (bottom) Lou Jones
151 (top) Andy Sacks / Tony Stone Worldwide
151 (bottom) Sylvain Coffie / Tony Stone Worldwide

**Chapter 6**

158 Corp Data
159 Courtesy Apple Computer, Inc.
160 Courtesy Logitech
161 Courtesy Levi Strauss
163 Courtesy Tim Trainor
164 (top) Courtesy Tim Trainor
164 (bottom) Courtesy Apple Computer, Inc.
165 Courtesy IBM
166 Zigy Kaluzny / Tony Stone Worldwide
167 (left) Bettmann
167 (right) North Wind Picture Archives
168 (top) Courtesy Tim Trainor
168 (left) Courtesy Signa
168 (right) Hank Morgan / Rainbow
170 Courtesy Epson
172 Courtesy IBM
173 Courtesy Hewlett-Packard
174 Bonnie Kamin
175 John Bagley
177 Courtesy Digital Equipment Corporation
178 Bill Strode / Woodfin Camp & Associates
179 Andy Sacks / Tony Stone Worldwide
181 Courtesy Microsoft
182 (top) Jim Brown / Offshoot Stock
182 (bottom) James Wilson / Woodfin Camp & Associates
183 (top) Courtesy Apple Computer, Inc.
183 (middle) Lou Jones
183 (bottom) Courtesy NASA

**Chapter 7**

191 Courtesy Seagate Technology
192 Bonnie Kamin
196 Courtesy Seagate Technology
197 Courtesy Quantum
198 Frank Muller / Woodfin Camp & Associates
199 Bonnie Kamin
201 Fredrik D. Bodin / Offshoot Stock
202 Courtesy IBM
203 Courtesy IBM
205 Bettmann
208 (top left) Fredrik D. Bodin / Offshoot Stock
208 (top right) John Coletti / Tony Stone Worldwide
208 (bottom left) Richard Pasley
208 (bottom right) Howard Sochurek / Woodfin Camp & Associates
209 Courtesy IBM
212 Courtesy Tim Trainor

213 Courtesy Tim Trainor
214 Courtesy Tim Trainor

**Chapter 8**

222 Russell Schleipman / Offshoot Stock
235 Courtesy Novell
237 Sepp Seitz / Woodfin Camp & Associates
243 (top) Courtesy Image Club Graphics
243 (bottom) John Curtis / Offshoot Stock
246 Courtesy Knight-Ridder Newspapers, Inc.
247 Robert E. Daemmrich / Tony Stone Worldwide
250 (top) Fredrik D. Bodin / Offshoot Stock
250 (bottom) Bonnie Kamin
251 (top) Craig Blouin / Offshoot Stock
251 (bottom) Tim Brown / Tony Stone Worldwide

**Chapter 9**

258 Courtesy Tim Roske / Nynex
265 (top) Courtesy Daniel Bricklin / The Software Garden
265 (bottom) Courtesy Robert Frankston
280 Howard Grey / Tony Stone Worldwide

**Chapter 10**

295 Courtesy Douglas Englebart
300 Courtesy Paragon[3]
302 Hollywood Pictures / Shooting Star
304 Fredrik D. Bodin / Offshoot Stock
305 Courtesy Microsoft
306 Courtesy Lawrence Livermore National Laboratory
307 Courtesy Apollo
308 (top) Courtesy University of Colorado Health Sciences Center
308 (bottom) Sarah Smith / Sports Science
310 (top) Golden Light Imagery
310 (left) Courtesy Tim Trainor
310 (right) Courtesy Mr. Screens
311 (top) Dave Wilhelm / The Stock Market
311 (middle) Courtesy Digital Image, Inc.
311 (bottom) Courtesy Mr. Screens
312 Courtesy NASA

**Chapter 11**

318 Bonnie Kamin
329 Alan Levenson
340 Frank Moscati
341 Elena Dorfman / Offshoot Stock
342 Courtesy Hewlett-Packard
343 (left) Courtesy Apple Computer
343 (right) Tom Tracy / The Stock Market
344 Bonnie Kamin
345 Fredrik D. Bodin / Offshoot Stock

**Chapter 12**

354 Richard Howard / Offshoot Stock
356 Russell Schleipman / Offshoot Stock
357 (top) Courtesy Hewlett-Packard
357 (bottom) Russell Schleipman / Offshoot Stock
362 Courtesy Lotus
366 Courtesy GM
367 Courtesy IBM
375 Jose Paelez / The Stock Market
376 (left) Courtesy Sharp
376 (right) Corp Data

**Chapter 13**

384 Courtesy NASA
387 (top) Bettmann
387 (bottom) Corp Data
388 Tim Brown / Tony Stone Worldwide
393 Courtesy The Charles Babbage Institute / University of Minnesota
395 Michael A. Keller / The Stock Market
410 Charles Thatcher / Tony Stone Worldwide
415 Roger Tully / Tony Stone Worldwide

**Chapter 14**

425 Courtesy Hewlett-Packard
435 Courtesy Lotus Media Services
437 Stuart Bratesman / Courtesy Dartmouth College
439 Courtesy Hewlett-Packard
443 (top) Courtesy Unisys
443 (bottom) Corp Data
444 Bonnie Kamin
445 Courtesy Lotus

**Chapter 15**

459 Courtesy Wang Laboratories
461 Courtesy Hewlett-Packard
462 Courtesy Ameritech
469 Courtesy Peter Norton
472 Courtesy Fingermatrix
473 Corp Data
478 Corp Data
479 Dana Downie / Photo 20-20
482 Roger Tully / Tony Stone Worldwide
483 (top) Jim Pickerell / Tony Stone Worldwide
483 (bottom) James Kegley / Offshoot Stock

**Chapter 16**

490 Courtesy Hewlett-Packard
491 Alexander Teshin Associates
493 James Wilson / Woodfin Camp & Associates
494 Dan McCoy / Rainbow
495 Courtesy Autodesk
499 Courtesy AT&T
502 Courtesy Compaq
503 Bettmann
504 Bonnie Kamin
505 Bonnie Kamin
506 Bonnie Kamin
507 (a) Courtesy NCR
507 (b) James Wilson / Woodfin Camp & Associates
507 (c) Courtesy Hewlett-Packard
507 (d) Jim Brown / Offshoot Stock
507 (e) Jeff Zaruba / Tony Stone Worldwide
507 (f) Courtesy Hewlett-Packard
507 (g) David Joel / Tony Stone Worldwide
509 Courtesy Hewlett-Packard
510 Courtesy TRW Inc.
512 (left) Biophoto Associates / Photo Researchers
512 (right) David Scharf
513 (top) Tim Pennington-Russell
513 (bottom) Corp Data
514 (top) Courtesy Timex
514 (bottom) Lawrence E. Manning / Westlight
515 (top) Corp Data
515 (bottom) Dan McCoy / Rainbow

# Contents Summary

# Contents

# Unit II Computer Hardware 121

# Unit III   *Software Tools*   **219**

## 8   Word Processing and Desktop Publishing   **220**

## 9   Electronic Spreadsheets   **256**

# Unit IV    *Information Systems*      **351**

## 12 Management and Decision Support Systems    352

## 13 System Design and Implementation    382

# 14 Software Development    420

# Unit V  *Technological Trends*    455

# 15 Privacy, Ethics, Crime, and Security    456

# Preface

**A**s we prepared to write the fifth edition of *Computers!*, we were again reminded of the speed at which technological change takes place. Expanding interest in the Internet and the new Windows 95 operating system has forced us to rethink how and when we embrace changes to our classrooms. Graphical user interfaces are the standard as local area networks become commonplace. This technological revolution has changed the core knowledge demanded of the productive worker and informed citizen. These issues and others are addressed in the fifth edition of *Computers!*

    *Computers!* is designed to help you convey to students *why* certain knowledge is essential, *what* is important, and *how* this information can be applied. The wealth of information available can be overwhelming. *Computers!* will help you show students how this information is relevant. It is written to be easy to understand by people young and old who have little or out-of-date technological experience. To these people, your students, we hope to provide an up-to-date guide to information technology.

## NEW TO THIS EDITION

We see in our own computer labs how often network concepts such as login procedures are intertwined with basic computer concepts like booting a PC. Furthermore, fax machines, electronic and voice mail, and tales from the Internet have become so commonplace that students need an early introduction to this aspect of information technology.

### Earlier Introduction to Networks

In the past, network and related issues have been relegated to a chapter at the end of the hardware unit. *Computers!* 5e places the network and data communication chapter in the introductory unit. The technical discussions of specialized communication hardware and related protocols are found later in the chapter on storage and communication hardware.

### Windows 95

We were a part of Microsoft's beta-testing program for Windows 95 and have incorporated screen captures, feature-by-feature comparisons to Windows 3.1 and

Macintosh's System 7.5 (A Closer Look, chapter 3), and a hands-on tutorial (Appendix C) you can use to introduce Windows 95. However, the focus of this book is not Windows 95, nor any specific software package or hardware. As with earlier editions of *Computers!*, the focus is on common features, how things work, and ways that computers make you more productive.

### Buyer's Guide to Personal Computers

The appendices link *Computers!* 5e to hands-on work with personal computers. An updated guide to buying a PC is now Appendix A. Appendix B provides a hands-on Windows 3.1 tutorial that introduces the same features shown in the Windows 95 tutorial (Appendix C). MS-DOS/PC-DOS is introduced in a similar way in Appendix D.

### Switching the Hardware and Software Units

The fifth edition of *Computers!* returns the detailed look at hardware concepts to Unit II, followed by the overview of common software tools, such as word processing and electronic spreadsheets, in Unit III. The first two editions successfully used this design, and moving hardware concepts forward facilitates an earlier introduction of network and data communication issues.

### Software Explorations

New with this edition are 16 software tutorials, called *Explorations,* that build on themes introduced in the text. For example, Exploration 4 walks students through a simulated Internet session while chapter 4 introduces the Internet and related network concepts. The complete set of 16 Explorations is available to adopters through our World Wide Web site *(http://mgh.willamette.edu/mgh/)* or on the Instructor's CD-ROM for distribution to students.

### Electronic Study Guide

The Windows-based *Interactive Study Guide for Computers!* can be bundled with the text for students. This guide provides a concise review of key concepts and terms along with crossword puzzles, drag-and-drop problem solving, and other interactive exercises. All of the Explorations are easily incorporated with the reviews and exercises provided by the guide. A powerful progress management program is also included to help students track their progress and pinpoint specific areas of difficulty.

### Visual Basic and QBASIC Supplements

The fifth edition of *Computers!* is slimmer than earlier editions. This was accomplished, in part, by replacing the BASIC appendix with programming supplements written by Jeff Stipes. These materials take an innovative approach to teaching Visual Basic *(A Quick Look at Visual Basic)* or QBASIC/QuickBASIC *(A Quick Look at QBASIC)* in six hours of class time or supervised lab time. Students learn to code by creating forms and subprograms that complete a campground registration program.

## KEY FEATURES

Educators who have used earlier editions of *Computers!* have said that its enduring strengths lie in its readability, comprehensive coverage, and modular design. We have tried to build on these strengths in the following ways.

### ■ Flexible Design

This textbook contains much more than just explanations of current computer concepts. You can deliver this information to your students by using different chapter combinations and a variety of teaching tools. A practical guide to purchasing a personal computer system is found in Appendix A. Hands-on introductions to Windows 3.1, Windows 95, and DOS round out the appendices. The Explorations provide a computer-based interactive learning experience which reinforces basic computer concepts. Furthermore, the Visual Basic and QBASIC supplements, along with more than three dozen tutorial lab manuals for popular application packages and user interfaces, can be integrated with the concepts covered in *Computers!*.

### ■ Pedagogy

As in previous editions, *Computers!* emphasizes the integration of terms and concepts with the students' need to apply this information to their present and future work. Each chapter contains the following pedagogical features to support this goal:

♦ Chapter Opener—topical outline of the chapter

♦ From the User's Point of View—aids students' continuous search for relevance in what they are asked to learn

♦ Chapter Facts—succinct presentation of the most important information in each chapter

♦ Terms to Remember—listing of key words and phrases

♦ Mix and Match—asks students to fill in key terms that fit related definitions

♦ Review Questions—objective questions about the principal points in the chapter, easily answerable from the text

♦ Applying What You've Learned—questions and projects requiring creative thought and independent research by the student

Additional exercises using Terms to Remember and Review Questions are provided in the *Interactive Study Guide for Computers!* and the printed *Student Study Guide*. Together, these materials will help to motivate and reinforce student learning.

### ■ Real-World Applications and Examples

The fifth edition includes many scenarios using technology in real situations. This alerts students to how all-encompassing technology really is. In addition, three features of special interest appear in each chapter:

**Did You Know?** These are short sidebar articles that highlight topics of practical or special interest to students.

**Who's Who?**   Each dossier presents a brief look at the people responsible for the technological innovations that change our lives:

- Chapter 1:   Blaise Pascal; Steve Jobs and Steve Wozniak
- Chapter 2:   John W. Mauchly and J. Presper Eckert
- Chapter 3:   William "Bill" Gates
- Chapter 4:   Mitch Kapor
- Chapter 5:   John Bardeen, Walter Brattain, and William Shockley; Robert Noyce, Marcian Hoff, and George (Gilbert) Hyatt; Jack Kilby
- Chapter 6:   Joseph Marie Jacquard
- Chapter 7:   Herman Hollerith; George Boole
- Chapter 8:   Bruce Bastian and Alan Ashton
- Chapter 9:   Daniel Bricklin and Robert Frankston
- Chapter 10:  Douglas Englebart
- Chapter 11:  Dr. Edgar F. Codd
- Chapter 12:  Thomas John Watson Sr.
- Chapter 13:  Charles Babbage; Augusta Ada Byron
- Chapter 14:  John G. Kemeny and Thomas E. Kurtz; Grace Murray Hopper
- Chapter 15:  Peter Norton
- Chapter 16:  Karl Alex Müller and J. Georg Bednorz

**A Closer Look at...**   Every chapter wraps up with an in-depth and graphical investigation of a topic presented in that chapter:

- Chapter 1:   Personal Computing
- Chapter 2:   Buying a Computer System
- Chapter 3:   Windows 3.1, Windows 95, and the Macintosh OS
- Chapter 4:   The Internet
- Chapter 5:   Manufacturing a Chip
- Chapter 6:   Environmentally Conscious Computing
- Chapter 7:   Upgrading a Personal Computer
- Chapter 8:   Selecting a Word Processing Package
- Chapter 9:   Designing a Better Worksheet
- Chapter 10:  Computer Art
- Chapter 11:  Hypermedia
- Chapter 12:  Presentation Software
- Chapter 13:  Project Management Software
- Chapter 14:  Programming Languages
- Chapter 15:  Privacy—Is It Still Possible?
- Chapter 16:  Emerging Technologies

The result, *Computers!* 5e, is a comprehensive, flexible multimedia package designed to help you introduce computer concepts and promote computer awareness to students with various backgrounds and needs.

## SUPPLEMENTARY MATERIALS

The following supplementary materials were developed to help customize *Computers!* to your unique teaching style and course objectives.

### Complete Instructor's Manual

The *Instructor's Manual* for this edition contains detailed support material for each chapter:

- Lecture outline
- Additional material for lectures not found in the text
- Teaching tips
- Definitions of Terms to Remember and related page numbers
- Complete answers to the Review Questions
- Suggestions for related lab assignments and class projects not included in the *Student Study Guide*
- Bibliographic list for additional research

### Instructor's CD-ROM

The accompanying CD-ROM combines electronic versions of material found in the *Instructor's Manual* with multimedia support materials, including PowerPoint presentations and stand-alone software explorations.

- PowerPoint presentations for each chapter
- Exploration software for each chapter
- Authors' lecture notes with teaching tips
- Answers to chapter Review Questions

### Student Study Guides

The printed *Student Study Guide* includes space for answering in-text Review Questions, projects with related worksheets, crossword puzzles, Mix and Match exercises, and references for each chapter. Answers are printed in the back of the *Student Study Guide*.

The *Interactive Study Guide* provides a concise review of key concepts and terms on disk, plus crossword puzzles, drag and drop problem solving, and other interactive exercises.

### Computerized and Printed Test Bank

More than 2,000 true/false, multiple-choice, and fill-in questions correspond to the Terms to Remember and Review Questions in the text. These are available in printed form and on disk with MicroTest's Windows-based test generator.

### Internet Home Page

Look us up on our World Wide Web home page at *http://mgh.willamette.edu/mgh/*. The *Computers!* Web site contains up-to-date information related to the text, updates on assignments and exercises, and provides a way to communicate with the authors.

### Broadcast Quality Videotapes

Ten 10-minute "lecture launcher" video clips on today's hottest computer topics and issues are available to adopters. Taken from the popular series by PCTV, Inc., *The Computer Chronicles*, they offer an exciting cutting-edge introduction to any lecture.

### Application Software Tutorials

A variety of hands-on tutorials are available, covering current versions of PC and Macintosh operating systems; word processing, spreadsheet, database, presentation, and integrated software; and commercial software and shareware. For a current list of these materials, contact your McGraw-Hill sales representative.

## SPECIAL ACKNOWLEDGMENTS

It is impossible for textbook authors to produce a book alone. Many people have been involved in this project. Some deserve our special thanks for their care and help. At the top of our list is Rhonda Sands of McGraw-Hill. Her quick wit and humor kept us going. The wonderful presentation of text is due to fine production experts including Gary Palmatier of Ideas to Images; Laurel Anderson of Photosynthesis; copyeditor Elizabeth von Radics; and Frank Ruggirello, Natalie Durbin, and Roger Howell of McGraw-Hill.

Our very dear friend Nina Davis provided innumerable insights into the real world of systems design and analysis that fine-tuned chapter 13. Many of the "conventional wisdoms" presented in Appendix A can be credited to Roger Carlson, whose own wisdom was a great contribution to this manuscript and earlier editions. Jeff Stipes's work on spreadsheets from *Software Tools in Business* (McGraw-Hill, 1991) was the inspiration for chapter 9. Nor can we forget David Kroenke's five-component model and insights about business systems. To each of these individuals, a very special thank-you.

Finally, we would like to thank these people for their assistance with *Computers!* in both this and previous editions: Geoff Alexander, Cabrillo College; Julius Archibald, Plattsburgh State University; Phil Anderson, Muskegon Community College; Gary Armstrong, Shippensburg University; Kathryn Baalman, St. Charles County Community College; Julie Barnes, Bowling Green State University; Dr. Bauers, Fairmont State College; Jim Blaisdale, Humboldt State University; Don Bogema, Muskegon Community College; Jack Breglio, Rancho Santiago College; Susan Brender, Boise State University; Harry Brown, Muskegon Community College; Bruce Burns, Fish-Are-Us; Keith Carver, Sacramento City College; Jane Cochran, Southwestern Community College; Lee Cornell,

Mankato State University; William Cornette, Southwest Missouri State University; Steve Deam, Milwaukee Area Technical College; Kent DeYoung, Muskegon Community College; Pat Fenton, West Valley College; Marie Flatley, San Diego State University; Stan Foster, Sacramento City College; Janet Gerth, Essex Community College; Gene Gordon, Bloomsburg University of Pennsylvania; Tim Gottleber, North Lake College; Professor Haag, University of South Florida; Larry Haffner, McKendree College; Terry Hamberger, York College of Pennsylvania; Rick Hamill, Beech Tree Farm; Cindy Hanchey, Oklahoma Baptist College; Frank Hannum, Eight-Bit Corner; Pat Harris, Mesa Community College; Greg Hodge, Northwestern Michigan College; Enid Irwin, Santa Monica College; Peter Irwin, Richland College; Maribeth King, Kigore College; Linda Knight, Northern Illinois University; Linda Lantz, Community College of Aurora; Robert Lingvall, Southwestern College; Thom Luce, Ohio University; James Mathews, Siena College; Lynn McAustin, Cuesta College; Paula McClurg-Ziemelis, Muskegon Community College; Marty Murray, Portland Community College; Richard Otto, David Chapmen Agency; Michael Michaelson, Palomar College; Blair Morrissey, Muskegon Community College; Patti Nunnally, John Tyler Community College; John Pfuhl, Monmouth College; Randy Pidhayny, Silicon Graphics; Robert Pobasco, University of Idaho; Daniel Randles, General Telephone; Herb Rebhun, University of Houston—Downtown; Joan Roberts, Front Range Community College; John Salzsieder, Phillips University; Bill Sias, Brunswick; Rosemary Skeele, Seton Hall University; Rod Southworth, Laramie County Community College; Jesse Sprayberry, Muskegon Community College; Roger Stoel, Muskegon Community College; Earl Talbert, Central Piedmont Community College; Nancy Tate, Washburn University; Antony Tiona, Broward Community College; Todd Trainor, Mailbox Etc.; Robert Vanderlaan, Muskegon Community College; Kenneth Walker, Weber State University; Randy Weinberg, St. Cloud State University; David Wen, Diablo Valley College; Dave Wenk, Martin-Marietta Corporation; David Whitney, San Francisco State University; Francis Whittle, Dutchess Community College; Louis Wolff, Moorpark College; and Bob Wright, Muskegon Community College.

Timothy N. Trainor
Diane Krasnewich
*Muskegon, Michigan*

# Information Technology

Throughout history people have turned to technology to help them solve problems. Chapter 1 discusses reasons for studying about computers and overviews how these problem-solving machines are used in society. It also examines the four-step cycle that computers and other tools employ when working. Additionally, the chapter explores situations in which the computer cannot or should not be used.

Computers are just one component of a unified system. Besides the actual machines, a computer system also requires people, procedures, data, and programs. Chapter 2 examines how these components fit together to increase the user's productivity. The five-component model is a common thread tying together the diverse applications for computer systems presented throughout this book.

The common properties of application and system software are the focus of chapter 3, which starts off by examining common user interfaces. Sources for computer programs and the need to choose software based on the user's needs and level of understanding are discussed at length. Chapter 4 concludes this unit with a study of data communication and networking applications. A mobile society requires that information travel with its members. For this reason, chapter 4 focuses on how processing power and information are distributed to users, no matter where they are.

# End-user Computing

# FROM THE USER'S POINT OF VIEW

**C**omputers are changing the way we work, play, and live. This chapter sets the tone of the book by introducing you to the fundamental computer concepts behind the input, processing, output, and storage cycle; programmable tools; and data communications. After we explain what computers can and cannot do, you are challenged to question what computers *should not* be asked to do.

## INCREASING YOUR PRODUCTIVITY

As John Morse and Sally Anderson watched, the building began to vibrate. The shaking was slight at first, then increased. Finally, as the building swayed, its main entrance crumpled and collapsed. After a few seconds, the vibrations stopped, leaving the building only partially standing. The two observers had watched in silence from the first shocks.

"Let's see if we can pinpoint the problem," Sally said. She made a few entries on a keyboard connected to a computer. They had viewed the simulated effects of an earthquake on the attached screen, similar to Figure 1.1. A printer also located in the small architectural office purred for several seconds. John snatched the sheet of paper that floated into the paper tray and showed it to Sally. "I'm not sure, but I think we need to beef up the strength of that crossbeam over the entrance. Let's send these results to Juan's computer downtown to see if he agrees."

Sally was enthusiastic. "This is great," she said, as she keyed in the downtown office's number. "With hand calculations, it would have taken us days to do this analysis. By using the computer, we have our answers in a matter of minutes. Better still, we can send the information across town or around the world."

"And we have more assurance that our building will be safe," John concluded. "It's hard to remember how we did things before computers." John stopped to think about how the computer had changed his professional life and had increased his personal productivity.

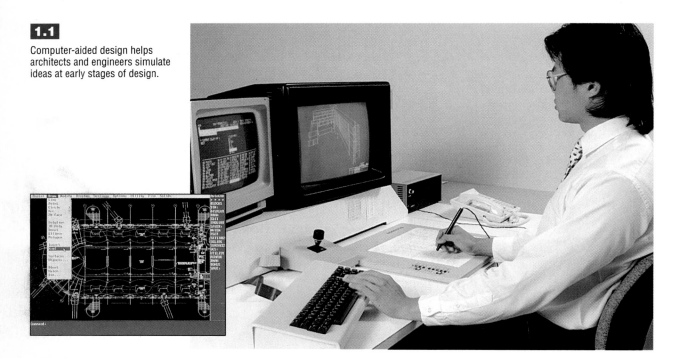

**1.1**

Computer-aided design helps architects and engineers simulate ideas at early stages of design.

Architects have known formulas to measure structural strength for more than 100 years. Computers have taken professionally accepted techniques and improved them. A computer can complete in minutes computations that used to take hours for people to do. People who use computers can concentrate on solving major problems without worrying about all the minor details. Previously, people were involved mainly in solving mathematical equations, or "crunching numbers." By doing the routine calculations for people, computers have allowed human creativity and productivity to increase.

By linking computers and communication technology, information and ideas fly among computer users at the speed of light. Delays that could handicap project coordination are minimized. Furthermore, this technology promotes critical communication between people even when they are separated by large distances.

Computers perform a variety of jobs. In John and Sally's office, secretaries and architectural assistants use word processing programs on computers for correspondence, to list structural specifications, to write proposals to clients, and for other jobs.

### ▦ Impact on Critical Thinking

Since the 1950s, people have turned to the computer for help in solving problems. A *computer* is a machine that processes facts and figures to produce information. Therefore, *information* is the result of processing facts and figures in ways that are useful to people. Through the years computers have become smaller, more powerful, and less expensive.

As more organizations bring computers into the workplace, more people become exposed to what computers can do and acquire more computer skills. As early as elementary school, children are using computers to write stories and do math. As a result, computers influence the way many people think about and approach problems. The

**1.2**

The speed with which computers collect and process data into useful information helps us track and forecast weather patterns.

average person depends on, is served by, or actually operates some type of computer several times each day.

It is obvious that computers are a part of everyone's life. Your future success requires a basic level of knowledge about computers and skill in using them. This book is designed to help you attain these goals. As you read and complete assignments in this text, you will learn to involve computers in your critical thinking. You should understand how computers affect your life and how they are used to solve everyday problems. You should be able to talk intelligently about computers. Equally important, you should be prepared for the changes computers will bring into your life.

Computers are installed in cars, toys, and appliances. They are used by musicians, waiters, artists, bank tellers, and teachers. Computers collect meteorological data, transmit it to other computers for processing, forecast the weather, and support the television and radio broadcasts of this forecast (Figure 1.2). People research, write, and edit books with the aid of computers. Then, with assistance from computers, they instantly print out the words many miles away. Doctors, lawyers, pilots, auto mechanics, and sales clerks all depend upon computers. Computers help people organize and save their thoughts. Thought itself can be stimulated by computers that serve as storehouses of facts and figures. These facts and figures—about people, things, ideas, and events—are called *data*.

## ▇ Promoting the Competitive Edge

With each passing year, computers become more powerful and less expensive. As more people use computers, new technological advances are introduced. Many of these improvements are intended to make computers easier to use, or more *user-friendly*. Computers allow you to become more competitive in the workplace and more efficient at home.

At home, computers are responsible for many comforts and conveniences. Microwave ovens, using computers and meat probes, turn themselves off when the proper internal temperature of the food is reached. Computerized clothes dryers continuously monitor the moisture level of clothes and shut off when a preset level of dryness is attained. These situations are examples of *process control*, where computers constantly monitor and adjust an activity without direct human intervention. Process control is just one of several labor-saving tasks computers perform.

Many forms of recreation also depend on computers. Some people spend their leisure time at video arcades using computer-driven games. Computer *simulations* generate images that imitate real-life or imaginary situations such as high-speed racetracks, jungle obstacle courses, or intergalactic battlefields. Animators use computers to produce the lifelike graphics found in movies, advertisements, and television shows. Architects, like John and Sally, simulate stresses caused by earthquakes or high winds on new building designs. Engineers simulate the performance of new aircraft and automotive designs before the products are actually built.

With the aid of computers, scientists perform *data storage and retrieval*. Data from current research can be stored on a computer, and computerized data libraries can be searched to find relevant reference materials. Sources of information often exist in different geographic locations and are accessed through standard telephone lines. Data is usually organized and cross-referenced in large collections called *databases*. With computers this kind of data retrieval takes only a fraction of the time required to find the same information by hand. Computers also can simulate scientific experiments, monitor instruments used in lab tests, and analyze collected data.

In health care, computers assist physicians in diagnosing illnesses by relating symptoms to information in a medical database. Computer-controlled surgical devices aid in delicate operations. Computers monitor the vital signs, such as heart rate, of critically ill patients. Other computers maintain a patient's medical history for attending health professionals. Computer technology has generated many new medical techniques.

The competitive business world requires that successful people use a computer's speed and accuracy for *data processing*. By utilizing computers to convert facts and

**1.3**

Information technology links together students in remote classrooms to exchange ideas and information.

figures into useful information, businesspeople can keep track of their inventory, have immediate access to sales information, and quickly identify potential customers.

Computers can meet the individual needs of students in a classroom. Computers can serve as tutors by presenting material to students and quizzing them later. These machines also are tools for students; they help them retrieve information for assignments, type and edit the papers, produce graphs and drawings, compute answers

**Who's Who**

# Blaise Pascal

(1632-1662)

From his earliest days, Blaise Pascal showed mathematical promise. By age 16 he had written an important book on geometry. In order to help his father, a tax commissioner, with a barrage of calculations, 18-year-old Pascal built a mechanical adding machine. Called "la Pascaline," it used cogged wheels to add and subtract up to eight-digit numbers. Its design was tailored to handle data in the form of the French monetary system.

Pascal's goal was to see his machine in every business and upper-class house of France. Unfortunately, it did not get the welcome he thought it deserved. La Pascaline was too expensive to be practical, although more than 500 models were made. Depressed by his lack of success, Pascal turned his life to religion. Sporadic forays into physics and mathematics left a legacy to the scientific community. He died young, still upset by the failure of his invention.

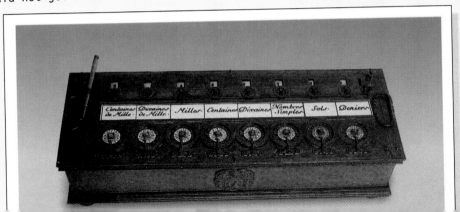

to problems, and simulate hazardous lab experiments or historical events. Behind the scenes, teachers use computers to grade tests and keep student records. As shown in Figure 1.3, computers even link together classrooms from remote locations to support the exchange of ideas and values.

Computers touch every aspect of your life. Understanding computers and learning how to use them is necessary both now and in the future.

## TURNING DATA INTO USEFUL INFORMATION

Computers help people save time and solve problems. As a problem-solving tool, the computer has much in common with other tools you use regularly. To illustrate, imagine you have just enjoyed a delicious dinner and now have a problem: dirty dishes.

### The IPOS Cycle

You have some options in deciding how to solve this problem. You can use a tool—a dishwasher—or do the dishes by hand. Prospective computer users often face the same kind of decision. They can use a computer to do a job or they can do it by hand.

Using the dishwasher and other tools involves four basic steps:

1. *Input.*  You put something into the device.
2. *Processing.*  The device changes the input in some way.
3. *Output.*  You take results out.
4. *Storage.*  You may save any results that have future value.

Assume that you decide to use the dishwasher. You know the result you want. You also know the pattern of events that has to take place. Your solution is easy:

1. *Input.*  You put dirty dishes and soap into a dishwasher. You press a button, and the dishwasher inputs the right amount of hot water.
2. *Processing.*  The dishwasher increases the water temperature and washes and rinses the dishes, changing them from dirty to clean.
3. *Output.*  You have the result you wanted—clean dishes.
4. *Storage.*  You complete the job by stacking the dishes in the cupboard.

This four-step process, diagrammed in Figure 1.4, often is identified by its initials: *IPOS.* All uses for a computer, called **computer applications**, or *apps,* conform to the first three steps of the cycle. The last step, storage, is included in many applications.

An activity as simple as ordering a cheeseburger at a fast-food outlet follows the IPOS cycle. As you place the order, the data is entered into a keyboard. The **keyboard** is an example of input equipment. Keyboards in fast-food outlets often have pictures of items on the menu. Pictures that represent data or a computer operation are known as **icons.** When the icon for a menu item on the keyboard is pressed, the computer retrieves the stored description and pricing information for that item. This immediate response of the computer to the user's request makes a computer application **interactive.** After all items have been ordered, the processing step begins.

The computer uses information input previously to calculate and print a receipt. This is done on a **printer,** output equipment that puts information on paper. The

**1.4**

The IPOS cycle defines the steps common to all information processing systems: input, processing, output, and storage.

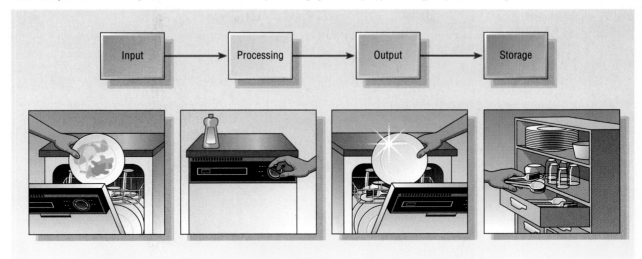

receipt includes descriptions and prices for all entered items. At the same time, the item descriptions and quantities are output in the kitchen, where cooks prepare the food. The computer also stores information on the order for later use. This completes the IPOS cycle.

By exchanging your money for the food, you have participated in a *transaction*, or exchange of value. At the end of the day, the computer processes all sales transactions to produce a sales report the manager can use. The report helps the manager order more supplies and schedule employees to match customer buying patterns.

## ...ABOUT COMMON TECHNOFEARS

If using a VCR or resetting the stations on your car radio makes you uncomfortable, relax. You've got plenty of company. According to a study by Dell Computer, 55 percent of Americans are uncomfortable using some kind of technology. In fact, one-fourth of all adults have never used a computer, set a VCR to record a television show, or programmed their car radios. Computers, which 23 percent of adults felt uncomfortable using, ranked third on Dell's technophobia scale. Car phones topped the list by intimidating 34 percent of adults, followed by programmable thermostats at 25 percent. Automatic teller machines ranked fourth (22 percent), followed by compact disc players (20 percent) and answering machines (15 percent). Few Americans were uncomfortable with VCRs (9 percent) or digital alarm clocks (8 percent).

*Source: PC Today,* October 1993, page 9.

The IPOS cycle for this system is easily identified:

1. *Input.* The counter person presses keys to identify ordered items and quantities.
2. *Processing.* The computer multiplies quantities by prices, calculates tax amounts, and determines a total.
3. *Output.* Items and totals are printed in the kitchen and at the counter. This information is used by cooks and customers.
4. *Storage.* Data on sales, by product and time of day, is stored for later use.

Keyboards commonly are used to type data directly into the computer. However, talking into a telephone or activating a sensor with light or heat are also ways to input data. Processing may involve sorting names into alphabetical order or applying mathematical functions to sets of numbers. When processing is complete, information is output in the form of a screen display or printed report. Output also takes several other forms. The action of a mechanical arm as it swings into place to tighten a bolt on a new motorcycle is another example of output. The processed data is then stored until needed on special computer-operated devices. Stored information may be used as input in other applications, putting the IPOS cycle into motion again.

### ▦ Computer Hardware

For a computer to complete a job requires more than just the actual equipment, or **hardware**, we see and touch. A keyboard and printer help with the input and output steps of an IPOS cycle. Other hardware, the computer, does the processing.

Much of the processing computers do can be divided into two general types of operations. *Arithmetic operations* are computations with numbers, such as addition, subtraction, and other mathematical procedures. Early computers performed mostly arithmetic operations, which gave the false impression that only engineers and scientists could benefit from computers. Of equal importance is the computer's ability to compare two values to determine if one is larger than, smaller than, or equal to the other. This is called a *logical operation*. The comparison may take place between numbers, letters, sounds, or even drawings. The processing step in the IPOS cycle is built around the computer's ability to perform arithmetic and logical operations.

## Computer Software

Instructions must be given to the computer, however, to tell it how to process the data it receives and the format needed for output and storage.

For example, suppose a chemistry student needs to convert a series of temperatures from Fahrenheit to Celsius. With an inexpensive calculator, the following formula would have to be entered repeatedly and new values keyed each time:

Celsius = (Fahrenheit − 32) × (5/9)

With this amount of repetition, the risk of error is high. With a computer, the equation, along with input and output steps, can be captured in a *computer program*. This program, also called *software*, provides a series of instructions followed in sequence to control the input, processing, output, and storage performed by the computer. Figure 1.6 shows a program that a chemistry student could use to complete the computation.

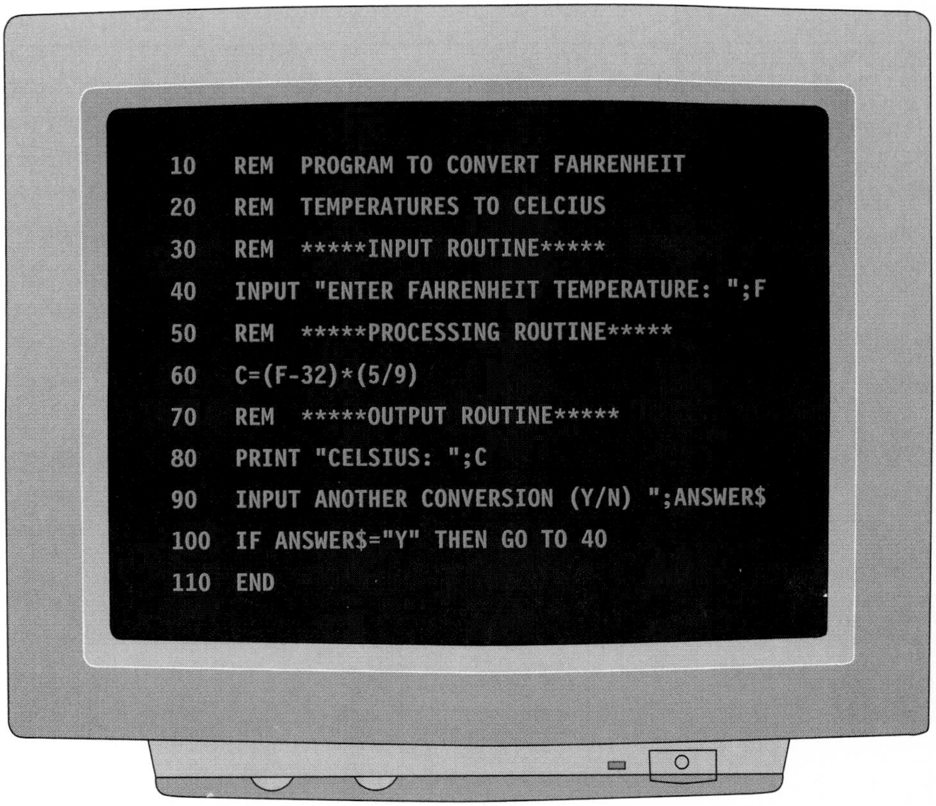

**1.6**

Computer programs make it possible for people to communicate with computers in statements understandable to both humans and machines.

```
10   REM  PROGRAM TO CONVERT FAHRENHEIT
20   REM  TEMPERATURES TO CELCIUS
30   REM  *****INPUT ROUTINE*****
40   INPUT "ENTER FAHRENHEIT TEMPERATURE: ";F
50   REM  *****PROCESSING ROUTINE*****
60   C=(F-32)*(5/9)
70   REM  *****OUTPUT ROUTINE*****
80   PRINT "CELSIUS: ";C
90   INPUT ANOTHER CONVERSION (Y/N) ";ANSWER$
100  IF ANSWER$="Y" THEN GO TO 40
110  END
```

When the program is in place, the student enters only the Fahrenheit temperature for each conversion. The resulting information is displayed on a screen. Output also could be printed on paper or stored for later use or both. In either case, if the hardware is directly connected and communicating with the computer, it is said to be *online*.

The ability to follow a program sets computers apart from most tools. However, new tools ranging from typewriters to electronic ovens have embedded, or built-in, computers. An *embedded computer* can accept data to use several options in its program; the program itself, however, cannot be changed. Although the tools are flexible, the embedded computers themselves are not.

## Types of Data

Historically, both computers and calculators used numbers as the primary form of input data. With the advent of new computing applications and hardware, the definition of data has expanded.

**Numeric**   *Numeric data* consists of numbers and decimal points, as well as the plus (+) and minus (–) signs. Both arithmetic and logical operations are performed on numeric data. This means that the numbers can be used for calculations as well as sorted, or compared to each other.

**Textual**   *Textual data,* or *text,* can contain any combination of letters, numbers, and special characters. Sometimes textual data is known as *alphanumeric data.* Usually, text is organized into words, sentences, and paragraphs. Term papers, labels, books, and correspondence are examples of textual data.

**Audiovisual**   Various forms of data that we can hear or see make up *audiovisual data.* Although computers have contained speakers for many years, recently we have seen the advent of data in the form of voices and music. The computer can produce spoken output as well as accept the human voice for input. Data can also take the form of graphs and drawings generated by both users and software. Existing visual images, such as photographs and video sequences, can be input into the computer and manipulated as data.

**Physical**   *Physical data* is captured from the environment. For example, light, sound, voice, temperature, and pressure are types of physical data. The temperature of the room in which you are sitting may be controlled by a computer. A thermostat is set to sense the air temperature. When the temperature exceeds a specified level, a cooling system is turned on. The warmth of the air is used as physical data input into a thermostat to regulate room temperature. In many large buildings, computer systems process several kinds of physical data to regulate operations. Computers can set off security alarms, control temperature and humidity, or turn lights on and off—all in response to physical data. These applications increase people's safety and save them time and money.

## Data in a Computer

As you can see, all types of data are stored and processed in the computer. Because computers run on electricity, the data is stored as a series of on and off patterns. Think of a row of light bulbs. Each bulb can be in only one of two states: on or off. By using different patterns of on and off bulbs, many unique combinations can be obtained. Each individual computer circuit also functions in one of two states: on (represented as 1) or

**1.7**

Data comes in different forms to accommodate a variety of input and applications.

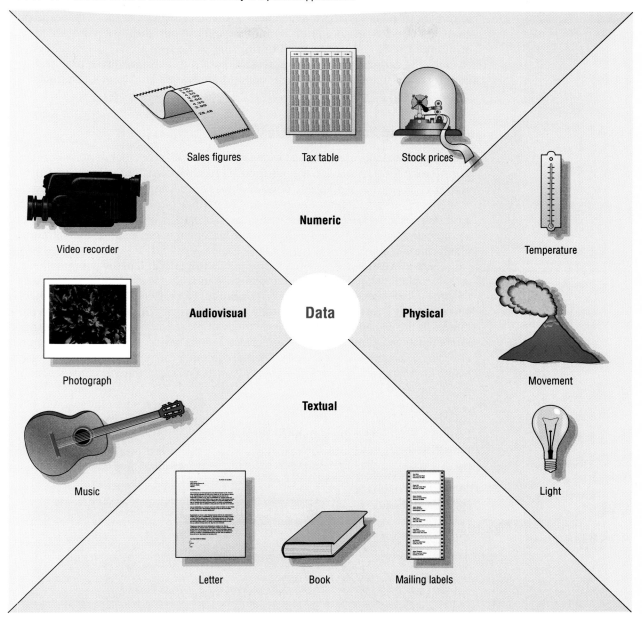

off (represented as 0). These two values are *binary digits*, or ***bits***. They are the building blocks for the ***binary code*** used to represent data and program instructions for computers. Binary means "consisting of two parts." Different patterns of bits in a binary code can be used to represent characters or operations. For example, the bit pattern 01000001 might represent the letter *A*, whereas 10111110 00100001 might represent an instruction to the computer to do addition.

## THE IMPACT OF INFORMATION TECHNOLOGY

Information technology is limited chiefly by the imaginations of the people who program and operate the computers. Computer applications already cover a wide range of human needs and wants, from optimizing cattle feed to navigating aircraft to customizing car production. Computers are powerful tools for solving problems and meeting needs in today's world. With support from human intelligence, computers can expand human capabilities.

### ■ Expanding Your Capabilities

Computers generally are equipped with vast storage capacities that permit easy access to great volumes of knowledge. Suppose a doctor receives a call from an anguished mother about a child who has swallowed a poisonous substance. The physician can be connected immediately to a computer database in Atlanta that provides exact information on antidotes, their dosages, and other treatment information. No matter how experienced a physician might be, it would be impossible for him or her to memorize such volumes of information and recall it instantly.

Fast processing speeds enable computers to perform lengthy computations or establish relationships among large amounts of data within seconds. Such speeds reduce the time people spend on routine tasks. The ability of a computer to process data quickly and accurately is invaluable for monitoring physical activity. Changes in a patient's pulse rate or in the radiation level at a nuclear power plant can be detected and reported immediately by a computer. If the correct instructions have been entered, the computer also can react automatically. For example, the computer can sound an alarm if a patient's health is endangered. If a nuclear reactor shows danger signs, the computer can initiate a shutdown sequence.

Computers also go where people cannot. In outer space, under the sea, and inside volcanoes, nuclear reactors, and oil refineries, computers monitor conditions and warn people when dangerous situations arise. Inside people, computers monitor body functions; inside machines, such as car ignitions or microwave ovens, computers control operations. By connecting computers together, *networks* are created that allow exchange

**1.8**

Computers increase our capacity to control the environment in many ways.

### How Can a Computer Help People?

- ■ Computers permit easy access to large volumes of data

- ■ Computers perform lengthy computations quickly and accurately

- ■ Computers identify relationships among large amounts of data

- ■ Computer-controlled devices go where people cannot

- ■ Computers can simulate human performance

**Who's Who**

# Steve Wozniak

(b. 1950)

# Steve Jobs

(b. 1955)

When Steve Wozniak was 13, he won first prize at a local science fair for a transistor-based calculator. Taught about electronics at an early age by his engineer father, Wozniak always wanted to be an engineer. While he was a teenager, circuitry became available to build computers at home. Wozniak and other computer hobbyists formed the Homebrew Computer Club. In 1971 Wozniak met Steve Jobs, then 16. They found a mutual interest in computing and guessed that a completely assembled, inexpensive computer would be in demand. Using money raised from selling personal possessions, Jobs and Wozniak formed a partnership in 1975 to make the computers in Jobs's attic. The computer was somewhat primitive; it had a little keyboard and no case. Yet at the time, people were impressed. The Apple I contained a $25 microprocessor and sold for $500. Only 175 of them were sold. By the end of 1977, the Apple II was

announced and it was highly successful. The partnership went on to become the Apple Computer Corporation. Wozniak left Apple in 1985 to start the CL9 (Cloud 9) Company. He later earned a degree in computer science under an alias. Presently, he runs a company that specializes in developing universal remote controls and other technological devices. Jobs resigned from Apple also in 1985 and formed the NeXT Corporation, a firm that designs computer programs.

of data and software over many locations simultaneously. Networks can link many users to the information provided by a strategically placed computer.

Further, some computers can simulate, or imitate, human performance: Voice synthesizers, computer-operated limbs, and Braille printers increase the ability of physically handicapped people to move about or to communicate. Computers increase the capacity of people to control their environment.

## ■ What Computers Can, Cannot, and Should Not Do

Since computers are products of advanced technology, they tend to be regarded as mysterious. People have attributed human, even superhuman, qualities to computers. This simply is not warranted. Computers are merely tools, designed by people, programmed by people, and used by people. A computer's most basic limitation is that it does no original or creative thinking. Any actions it takes, problems it solves, or decisions it makes are controlled by programs written by people.

Computers are, however, useful in organizing information to expedite problem solving and decision making by people. By following well-written programs, computers can do amazing things. But people must do the thinking necessary to write the software.

Computers exist to benefit and assist people, not replace them. Computers cannot, for example, make emotional judgments, disobey instructions entered by humans, or replace interpersonal relationships. On the contrary, people must be extremely explicit when instructing a computer to perform even the simplest activities. What computers can do, however, is extremely helpful. They can:

♦ Store data in vast amounts

♦ Process data quickly, accurately, and tirelessly

♦ Graphically represent numbers

♦ Simulate possible outcomes based on a given set of conditions

♦ Recommend or take action based on output

Computers cannot be effective unless the people using them are able to identify the output they need, the input required, and what processing should be used to achieve those results. Ultimately, computers are dependent upon people.

Accordingly, people should not relinquish their decision-making responsibilities to computers. Humans need to be on hand to interpret conditions reported by computers, particularly if medical treatment, national defense, air traffic control, or even loan processing are involved. Non-programmable, human factors must complement computer readouts for a complete and fair analysis.

At times computers may appear to make decisions. In monitoring a building's temperature, for example, a computer might trigger a fire extinguishing system. Another computer, used for monitoring vital signs, might regulate the flow of oxygen to a patient. More-complex programs that simulate human responses and decision making are said to have *artificial intelligence*. In all these cases, however, although the computer initiates action, it does not make a decision. Rather, the decisions of these process control systems were made by the human beings who programmed the machines to respond to a particular set of conditions. Therefore *people must take complete responsibility for a computer's actions*. They must anticipate all potential problems and direct computers to avoid them.

Though computers may be able to enhance a person's capabilities, they can never adequately replace interpersonal relationships. Even the most sophisticated computing

**1.9**

Although computers help students check their spelling and grammar when writing a report, they cannot replace a teacher's smile or a heartfelt compliment.

machinery cannot supplant parent-to-child and teacher-to-student interaction. Similarly, the rapport between physician and patient is essential for successful treatment.

People are an integral part of any computer system that accepts input, processes it, and delivers output. People control computer systems through program design, by monitoring operations, and by making final decisions based upon computer output. They should not give up decision-making responsibilities because the human qualities of analysis, reasoning, and compassion are required to interpret computer-delivered results. Computers cannot operate independently; humans are the driving force behind computer processing.

## ■ Mastering Change

Change is a way of life for people in today's society. The average adult, according to some estimates, will change jobs four to seven times. To cope successfully with a changing world, you must recognize that change can be constructive. People who resist change because they fear new technology undermine their potential to become more effective. Still, people fear computers for many reasons:

♦ Some people don't understand how computers work. The "magical box" that performs seemingly amazing operations is viewed as mysterious and terrifying. The qualities of the computer are not mystical, however. Computers should be regarded as tools to be manipulated by people. The more a person understands what a computer can do, the more comfortable the user is with the computer.

♦ People think computers will take away their jobs. The computer is more predictable and more efficient than humans. Often it is responsible for employee displacement. Actually, the introduction of computers and automation can increase the number of jobs within a company—but the new jobs often require computer knowledge. Because the automation of manual labor jobs is likely to continue, people should learn to make computers work for them. Few benefits can be gained by rejecting computers out of fear or resentment.

♦ People think computers will replace free will and decision making. Fears that a machine can assume control of human thinking are unfounded. At all times people instruct computers. When computers provide information and advise decision makers, they do so according to criteria specified by people. However, computers do identify and assemble decision-related information quickly and efficiently. By using computers, decision makers can be more efficient.

♦ Humans are reluctant to give up old habits. Some people think change is bad. Often using new computer technology requires learning new procedures. This requirement can disrupt the "comfort level" in a job. Once people are willing to discard outdated procedures, they can promote progress. They increase their productivity, and may be able to make their lives easier, by allowing computers to take up some of their work load.

By overcoming the urge to cling to the status quo, people can accept computers as an integral part of their lives. Many opportunities follow such acceptance. Computers

**1.10**

Keeping up with change is a necessary part of living in modern society.

# A Closer Look at Personal Computing

**You may be asking yourself:** What does this mean to me? It means you should try to become a proficient **end user**. In the broadest sense, an end user is a person who knows how to use a computer and communication technology to organize data, stimulate new ideas, solve problems, and communicate the results to others. At a personal level, a wide variety of activities fit into this description. As end users, teachers and students employ a different mix of computer skills, equipment, programs, and data than is required for users in law, medicine, business, and government. The following questions are often asked by people as they learn how to become proficient end users.

**Q: Is it difficult to operate a computer?**

**A:** Operating computer equipment is as simple as learning how to turn it on and complicated enough to be a part of everyone's lifelong learning.

**Q: How will I know what to do?**

**A:** Computer programs are designed to guide you through operations by providing prompts and menus with possible options.

## Word Processor Menu

What do you want help with?

> **Essentials like moving this Cue Card**

> **Typing or revising text (incl. tables and footnotes)**

> **Changing how text looks**

> **Margins, page numbers, and other page settings**

> **Mass mailings: letters, labels**

> **Pictures**

> **Files: opening, finding, etc.**

> **Saving and printing**

< | Menu | Close

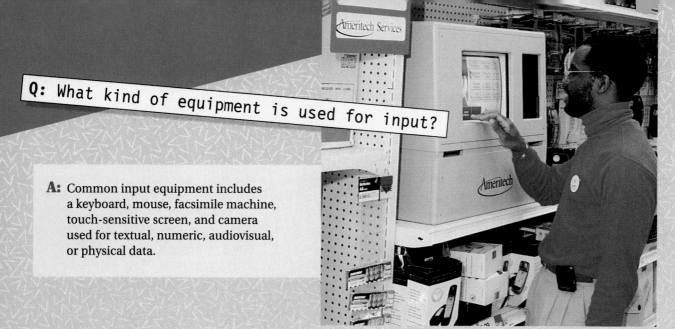

**Q: What kind of equipment is used for input?**

**A:** Common input equipment includes a keyboard, mouse, facsimile machine, touch-sensitive screen, and camera used for textual, numeric, audiovisual, or physical data.

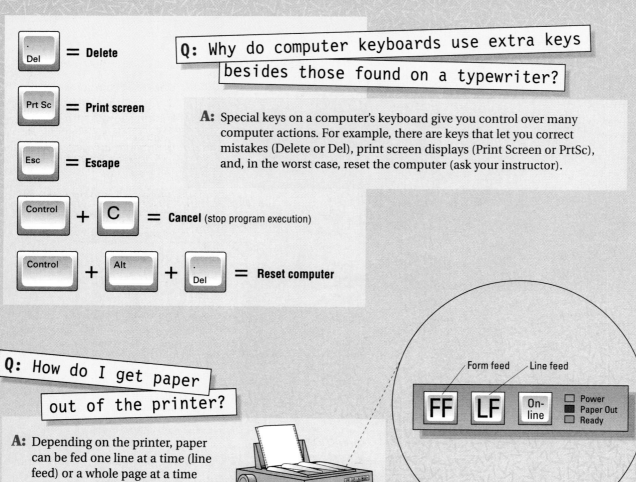

. | Del = **Delete**

**Q: Why do computer keyboards use extra keys besides those found on a typewriter?**

Prt Sc = **Print screen**

**A:** Special keys on a computer's keyboard give you control over many computer actions. For example, there are keys that let you correct mistakes (Delete or Del), print screen displays (Print Screen or PrtSc), and, in the worst case, reset the computer (ask your instructor).

Esc = **Escape**

Control + C = **Cancel** (stop program execution)

Control + Alt + Del = **Reset computer**

**Q: How do I get paper out of the printer?**

**A:** Depending on the printer, paper can be fed one line at a time (line feed) or a whole page at a time (form feed) when it is *offline*—not communicating with the computer.

Form feed   Line feed

FF   LF   On-line

☐ Power
■ Paper Out
☐ Ready

**Q:** What do I do with the disks when they are not being used by the computer?

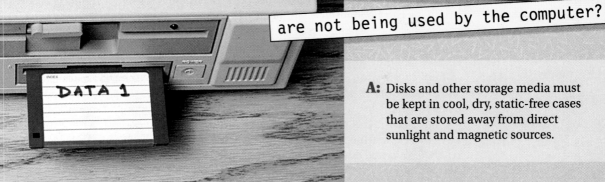

**A:** Disks and other storage media must be kept in cool, dry, static-free cases that are stored away from direct sunlight and magnetic sources.

**Q:** How can I guard computer equipment from physical harm or theft and protect myself from loss of data or electronic invasions?

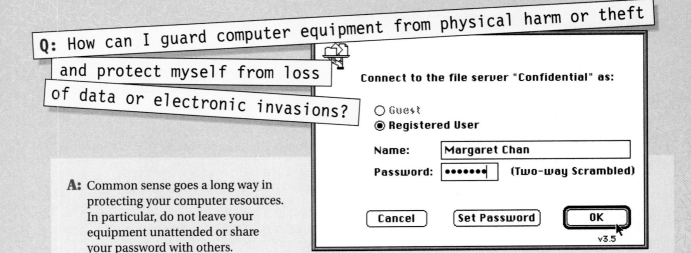

Connect to the file server "Confidential" as:

○ Guest
● Registered User

Name: Margaret Chan
Password: •••••••  (Two-way Scrambled)

[ Cancel ]  [ Set Password ]  [ OK ]

v3.5

**A:** Common sense goes a long way in protecting your computer resources. In particular, do not leave your equipment unattended or share your password with others.

**Q:** Where do I go to get answers to problems?

**A:** Manuals, telephone help lines, and knowledgeable friends or colleagues can help answer questions.

provide people with more information in less time. Databases can be changed immediately, allowing people to act on the most current information. With fast feedback, problems can be identified and dealt with promptly. The efficiency of any operation can be enhanced with increased access to information—the primary output of computers.

Computers provide access to hundreds of information sources. Tapping these sources can provide new insights, or even prevent the waste of time and effort involved in duplicating work. For example, during the early days of the U.S. space exploration program, $250,000 was spent on a metallurgic study. It was then discovered that the same research already had been conducted by Soviet scientists and reported in a Soviet journal. Had the U.S. scientists been aware of Soviet contributions in the field, they might have built upon the available knowledge. Instead, they duplicated it, an action that resulted in wasted money, effort, and time. In cases such as this, access to diverse sources of information is extremely valuable.

## CHAPTER FACTS

- Computers process facts, figures, and images. They have been used as problem-solving tools since the 1950s. As computers have become more user-friendly, they have been adapted for a variety of applications by many levels of users.

- The facts, figures, and images a computer uses to solve problems are called data. Data is processed into useful information.

- Many computer applications take the form of process control, simulations, data storage and retrieval, and data processing.

- Computers and other tools operate under the four-step IPOS cycle: input, processing, output, and storage. Once it is completed, the cycle can be repeated with different input data.

- When a user's request from a computer is immediately acted upon, the exchange is considered interactive.

- Data can be input into a computer through hardware such as a keyboard, a telephone, a mouse, or through cameras and sensors. Any transaction can produce useful data.

- Computer output can be a screen display, report from a printer, action of a mechanical arm, various sounds, and visual images.

- Computers perform both arithmetic operations and logical operations in the IPOS cycle. Arithmetic operations involve mathematical computations whereas logical operations do comparisons of data values.

- A computer program or software is a set of instructions that is followed to produce a desired result.

- Data can be numeric, textual, audiovisual, or physical. All four types of data may be input to or output from a computer.

■ Computers use binary codes to represent all four types of data. Each letter, number, or sound, for example, is assigned a unique combination of on or off bits that make up the binary code for that piece of data.

■ The chief limitation of computers is that they do not perform any type of original or creative thinking. They also cannot replace the decision-making power of people, make emotional judgments, or disobey their programming.

■ Computers effectively store large amounts of data, perform processing quickly and accurately, simulate outcomes on the basis of given conditions, and recommend actions.

■ Computers depend upon people to provide correct data and instructions. Computer output must be interpreted by people as a basis for making decisions.

■ Some misunderstandings arise when people don't realize how computers work. People may feel that computers will replace them on the job or make decisions previously made by humans. Also, some people are reluctant to change to innovative technology, even if the new methods will increase their productivity.

■ Proficient end users can perform common tasks with their computers.

## TERMS TO REMEMBER

| | | |
|---|---|---|
| arithmetic operation | data storage and retrieval | online |
| artificial intelligence | end user | physical data |
| audiovisual data | hardware | printer |
| binary code | icon | process control |
| bit | information | simulation |
| computer | interactive | software |
| computer application | keyboard | textual data |
| computer program | logical operation | transaction |
| data | network | user-friendly |
| database | numeric data | |
| data processing | offline | |

## MIX AND MATCH

*Complete the following definitions with the Terms to Remember.*

1. A(n) _____ is a picture of an item, action, or computer operation.

2. The pattern of on/off bits used to represent data in computer memory is referred to as _____.

3. A(n) _____ is an exchange of value, resulting in usable data.

4. Processed data is collectively known as _____.

5. A(n) _____ is a computer-generated environment that mimics a real-life or imaginary situation.

6. _____ is data containing only numbers (0–9), decimal point, and plus (+) and negative (–) signs.

7. A system of computers and hardware sharing data and software over communication lines is called a(n) _____.

8. A(n) _____ is a machine that allows input of facts and figures, processes them, and outputs useful information.

9. _____ is an attribute of computers meaning "easy to use."

10. When hardware is not communicating with the computer, it is _____.

11. A situation wherein a computer constantly monitors and adjusts an activity is referred to as _____.

12. _____ is a complex computer program that simulates human responses and decision making.

13. Output hardware producing printed information on paper is called a(n) _____.

14. A(n) _keyboard_ is input hardware containing typewriter-like keys which the user presses.

15. The computer and other associated equipment is collectively referred to as _____.

---

## REVIEW QUESTIONS

1. Define the Terms to Remember.

2. Provide an example of each of the following tasks that computers perform every day: process control, simulations, data storage and retrieval, and data processing.

3. What is the four-step cycle used by computers and other tools?

4. Describe two processing operations that computers perform.

5. Why do embedded computers make tools more flexible?

6. What are four types of data computers can use as input?

7. What are five ways in which computers increase the capacity of people to control their environment?

8. What is the chief limitation of computer technology?

9. List three activities that computers cannot perform.

10. List five general activities that computers can do well.

11. Why should people avoid giving up decision-making responsibilities to computers?

12. What are four misunderstandings that people have about computer technology?

13. Identify eight questions and the associated answers new end users often ask.

---

## APPLYING WHAT YOU'VE LEARNED

1. Computers are being used as tools in many jobs. In fact, few areas of work are untouched by computer technology. How could computers be used in your future career? If you don't think computers could be involved, why not?

2. Identify five occupations that *do not* involve computers in any way. Are they high-paying jobs with potential for growth? Why or why not? Are they likely to be replaced by automation? Why or why not?

3. The IPOS cycle is found in the application of many tools. Pick a tool not mentioned in the text and identify the four steps in its IPOS cycle. What types of data are used? How is data input? What form does the output take?

4. Two common forms of output are reports and screen displays. Describe three situations in which a printed report is more useful than a display. Describe three situations in which a screen display is more useful.

5. Identify which type(s) of data (numeric, textual, audiovisual, or physical) would be used in these situations:
   a. writing a term paper on a computer
   b. monitoring a baby for continuous breathing
   c. playing a video game
   d. sensing earthquake tremors
   e. providing computerized telephone directory assistance
   f. mixing voices, instruments, and recorded dancing on a music video
   g. calculating income tax through use of a computer

6. Embedded computers are found in many devices you use each day. Name a tool you use that could be improved by embedding a computer. What type of data would the computer use? What kind of processing would it do?

7. Despite the many applications for computers, they are not the solution to all problems. Describe three situations in which use of a computer would be unethical, impractical, or pointless.

# Computer Information Systems

**E**ach technological development seems to bring with it new terms and concepts. To make sense out of these new ideas, as well as what we already know about computers, it helps to have a logical framework for organizing related facts. The five components of a computer information system (people, data, procedures, hardware, and software) form such a framework. Every concept and term discussed throughout this text can be associated with one or more of these components.

## SYSTEM COMPONENTS

Computers come in many sizes—from computers that occupy entire rooms, to notebook-sized computers, to computers as small as your fingernail. Although computer hardware is the most visible part of a computer, it is merely one part of a *computer system*. A system is a collection of elements that work together to solve a specific problem. Regardless of size, every computer needs the other components of the system to produce results. The components of a computer system are:

- ◆ People
- ◆ Data
- ◆ Procedures
- ◆ Hardware
- ◆ Software

These components are integral to every computer system, as illustrated in Figure 2.1. Every time you use a computer to generate information, you become one of the five system components.

**2.1**

People use procedures to control data that is processed by hardware following detailed software instructions. These are the five components of every computer system.

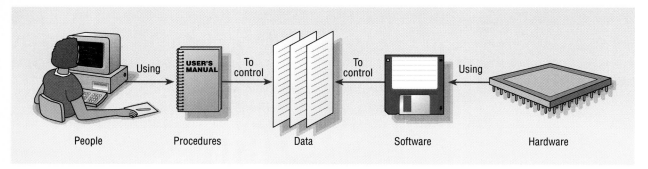

| People | Procedures | Data | Software | Hardware |

## PEOPLE

Computer systems are developed by people and for people. People build and control computer systems to help them make decisions, solve problems, and be creative. The components of a computer system are brought together by people. These people fall into two categories: computer users and computer professionals.

### Computer Users

The driving force behind the development of computer systems are the computer users. Users identify problems and then direct the computer system to produce information that supports solutions. People's demands for answers and assistance push forward the development of new computer technology.

A computer user applies the information produced by a computer. For example, users include anyone who requests a phone number from directory assistance, withdraws money through an automatic-teller machine (ATM), or watches a movie animated by a computer. At times you may become a computer user by circumstance rather than by choice. For example, choosing an outside activity according to the weather report is an action that depends on a computer. Weather forecasts result from computer analysis of weather data. Indirectly, the information a computer provides influences your decision. In many situations like this, you are a user, but not by direct choice. You can, however, choose whether or not you will be an *informed user.*

Informed users understand how the components of a computer system work together to perform a task. They know the capabilities and limitations of a computer. Most important, informed users can employ computer output for their own benefit and for the benefit of others.

Increasingly, users in all types of jobs are satisfying their computer needs without the need for specialists through *end-user computing.* This implies that the end user is responsible for data entry, computer operations, and utilizing the resulting output. Many of these people go on to become *user-developers,* who design and test their own computer applications. As a result, end-user computing has allowed them to meet their own processing needs with minimal aid from computer professionals.

**2.2**

An informed user takes responsibility for all aspects of the IPOS cycle, gaining total control over the information produced.

## Computer Professionals

*Computer professionals* are people who work directly with the development and operation of computer technology. Some computer professionals help users design computer-assisted solutions. Others operate and repair the computer equipment. Management of data, end-user training, and all computer acquisitions in an organization are the responsibilities of computer professionals. Interesting computer-oriented career opportunities are found in systems development, operations, and management.

## Systems Development

The components of a computer system can be brought together in various ways. Local computer stores provide knowledgeable *computer salespeople* to help new users decide which software and hardware best meet their needs. The Closer Look at the end of this chapter details several questions you should ask when shopping for a new computer system.

Systems analysts are employed by larger organizations to work with users in developing computer systems that satisfy specific requirements. The analyst is the link between users and new technological innovations that improve personal productivity. Users describe what they need to an analyst, who then coordinates the development of a new system. This process could involve purchasing new computer software and equipment. Other times it means linking existing hardware into a computer network. In this way users and systems analysts work together to build productive computer systems.

When new information is needed, *programmers* translate program specifications and requirements, written by a team of analysts and users, into computer programs. Their primary duties are writing and testing the instructions to be used by the computer.

**2.3**

Programmers write and review system documentation as a basis for their work in creating new software or modifying existing programs.

To accomplish this, programmers first determine what kinds of processing must be performed. Then they construct a sequence of computer operations that complete those processing requirements, and code the operations in a programming language. Finally, they thoroughly test the program to check for errors in logic or coding.

Sometimes it is more efficient and cost-effective to adapt an existing program to meet new needs, rather than write an entirely new program. These *program revisions* are often made to improve an application or bring it into compliance with changing laws or company policies. In fact, 50 to 75 percent of the lifelong cost of a program occurs in keeping it up-to-date.

## Operations

To support end-user computer operations, many organizations have **help desks** staffed by computer professionals, who answer questions users may have about computer operations, software applications, and hardware problems. Job responsibilities also include responding to emergencies, such as recovering lost data or restarting a computer after a power outage.

In a *computer center,* organizations can centralize computer professionals and hardware resources. Computer centers employ a variety of specialized operations personnel to oversee the daily IPOS cycles. Larger computer centers also have *service technicians* on staff, who perform repairs and maintenance. Operations personnel work at several different levels of responsibility: data entry, computer operations, and the control of computer center equipment and output. When the computer resources are shared in a network, specially trained *network engineers* are responsible for keeping hardware and software working for connected users.

The work performed within a computer center follows the IPOS cycle common to all computer systems. Although user-developers may be working on their own, an organization has many large or routine processing jobs, such as payroll or sales reports, that require operations personnel. In these cases, *control clerks* supply data to *data entry operators,* who input the data into the computer. *Computer operators* ensure that all equipment is functioning properly and are responsible for daily maintenance of storage devices and printers. They also make sure that scheduled computer programs are run on time. Output from the programs is given back to the control clerk, who delivers the information to the appropriate users and schedules when programs are run. Finally, *data librarians* catalog and store important tapes and disks in fireproof tape/disk libraries when not in use. The entire IPOS cycle is reflected in the tasks of operations personnel.

## Management

Responsibility for ensuring that the computer resources of an organization are used effectively belongs to the *information systems manager* (Figure 2.4). This person coordinates employees so that computing jobs are completed on schedule and within

An information systems manager oversees an organization's computer resources.

## DID YOU KNOW?
### ...ABOUT TROUBLESHOOTING TIPS

When you're having computer problems, the last thing you want to do is thumb through pages and pages of information, looking for a solution. So here are some quick, basic tips to put you on the road to repair:

- Walk away from the problem momentarily to clear your head. Relax, take a walk, order a pizza—anything to take your mind off the situation for a while.

- Look for the obvious. Are all cables plugged in securely? Is there paper in the printer? Is there a diskette in the diskette drive you're trying to use? Is the monitor turned on?

- Look for clues in locating the problem. (Remember, the main components are the computer case, the monitor, the keyboard, and the printer.) If the computer will not boot up at all, it is probably a hardware problem. If only one key on the keyboard is not working and the others are, the keyboard is probably faulty.

- Reboot. If you cannot locate the source of the problem, try starting all over again. The problem may even solve itself.

- If you can't locate the problem yourself, don't be afraid to ask for help. Bring a friend to your computer, call a technical support line, or take your computer to a repair shop.

*Source: PC Novice,* Premium Issue, December 1, 1992, vol. 3, page 62.

budget. Managers also analyze computer operations to detect inefficiencies and improper or illegal uses of the system, and they look at opportunities for improvement. In most organizations, information systems managers work closely with top-level executives on decisions concerning computer resources and operations throughout the organization.

Organizations manage their information technology in many ways. Unfortunately, in some cases no one is officially responsible for the computer technology and associated information resources. This lack of management can result in inefficient, improper, or illegal use of computer hardware and software. Once an information systems manager is designated, other related management positions are added as the organization's information system grows. Often database and network administrators are hired to work with end users in managing the sophisticated computer systems found in larger organizations.

People—whether they are users, analysts, programmers, operators, or managers—must all work together to make a computer system function properly. At times, one person may perform several jobs. When using a personal computer system, one person often does everything. In larger operations several people are involved with a computer system. For the successful operation of that system, coordination of effort is imperative.

### DATA

The second component of a computer system, data, represents facts about people, things, ideas, and events. For example, glasses, a video of a bicycle race, brown hair, Lincoln's Gettysburg Address, and six feet tall all are items of data. Taken individually, they have little to do with each other. When data items are combined and processed to form information, however, these items have meaning for people. From the above list, glasses, brown hair, and six feet tall can be extracted. Combined on a driver's license, these data items could form a partial description of your brother. These same pieces of data in another situation could be describing Abraham Lincoln. If Lincoln's Gettysburg Address is heard while pictures of Civil War battlefields are shown, this information can make a history lesson more interesting. The racing video combined with the coach's comments describing the cyclists' styles could be used to improve an athlete's performance or teach racing techniques to others.

## ▧ Organizing Data

For processing by a computer, data is organized into bits. People, however, have historically organized numeric and textual data into a convenient hierarchy. The most fundamental unit of text or numeric data is the character, represented in Figure 2.5 by a single letter, number, or symbol. A related group of characters is referred to as a *field*. A related group of fields is known as a *record*. Records that reflect a common meaning or use are grouped together to form a *file*. To understand these relationships, consider how the data on your driver's license is organized. The license number, CO248615 (Figure 2.5), is a field made up of numeric and alphabetic characters. Sometimes a single character, such as M or F—indicating the gender of the driver—can be used as a field. Your photograph on the license can be another field. Additional fields hold data about physical descriptions, including hair color, height, weight, and need for corrective lenses. When combined into a record, a driver's license, these data relationships become apparent. In this case, the record provides information about the driver's identity and appearance.

When several driver's licenses are brought together, they can be analyzed to produce even more information. This collection of licenses—or records—constitutes a file. A file groups similar records that can be summarized to increase knowledge. For example, examination of all licenses in California can show how many drivers in the state are over 65 years old. Additional information can be obtained by processing related records as a file.

At times people must use several files to meet their information needs. Information contained in one file is often related to information in several other files. For example, the file of traffic violations and the file of licensed drivers have license numbers in common. The use of data from both files would help state agencies identify the names and addresses of drivers with outstanding tickets.

Computer systems allow people to share, modify, and manipulate files to increase their knowledge. Cross-referencing files is made easier with the aid of a database program that integrates related files into a common database. Users of databases are able to access information selectively, according to their specific needs.

Data is not always organized into databases or even fields and records. Audiovisual and physical data are often stored as files. Many times, further subdivision is not

## 2.5

A database contains related files which are organized into records. Each record contains text and numeric data organized into fields.

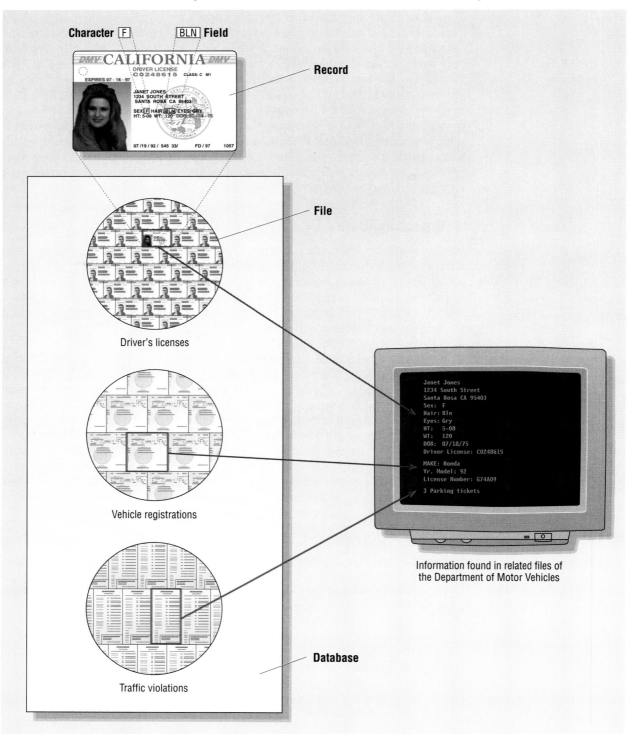

Character F        BLN Field

Record

File

Driver's licenses

Vehicle registrations

Traffic violations

Database

Information found in related files of
the Department of Motor Vehicles

**2.6**

Movies, music videos, and other audiovisual data can be edited using a computer and special software.

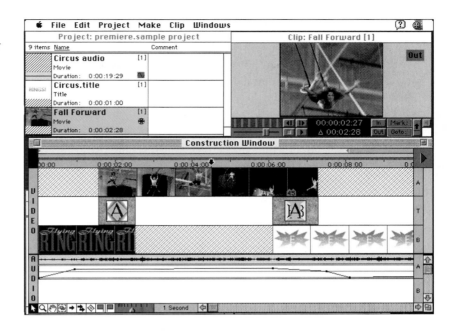

practical or useful. Self-contained data items that have meaning by themselves are sometimes referred to as an *object*. A photograph, song, or movie becomes an object when it is converted to a computer-usable format. Objects can be inserted into other objects or files. For example, photographs are inserted into a text file when writing a newspaper article.

## Data Versus Information

Complete, correct, and timely data is essential to the successful completion of the IPOS cycle. Computers have impressive capabilities, but they do not have the intuition or judgment to find data entry errors. Data entry personnel must check the correctness of input data. The accuracy of information depends on the quality with which the data is input. This notion is the basis for what computer professionals refer to as *GIGO:* garbage in, garbage out.

As data is accumulated and processed, it becomes information, a valuable product in its own right. People use computers to obtain information, and the foundation of information is data. Without information, many human and organizational functions would be stymied. If your school lost all its student records, for example, you would have a difficult time proving you completed required courses. If your bank's data files were destroyed, there would be no record of your accounts, and all your savings could be lost. Loss of data on an airline reservation system could cause chaos all over the world. As you can see, collections of data are major assets in large organizations and for individuals. It is necessary that the data be kept secure.

There are costs to creating information from data. Besides the obvious price of buying hardware and software, training users, and maintaining the computer system, there is one nonfinancial cost. When data is processed into information, it is no longer presented its original form. The data may be summarized into a total or a chart. At the cost of reducing the data that we see, information may be clearer and more useful.

## PROCEDURES

*Procedures* are the third component of a computer system. They are systematic courses of action that help people use software, data, and hardware. Procedures identify what needs to be done and how to do it properly. They also help new users understand how to work with computer systems and what to do if something goes wrong. A typical set of procedures for a session with a personal computer might include the following:

- Turning on all the hardware components of a computer system
- Formatting a new disk
- Running an application program
- Inputting text and scanning related photographs
- Verifying the correctness and completeness of the data entered
- Saving the input on a formatted disk
- Preparing the printer for output
- Printing a document
- Copying data files onto a second disk as backup
- Turning off the hardware

### Operating Procedures

Anyone owning or operating a personal computer must follow procedures. Before a computer can be put to work, *operating procedures* are used to turn on the machine. Other operating procedures include instructions on locating, copying, and erasing files on a disk. They are, in fact, the rules for using any hardware or software correctly. *Communication procedures* are used to link one computer to others and facilitate sending data among them.

Procedures exist for every computer application. Once equipment is on, users need *data entry procedures* that describe the preparation and input of data. This would include a manual check of data before entry to ensure it is accurate and complete. The term *verification* is used when the data entry operator is responsible for checking data for errors. Data should be verified after it is entered and before it is processed.

When computer programs check for errors as part of data entry procedures, this is called *error detection*. For example, the data entry operator visually verifies that every address entered is correct, while a computer program performs error detection by checking each telephone number field for nonnumeric characters. Responding to and eliminating processing errors requires *error recovery procedures*. For example, changing a grade that was incorrectly entered is an error recovery procedure. Service technicians and users follow *preventive maintenance procedures* when cleaning equipment and running checks on computer circuitry. Preventive maintenance procedures help keep the computer and other hardware in good operating condition. A task as simple as cleaning a computer keyboard should be regarded as important. Another maintenance procedure is cleaning the disk drive's read/write heads, which input and output disk-stored data. Printers, too, must be cleaned regularly.

In addition, informed users and operators should protect their computer files by following *backup procedures*. Making a copy, or *backup,* of data and information onto a tape or second disk minimizes the possibility of losing data.

J. Presper Eckert (far left) and John W. Mauchly (fourth from right) with the ENIAC development team.

# John W. Mauchly

(1907-1980)

The war effort of the early 1940s and the increase in the level of sophistication of circuitry influenced several research groups to attempt to build an electronic computer for aiding the armed services. In England the war brought the need to break German military codes faster than could be done manually. The end of 1943 marked the initial operation in England of the Colossus, the world's first working electronic computer. It could decode messages 12 times faster than any previous machine.

At the same time, the U.S. government signed a contract with the University of Pennsylvania to develop an electronic computer for calculating artillery trajectories. John W. Mauchly and J. Presper Eckert met at the University of Pennsylvania while Mauchly was a professor and Eckert a lab instructor. Together they designed and built the Electronic Numerical Integrator and Calculator (ENIAC), completed in 1946. The ENIAC weighed 30 tons and contained 17,000 vacuum tubes, 70,000 resistors, and 5 million soldered joints. ENIAC was able to perform 5,000 additions per second and used so much power it caused the lights to dim in one section of Philadelphia.

# J. Presper Eckert

(1919-1995)

Unlike the Colossus, the ENIAC was considered a general-purpose computer because it was able to perform a wide variety of jobs very quickly. However, it was not programmable by today's definition. To change ENIAC's program, it was necessary to rewire the master program circuits, requiring much expertise and time. Their later collaboration, the UNIVAC, was used by the Census Bureau in 1951. Mauchly went on to found ACM (Association of Computing Machinery) and worked for Remington Rand. Always good at conceptualizing new ideas, he later formed his own firm, Dynatrend, which forecasts the weather and stock market trends. Eckert continued work in the electronics field, receiving 85 patents and the National Science Foundation's National Medal of Science.

**2.7**

At this center a technician follows troubleshooting procedures to help users solve equipment problems.

### Emergency Procedures

Users handle a computer *crash*, or failure, with *emergency procedures*. These procedures may enable people to recover important data and start the system working again. Often, standardized emergency procedures are included in computer manuals. Many computer manufacturers have established emergency telephone numbers where experts answer users' questions in the event of a crash.

People use *troubleshooting procedures* to locate the cause of a crash, One of the most important troubleshooting procedures involves using *diagnostic software* to track down malfunctioning components in a computer. With diagnostic software, a user can detect and eliminate some problems before more damage is done.

Procedures are essential to the upkeep of any computer system. The cost of implementing these procedures is far less than the potential costs of repairing neglected systems or recovering lost data.

### HARDWARE

The fourth computer system component, hardware, comes in many configurations, depending on what the computer system is designed to do. Hardware can fill several floors of a large office building or can fit in a notebook. Different types of hardware are used for each step of the IPOS cycle.

**2.8**

The keyboard and mouse are common types of input hardware.

## Input Hardware

Input hardware is used to enter data into the computer. The keyboard at the ticket outlet where you reserve seats for a concert is a type of input hardware. In Figure 2.8, a draftsperson uses a mouse to create drawings for blueprints. A *mouse* is an input device that a user moves around on a flat surface. Its movements become input and are duplicated on-screen. The user locates program options by using the mouse to point to the related screen icon. Pressing a button on the mouse activates the desired option.

Even small grocery stores are using specialized input devices. A cashier uses a scanner to enter your grocery items directly with input hardware that is either handheld or part of a cash register. The device sends the data into a computer that prints your receipt and reorders stock.

## Processing Hardware

The computer itself is considered processing hardware. As shown in Figure 2.9, a computer is composed primarily of a memory unit and a processing unit. The memory unit, or *memory*, provides temporary storage for input data, programs, and the results of processing. The processing unit, or *processor*, interprets the program instructions in memory, controls the flow of data into and out of memory, and performs arithmetic and logical operations. The processor fetches the program instructions one at a time from memory, along with any needed data. After that instruction is followed, results are sent to memory and the next instruction is fetched. This cycle is repeated until the program is completed.

**2.9**

A computer uses program instructions in memory to perform calculations and comparisons by an internal processor.

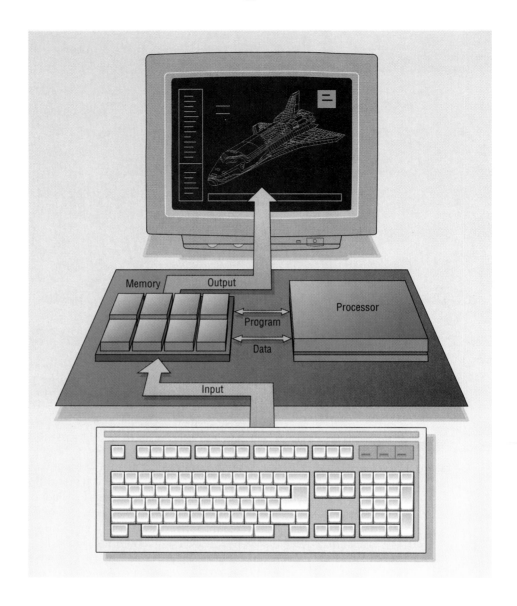

Processing hardware can be a small embedded computer performing a single task or a large *mainframe* working on many concurrent tasks. Describing the most powerful computers as mainframes dates back to a time when computers were filled with racks of vacuum tubes and miles of wire. This term is used today to describe very powerful machines that often house several processors and large amounts of memory. Mainframe computers can handle the different processing needs of many users at the same time.

*Minicomputers* service a different user need. A minicomputer can handle a limited number of users and programs at the same time using a single processor. Often this is all a small business, laboratory, or workgroup of users would need. Sometimes a network of minicomputers is used in place of a single mainframe.

Computer systems designed to be used by one person at a time are called ***personal computers***, or ***PCs***. Many personal computers are portable and some even operate on rechargeable batteries. Personal computers are also referred to as *microcomputers*. Other common names for personal computers are discussed in chapter 5.

## ■ Output Hardware

Processed information is provided to the user through output hardware. The two primary forms of output hardware are monitors and printers. A ***monitor*** displays information on a screen for temporary use. Directory assistance operators, for instance, enter a name into a computer, which displays the telephone number on a monitor. On the other hand, printers deliver copies of output on paper for distribution or long-term use. Printed output include grade reports, bills, and junk mail.

## ■ Storage Hardware

Storage hardware is necessary because the computer's memory is temporary and has only a limited capacity for holding data. The two most common types of storage hardware are ***tape drives*** and ***disk drives***. These drives can save (write) data on a tape or disk and copy (read) it back into the computer's memory upon command. Computer systems are much like stereo systems in this regard. In both systems, when the machinery is not in use, the music or the data must be stored in a common machine-readable format for later use.

There also are similarities in the storage media. Both music and data can be stored on a ***compact disc (CD)***, as shown in Figure 2.10. This information is permanent, however, and cannot be changed. When users need to save their own data, they use a

**2.10**

Compact discs, also called CD-ROMs, store text, music, photographs, and video images.

**2.11**

A computer system includes input, processing, output, and storage hardware.

## Common Computer Hardware

■ **Input Hardware**

Keyboard

Mouse

Scanner

■ **Processing Hardware**
*(contains memory and processor)*

Embedded computer

Personal computer

Minicomputer

Mainframe

■ **Output Hardware**

Monitor

Printer

■ **Storage Hardware**

Disk drive

Tape drive

tape, floppy disk, or hard disk; these are recordable storage media. *Floppy disks (diskettes)* are removable, and a diskette drive uses any number of disks, one at a time. Hard disk drives are built inside the computer, and the *hard disk* is usually not removable. Unlike most CDs, diskettes and hard disks may have data erased and recorded on them many times. Hard disks hold more data and are more expensive than floppy disks. In addition, hard disk drives provide faster access to the data on disk than do diskettes. Future technology holds the promise of inexpensive CDs that can be recorded and erased by the average user.

Thus, each step of the cycle—input, processing, output, and storage—has an accompanying set of hardware (see Figure 2.11). A computer is the traditional equipment used for processing. Attached equipment used for storing, entering, and outputting data are generally referred to as *peripherals*.

## SOFTWARE

Software is the final computer system component. These computer programs instruct the hardware how to conduct processing. The computer is merely a general-purpose machine that requires specific software to perform a given task. Computers can input, calculate, compare, and output data as information. Software determines the order in which these operations are performed. Like data, programs are stored on tapes or disks when not in use. When needed, the computer reads the programs from storage hardware into the computer's memory. The instructions in the programs then direct processing. Programs usually fall into one of two categories: application software and system software.

## ■ Application Software

*Application software* is a type of program that solves specific user-oriented processing problems. Business applications include payroll, accounting, inventory, budgeting, and personnel management. Video games and checkbook-balancing programs are personal applications.

Another type of application software is personal productivity programs. This software allows the user to apply the computer to common problems and tasks an individual may have, even if not part of an organization. Often, personal productivity software is sold in packages that contain the program itself, a copyright agreement, and a user's manual with operating instructions, as shown in Figure 2.12. The most popular personal productivity programs fall into four basic categories: word processing, electronic spreadsheet, graphics, and database.

**Word Processing Programs**   *Word processing programs* expedite report and letter writing. They enable the user to insert, move, copy, and erase words, sentences, and paragraphs on a monitor. The programs will center headings, number pages, and double-space a document when instructed by the user. The software allows the user to control the printed form of the document as well.

**2.12**

A software package contains the storage medium (disk or CD) with the program, user's manual, copyright agreement, and operating instructions.

**Electronic Spreadsheets** *Electronic spreadsheet* software creates documents containing numbers organized into columns and rows for processing and analysis. Financial data, such as budgets or monthly income statements, are often organized this way. An electronic spreadsheet could also be used as a gradebook by a teacher. Because the spreadsheet software formats data and performs arithmetic operations or complicated formulas, it is a valuable timesaving tool.

**Graphics Packages** *Graphics packages* generate pictures, drawings, charts, and diagrams on-screen or on paper. Some graphics software is guided by information produced from electronic spreadsheets. Numbers from the spreadsheet can be used to draw bars on a graph, points on a diagram, or slices of a pie chart. Other graphics software enables users to draw pictures. The screen becomes a blank canvas, and a mouse or other input device becomes a paintbrush. Graphics software often enables users to select shades and colors for the drawings. Specially equipped printers can paint the computer-generated drawings on paper or film.

**2.13**

Personal productivity software helps people use a computer to write letters (word processing), manage budgets (electronic spreadsheet), create charts and graphs (graphics package), or organize related data (database program).

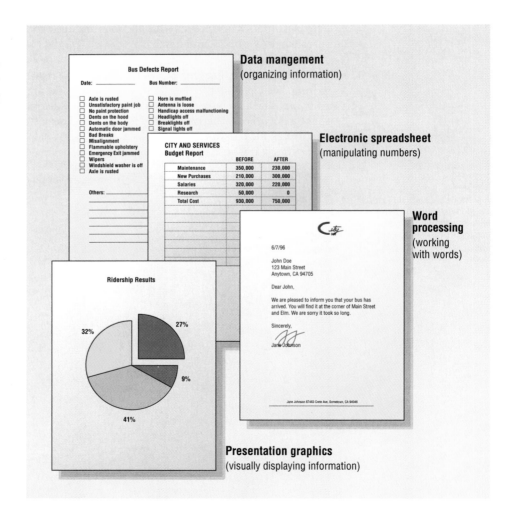

**Data mangement**
(organizing information)

**Electronic spreadsheet**
(manipulating numbers)

**Word processing**
(working with words)

**Presentation graphics**
(visually displaying information)

**Databases**   Software that sets up and maintains related data files is called a *database program.* Database programs assist users in organizing data to answer questions and solve problems. Database software provides capabilities for loading and modifying databases. These packages enable users to extract, format, and print pertinent data with ease. A school's registrar, for example, could request information from a database instead of sifting through file cabinets full of student records. The registrar might ask such questions as: Which classes filled during the first week of registration? How many out-of-state students are enrolled? Which classes still have empty seats? Within seconds, a database program could provide lists of students or classes meeting the specified conditions. Building or using a database requires an understanding of the many ways in which data is interrelated and how the data can be used.

## 2.14

System software controls the flow of application software and related data in and out of the computer's memory.

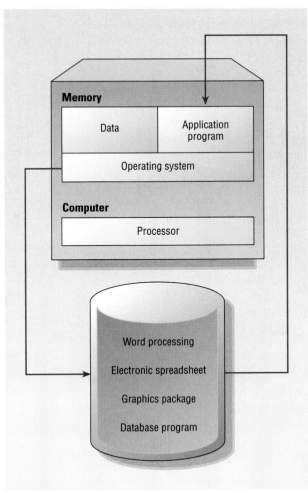

## System Software

The second type of software, *system software,* controls internal computer activities. An *operating system,* for example, is a collection of system programs that aid in the operation of a computer regardless of which application software is being used. When a computer is first turned on, one of the system programs is *booted,* or loaded, into the computer's memory. This software contains information about memory capacity, the model of the processor, the disk drives to be used, and more. Once the system software is loaded, the application software can be brought in (Figure 2.14).

System programs are designed for specific pieces of hardware. These programs coordinate peripheral hardware and computer activities. For example, microcomputers primarily use disks for storing data and programs. Therefore, personal computer users initially use a disk with the *disk operating system (DOS)* to boot their equipment. When the computer is turned on, one system program from the DOS disk is loaded into memory. As the user works with the computer, DOS will transfer input from keyboard to memory, then from memory to storage, and allocate storage space on disks for data files. Later, DOS may transfer data from memory or a disk to a printer. Many of the services provided by DOS are transparent to users; that is, the services are performed without users being aware of this support.

Data communications within and among computer systems is handled by system software. *Communication software* transfers data from one computer system to another. These programs usually provide users with data security and error checking along with physically transferring data between the two computers' memories.

# A Closer Look at Buying a Computer System

**P**urchasing your first personal computer system can be a little intimidating. Approach this purchase as you would that of any household appliance. First and foremost, you should have a good idea of how you would use a personal computer. If you don't know how you would use a computer, perhaps you don't need one yet. In addition, establish a budget and work within it. What follows are a series of questions users often ask when buying their first computer system.

**Q: What comes first—hardware or software?**

**A:** Software drives hardware. Look at your application needs and talk to others about what programs they use. Once you have decided on which application packages you want, their use will dictate minimum hardware requirements.

**Q: Should I be concerned about compatibility?**

**A:** Yes, keep in mind the people with whom you will be sharing data, ideas, and information. Existing systems at school or work, and those belonging to friends, can influence your decisions. Compatibility concerns the sharing of programs, data, and operating procedures among hardware components.

**A:** Reading computer magazines and talking to friends can help you focus on reliable computer software and hardware. Computer magazines often contain consumer reports on selected software and hardware, which identify important features and test comparable products.

## Summary of Features—Personal/Workgroup Lasers

| In alphabetical order by company | Apple LaserWriter Select 360 | Brother HL-630 | Canon LBP-860 | C. Itoh ProWriter CI-8Xtra | HP LaserJet 4M Plus |
|---|---|---|---|---|---|
| Dimensions (HWD, in inches) | 8×15×18.3 | 7.2×14.4×14.3 | 12×17×16 | 8.6×15.5×15.9 | 11.7×16.6×15.9 |
| Weight (pounds) | 26 | 16.6 | 37 | 11 | 37 |
| Engine type/Rated speed (pages per minute) | Laser/10 | Laser/6 | Laser/8 | Laser/8 | Laser/12 |
| Instruction set | RISC | CISC | RISC | RISC | RISC |
| Standard/maximum RAM | 7 MB, 16 MB | .5 MB, 2 MB | 2 MB, 34 MB | 4 MB, 20 MB | 6 MB, 38 MB |
| **INTERFACES** | | | | | |
| Parallel/serial port | ■ ■ | ■ Optional | ■ ■ | ■ Optional | ■ ■ |
| Bidirectional/ECP parallel support | ■ ■ | ■ □ | □ □ | ■ □ | ■ □ |
| LocalTalk/SCSI port | ■ □ | □ □ | ■ □ | □ □ | ■ □ |
| Automatic interface switching | ■ | ■ | ■ | ■ | ■ |
| Simultaneously active ports | ■ | ■ | ■ | ■ | ■ |
| **PAPER HANDLING** | | | | | |
| Capacity of each standard cassette (sheets) | 250 (letter), 50 (multipurpose) | 200 (adjustable: holds sizes from 3×5 inches to 8.5×14 inches) | 250 (letter), 100 (multipurpose), 75 (envelope) | 250 (multipurpose) | 250 (letter), 100 (multipurpose) |
| Rated maximum paper weight (pounds) | 32 | 36 | 28 | 32 | 36 |
| **FONTS AND FEATURES** | | | | | |
| PostScript support | Adobe Level 2 | N/A | Adobe Level 2 (optional) | N/A | Adobe Level 2 |
| Maximum resolution in PostScript (dpi) | 600×600 | N/A | 600×600 | N/A | 600×600 |
| Number of Type 1 fonts | 35 | N/A | N/A | N/A | 35 |
| Resolution enhancement | ■ | □ | □ | ■ | ■ |
| **CUSTOMER SUPPORT** | | | | | |
| Toll-free technical support | ■ | ■ | ■ | ■ | ■ |
| BBS or online service | □ | ■ | ■ | ■ | ■ (CompuServe) |
| Warranty (parts and labor) | 1 year | 1 year | 2 years | 1 year | 1 year |

■ = YES    □ = NO    N/A = Not applicable: The product does not have this feature

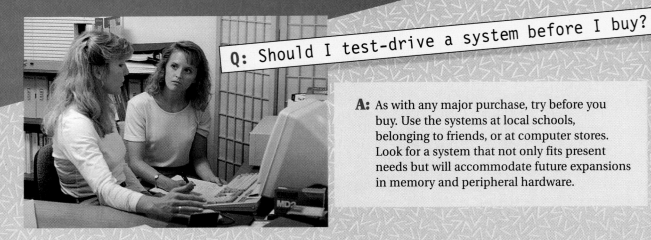

**Q: Should I test-drive a system before I buy?**

**A:** As with any major purchase, try before you buy. Use the systems at local schools, belonging to friends, or at computer stores. Look for a system that not only fits present needs but will accommodate future expansions in memory and peripheral hardware.

**Q: How can I get the best deal on a system?**

**A:** When it comes time to buy, the training and service provided by a local full-service computer store must be balanced against the lower costs offered by discount stores and mail-order houses. Check to see if any system and application software is included in the price. Compare the length of time the warranties are valid. Also check whether repairs can be made at your home (on-site) or if you must take the faulty hardware to a service center.

**Q: Do I need a special room or any extra equipment to set up the system properly?**

**A:** Most rooms with a desk and available electrical outlets can serve as your new computer center. Set up the system in a relatively clean, cool, dry place. You may want a surge protector to minimize damage due to power fluctuations. Give yourself plenty of work room, good lighting to avoid glare, and storage space for easy access to disks and manuals.

**Q:** Once the system is set up, who will help me get started?

**A:** Training sessions can help you learn about backup, maintenance, troubleshooting, and other procedures. Special classes may be offered or included with the software applications you have purchased. Otherwise, check local computer stores, user groups, colleges, and community education centers for classes.

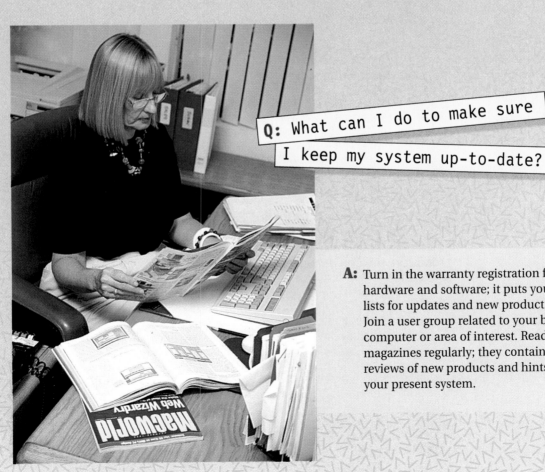

**Q:** What can I do to make sure I keep my system up-to-date?

**A:** Turn in the warranty registration for your hardware and software; it puts you on mailing lists for updates and new product information. Join a user group related to your brand of computer or area of interest. Read computer magazines regularly; they contain helpful reviews of new products and hints on using your present system.

## CHAPTER FACTS

- A computer system comprises five components: people, hardware, software, data, and procedures.

- People can be users or computer professionals. A user applies information produced by a computer. Informed users participating in end-user computing understand a computer's uses and limitations. User-developers can set up and program their own computers.

- Computer professionals work directly with computer technology. They can be involved with systems development, operations, or management.

- Professionals who are a part of the systems development process include salespeople, systems analysts, and programmers.

- Operations-oriented professionals help end users solve problems, enter data, operate equipment, control the flow of data into and out of the computer center, store unused tapes and disks in libraries, maintain networks, and service equipment.

- Information systems managers supervise work and personnel in a computer center.

- Text and numeric data are often organized into fields, which make up records. Records are combined into files. Related files may be organized into databases.

- Audiovisual or physical data, such as video recordings or sounds, are referred to as objects when in a computer-usable format.

- Procedures are instructions to help people use data, software, and hardware. They can relate to data entry, error recovery, preventive maintenance, operating, communications, backup, emergencies, and troubleshooting.

- Hardware is classified by the IPOS cycle. Input hardware may be a keyboard, mouse, or scanner. Processing hardware consists of the memory unit and processing unit within all sizes of computers. Output hardware may be a monitor or printer. Storage hardware is usually a disk drive.

- Software is divided into two categories: application software and system software. Application software solves users' specific processing problems. System software is the series of programs that control the computer's resources.

- Four common types of application software are word processing programs, electronic spreadsheets, graphics packages, and database programs.

- Disk operating systems and communication software are types of system software.

---
**TERMS TO REMEMBER**
---

| | | |
|---|---|---|
| application software | electronic spreadsheet | mouse |
| communication software | field | object |
| compact disc (CD) | file | peripheral |
| computer center | floppy disk | personal computer (PC) |
| computer system | graphics package | procedure |
| database program | hard disk | processor |
| diagnostic software | help desk | record |
| disk drive | mainframe | system software |
| diskette | memory | tape drive |
| disk operating system | minicomputer | word processing program |
| (DOS) | monitor | |

---
**MIX AND MATCH**
---

*Complete the following definitions with the Terms to Remember.*

1. A group of related fields is called a(n) _____.

2. _____ is the term meaning the screen as output hardware.

3. Software that helps users write reports and letters is referred to as a(n) _____.

4. A group of related records is a(n) _____.

5. A(n) _____ is processing hardware that handles a limited number of users and programs simultaneously using a single processor.

6. The centralized location for computer hardware and related professionals is called the _____.

7. Computer _____ is the circuitry inside the computer that temporarily stores data and programs.

8. A(n) _____ is a systematic course of action.

9. A computer program that generates drawings and diagrams is referred to as a(n) _____.

10. Equipment attached to processing hardware for input and output is known as a(n) _____.

11. The _____ is the circuitry inside a computer that performs arithmetic and logical operations.

12. Software that organizes and maintains related data files is a(n) _____.

13. A(n) _____ is a large computer that houses several processors and vast amounts of memory.

14. Computer programs that control internal computer activities and external resources are called _____.

15. A(n) _____ is a program that organizes numbers and associated text into rows and columns.

## REVIEW QUESTIONS

1. Define the Terms to Remember.

2. What are the five components of a computer system?

3. How do the skills of a user-developer differ from those of an informed user?

4. What career options are available to computer professionals?

5. Why are program revisions made to working software?

6. What type of data is organized into fields and records?

7. Data must have what three characteristics for successful completion of the IPOS cycle?

8. How are each of these procedures used: operating, data entry, error recovery, preventive maintenance, backup, emergency, and troubleshooting?

9. How is verification different from error detection?

10. Identify one type of input hardware, processing hardware, output hardware, and storage hardware.

11. What is included with a personal productivity software package?

12. What are the functions and types of data used for each of these application programs: word processing, electronic spreadsheet, graphics, and database?

13. What happens when you boot a computer?

14. Why would a user want to select application software before purchasing new hardware?

## APPLYING WHAT YOU'VE LEARNED

1. Identify three examples of computer systems you have seen or used. What are the five components of each system? If you are unsure of a component or the correct term to be used, describe what is included in that component.

2. Find several ads for one of the computer professional positions mentioned in the text. Remember that the actual name of the position may be different. Summarize requirements for experience and education, as well as pay and benefits offered.

3. When a computer system does not work properly or incorrect output appears, you often hear the excuse "It's the computer's fault!" In light of GIGO and the need for good procedures and well-trained people, what could be some possible causes of the following situations?
   a. This month's telephone bill is $35,600.
   b. Your mother's flight reservation back from Mexico is not listed on the airline's computer reservation system, but she has a ticket.
   c. When she applies for a loan, your sister is told she has a bad credit rating (but she has never applied for credit before).
   d. A computer-controlled heating/cooling system turns up the furnace when the temperature outside is 90 degrees.

4. Identify the content of the fields, records, and files for these applications:
   a. information about a patient entering a hospital for the first time
   b. a university's collection of data about currently enrolled students
   c. the customer ordering system for a fast-food restaurant

5. There is always the potential for trouble when procedures are not written down or when they are ignored. Some people say, "If at first it doesn't work, read the instructions." Make a list of procedures necessary in one of these situations or in a situation of your own choosing.
   a. using and maintaining a new car
   b. operating a special tool or piece of equipment you know how to use
   c. installing an electrical outlet or replacing a fuse
   d. cooking an involved dish such as baked Alaska

6. Find an article in a computer magazine that compares similar hardware, for example, two computers or two printers. What features or options are available? What testing procedures or comparisons were used? If several features are available, how would you rank these features from most important to least important? Which of the products would you purchase? Explain your reasoning.

# CHAPTER 3

# Software Interfaces

# FROM THE USER'S POINT OF VIEW

The software you purchase reflects not only your computing needs but your personal tastes as well. Whether you use a mouse or keyboard for input, there are common procedures for accessing data, selecting program options, and printing results. Being familiar with the common user interfaces discussed in this chapter makes learning to operate new software packages easier. You can minimize frustration when recovering from mistakes by understanding these basic software concepts.

## USER INTERFACES

General-purpose computer hardware is turned into a tool that solves specific problems through software. The specific instructions of a program determine how easy a computer system is to use, what gets done, and how the final results are presented. The combination of menu options, icons, and commands you use when working with a computer program is called the *user interface*.

Experienced end users feel comfortable using several of the common user interfaces. For example, Nancy Mitchell and friend Linda Frye just purchased a new adventure computer game on disk that explores a haunted house. Both friends were anxious to get the software running on their personal computers—they have a friendly competition to be the first to find the hidden key or trap door. Although their computer hardware is basically the same, the procedures Nancy and Linda use to explore the program features are quite different. They work with different user interfaces. Common user interfaces fall into one of four categories: command-driven, shell, graphical, or natural language.

## 3.1

Users interact with a program's user interface through a keyboard by entering commands or with a mouse by selecting menu options and activating icons.

## Command-Driven Interfaces

Nancy's computer system uses a ***command-driven interface*** for its system software. This interface recognizes a special set of keywords, symbols, and commands that initiate program options and operations. A ***screen prompt*** is used by most command-driven interfaces to indicate when the system is ready to accept a new command. A blinking ***cursor*** highlights where the computer is going to display what the user is typing. Specific key combinations entered through the keyboard allow the user to control the cursor location on-screen (see Figure 3.2).

Figure 3.3 shows a screen display of both the DOS prompt and the command Nancy uses to display the directory of her Haunted House disk. A ***disk directory*** contains the name, size, creation date, and creation time of each data file or program saved to the disk.

To find out how to start the game, Nancy could read the printed version of the user's manual or display an electronic copy of the manual on-screen. Instead she displays the ***readme file*** that often accompanies professionally developed software. Nancy knows that the readme file listed in the disk directory of Figure 3.3 will provide enough instructions to get her started and perhaps provide additional information about the program.

## 3.2

The special keys on the keyboard control cursor movement and other functions.

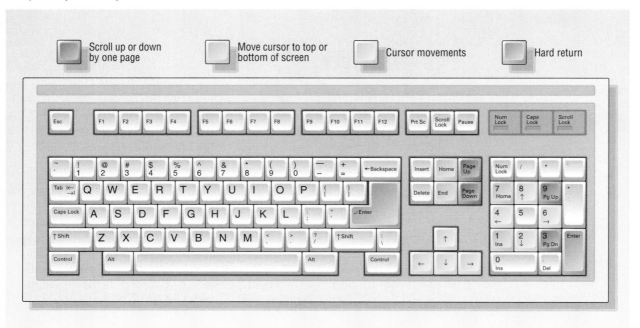

Before playing her new game, Nancy needs to install, or set up, the program on her computer system. She follows *(executes)* the installation program, answering questions about her computer system. These questions include information about the specific printer model, screen type, mouse type, and memory capacity of the computer. Many times these questions can be answered with single-character input such as Y (yes) or N (no). Once the game program is installed, Nancy starts Haunted House by typing the program name, haunt, after the screen prompt. Pressing the Enter key initiates program execution.

**3.3**

User interfaces let people control their computer systems by selecting various program options using menus, commands, or icons.

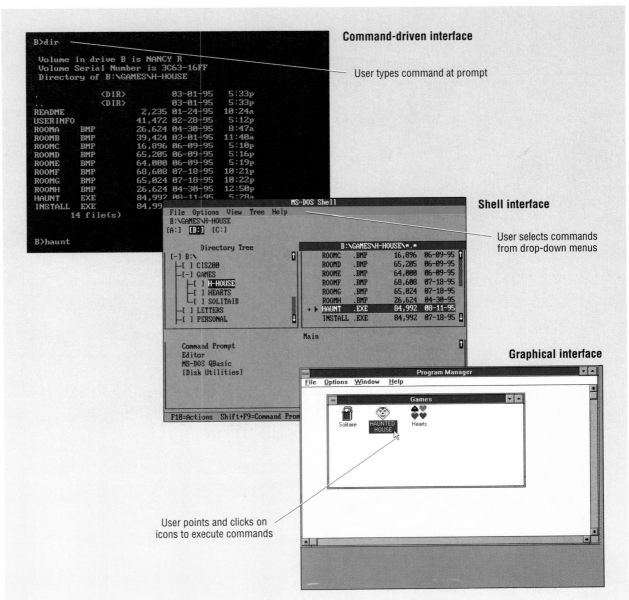

**Command-driven interface**

User types command at prompt

**Shell interface**

User selects commands from drop-down menus

**Graphical interface**

User points and clicks on icons to execute commands

What Nancy sees after starting the game is a series of color graphics depicting different rooms. She navigates through the rooms by entering different keywords. The game accepts commands such as West and Door or Pickup and Key. The user's manual and on-screen help displays list many of the key commands. Part of the game is to find commands that work in certain situations.

Command-driven interfaces date back to when users entered data primarily with a keyboard. Experienced users become extremely proficient with these commands. New users do not find memorizing commands very user-friendly, however. This is true in part because each command-driven interface has its own word order, spacing, abbreviations, and special symbols that make up the command *syntax*.

## ...ABOUT DESKTOP OPERATING SYSTEMS

### Windows 95

*Strengths:* Windows 95 combines the power of multitasking and memory management with improvements to the Windows 3.1 interface. New features include plug-and-play capabilities, support of workgroup computing, and improved network support.

*Weaknesses:* The first release may lack the maturity and stability of its competitors. When compared to Windows 3.1/DOS, Windows 95 requires substantially more memory and disk space.

### OS/2 (IBM)

*Strengths:* Runs several processing tasks simultaneously and doesn't crash when an application crash occurs. Serves as a highly stable and reliable platform.

*Weaknesses:* Requires substantial memory and disk space, and it operates only on Intel-based microprocessors. Native OS/2 applications are limited.

### UNIX

*Strengths:* User-friendly interfaces are now available, which put a familiar face on UNIX's powerful but difficult-to-use features, such as multitasking and multiuser support.

*Weaknesses:* Expensive compared with other operating systems. Can be complicated to install and administer.

### System 7.x (Mac OS)

*Strengths:* High stability and ease of use. Applications easier to master because of the consistent interface. Exhibits the best handling of graphics applications, compared with other systems.

*Weaknesses:* Requires state-of-the-art Macintosh hardware. Difficult to integrate into the Intel-oriented business world.

### Shells

A software *shell* helps users avoid memorizing different command syntaxes. A shell interfaces application programs with DOS. This allows users to perform common operating system functions, such as saving data or displaying a directory, without leaving the application software. Popular command-driven systems and application software often have compatible shells. Users navigate through a shell by selecting menu options, as shown in Figure 3.3. Menu options are highlighted by using the mouse or designated keys on the keyboard.

Menus are often used in application software as well, listing key commands for the program. The Haunted House program has menus labeled Door and Window. North, South, East, and West are options within the Door menu. When a menu option appears in a light color on-screen, the related activity is not available. If the room Nancy is in does not have a door in the north wall, for example, the menu option North is not highlighted when she is in that room.

### Graphical User Interfaces

In contrast, Linda's computer system uses a ***graphical user interface (GUI)***, pronounced "gooey." A mouse is used to control the location of a ***screen pointer*** within a GUI. Linda installs the Haunted House program by starting up the install program that comes on the program disks. Further instructions are in the user's manual.

Linda uses the mouse to move the pointer on top of the menu option or icon she desires, then *clicks* (presses) a mouse button to activate it. She runs the program by positioning the mouse pointer on the HAUNTED HOUSE icon (see Figure 3.3) and *double-clicking*—quickly pressing the mouse button twice. Users execute, or *launch*, programs by double-clicking on the associated icon.

Linda navigates through different rooms by using other features of a graphical user interface. To exit through a selected door, she clicks on the doorknob. When Linda wants to *drag*, or move, an object on-screen, she points to the object with the mouse, holds down the mouse button while moving the icon to a new location, and releases the button when the object is properly placed. For example, when Linda uncovers the skeleton key, she drags it across the screen and into her basket (icon) of goodies.

Using system software with a GUI also involves dragging and dropping icons into new screen locations. Linda can back up data files by duplicating the icon for that file and dragging one of the copies to a different disk icon. An outdated data file is removed from a disk by dragging its icon to the trash can (see Figure 3.4) or recycle bin icon. Many of the icons used with graphical user interfaces represent desktop accessories. Besides a bin, you will find icons representing file folders, calendars, calculators, clocks, and address books.

### Natural Language Interfaces

Technology is developing that allows users to activate program options by writing or speaking in their native languages. These ***natural language interfaces*** recognize the syntax of a language such as English or Japanese for increased user-friendliness. Interfaces that recognize spoken words are not widely available, although you can find natural language interfaces that accept keyboard entries. The Haunted House program with a natural language user interface must be extremely flexible to be effective. For instance,

**3.4**

Icons are dragged to new screen locations or dropped onto other icons to initiate program operations.

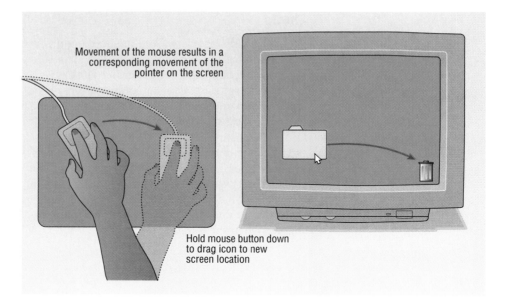

Movement of the mouse results in a corresponding movement of the pointer on the screen

Hold mouse button down to drag icon to new screen location

it should understand and act upon the entry, "let's see what's on the other side of that door by the lamp", regardless of the accent (or grammar skills) of the speaker. Currently, these systems are restricted to a specific domain, such as a game, and are limited in the number of words they recognize.

## EVALUATING SOFTWARE FEATURES

Properly designed software is user-friendly because it is self-explanatory and handles situations in a comfortable, common-sense approach. By selecting software you need and feel comfortable using, you can personalize your computer system.

The features of computer programs differ with the individual job performed and results desired. Some support specific user needs, others make the software easier to use. When evaluating different application packages, you should ask yourself these questions:

- Are the program and associated procedures easy to use?
- On which computers does the software work?
- Does the software come with help features, manuals, and other forms of easy-to-read documentation?
- Is there a telephone number I can call when the manuals and other documentation do not answer a question?
- Can this software access data stored by other programs and vice versa?
- How flexible is the program, and can it be used for more than one application?
- Does the software require special input or output hardware?
- How much memory does the program require?
- How much disk storage space is required to save it?

**3.5**

People look for flexible, user-friendly software packages that can share data with other programs.

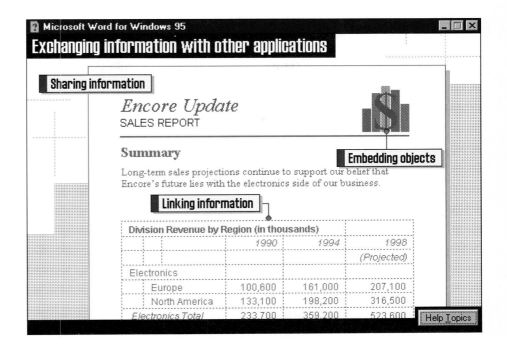

These features help us learn how to use the software effectively, minimize frustrations, and provide insights into future applications for the package.

## File Conventions, Suites, and Groupware

Some application packages stand alone. That is, they are not designed to share data with other programs. As use of computers increases, demand has grown for software that can share data with other applications. People discovered that spreadsheets could support information presented in a textual document. Also, a bar chart can clarify figures laid out in a spreadsheet. In short, people need the capability to combine formerly independent applications through use of common data files and objects.

The need to share data and objects led to the emergence of standards for text, database, and worksheet files as well as audio, film, and graphic objects. The *filename* uniquely identifies the file or object. A three-letter *filename extension* is added to the filename to identify the format of the data. Figure 3.6 identifies common file formats and their filename extensions.

Software developers have also addressed the need to share data through the development of *integrated software*. A single software package provides user interfaces for word processing, spreadsheet, and data management applications, which permits users to share data among those applications. The word processing feature of an integrated software package, however, could not be purchased separately.

In contrast, software manufacturers are now marketing *suites,* collections of separate application packages sold together that easily share common data and objects. A typical suite would contain word processing, spreadsheet, database, and communication programs as well as a program to aid in creating outlines and slides for presentations.

**3.6**

Three-letter filename extensions are added to the filename to identify the file format.

| Extension | Software | Description |
|---|---|---|
| .ASC | Many products | American Standard Code for Information Interchange (ASCII) |
| .BMP | Paintbrush | Bitmap graphic |
| .CAL | Calendar | Data—text |
| .CBT | Many products | Computer-based training data file |
| .COM | Many products | Command file |
| .CRD | Cardfile | Data—text |
| .DB | Paradox | Database file |
| .DBF | dBASE | Database file |
| .DOC | Many products | Data—text |
| .DOT | Word (Windows) | Document template |
| .DWG | AutoCAD | Data—3D drawing |
| .EXE | Many products | Executable file |
| .GIF | Many products | Internet Graphic Interchange Format |
| .PCX | Paintbrush | Data—graphic |
| .PIC | Lotus | Data—graphic |
| .TIF | Many products | Data—typeset |
| .TXT | Notepad | Data—text |
| .XLC | Excel | Data—graphic |
| .XLS | Excel | Data—spreadsheet |

Personal computer users connected through a network can be supported by *groupware*. These packages provide compatible data formats and integrated software, facilitating data and object sharing throughout the network. Groupware applications include common calendars and appointment scheduling, electronic mail, interactive conference calls, document sharing, and editing sessions with several users (Figure 3.7). This type of network application is discussed in chapter 4.

## ■ Object Linking and Embedding

When people working on common tasks can share data, everyone benefits from increased productivity. A salesperson might use a spreadsheet program to track personal sales, saving the spreadsheet in a file. The department manager can combine the sales data from several spreadsheet files in a graphics program, producing a chart showing

**3.7**

Computer users linked to a network use a groupware package to support common appointment calendars, document sharing, interactive conference calls, and group editing sessions.

increasing sales in the past year. While preparing a report to stockholders, someone in public relations could include the sales chart into a word processing document. If the original sales spreadsheet is changed, how does this affect all other copies of the data in other programs?

An object from one application program can be brought into another program in three ways: copying, embedding, and linking.

*Copying* simply makes a duplicate of the original object in another program, such as copying a company's trademark to the top of a report. When the original is altered, the copy is not affected; neither can the copy can be altered by the user.

When object *embedding* is done, a duplicate of the original is made in another program along with information on the application from which the original comes. When the original is altered, the embedded object stays intact. However, a user can edit the embedded object within the application program where it was embedded by calling up the original application program. For example, public relations embeds the sales chart in the shareholders' report and changes its colors by using a graphics package called from within the word processing program (see Figure 3.8).

To maintain an active connection between an original object and a duplicate of it in another document, object *linking* is used. In this case, a reference to the original object is maintained by the second application program. When the original object is modified, the user is given the option of automatically updating the linked versions in other documents or not updating the duplicates. The sales manager would want updated

**3.8**

Objects can be duplicated in other application programs by copying, object linking, and object embedding.

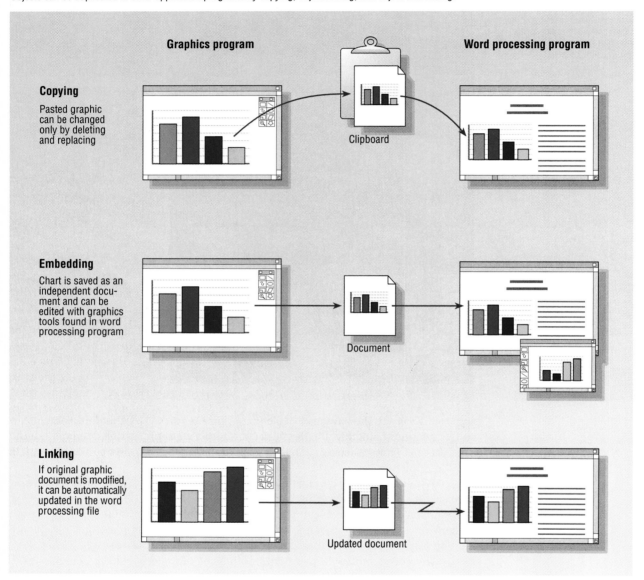

| | Graphics program | Clipboard | Word processing program |
|---|---|---|---|

**Copying**

Pasted graphic can be changed only by deleting and replacing

Clipboard

**Embedding**

Chart is saved as an independent document and can be edited with graphics tools found in word processing program

Document

**Linking**

If original graphic document is modified, it can be automatically updated in the word processing file

Updated document

data from salespeople until, perhaps, the end of the month. Then the link between a salesperson's spreadsheet data and the manager's chart could be disconnected. Next month's data would appear in a different chart.

## Windows and Multitasking

Integrated software and suites often are powerful enough to allow users to switch between two or more activities with a simple keystroke or click of the mouse. The operating systems

**3.9**

With multitasking, a computer can maintain operation of several tasks concurrently.

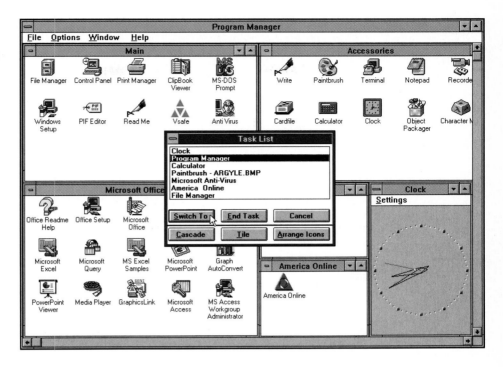

of some computers support *multitasking,* which enables the computer to maintain the operation of two or more independent programs concurrently. To track and allow user control over multiple operations, the computer screen is divided into sections, or *windows* (see Figure 3.9). Each window displays a menu or status report on a separate program or activity. Programs used to create a financial statement, for example, might use three windows. One would display the text of the report, generated through word processing software. The second could hold a spreadsheet. Graphics tying together the words and the numbers might occupy the third window. The windows allow the user to view activities in the programs while the links created through object linking would keep data in all three programs current (see Figure 3.9).

*Terminate stay resident (TSR)* programs are commonly found in operating systems using windows. The TSR program stays inactive, but in memory, while other applications programs are in use. A desktop program is a widely used TSR application. This program provides resources commonly found on a person's desk, such as a calendar, calculator, telephone directory, appointment schedule, and notepad. When the user needs a calendar to schedule a meeting, the desktop TSR can be accessed without exiting the active application program.

Imagine, for example, someone interrupted by a telephone call as he is trying to write a report with a word processing program. The caller is requesting the rescheduling of an important meeting. The user can activate the desktop TSR calendar and appointment schedule without interfering with the work in progress (see Figure 3.9). By pressing a combination of keys, the TSR program is activated. A menu appears in a window, and the user selects the calendar and appointment scheduling options. Once the meeting time is changed on the calendar, he deactivates the desktop TSR and continues working on the report. The scheduling activities take place within windows on-screen and do not affect the report.

**3.10**

A dialog box prompts the user for input through text boxes, list boxes, and buttons.

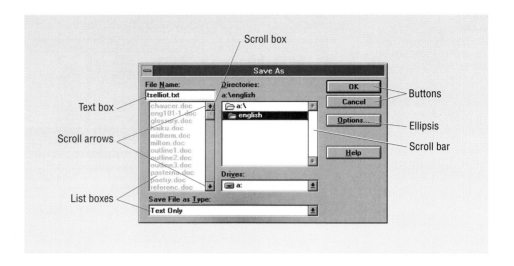

## Menus and Dialog Boxes

Menus are used in a variety of user interfaces. Shells use menus almost exclusively. Full-screen menus stay on-screen until the user selects a menu option. Some programs use *drop-down menus,* sometimes called pull-down menus, to minimize space used on-screen. In this case, the menu stays at the top of the screen, hidden in a menu bar until selected by the user. An activated menu opens to list program options. Once an option is selected, the menu rolls back, out of the way.

Some menu selections open a dialog box, which asks for additional data. A *dialog box* prompts the user to enter text, select names from a list, or click on a *button* icon which confirms a selection or cancels the operation. Each button is labeled to identify the associated operation, such as OK, Cancel, Browse, or Help. A common convention is to add three periods, called an *ellipsis,* to menu options that invoke a dialog box.

The dialog box in Figure 3.10 includes a text box, list box, OK button, and Cancel button. Data may be entered into *text boxes* using the keyboard. For example, the user could type a new filename for data being saved to disk. A *list box* is used to display options, in this case the names of files in a list or disk directory. The *scroll arrows* roll the list up and down within the list box. When information is hidden from view, a window or list box can move, or *scroll,* the view left and right or up and down. Another way to scroll through a list is to drag the *scroll box* within the *scroll bar* (see Figure 3.10). The scroll box moves up and down with the list when you click on the associated scroll arrow or drag the box with the mouse. To select an item, the user scrolls the desired item name into view within the list box, positions the pointer on it, and clicks the mouse button.

## Manuals and Help Screens

Becoming proficient with a new application program may require that the user learn a new interface. When users of unfamiliar software face problems or uncertainty, they look to the *user's manual* for answers. The user's manual provides information on how to operate the program, descriptions of program features, an explanation of error messages, and a telephone number for customer support services. This same

**3.11**

Context-sensitive help screens, instead of manuals, can often answer user questions.

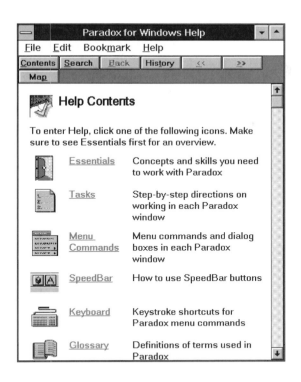

information is available on the ***help screens*** users can activate through a keystroke or by clicking a mouse button.

Help screens, like the one illustrated in Figure 3.11, put answers at users' fingertips. Some help screens are even *context-sensitive*—displaying information directly related to the program options that were available when the user asked for help.

Each user interface supports a different way to access help screens. Some programs require use of a particular function key whereas others list a help directory on a menu. Still others require that users ask for assistance by typing "help" or by clicking on a Help button. Many software developers standardize access to help screens via the F1 function key.

## SYSTEM SOFTWARE

Application software is designed to work with a computer's system software. This relationship did not always exist, however. The earliest forms of application software were executed without the assistance of system software. Computer operators and programmers did all of the setup for each application—scheduling jobs, controlling devices, allocating memory, and directing processing. In effect, these people were responsible for system control, but requiring them to prepare the computer for each job was inefficient.

Every computer manufacturer soon provided system software to help people communicate more easily with their computers. Three types of system software can be identified: operating systems, utilities, and language translators.

When users first turn on their computers, they deal with an ***operating system (OS)***, a collection of system programs that oversee the control and coordination of a computer system's resources. Another form of system software, called ***utility software,*** performs special processing tasks, such as transferring data by using a telephone along with optimizing hardware. A ***language translator*** is a system program that converts the English-like instructions used by computer programmers into the machine-readable code used by the hardware. Programs written in languages such as BASIC, Pascal, C, or COBOL must be converted into the appropriate machine language.

## ■ Operating Systems

As its name implies, the operating system is a collection of programs that oversees all computer operations. Before any processing can occur, the main command program, or ***supervisor,*** is booted into the computer's memory. Two methods are available for booting the operating system into memory. When a hard disk is available, the supervisor is automatically loaded from it. In other situations, the user places the operating system

**3.12**

Although most computer systems boot the operating system's supervisor program from disk, a few computers have it hardwired into memory.

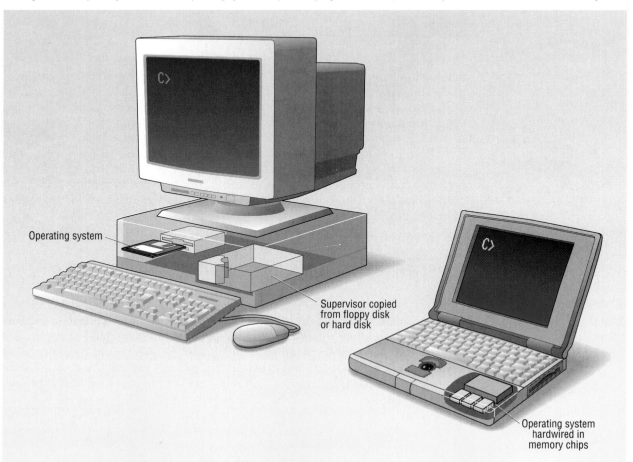

Operating system

Supervisor copied
from floppy disk
or hard disk

Operating system
hardwired in
memory chips

disk into a floppy disk drive and turns on the computer. Without further instructions from the user, the computer transfers the operating system into the computer's memory, preparing the machine to begin processing. In larger computer systems, this booting process may require several steps to identify each attached peripheral. Mainframe operators often refer to the booting process as the *initial program load (IPL).*

# William (Bill) Gates

(b. 1955)

Bill Gates taught himself programming at age 13. As a Seattle teenager, he and his friends would ride their bicycles to a local computer company to help them look for programming errors. In 1962 he took a leave from high school when TRW offered him a job at $20,000. With a friend, Paul Allen, he did system programming for Honeywell Corporation. Together they wrote a BASIC interpreter for the Altair microcomputer based on the Intel 8008 chip.

In 1975 he formed Microsoft Corporation, which wrote system programs for Altair and Apple microcomputer and expanded BASIC for other computers. IBM asked Gates to write an operating system for its new PC machine. The result was MS-DOS, one of the widest-selling operating systems in the world. Gates also directed software development for the MacIntosh and Radio Shack Model 100 microcomputers. Microsoft kept producing winning software such as Word, Works, and Flight Simulator.

In 1987 IBM chose Microsoft's Windows for the PS/2 computer. Windows has since become a new standard. Bill Gates is one of the richest men in America.

**Who's Who**

During the second method of booting, the operating system requires that the operating system already be programmed in permanent memory. The operator need only switch on the computer, and the built-in operating system is activated. Hardwired operating systems need not be loaded physically into the computer because they are permanently stored within it.

Once the supervisor program is loaded into memory, it activates other programs from the operating system to oversee resources, manage files, and control tasks. If the computer is attached to a network, a *network operating system* may be in control of shared input/output hardware and memory resources.

**Resource Management**    A major responsibility of any operating system is to make sure each hardware component is receiving and sending data and software in an error-free manner. Resource management would include formatting new disks, system security, transferring error-free data between system components, and displaying error messages when problems occur. An operating system even detects such "error" conditions as an open disk drive door or a printer that has run out of paper.

The operating system also sets up system *defaults*, or standard hardware connections and formats the computer uses unless otherwise instructed. By presetting computer resources to operate in a certain way, default values save the user time. Many defaults get set up by specific system files or when an application program is installed. During booting, the supervisor reads different device drivers from disk. When users connect equipment to the system, they "install" that equipment by copying the related device driver file to the boot disk. The *device driver* file identifies operating characteristics of such peripherals as a mouse, printer, or scanner.

Data and programs reside in memory, making memory one of the most important resources an operating system manages. When multitasking is possible, the operating system must keep track of several programs and associated data at the same time. The operating system also checks everything coming into the memory for transmission and storage errors. This helps ensure that programs and data will run properly. When errors are found, the operating system reads the data or program again from the input device, asks the user to reenter it, or displays an error message.

Computers with limited amounts of memory cannot store large computer programs. Because only a small portion of a program can be processed at any given moment, most of the program and memory are unused at any given time. Yet the entire program takes up space in memory during processing. Some operating systems support *virtual memory* as a way of bypassing this resource limitation. The operating system uses disk storage as an extension of memory. In other words, the processor treats storage on a disk drive as part of memory. Figure 3.13 depicts a large program that is broken down into sections, called *pages*. Pages that are not currently being used by the processor are stored on disk. When a page is needed, the operating system swaps it into memory by replacing a completed page. One drawback is slower processing speeds because of the time it takes to transfer pages between the disk drive and memory. However, virtual memory increases the versatility of the processor by letting it handle programs that exceed its memory capacity.

**File Management**    When storing programs and data on tape or disk, the operating system prompts the user to enter a unique filename. The filename along with the current date and time is then added to a disk directory or tape label. The file management responsibilities of an operating system are keeping track of these files and moving them from storage into memory and back again.

**3.13**

Virtual memory operations use disk drives as extensions of the computer's memory.

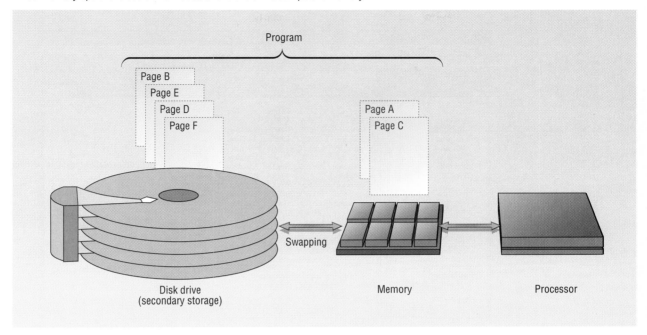

Users interact with the operating system to change a filename in the disk directory, copy it to another disk, delete it, or protect it from accidental deletion. When the operating system designates a file as *protected*, or *read-only*, the file can be used and copied, but not altered or erased. Before the operating system can remove a file from disk, the user must turn off the file protection.

An operating system's file management features can also be used to organize and store data. Files are stored sequentially one after another on tape. Disk files are independently accessed and stored in different disk directories. It is recommended that you store application programs with their associated data files in separate disk directories. By doing so you make it easier to back up files in the data directory on a regular basis. Files in the program directory get copied to another disk as backup and protected to prevent accidental erasure. When program revisions occur, you unprotect the old program files, erase the directory, and install the new program while leaving the data files alone.

System software using a graphical user interface displays disk directories as file folders. In this case, programs and data are kept in separate file folders. In addition, file folders can be stored inside other folders. For instance, Linda has a Games file folder on her hard disk. When she installed the Haunted House program, she created a new file folder, H-House, in the Games folder. Linda's Games folder has two other file folders: Solitaire and Hearts.

Nancy's system works the same way. When installing the Haunted House game, she added a directory labeled H-House to the Games directory. Figure 3.14 shows the relationships among the Games directory, H-House directory, and other related directories. These directories are called *subdirectories* because they are added after a disk is formatted and are subordinate to the original disk directory known as the *root directory*.

**3.14**

Users make or remove subdirectories as computer-based projects come and go. Only the root directory remains on the disk permanently.

Root directory

Subdirectories

Data and program files

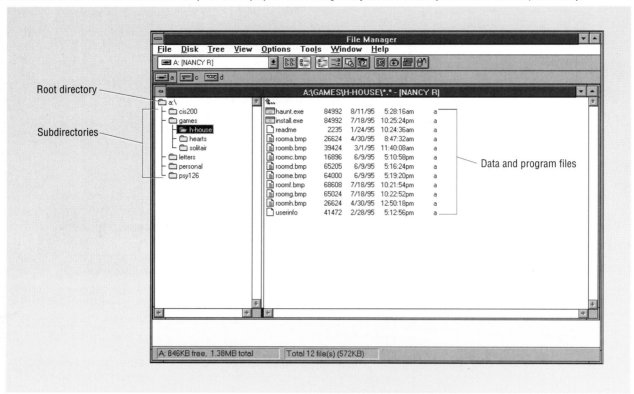

**Task Management**   Any operation performed by a computer system is a *task*. Printing a document, copying a file, or computing the volume of concrete needed for a bridge footing are all examples of tasks. A single-task operating system can handle only one operation at a time. Early computer systems and some personal computers use single-task operating systems.

Mainframe, minicomputer, and many personal computer systems are often asked to perform several processing jobs at one time. Because modern computers perform operations for most applications with time to spare, the operating system can divide the computer's processing power among different applications and users. As a result, multitasking and timesharing are two features that allow users to take advantage of the computer's power.

As you may recall, multitasking is the ability of a computer system to handle several programs concurrently. Actually, each program is given a priority. The program with top priority is processed until the computer has to wait for input or output. Operating systems with multitasking capabilities shift to the program with the next highest priority instead of standing idle. The computer resumes processing the instructions from the top-priority program when the input or output for the first program is complete.

For example, a mail-order business with a minicomputer may find that the computer is not utilized to its full capacity when order clerks enter phone orders on it. With multitasking capabilities, however, the computer can work on weekly sales reports

**3.15**

Timesharing is a type of multitasking in which the computer system skips between different application programs and gives each user roughly the same amount of processing time.

when no orders are being taken. Since the order entry program has top priority, the operating system will interrupt the report program and return to order entry when an operator begins to enter a new order.

*Timesharing* is another type of task management. Instead of one program getting priority over others, timesharing assigns each program a slice of time. The programs are then processed in a round-robin pattern, each user being served individually and unaware that others are being served at the same time. Operators using a catalog company's mainframe computer system find themselves timesharing the computer with dozens of other operators. Because each operator is given a time slice, it seems as though each has the computer to himself or herself (Figure 3.15).

## Utilities

Utility software performs jobs the operating system does not automatically handle (Figure 3.16). For example, a variety of file conversion utilities exist to convert data into another format. Users might run a file conversion utility to convert a database file into a text file or to change drawings from one graphic format to another.

Some utility programs help users optimize their computer hardware. By stripping out unnecessary spaces and by performing other data compaction methods, data compression utilities reduce the amount of disk space a file uses. The same software restores the file to its original form when the data is read from the disk. Other utility programs reorganize files on disk to optimize data access and retrieval times. Still others may be used to find errors in the operating system or change the OS environment.

A common utility program is used to save time when printing large documents. A *SPOOLer* (Simultaneous Peripheral Operation OnLine) utility coordinates the transfer of data between the computer and other peripherals, in this case the disk drive and printer. The user can work with other programs and files, instead of waiting for the

## Jobs Performed by Utility Programs

- Backup and restore

- Data communication within a network

- Data compression/decompression

- Disk optimization

- Emulation of other equipment

- File conversions

- Screen savers

- Software guides

- Spool data between computer and peripherals

- Text editors

- Miscellaneous (merges, sorts, searches)

document to be printed. The SPOOLer transfers the document from the computer to the disk drive and handles the printing of the document. SPOOLers are especially important in networks where several users share output hardware.

By using communication software, also a utility, users can link their computers with other computers over telephone lines. Once the user stores the appropriate data formats and telephone numbers, the communication software oversees the telephone call, linkage between computers, and transmission of data.

Sometimes a user wants one piece of equipment to act like another. Consider, for instance, trying to output a document saved in a file format used by an out-of-date printer. By using a printer emulation utility on your computer, a different printer can still output the file. *Emulation* programs mimic the operation of hardware.

## Language Translators

In its simplest form, a computer program indicates which switches inside the computer are on and off, which circuits flow with electricity, and which do not. It is not very efficient for a programmer to write programs in this *machine language*, however. Programmers are most efficient when they can work with discrete operations, such as sorting, adding, or copying. Data structures are easier to organize when expressed as objects and files instead of binary codes composed of 1's and 0's.

In the 1950s computer professionals realized that they needed to develop their own computer programming languages. Over the years different *high-level languages* have developed. The command syntax of these languages resembles human language. High-level languages eliminated the need for programmers to memorize unique codes

**3.17**

This high-level program is written in the FORTRAN programming language. After it is translated into the computer's machine language, it will input two numbers and add them together.

```
      INTEGER NUM1, NUM2, SUM
      READ (5,10) NUM1, NUM2
  10  FORMAT (I4,I4)
      SUM = NUM1 + NUM2
      WRITE (6,20) NUM1, NUM2, SUM
  20  FORMAT (10X, 'THE SUM OF', I4, '+', I4, 'IS', I5)
      STOP
      END
```

for different computer operations or memory locations. As shown in Figure 3.17, IBM's FORTRAN, or FORmula TRANslator, language uses words such as READ, WRITE, and STOP as programming statements. FORTRAN also is capable of dealing with complex mathematical formulas. This language was introduced in 1957 and came into widespread use during the 1960s. Because FORTRAN eases the transition from mathematical notation to computer programming, it is still used today for engineering, mathematics, and graphics applications. Other popular high-level languages are BASIC (see Figure 1.6), COBOL, C++, RPG, and Visual BASIC.

Before it can be run, each program written in a high-level programming language must be translated into the computer's machine language. To write a FORTRAN program that works on a personal computer, you need a system program that translates FORTRAN instructions. The FORTRAN translator converts the English-like FORTRAN into the personal computer's own machine language.

## WHERE TO FIND SOFTWARE

Software can be developed by employees, leased, bought, or shared. With the abundance of prepackaged software on the market, development by computer professionals is usually reserved for customized programs. New systems and application packages are announced every week, and rumors abound about others that are not yet available to consumers. Software associated with these rumors becomes *vaporware* if it is never released or becomes delayed due to programming problems.

Leased or purchased software provides needed capabilities for most applications at minimum cost. Inexpensive or free software is distributed through networks and among users with similar interests. The most popular software sources are described in the following section.

### Retail Stores and Computer Manufacturers

Many users purchase off-the-shelf software packages at retail computer stores. These outlets provide hardware, supplies, magazines, and manuals—in addition to vast selections of software. Purchasing software through retail stores has a distinct advantage. Most retailers will permit you to test application programs before you purchase them. Also, salespeople usually are on hand to describe software features and review user's manuals.

Before you buy a software package, you should test it to see if it meets your needs. Friends and family members with their own computer systems can often help by letting you try computer programs they use and like.

Manufacturers of computer hardware usually provide compatible system software; some make application programs available as well. Because many users base their hardware decisions on availability of a specific software package, computer manufacturers often package personal productivity software with their hardware as a sales incentive. For example, a new user may purchase a personal computer specifically for its word processing ability. If he or she is working with a limited budget, hardware packaged with a compatible operating system and word processing program could be highly desirable.

## Magazines

Computer trade magazines are an inexpensive source of information on programs, often reviewing competing software packages and providing feature-by-feature comparisons, as shown in Figure 3.18. Hundreds of magazines and newsletters publish articles geared toward personal computer use. Many magazines specialize in reviewing software compatible with one or two brands of computers. Also, special-interest magazines, such as periodicals about sports, music, or entertainment, may review technology and software of interest to their readers.

Advertisements for software are also contained in magazines. Although ordering computer programs through the mail may seem like a convenient way to acquire software, purchasing anything sight unseen has its risks. Mail-order customers should try to review the software before buying it. *Promotional software* is sometimes available, allowing people to try out programs with limited amounts of data or not allowing the user to save results. For example, a promotional database program might limit the user to 30 records. Promotional copies are not useful for regular workloads, but they do allow the user to become familiar with the program before buying the package.

## Public Domain Software and Shareware

Some software is available to interested computer users free of charge. This *public domain software* is distributed through networks and by trading software with other computer users. Several magazines even operate reader services that provide lengthy catalogs of public domain listings. However, there is no guarantee that the program is useful or error-free. Pages full of utility and application software are made available to anyone who requests them. You could build a library of application programs without purchasing commercial software.

Great care should be taken when using public domain software. In some cases, public domain software harbors a *virus* or *worm* that can erase data or damage equipment. To protect yourself, acquire public domain software only from reliable sources, such as friends or local user groups. Utility programs are also available that check for and neutralize infected software before it causes any problems.

Public domain software is a "take it as it is" proposition. You can copy it or change it at will. Some software programmers continue to make improvements on their programs. To support this work, they allow users free use of and copying rights on the software for a limited time. When the time limit is up, the user is legally obligated to register by paying a small charge. Typically, information about the copyright is included in a message

**3.18**

Computer magazines provide readers with comprehensive software reviews.

## Summary of Features—Whiteboard Software

| Products listed in alphabetical order | Intel ProShare Personal Conferencing Software Standard Edition | Person to Person for Windows | Smart 2000 Desktop Conferencing Software | TalkShow |
|---|---|---|---|---|
| Number of licenses required | 1 per conference | 1 per user | 1 per user | 1 per conference |
| Guest copy included/Self-downloading | ■■ | □□ | □□ | ■□ |
| Online help | ■ | ■ | □ | ■ |
| Vendor offers videoconferencing upgrade | ■ | ■ | ■ | □ |
| **COMMUNICATIONS** | | | | |
| Modem speeds (Kbps) | 2.4–19.2 | 9.6–57.6 | 2.4–57.6 | 1.2–57.6 |
| ISDN | ■ | ■ | ■ | ■ |
| **File transfers:** | | | | |
| Via Clipboard | □ | ■ | □ | □ |
| Pauses other activities | □ | □ | ■ | ■ |
| **CONFERENCING FEATURES** | | | | |
| Maximum number of attendees | 2 | 8 | 64 | Unlimited |
| Peer-to-peer meetings | ■ | ■ | ■ | ■ |
| Chaired meetings | □ | □ | ■ | □ |
| Roster can change after meeting starts | N/A | ■ | ■ | ■ |
| Software announces requests to join | N/A | □ | ■ | ■ |
| Application sharing/remote control | □□ | □□ | ■■ | □□ |
| Undo | ■ | □ | □ | ■ |
| Slide sorter/Presenter | □□ | □□ | ■□ | ■■ |
| Passwords | □ | □ | ■ | □ |
| **Whiteboard work space:** | | | | |
| Maximum number of private/shared work spaces | 1/1 | Unlimited/Unlimited | None/1 | 2/1 |
| Pages per private/shared work spaces | Unlimited/Unlimited | 1/1 | None/300 | Unlimited/Unlimited |
| **Annotation tools:** | | | | |
| Number of markers and pens | 3 | 1 | 2 | 2 |
| Text tool | ■ | ■ | ■ | ■ |
| Graphics drawing tools | □ | ■ | ■ | ■ |
| Other annotation tools | Object select, remote pointer | Erasers, remote pointer | Screen blank, clear annotations, remote pointer | Grabber, object select, remote pointer, eraser |
| Tools can edit typed text | ■ | □ | □ | □ |
| **SUPPORT** | | | | |
| Toll-free support line | □ | ■ | □ | □ |
| Other available support | CompuServe forum, private BBS, fax, toll-free fax-back | CompuServe forum | Private BBS | Private BBS |

■ = YES   □ = NO

# A Closer Look at Windows 3.1, Windows 95, and the Macintosh OS

**T**he existence of a wide variety of user interfaces has created a demand for a common standard. New users find it frustrating to have to learn different menus and new icons every time they launch another software package. Informed users want to use skills they have already mastered on new application packages. In both cases, having a common user interface reduces the amount of time it takes to learn new applications.

We will examine three user interfaces for system software. Microsoft's Windows 3.1 and Windows 95 graphical user interfaces are popular alternatives to the command-driven DOS interface used by IBM and Intel-based personal computers. The Mac OS, the graphical user interface used by the Apple Macintosh, has set a standard for user-friendliness. The design and layout of these interfaces has in turn established a look and feel that many application packages use. By standardizing on common menus and screen layouts, users spend less time learning the interface and more time exploring software options. What follows are screen displays of each interface handling common file management tasks.

Q: How do you display the root directory of the floppy disk in drive A?

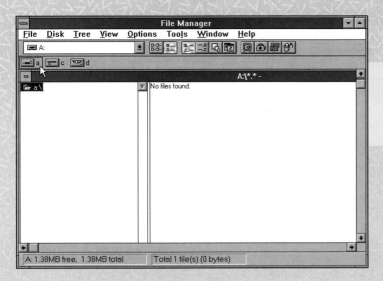

**A:** *Windows 3.1:* Launch the File Manager from the Main group and click on the drive A icon.

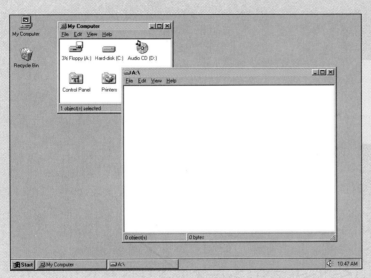

**A:** *Windows 95:* Double-click on the My Computer icon, then 3½ Floppy [A:].

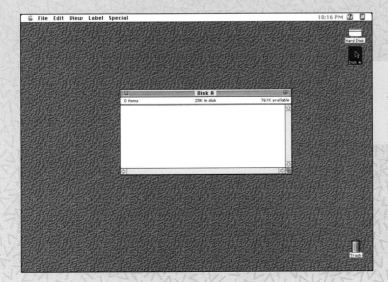

**A:** *Macintosh OS:* Double-click on the floppy disk icon on the desktop.

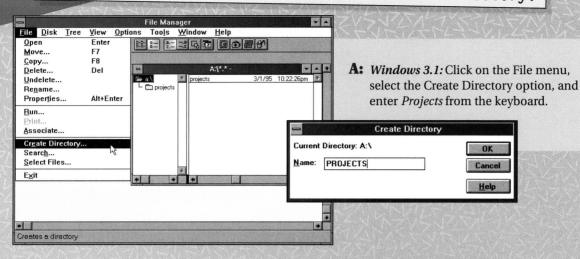

**A:** *Windows 3.1:* Click on the File menu, select the Create Directory option, and enter *Projects* from the keyboard.

**A:** *Windows 95:* Click on the File menu, select New, select Folder, then enter *Projects* from the keyboard.

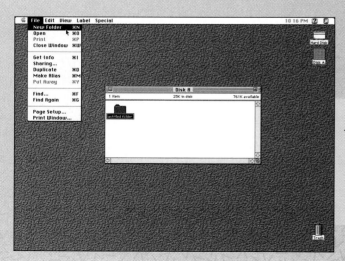

**A:** *Macintosh OS:* Click on the File menu and select New Folder to display an untitled file folder. Entering *Projects* from the keyboard creates a new file folder title.

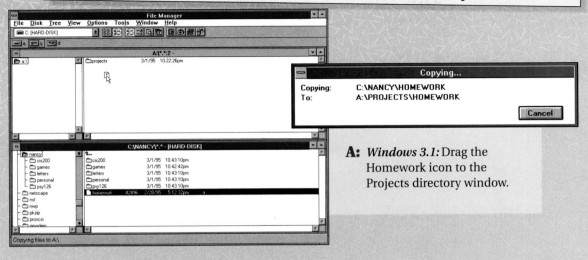

**A:** *Windows 3.1:* Drag the Homework icon to the Projects directory window.

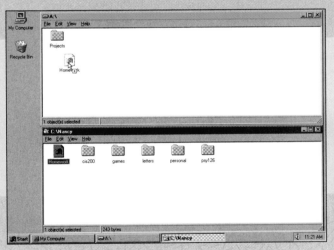

**A:** *Windows 95:* Drag the Homework icon to the Projects directory window.

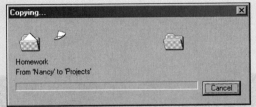

**A:** *Macintosh OS:* Drag the Homework icon to the Projects file folder and release the mouse button.

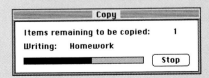

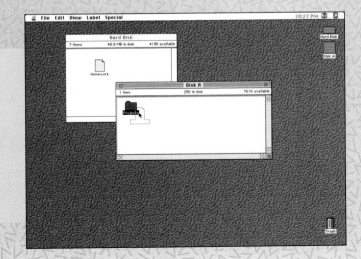

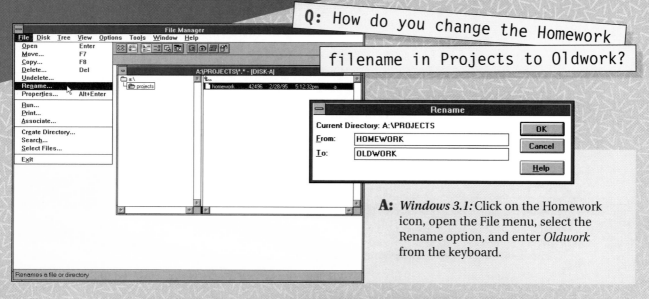

Q: How do you change the Homework filename in Projects to Oldwork?

A: *Windows 3.1:* Click on the Homework icon, open the File menu, select the Rename option, and enter *Oldwork* from the keyboard.

A: *Windows 95:* Click on the Homework icon, open the File menu, select the Rename option, and enter *Oldwork* from the keyboard.

A: *Macintosh OS:* Click on the Homework icon's title and enter *Oldwork* from the keyboard.

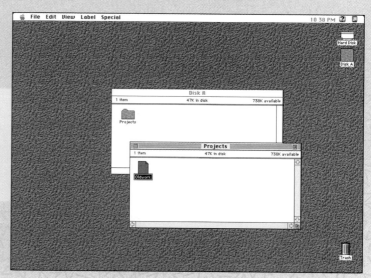

**Q:** How do you delete the file Oldwork from disk?

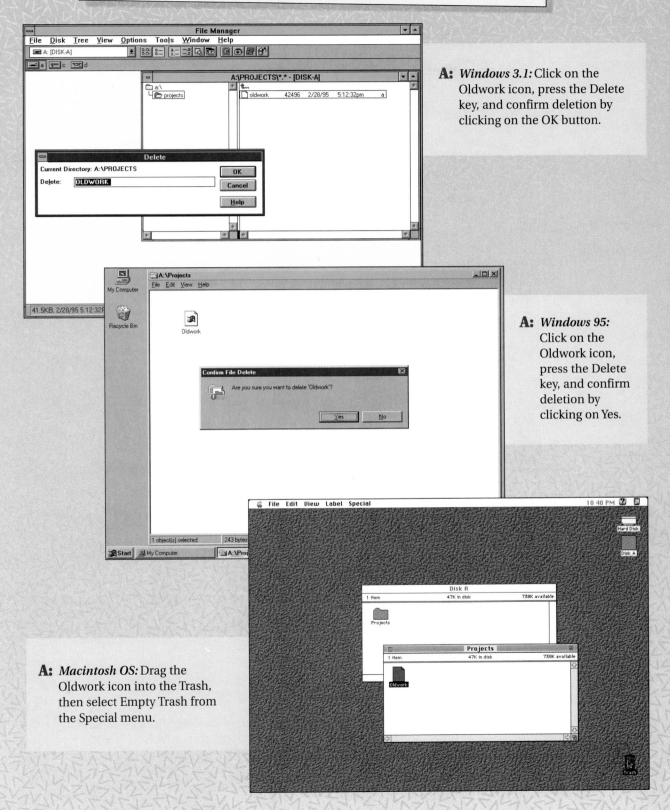

**A:** *Windows 3.1:* Click on the Oldwork icon, press the Delete key, and confirm deletion by clicking on the OK button.

**A:** *Windows 95:* Click on the Oldwork icon, press the Delete key, and confirm deletion by clicking on Yes.

**A:** *Macintosh OS:* Drag the Oldwork icon into the Trash, then select Empty Trash from the Special menu.

preceding the program, which also asks people to pass copies to others. This type of "try before you buy" software is known as *shareware*. People who support shareware programmers with a monetary donation usually receive a manual, as well as the next version of the program when it is ready.

## User Groups and Professional Associations

User groups can provide fellowship among users who share an interest in computers. They also are good sources for public domain software, shareware, and programs developed by users themselves. Usually, user groups consist of people interested in the same brand of computers, who meet to discuss shared problems and new ideas. Users who join these groups can learn about the latest software and hardware developments for their machines.

The interest in different types and sizes of computers has resulted in a variety of user groups. Personal computer users generally form groups locally; national user groups bring together users of large systems. In both cases, computer interests spawn homemade programs that can be shared by all members of the group. Some programs are circulated among club members free of charge; others are sold for the cost of the disk. In general, the distribution of software by user-developers is not for profit.

---

### CHAPTER FACTS

- User interfaces include features such as windows, menus, icons, dialog boxes, and help screens to increase user-friendliness.

- User interfaces can be categorized as command-driven, shell, graphical, or natural language.

- Command-driven interfaces rely on keywords and common syntax to initiate computer processing.

- Software shells display program options as menu options. Users choose the options through a mouse or keyboard.

- Graphical user interfaces with icons and menus are designed to use a mouse as the primary input device.

- Clicking, double-clicking, and dragging are all input operations performed with a mouse.

- Natural language interfaces accept spoken or typed instructions in the user's native language.

- Software drives hardware, and as a result users should evaluate programs and determine software needs before making hardware decisions.

- Standards exist for naming files and objects to be shared among application programs.

- Integrated software, suites, and groupware all facilitate sharing data and objects.

- A duplicate of an object can be copied to, embedded in, or linked to another document.

- The ability to share data with other software, work concurrently with other programs, and comprise easy-to-understand user interfaces and manuals are all desirable features of a software package.

- System software monitors the computer's internal operations. Operating systems, language translators, and utilities represent different kinds of system software.

- An operating system is a collection of programs, coordinated by the supervisor, that controls hardware and memory resources, manages files using peripherals, and coordinates task processing.

- An operating system may support multitasking, the concurrent operation of two or more programs.

- Utility software performs such standard processing tasks as file conversion, spooling, emulations, and data compression.

- Language translators convert high-level languages understandable to people into machine language, usable by computer circuitry.

- Software is available from retail computer stores, manufacturers, magazines, networks, and user groups.

## TERMS TO REMEMBER

| | | |
|---|---|---|
| command-driven interface | language translator | shareware |
| cursor | linking | shell |
| default | machine language | supervisor |
| dialog box | multitasking | task |
| disk directory | natural language interface | terminate stay resident |
| embedding | operating system (OS) | (TSR) |
| filename | public domain software | timesharing |
| graphical user interface | root directory | user interface |
| (GUI) | screen pointer | user's manual |
| help screen | screen prompt | utility software |
| high-level language | scroll | window |

## MIX AND MATCH

*Complete the following definitions with the Terms to Remember.*

1. Programs that are distributed free of charge as known as _____.

2. A(n) _____ relies on mouse or keyboard input to select menus or icons.

3. A collection of system programs that oversees a computer system's operations is called a(n) _____.

4. A(n) _____ is a window that prompts the user to enter text, select names, or click on an icon to initiate or cancel a program option.

5. A unique set of letters, numbers, and symbols that identifies a data file or program constitutes a(n) _____.

6. A(n) _____ is an icon that is controlled by the movement of a mouse or some other pointing device.

7. The system program that is loaded into a computer's memory from the start to coordinate all processing activities within the computer system is the _____.

8. A(n) _____ uses keywords and syntax to initiate program options.

9. _____ performs processing tasks not under the control of the operating system.

10. A(n) _____ is a subdivision of a screen display, allowing the user to look at several menus, dialog boxes, or status reports from more than one program.

11. A standard assumption that a computer system uses unless otherwise instructed is called a(n) _____.

12. The _____ is created when a disk is formatted.

13. Duplicating an original object in another application package and creating an active connection that enables the user to update the duplicate when the original is changed is known as _____.

14. _____ is the operating language unique to each computer that is made up of bits (0 or 1) representing electronic switches (off or on).

15. The blinking line or box showing where the computer will display next keyboard entry is called the _____.

## REVIEW QUESTIONS

1. Define the Terms to Remember.

2. What are the four basic categories of user interfaces?

3. What determines where input commands and data are located on-screen when using a command-driven interface?

4. What type of data does an installation program accept from the user?

5. What does it mean when a menu option appears as a light color (dimmed)? What does an ellipsis (...) indicate?

6. How are the procedures for getting a program up and running different between command-driven system software and software using a graphical user interface?

7. What makes software user-friendly?

8. Name one advantage and one disadvantage of virtual memory.

9. Identify nine questions users should ask when evaluating new software.

10. How can a user tell if a file is in one of the standard formats?

11. What are three types of software that manufacturers sell to facilitate sharing of data and objects?

12. What are the differences between copying, object linking, and object embedding?

13. What are three different methods a dialog box uses to prompt user input?

14. How are the scroll arrows used when selecting an item from a list box?

15. What type of information is found in a user's manual?

16. What are the two methods for booting an operating system into memory?

17. Describe three responsibilities of an operating system.

18. What are six jobs performed by utility software?

19. How can you try software before buying it?

20. How do you protect yourself from problems associated with public domain software?

21. What are six sources for computer software?

## APPLYING WHAT YOU'VE LEARNED

1. Try one of the application packages available to you at school or home. What type of user interface does it use? Does it have a tutorial or help features? What came with the package (user's manual, and so on)? List the features that make it user-friendly.

2. Look at the user's manual for the operating system used on a school or home computer. What type of user interface is used? Are help screens available? How do you display a disk directory and copy, rename, or delete a file? What type of device drivers come with the operating system? Is multitasking available?

3. The price of a software package varies greatly depending upon its source. Choose a popular application package, such as a word processing program or a suite. Find out its current price by checking several computer stores and looking for mail-order advertisements in magazines. Check if a student edition is available. From whom would you order the software if price was not an issue?

4. A wide variety of utility programs are available for popular personal computers. Research one type of utility program to find out where you can get it, what it does, and how much it costs.

5. What language translators are available for computers at your school? For what type of application is each language used?

# Linking Information Technology

# FROM THE USER'S POINT OF VIEW

Informed computer users seem to go through stages as they become comfortable using computer technology. At first, new operating procedures and application packages hold your attention as you learn how to use them. Next you want to share your computer-generated words, graphs, and other information with colleagues and friends, or explore the web of interconnected computers to meet new people and find things of interest. At this time you will want to learn about data communication hardware, software, and procedures. Linking your personal computer to other computers in a network opens up opportunities to improve personal productivity, explore new ideas with others, and communicate with people all over the world. As you might expect, a whole new vocabulary is necessary to explain the communication options available.

## DATA COMMUNICATIONS

Astronomer Neil Janson pointed to the chart coming out on the printer. "I'm just not sure," he said. "It may be a supernova—or just an astronomical aberration!" Neil's assistant, Jamal Manot, nodded without taking his eyes off the output. "Maybe we should send this stuff to Dr. Baranson. It's 4 A.M. here, but it's noon in England, and she told us to let her know if we find something significant."

With a series of commands, Neil requested the transfer of data from the Rathmore Observatory in the California desert to an office 8,650 kilometers away in Greenwich, England. But the transmission was not direct. First a message was sent to the observatory's minicomputer with instructions to connect to the research network. The message traveled

**4.1**

By using data communication, astronomers can transmit data about celestial phenomena around the world.

through telephone lines from California to another computer in Boston. Using a communication satellite, the message then traveled to the Greenwich research computer. When Dr. Baranson was notified via electronic mail that a priority request was waiting in her mailbox, she immediately brought it up on her PC's screen. The data from California was in England for analysis in a matter of seconds (Figure 4.1).

## Telecommunications

Regardless of how computers are used, people find an increased need to share information with others. The headquarters of a manufacturing firm must communicate with its regional factories. A university uses television broadcasts to teach students living too far away to commute to campus. A computer user at home would like to talk to other users about a new software package. All of these applications involve communication of electronic messages over a long distance—*telecommunication*. When a computer is involved, the transmission of textual, numeric, audio, or video data is called *data communication*.

For effective data communication, all five components of a computer system are necessary:

♦ *Data:* the message itself

♦ *Procedures:* a mutually agreed upon method of communication

♦ *Hardware:* equipment doing the sending, receiving, and storing

♦ *Software:* instructions for data transmission and network operations

♦ *People:* users and computer professionals

In a simple personal communication, two people will talk to each other in a language they both understand. The means of connection can be face-to-face talking, the telephone, or a letter. The most common means of communicating over long distances involves the telephone.

For the successful marriage of computers and telephones, data must be coded in a form compatible with both technologies. Computers transmit data as *digital signals* by representing bit patterns as changes in electrical voltages from positive (+), to zero (0), and negative (–). Telephones and other communication devices use *analog signals,* which express data as patterns of continuous sound frequencies, such as a human voice (see Figure 4.2).

**4.2**

Computers generate digital signals representing bit patterns, whereas standard telephone lines were designed to handle analog signals in the form of voices and other sound patterns. To use a telephone for data communication, digital signals need to be converted to an analog format.

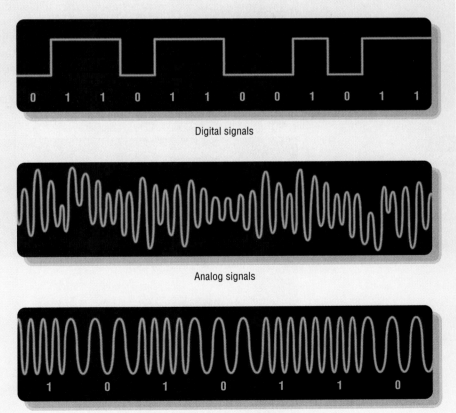

Digital signals

Analog signals

Digital signals converted to analog signals by modem

People who want to establish data communication links using a telephone, therefore, have to make a choice. One option requires purchasing digital communication equipment that transmits the computer's digital signal over standard telephone lines. One agreed upon standard is the *ISDN (Integrated Services Digital Network)* format. The other option is to convert the computer's digital signal into an analog format used by common telephone hardware.

## ▓ Facsimile Machines

For many organizations the ***facsimile machine***, or ***fax***, has become an increasingly popular way to transmit ideas and important information. Just as a telephone transmits voice messages, a fax machine transmits images of printed material. The data can be a drawing, a photo, a handwritten document, or even your take-out lunch order (see Figure 4.3).

After dialing up a receiving fax machine, the user inputs the document into the sending fax machine. The machine converts the document into analog signals that are sent to the receiving fax machine via telephone. The quality of the sending machine and printing equipment determines the resolution (clarity) of the output. Early facsimiles were rather grainy and printed on light-sensitive thermal paper that deteriorated with age. More-expensive fax machines transmit a page in less than a minute and output it on plain paper with a resolution similar to that of a printer.

Stand-alone fax machines are inexpensive and easy to operate. They can even substitute as a copy machine by sending a document to itself. A disadvantage of stand-alone fax machines is that the hard-copy output cannot be edited or stored on a computer without being reentered using a keyboard or other input device.

An alternative is the internal *fax board* that is added to a personal computer. This device connects the computer to the telephone line using a standard telephone wall jack. Once the fax board is installed, the PC can send, receive, and edit documents without

Many businesses, like this delicatessen, use a fax machine to receive customer orders.

ever producing a paper copy. The disadvantage of this approach is that the user must leave the computer on in order to receive incoming faxes. In addition, an independent scanner is needed to convert images and other information that is originally in a printed format. For this reason, you can find stand-alone hardware that combines the features of a scanner, printer, fax, and copy machine into a single peripheral.

The speed of data transmission and the diversity of documents that can be sent are advantages of facsimile machines. Signatures that have been faxed are in many cases considered as legally binding as those on original documents. For example, some police cars are equipped with fax machines so that signed search warrants can be immediately sent from the judge to the investigating officers.

## Modems

Compatibility between the digital signals of computers and the analog signals used by telephones requires special devices for encoding and decoding data. These devices are known as ***modems,*** a term coined from the functions they perform: *mo*dulation and *dem*odulation. Modems permit two computers linked by analog telephone equipment to exchange data. A sending modem modulates digital data into analog form for transmission over standard telephone lines. A modem at the receiving end demodulates the analog signals back into digital form for input to the receiving computer (see Figure 4.4).

A modem usually connects to the telephone jack, officially called a *RJ45 jack,* in the wall. Some modems, called *internal modems,* are built into circuit boards and housed inside the body of the computer. A stand-alone modem called an *external modem* is shown in Figure 4.4. It uses one cable to connect to the computer and another cable to connect to the telephone wall jack. A person wishing to transmit data need only dial a number to establish the connection. Modulation and demodulation take place within the circuitry of the modem. Either type of modem provides data communication that is unhindered by noise interference from the surrounding area.

## Data Transmission Speeds

The rate of data transmission is often measured by the number of ***bits per second (bps)*** sent through communication equipment. The speed of data transmission can also be represented by its ***baud rate,*** or the number of times the transmitted signal changes

**4.4**

A modem modulates bit patterns into an analog signal for transmission over standard telephone lines. Another modem then demodulates the signal back into its original digital form.

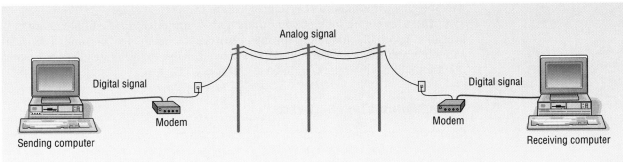

**4.5**

Portable computers combined with a cellular fax-modem become personal communication devices you can use anywhere at any time.

within a second. The term *baud* is derived from Baudot, the Frenchman who developed a coding scheme for telegraph communications.

Often the terms *baud rate* and *bps* are incorrectly interchanged. Baud rate varies with the communication hardware used. The speed at which a signal changes is not necessarily equal to the number of bits being sent. At low speeds, such as 300 bps, the baud rate is typically also 300. For higher speeds, data transmission hardware and software make it possible for more than 1 bit to be transmitted with each signal change. Baud rate is best used to compare transmission characteristics of communication hardware, whereas bits per second is a better measurement of data transmission speeds. At 300 bps it would take 20 minutes to transmit a 10-page single-spaced document. The same document would be sent in 25 seconds at 14,400 bps.

### ■ Personal Communication Devices

The popularity of modems and facsimile machines has led to the development of *fax-modems*. These machines combine the data communication capabilities of a modem with the image transmission capacity of a fax machine.

Other combinations of computers and communication technology are also available. A portable computer with an internal cellular fax-modem becomes a personal communication device. When linked into a network, informed users literally have a world of information in their purse or briefcase (Figure 4.5).

### ■ Communication Software

Communication software is the user's interface with the modem or internal fax board. These programs aid the user in dialing up the receiving computer, redialing the number when it is busy, providing online help, maintaining file security, and performing other

# Mitch Kapor

(b. 1951)

Before becoming involved with computers, Mitch Kapor worked for a short time as a counselor in a mental-health clinic. He also tried being a stand-up comic, disc jockey, and instructor in transcendental meditation. His life changed when he obtained an Apple II in the late seventies. After teaching himself to program, he worked as a consultant for the Apple Corporation. By the mid-eighties, Kapor had founded Lotus Development Corporation, which sold the immensely popular Lotus 1-2-3 electronic spreadsheet software. In 1986 Kapor surprised the computer world by resigning from Lotus. Although the company was at the height of its success, Kapor was bored with corporate life and the cutthroat business of computer software.

In 1990 Kapor joined with John Perry Barlow, lyricist for the Grateful Dead and computer hacker, to form the Electronic Frontier Foundation (EFF). The original intent of EFF was to defend the civil liberties of hackers and network users, however EFF has broadened its role. As its name implies, EFF fosters the idea that the electronic superhighway is really a frontier, an uncharted territory. Kapor believes that, like homesteading in the late 1800s, there will be struggle for ownership of cyberspace. He sees large companies vying for exclusive control of the telecommunications industry, and bringing with them restriction of use.

To Kapor, it is essential that the Internet and other online services remain available to everyone for every purpose. Especially important are the open forums, if control can remain in the hands of the people and individual liberties can be maintained. Since EFF is funded, in part, by some of the hardware and software manufacturers, its ideas have not been ignored. By discussing the future of computers and communications now, Mitch Kapor believes, society can hopefully steer toward a civilized cyberspace. The Electronic Frontier Foundation is available through e-mail at: eff@eff.org.

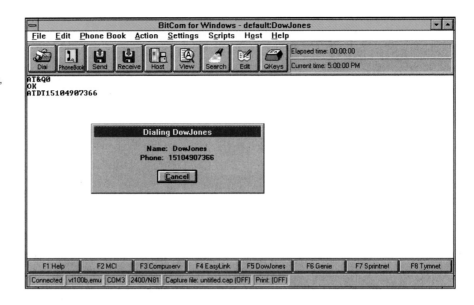

**4.6**

Communication software helps users link their PCs through a modem and telephone line into computer networks. In this case, the latest stock market closings can be received from a financial network.

operations related to data communications. Many communication programs can automatically connect to other computers at a specified time to transfer data. For example, in Figure 4.6 an investor with a PC and modem is dialing up and transferring current stock and bond prices into her personal database software just after the markets close. The investor does not even have to be present when the transfer of data occurs.

## DISTRIBUTED PROCESSING

Computer networks support data communication between two or more computer systems. A dozen PCs in an office linked together to share files and electronic mail is a small-scale network. On a larger scale, multicontinent satellite links enable banks in the world's financial centers and your hometown to exchange data. The system software that coordinates the flow of data around a network is the *network operating system*. It takes responsibility for the internal workings of the network, just as the disk operating system is responsible for the internal workings of a personal computer.

There is a great deal of flexibility in the ways data processing is handled on a network. A variety of configurations support *distributed processing*. By having several computers connected together to share data and processing responsibilities, computer-based processing is distributed back to the workplace where the data originated. The physical placement of each computer is tailored to personal and organizational needs. The following cases demonstrate typical network configurations.

### ▧ Local Area Networks

Although Harrington College serves a growing urban area, its faculty and students have modest data communication requirements. Each faculty member uses a workstation in his or her office to write assignments and access student records. Personal computers

**4.7**

In this local area network, PCs in each office share high-speed printing and a database maintained by a server in the computer lab.

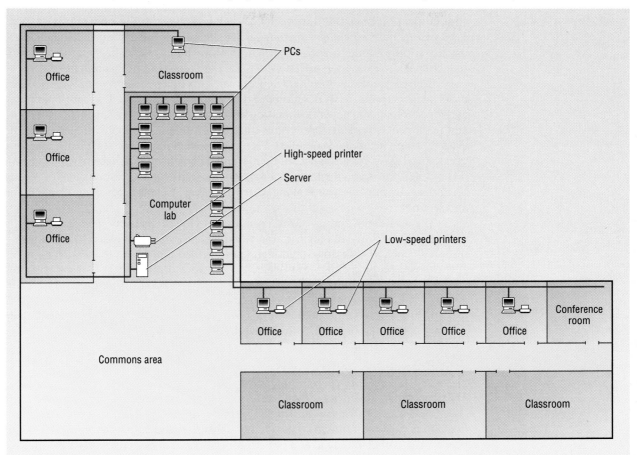

working within a network are often referred to as ***workstations.*** An on-campus computer lab with 40 PCs was created for students by knocking out a common wall between two classrooms. The faculty and lab PCs are separate from each other, though they all are located in one building (see Figure 4.7). Harrington chose to link its computers together into a ***local area network (LAN).*** This type of network is usually privately owned and connects computers within a confined service area.

The students share access to a high-speed printer, personal productivity software, and a database of assignments set up by the faculty. When hardware, programs, and large amounts of data must be shared by network users, a dedicated computer called a ***server*** is employed. There are many types of servers, including file servers, database servers, and print servers. The server acts as a clearinghouse for expensive hardware resources, such as a high-speed printer, or distributes data and programs to other workstations in the network. The server operates under the control of the network operating system and usually has a large amount of disk storage capacity.

To connect to the LAN, each computer has a *network card* added to the internal circuitry of each computer. This special type of expansion board, discussed in more detail in chapter 5, contains the circuitry and connectors needed to physically connect to the communication lines that interconnect each computer in the network. Local area networks are most efficient when they service a large number of users in a limited area, usually within a mile of each other. Large office buildings, college campuses, and industrial complexes often use LANs to fulfill their data communication needs.

Each computer in a local area network can work independently of the others. When users need to access network resources, they follow a *login script*. This script identifies and links users to the network operating system after they enter a specified user name and password. A student's user name could be a student number or the name of the class in which he or she is enrolled. Faculty members might use their last name as a user name. Passwords are kept confidential and do not display on-screen when entered. A computer professional known as a **network administrator** is responsible for setting up user names and passwords along with overseeing all aspects of network operations and security.

The user name and password do more than identify a user's workstation to the network. Given a specific login script, the network *maps* (identifies) local hardware resources, such as disk drives and high-speed printers, to which the workstation has access based on predefined user needs. The network administrator is responsible for creating and maintaining login scripts and maps. A student using a PC and LAN in Harrington College's computer lab can access a word processor on the file server's hard disk and the network printer. Students do not have access to the disk drive that maintains system documentation used by the network administrator.

## Wide Area Networks

The observatory at which Neil and Jamal work is just one part of a **wide area network** **(WAN)** illustrated in Figure 4.8. The WAN connecting Neil's California observatory to England is called the *Internet*. This type of network spans large geographic areas and uses a variety of commercial and private communication lines to connect computers. The Internet connects universities, research centers, and businesses from hundreds of countries all over the globe. The Closer Look at the end of this chapter examines ways you can explore *(surf)* the Internet.

Each computer system within a WAN or LAN is called a *node*. Nodes include direct input from mainframes, PCs in labs, and laptops used by traveling businesspeople. Like LANs, login scripts are used to gain access to WANs.

Your local telephone company is a part of a WAN. The computers at each telephone exchange connect to other exchanges to allow you to talk to people all over the world. Although you do not log in when using your telephone, the associated area code and telephone number serves as your user name in this type of WAN.

## Value-Added Networks

Wide area networks provide innovative businesspeople the opportunity to offer additional services to network users for a fee. These services include access to databases, electronic mail, games, and even timesharing with mainframe computers. Businesses that add services to current WAN capabilities create a **value-added network (VAN)**.

**4.8**

Rathmore Observatory is part of a wide area network that connects people and computers over geographically dispersed areas.

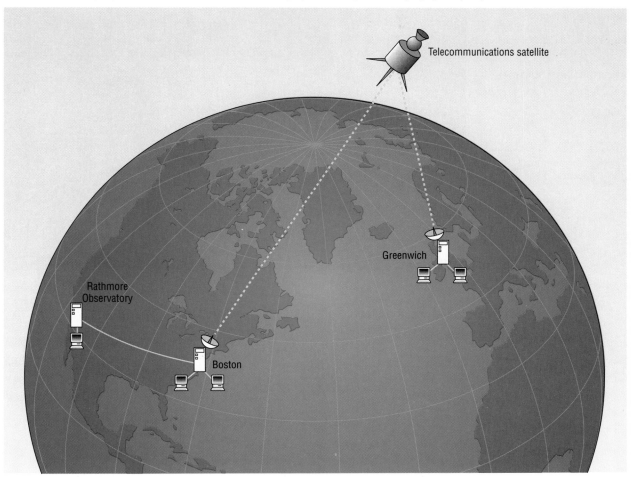

For example, VANs for telephone users may be assigned a 900 area code. Telephone numbers serviced by this area code could provide tax or financial advice. Several of these pay-by-the-minute VAN services have become very controversial because of the type of information they deliver to users.

In many countries VANs are under government regulation and are classified as either public or private. Public VANs are available to anyone with communication hardware and the ability to pay service fees. Public VANs, sometimes called information services, are discussed in more detail later in this chapter.

## Client/Server Computing

Every organization has its own data handling and data processing requirements. A variety of network designs have been developed to meet these needs. For instance, data communication at Northern Bank requires sharing data among three branch offices,

**4.9**

A client/server design used by this bank supports greater network flexibility because each teller computer or ATM, the client, is intelligent enough to perform tasks usually taken on by the server in more-traditional network setups.

## DID YOU KNOW?
### ...ABOUT E-MAIL DOs AND DON'Ts

- Format your messages. Narrow columns are easier to read than those that span the width of the screen.

- If you write an e-mail message with your word processor, save it as an ASCII file. Otherwise, the formatting codes of your word processor will produce unexpected results on your addressee's screen.

- Think before you write. E-mail's convenience prompts some users to dash off several hasty notes, when, with a little forethought, one message would have done the job.

- Don't type in all-capital letters.

- Don't send cutesy messages.

- Be concise, but avoid choppy, staccato sentences.

- Attach a meaningful headline. This gives the recipient an idea of the message's content before he reads the entire opus.

- It's a nice touch to sign your name, even though most e-mail systems automatically identify the sender.

*Source: PC/Computing,* October 1988, page 196.

located in two adjacent towns, and a credit card authorization center. Automatic teller machines (ATMs) and workstations similar to those shown in Figure 4.9 are hardwired with telephone lines to a server in each branch. Data processed in the branch office is transmitted by the server to a computer in Northern's main office.

Northern Bank uses a flexible *client/server* network design. In a client/server network, the user's computer, the client, takes on more responsibility than it does in a traditional server-oriented network. The client computer most often handles the user interface software. Northern's ATMs and personal computers are used for displaying menus and accepting data. The tellers use a specific type of personal computer without disk drives, known as a *diskless workstation,* because the data is stored and maintained by the server.

A client/server network is a classic example of distributed data processing. Each client on the network handles its own data entry and error checking. This approach improves network performance by freeing the server to handle other network responsibilities, such as accessing the customer database maintained across town at the main office. Furthermore, more ATMs or teller workstations can be added to the network before compromising system performance, because each system takes responsibility for its own user interface and data handling.

## ■ Teleprocessing

Before the advent of inexpensive personal computers, many organizations purchased *terminals,* which contained a keyboard for input and a screen or printing mechanism for output. Although it looked like a PC, a terminal did not have any processing or storage capacity of its own. Data input through the terminal was immediately sent to an attached computer for processing, and results were then sent back to the terminal for output.

An important problem for many organizations at this time was where processing power should lie when data was shared over a large geographic area. One popular solution was *teleprocessing*. In a teleprocessing system, communication lines connect remote terminals and printers to a centralized computer center. Transaction-intensive applications that required the input and tracking of hundreds of thousands of credit card charges, billings for insurance policies, and the like needed high-speed centralized computing power.

Airline reservation systems were a perfect application for teleprocessing. Thousands of people at hundreds of locations need to reserve seats, often months in advance. Coordination of reservations needed to be centralized. Terminals at travel agencies were linked, as part of a teleprocessing system, to a high-speed computer. The central computer would keep track of each ticket request and update flight information using a database management system. As a result, travel agents could provide up-to-the-minute information on flight schedules. When they booked seats on particular flights, that information was sent through communication lines and recorded immediately to prevent overbooking.

These high-volume teleprocessing systems have slowly evolved as new technology becomes available. Personal computers replaced terminals, and now many of these organizations are using their centralized high-speed computers as servers in a client/server network.

## NETWORK TOPOLOGIES

A computer network can be as simple or as complex as user requirements dictate. Three fundamental designs, known as **network topologies**, are used for organizing computer networks: the bus topology, the ring topology, and the star topology.

**4.10**

The bus topology connects computers along a common network cable.

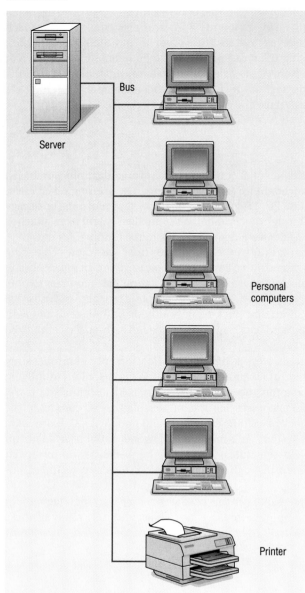

Server

Bus

Personal computers

Printer

### Bus Topology

A *bus topology* connects several computers, or nodes, with a single network cable. Just as a bus services all the stations along its route, in a bus topology all messages move over a single communication line to which all nodes are connected. Each node is capable of establishing direct communication through the bus line with every other node in the network. Figure 4.10 shows an example of a bus topology.

Consider, for instance, a group of civil engineers and support personnel working within the same office and using a bus network. Design ideas, building schedules, and other data entered into individual PCs would be stored on the database server where others could access it as needed. Everyone also has access to the color printer connected to the server. The bus topology promotes efficient person-to-person communication and the sharing of data.

### Ring Topology

Direct communication between nodes is also possible in a *ring topology*. Each node in a ring network is connected to two others, ultimately forming a large circle. An electronic message typically must travel from one node to the next, around the ring, until it reaches the appropriate destination (see Figure 4.11). Electronic messages and other transmissions always travel in the same direction. A ring topology may be used to connect computers at several large universities. Ideas and research can be passed around the network as needed. Institutions do not need to be directly connected to all others for information to be effectively shared.

### Star Topology

At the hub of *star topology* is a central controlling computer that routes all communication requests. As shown in Figure 4.12, each node is linked solely to the central computer, called the *host*. Since no internode connections exist, direct computer-to-computer communication is impossible without going through the host. Instead, the host intervenes to deliver messages to specified

**4.11**

Ring networks connect one computer to two others as part of peer-to-peer communication.

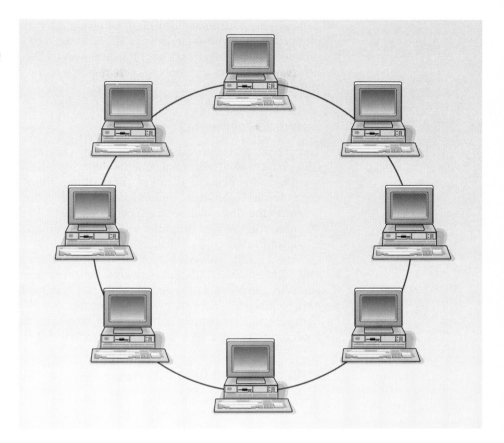

**4.12**

Star networks form around a central computer system (host), which coordinates communications between the various computers.

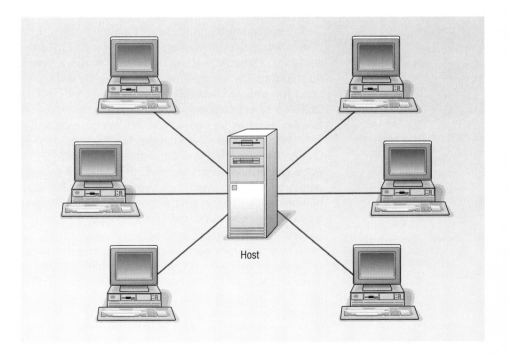

Host

destinations. A manufacturing plant with computers coordinating different phases of production could use a star network. The host would coordinate activities and maximize production schedules by acting as the intermediary between the other computers. One disadvantage of the star topology is that failure of the host computer shuts down the entire network.

## Hybrid Topologies

Two or more topologies can be linked to form a *hybrid topology*. For example, Rathmore Observatory links Neil, Jamal, and the other scientists together on a LAN using a bus topology. This network is linked through the Internet to a network of university computers in Boston that employs a ring topology. From there Neil and Jamal's message is sent to the Greenwich research computer that also serves as a host computer in a star network. The host computer then passes the message along to Dr. Baranson's PC, as shown in Figure 4.8.

As a result, one way to describe the Internet is as a WAN using a hybrid topology. The point at which different networks are linked together is called a ***gateway***. This hardware contains circuitry and communication software to aid in linking two networks or in connecting a network to a teleprocessing system. Differences in communication hardware and procedures between the systems are handled by the gateway. A data communication specialist would be needed to install the gateway.

## Coordinating Data Communication

When computers share a communication channel, arrangements must be made to prevent overlapping data transmissions *(collisions)*. To avoid collisions and other data communication problems, a network uses a set of communication ***protocols***—predefined procedures for establishing, maintaining, or terminating data communication between nodes.

Two common protocols for computers sharing a communication channel involve contention and token passing. These protocols establish procedures that minimize data collisions. These procedures are similar to those used by people when they talk with one another. For example, people sharing the same telephone line (party line) in rural areas run into problems when two people try to use the telephone at the same time. Collision detection occurs when each caller hears the other dialing. One way to handle this *contention* is for both callers to hang up, wait, and try again.

When computers in a network have a similar problem, a contention protocol called CSMA/CD (carrier sense multiple access with collision detection) is used. In other words, when contention occurs as two computers start to transmit simultaneously along the communication channel, they both stop and wait a randomly assigned amount of time before retrying. That is, each node waits a slightly different period of time as a means of resolving the contention problem. The popular Ethernet protocol commonly found with LANs utilizes CSMA/CD, as shown in Figure 4.13.

Have you ever been to a meeting where everyone tried to talk at once? One way to handle this problem is to make a rule that only the person with the designated token (gavel, stick, and so forth) can talk. When one person has had his or her say, the token is passed to the next person. This procedure is repeated until everyone has had a chance to speak. *Token passing* protocols use similar procedures. An electronic signal (token) is sent continually from one node to another. Network nodes cannot transmit any data

**4.13**

These common network types use different topologies and communication protocols.

## Common Network Types

| | Communication Protocol | Topology |
|---|---|---|
| **Ethernet** (802.3) | CSMA/CD | Star or bus |
| **Token Ring** | Token passing | Star |
| **ARCNET** | Token passing | Star or bus |
| **LocalTalk** | CSMA/CA (collision avoidance) | Bus |
| **FDDI** | Token passing | Ring |

until they receive the token. The token carries the message from node to node until it reaches its destination in the network.

These communication protocols and network topologies are combined in different ways as shown in Figure 4.13. Network administrators choose from these competing network types when linking computer technology. They consider the number of users and their needs along with current hardware and the physical characteristics of the workplace.

In the final analysis, the network operating system controls the flow of data between network nodes. It does this by using either a server-based or peer-to-peer approach to data communication. As you might expect, a *server-based network operating system* relies on system software running on a database or file server. The server handles all network communication. The number of nodes connected to the server is limited by the volume of data communication handled by the server and its processing speed. Some high-performance network operating systems work on servers with multiple processors.

*Peer-to-peer network operating systems* become practical when fewer than 25 computers need connecting. A peer-to-peer approach evenly distributes network tasks involving communication protocols among all the computers, not just one. Every computer on the network communicates directly with the others. As a result, users easily share such system resources as disk space, printers, and scanners. As you can imagine, connecting too many computers using this approach creates performance problems because network responsibilities become too demanding.

## NETWORK APPLICATIONS

Networks—whether wide area or local—expand our ability to use computers as problem-solving tools. Numerous public and private networks now bring a variety of services into corporate offices and private homes. In fact, it is relatively common for organizations to enhance interoffice data communication by linking people together through user-friendly computer networks. Here is a review of some of the most common types of network applications.

### ▇ Bulletin Board Systems

A public access message system, known as an electronic ***bulletin board system (BBS)***, allows users to communicate with one another, often without charge. By signing on to

**4.14**

Games and software can be downloaded from a BBS or information service to online personal computers.

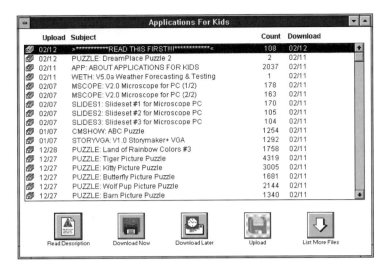

a bulletin board service, users can share programs, data, and messages with other bulletin board members. Participants in a BBS use modems to gain access to the service. They can scan bulletins left by other users or compose their own messages.

Initially, bulletin boards were used by computer hobbyists, who exchanged information about new technologies and applications for computers. Since then the number of BBSs has grown to accommodate all types of callers; DNA researchers swap information via bulletin boards, as do engineers, physicians, and marine biologists.

Members of a BBS also have access to noncommercial, public domain software and shareware, as shown in Figure 4.14. The programs are uploaded to the bulletin board computer. To **upload** is to transfer data or programs to another computer. Once the bulletin board receives the public domain software, it can be copied by any user in the network. This process, the receiving of a program or data from another computer, is called **downloading**.

Despite the low or nonexistent service fee, bulletin boards still require some human intervention. A *system operator,* or *sysop,* is responsible for maintaining the bulletin board operation, checking that no questionable data or copyrighted software appears on the BBS for downloading, and providing assistance to members.

## ■ Information Services

The growth in popularity of personal computers has spawned the development of VANs that provide users with access to expansive databases. These commercial services are known as **information services** or *information utilities* and are accessible to anyone with a computer, modem, and telephone. Information services offer convenient access to huge stores of information.

Information services require payment of a minimum monthly fee or a one-time subscription fee, plus charges for time spent online with the network, as well as other possible telephone charges, usually determined by the time of day and duration of access. Access is most costly during business hours.

Information services such as CompuServe, Prodigy, and America Online offer news and business bulletins, banking services, and online forums, as shown in Figure 4.15. An information service or BBS may support several *forums,* which promote

**4.15**

Online forums promote the open discussion of topics concerning a variety of special-interest groups.

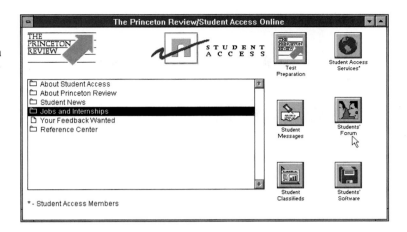

the real-time interchange from different users on selected topics. Also, reviews of films, plays, books, and restaurants can be accessed, along with airline schedules and video games. These services provide customer access to software packages, text editors, and programming languages. There is even an online shopping service that lets subscribers purchase sporting goods, appliances, and clothing at a discount. Information utilities target a broad audience and provide information on many subjects.

The Dow Jones News/Retrieval Service, for example, is an information service geared to the needs of businesspeople. The service offers stock market quotations, reports on business and economic news, and profiles of companies. Nonbusiness information provided by the Dow Jones service includes general news stories, weather reports, and online encyclopedias.

In addition to these information utilities, a number of specialized dial-up services have emerged. Career opportunity networks assist people who desire new jobs, and even provide career counseling to network users. Dating services target the social interests of users. Other special-interest information services provide news in such fields as medicine, law, education, and entertainment.

## ■ Telecommuting and Teleconferencing

The ability to access information networks from home has forced many people to reevaluate how training and work are done. Already, some people's work takes them outside the office. With the ability to link workers together through computer networks, **telecommuting** is now feasible. A wide range of productivity software, combined with portable computers, allows "telecommuters" to work at home or at other locations.

Some professionals, such as architects, writers, and computer programmers, can work at home, using a personal computer. By logging into the office network from home, they can use *electronic mail*, or *e-mail*, to keep in touch with their office. E-mail replaces or enhances the traditional interoffice mail system. A memo can be sent to one person, several people, or everyone connected to the network. The e-mail message found in the Closer Look at the end of the chapter is ready to go to the president of the United States.

Some systems assign a personal disk file, or *electronic mailbox,* to each user. The originator prepares a list of recipients for each document. The e-mail program uses the list to identify the mailbox destinations to a computer, which delivers the memo by

Teleconferencing between two or more users is possible by installing video cameras on the top of everyone's personal computer.

copying it into the specified mailbox files. People can read their messages each time they check their electronic mailboxes. They can use e-mail to respond immediately to the memo if necessary.

The e-mail system also delivers messages, electronic worksheets, and work assignments to the employee's home computer. If additional data is needed from work, employees can download it to their personal computers. The work is completed at home and transmitted back to the office through the same system.

This type of flexibility provides a solution to workers in special situations. Working at home can appeal to people with small children; they can stay at home and raise a family without sacrificing their careers. Working at home can also appeal to employees with physical disabilities who find it difficult to commute daily to an office.

As you can see, the office environment is no longer bound by walls or limited to a single building. Through computers many of these activities can take place in the home. By using communication networks, individuals at different locations can hold conferences. *Teleconferencing* enables businesspeople to participate in seminars given by experts located around the world without the inconvenience and expense of physically traveling to the seminar. In other cases, the conference may involve a quick discussion between two people trying to solve a specific problem, as shown in Figure 4.16.

## Workgroup Computing

Linking computers to form networks is changing the way people work in other ways as well. E-mail reduces the time and expense of sending documents or messages through conventional delivery services. Users can send messages to any other user or to everyone in the mail network; thus, they can receive from any other users as well. *Voice mail* is the verbal equivalent of e-mail. Messages are recorded and routed to an individual's electronic mailbox and played back as needed; responses can then be sent to the appropriate person.

**4.17**

Groupware is designed to support workgroup computing.

## Workgroup Computing Using Groupware

■ **Electronic Mail and Voice Mail**

Private and public mailing lists

Automatic acknowledgment of mail

Built-in word processing

Fax support

Password security on mailbox

Message filtering

■ **Bulletin Board**

Allows response to posted messages

Allows downloading and uploading
of data and software

Virus protection

■ **Teleconferencing**

Supports video broadcast of participants

Electronic whiteboard

Supports mediation from a designated facilitator

Electronic voting

■ **Calendar and Scheduling**

Ability to lock out selected times

Automatic checking for common meeting times

E-mail notification of meeting

E-mail meeting confirmation

■ **Shared Documents**

Private and public files

Password security on files

Supports complex documents

Supports group editing

Maintains readers' log

E-mail and voice mail are important features of workgroup software, or *groupware*, which also incorporates public calendars and scheduling, interactive conference calls, electronic voting, and document sharing (see Figure 4.17). Groupware works within a network to help people communicate ideas and resolve problems. It coordinates the flow of information between people to support *workgroup computing*. People working in different time zones can use groupware features on wide area networks to minimize problems associated with different working hours.

For example, researchers like astronomer Neil Janson use groupware to share information. At the beginning of this chapter, Neil used an e-mail system within a wide area network to contact Dr. Baranson in England. After the initial findings were posted on one of the Internet's electronic bulletin boards, other astronomers responded with dozens of e-mail messages, asking for more information. To handle this increase in e-mail messages, Neil used the groupware's message-filtering feature to redirect all e-mail about the aberration to a particular mailbox. *Message filtering* allows a groupware user to automatically sort incoming mail based on personally selected keywords; any e-mail using a keyword is sent to a specific mailbox. Some groupware packages will even signal the user when "priority" mail arrives from a specific person or company.

Many of the e-mail messages requested a teleconference with Neil. During the teleconference the groupware's user interface supported the questions and answers using an *electronic whiteboard*. Participants posed questions by typing on their keyboards; Neil answered questions in the same way. The electronic whiteboard posted each question and related answer on a designated area of everyone's PC screen. Photographic images taken by Neil's telescope and computer-enhanced could be displayed on command by any of the groupware users.

As Neil worked with others in collaborating his findings, he started writing an article about it for an important scientific journal. The groupware document-sharing feature helped Neil distribute rough drafts of the article to colleagues working at the observatory as well as others located at different universities. Furthermore, the groupware's *readers' log* kept track of who had accessed, and hopefully read, the paper. Another groupware feature allowed the readers to make editorial comments about the article. These suggestions were independently stored in separate files that Neil could recall when writing the final draft.

## ■ Electronic Funds Transfer

When you cash a check, another network of computers comes into play. The banking industry has developed a WAN that helps minimize the work involved in transferring money between banks. An *electronic funds transfer (EFT)* system handles financial transactions through a computer network rather than by exchanging cash. Through the use of electronic passwords and credit cards, buyers and sellers can advise a bank that a transaction has been completed. The bank completes the transaction by automatically moving the money from the buyer's account to the seller's.

An EFT system provides a solution for problems that continually have plagued buyers, sellers, and banks. Without the use of EFT, buyers have had limited purchasing

**4.18**

Without electronic data interchange, purchase orders, bills, and other transactions must be manually processed.

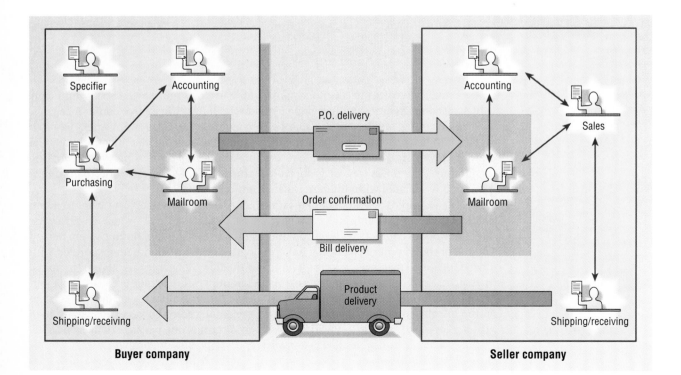

power outside of their local community; out-of-town stores would not always accept their checks. Also, many stores do not have credit plans available for major purchases. Sellers, in turn, always had to be on the outlook for stolen or uncashed checks. There was also a delay between the time a buyer wrote a check and the time a seller actually received the money. Banks were caught in the middle, handling millions of checks per day. An EFT system minimizes the need to write checks and for the bank to process the paper involved.

Currently, the French are leading the way in using a new type of credit card that will help minimize fraudulent electronic transactions. Called a *smart card*, this credit card contains a processor and memory chip that stores and updates the owner's credit information. Every time a transaction is made using this smart credit card, the transaction immediately becomes part of the owner's credit history. If a stolen card is used, the memory chip is wiped clean by a credit card reader. Erasing occurs when the merchant tries to verify the customer's credit through the bank's central computer system.

### ■ Electronic Data Interchange

For organizations, *electronic data interchange (EDI)* is the electronic exchange of specially formatted business documents for ordering new supplies. Business computers transfer data directly instead of people using paper forms sent through regular mail, as illustrated in Figure 4.18. Electronic data interchange takes place when a catalog company electronically sends a summary of its customer orders to its suppliers' computers. When EFT is linked to EDI, bank statements are sent to the organization, and bills are paid electronically. By using EDI, an organization can cut down on paperwork, reduce data entry errors, and more efficiently manage its data.

**4.18** *(continued)*

EDI automates this process by connecting the buyer's and seller's computer systems.

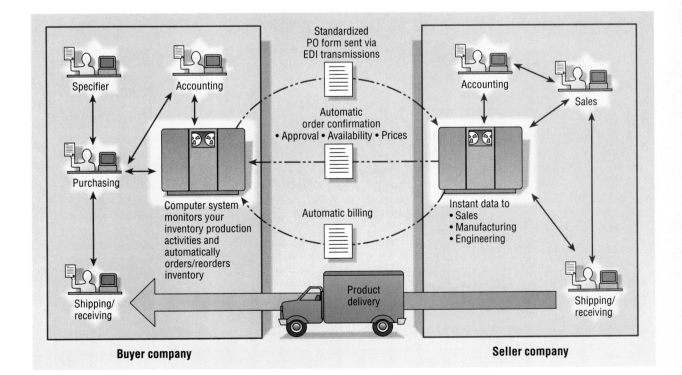

# A Closer Look at The Internet

**The Internet** has turned out to be more than the "information superhighway" that then U.S. Senator Al Gore described in 1989. It is also the information back alleys and side streets. It is a web of computers interconnecting a few PCs in cozy labs strung together by cable to international telephone networks connecting high-speed computers by bouncing digital signals off satellites. Many of these pathways are open to electronic wanderers with the time and patience to explore new frontiers.

**Q: How do I link up with the Internet?**

**A:** The two traditional Internet ports-of-entry are either an information service or a LAN already connected to an Internet gateway. A PC and modem with a valid user name and password for Prodigy, CompuServe, America Online, or other Internet provider gets you in automatically. At many schools, access to the LAN also provides access to the Internet.

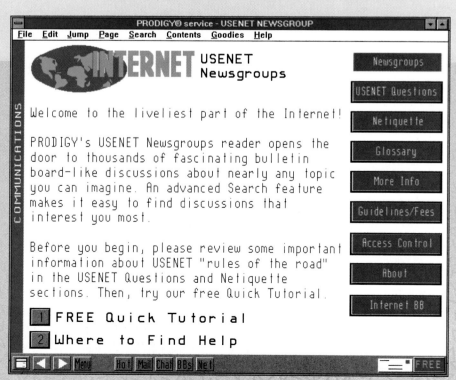

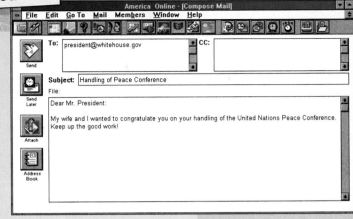

**A:** You can use the Internet to communicate with anyone with an *electronic
mail address*. There are three basic parts:

*username@useraddress*

No spaces are allowed in the address.
The user name is the same one used
during login and ends with the @ symbol.
The user address most often contains
location, organization identifier, and
country identifier (dropped in the U.S.)
separated by periods. A few samples follow:

@whitehouse.gov (gov = government organization or department)

@microsoft.com (com = commercial organization)

@umn.edu (edu = education, in this case the University of Minnesota)

@cern.ch (ch = Switzerland, in this case the European Particle Physics Lab)

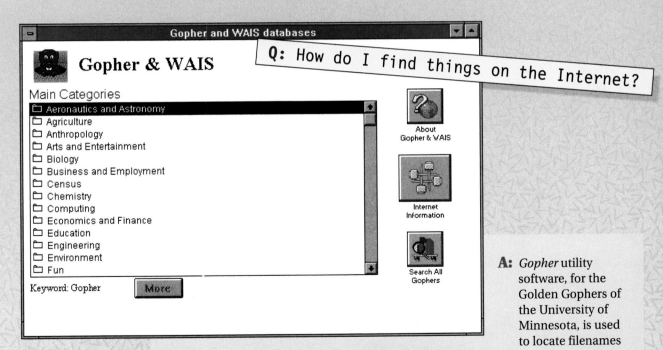

**Q: How do I find things on the Internet?**

**A:** *Gopher* utility
software, for the
Golden Gophers of
the University of
Minnesota, is used
to locate filenames

of interest. Often a brief description of the file's contents is available. Other popular
options are *WAIS (Wide Area Information Servers)*, pronounced "ways," which help
you search through database indexes for topics of interest.

**Q:** What can I do with information when I find something interesting?

**A:** The sharing of data is what the Internet is all about, and many host computers have *FTP (file transfer protocol)* servers to support downloading files to your PC. Special utility software called *archies,* like the comic book character, are used to locate files stored on FTP servers.

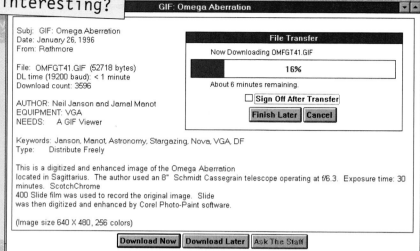

**Q:** How does the World Wide Web work?

**A:** The *World Wide Web,* or *WWW,* uses a hypermedia data organization that allows users to easily jump from one Internet server to another (see chapter 11). Users need a WWW user interface, called a *browser,* to jump from topic to topic. By utilizing a mouse to select buttons or designated areas on-screen, the WWW browser lets people explore Internet connections by following various hypermedia links.

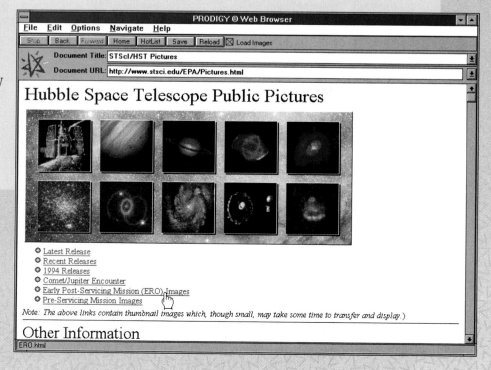

**Q:** What are some of the basic tools for surfing the Internet?

**A:** Software that people commonly need to access the Internet include an e-mail handler, GIF (graphical interchange format) viewer, World Wide Web browser, and data compression/decompression utility software. A local telephone number or LAN gateway and a willingness to make mistakes while exploring are also necessary. Information services often provide all or some of these software tools.

**Q:** Should I have any concerns when using a public network?

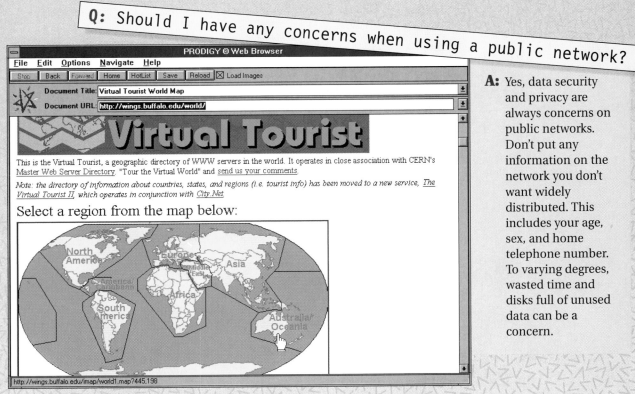

**A:** Yes, data security and privacy are always concerns on public networks. Don't put any information on the network you don't want widely distributed. This includes your age, sex, and home telephone number. To varying degrees, wasted time and disks full of unused data can be a concern.

## CHAPTER FACTS

■ Telecommunication is electronic communication over long distances. Data communication is the electronic sending and receiving of data.

■ Data coming to and from computers is in digital form. This is converted to analog signals to be sent over voice-oriented telephone hardware.

■ Facsimile (fax) machines work like modems by converting and transmitting paper-based images over telephone lines for printing or storage on another machine.

■ Digital/analog conversion is done by modems, which take bit patterns representing data and convert them to sounds for transmission using telephone lines. A modem at the receiving end converts sound back into original bit patterns.

■ Portable computers with cellular modems become personal communication devices with great flexibility.

■ Distributed processing involves several computers linked together to share data processed by end users.

■ Local area networks (LANs) serve a confined area such as an office complex, whereas wide area networks (WANs) can cover large geographic areas.

■ Networks with services beyond data communication are called value-added networks (VANs).

■ Powerful personal computers now support client/server network designs, where the PCs take over processing once done by the server.

■ The sharing of a single computer's processing power by several terminals over communication lines is teleprocessing.

■ Network topologies fall into three basic categories: bus, ring, and star.

■ A single communication channel links computers within a bus network.

■ Computers within a ring network are linked to two others forming the ring.

■ Star networks rely on a host computer to coordinate data communication.

■ Predefined procedures for transmitting data are known as communication protocols.

■ Gateways link networks with different protocols.

■ Network operating systems support data communication through peer-to-peer or server-based connections.

- Bulletin board systems (BBSs) serve as centers for leaving public messages and sharing public domain software.

- By accessing an information service, a user can tap into a variety of online services, such as reservation systems, reviews, market quotes, and forums.

- Working people can use computer technology to work at home or reduce travel time through telecommuting and teleconferencing.

- Workgroup computing is made possible with groupware features that support electronic mail, voice mail, public calendars, meeting schedulers, electronic voting, teleconferencing, and document sharing.

- Electronic funds transfer (EFT) uses a computer network to handle financial transactions between banks, buyers, and sellers.

- Electronic data interchange (EDI) allows the exchange of business documents between two or more organizations.

- Internet users use e-mail addresses to locate people and send them messages.

- Gophers, wide area information servers, and archies are used to locate information on the Internet.

- World Wide Web browsers allow users to jump from topic to topic.

- Data security and privacy is always a concern when working on public networks like the Internet.

## TERMS TO REMEMBER

| | | |
|---|---|---|
| baud rate | electronic mail (e-mail) | server |
| bits per second (bps) | facsimile (fax) machine | telecommunication |
| bulletin board system (BBS) | gateway | telecommuting |
| client/server | groupware | teleconferencing |
| data communication | information service | teleprocessing |
| distributed processing | local area network (LAN) | upload |
| download | modem | value-added network (VAN) |
| electronic data interchange (EDI) | network administrator | voice mail |
| electronic funds transfer (EFT) | network operating system | wide area network (WAN) |
| | network topology | workstation |
| | protocol | |

## MIX AND MATCH

*Complete the following definitions with the Terms to Remember.*

1. _____ answers telephone calls and saves callers' messages for later playback.

2. A(n) _____ sends and receives paper-based images over communication lines.

3. An online meeting of people using network technology is known as _____.

4. When you _____, you receive data or programs directly from another computer.

5. The person responsible for overseeing network operations and security is known as the _____.

6. A(n) _____ is a commercial VAN wherein users pay for access.

7. The description of how computers are interconnected within a network is known as the _____.

8. _____ is the act of sending data electronically from one location to another.

9. The practice of exchanging bills and banking information using data communication technology is known as _____.

10. A(n) _____ is a public access message system that allows users to leave or read messages.

11. Sending data or programs directly to another computer is known as _____.

12. A(n) _____ is a node within a network that handles particular tasks.

13. The device that converts a single data transmission from analog to digital signals and back is a(n) _____.

14. Personal messages sent and received through a computer network are known as _____.

15. A(n) _____ comprises interconnected computers within a confined service area.

## REVIEW QUESTIONS

1. Define the Terms to Remember.

2. Why would someone want to send data using the Integrated Services Digital Network (ISDN) format?

3. What are the advantages and disadvantages of using a fax board versus a stand-alone fax machine?

4. Why are modems needed for data communication?

5. When is a computer a personal communication device?

6. What are five services that data communication software provides computer users with modems?

7. How are personal computers connected to a local area network?

8. What happens when you log in to a network?

9. What is the difference between a teleprocessing computer system and a computer network?

10. What are the characteristics of the three basic network topologies?

11. Describe two different methods for avoiding data collisions on a network.

12. What are the limitations of server-based and peer-to-peer network operating systems?

13. What are the responsibilities of a bulletin board's sysop?

14. How do information services charge users?

15. What are seven groupware features that could be used for workgroup computing?

16. How are electronic funds transfer and electronic data interchange similar?

17. How are electronic mail addresses, gophers, wide area information servers, file transfer protocols, archies, and browsers used on the Internet?

18. What are the concerns of public network users?

## APPLYING WHAT YOU'VE LEARNED

1. Communication software is a critical component of any data communication system. Compare two commercial and/or shareware packages. Identify costs for acquiring the software and list any special features you find interesting or useful. Don't forget to look at software available on local BBSs and through information services.

2. If you wanted to join all the computers in your school into a network, which of the topologies would you use? Make a simple drawing of the network, label each node, and identify its location.

3. Educators have been speculating how groupware can change the way classes are taught. Pick a grade and subject, then describe how students and teachers could use groupware to improve the quality of instruction in their classroom.

4. An electronic mail or voice mail system uses a computer to store correspondence. Potentially, this could make it available to anyone with access to the system.
   a. What could be done to protect the privacy of a person's business or academic correspondence?
   b. What other losses of privacy could occur if e-mail is used in all departments of a large organization?

5. Telecommuting is slowly becoming accepted in business, but it does have its disadvantages. Name five jobs where telecommuting would not be possible. What are five jobs where telecommuting is not only possible but could be advantageous to both workers and employers? What are some additional responsibilities that a telecommuter has?

6. Describe how a consumer-oriented EDI system would work. Do you know of any companies that are allowing PC users to use such services?

7. Any and all types of data, photographs, music, and videos are available on different networks. Should consumers be able to "lock out" their computers and telephones so children cannot access some of these resources? Do you think VANs should be regulated? Explain your rationale.

# Computer Hardware

**U**nit II explores how computer technology works internally. Chapter 5 explains the different types of processing hardware. Ranging in power from a single-purpose microcomputer to a high-capacity mainframe or supercomputer, the processing hardware is the controlling element. Characteristics of each type of processing hardware are examined along with the problems they best solve. Also, this chapter examines closely how people can upgrade their own personal computer.

Computer-generated information is only as useful as the input data and output information. Chapter 6 looks at the different types of input and output hardware involved in a variety of applications. Different techniques exist for entering data of varying types. Peripherals also come in diverse forms to support temporary, permanent, and action output.

People use a variety of equipment to store and transfer data in a computer-readable format. Chapter 7 explores magnetic tape and disk media as well as innovations in optical storage. Specific procedures and hardware for maximizing disk utilization, minimizing storage and transmission errors, transferring data, and optimizing communication channels are examined as well.

# Processing Hardware

# FROM THE USER'S POINT OF VIEW

**A**s with any technology, present-day computers are built on the hardware designs of the past. Even if you never look inside your personal computer system, it is important that you understand how the computer itself works. As an automobile driver, it is not necessary that you know the internal workings of an engine, but this knowledge helps you understand the limits of the vehicle and explain performance problems to technicians. Likewise, understanding the processing components of a computer system helps you troubleshoot problems or, at least, adequately explain difficulties to a computer professional. Also, knowing the options available to speed up processing helps you become a knowledgeable consumer when purchasing new computer equipment.

## PROCESSING IN THE PAST

Although the input and output components of a computer system—such as the keyboard and monitor—may be most familiar to the average user, the real power lies unseen within the processing hardware. The power and speed of processing hardware has increased astronomically since the first computers were built. Over the past 50 years, several unique forms of processing hardware have led people who study computing history to break it into five generations.

### First Generation

Before the 1940s there were several attempts to build mechanical computing machinery. Charles Babbage (Who's Who, chapter 13) and Blaise Pascal (Who's Who, chapter 1) both attempted and succeeded to varying degrees using springs and gears.

Even as late as 1944, an electromechanical calculator, the MARK1, incorporated mechanical and electrical components to perform simple arithmetic on data. The Colossus, developed in England in 1943, was used to decode German military codes during World War II. It is considered the first working electronic computer.

Back in the United States, J. Presper Eckert and John W. Mauchly were building the ENIAC (see Who's Who, chapter 2). Its processing hardware consisted of 17,000 vacuum tubes, 70,000 resistors, and 5 million soldered joints. *Vacuum tubes*, with their ability to turn off and on, were the components that stored the data and results as they were processed. Each vacuum tube was made of glass and contained electronic circuitry. Other computers, such as the UNIVAC I (shown in Figure 5.1), and radios and televisions of the day, depended on vacuum tubes. These tubes were unreliable, however, because the tremendous heat they generated shortened the working lives of the tubes and associated electrical equipment. Replacing tubes slowed processing.

## Second Generation

The late 1940s brought an invention that would revolutionize not only the computer industry but the entire world of electronics—the *transistor*. It was a small component that could transfer an electronic signal across a resistor. When transistors were used as the basis for a computer's processing hardware, the problems of heat production and unreliability were significantly reduced. Use of the transistor, developed by William Shockley, John Bardeen, and Walter Brattain (see Who's Who in this chapter), quickly spread to radios and other electronic devices.

### Third Generation

Although people found new uses for the transistor, it still produced too much heat for use in small or enclosed equipment. In 1959 Jack Kilby tested the first *integrated circuit,* or *IC* (see Who's Who in this chapter). The IC is a solid-state circuit made from a semiconducting material. The wafer-sized ICs could hold the equivalent of hundreds of transistors. The wafers, called *chips,* made computers smaller, faster, and lighter than their predecessors. The Closer Look at the end of this chapter explains how chips are manufactured.

### Fourth Generation

The miniaturization of computer processing hardware continued with the invention of the *microprocessor* by Gilbert Hyatt and Marcian Hoff (see Who's Who in this chapter). Initially designed for use in video controllers, microprocessors found instant success in the computer market. Previously, computer processing capabilities were distributed among several integrated circuits. Microprocessors combined circuits for processing, limited memory, and input/output control on a single chip. The first commercially developed microprocessor—the Intel 4004—was introduced in 1971. A few years later, the Intel 8008 expanded the capacity of the original version by providing multiuse arithmetic and control circuitry. The computing power that occupied an entire room during the 1950s can today reside on a slice of silicon smaller than a penny (see Figure 5.2).

**5.2**

The first four computer generations are represented here by their processing hardware: **(a)** the vacuum tube and **(b)** the transistor, **(c)** integrated circuits on the head of a pin, and **(d)** the microprocessor.

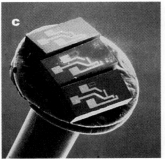

### Fifth Generation

The microprocessor is still the processing hardware of choice for many computers. However, research into faster ways of processing volumes of data has led to alternatives for this fourth-generation hardware. By combining rows of microprocessors, computer scientists are leading the way into the fifth generation through *multiprocessing*, also called *parallel processing*. In *asymmetrical multiprocessing* each program is assigned its own processor. When using *symmetrical multiprocessing*, a computer program is broken down into several modules and processed simultaneously by parallel processors. Efficiency and speed are considerably increased.

## BINARY CODES FOR DATA AND INSTRUCTIONS

Even from the earliest days of computing, the processing hardware of every computer generation used bits (binary digits of 0 or 1) and bit patterns to internally represent data and programs. George Boole held that all logical conditions could be described as either true or false (see Who's Who, chapter 7). Computer circuitry is an application of this theory. When electricity is present, circuits or paths through the computer's processing components may be either open or closed to the electrical pulses. Bit patterns, or combinations of these on/off bits, are how data and programs are processed and stored.

### Machine Code

Computer programming languages using English words or abbreviations must be translated into binary codes. When processing hardware is manufactured by different companies, each may have its own binary machine language, or *machine code*. Machine code represents the processor's internal switches with a 0, designating an open switch, and a 1, designating a closed switch. Different switch settings perform different operations.

Figure 5.3 shows how one line from a program written in the BASIC programming language might be translated into several lines of machine code. This line of BASIC code is one of many that make up a complete program. It is used to figure a total price when purchasing a designated number of tickets at a specified cost. The first two binary codes in Figure 5.3 identify the location in memory of the number of tickets sold and the cost of each ticket. The next line of machine code tells the processor to multiply TICKETS by COST. The last binary instruction indicates where the results, called TOTAL, are stored in memory.

### Standard Codes for Data

As with program instructions, data is also expressed as binary code. All input, whether a keystroke from a keyboard or a scan from a scanner, is converted to zeros and ones. Keystrokes can be an alphanumeric symbol or a *control character*, which represent special instructions for cursor movement, tabulation, carriage return, and so on. A scanner converts a photograph into a computer-usable format by organizing the image into rows and columns of dots whose location and color are represented in binary code. Music is

**5.3**

One instruction in the high-level programming language BASIC actually translates into several lines of machine code.

| Machine Code | | |
|---|---|---|
| **One high-level program instruction** | **=** | **Several machine language instructions** |

|  |  |
|---|---|
|  | 1011  0011  1001  0100<br>*Moves TICKETS from memory to processor* |
|  | 1111  0101  1101  1100<br>*Moves COST from memory to processor* |
| TOTAL = TICKETS * COST | 0001  1000  0010  1001<br>*Initiates multiplication* |
|  | 1110  1010  0110  0100<br>*Moves answer (TOTAL) from<br>processor to memory* |

converted to bit combinations to indicate the pitch and duration of individual notes. Different combinations of bits represent textual, graphical, and audio data. Computers that process data converted to binary digits are called *digital computers*.

A group of bits forms a bit pattern, known as a **byte**, which represents a single alphanumeric or control character. Several standard binary codes exist to represent textual data. As a result, no single standard has been established for all computers. Typically, computers use codes that assign either 7 or 8 bits per byte. Codes vary according to the type of computer system used.

Most smaller computers use a 7-bit code called the American Standard Code for Information Interchange, or *ASCII* (pronounced "*as*-kee"). ASCII was used originally by the communication industry for transmission over telegraph lines. This code has been adopted as the standard for many computers, particularly PCs. With ASCII, users can transmit data from one computer to another, even if the machines have different internal coding systems. Non-compatible data from one computer is converted to the widely compatible ASCII code for transmission. The second computer receives the ASCII data and converts the data to its own internal code. Software also exists to convert data to an ASCII file for storage on disk.

As a result, the use of ASCII increases opportunities to share data. A more recent version of ASCII uses 8-bit bytes. This expansion increased the number of bit combinations possible from 128 to 256 and therefore the number of characters that could be represented. For example, the bit pattern for the uppercase letter *A* in 8-bit ASCII is 01000001, a dollar sign is represented by 00100100, and the control character TAB is 00001001 (see Figure 5.4).

Larger computers typically use an 8-bit code called Extended Binary Coded Decimal Interchange Code, or *EBCDIC* (pronounced "*eb*-sih-dik"). The letter *A* in EBCDIC is 1100 0001, and a comma is encoded as 0111 1101. Whereas ASCII is used most commonly

**5.4**

Eight-bit ASCII is a binary code used in most personal computer systems to represent alphanumeric and control characters. Also shown is the EBCDIC equalivant used by mainframe computers.

| Eight-Bit Codes for Storing Data | | |
|---|---|---|
| **CHARACTER** | **ASCII** | **EBCDIC** |
| 0 | 00110000 | 1111 0000 |
| 1 | 00110001 | 1111 0001 |
| 2 | 00110010 | 1111 0010 |
| 3 | 00110011 | 1111 0011 |
| 4 | 00110100 | 1111 0100 |
| 5 | 00110101 | 1111 0101 |
| A | 01000001 | 1100 0001 |
| B | 01000010 | 1100 0010 |
| C | 01000011 | 1100 0011 |
| D | 01000100 | 1100 0100 |
| E | 01000101 | 1100 0101 |
| a | 01100001 | 1000 0001 |
| b | 01100010 | 1000 0010 |
| c | 01100011 | 1000 0011 |
| d | 01100100 | 1000 0100 |
| e | 01100101 | 1000 0101 |
| space | 00100000 | 0100 0000 |
| # | 00100011 | 0111 1011 |
| $ | 00100100 | 0101 1011 |
| * | 00101010 | 0101 1100 |
| ? | 00111111 | 0110 1111 |

with PCs and data communication, EBCDIC is used primarily for internal data handling by larger computers.

Eight-bit codes such as ASCII and EBCDIC have 256 different binary combinations. These coding systems adequately cover all the written characters traditionally used in English and other Indo-European languages; however, they do not take into consideration other languages, such as Chinese and Japanese, that employ thousands of characters. A new 16-bit coding system called *Unicode* supports 65,536 different binary combinations. Unicode is designed as a way for computers to process and store text in every known written language.

# William Shockley

(1910-1989)

## John Bardeen

(b. 1908)

## Walter Brattain

(1902-1987)

In the 1940s, computers and other electronic equipment had reached a physical impasse. They processed data by means of vacuum tubes, which were bulky, hot, undependable, and consumed a lot of power. Scientists William Shockley, John Bardeen, and Walter Brattain worked together at Bell Laboratories, looking for a more reliable replacement for the vacuum tube. After many tests, Shockley theorized that applying an external electrical field to a block of quartz with semiconducting film on one side and a metallic conductor on the other would provide the needed medium. They produced a "junction transistor" and revealed it to the scientific world in 1948. Acceptance was not immediate for the solid-state transistor. Although easier to mass produce than the vacuum tube, transistors did not fit into the vacuum tube connections of existing machines. Use of the transistor in telephones, hearing aids, and radios, however, brought the three men recognition. In 1956 Shockley, Bardeen, and Brattain were awarded the Nobel Prize for Physics. Just 10 years after its invention, the transistor technology was supplanted by a new idea—putting an entire circuit on a single piece of silicon—the integrated circuit.

## INSIDE A COMPUTER

Once data has been converted into binary form, it is ready to be processed. Manipulating data to obtain information occurs within the computer's processing unit. The processing unit provides all the computational and internal system control functions of a computer within two major components: the processor and the memory.

The processor combines arithmetic, logic, and control/communication operations on one or more chips, depending on the type of computer. Memory requires several chips to store data and programs during a specific IPOS cycle. Operations executed (performed) within the processor and memory are synchronized by an internal clock. The clock emits electrical pulses or cycles at a fixed rate. For example, the clock speed determines if a processor in a personal computer runs at 90 *MHz (megahertz)* versus 33 MHz. Each megahertz is equal to a million clock cycles per second. These pulses are used to coordinate program execution.

### Processor

Data manipulation, although seemingly sophisticated, is actually based on a simple premise. Computers can add and compare values. These operations take place at tremendous speeds within the processor. The speeds are measured in fractions of a second as *milliseconds* (thousandths), *microseconds* (millionths), *nanoseconds* (billionths), and *picoseconds* (trillionths). Instead of executing highly complex operations, a computer conducts many simple operations very quickly. This is the essence of computer processing power.

The processor, also called the ***central processing unit***, or ***CPU***, performs three basic operations: arithmetic, logic, and control/communication.

**Arithmetic Operations**    All the mathematics a computer performs is, essentially, addition. The computer can add two numbers to obtain a sum. Subtraction is actually negative addition, multiplication is repeated addition, and division is repeated negative addition. That is, a computer will use addition to find solutions to the following problems:

| SUBTRACTION | MULTIPLICATION | DIVISION |
|---|---|---|
| $6 - 3 = n$ | $6 * 3 = n$ | $6 / 3 = n$ |
| $6 + (-3) = 3$ | $6 + 6 + 6 = 18$ | $6 + (-3) + (-3) = 0*$ |

*Here the computer determines the answer (2) by counting the number of −3s that must be added before 0 is reached.

Simple addition, therefore, enables the computer to solve complex mathematical problems. Repetitions of arithmetic functions take very little time, because millions of instructions can be processed every second.

**Logical Operations**    Computer logic is, simply, comparing two values by determining whether a value is equal to, greater than, or less than another value. Although this idea is simple, it holds the potential for great processing power. For example, computer logic

**5.5**

This BASIC program uses a computer's ability to make logical comparisons to compute weekly overtime pay when an employee works more than 40 hours.

**BASIC Payroll Program**

```
100   REM *** PROCESSING SECTION OF PAYROLL PROGRAM ***
110   REM PROGRAM CODE TO COMPUTER REGULAR AND OVERTIME PAY
120   OVERTIME = 0
130   IF HOURS > 40
132      THEN REGPAY = RATE * 40
134          OVERTIME = (HOURS - 40) * (RATE * 1.5)
138      ELSE REGPAY = RATE * HOURS
140   GROSSPAY = REGPAY + OVERTIME
```

**Example A**

Rate = $5.00 and Hours = 40

Since 40 is not greater than 40

REGPAY = 200 (5.00 × 40)

OVERTIME = 0

GROSSPAY = **$200** (200 + 0)

**Example B**

Rate = $5.00 and Hours = 45

Since 45 is greater than 40

REGPAY = 200 (5.00 × 40)

OVERTIME = 37.50 [(45−40) × (5.00 × 1.5)]

GROSSPAY = **$237.50** (200 + 37.50)

can determine whether the number of tickets sold is equal to the number of seats in a theater. If so, the show is sold out. Computerized inventory systems depend on this type of logic.

Payroll processing also makes use of computer logic. If the number of hours an employee has worked in a week is greater than 40, the computer can adjust the pay scale to reflect overtime. The program in Figure 5.5 shows how this logic is coded in the BASIC programming language to compute overtime. The resulting values would be the employee's gross earnings.

Computer logic also can be used to sort data into alphabetical or numeric order. As with arithmetic, the computer executes logical functions at ultrahigh speeds, performing millions of instructions per second, or *MIPS*.

**Control/Communication Operations**   The processor, under control of the operating system, uses its control/communication operations to direct the flow of data into and out of memory. It also coordinates arithmetic and logic operations. To perform these operations, instructions and related data are sent along wires or bus lines. The **bus** is the path (circuitry) that connects the CPU with internal and external components. Peripheral hardware is connected to the CPU through an *expansion bus.* To send machine code along a bus line, bits or bytes may be collected into *words.* Each word is the number of bits that the CPU can use at a time. A 32-bit computer (a CPU that uses 32 bits per word) can process data faster than an 8-bit or 16-bit computer.

### Expansion Bus

Figure 5.6 illustrates how data is processed and returned to memory through control/communication operations performed by a processor using the bus to move the machine code and related data. Control/communication operations also initiate the arithmetic

**5.6**

Data and programs move from memory and peripheral hardware to the processor and back through bus lines.

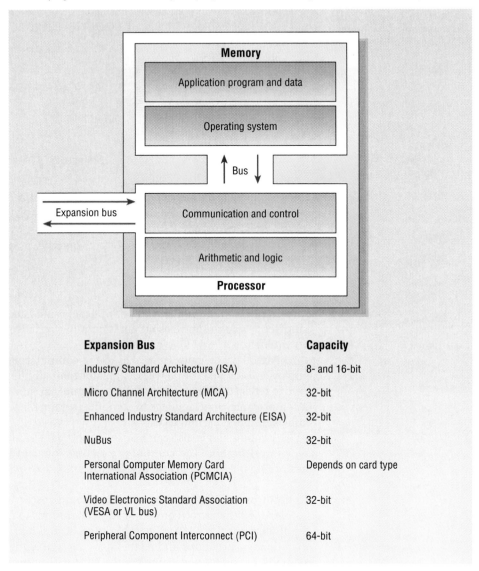

| Expansion Bus | Capacity |
|---|---|
| Industry Standard Architecture (ISA) | 8- and 16-bit |
| Micro Channel Architecture (MCA) | 32-bit |
| Enhanced Industry Standard Architecture (EISA) | 32-bit |
| NuBus | 32-bit |
| Personal Computer Memory Card International Association (PCMCIA) | Depends on card type |
| Video Electronics Standard Association (VESA or VL bus) | 32-bit |
| Peripheral Component Interconnect (PCI) | 64-bit |

and logic operations of the processor when needed. Results are then sent back to memory by the processor. As explained later in this chapter, the processor communicates with other hardware by sending out electrical pulses along an external bus line. Popular expansion bus standards and their related transmission capacities are shown in Figure 5.6.

Over the years the microprocessors controlling personal computers have become increasingly powerful as processing speeds have increased. For example, the original IBM personal computer used an Intel 8088 microprocessor that ran at 4.77 MHz. The

**5.7**

The processing speed of a microprocessor is measured in megahertz (MHz) with 1 MHz equal to 1 million clock cycles per second.

| Microprocessor Speeds | | | | | | |
|---|---|---|---|---|---|---|
| **Typical Computer** | **Processor ID** | **Processing Speed (MHz)** | **Word Size (bits)** | **Expansion Bus (bits)** | **Internal Bus (bits)** | **Max RAM** |
| *INTEL-BASED MICROPROCESSORS* | | | | | | |
| IBM PC | 8088 | 4.77 | 16 | 8 | 16 | 1 MB |
| IBM PC/AT | 80286 | 8+ | 16 | 16 | 24 | 16 MB |
| IBM PS/2 Model 80 | 80386 | 25+ | 32 | 32 | 32 | 32 MB |
| IBM PS/2 Model 90 | 80486 | 33+ | 32 | 32 | 32 | 32 MB |
| IBM PC300 | Pentium | 66+ | 32 | 64 | 32 | 4 G |
| HP Vectra VT | Pentium Pro | 150+ | 32 | 64 | 32 | 4 G |
| *MOTOROLA-BASED MICROPROCESSORS* | | | | | | |
| **Apple Macintosh** | | | | | | |
| Classic | 68000 | 8+ | 32 | 16 | 24 | 16 MB |
| L/T | 68020 | 16+ | 32 | 32 | 32 | 32 MB |
| SE/30 | 68030 | 20+ | 32 | 32 | 32 | 32 MB |
| Apple Quadra | 68040 | 33+ | 32 | 32 | 32 | 32 MB |
| *RISC-BASED MICROPROCESSORS* | | | | | | |
| Apple/IBM | PowerPC 604 | 133+ | 64 | 64 | 64 | 16 G |
| DEC | Alpha | 150+ | 64 | 64 | 64 | 16 G |
| Silicon Graphics | MIPS R10000 | 150+ | 64 | 64 | 64 | 16 G |

latest generation of microprocessors runs at 100 MHz or faster. Figure 5.7 shows the different microprocessors used by popular microcomputer manufacturers and their related processing speeds and bus capacities. We should point out that when you hear people refer to an Intel-based (or IBM-compatible) microcomputer as a 486 or Pentium machine, they are referring to the type of microprocessor used by the computer. A 486 computer has an Intel 80486 or compatible microprocessor, whereas a Pentium computer uses an Intel Pentium microprocessor.

## Coprocessors and RISC

For applications requiring high-speed mathematical computations, a specialized microprocessor, called a *math coprocessor,* is often available. This component supports the CPU by performing the calculations more rapidly than the primary processor while being controlled by the primary processor. Other specialized coprocessors support high-speed video.

Some chip manufacturers take a keep-it-simple approach when designing processors to boost processing speeds. The resulting ***reduced instruction set computing (RISC)*** processor uses fewer machine codes, which enables it to achieve faster processing speeds (see Figure 5.7) by eliminating intermediary steps. Applications calling for real-time graphic displays, such as the flight simulator shown in Figure 5.8, are currently taking advantage of RISC technology.

## Memory

In memory, data and programs are held only temporarily, just before and after processing is completed. Application programs instruct the computer to execute specific tasks. The machine code for these instructions and the necessary data are loaded into memory, where they stay until the processor needs them. After the processor conducts any required arithmetic and logic operations, it returns the results to memory for temporary storage. In general, memory should be thought of as temporary storage.

The relationship between memory and the processor is analogous to you sitting at your desk next to a file cabinet. You (the processor) are processing information found on your desk (temporary storage). Your in and out baskets are the means by which you receive (input) and send (output) data. Once you have processed information, it is either thrown away (erased) or filed in the cabinet (permanent storage). Disks provide a computer system with permanent storage.

The contents of a computer's memory, in most cases, are temporary and constantly undergoing change. This type of memory is known as *volatile memory.* The contents of volatile memory are subject to loss when the power is turned off. Thus, a constant electrical power supply is needed to retain data and instructions in volatile memory. Of course, data, program instructions, and the results of processing can be retained on storage media such as tapes and disks, which are discussed in chapter 7.

In general, memory chips fall under one of two categories: ***read-only memory (ROM)*** and ***random access memory (RAM).*** Special-purpose programs are built into ROM chips during manufacturing. Because programs stored in ROM are etched into memory circuits, these programs do not have to be loaded into memory from disk. This permanent software in ROM is called *firmware.* ROM is a form of *nonvolatile memory,* so it is typically used to hold system programs and language translators. For example, the BIOS (basic input/output system), which provides the operating system with a description of the hardware used by a computer, is found in ROM.

In contrast, RAM is a form of volatile memory used for temporary general-purpose storage. When we think of computer memory, we usually have RAM in mind. Programs and data must be loaded into RAM from outside sources, such as disks. If the power to the computer fails, RAM is completely erased. Programs and data must then be loaded again.

To locate needed data or instructions for processing, the computer assigns a number, or ***address***, to each byte position in memory (see Figure 5.9). Programmers working with high-level programming languages use words or symbols to assign labels (field names) to data needed from memory. The computer then associates these labels with its own internal addresses. Once the assigned address is located, the computer retrieves the specified data.

The storage capacity of memory is measured by the number of characters, or bytes, it can hold. Typically, memory is measured in thousands or millions of bytes.

**5.9**

RAM chips temporarily store data and programs. Each byte (character) is assigned a unique location in memory, identified by its address.

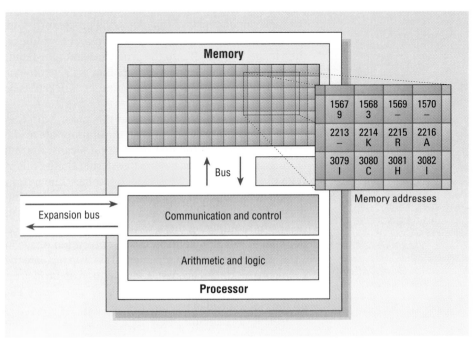

A *kilobyte (K)* represents 1,024 bytes, which is often rounded to 1,000 bytes. A computer with 512 K memory, therefore, provides storage for exactly 524,288 bytes, rather than 512,000. The confusion is a result of rounding 1,024 down to 1,000 before calculating memory capacity. Memory capacities in newer personal computers are measured in *megabytes (MB),* or millions of bytes, and larger computers have several *gigabytes* (*GB—* billions of bytes) of primary memory. Future computers will have *terabyte* (*TB*—trillion-byte) capacities.

Although internal processing speeds are fast, it is comparatively slow for the processor to acquire the necessary data from storage such as a disk. Because of this, the CPU may sit idle during some of the time a program runs.

To minimize waiting time for the CPU and speed up processing, users can now purchase computers, or enhance their existing computers, with a feature called **cache memory**. Cache (pronounced "cash") memory is a part of RAM that holds the data most likely to be needed next by the CPU. When data is retrieved from disk, it is loaded with the other data in that disk area into cache memory. In some cases, cache memory can exceed 512 K of storage. As a result, there is a good chance the next data the computer needs for processing is already in cache. Using cache memory supports faster processing because retrieving data from the cache is thousands of times faster than retrieving it from disk.

The data contained in cache memory is not always the data needed, but cache is judged by its hit ratio, similar to a batting average. Hit ratio is the percent of times the correct data is in the cache (a hit) divided by the number of times the CPU goes to the cache looking for data. Effective cache memory has over a 90 percent hit ratio.

## ■ CPU Operations

The question now arises: How does the processor orchestrate all of the actions involved in running a program? All processing, regardless of the operation, is broken into two phases: the instruction phase and the execution phase.

During the *instruction phase,* the processor's control/communication operation identifies the next program instruction and its address in memory. The instruction is then loaded (fetched) into the processor and translated in an action the processor can perform. For example, in Figure 5.10 four instructions compute ticket sales for a concert. The first instruction, locating the number of tickets, is recalled. This completes the first instruction phase in the figure.

The *execution phase* starts at this point, with the processor transferring related data from memory or performing the appropriate arithmetic or logic operation on the data. In Figure 5.10 the first instruction locates the value 4 (tickets sold) in memory. During the execution phase, 4 is transferred along a bus from memory into the processor. With the completion of this execution phase, the next instruction phase begins.

The instruction/execution cycle is repeated for the single-ticket cost of $20. Once the cost and number of tickets are in the processor, the next instruction/execution cycle results in multiplying these values. When the result, called TOTAL, is returned to the designated memory address, the last execution phase in this example is finished.

The processor uses the internal clock to regulate the transfer of data or instructions so the phases do not overlap. The repetition of the instruction/execution cycle continues until all program instructions have been processed. The speed of processing depends on the clock speed of the processing hardware.

The CPU circuitry that once required a roomful of vacuum tubes connected by miles of wire now resides on several small silicon chips. A microcomputer's

**5.10**

Four instruction/execution cycles go into computing the purchase price for concert tickets.

## Processing Phases: Instruction and Execution

When the computer processes the machine language instructions for

```
TOTAL = TICKETS * COST
```

four instruction/execution cycles are performed:

**Memory** **Processor**

**1.**   *INSTRUCTION*

1011 0011 1001 0100
Fetch instruction locating
TICKETS in memory

*EXECUTION*
Move 4 to processor

**2.**   *INSTRUCTION*

1111 0101 1101 1100
Fetch instruction locating
COST in memory

*EXECUTION*
Move 20 to processor

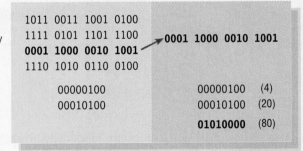

**3.**   *INSTRUCTION*

0001 1000 0010 1001
Fetch instruction to multiply
TICKETS by COST

*EXECUTION*
Multiply 4 by 20 giving 80

**4.**   *INSTRUCTION*

1110 1010 0110 0100
Fetch instruction locating
a memory address for
answer TOTAL

*EXECUTION*
Move 80 to memory

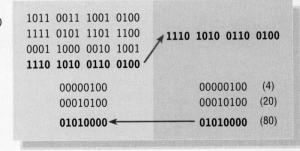

**5.11**

Bus lines, expansion slots, and input/output (I/O) ports connect the processor to memory and a variety of hardware, expanding the capabilities of a computer system.

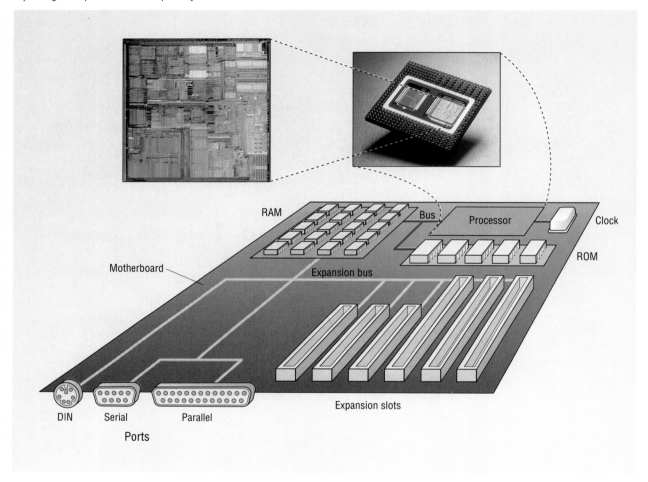

microprocessor, RAM modules, ROM, clock, and other supporting circuitry are interconnected on a single circuit board called the *motherboard*. An example of a motherboard is shown in Figure 5.11.

### Expansion Slots and Cards

When microcomputer users need to increase their computer's functionality, they can add new features to the processing hardware through *expansion slots* on the motherboard. Expansion slots are connectors on the expansion bus that link the processor to circuit boards or *expansion cards*, which fit into the slot (see Figure 5.11). Expansion cards are available for adding disk storage, installing a fax and/or modem, connecting to a network, providing multimedia capabilities such as sound and video, and installing cache memory. Personal computers will have from three to eight expansion slots on the motherboard.

# Jack Kilby

(b. 1923)

# Robert Noyce

(1927-1990)

# Marcian Hoff

(b. 1937)

# Gilbert Hyatt

(b. 1938)

Just a few years after the invention of the transistor, two groups of scientists were competing to produce its successor. Jack Kilby worked at Texas Instruments in research. He succeeded in 1959 in building the first working circuit on a chip—an integrated circuit, or IC. Robert Noyce and fellow scientists at Fairchild Semiconductors layered these chips and isolated them with insulating material. Despite their independent work, Kilby and Noyce are recognized as the co-inventors of the integrated circuit, precursor to the microprocessor. Noyce and two colleagues left to form their own company to manufacturer integrated circuits—Intel.

In 1971 Marcian Hoff, a researcher at Intel, and his coworkers used the idea of the integrated circuit to develop the first working microprocessor, the 4004; the following year they produced the 8008. Although Hoff and his team were credited with the invention, an engineer named Gilbert Hyatt actually had a patent on the single-chip microprocessor in 1970, before Hoff's model. A recent court decision awarded Hyatt the recognition as inventor of the microprocessor.

*Clockwise from top right: Jack Kilby, Robert Noyce, and Marcian Hoff with the first integrated circuit (below).*

Installation of new expansion cards is quite easy. For example, users wishing to add enhanced graphics need only purchase a super video graphics array (SVGA) board to replace a video board currently in an expansion slot. New expansion boards are often accompanied by a disk containing a related device driver. The driver must be installed with the system software on the hard disk. The new graphics capabilities become immediately available after rebooting the computer, although related software packages sometimes need to have the monitor driver installed again.

### Input/Output Ports

Regardless of the application, the data is input to the computer from hardware external to the CPU. Output is also sent outside of the processing hardware. To accommodate different types of input, output, and storage hardware, a computer has several places where hardware is connected to the processing unit. These places, connected to the motherboard, are called *I/O (input/output)* ports. Two types of I/O ports are available: serial and parallel, as shown in Figure 5.12. Data is sent between the computer and the

**5.12**

Serial and parallel ports allow I/O hardware to be connected to the processing hardware of a computer.

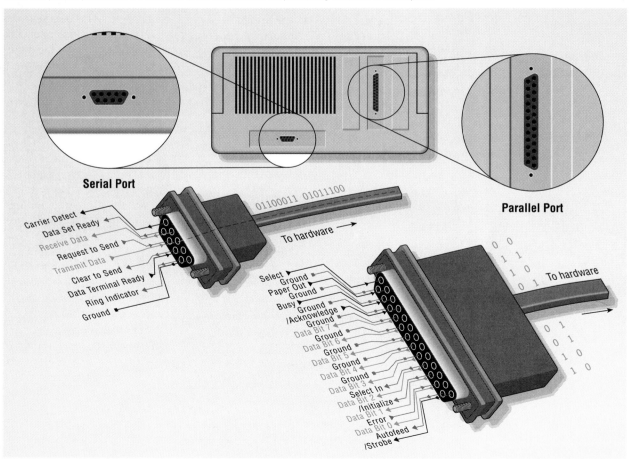

attached hardware 1 bit at a time with a *serial port*. When a *parallel port* is used, the entire bit pattern for a single character is sent at the same time (see Figure 5.12). The I/O ports, often found on expansion boards, provide a point of connection between peripheral hardware and the bus line.

Different peripheral devices will have different I/O port requirements. The advantage of using a parallel port is that it is faster, since it sends several bits simultaneously; however, the I/O and storage hardware must be physically close to the computer. And though serial ports do not provide as high a transmission speed, the peripherals can be farther away. A mouse is often attached to a serial port. Serial ports are also used to help send data over telephone and other communication lines. Part of the decision in buying a computer is to be sure sufficient I/O ports and expansion slots are available to handle current and future hardware and processing needs.

## COMPUTERS TO SOLVE DIFFERENT PROBLEMS

Computers come in various sizes to address all kinds of problems. Just as operating systems have capabilities to solve different problems, processing hardware also is diversified. In general, processing hardware is characterized by cost, size, storage capacity, number of users, and processing speed. In many cases, there is a considerable amount of overlap among groups. Three of the most commonly used terms for describing processing hardware are: mainframes, minicomputers, and microcomputers.

### Mainframes and Organizational Systems

Mainframes are large, relatively expensive machines that offer extensive problem-solving capabilities. Mainframes can have memory capacities measured in gigabytes and more. The largest mainframes can process well over 100 MIPS and often incorporate several processors. Their operating systems usually handle multiple applications within a timesharing environment. This provides many users with the ability to perform different processing tasks. Data storage is primarily on hard disks, with tapes used as backup.

Mainframes can serve as the heart of a teleprocessing system with remote connections all over the world. In other configurations computers of all sizes can be linked to mainframe computers as part of a network, or the mainframe may act as a database server. Few individuals or departments within a business require the massive processing capabilities offered by mainframes (see Figure 5.13). These machines are used primarily by government, universities, and large businesses. Such organizations have extensive processing needs as well as the financial means to purchase or lease costly mainframes.

People use mainframes for complex problems or large-volume jobs. Major banks can process bills for credit card holders all over the world with the aid of a mainframe. Insurance companies use mainframes to process millions of policies. Large research projects, such as the Human Genome Project, use the vast mainframe memory, storage capacities, and fast processing speeds to conduct tests and coordinate operations. Thus, mainframes have met the hefty processing demands of larger organizations.

**5.13**

Computers come in many sizes with various capabilities: **(a)** Expensive supercomputers perform incredibly complex calculations, such as modeling global weather patterns. **(b)** Mainframe installations occupy entire rooms; their size and cost limit their use to large corporations, government agencies, and universities. **(c)** Minicomputers are scaled-down versions of the mainframe and usually serve a number of network users. **(d)** This desktop engineering workstation is a powerful micro-computer. **(e)** The now-familiar PC, or personal computer, has brought the power of electronic data processing into the home, the schoolroom, and the workplace. **(f)** Laptops allow users to bring their computers almost anywhere. **(g)** The ultimate in portable computing, the personal digital assistant (PDA) can be configured to recognize handwritten notes and telecommunicate from remote locations.

## ■ Minicomputers and Workgroup Systems

The minicomputer is a scaled-down version of the mainframe. Both the processing power and cost of minicomputers are less than that of the mainframe. Yet minicomputers have larger memory sizes and faster processing speeds than most microcomputers. They are well suited to the needs of smaller workgroups of specialists within large organizations, a smaller business subsidiary, or a medium-sized independent business or laboratory. Because minicomputer prices range from about $25,000 to several hundred thousand dollars, many companies prefer to lease rather than buy them.

Memory capacities in current minicomputers are measured in megabytes and can easily range into gigabytes of temporary storage. Minicomputers have fast processing speeds and operating systems with multitasking and network capabilities enabling them to serve more than one user (see Figure 5.13). They can be equipped with drives for diskettes and tape, as well as for hard disks. Tapes and floppy disks are inexpensive media for backing up important data files and programs.

A minicomputer serves as a centralized storehouse for a cluster of workstations or as a network server. For example, a team of architects working on different subsystems within the same building design could be directly linked to the office minicomputer

that maintains everyone's files and documentation. A manufacturing plant might use a minicomputer in the front office for on-site inventory tracking and process control. Researchers working at different labs who need to locate and share data might set up a minicomputer as a World Wide Web server on the Internet. Many organizations use several minicomputers in a network instead of one mainframe. The advantage to this design is that not all processing power is dependent on a single machine.

## ■ Microcomputers and Personal Systems

Advancing computer technology has brought computers into the home, the schoolroom, and the workplace. Called home computers, laptops, personal digital assistants, personal computers, microcomputers, or micros, these machines are powerful, yet easy to operate.

Every microcomputer is capable of performing jobs once handled by only the largest computers. Purchase prices for micros range from $500 for home units to $10,000 or more for professional models. A typical microcomputer memory unit stores up to 64 MB of data. Processing speeds of microcomputers are measured in megahertz instead of MIPS. A microcomputer running at 90 MHz is faster than one running at 33 MHz and works at approximately 90 MIPS.

## DID YOU KNOW?

### ...ABOUT THE SPEED OF TECHNOLOGICAL ADVANCEMENT

- Every 18 months, advances in technology virtually double the amount of computing power a dollar will buy.

- In the past 35 years, computer performance has increased by a factor of 1 million, while the entry-level price of a computer has decreased by a factor of 1,000.

- If automobile development had moved at the same speed, your luxury car would cruise comfortably at 1 million miles per hour, get a half-million miles per gallon of gas, and sell for just under $2.40!

Microcomputers are designed to be operated by one user at a time, using the keyboard or mouse for data entry and a monitor or printer to display output. Disk drives are used to store data. When the computer housing with disk drives is placed vertically on its side, as shown in Figure 5.14, it is in a *tower* configuration. Some microcomputers, such as cash registers, are dedicated to one job. Others perform a variety of work directed by application programs.

Millions of people have used microcomputers to solve a wide range of problems and to increase their personal productivity. Many user interfaces provide applications

**5.14**

Microcomputers in a tower configuration are placed under a desk instead of on top of it.

that mimic tools found in an office. Typically, they provide clocks, calendars, calculators, daily schedule reminders, and scratch pads—all brought to the screen by pressing a few keys. In recent years design changes have reduced the size of some microcomputers, making computer technology portable and affordable.

*Laptop computers* (see Figure 5.13) are roughly the size of a large notebook. Their power source—a battery—is completely self-contained yet can be recharged from an electrical outlet. Laptops, sometimes called *notebook computers,* can contain more than 500 MB of hard disk memory, 16+ MB of RAM, floppy disk drives, keyboard, mouse, and a color monitor. Power adapters can be used to plug into any electrical outlet throughout the world. Other snap-in modules facilitate connection with an additional battery or serial port, a network, or fax equipment. You can even plug a laptop into a car cigarette lighter and power it with a car battery! Obviously, not all laptop computers have all these features, and many of the modules are expensive, but a user need not suffer loss of processing power when downsizing to a laptop.

Even smaller than the laptop computer is the ***personal digital assistant*** (**PDA**), a computer using a pen, or *electronic stylus,* rather than a keyboard for input. As shown in Figure 5.15, the monitor is rather small and the only apparent form of output. Tremendous capabilities are hidden in this personal digital assistant, however. It can recognize hand-printed text, storing it as a business letter, note, or other document.

**5.15**

A personal digital assistant uses a pen and human voice for input instead of a keyboard and mouse.

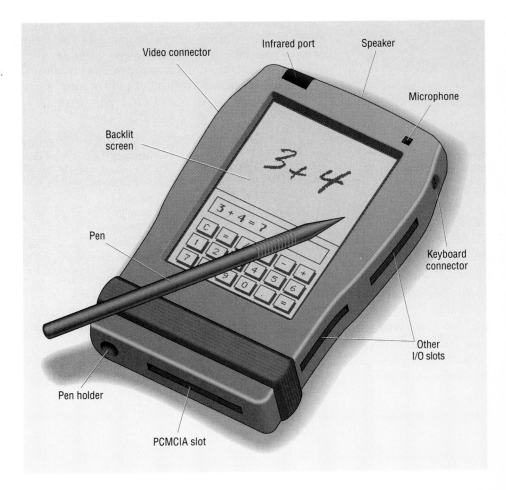

Video connector

Infrared port

Speaker

Microphone

Backlit screen

Pen

Keyboard connector

Other I/O slots

Pen holder

PCMCIA slot

Rough sketches can be converted to more precise graphic output, such as charts and diagrams. Basic mathematics problems, such as addition and multiplication, are calculated when the problem is written on the screen (see Figure 5.15), and personal productivity software, such as day-at-a-glance calendars, are available. Special I/O ports allow a full-sized keyboard and monitor to be attached. A PDA can also be connected to a printer, fax machine, pager, or disk drive to output or store data. The processing hardware is based on RISC technology. Many people see PDAs as changing the way we do personal computing.

## ▦ Specialized Processing Hardware

Although microcomputers, minicomputers, and mainframes cover a wide range of sizes, power capabilities, and applications (Figure 5.16), they may not be sufficient to handle some processing requirements. As a result, newer and more specialized processing hardware has been developed, which includes embedded computers, supercomputers, and fault-tolerant computers.

**Embedded Microprocessors**    Your new refrigerator, microwave oven, or stereo system probably is equipped with its own microprocessor. These appliances, like many other products, are now being manufactured with embedded computers. An *embedded computer* is a microprocessor designed to operate within another tool. Embedded computers are, of course, not as flexible as general-purpose computers. They use microprocessors but are not microcomputers. The microprocessors used by embedded computers contain only one preset program (firmware). In addition, these microprocessors do not use standard input, output, and storage hardware. The microprocessor in your refrigerator will not help you write a letter, but it will regulate

**5.16**

Comparison of processing hardware features from small microcomputers to large mainframe computers.

| Cost | Size | Memory | Number of Users | Processing Speeds |
|------|------|--------|-----------------|-------------------|
| *MICROCOMPUTER* | | | | |
| $500 to $10,000 | Fits on desktop | 64,000 to 64 million characters | 1 | Up to 100 million instructions per second |
| *MINICOMPUTER* | | | | |
| $25,000 to $250,000 | Fills a closet | 4 million to 1 billion characters | 100s | 50 million or more instructions per second |
| *MAINFRAME COMPUTER* | | | | |
| $250,000 and more | Fills a room | 32 million characters or more | 1,000s | 100 million or more instructions per second |

the refrigerator's temperature to keep your food fresh. The purpose of embedded computers is to expand the capacities of the tools you use.

**Supercomputers**   The most advanced and expensive type of computer is the *supercomputer*. Processing speeds in supercomputers are 1,200 MIPS and faster. The Cray supercomputer shown in Figure 5.13 can process about 1.2 billion mathematical calculations every second. With a price tag that is equally tremendous, from $5 million to $20 million, supercomputer use is usually limited to such organizations as large oil companies, government agencies like the U.S. Department of Defense, and research organizations such as the National Aeronautics and Space Administration (NASA). Probably the largest commercial users of supercomputers are in the entertainment/advertising industry.

Supercomputers are designed using multiprocessing to achieve much faster processing speeds than mainframes, but they use this processing power to work on just one complex problem at a time instead of sharing processing time with many users. For example, the U.S. Weather Bureau uses the fast processing speeds of a supercomputer for a single purpose—forecasting the weather. To analyze data from satellites and from hundreds of weather stations, forecasters need a supercomputer's speed.

Oil companies use supercomputers for petroleum exploration by analyzing rock formation and samples. Military strategists use them to simulate defense scenarios. Cinematic specialists use them to produce sophisticated movie animations. Supercomputers are powerful, but they are special-purpose tools.

**Fault-Tolerant Computers**   Many organizations cannot afford to be without their computer, even for a few minutes. As a result, a few computer manufacturers specialize in building *fault-tolerant computers*—machines designed to never crash. To achieve this, the manufacturer duplicates all important components of the processing hardware. Fault-tolerant computers have at least two memories, processors, and disk drives, with duplicate wiring to all these parts. Sources of emergency electrical power, such as batteries and generators, are also part of the fault-tolerant computer system.

The operating system is designed so that the processing and storage hardware is never used at more than half its capacity. Therefore, when hardware problems occur, the operating system automatically switches processing to the remaining hardware without interruption. Fault-tolerant computers are especially useful in hazardous environments or in situations where an organization cannot afford to be without processing power. Although fault-tolerant computers are more expensive than standard computers, hospitals (see Figure 5.17), scientific laboratories, and nuclear power plants need the hardware duplication and backup they provide.

**5.17**

Fault-tolerant computers are designed with duplicate hardware so an organization, such as this hospital, is never without processing power.

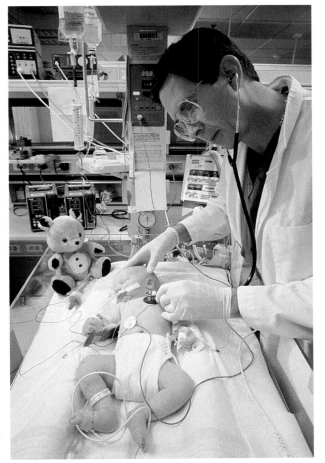

# A Closer Look at
# Manufacturing a Chip

**H**ow is a microprocessor made? Even a look under a microscope at a microprocessor does not reveal the numerous steps required to take a hunk of quartz rock and transform it into the wafer of silicon holding the brain of a computer.

**Q:** The circuitry on a microprocessor is so small. Does it start out that way?

**A:** Large detailed drawings of the circuitry are made, usually drawn using a computer. Each circuit is hand-checked. Then the drawing is made into a photographic image and reduced to microscopic size.

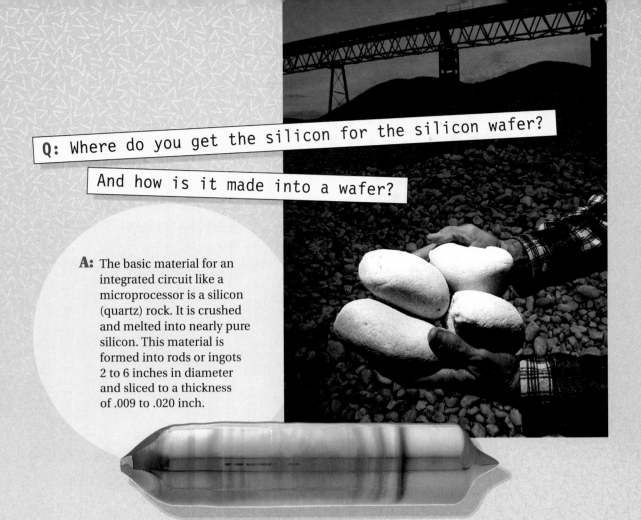

**Q:** Where do you get the silicon for the silicon wafer?

And how is it made into a wafer?

**A:** The basic material for an integrated circuit like a microprocessor is a silicon (quartz) rock. It is crushed and melted into nearly pure silicon. This material is formed into rods or ingots 2 to 6 inches in diameter and sliced to a thickness of .009 to .020 inch.

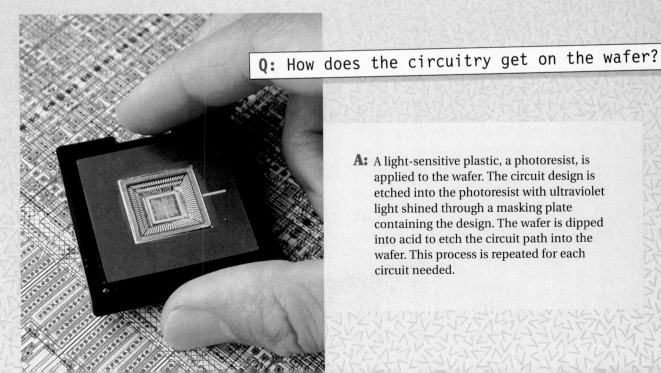

**Q:** How does the circuitry get on the wafer?

**A:** A light-sensitive plastic, a photoresist, is applied to the wafer. The circuit design is etched into the photoresist with ultraviolet light shined through a masking plate containing the design. The wafer is dipped into acid to etch the circuit path into the wafer. This process is repeated for each circuit needed.

**A:** A wafer contains several hundred microprocessors. When etching is completed, the wafers are cut with a diamond saw into individual microprocessors, each less than 1/8 inch square.

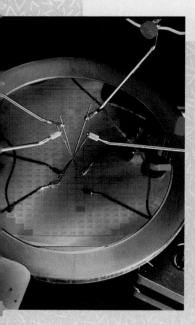

**Q:** Why are microprocessors manufactured in clean rooms?

**A:** A particle of dust can ruin an entire processor. To avoid this, work is done in a "clean room," where much of the handling of the wafers is done by machines. People in the clean room wear protective clothing, which guards them from caustic chemicals and guards the wafers from dirt and moisture.

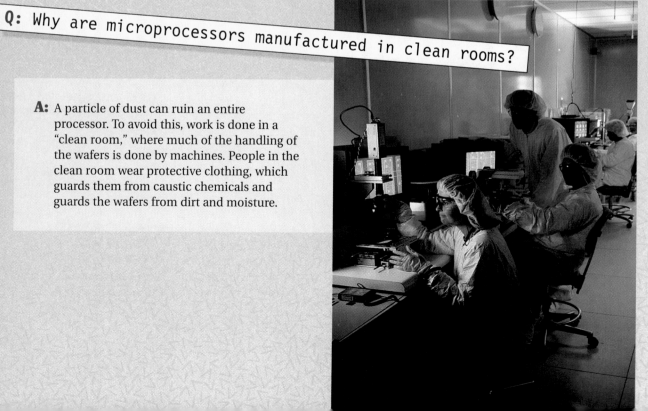

**A:** After each series of etchings, the wafer is examined under a microscope. Defective wafers are removed from production. Microprocessors are also tested electronically several times during production.

**Q:** How do the microprocessors fit into the computer?

**A:** Individual microprocessors are attached and wired onto frames. They are then installed on boards that are assembled with other integrated circuits to become the finished microcomputer motherboard.

## CHAPTER FACTS

- First-generation computers used vacuum tubes for processing hardware.

- Transistors were invented by Shockley, Bardeen, and Brattain in the mid-1950s and became the processing hardware for second-generation computers.

- Third-generation computers used integrated circuits (ICs), which were first tested in 1959 by Jack Kilby.

- Computers from the fourth generation combined many integrated circuits into a microprocessor. This technological breakthrough in the late 1960s is credited to Hyatt and Hoff.

- In the fifth generation, computers become more powerful through the development of multiprocessing hardware using parallel processors.

- All processing hardware works on Boole's two-state logic. In digital computers, instructions are put into a binary code called machine code, represented by 1 (presence) and 0 (absence) of electricity.

- Standard 8-bit binary codes, ASCII and EBCDIC, enable computers to encode data and transfer it over bus lines. Unicode is a new 16-bit coding system for digitizing data representing a wide variety of written languages.

- The processor, or central processing unit (CPU), performs communication/control, arithmetic, and logical operations. Programs and data are temporarily stored in memory before and after processing.

- Processing speeds are measured in fractions of a second: millisecond (one-thousandth), microsecond (one-millionth), nanosecond (one-billionth), and picosecond (one-trillionth).

- Within the processor, control/communication operations direct the flow of data and instructions along bus lines.

- The speed of the processor is also measured in megahertz (MHz)— a million clock cycles per second.

- Random access memory (RAM) is temporary storage. Read-only memory (ROM) is preset during manufacturing.

- Data is retrieved in the processing hardware according to its memory location, or address.

- Memory capacity is measured by number of bytes. A kilobyte (K) is approximately 1,000 characters. A megabyte (MB) is 1 million characters. Large computer systems have memory capabilities in billions (gigabytes) and, in the future, trillions (terabytes) of characters.

- Processing consists of two phases: the instruction phase and the execution phase. These are coordinated by an internal clock.

- Expansion slots on the motherboard allow additional hardware capacity to be added to the computer's circuitry.

- Serial and parallel input/output (I/O) ports provide a place where peripheral hardware can be connected to the motherboard.

- Mainframes are large, high-speed computers with billions of characters of memory.

- Minicomputers are smaller than mainframes, but have many megabytes of memory and processing speeds measured in MIPS (millions of instructions per second).

- Microcomputers are small but powerful machines. They usually serve only one user at a time but in varying applications. Their processing speeds are measured in megahertz.

- Laptop computers allow true portability of processing power. Personal digital assistants are even smaller and rely on pen input to process written text.

- Embedded computers are microprocessors built into appliances and tools. They are permanently programmed to expand the device's capabilities.

- Supercomputers are powerful machines with large storage capacities. They are expensive and used only in applications requiring fast processing of large amounts of data.

- Fault-tolerant computers contain duplicates of all important hardware components. Each component is used only to half capacity. When a component fails, the duplicate takes over.

---

## *TERMS TO REMEMBER*

| | | |
|---|---|---|
| address | integrated circuit (IC) | random access memory (RAM) |
| bus | laptop computer | |
| byte | machine code | read-only memory (ROM) |
| cache memory | microprocessor | reduced instruction set computing (RISC) |
| central processing unit (CPU) | motherboard | |
| | multiprocessing | serial port |
| expansion card | parallel port | supercomputer |
| expansion slot | personal digital assistant (PDA) | transistor |
| fault-tolerant computer | | vacuum tube |

## MIX AND MATCH

*Complete the following definitions with the Terms to Remember.*

1. A(n) _____ is a portable computer that uses pen-based input instead of keyboard.

2. A powerful, high-speed special-purpose parallel processing computer capable of handling enormous amounts of data is known as a(n) _____.

3. A small, solid-state _____ is placed with other electronic components on a silicon wafer.

4. A(n) _____ has duplicate processing components.

5. A group of bits representing a single character is known as a(n) _____.

6. Small portable computers containing keyboards are collectively referred to as _____.

7. A(n) _____ is a single chip containing I/O control, processing, and some memory circuitry.

8. The simultaneous processing of the same program through the use of several processors is known as _____.

9. A(n) _____ is circuit board designed to fit into a slot on a microcomputer's motherboard.

10. The unique number assigned to each memory location within a computer's processing hardware is called a(n) _____.

11. A(n) _____ port can send or receive data 1 bit at a time.

12. The primary circuit board in a microcomputer is called the _____.

13. The _____ is a small electronic component that is the basis of the second-generation computer.

14. A(n) _____ port can send or receive data 1 byte at a time.

15. Cards are plugged into _____ in the motherboard's expansion bus.

## REVIEW QUESTIONS

1. Define the Terms to Remember.

2. What is the characteristic processing hardware for the first, second, third, fourth, and fifth computer generations?

3. Describe how Boole's two-state mathematics is applied to computer-based instructions and data.

4. Explain how programs are assigned to different processors when using asymmetrical versus symmetrical multiprocessing.

5. How is Unicode different from ASCII and EBCDIC?

6. What operations are performed by the central processing unit?

7. How is a microprocessor's processing speed measured?

8. What is the difference between a millisecond, microsecond, nanosecond, and picosecond?

9. Under what simple premise does the processor work?

10. What are the uses of these specialty processing hardware: cache memory, math coprocessor, and RISC?

11. What is stored in RAM?

12. Explain how the processor uses memory addresses to locate data and instructions.

13. How are expansion cards and I/O ports used to add to a microcomputer's capabilities?

14. What are five ways to group processing hardware? Use these characteristics to differentiate among microcomputers, minicomputers, and mainframes.

15. Identify two types of portable microcomputers and explain how they differ from each other.

16. What are three applications for supercomputers and embedded computers?

## APPLYING WHAT YOU'VE LEARNED

1. Look at the instructions that come with the school or home computer you use. How fast is the processor? How much RAM does it have? How many expansion slots does it have? What type of disk and tape storage is available? *Note:* Some Intel-based systems have a utility program called MSD (Microsoft Diagnostics) that can also be used to find these answers.

2. Classify each processing job by the type of operation it would require: arithmetic, logical, or control/communication. Some problems may require more than one processing operation.
   a. finding a square root of a number in memory
   b. checking the breathing rate of a patient
   c. loading into memory visual data read by a scanner
   d. calculating how many males and how many females are in an employee file
   e. sending to a distant terminal the names of only those customers with unpaid bills

3. What are the advantages and disadvantages of pen-based computing used by PDAs? For what type of applications would you use a PDA?

4. Compare and contrast the cost of two personal computers in a newspaper or magazine advertisement. Identify the processor, processing speed in MHz, RAM capacity, and expansion bus type for each computer. If possible, find out how much ROM and how many expansion slots both computers have.

5. Bubble memory was once announced as the memory of the future. Research on it has slowed. Read an article on it. Why is it not more popular? What are its advantages? Is another type of nonvolatile memory being developed instead?

6. Besides those mentioned in the text, what are five machines or tools that would benefit from having embedded computers?

# Input and Output Hardware

**E**very day you
may be pushing buttons, using a
mouse, or searching a screen for
information. You can customize your
computer system for special input and
output needs with a staggering array of
input/output hardware. We will take a look
at hardware available and discuss the
applications for which they are used.
Each I/O peripheral has one thing
in common: When used properly,
it helps you become
more productive.

## LINKING PEOPLE AND HARDWARE

What concerns users most, despite the variety of processing and storage hardware available, is the input of data and the output of information. For many, the keyboard, mouse, monitor, and printer are the most easily recognized peripherals—hardware related to I/O operations. Input/output operations are where computers and people meet. People can enter data or create objects through input hardware; they then receive results of processing through output hardware.

In chapter 5 we saw that expansion cards and I/O ports were used to connect peripheral hardware to a computer. When an expansion card is added to a system, related device driver software is installed on the system's hard disk. Then the system is rebooted to make the hardware available.

New *plug-n-play* hardware supports easier installation. When this type of expansion card and connected hardware are plugged in, installation information becomes available to the operating system. This information could include the type and model of the peripheral as well as the filename of the device driver software. The system then automatically searches for the device driver and installs it if available. For example, the system could find the file on another computer in a network and install it from there.

If the driver is not available, the system activates a *software guide*. The guide, sometimes called a wizard or expert, asks the user specific questions about the hardware and may instruct the user to insert a disk containing the device driver to be installed. These leading questions will allow the system to make the I/O hardware available for use involving minimal user effort—and frustration.

## INPUT HARDWARE OPTIONS

User-friendliness is most important wherever user/computer interaction is most frequent. *Real-time processing* requires a dialog between the user and the computer. When the user requests service from the computer, the computer responds, often by producing a dialog box, menu, or other screen display. The user enters data by responding to these prompts. The computer continues processing, prompting the user for more data or instructions as necessary. This series of exchanges is characteristic of interactive input and real-time processing. Different types of input peripherals are available to support different user needs. The following are the most commonly used devices.

### ■ Keyboards

Almost every computer system contains a keyboard, still the most widely used input hardware. Most keyboards have some features in common. They have typewriter-like keys for inputting letters, numbers, and other symbols. Cursor-control keys manipulate the cursor up, down, left, and right. In addition, *function keys* (Figure 3.2) can activate particular software features, such as centering in a word processing program, or locating the first worksheet cell. Many software packages allow users to define the activities associated with function keys. These keys let users control several operations by pressing just one or two keys instead of selecting menu options or entering commands.

Numeric keypads are on many keyboards for easy input of numeric data. On other keyboards, the keys represent icons rather than alphanumeric symbols. These are useful in fast-food restaurants, where the icons represent food items, or in teaching children who cannot yet read. Also, keyboards are available for foreign languages, as shown in Figure 6.1, and can include keys with Braille or scientific characters.

**6.1**

A stylus is used to indicate on the keyboard which Chinese character to input.

When a key on a keyboard is pressed, electrical circuitry below the key changes and is detected by a microprocessor in the keyboard. The binary code for that character is sent through an I/O port, down the bus line, and into the central processing unit. Some keyboards have small temporary storage areas to allow users to type ahead of the computer system. Characters saved in this *buffer* are processed as the CPU becomes available, usually within a fraction of a second.

### ■ Pointing Devices

Although the keyboard is an efficient way to input text, it can be a deterrent to nontypists using a command-driven operating system. Due to the increase of graphical user interfaces, most of the software now developed permits (or requires) use of a mouse. As mentioned in chapter 3, the user controls a screen pointer by moving a mouse across a flat surface—the desktop; the motion is converted to similar movement on a monitor. When a button on the mouse is clicked, the location of the mouse in relation to icons or menus on a monitor is sent through an expansion bus to the CPU. This will initiate an action, such as opening a file or displaying a menu.

Despite the mouse's ease of use, it has a disadvantage. In a small work area, room to move the mouse may be limited. Also, people with restricted arm movement may find using a mouse difficult. The ***trackball*** is an alternative input peripheral which looks like an upside-down mouse. Rather than move a mouse across a surface, a trackball user rolls a ball mounted in a stationary housing (see Figure 6.2). Like a mouse, a trackball also has buttons for fixing the cursor position on-screen and initiating actions. A trackball can be installed in any I/O port that can support a mouse.

Because trackballs require minimal workspace, manufacturers have been including them with laptop and smaller computer systems. Some trackballs are temporarily mounted at the side of the computer and removed when necessary. Others are permanently placed in the middle or at the side of the keyboard itself, or even at the side of the monitor. Still others can be held in the hand and the ball moved with the thumb. For less portable personal computers, larger trackballs are available. A recent development is the wireless mouse, or *remote mouse,* which works on transmission of infrared or radio waves.

**6.2**

Trackballs, either built into a portable computer or attached to its side, provide an alternative to the mouse.

**6.3**

The handheld scanner and page scanner facilitate direct input of documents and graphical objects.

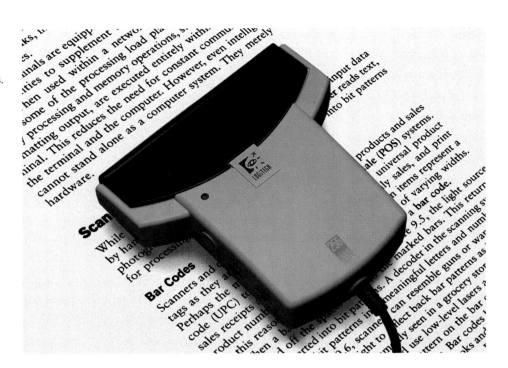

## Scanners

Whereas a keyboard, mouse, or trackball requires manual input of data, scanners allow input of printed data. A *scanner* reads text, photographs, and graphics from paper which are then converted into bit patterns for processing, storage, or output. The handheld scanner in Figure 6.3 can scan a few lines of text or a small photo in one sweep; a page scanner inputs a standard-sized page. Another type of scanner, the flatbed, can read oversized documents or book pages. Though the applications of scanners vary, each requires specific software to convert data to binary code.

Scanners are available for inputting graphical objects such as drawings, photographs, and maps. As the image is scanned, it is converted into light and dark picture elements, or *pixels,* similar to a newspaper photo. Color scanners can assign a specific color to a pixel. The pixels are then stored as bit patterns. This technique makes the images usable by word processing, desktop publishing, and graphics packages. Law enforcement services can scan fingerprints and store them on file. Analysis programs compare sets of prints to find probable matches among millions of fingerprint records.

**Bar Codes**    Scanners and other devices that collect data from products and sales tags as they are purchased are part of ***point-of-sale (POS) systems.*** The most familiar POS system, which uses the universal product code (UPC), helps update inventory, track daily sales, and print sales receipts at grocery stores (see Figure 6.4). The UPC markings on items represent a product number and consist of a series of bars of varying widths. For this reason the UPC often is referred to as a ***bar code.***

When a bar code is scanned, the light source is reflected off the spaces between the marked bars. This returned light is then converted into bit patterns. A decoder in

**6.4**

Bar-code scanners initiate a six-step IPOS cycle that updates inventory records and prints grocery receipts.

## Six Steps to Printing a Receipt in a UPC System

◾ Bar code scanned, identifying key field

◾ Computer searches inventory file using key field

◾ Match found—computer updates inventory, then transfers price and description back to computer

◾ Computer sends data to terminal at checkout counter

◾ Register figures sales price and tax

◾ Register prints price, tax, and product descriptions on receipt

**6.5**

A handheld scanner can input bar codes from a price tag.

the scanning system translates the bit patterns into meaningful letters and numbers. As shown in Figure 6.5, scanners can resemble guns or wands, which send out a beam of light to reflect back bar patterns as input. Other scanners, such as those commonly seen in a grocery store, are built into checkout counters and use low-level lasers as the light source.

The UPC system requires the pattern on the bar-code label to represent a manufacturer's product code. Bar codes have been put to many other uses. For example, library books and library cards are marked with bar codes to expedite checkout. Bulk mailings sent by businesses contain bar codes related to the address and zip code at the bottom of an envelope to speed up processing by the post office.

As an inventory control application, the bar codes identify a stock number. This number is the key field for records in the inventory file. By using the bar code, the computer locates the record associated with that stock number. The record contains such information about the product as name, current stock levels, and price fields. These fields are used to generate a customer receipt. This method allows stores to offer sale prices without having to change each price tag. Instead, a single change is made to the price field in the correct record of the inventory file. Figure 6.4 shows the steps used to print a receipt in the POS system. A log of all transactions is stored on disk or tape as they are processed. The computer later uses this log to produce reports that help balance cash in the registers and reorder merchandise for the store.

**Optical Mark Recognition**    Handwritten characters and marks can be read with scanners and specialized software. The scanners for *optical mark recognition (OMR)* methods sense the presence of a pencil mark by the way light reflects off of it. Popular uses for optical mark recognition are standardized tests, surveys, and questionnaires. On some of these forms, scanners can distinguish plus and minus signs, check marks, and other symbols. Handwritten characters must be made in a certain way to enable the scanner software to recognize and translate that character to binary code.

**Optical Character Recognition**    *Optical character recognition (OCR)* permits users to input printed or typewritten documents with a scanner. Entire pages of text are read rapidly by scanners and converted to bit-mapped graphic images, some of which may be blurry. The patterns of white space on the page are used by the scanner software to determine margins, columns, and paragraphs. Then the scanned images are matched to character templates found in the software and converted to text. If no match is found, the user may be asked to supply the missing characters by typing them in or consulting an online dictionary.

Many publishers and archives use OCR scanners. For example, books that are starting to deteriorate may be scanned into typesetting computers. Type for newer editions of books can be set by scanning pages from previous editions. Law firms scan old contracts to make online revisions. Reference services scan current books and magazines to update their holdings. This type of scanner is also used to track packages sent by international delivery services.

There are OCR scanners available for personal computers as well. When a user scans text, it is input directly into standard word processing formats for later editing. This eliminates the need to retype a document already in a printed form from some other medium, such as a newspaper, or from an incompatible word processing program.

**Magnetic Ink Character Recognition**    Similar to OCR, *magnetic-ink character recognition (MICR)* employs computer-readable symbols; however, MICR requires the use of special magnetic ink to record the symbols, as shown in Figure 6.6. This type of coding is used primarily in banking operations to enter data from checks and deposit slips. These banking documents are imprinted along the bottom with MICR symbols that indicate customer account numbers, bank identification, and dollar amounts. An MICR scanner, also shown in Figure 6.6, reads the MICR character data for routing between banks as storage on tape or disk for subsequent processing.

**6.6**

MICR scanners input the bank's and customer's account numbers from a check along with the check amount.

MICR characters

## Other Input Devices

Although the keyboard, mouse, and scanner are the most familiar devices for input, other input peripherals are used for particular applications. Joysticks replace keys and a mouse for cursor control in playing computer games. The *joystick* looks like an automobile stick shift. By moving the joystick's arm, players can control the movement and action of characters on-screen. Some drawing software permits use of a joystick for input instead of a mouse.

**Light Pen** A *light pen* is a handheld, light-sensitive stylus attached to a computer that accepts the stylus position on the monitor as input. The user moves the pen across a screen to make menu selections or draw shapes (see Figure 6.7). Because the user holds the pen up to the monitor for input, this method can be tiring after a long period.

**6.7**

By using a light pen, a user chooses a response without typing.

**Pen-Based Computing**    The input of handwriting as data is a boon for many nontypists. *Pen-based computing* involves the use of a special pen on a monitor surface, as with a PDA (personal digital assistant). The tip of the pen creates an electromagnetic field when passed over the screen. The screen itself contains a current flowing either through a grid of wires or from top to side on a metallic screen. Touching the screen disturbs the current and allows the computer to sense where on the screen the pen is located. Pen-based computing can be used for note taking, on-site inventory, or editing a word-processed document directly on-screen, using common proofreading symbols. Figure 6.8

**6.8**

Software within a pen-based computer or personal digital assistant (PDA) will accept handwriting as input for editing text on-screen.

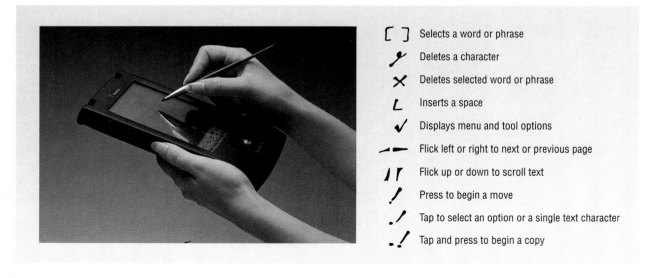

[ ]    Selects a word or phrase

   Deletes a character

✗    Deletes selected word or phrase

L    Inserts a space

✓    Displays menu and tool options

╼    Flick left or right to next or previous page

⁒    Flick up or down to scroll text

⁄    Press to begin a move

⁘    Tap to select an option or a single text character

⁙    Tap and press to begin a copy

**6.9**

Touching the screen breaks a matrix of infrared beams, which are used to locate the screen position for input.

displays some of the proofreading symbols used in pen-based editing. Individual differences in handwriting have posed problems for PDAs, but hardware and software engineers are researching solutions.

**Touch-Sensitive Screen**   Similar in use to the light pen is the ***touch-sensitive screen***, which enables users to input instructions by merely touching on-screen prompts (see Figure 6.9). These screens are sensitized so the pressure of a finger, pencil, or stylus initiates input. Another type waits for a touch to interrupt infrared light beams criss-crossing in front of the screen. The combination of light beams that are interrupted determine the screen area used for input. Such screens are especially helpful when people are unfamiliar with computers. Information systems in shopping malls, airports, and amusement parks are now being developed using touch-sensitive screens as the only input hardware.

**Tablet**   Drafting or drawing ***tablets*** work on a similar principle. A stylus, or *puck,* with crosshairs and buttons is run across the surface of a flat, pressure-sensitive or magnetically sensitive tablet (see Figure 6.10). The pattern of pressure or position of the puck when a button is pushed is sensed by wires under the surface of the tablet, then ***digitized;*** that is, the location of the stylus/puck is expressed as an XY coordinate and transmitted to the computer. The image "drawn" or "traced" on the drafting tablet is echoed on-screen.

By using tablets or light pens, people can input structural drawings into the computer. The drawings then can be viewed and manipulated as if the objects they represent actually existed. An aircraft engineer can design a plane and input the specifications into the computer; software then creates a three-dimensional computer drawing which can be tested like a model of the aircraft. Test flights can be simulated and design features evaluated—all under control of the computer. This enables users to detect problems in a product and modify designs before the product is made.

**6.10**

As the puck is moved across a blueprint, the graphical data is digitized and input into the computer.

**Digital Camera**   On the outside, the *digital camera* looks like a regular camera: The user focuses, aims, and shoots a scene. Instead of being stored on photographic film, however, the image is digitized and stored on a small disk within the camera. This disk can then be removed and read by a computer. The images on the disk can be transferred for use within graphics software or displayed on a monitor or projector. The same disk can be used many times over.

**Telephone**   A telephone with tone dialing is used widely as an interactive input device. A user can pay utility bills at home by dialing a number that establishes a connection to a bank computer. Then the user's bank account number, utility account number, and amount are entered via the telephone keypad. The computer generates a vocal response, verifying that the bill has been paid. Current account information on credit cards is available by entering an account number and PIN (personal identification number) with a touch-tone phone. A similar system is used to inquire about airport arrivals and departures by keying in the flight number, day, and flight destination, which results in a vocal listing of flight information.

**Credit Card Reader**   The credit card reader used by merchants, restaurants, hotels, and gas stations is another type of input peripheral. The credit card is passed through a slot containing a magnetic-tape reader. The strip of magnetic tape on the back of the credit card is read to obtain the credit card number. The amount of the sale is entered through a keypad. The computer responds with an approval or disapproval of the sale based on the customer's current credit status.

**Punched-Card Readers**   *Punched-card readers* of various types date back to Herman Hollerith's (Who's Who, chapter 7) original punched card. Instead of magnetic strips, these cards had holes punched by *keypunch* machines. Different combinations of holes represented text and numbers. Data entry operators used a keyboard on a keypunch machine to punch data on the cards. Computers output data on punched cards by using a *cardpunch*. For instance, utility companies sometimes included punched cards with their bills. Customers returned the punched card with payments, and the billing data was read into the computer from the cards by a card reader.

**Who's Who**

# Joseph Marie Jacquard

(1752-1834)

Joseph Marie Jacquard grew up in pre-Revolutionary France the son of a weaver and a pattern maker. In his youth he spent many boring hours as a drawboy, lifting the warp strings on a loom for the master weaver to draw the shuttle through them. In 1790 he had an idea to mechanize the loom, but the French Revolution intervened. In 1801 Jacquard developed a loom that used punched cards to control its operation. Needles fell through holes in the cards and lifted the warp strings; different combinations of punched holes created different designs and patterns in the woven material. Fabric designs and quality improved dramatically.

The weavers saw the innovation as loss of their jobs, however. They burned the looms and attacked Jacquard. The government, recognizing value of the loom, gave Jacquard in 1806 a pension and royalties. This allowed others to manufacture the looms, which quickly spread across Europe. Punched cards were to reemerge in information processing more than 80 years later in the United States.

**6.11**

A voice-recognition device translates the human voice into digital signals. Clear and careful speaking is required when using this input peripheral.

**Voice Recognition**    Spoken commands become input through the use of *voice-recognition devices* (Figure 6.11). In one typical application, a computer using a voice-recognition device accepts spoken commands from a person confined to a wheelchair. The individual need only announce the direction and speed. The computer recognizes the spoken words and converts them to output, guiding the wheelchair. Other such devices serve as security systems by admitting only those people whose voice can be recognized by the system.

High-tech dictation machines for business exist where voice input immediately is sent to a word processing program; however, voice-recognition devices still have many drawbacks. Only a limited vocabulary is understood by the devices, and users often have to talk slowly. In addition, computers must be programmed to recognize the speech patterns of those people who will be using the equipment. Currently, many such systems require that users read a list of key terms into the computer to establish a working vocabulary. Still, as hardware specialists continue to refine voice technologies, voice input has the potential to come into wider use. Eventually, computers are expected to accept all voice input. People talking to the computer on their wrist will be a common sight.

**Sensors**    In many scientific applications, data input is done through a *sensor,* as in Figure 6.12. When coupled with specialized application programs, these input devices allow data—such as the chemical makeup of a material, blood components, the movement of land along an earthquake fault, changes in radioactivity, or an automobile engine's performance measurements—to be sent to a computer for analysis. No matter what the application, the input peripherals in Figure 6.13 are being developed to make data acquisition timely and accurate.

**6.12**

This imaging system acts as a sensor using different densities of tissue in the skull as input data.

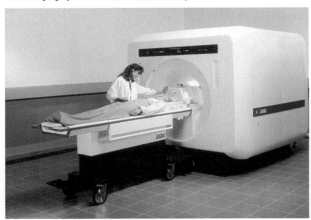

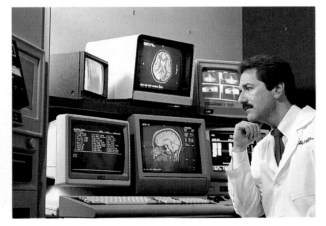

**6.13**

Input peripherals are designed to work with a variety of data and user participation.

| Input Device | Description |
|---|---|
| Keypunch | Puts holes representing data into punched cards. |
| Credit Card Reader | Reads magnetic tape on back of credit card. |
| Digital Camera | Places "photographs" on disk for computer input. |
| Keyboard | Most popular data entry device. Some come with optional numeric keypads, function keys, and cursor-control keys. Some have built-in trackballs and ergonomic designs. |
| Image Scanners | Accepts graphical data and converts it to pixels (digitizes). |
| Light Pen | Handheld hardware used to control cursor for graphic input. |
| Mouse, Trackball, Joystick | Used with graphic displays to control cursor. A mouse can be guided by remote control. |
| Punched-Card Reader | One of the oldest types of input devices, reads data from punched cards. |
| Scanner | Accepts a wide variety of machine-readable characters, which include optical marks, optical characters, magnetic-ink characters, and bar codes. |
| Sensor | Allows direct input of physical data. |
| Tablet | Supports graphic input through freehand drawing or tracing. |
| Telephone | Used to input numeric data from long distances; some voice-recognition hardware is used with telephone input. |
| Touch-Sensitive Screen | User touches on-screen prompts to control input; no additional hardware needed. |
| Voice-Recognition System | Activated by user's voice after voice has been programmed into the computer; currently accepts limited number of vocal commands. |

## OUTPUT HARDWARE SOLUTIONS

The most visible role of computers as problem-solving tools is when users receive and apply the actual results of computer processing. Output peripherals support a large diversity of applications. Generally, output hardware falls into three categories: permanent output, temporary output, and action output.

### Permanent Output

Computer-processed information in the form of printed documents, drawings, and microfilm are examples of permanent output. A vast selection of hardware is available for its production. When different types of permanent output are used together, they provide broad support for professional and personal applications. An architect's office, for example, might make use of reports, graphics, and microfilm for daily support of operations. The following sections introduce the most common types of permanent output hardware.

**Printers**  Permanent output is produced by many organizations for routine business correspondence, payroll processing, billing, and accounting. Many of these applications require the use of a printer. For example, architects deliver cost estimates and formal bids to clients as professional documents. The method used to produce the output as well as the speed and type of character printed are used to categorize printers.

Either impact or nonimpact methods are used by printers to transfer information to paper. Impact printers contain print elements that strike a ribbon which hits the paper. A popular type of impact printer for personal computer systems uses *dot-matrix characters*, which are formed as a pattern of dots within a matrix. The dot-matrix printer transfers the dots to paper using a print head that contains several pins (usually 9 or 24), as shown in Figure 6.14. Different combinations of pins strike an inked ribbon. As

**6.14**

Draft-quality printers use either 9- or 24-pin print heads.

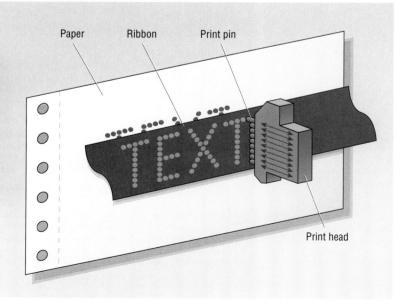

Paper  Ribbon  Print pin

Print head

## ...ABOUT IMPORTANT MAINTENANCE TASKS

- Wash your monitor screen
- Clean the disk drive head
- Delete hard disk files you no longer need
- Clean the printer's insides
- Change the printer ribbon/toner

*Source: Personal Computing,* October 1986, page 121.

the print head moves across the paper, the pattern of dots required for each character is printed on paper. If a document includes charts or drawings, these objects can also be printed as patterns of dots. Double-printing the dots creates *correspondence-quality characters.*

Impact printers that use *full characters* produce a top-quality output suitable for almost any business application. Each number, letter, and symbol available in a full-character printer is solid, like typewritten characters (see Figure 6.15). These printers may not be able to print graphic objects adequately, but can handle applications such as accounting, personnel, and payroll very well.

**6.15**

Printers produce either draft-quality (dot-matrix), correspondence-quality, or full characters.

Draft Quality

Correspondence

Full Charac

**6.16**

Line printers are the fastest form of impact printing.

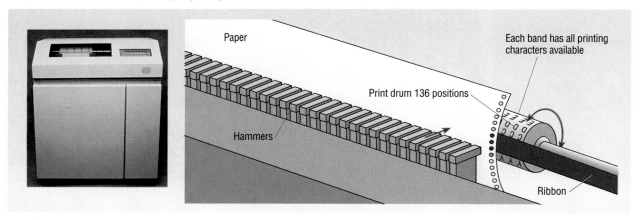

Paper

Each band has all printing
characters available

Print drum 136 positions

Hammers

Ribbon

Line printers represent the fastest form of impact printing. By using either a rotating drum or chain containing every possible letter, number, and special character, a line of print can be quickly formatted. A printed line is created by striking an inked ribbon and paper against the drum or chain with small hammers, as shown in Figure 6.16. Line printers are frequently used with minicomputers and mainframes needing reliable and continuous operation from a printer.

Nonimpact printers form characters without using an inked ribbon. *Ink-jet printers*, for example, spray tiny drops of ink to form character and object shapes on paper. Ink-jet printers are technically dot-matrix printers, since characters are formed as a pattern of dots, however the quality of output is generally much higher from an ink-jet printer than from most draft-quality dot-matrix printers. Color ink-jet printers are now available with jets that can be filled with three different ink colors. The mixing of these colors can result in thousands of different hues for printing text and objects. Although a complex color printout may be slow to produce on an ink-jet printer, the clarity and quality of color are extremely high.

Other nonimpact printers form characters with such elements as heat and electricity. A *thermal printer* uses heated dot-matrix wires to print output on specially treated paper. *Electrostatic printers* emit electrical impulses that are reproduced as characters on electrostatic paper. Some fax machines use techniques similar to thermal printers to produce documents on heat-sensitive paper. Output on thermal paper fades quickly when exposed to light, but the hardware is often inexpensive.

A nonimpact printer that produces high-quality output at very high speeds is the *laser printer*. Laser printers operate much like copy machines. A controlled beam of intense laser light forms images on an electrically charged drum (see Figure 6.17). These images attract toner particles. The particles, arranged as the images, are transferred to paper, where heat is used to fuse the particles to the page. Laser-created documents feature a high-quality print with high resolution one page at a time. This allows users to print their own letterheads, logos, and graphic objects along with the text, instead of using preprinted forms. Costs for laser printers have steadily declined. As they become more affordable, they are in demand by both individual and commercial users who need high-quality printing at fast speeds.

**6.17**

Laser printers contain a laser that scans across an electrically charged drum, creating output rivaling traditional typesetting.

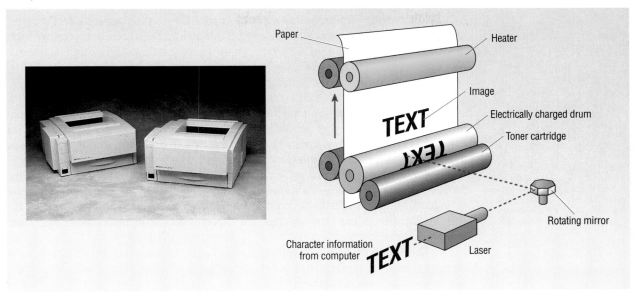

**6.18**

A plotter produces drawn, rather than printed, output.

With new developments in laser print technologies, color laser printers have been developed. Of highest quality is the *dye sublimation printer,* which fuses a gaseous form of colored ink onto special paper. The quality of output equals that of photographs.

**Plotters**    Within an architectural firm, many computer applications require large graphic output in the form of graphs, maps, charts, and drawings. An architect's designs, for example, require sketches instead of text. One kind of device that produces permanent graphic output in large sheets is the ***plotter*** (see Figure 6.18). Directed by signals from the computer, the plotter moves a pen across a piece of paper. A plotter equipped with more than one pen can produce multicolored graphic output.

There are two basic types of plotters available. The flatbed plotter holds a sheet of paper on a flat surface, then moves a pen across the sheet to form images. On a drum plotter, the paper is wound around a drum; then the paper's rotation and pen movement are computer-coordinated to produce an image. Plotters can plot drawings from the size of standard letter paper up to 3 feet by 4 feet. Some drum plotters are capable of producing longer continuous drawings. With both flatbed and drum plotters, two- or three-dimensional graphics can be created. Plotters producing color output are also available.

The technology used in plotting drawings also makes available output peripherals that will cut templates for signs, or etch plastic surfaces with the same accuracy that a plotter produces in drawings.

Plotters and related hardware are high-quality, low-volume devices ideal for output of large drawings, maps, and other detailed graphics. In other words, they produce high-quality output for specialized purposes, but the process is time-consuming. As a result, plotters are unable to mass-produce graphic output efficiently.

**Microfilm and Microfiche**    Large volumes of information can be held in rolls *(microfilm)* or sheets *(microfiche)* of film on which miniature images are recorded. High-capacity microfilm enables users to access a high quantity of full-page images quickly and conveniently. In addition, microfilm is used for permanent preservation of printed information, since data on film is more durable and more compact than paper.

With ***computer output microfilm (COM)*** techniques, the results of computer processing are transferred—in miniature form—directly onto microfilm or microfiche. On microfilm, pages of data are imaged sequentially on a reel of film. Microfiche is a sheet of film often measuring 4 inches by 6 inches and carrying information equivalent to a 200-page report (see Figure 6.19).

Microfilm output is used for distribution of airline schedules, automotive parts catalogs, medical X rays, and lists of books in print. It also is ideal for storing back issues of newspapers and magazines as well as keeping archival records for hospitals, businesses, and universities. An architectural firm can use microfilm resources to access information on old blueprints, building codes, and zoning laws.

Recently, the *CD-R (compact disc—recordable)* has been used instead of COM for storing certain types of permanent output. Although contract addendums can be signed

**6.19**

A COM system produced the microfiche page being examined on this reader.

and modified tax returns submitted, the original signed contracts and tax returns will not be changed. These are ideal for storage on CD-R.

### ◼ Temporary Output

Video displays and audio responses serve as effective, yet temporary, output in applications that do not require permanent output. Computer technology brought with it an onslaught of permanent documents. The resulting "paper avalanche" became a hindrance to information retrieval. Computer technology soon enabled users to locate needed files directly and to receive real-time service. Users find that output used for reference does not have to be printed on paper. Video displays for temporary output have reduced this paper avalanche.

When the information changes rapidly, temporary output becomes a necessity. In airports, screens display up-to-the-minute flight information. At a football field, scoreboards provide temporary output reflecting current scores and statistics. In addition to screen output, audio response and interactive devices also provide output for immediate, temporary use.

**Video Display Output**   Monitors, also called *video display terminals* (*VDTs*), provide the same information as a plotter or printer, but in a temporary form. They are usually connected to the computer through a video controller card inserted into one of the computer's expansion slots. Monitors are either *cathode ray tubes (CRTs)* or flat screens. Cathode ray tubes operate much like television picture tubes: The computer generates signals that move an electron beam row by row across the phosphorus-coated face inside the CRT. The change in signals results in some very small areas of the row being activated (lit) and others not. *Pixels* (or picture elements), as these areas are known, are arranged in rows and columns. There may be a thousand pixels in each row of the screen (as shown in Figure 6.21), and a screen is rescanned or refreshed more than 25 times per second. This technique, known as *raster scanning*, permits clear but ever-changing images on-screen (see Figure 6.20).

**6.20**

The display on a monitor is made up of many pixels differing in color and intensity.

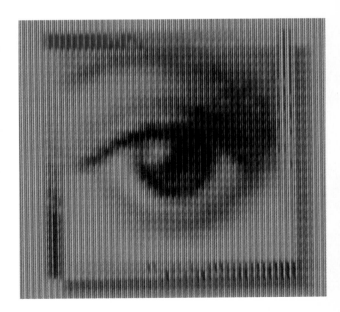

Flat screens can be made more compact than other designs and are used with laptop and pen-based computer systems. A row-and-column arrangement of pixels is also involved. Flat screens for portable computers may employ a *liquid crystal display (LCD),* in which an electrical field causes liquid crystals to change intensity and align in a predetermined configuration, creating output objects. Such monitors are very flat, compact, and lightweight.

Many flat screens and CRTs have a *sleep mode* option. When left on but idle for some time, the monitors powers down to a lower energy level, 30 watts or less to meet EPA (Environmental Protection Agency) standards. The user can set the time interval before sleep mode begins. Full power is restored with a simple touch of the mouse or keyboard. Another energy-saving option is a **screen saver** utility program, which replaces an idle monitor's display with a moving image. This prevents the image from being burned into areas of the monitor. Like sleep mode, a screen saver is disabled when the user initiates input.

Images might be displayed on *monochrome,* or single-color, monitors. Typically, monochrome screens display output in green, white, or amber colors on a black background. Multicolored output can be produced by **RGB monitors,** which use red, green, and blue components in each pixel to form full-color images. Many LCD monitors are monochromatic, although color monitors are available. Color LCD monitors are expensive because each of the color components for a single pixel is controlled by a separate transistor—almost a million transistors per screen.

Standards have been developed for color monitors over the years, as summarized in Figure 6.21. These standards are based on the screen resolution and the number of

**6.21**

The standards for color monitors differ in the number of colors displayed as well as the screen resolution.

| Monitor Type | Resolution (pixels) | | Number of Colors | |
|---|---|---|---|---|
| **CGA** (color graphics adapter) | 640 × 200 | | 16 | |
| **EGA** (extended graphics adapter) | 640 × 350 | | 16 | |
| **VGA** (video graphics array) | 320 × 200 | | 256 | |
| **Super VGA** | 1,024 × 768 | | 256 | |
| **XGA** (extended graphics array) | 1,024 × 768 | | 65,536 | |

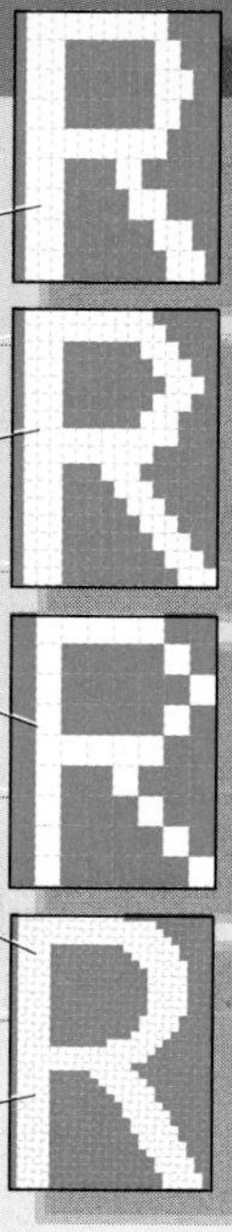

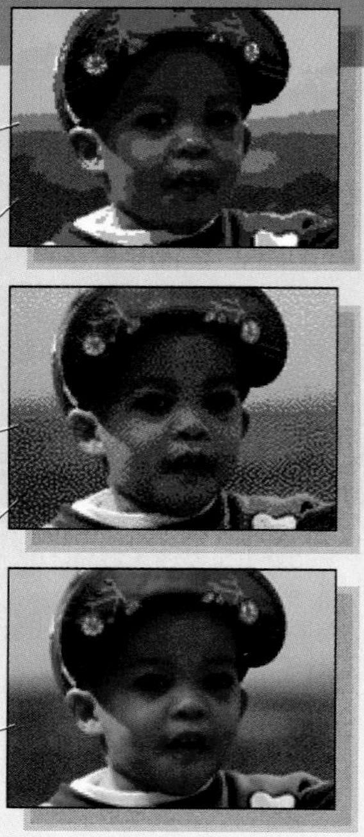

colors available. Older monitors with a *CGA (color graphics adapter)* can display up to 640 (width) by 200 (height) pixels per screen in 16 colors; *EGA (extended graphics adapter)* increased the screen display to 640 by 350 pixels with 16 colors available. When *VGA (video graphics array)* was introduced in 1987, it astounded people by its near-photograph-quality display. Monitors with VGA can display from a range of 262,144 colors (up to 256 colors at a time) in any of the 320 by 200 pixels on the screen. *Super VGA*, released two years later, displays 256 colors in 1,024 by 768 pixels and is the current standard for personal computers. *XGA (extended graphics array)*, developed in 1990, permits displays in an incredible 65,536 colors on screens with 1,024 by 768 pixels. It is easy to see that future developments in this area can only enhance the lifelike quality of graphic displays.

For presentations to audiences, large-screen formats are available. One example is a CRT television screen with a 35-inch-diagonal screen. Another alternative is the *projection plate,* which is a semitransparent plate that fits on top of an overhead projector and is directly connected to a computer. The image that normally appears on the computer's monitor is transmitted to the plate and projected on a large screen. Also, output can be sent to an RGB projector that shows the image on a large screen.

**Speech Synthesizers**   *Speech synthesizers* create messages as temporary output that computer users hear (see Figure 6.22). The most familiar form of audio output is heard in telephone recordings for the weather, time, or common operator messages.

New applications for speech synthesizers are constantly being found. Often delivered through telephones, speech output has been used to provide information about stock market prices and flight departure times. In late-model cars, a voice output reminds the driver to turn off headlights or add fuel to an almost-empty tank. Because audio

**6.22**

A speech synthesizer enhances the ability of these children to learn spoken language.

output requires only the ability to hear, it can be of great value to people with visual handicaps and reading disabilities. For example, computers and calculators are available where all output can be heard, if needed.

## ◼ Action Output

The information provided by temporary and permanent output hardware requires the sight or hearing of people for interpretation and use. Action output, on the other hand, consists of processing data to initiate some form of movement or process control activity.

One type of action output is produced by ***computer numerical control (CNC) machines.*** These devices accept numeric specifications as input. They produce machine parts that meet those specifications precisely as output. Programmable drill presses and lathes are CNC machines from which a cutting action is output. People who once operated manual tools may now program CNC machines to produce desired results (see Figure 6.23).

For technicians and engineers, *CAD (computer-aided design)* technologies support ***computer-aided machining (CAM).*** Computer-aided machining links numerical control capabilities directly with computer-generated designs by converting CAD designs into specifications used by CNC machines. This communication between design and manufacturing equipment is known as ***CAD/CAM.*** Large metalworking machines are used under CAM systems to prepare tools for the stamping of automotive parts or the fabrication of mobile homes based on CAD designs.

In ***robotics*** systems, computer-driven machines are programmed to perform work (Figure 6.24). Robot output can be determined solely by computer programs. In other cases, output is a result of the input of physical data. Some robots are attached to cameras that allow them to "see" their surroundings and adapt their action output according to what they view.

Robots can do high-risk jobs, such as working among toxic fumes or handling radioactive materials, with no ill effects. The earliest robots were used to do these health-

Precision part production depends on the programmability, accuracy, and flexibility of CNC machines.

**6.24**

Linking robots on an assembly line creates a manufacturing system that performs complex operations.

threatening duties. In recent years people have put robots to many labor-saving uses. For example, a robotic engine-manufacturing tool might perform a series of functions: sizing holes in a block, inserting pistons, and putting the engine block head in place. The robots sense the size of each hole, then locate and insert pistons that fit the holes to 0.0001 inch.

The field of medicine has found several uses for action output. In hospital emergency rooms, computers with sensors monitor a patient's vital signs and, as action output, regulate the flow of oxygen or medication to the patient. Embedded microprocessors can send small electrical shocks to muscles to stimulate movement in paralyzed limbs; computerized pacemakers stimulate heart muscles. In both cases, muscle movement is the action output.

## PERIPHERAL DESIGN AND SAFETY

Some particular health concerns for users have arisen due to the increased use of input and output peripherals in the past two decades. When people used only typewriters and pens for business paperwork, there were always breaks in the action. For example, the typewriter carriage had to be returned at the end of each line, paper needed to be changed, and errors had to be manually corrected. With the advent of computers, especially word processing programs, it was possible for a person to spend several hours typing at a keyboard and looking at a monitor with little change in hand or body position. It wasn't long before workers were complaining about pain in their wrists and hands, back and neck aches, and headaches due to eyestrain.

## Repetitive Strain Injuries

Doctors and researchers have found several causes for many of these symptoms. *Repetitive strain injury (RSI)* can result from continuous typing on a keyboard or use of a mouse. In an RSI, the tendons in the arms become inflamed and squeeze the nerves. This causes numbness and pain. Unless the RSI is diagnosed and treated, serious long-term disabilities can develop. Carpal tunnel syndrome, an RSI of the wrist, can cause permanent damage, seriously limiting use of one or both hands. Over half of workplace illnesses in private industry can be attributed to RSI.

## Low-Frequency Emissions

Since monitors were introduced in the late 1970s, people have been concerned about the effects of the extremely low-frequency (ELF) emissions from these screens. Rumors of miscarriages and brain tumors caused by VDT emissions have yet to be substantiated by medical researchers. At the very least, many users find that the glare from a screen causes eyestrain and headaches. Other workers complain of continuous back or neck pain that seemingly cannot be relieved with routine pain medicine.

## Ergonomics

Some of these health problems are due to the design of computer equipment and its related workspace. Since most hardware is mass produced, there was little consideration at first for the need to fit an individual. *Ergonomics* is the study of how the tools and equipment we use can be designed to fit the way the human body moves and works. Health researchers, hardware engineers, office furniture designers, and people who set up the work areas for computer users all are considering ergonomic features when they create a new product (Figure 6.25).

For example, to reduce the number of repetitive strain injuries, designers and medical experts have come up with a variety of solutions. Doctors have designed splints to put around wrists to prevent injury-causing movement; surgery has relieved some sufferers of carpal tunnel syndrome. Hardware designers are attempting to create keyboards that better fit the human hand. These designs include pads on which to rest your wrists, letters in different locations on the keyboard, and keyboards that are curved, as illustrated in Figure 6.26. There are even keyboards shaped like an inverted V, where the hands are placed at the sides, rather than on top.

To reduce the perceived dangers of monitors, antiglare screens and changes in screen colors are being used. For those who would like to protect themselves from emissions, there are leaded aprons that can be worn, similar to those used by X-ray technicians. Many European countries have adopted strict standards on monitor emissions. Although scientists are constantly trying to reduce the emissions from VDTs, manufacturers claim that there has been no definitive proof that continued exposure to these emissions is harmful.

Many of the complaints of back pain and general fatigue are due to the workspace itself, not the I/O hardware. Bad posture due to sitting on poorly designed chairs or at

**6.25**

A safe and comfortable workspace should be designed with ergonomics in mind.

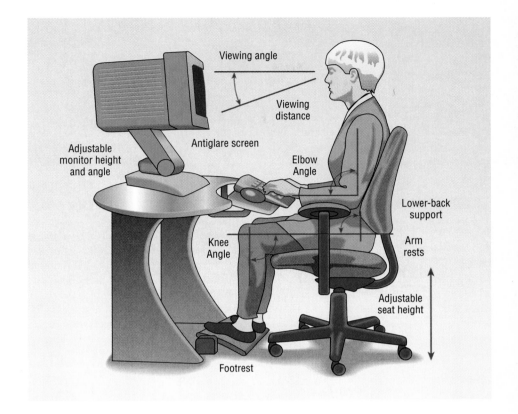

**6.26**

Keyboards are being redesigned to reduce the likelihood of RSI (repetitive strain injury).

# A Closer Look at
# Environmentally
# Conscious Computing

**C**omputers have made society more productive but brought a variety of environmental concerns. Increased energy use, piles of obsolete hardware, and work areas buried under paper are just a few problems. Here are some suggestions for environmentally conscious, or *green*, computing.

**Q:** Can I slow down paper proliferation in my work area?

**A:** Although the final copy of many documents must be perfect, you can reduce paper use by editing a document online and using the software's print preview option, rather that editing a draft paper copy. Many memos can be sent via electronic mail instead of in an envelope. Recycle used paper if possible.

**Q:** What is a green computer?

**A:** A green computer system has a CPU and monitor that both meet the EPA standard of 30 watts or less during sleep mode.

**Q:** How can I tell if a computer has been designed for energy efficiency?

**A:** Look for the Environmental Protection Agency (EPA) Energy Star logo on both monitors and computers. Lower wattage means lower energy costs and less heat generated by the equipment, translating to fewer electrical problems.

energy

**EPA POLLUTION PREVENTER**

**Q:** What can I do with old or obsolete computer hardware? Can it be recycled?

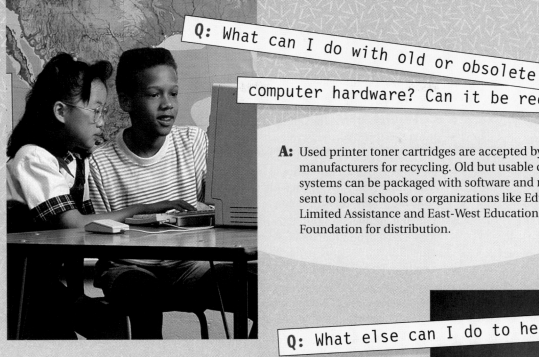

**A:** Used printer toner cartridges are accepted by some manufacturers for recycling. Old but usable computer systems can be packaged with software and manuals and sent to local schools or organizations like Educational Limited Assistance and East-West Educational Foundation for distribution.

**Q:** What else can I do to help?

**A:** Turn your computer off at the end of a work session. If you don't own a green computer, retrofit your system with *power management software* to include sleep mode. Use a simple screen saver, which is more energy efficient than multicolored designs, to further reduce energy consumption. Look for portable computers that use recyclable or rechargeable batteries. Format and reuse old diskettes.

**Q:** What does the future hold for environmentally conscious computing?

**A:** Look for all computers to be green in the future. And don't be surprised if other office machines, such as printers and copiers, are soon required to meet the EPA's Energy Star requirements as well.

desks raised to an improper level, or working under insufficient lighting can cause many of these complaints. Here are some suggestions to help you achieve safe computing:

♦ Sit on a chair with rollers that is built for your height. Your back should be straight but supported, lower arms and thighs parallel to the floor, and feet flat. Chair and desk heights should be adjustable. A footrest may be necessary.

♦ The top of your monitor should be even with your eye level and 24 to 26 inches away. Any documents from which you are typing should also be at that level. Adjustable monitor arms and copy holders are available.

♦ By using indirect lighting, screen glare can be reduced; there are also antiglare screen covers on the market. Be sure adequate light is available on all surfaces you read.

♦ Take a break for at least 15 minutes every three hours. Move around, stretch, and do other activities to vary your arm and body positions. At a minimum, stretch your arms every hour or so. Even while working, occasionally look away from the screen and focus on a distant object.

♦ Warm up your hand muscles before a long typing job. Suggested exercises include clenching and releasing your hands, stretching your fingers, and massaging your palms.

♦ Create a working environment that is as stress-free as possible. Personalize your workspace and set up an efficient flow of paperwork and information within your work area.

As we increase the use of input and output hardware in our work environments, both workers and designers have reached the same conclusion: We must adjust the equipment to fit our individual needs, not adjust our bodies to fit the equipment.

## CHAPTER FACTS

▪ Input/output (I/O) hardware is the link between computers and people.

▪ Keyboards may contain character keys, function keys for activating software features, numeric keypads, or icons.

▪ Pointing devices, such as a mouse or trackball, provide an alternative to the keyboard for data input.

▪ Scanners are used to transfer images and user-recognizable characters into binary code. They can scan bar codes, optical marks (OMR), optical characters (OCR), magnetic-ink characters (MICR), or graphic images.

▪ Sensors allow direct input into computers of such physical data as chemical makeup or radioactivity levels.

▪ Users can input data with a joystick, light pen, or touch-sensitive screen, or by drawing on a tablet.

▪ Voice-recognition systems allow vocal input based on a preprogrammed vocabulary.

■ Input also can be sent through telephone tone dialing, a credit card reader, or punched-card reader.

■ Output hardware can be permanent, temporary, or result in action.

■ Permanent output is usually in printed form. Printing can be accomplished by impact or nonimpact methods.

■ Plotters can produce drawings, maps, and pictures as another form of permanent output.

■ Photographically reduced images can be stored on microfiche (pages of film) or microfilm (reels of film); COM is high-volume, durable, permanent output.

■ Monitors or video display terminals provide temporary output. Graphics and text are presented through patterns of pixels or by using liquid crystal displays (LCDs).

■ Energy-saving options such as sleep mode and screen savers are available for monitors.

■ Output can be presented on monochrome or RGB monitors. Standards for color monitors are CGA, EGA, VGA, Super VGA, and XGA.

■ Speech synthesizers output spoken words.

■ Action output is produced through the programming of robots or by computer numerical control (CNC) machines.

■ Action output is used to monitor and stimulate muscles connected to artificial or paralyzed limbs.

■ Safety in computing involves protection against repetitive strain injuries and low-grade emissions from monitors. Work areas should be designed with ergonomic considerations.

## *TERMS TO REMEMBER*

| | | |
|---|---|---|
| bar code | function keys | RGB monitor |
| buffer | ink-jet printer | robotics |
| CAD/CAM | laser printer | scanner |
| computer-aided machining (CAM) | light pen | screen saver |
| | pen-based computing | software guide |
| computer numerical control (CNC) machine | plotter | tablet |
| | plug-n-play | touch-sensitive screen |
| computer output microfilm (COM) | point-of-sale (POS) system | trackball |
| | real-time processing | video display terminal (VDT) |
| digitize | repetitive strain injury (RSI) | voice-recognition device |
| ergonomics | | |

## MIX AND MATCH

*Complete the following definitions with the Terms to Remember.*

1. A small temporary storage area in memory or I/O hardware is called a(n) _____.

2. A(n) _____ is an output device that produces line drawings by moving a pen across paper.

3. _____ are used to activate particular software features.

4. The study of how tools, furniture, and equipment can be designed to fit the human body is called _____.

5. A(n) _____ is a machine-readable collection of stripes of varying width used to identify items.

6. The capability to connect I/O hardware with minimum user involvement is referred to as _____ technology.

7. A computer-controlled mechanical arm or device that can be programmed to do repetitive movements is an example of _____.

8. A(n) _____ is an input peripheral used to sense patterns of bars, dots, images, or characters and convert them into digital data.

9. A(n) _____ forms characters on a drum; the image on the drum is developed, as in a copy machine, and the characters are printed on paper.

10. A(n) _____ uses red, green, and blue pixels to form a variety of colors.

11. Output onto microfilm or microfiche of computer-generated data is known as _____.

12. A(n) _____ asks leading questions and makes requests of a user to facilitate easy completion of hardware installation or other task.

13. A monitor that becomes an input device when a user touches it is called a(n) _____.

14. _____ use programs representing numeric specifications to produce precise machine parts.

15. A(n) _____ produces a moving screen display to prevent burning in a single design on an idle screen.

## REVIEW QUESTIONS

1. Define the Terms to Remember.
2. How does plug-n-play hardware make a computer more user-friendly?
3. What are two pointing devices used for data input, and how do they work?
4. Define four types of machine-readable data read by scanners, and describe an application for each.
5. How does a touch-sensitive screen work, and where could it be used?
6. Describe how a digital camera saves photographic images, and identify an advantage of creating photographs this way.

7. How can a telephone and credit card reader be used as part of input operations?

8. Describe an application for voice-recognition devices, and identify three current limitations to it.

9. How is a sensor used as an input peripheral?

10. How do ink-jet, thermal, electrostatic, and laser printers work?

11. What are the pros and cons of using a plotter for output?

12. Why would an organization use computer output microfilm?

13. Describe two ways of storing reduced images by using COM.

14. Name and describe the differences among the five standards for color monitors.

15. Describe an application for speech synthesizers.

16. What determines the movement (output) of a robot?

17. What are two major health concerns for users of computer systems?

18. How can people help make computing safe and comfortable for themselves?

19. Identify two ways people can save energy when using their computer.

## APPLYING WHAT YOU'VE LEARNED

1. What input and output peripherals would be most suitable for these examples of data processing?
   a. updating fast-food restaurant inventories
   b. grading a college entrance exam and reporting the results to the students
   c. spray-painting motorcycles on an assembly line
   d. checking driving records for a driver's license renewal

2. How could voice-recognition devices and sound/speech synthesizers aid in these situations?
   a. a wheelchair for a paraplegic
   b. a computer used by a child who cannot read
   c. danger and fire alarms for a blind person
   d. a computer used by a person learning English
   e. safety features in a building during a power blackout

3. Visit a local computer store and compare the price and quality of a dot-matrix, ink-jet, and laser printer. Discuss your findings and obtain copies of output from each printer.

4. What are five applications for a robot other than those mentioned in the text?

5. Some I/O hardware buyers believe in getting the biggest and fastest hardware they can afford.
   a. What are the disadvantages of this approach?
   b. What are the disadvantages of buying the least expensive hardware?
   c. Would it be better to delay purchasing necessary hardware equipment until the price comes down or to buy the newest equipment now?

6. On the horizon for video equipment is high-definition television. Write a short research report on this upcoming technology. How does it differ from present television? What timeline (and prices) are expected for its release? Are standards established for this technology?

# Storage and Communication Hardware

**H**ours worth of work can be saved, transmitted across the country, or lost in the blink of an eye when using a computer system. One of the most common mistakes new computer users make is forgetting to copy important data and programs to another tape or disk. Without a duplicate, you could lose valuable information or software if the original is lost or destroyed. You can minimize problems by learning backup procedures and how to properly handle different storage media. Once you appreciate the importance of storage hardware, proper data handling procedures will become second nature.

One of the most common frustrations users have is trying to establish a data communication link to another computer. Understanding how modems use communication technology and what to look for when linking to an information service will make you a knowledgeable consumer of these products and give you a fighting chance of getting the job done with a minimum amount of fuss and time.

## STORAGE MEDIA

The right mix of I/O hardware is essential to a user-friendly computer system. Of equal importance is choosing the correct type of storage media and hardware. Storage media hold data before processing and store the results of processing. The term *storage media* refers to the material on which data is recorded; tapes and disks are the most common.

When data and program files are constantly changing, magnetic storage media are most often used. Magnetic-tape or -disk drives record data by magnetizing small

**7.1**

Microscopic particles on the surface of magnetic disks or tape are magnetically aligned to represent data and program instructions as bit patterns.

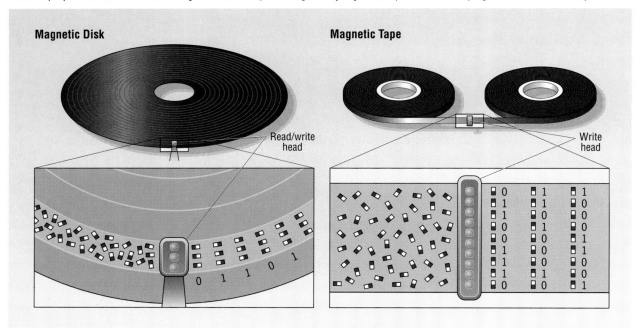

areas on the storage media (see Figure 7.1). These magnetized areas store the binary codes representing data or program instructions. When the file is no longer needed, the storage hardware overwrites the binary code and records new information in its place.

Disks are the most commonly used storage media because they support direct access to data. Unlike tapes, on which data is *written* (recorded) and *read* (playedback) in a preset order, disks allow independent pieces of data, such as a record or sound clip, to be read and written. Magnetic disks are popular because they can be erased and reused.

## MAGNETIC-DISK STORAGE

Disk drives are equipped with read/write heads that convert the magnetized spots on disk into a binary code. As the disk spins inside the drive, the read/write head passes over the surface of the disk. The head writes data on the disk by magnetizing spots on the disk's tracks or retrieves data from the disk by reading magnetized spots already there. The disk drive reads the bits as a continuous stream of data. Since each byte of data consists of 8 bits, the computer then organizes the bits into bytes.

Moisture and extreme heat or cold are bad for any disk. Magnetic fields associated with electrical equipment such as telephone receivers or with paper clips kept in a magnetized holder can erase any magnetic storage media. Dirt and dust damage both the read/write head and the disk surface, if caught between the two (see Figure 7.2). As a result, removable disks must be handled with care and stored in a cool, dry location out of direct sunlight. Disks should never be left in a hot car during the day or a cold car overnight.

**7.2**

A disk drive's read/write head is extremely vulnerable to common contaminants that can damage the mechanism and destroy stored data.

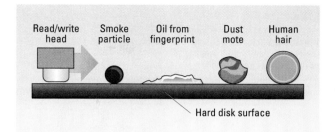

## Hard and Floppy Disks

The primary types of disk drives use either hard disks or floppy disks. When compared with floppy disk drives, hard disks provide users with fast access to stored data. Storage capacities can exceed 1 billion bytes (gigabyte). Hard disks come in a variety of sizes, from about a 14-inch diameter for minicomputers and mainframes to a 1.3-inch diameter for portable personal computer systems (shown in Figure 7.3).

To achieve fast access speeds, the read/write head does not actually touch the hard disk surface, but floats over it. And though hard disks are sealed to protect the disk from dirt and dust, a sharp blow during operations can cause a head crash. ***Head crashes*** occur when the read/write head touches the surface of the hard disk, resulting in damage to both the disk and disk drive.

*Floppy disks,* or *diskettes,* are round, flat, flexible pieces of plastic used primarily for data storage and backup in personal computer systems. Typical diskette sizes are 5.25 inches and 3.5 inches. In the past, 8-inch floppy disks were used; 2-inch diskettes are available, but not widely used. Windows in the diskette cover permit access to the surface for reading or writing of data. Because the read/write heads are designed to physically touch the diskette's surface, diskettes can wear out. As a result, it is very important for users to back up data and programs on diskettes.

**7.3**

This hard disk is 1.3 inches in diameter and is designed to work within handheld personal computers.

**7.4**

The most commonly used floppy disks are 3.5 inch or 5.25 inch. Their storage capacities depend on the data's storage density (double or high).

Diskettes are distinguished not only by size, but also by their storage capacity. Storage capacity is measured by the ***density*** (bytes per inch) in which data is written on the disk. These disks generally fall into one of three categories: single, double, and quad (high-capacity) density (see Figure 7.4). Diskettes manufactured with only one usable side are considered single-sided, whereas double-sided disks use both sides.

To safeguard data from accidental erasure, the ***write-protect notch*** on a 5.25-inch floppy disk can be covered, as shown in Figure 7.5. The smaller 3.5-inch diskettes have a ***write-protect window***, which is opened to protect programs and files from deletion. In both cases, data can be read or input from the disk, but the disk cannot be used to store new output. Data stored on disk can also be write-protected by having the operating system designate selected files as read-only.

## ■ Disk Storage

Disk drives store data on disks in concentric circles called ***disk tracks***. Note in Figure 7.6 that tracks are subdivided into storage locations called ***sectors***. Individual sectors hold one record or group of records called a ***block***. The computer locates a record by its track and sector number.

On hard disks a special magnetized code marks the beginning of each track. Diskette tracks and sectors are established according to a sensing hole (see Figure 7.6). ***Soft-sectored diskettes*** have one sensing hole which physically identifies the beginning of each track. Track sectors on a soft-sectored diskette are identified by the disk drive through formatting.

During the ***formatting*** process, a system program controls the disk drive as it eliminates any old data and sets up each track and sector. The disk's root directory is also created during formatting. It and other directories added by the user catalog the contents of the disk by filename and file size. The date and time each file was saved to

**7.5**

Data on a 5.25-inch disk is protected from accidental erasure by covering the write-protect notch. Opening the write-protect window of a 3.5-inch disk protects data and programs.

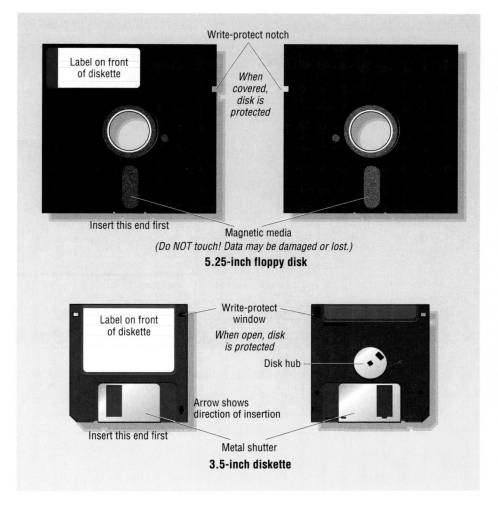

Write-protect notch

*When covered, disk is protected*

Label on front of diskette

Insert this end first

Magnetic media
*(Do NOT touch! Data may be damaged or lost.)*
**5.25-inch floppy disk**

Label on front of diskette

Write-protect window
*When open, disk is protected*

Disk hub

Arrow shows direction of insertion

Insert this end first

Metal shutter
**3.5-inch diskette**

**7.6**

Computer users format new disks to set up tracks and sectors. A single sensing hole on a soft-sectored diskette determines where tracks begin and end. Files using non-continuous sectors are said to be fragmented.

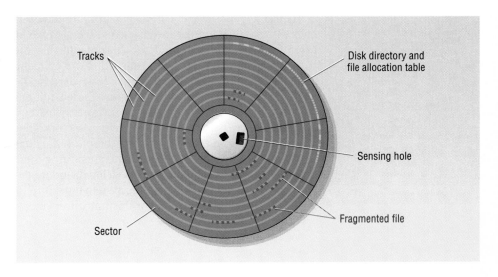

Tracks

Disk directory and file allocation table

Sensing hole

Fragmented file

Sector

7.7

The disk directory identifies the location of the file Eng101-1.doc in the English folder (or subdirectory). The file's size, date of last change, and other attributes are found in the directory.

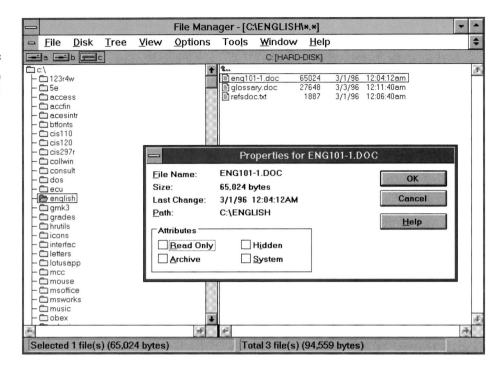

the disk are also stored, as shown in Figure 7.7. A separate *file allocation table (FAT)* identifies, by sector number, where the file is found on the disk. The disk sector number becomes the file's **disk address**. When a user requests access to a file on a certain disk, the operating system uses the disk drive to look for the filename in the disk directory. When a match is found, the operating system locates the file by accessing the sector number provided by the FAT.

For example, a user might open the Eng101-1.doc report file on a hard disk. The personal computer operating system (OS) would search the English directory to find Eng101-1.doc. It would then use the disk address found in the file allocation table to locate the start of the file. The OS would move the disk drive's read/write head to the track with the disk address and check that sector for an identifying label for the Eng101-1.doc file. If the match is found, the OS copies the file into memory one sector at a time.

Since Eng101-1.doc is not finished, the user might add several new pages before saving the file to disk again. The larger file needs more disk space, and the FAT identifies open sectors that can be used. Rarely are these additional sectors located on the same track as the original file. When the file is saved again, the operating system starts writing over the old sectors, then jumps to the new sectors. The OS uses an internal pointer to link to two areas together. This is an example of *file fragmentation,* which is illustrated in Figure 7.6. It is a practical way for the operating system to handle the dynamic use of disk storage space as files are added, deleted, and modified.

As a disk fills up, the operating system must turn to file fragmentation more often to allocate the available space. At this time, users might notice that it takes longer to open and save files. *Defragmentation utility programs* are available to reorganize the sectors used by files. This type of system software rewrites files on the disk so they use continuous sectors, thereby allowing faster reading and writing.

## ▨ Disk Controller

Storage hardware varies in the *access time*—the time it takes to locate data on storage media. It also varies in the speed at which data can be input or output—the *transfer rate*. Figure 7.13 shows the access times and transfer rates for disk and tape drives. When compared to those of hard disk drives, access times are slower for floppy disk drives, because the disk does not spin as fast.

The speed in which the disk turns is just one factor that determines how fast data can be read and written. The type of *disk controller* used to connect the disk drive to the computer's internal circuitry is another factor. A disk controller is connected to a computer's expansion bus in several ways. On some computers the controller is found on the computer's motherboard; in other configurations the disk controller is on an expansion card that slips into one of the motherboard's expansion slots (see Figure 7.8).

### 7.8

Disk controllers coordinate the flow of data to and from the computer and disk drive. They are often connected to the system as an expansion card and can control the flow of data to several drives.

| Disk Controller Technology | Storage Capacity | Transfer Rate | Comments |
|---|---|---|---|
| MFM (Modified Frequency Modulation) | 127 million bytes | 655 K per second | Old standard |
| RLL (Run-Length Limited) | 200 million bytes | 800 K per second | Old standard |
| IDE (Integrated Drive Electronics) | 528 million bytes | 1 MB per second | Inexpensive and reliable |
| ESDI (Enhanced Small Device Interface) | > 1 billion bytes | 3 MB per second | Limited popularity |
| Enhanced IDE (Integrated Drive Electronics) | > 1 billion bytes | 2–3 MB per second | Expands capacity of popular standard |
| SCSI (Small Computer System Interface) | > 1 billion bytes | 3 MB+ per second | Popular standard that links up to 7 peripherials on the same cable |

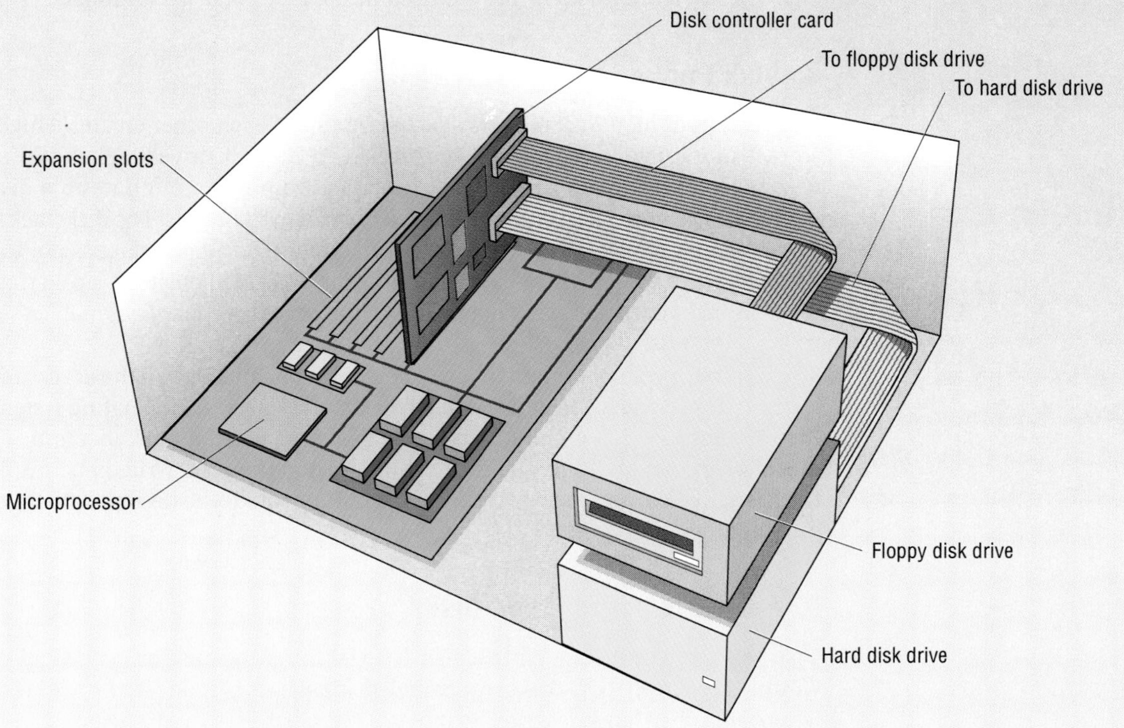

**7.9**

Direct access to data on a disk is accomplished through a movable read/write mechanism that can access data on one cylinder at a time.

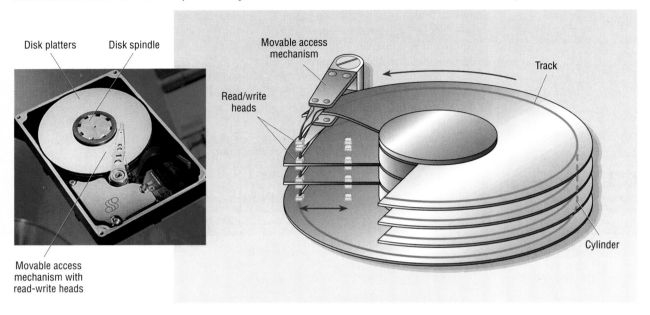

Disk platters    Disk spindle

Movable access mechanism

Read/write heads

Track

Cylinder

Movable access mechanism with read-write heads

Most disk controllers are designed to handle one or two hard disks as well as two floppy disk drives. Figure 7.8 identifies some common types of disk controllers.

### Disk Packs

A collection of hard disk platters stacked on top of each other creates a high-capacity storage unit called a *disk pack* (see Figure 7.11). The disk drive that handles a disk pack uses several read/write heads to retrieve data from or output data to a disk surface. Figure 7.9 shows the access mechanism with read/write heads. The disk pack illustrated in the figure provides seven recording surfaces; the bottom surface is not used. When the read/write heads, which move as a unit, are in a given position, seven tracks can be read—one on each surface. Repositioning the access mechanism enables seven more tracks to be read.

The collection of tracks that can be read at one position of the access mechanism is called a **cylinder**. To locate a specified file on a disk pack, the operating system searches the directory for a matching name and its corresponding disk location. The access mechanism moves to the specified cylinder. Then the read/write head for the correct track is activated, and the beginning of the file is located. The desired data then is copied into memory.

### Removable and Fixed Disks

Disk packs can be inserted into a disk drive for temporary use or installed permanently within the drive. Such disks are called *removable disks* or *fixed disks,* respectively. Removable disks lend versatility to disk use. Because disks can be inserted and removed,

**7.10**

Hard disks fixed inside a hard card are easily installed into a personal computer's expansion slot on the motherboard.

the number of disks available for use with a drive is countless. Inside a disk drive the removable disk is less vulnerable to dirt and destructive elements in the environment.

Fixed disks are built inside the computer case and sealed from the outside environment to protect the disk. An access light on the front panel is turned on when data is being read or written. Users are advised to *park* the drive before moving a computer with a fixed hard disk. Parking the access mechanism, shown in Figure 7.9, locks the disk drive's read/write heads into place so the arm does not move after the computer is turned off.

One way of installing a fixed disk into a PC is to insert a hard card (Figure 7.10) into an open expansion slot on the computer's motherboard. A *hard card* is an expansion card with a small fixed disk built inside. The disk drive shown in Figure 7.3 is found inside a hard card that uses a PCMCIA (Personal Computer Memory Card International Association) expansion slot to snap into a computer's expansion bus. (For more information on the PCMCIA expansion bus, see Figure 5.6.) These cards provide an easy way to expand a PC's hard disk capacity and are often used with laptop computers and PDAs. Storage capacities range from 20 MB to more than 100 MB. Another way to increase disk capacity is to install an *external disk drive*. These removable or fixed disk drives usually connect to one of the computer's parallel ports.

Personal computer systems with fixed disks usually have an additional disk drive that handles floppy disks to back up critical data and programs, but they can also be equipped with *disk cartridges*. Cartridges are hard disks that are mounted and removed from disk drives. These storage media are compact, often measuring only 3.5 inches in diameter, but store more than 20 MB of data. Cartridges, like disk packs, provide portable, interchangeable, high-capacity hard disk storage (see Figure 7.11).

Some cartridge disk drives employ a physics principle observed by eighteenth-century physicist Daniel Bernoulli. Aerospace engineers use Bernoulli's Law when designing airplane wings, because it deals with the actions of air or liquids when they

**7.11**

Removable disks come in the form of disk packs and disk cartridges.

are flowing at varying speeds over different surfaces. Bernoulli disk drives use this principle to bring the read/write heads and disk surface together when the disk is spinning. When the power is turned off, they drop away from each other, which automatically protects the disk from harm.

## OPTICAL DISK STORAGE

The computer industry is always looking for more-efficient ways of saving data. New storage technologies using optical disks exceed the storage capacities currently available with magnetic disks of the same size. Optical storage techniques used by computers are basically the same as those used to record music on compact discs. Each employs lasers and is most often used to store data/music on a permanent basis. *Optical disks* differ from magnetic-disk storage by the way data is stored and read from the storage media. A laser beam is used to write and read data on these reflective disks, so they are also known as laser discs. Optical disks support direct access to data and have more storage capacity than magnetic disks. There are three different types of optical disks in common use: read-only, recordable, and erasable.

**7.12**

A laser can read an optical disk's surface, where pitted areas represent binary 1's and smooth areas represent binary 0's. A clear protective layer is applied to the surface to minimize damage due to rough treatment.

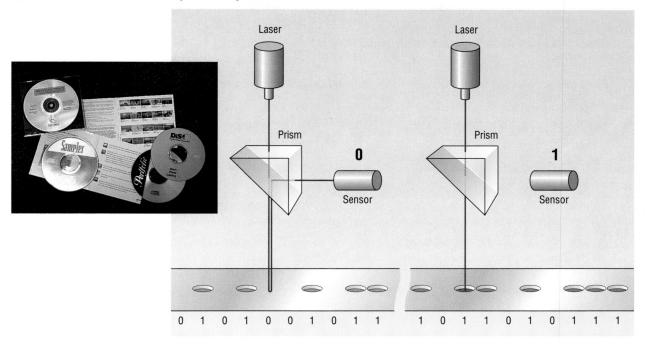

To record data on an optical disk, a high-powered laser burns small pinpoint pits into the disk's surface to represent bit patterns (see Figure 7.12). Therefore, read-only and recordable disks are written on only once. A lower-power laser scans the optical disk's surface to read the bit patterns.

In the form of videodiscs or compact discs (CDs), optical disks represent a new trend in small, high-capacity storage of images and sound. A single optical disk stores nearly 1 GB of data on one side. To put this storage capacity into perspective, an optical disk can hold 800 television-quality images or 60 minutes of high-fidelity music. The Kodak film company has even established a Photo CD standard for storing photographic images.

## Read-only Disks

Optical disks for data storage include the *CD-ROM (compact disk—read-only memory),* which is expensive to produce initially but is easily and inexpensively reproduced. This is an ideal way to distribute large amounts of data, such as an online encyclopedia or multimedia presentations. Computer programs and associated user manuals are often distributed on CD-ROMs.

Over the years CD-ROM drive performance has improved as the hardware technology provided faster access speeds. The original single-speed CD-ROM drives are now considered obsolete. Double-speed (2X) and quad-speed (4X) CD-ROM drives currently offer the best performance for the price, with access speeds at 300 milliseconds or less (see Figure 7.13). Faster drives (6X+) are on the drawing board.

**7.13**

Data storage is available on a wide variety of media. Each storage medium has different access speeds, transfer rates, and storage capacities.

|  | **Access Time** | **Transfer Rate** | **Storage Capacity** |
|---|---|---|---|
| **Removable disk pack** | 15 to 100 milliseconds* | 150,000 to 2 million characters per second | 65 million to 32 billion characters |
| **Fixed disk** | 5 to 30 milliseconds | 200,000 to 2 million characters per second | 10 million to 8 billion characters |
| **Floppy disk** | 70 to 500 milliseconds | 30,000 to 100,000 characters per second | 180,000 to 1.4 million characters |
| **Tape** | 10 milliseconds to several seconds | 18,000 characters per second | 10 million to 60 million characters |
| **CD-ROM** (double-speed) (quad-speed) | 265 to 400 milliseconds 150 to 240 milliseconds | 300,000 characters per second 500,000 to 600,000 characters per second | Up to 1 billion characters Up to 1 billion characters |

*millisecond = $\frac{1}{1,000}$ of a second

Since CD-ROMs have the storage capacity to hold lots of high-quality images, this type of storage is well suited for structural drawings used by architects and engineers. Music lovers are drawn to the clear, crisp sound quality available from CDs, which reproduce music free of the characteristic tape hiss of magnetic-tape recordings. Video sequences and library references are also recorded for educational applications. Unfortunately, CD-ROM drives, like the one in Figure 7.14, can only read disks; online recording and editing are not yet economically practical. The original data recorded on a CD-ROM cannot be changed.

## Recordable Disks

Originally, *WORM (write once read many)* disks were the only type of recordable optical disk. WORM drives record data on a blank disk, and the data is permanent once it has been recorded. These disks cost more than $10 each and are not compatible with CD-ROM drives. More recently, a less expensive *CD-R (compact disk—recordable)* format became available which is compatible with CD-ROM drives. As a result, personal computer users with a CD-R drive can create permanent, unerasable disks that can act as masters for CD-ROMs.

Practical applications for recordable optical disks often involve archiving data. Banks and brokerage houses must keep permanent records of every business transaction in which they are involved. WORM disks or CD-Rs provide large storage capacities for data that should not be changed for security or legal reasons.

## Erasable Disks

Like magnetic hard disks, erasable optical disk drives can overwrite data and are the most flexible type of optical storage media. Some of these optical disks are called *magneto-*

**7.14**

CD-ROMs store video-quality images and sounds as well as text. They are used for video games and can store the contents of an entire encyclopedia on a single disk.

*optical disks* because the bit patterns are aligned magnetically on the disk. Because the magnetized 1 and 0 bits reflect light differently, the bit patterns are optically read using a laser, hence the name *magneto-optical.*

The hardware cost and slow transfer speeds currently associated with eraseable optical disks have kept them from economically competing with magnetic hard disks. The increased storage capacity of optical disk technology gives it great potential as a popular type of storage hardware. Although research continues to improve erasable optical disk technology, magnetic storage media are still the storage workhorses for most computer systems.

## MAGNETIC-TAPE STORAGE

Tape drives, which operate like tape recorders/players, provide a low-cost, high-capacity means of sequentially storing and accessing data. The very nature of a strip of magnetic tape dictates that data is written and read in a preset order. For example, when music is stored on an audiotape, you cannot hear the fifth song on the tape until you listen to the preceding four songs or fast-forward past them. Unlike data on disk that is quickly accessed by the movement of an arm holding the read/write heads, tapes must be wound and rewound past stationary read/write heads. Therefore tape access speeds are on average always slower than disk. Access speeds can vary between a fraction of a second using a disk or several seconds using a tape (see Figure 7.13).

Many computer applications, however, do not require the fast access speeds. Backing up the contents of a hard disk to protect valuable data is easily and inexpensively accomplished using tape. Businesses use tapes to archive financial or legal data. Information services keep disk space available for new e-mail and forum conversations

**7.15**

Tape storage is done with reels or cartridges. In either case, data can be accessed only sequentially.

by moving old mail and comments to tape. If users need to recall backup or out-of-date data, they are usually willing to wait a few seconds to access it.

## Reel-to-reel Tapes

Large computers use tape drives to store and read data on reels of tape, as shown in Figure 7.1. A reel of magnetic tape is a half inch wide and can store 1,600 to 6,400 characters per inch on its half-mile length.

Tape drives record data as magnetized bit patterns. The orientation (polarity) of the magnetized areas on the tape's recording surface represents either a binary 1 or 0. Running down the length of tape are eight or nine *tape tracks*, or channels, in which bits are held. Combinations of bit positions that cross the tracks represent individual bytes. Figure 7.17 illustrates how data is typically stored on a tape.

Like magnetic-disk drives, tape drives are equipped with read/write heads. To read tape-recorded data, the read/write head senses magnetic spots, then transfers the data to memory. The read/write head also records magnetic areas in track locations to write data on tape. Like disks, tapes are write-protected when data should be used on a read-only basis.

## Tape Cartridges

Tape drives attached to early personal computers used cassette tapes similar to those used with home or car stereo systems. Cassettes and reels are now being replaced by *tape cartridges*. These cartridges are self-contained in hard plastic shells that are easy to mount in a tape drive and store when not in use (see Figure 7.15). They hold between 40 MB and 10 GB of data. Personal computer users utilize tape cartridges to back up important programs and data.

As you might expect, tape cartridges are sold in several formats. Two of the most popular cartridge formats are *QIC (quarter-inch cartridge)* and *DAT (digital audiotape)*. A wide variety of tape manufacturers sell QIC tape drives because industrywide standards have been established for some time. Newer DAT drives are higher capacity and faster than QIC drives because they use a tape-recording method similar to videocassette recorders (VCRs). Cartridge size and tape length vary, depending on the tape storage capacity needed by the user.

## SPECIALIZED STORAGE HARDWARE

Storage technologies have evolved to solve problems traditional tape and disk storage techniques cannot handle. Sometimes extremely dirty or electronically charged environments damage or erase magnetic storage media. Some industrial environments are so harsh that paper tapes, rather than magnetic tapes, store the program instructions for the computer-controlled machining tools. Large amounts of data or fast access speeds may require specialized hardware.

### Mass Storage

Some organizations, such as government offices, insurance companies, and historical archives, require storage and retrieval of extremely large volumes of data. One type of mass storage contains a honeycomb arrangement of data cartridges that each contain a strip of magnetic tape, as shown in Figure 7.16. A mechanical arm goes to the cartridge required and loads the tape within it onto a drum. From there the data on the tape is copied to a magnetic disk for faster access. Retrieval of the cartridge is slower than other storage methods but makes access of vast amounts of data possible. Furthermore, increased storage capacity is relatively easy to add.

**7.16**

Each cell of this mass storage system contains a length of magnetic tape, allowing retrieval of huge amounts of data.

## ...ABOUT CARING FOR YOUR FLOPPY DISKS

- Always place 5.25-inch diskettes back into a disk envelope when not in use
- Never place diskettes near magnetic devices
- Do not use paper clips on disks
- Store and use at temperatures between 50° and 110° F
- Keep diskettes away from the telephone
- Never bend floppy disks
- Never touch the floppy disk media
- Do not place heavy objects on a disk
- Store diskettes in a safe place
- Always make backup copies of your data

## RAID Drives

Another mass storage technique on a smaller scale combines several fixed hard disk drives, similar to those found in personal computers, into a *RAID (redundant array of inexpensive disks) drive*. This type of storage technology can be configured to support different system requirements. A RAID system needing to support a fault-tolerant computer provides duplicate file copies on different drives. When fast access speeds are a priority, RAID drives spread the contents of a file over two or more disks, which allows several read/write heads to access data simultaneously. Special disk controllers are needed to create RAID drives.

## RAM Drives

When users need the fastest possible access to data or when additional disk space is not immediately available, RAM memory is set aside to temporarily replace disk storage. A computer's operating system creates a *RAM drive* by setting aside a designated amount of memory, usually when the computer is booted. Memory used by a RAM drive reduces the amount of memory available to application programs.

In other instances, the RAM drive is a separate piece of hardware that connects to the computer through a parallel port or expansion slot. An independent RAM drive contains a circuit board filled with high-speed RAM chips; it is purchased when access speed is critical. This type of storage can be thousands of times faster than a diskette drive. A RAM drive is not a permanent storage solution, however, because RAM memory is volatile. In other words, all the data is lost when the power is turned off. Therefore, backup procedures are even more important when RAM drives are used.

### ■ Flash Memory

Recently, a type of *programmable read-only memory (PROM)* has been used as an alternative to RAM drives. These memory chips are nonvolatile and are therefore a true replacement for disk storage. Known as *flash memory,* the contents of these chips can be altered by the computer, and the data retained when the power is turned off. Access to data in flash memory is not as fast as a RAM drive, but is still many times faster than retrieving data using a disk drive. Flash memory cards use a PCMCIA expansion bus to connect to the computer's CPU.

Because flash memory does not use any moving parts that draw power, it is used when power consumption must be kept to a minimum. This is particularly important for portable computers relying on batteries. Flash memory is not likely to replace disk drives in other situations because it costs more and physically takes up more space.

The primary purpose of any storage hardware is to safely and accurately store data in the least amount of space. To ensure accuracy and to identify compromised data as soon as possible, a great deal of emphasis must be placed on error checking. This is one of several areas in which storage and communication technology have data handling procedures in common.

## George Boole

(1815-1864)

The logical design on which modern computer circuitry and data communication is based was developed by a nineteenth-century self-taught mathematician named George Boole. Boole's theory of logic was that any mathematical expression was in one of two states: true or false. Boole called it zero-one logic; we call it Boolean algebra. By combining many elements, each with two states, complex problems could be solved. Boole's life was dedicated to showing that logic had a strong place in mathematics, not just philosophy. His theories also made the design of Babbage's difference engine possible.

**Who's Who**

## MAXIMIZING HARDWARE PERFORMANCE

Communication hardware is primarily responsible for transferring data between two points. As with storage hardware, transfer rates and data integrity are of primary importance. To minimize data communication errors, computer systems use different error-checking routines. One of the most common is parity checking.

### Parity Checking

Data communication between computers requires error checking just as much as reading and writing on storage media. A common approach adds an additional bit to every bit pattern to check the data's integrity. This new bit is the *parity bit*.

A coding scheme such as ASCII requires 8 bits to make up each byte. When processing data, the computer uses 8 bits to represent 1 byte of data, with an extra (ninth) parity bit added in. The parity bit helps verify that data is encoded correctly. To do this, the computer instructs the modem or other hardware to maintain either an even or an odd number of 1 bits in each byte. The parity bit then takes on either a 1 or 0 value to meet that condition. This type of error-checking procedure is known as ***parity checking***.

In an example of parity checking, the letter *A* in ASCII is encoded with an even number of 1 bits: 0100 0001. The computer identifies that two 1 bits are used with the letter *A*. In an odd-parity-checking scheme, the parity bit is transmitted or stored as a 1, bringing the total of 1 bits to three, an odd number. The letter *C*, coded 0100 0011, would require a 0 parity bit to retain the odd number of 1 bits already in the bit pattern. Figure 7.17 shows the byte structure of the ASCII code format with odd-parity checking.

By using this odd-parity-checking scheme, the computer would check that each byte contains an odd number of 1 bits as a transmission is received or data is read from some storage medium. If a byte contained an even number of 1 bits, the computer would ask that the data be sent again. If errors continued to show up after several attempts, communication hardware will often slow down the transmission speeds. For example, a 9,600 baud modem might slow down to a 4,800 baud rate. Repeated parity errors when reading data from a disk would force the operating system to display an error message like "unable to read disk in drive A".

### Data Compression

Many computer users experience long waits when storing or transferring files that are hundreds of thousands of bytes in size. It is not uncommon to wait 10 or more minutes when uploading or downloading large programs, complex images, or video sequences off a network. Using a ***data compression*** utility program to compact data before it is transmitted can save time as well as disk space.

Most data compression techniques rely on the simple assumption that bit patterns are often repeated in data files. You see this repetition in the two *t*'s in the word *letter* or blank spaces in unused areas of a line graph. Graphic data usually has more redundancies than textual data. The data compression software looks for such a redundancy and puts a notation in its place. For instance, instead of repeating a binary code 10 times for 10 spaces, data compression software writes a notation that essentially says "10 spaces go here." When the notation is read from disk, the data is converted back to 10 independent spaces.

**7.17**

The parity bit is magnetized only when an odd number of magnetized 1 bits is needed. Computers then use parity checking to look for input or transmission errors. An even number of 1 bits indicates an error.

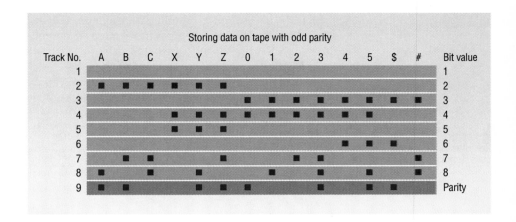

The types of redundancies and what to do with them vary among different data compression schemes. Sometimes expansion cards with a coprocessor and additional RAM chips acting like a disk cache work with the compression software. Data compression techniques supported by a specialized coprocessor are faster than techniques that rely only on terminate stay resident (TSR) software. In either case, the result is a 40 to 60 percent reduction in the size of a file.

As you might expect, data compression can also help computer users when storage needs exceed the capacity of their hardware. Using a data compression utility when reading and writing on disk is an alternative to upgrading your storage hardware.

## ■ Communication Channels

As mentioned in chapter 5, computers support two types of input/output ports: serial and parallel. The ribbon cable that connects a disk drive to the disk controller has nine different wires that carry the eight data bits and the parity bit. This is an example of a parallel cable and connection. Data communication between computers usually passes through a serial port which connects it to different types of communication channels.

The *communication channel* is the medium by which data communication takes place. The type of channel used dictates how the hardware is connected to the computer and the transmission speeds. Telephone lines, network cables, optical fibers, and communication satellites represent different types of communication channels.

In a local area network, a *twisted pair* of wires, similar to a standard telephone line, often connects the computers. Telephone (twisted-pair) wires are a common communication channel for connecting PC modems to information services and local bulletin board systems. One pair of twisted wires can handle only one telephone conversation or data transmission, as shown in Figure 7.18.

Computer hardware using digital signals transmitted using an *ISDN (Integrated Services Digital Network)* format can maintain 64,000 bps transmission speeds on standard twisted-pair telephone lines. Twisted-pair channels directly connecting two computers in a local area network can transmit data at speeds up to 10 million bps for distances up to 300 feet. This type of channel can maintain transmission rates of 2,400 bps for up to 10 miles. For greater distances the telephone company inserts hardware in the twisted-pair line that boosts the signal.

*Coaxial cables,* similar to those used in cable television networks, accommodate transmission speeds exceeding 400 million bps for short distances. When coaxial cable covers distances from 2 to 3 miles, transmission speeds of 10 million bps are common. The signal must be amplified to travel more than a mile, but each cable can transmit the equivalent of 80 sets of twisted pairs. Because the cables are insulated, fewer transmission errors are encountered.

Wireless communication channels are available that use infrared or radio frequencies to transmit data. The same radio technology used with cellular telephones

**7.18**

Data communication uses a wide variety of media (channels) to transmit data around the world.

| Communication Channels | |
| --- | --- |
| **Channel** | **Simultaneous Transmissions** |
| Telephone (twisted pair) | 1 |
| Coaxial cable | 80 |
| Microwave | 672 |
| Fiber-optic cable | 2,016 |

# Herman Hollerith

(1860-1929)

In the late 1880s, the U.S. Bureau of the Census was headed for trouble. Using methods available, Census Bureau employees took more than seven years to complete the 1880 count of 50 million. With the population burgeoning to 60 million, it was estimated the 1890 census would require more than 10 years to finish. Dr. Herman Hollerith of the Bureau searched for a better method. As he watched a train conductor punch the tickets of riders with their destination, he was reminded of Jacquard's method of using punched cards to dictate intricate weaving patterns. Inspired, he developed a series of machines that compiled the 1890 census information mechanically. The 1890 census count took only six weeks, but results were not announced until December 1890 in order to double-check the results and assure the public.

Numeric data was punched onto cards; it was represented by a hole in a designated area of the card. Combinations of two holes represented letters of the alphabet. Each card could store 24 digits or letters with 12 places for holes in each column. As the Hollerith machine processed a card, a pin would fall through each card hole into a pan of mercury. This action closed an electrical circuit and registered the count on a meter, so punched holes were translated into meaningful information. Also, using punched cards made it possible to record census data only once and retain the data for future use. This eliminated the need to duplicate work and increased the productivity of the Census Bureau employees.

Hollerith received a patent for his device in 1884. He formed his own company, TMC (Tabulator Machine Company), which produced card systems used in accounting and railroad car inventory. After several business ventures, his company CTR merged in 1924 into International Business Machines (IBM), the world's largest computer manufacturer.

**7.19**

Asynchronous data transmission sends a single character at a time, whereas synchronous transmission sends several characters at a time.

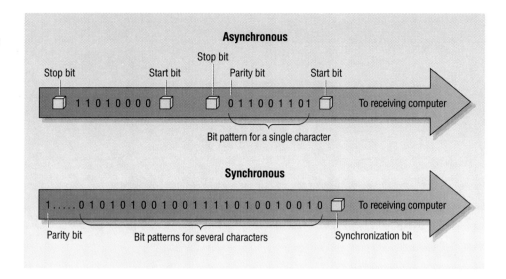

can be used to set up wireless computer networks. Fast transmission speeds supporting simultaneous data transmissions are possible using high-frequency radio waves called *microwaves.* This type of communication channel sends data signals at speeds up to 300 million bps through open space. Many long-distance telephone calls involve the use of microwave transmissions. As shown in Figure 7.18, a single microwave channel can carry more than 670 independent data transmissions. Microwave signals bounced off communication satellites can carry many voice and data signals simultaneously over great distances.

Developments in optical fibers using laser technologies provide ultrahigh-speed data transmission with speeds reaching 1 billion bps. A *fiber-optic cable,* shown in Figure 7.18, is a collection of spun-glass filaments that conduct laser beams. Although expensive, one fiber-optic channel can carry more than 2,000 simultaneous data transmissions.

### Asynchronous Versus Synchronous Transmissions

When a computer sends the data bits and parity bit down the same communication channel, both the sending and receiving hardware must be ready to accept data according to a predetermined spacing of bit patterns. Most commonly, data transmission patterns are *asynchronous.* That is, data is transmitted a single character at a time, byte by byte. A start bit and at least one stop bit are included in every byte transmitted (see Figure 7.19). This enables the receiving computer to recognize when each byte (character) has been transmitted. Asynchronous transmissions generally are used for PC communication with information services.

Providing speedier data communication are *synchronous* transmissions, which group data into blocks for transmission. A synchronous data transmission sends several characters at a time, as shown in Figure 7.19. Each block is preceded by one or more synchronization bits that serve as a timing mechanism. When the receiving computer encounters the synchronization bits, it is prepared for the arrival of a new block of data. Thus, separate bytes need not be identified by start and stop bits. Synchronous transmissions require buffers for holding blocks of incoming data. Fast, efficient

**7.20**

Data is transferred between two computers in one of two ways: Half-duplex means only one computer can send data at a time; full-duplex means both computers can communicate simultaneously.

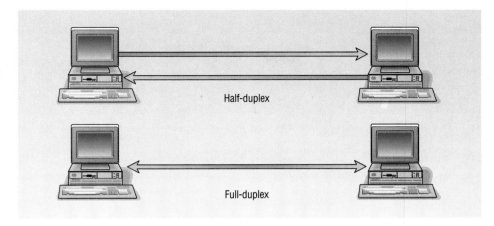

Half-duplex

Full-duplex

synchronous communication is used when data transmission speeds exceeding 20,000 bps are required.

### Data Transmission Modes

Data transmissions between computer hardware operate in one of two modes, as shown in Figure 7.20. *Half-duplex transmission* permits two-way communication over a communication channel, but data is transmitted in only one direction at a time. A CB radio, for example, provides half-duplex service. If one party is speaking, the other cannot respond until the message is completed. Half-duplex data communication often is used with peripheral hardware. The receiving hardware will respond only when it senses that all of the data has been sent. A printer, for example, will wait to receive text and other printing codes; when the line is clear, it will send back to the computer an acknowledgment that the text was received.

Simultaneous two-way communication is accommodated by *full-duplex transmission.* This mode allows computers to send and receive data concurrently. A telephone conversation is a familiar example of full-duplex transmission. Parties at both ends of the connection can speak or listen at any time during the conversation. Full-duplex communication is primarily used for interactive input.

### Multiplexing

Faster is usually better when it comes to data communication. However, high-speed communication channels are expensive. Furthermore, there is a point of diminishing returns where computer users cannot transmit data any faster even if higher-speed channels are available. One way to efficiently utilize a high-speed communication channel is to share it with other users. *Multiplexing* is the process of routing data transmissions from several sources through the same communication channel to a common destination.

To handle peak data communication demands, devices known as multiplexers were developed. A *multiplexer* receives signals from several computers, combines them, and retransmits them through a single communication channel. In effect, the multiplexer is a switching station. One approach is to have the multiplexer assign a fixed time interval (time slice) to every incoming transmission. As much data as the time slice permits is

# A Closer Look at
# Upgrading A Personal Computer

**S**ooner or later everyone needs to upgrade their personal computer. Many of these upgrades, from adding more memory to installing new expansion cards, can be accomplished at home. Popping the top off your PC may sound intimidating; however, even a novice can add a new expansion board to his or her system in a few hours. Although not for everyone (check to see if your warranty permits it) upgrading your own computer can be very straightforward and often cuts the cost in half. What follows are a few questions people often ask when interested in expanding their computer's memory and installing a CD-ROM drive.

**Q: How do I find the parts I need for upgrading my computer?**

**A:** Catalogs or stores that specialize in electronic components are a good source for parts. In many cases, they offer kits that combine compatible components into one package. For example, multimedia kits contain a sound card, speakers, CD-ROM drive, and disk controller.

**Q: Do I need special tools?**

**A:** Often the only tool you will need is a screwdriver.

**Q:** How do I know which memory chips to use?

**A:** The memory chips and microprocessor must work at the same clock speed. You can obtain this information from codes on memory chips currently in the computer or by checking the service manual. Shown here is a 4 MB SIMM (single inline memory module) board being inserted into a socket on the motherboard.

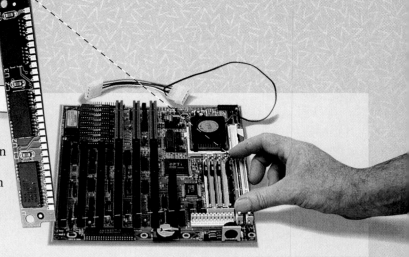

**Q:** Which expansion board goes into which expansion slot?

**A:** Expansion slots come in different lengths to accommodate different expansion bus capacities, that is, 16-bit versus 32-bit buses. The installation instructions for the expansion card indicate which expansion slots should be used. Generally, long cards go into long slots and shorts cards into short slots.

**Q:** What precautions are necessary when working with expansion cards and other hardware?

**A:** Computer maintenance and repair should take place in a clean, dust-free work area. Eliminate static electricity that could damage chips by grounding your hand, for example, on a metal pipe or the power supply. The technician in these photos is using a grounding wire attached to his wrist.

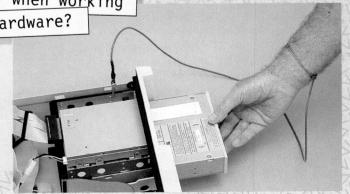

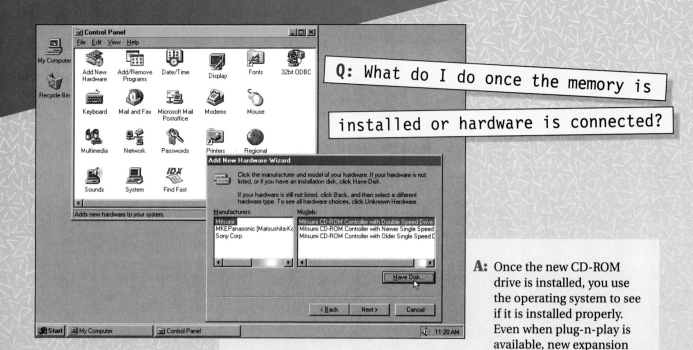

**Q:** What do I do once the memory is installed or hardware is connected?

**A:** Once the new CD-ROM drive is installed, you use the operating system to see if it is installed properly. Even when plug-n-play is available, new expansion boards often come with a disk containing an install or setup program that creates system files and copies needed utilities to the computer's hard disk. Consult the manual for specifics.

**Q:** What do I do if the computer doesn't work when I turn it on?

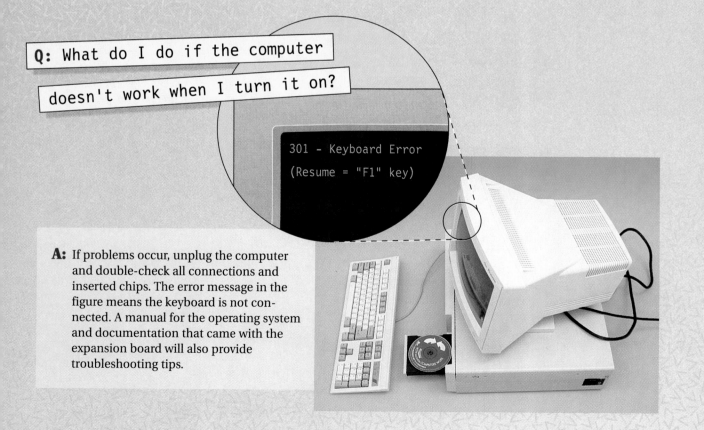

**A:** If problems occur, unplug the computer and double-check all connections and inserted chips. The error message in the figure means the keyboard is not connected. A manual for the operating system and documentation that came with the expansion board will also provide troubleshooting tips.

**7.21**

Multiplexers send data from several workstations through a single communication channel. Another multiplexer at the other end separates the signals back into their original format.

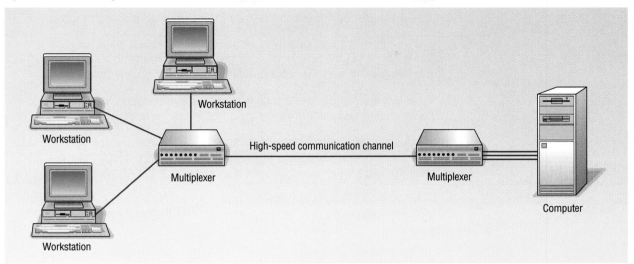

Workstation

Workstation

Workstation

Multiplexer

High-speed communication channel

Multiplexer

Computer

transmitted. By switching very quickly from one device to the next, all incoming transmissions are sent through the same communication channel (see Figure 7.21).

For example, a large office building with the computer center in the basement and many users on each floor might require a separate cable between each user and the computer. To reduce the number of cables, a multiplexer allows all users on one floor to share a single communication line. The users can operate a variety of I/O hardware simultaneously. Another multiplexer in the basement separates combined signals back into their original format. Rarely would any user notice a slowdown in their work.

### CHAPTER FACTS

- Data is captured on storage media for further processing. Tapes and disks are the most common storage media.

- Magnetic-disk storage is either on hard disks or floppy disks. Data is coded as magnetized spots by the disk drive on the disk's tracks. Tracks are divided into sectors.

- Data must be copied to other media as backup in case the original is lost.

- Disks must be protected from strong magnetic fields, extreme heat or cold, dirt, and dust. Users should never touch a disk's recording surface.

- The disk directory and file allocation table (FAT) list disk contents and starting locations of files and programs. Sector numbers or cylinders are used to locate the files and programs.

▨ Disks are either removable or fixed. Disk cartridges are small, removable hard disks used by microcomputers.

▨ Storage hardware varies by the access time needed to locate data on the hardware, and the transfer rate for input or output of that data.

▨ Data is read from an optical disk using a low-power laser; CD-ROM, CD-R, and WORM optical disks store data permanently as holes burned into the disk. Erasable optical disks are just becoming available.

▨ Tape storage media are either reels of tape, cassettes, or cartridges. As on disks, data is stored on tape tracks as magnetized spots.

▨ Mass storage through data cartridges is also available for use with large amounts of data. Redundant arrays of inexpensive fixed disks are also used for high-volume, high-speed storage.

▨ Flash memory and RAM drives store data in integrated circuits. Flash memory retains data through use of PROM chips, whereas RAM drives lose data when power is turned off.

▨ Parity checking ensures that data is correctly written and read by the storage hardware.

▨ Users can increase the storage capacity of media and decrease data transfer time by using data compression software, which replaces data redundancies with space-saving notations.

▨ The communication channels available for data communication differ in their transmission capacities. Telephone lines carry one call (transmission) at a time, with coaxial cables, microwave systems, and fiber-optic cables progressively handling more calls at the same time.

▨ Transmissions of data can be in asynchronous or synchronous patterns.

▨ Common computer-based transmission modes are half-duplex (one way at a time) and full-duplex (two ways at the same time).

▨ Multiplexers merge several signals for transmission over a single high-speed communication channel to and from a remote computer.

## TERMS TO REMEMBER

| | | |
|---|---|---|
| access time | disk controller | sector |
| block | disk track | soft-sectored diskette |
| communication channel | formatting | storage media |
| cylinder | head crash | tape cartridge |
| data compression | multiplexing | transfer rate |
| density | optical disk | write-protect notch |
| disk address | parity checking | write-protect window |
| disk cartridge | park | |

## MIX AND MATCH

*Complete the following definitions with the Terms to Remember.*

1. A hard disk designed to be inserted and removed from the disk drive is called a(n) _____.

2. A(n) _____ is a floppy disk with one alignment hole.

3. A(n) _____ consists of tape within hard plastic shell.

4. The medium by which data communication takes place is referred to as the _____.

5. _____ reduces data storage requirements by replacing data redundancies with specific notations.

6. The time it takes the read/write head to find requested data on storage media is referred to as _____.

7. A(n) _____ is a collection of tracks on a disk pack that can be read at one position of the access mechanism.

8. The speed at which data can be input to or output from the computer's memory and storage media is the _____.

9. Preparing a new disk by creating a disk directory and file allocation table is called _____.

10. _____ is the process of routing data transmissions from several sources through the same communication channel to a common destination.

11. Locking the disk drive access arm in place is known as _____.

12. A(n) _____ is a sliding tab on a 3.5-inch diskette.

13. A(n) _____ is read using a low-power laser.

14. The error detection technique that looks for either an even or odd number of 1 bits is called _____.

15. A(n) _____ is one of the concentric circles on a disk surface where data is stored.

## REVIEW QUESTIONS

1. Define the Terms to Remember.

2. Why are magnetic disks the most commonly used storage media?

3. What types of environmental hazards can damage a magnetic disk or accidentally erase data?

4. What causes a hard disk head crash?

5. What are two distinguishing features of a floppy disk? Give an example of each feature.

6. How can data on 5.25-inch floppy disks and 3.5-inch diskettes be protected from accidental erasure?

7. What happens when a disk is formatted?

8. How are the disk directory and file allocation table used to locate a file on disk?

9. How do you protect a fixed hard disk from a head crash when moving a computer system?

10. How do the three types of optical disks differ? Give an example of each type.

11. What is the current limitation of erasable optical disk storage?

12. What are the advantages and disadvantages of using magnetic tape?

13. When is magnetic-tape storage used?

14. What type of situations would call for mass storage, RAID drives, RAM drives, and flash memory?

15. What type of problems does parity checking detect?

16. Why would someone want to use data compression?

17. Name four types of communication channels and identify the transmission capacity associated with each.

18. What is the difference between a synchronous and an asynchronous data transmission?

19. How do half-duplex and full-duplex transmissions work?

20. What does a multiplexer do?

## APPLYING WHAT YOU'VE LEARNED

1. Some storage hardware buyers believe in getting the fastest and highest-capacity hardware they can afford.
   a. What are the disadvantages of this approach?
   b. What are the disadvantages of buying the least expensive hardware?
   c. Would it be better to delay purchasing equipment until the price comes down or to buy the newest equipment now?

2. Look at the storage hardware available to you in school or at home. What kind is it? Are the storage media fixed or removable? How much data (in bytes) can the media hold? Is access of the data sequential or direct? How fast can the data be accessed? You may need to check manuals for this information.

3. Look up the procedure for formatting a diskette on home or school equipment. Write a user's guide explaining the procedure to new students. Include any necessary pictures and warnings. Exchange this guide with a fellow student to see if it is clearly written.

4. Use the Extended ASCII chart (Figure 5.4) to determine the bit patterns for the characters in Abe? 5554132. List what the parity bit would be for each character if parity is odd.

5. Explore how optical disks are being presently used in education, training packages, advertising, music, or another field. Write a short report on your findings.

6. New data compression techniques are needed if movies and other video images are to be economically stored on a compact disc. Find out what compression techniques are currently being used to digitally store movies and music videos. What lies ahead? Write a short report on your findings.

# Software Tools

**C**omputer software turns a general-purpose system into a specialized problem-solving tool. Chapter 8 provides an in-depth look at word processing and desktop publishing software. Applications for these popular personal productivity tools are highlighted throughout the chapter. In addition, the features users need to create and edit documents are explained in detail. The chapter concludes with a discussion of questions to ask when purchasing a word processor.

The manipulation of numeric data through electronic spreadsheets is the focus of chapter 9. The standard procedures for entering and organizing data in a spreadsheet's row-and-column format are discussed at length. Common applications are presented throughout the chapter to illustrate the versatility of this personal productivity package. A review of good design features for worksheets concludes the chapter.

Computers can help users create spectacular drawings and graphics. They can also let a non-professional integrate textual, audio, and video data. Chapter 10 overviews graphics packages that support the development of graphs and charts using a four-step process. Free-drawing graphics software turns the computer monitor into an electronic canvas. Integration of different types of data is made possible with the features of multimedia software. The broad nature of visual and audio data is seen through the examples.

The file and database management programs discussed in chapter 11 represent some of the most powerful applications of computers. This chapter shows how data is organized and cross-referenced to provide useful information to users. The merging of multimedia techniques with data management into hypermedia applications is examined in detail.

# Word Processing and Desktop Publishing

# FROM THE USER'S POINT OF VIEW

The impact word processing can have on your writing is profound. Whether you write letters, research papers, newsletters and brochures, or even an occasional poem, word processing simplifies the process of both writing and editing. The ease with which text can be changed and spelling checked makes users better writers. Because a document does not have to be completely retyped to produce an error-free copy, you do not have to hesitate to make modifications. Once the words look right, you can add graphics and other objects by using sophisticated word processing or desktop publishing software. The final result can be a professional-looking document that effectively presents your ideas.

## WORD PROCESSING

Writing is an integral part of almost every occupation. Students, educators, business-people, and researchers write to present ideas in an organized manner (see Figure 8.1). "Putting it in writing" enhances the concreteness and legality of our work. Even the television and movie industries require many written documents, including scripts, contracts, and press kits. These documents are not seen on the movie screen, yet they are integral to the production of the show.

Every day in homes, schools, and offices, more than 2 billion pages of documents are exchanged. Creating documents has become a huge part of the operation of most organizations. Word processing software facilitates this process by making it easier for people to write. These programs also help writers to edit, store, and print their words.

**8.1**

Word processing increases everyone's personal productivity.

Hardware involved in word processing includes a computer, keyboard, monitor, and printer, as well as a scanner and mouse. Sometimes this hardware is combined into dedicated office equipment, called stand-alone word processors or intelligent typewriters, which are used exclusively to create and edit text documents. In other environments PCs run word processing software as well as programs for data processing. Operations performed by users and software while doing word processing can be organized into two major categories: editing and formatting.

Felicia Thompson is a freelance writer who is preparing a script for a popular TV mystery series. She writes her scripts using a word processing package on her home computer. Although precise operating procedures for word processing operations vary from package to package, Felicia's software contains many of the most common features.

Felicia must boot her computer with system software before she starts to work on the script. This procedure, as explained in chapter 3, prepares the computer to begin processing. Once the operating system is booted, Felicia loads word processing software from her hard disk. The word processing software helps her create, change, and save documents through the use of menus, help screens, *icon bars,* and *keyboard overlays.* Menus, icon bars, and help screens appear directly on a monitor (see Figure 8.2). Icons on the icon bar provide an alternative to selecting menu commands. Keyboard overlays are paper or plastic forms cut to fit around a keyboard, showing key combinations that are alternatives to selecting options from a menu with the mouse. The following sections review the editing and formatting operations Felicia uses to complete the document.

## Editing

Felicia primarily uses a keyboard to create the original script. Some features, described later, are easier done with a mouse or trackball. The word processing software makes *editing,* or revising, the text easier and more efficient.

## 8.2

The screen display includes menus and icon bars. The word wrap feature automatically moves *macabre* to the next line because it will not fit on the current line. A soft return is inserted after *a*. A hard return is inserted when the user presses the Enter key, as after the title.

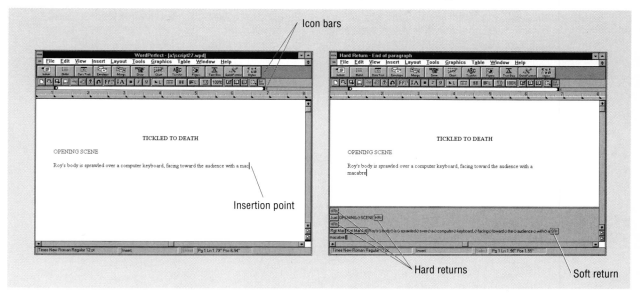

Icon bars

Insertion point

Hard returns

Soft return

**Word Wrap and Cursor Control**   With *word wrap,* Felicia can write in a continuous flow of sentences without entering a carriage return at the end of each line. The cursor is sometimes called the *insertion point* because new characters are inserted into the text at the cursor's current location. When Felicia types a word that goes past the right margin, the software enters a ***soft-return*** code, which automatically moves the cursor and word being typed to the next line (see Figure 8.2). Soft returns are carriage returns added or deleted by the word processing software to keep text within specified left and right margins.

Word processing software performs word wrap as a default operation, so Felicia can concentrate on being creative when she writes, rather than worry about the physical placement of words on the screen. The Return or Enter key on the keyboard is used primarily to create a blank line or to indicate the end of a paragraph, title, or heading with a ***hard return***, as shown in the lower portion of the screen in Figure 8.2. Hard-return characters are entered by the user and are not subject to change by the software.

Once Felicia has completed her first draft, she can scroll through the script, correcting typographical errors and making content changes as she goes. She can easily move the cursor to the next word, paragraph, or page by using the cursor-control keys. Other operations send the cursor to the beginning or end of a line, page, or document. Felicia manipulates these operations to move quickly to sections of the script she wants to edit.

**Delete and Insert**   Text can be erased within a document using the *delete* operation. Felicia has the choice of deleting a character, word, paragraph, or entire sections of the script. To delete a few characters, Felicia can place the cursor at the point where the delete is to begin, then press the Delete key for each character she wants to erase.

**8.3**

The highlighted words *from behind* were deleted from the script. Actions such as deletion can be reversed by "undoing" the previous command.

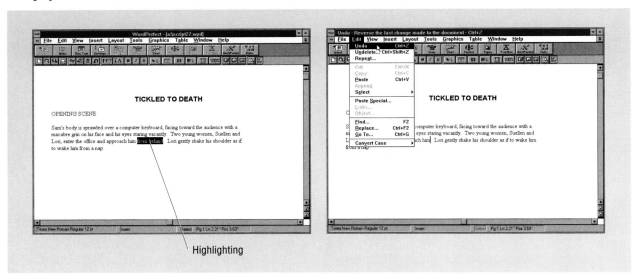

Highlighting

Alternatively, she can use the mouse to *highlight* from one character to large sections in the document and then press Delete to erase them. Highlighting changes the intensity of the text on-screen and is used to define a *block*, or section, of text (see Figure 8.3). In addition to being deleted, a block of text can be moved, copied, or printed at Felicia's discretion.

Felicia can add text anywhere in the script by using the *insert* operation. She places the cursor at the point where text is to be inserted, then types in the new text. The word processing software makes space available at this point in the text for a new character, line, paragraph, or several pages. If Felicia presses the Insert key, the insert operation is turned off. With the insert operation off, any new text entered *overwrites,* or replaces, text currently on-screen. Another press of the Insert key disables the overwrite and returns to insert mode. The Insert key is one of the features that can be *toggled* on and off—a press of the key toggles a software feature on and a second keypress toggles it off. In most word processing packages, word wrap automatically readjusts the inserted text to fit the established margins.

**Undo**   Although deleting blocks of text in a document may seem permanent, the action can be reversed. While Felicia was editing the third line of the opening scene, she deleted the phrase *from behind.* When she reread the sentence, she changed her mind and wanted to restore what she had deleted. Fortunately, Felicia's word processing package has an *Undo* command. By choosing the appropriate command from a drop-down menu, Felicia was able to reverse, or undo, the previous command that had deleted the words (see Figure 8.3). There is one limitation to undoing commands: The action must be taken directly after an error is made. Some word processing software can save and undo a series of commands, but if a serious mistake is found much later, the user may have to exit the document without saving it and reload the backup version of the document and start again.

## ...ABOUT IMPROVING YOUR COMPUTER COMMUNICATION

*Scenario 1:* "Oh, no, I'm not busy, not at all," she said lightly, motioning me into her office.

*Scenario 2:* "Oh, no, I'm not busy, not at all," she said sarcastically. I could almost see the icicles hanging from her words as she slammed her office door in my face.

Tone of voice and body language can be as important as the words we use. Computer-to-computer communication, however, is limited to what we can type. This limitation can cause misunderstandings, sometimes serious ones.

Over the past few years, an interesting solution has evolved among users of electronic mail and bulletin board systems. They employ a series of symbols to supplement the written word. These symbols are emoticons (from emote icons) or smileys, since they are based on the ubiquitous smiling-face drawing, placed sideways. Here are some examples:

| Symbol | Meaning |
|---|---|
| :) or :-) | smile; happy |
| :( or :-( | frown, sad |
| ;) or ;-) | wink; shyness; sarcasm |
| ;-0 | surprise; shock; boredom |
| :* | kiss |

Smileys also can be supplemented by abbreviations. Some of these also express emotions, whereas others are merely a form of shorthand.

| Abbreviation | Meaning |
|---|---|
| B4 | before |
| CUL8R | see you later |
| <g> | grin |
| NBD | no big deal |
| ROFL | rolling on the floor laughing |
| FWIW | for what it's worth |
| IMHO | in my humble opinion |
| BTW | by the way |
| FAQ | frequently asked questions |

These are only a sampling, and more turn up all the time. Watch for them, adopt them, and invent your own. Using them will improve your computer communication and mark you as a full-fledged e-mail or BBS aficionado.

**Copy, Cut, and Paste**   When text in a document needs to be rearranged, it is not necessary to delete the text and retype it elsewhere. Felicia can use a cut-and-paste operation to reorder paragraphs, move sentences within a paragraph, and switch words within a sentence. The text to be moved is highlighted using the mouse or various keystrokes. She "cuts" the highlighted text from the script by choosing that command from the Edit menu or by clicking on the Cut icon. Although the text disappears from the document, it is being temporarily stored in a buffer by the software. Felicia then locates the cursor where she wants the text inserted and selects an icon or menu option to "paste" what is in the buffer to the new location. This operation is referred to as *cutting and pasting* because these tasks actually had to be done manually on typewritten documents before the advent of word processors.

Another way to move text within a document relies on the mouse. Some word processing software allows users to click on highlighted text and drag it to another location within the document. This action is called *drag and drop.*

Portions of Felicia's script can be duplicated with the aid of the *Copy* command. A block highlighted within the document may be copied to another location in the same file. The block could also be copied as a separate file onto disk, and then later inserted into a different document, a procedure known as an **external copy**.

Felicia had used another word processing package to write previous scripts using her current theme and she saved each as a separate file on disk. Later she was able to **import** this previously written dialog into her current script. When importing text created by other software, the word processor usually converts the text to its own *(native)* formatting codes. A researcher could use the copy operation to import a bibliography or outline, kept as a separate file, into a report. By importing the contents of a spreadsheet sales report into a word-processed business letter, a contractor can easily produce a follow-up letter to send to a supplier. As we will see later, other objects such as graphics can also be imported.

**Find and Replace**   When Felicia uses the *Find* command of her word processor, she is able to locate a single symbol or a group of symbols anywhere in the document. As she finds out more information about the drug used in the murder, she wants to alter references to the drug's characteristics throughout a script of several hundred pages. When Felicia issues the Find command (sometimes referred to as a Search command and usually available in the Edit menu), she is prompted for the phrase to be found. After she enters the drug name, the word processor looks through the text from the beginning, stopping where that word is found. Felicia can now make any changes that she wishes. Subsequent Find commands result in locating subsequent occurrences of the word throughout the script.

The *Replace* command enables Felicia to make the same change several times within a document. When her script was almost complete, she found out that the new producer of the TV series was named Roy, the same name as her murder victim. She needed to change all occurrences of *Roy* to *Sam.* Instead of scanning the report line by line to change the name manually, Felicia uses the Replace command.

First, Felicia requests the replace operation by pressing appropriate keys or clicking on a menu option. As shown in Figure 8.4, the software guide prompts for the text to be searched, so Felicia enters *Roy.* She is then prompted for the replacement text and types in *Sam.* The computer then locates every instance of *Roy* and replaces it with the correct name. In a *global replace,* the computer automatically takes care of all word substitutions. In a *discretionary replace,* the computer finds the desired word and then waits for user confirmation before making each replacement. Felicia is careful when using the global

**8.4**

By using a Find and Replace command sequence, a user can locate and change all occurrences of a word or phrase in a document.

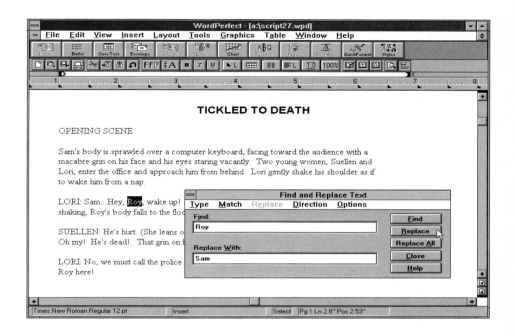

replace feature: Changing *Roy* to *Sam* throughout a text could result in *Royal Theater* being changed to *Samal Theater!*

**Go To and Bookmarks**   In a large document such as a research paper or script, writers often need to jump back and forth between certain sections. A student may need to add to the references or bibliography as the body of the text develops. Felicia finds herself constantly moving from the current page of the script she is editing to the cast of characters at the beginning of the script to production notes at the end. Users of word processing software can use the *Go To* command to quickly access areas of text without scrolling through the pages. Some of these areas, such as beginning and end of the text or specific page numbers, are preset by the software. Other user-determined points in the text, called *bookmarks,* can be set and given relevant names such as *References* or *Notes.* The Go To feature, accessible from a menu, is used to move the cursor to the desired section of text. The locations of the bookmarks can be changed as needed and are saved with the text but are not printed.

**Save and Open**   A user must assign a unique filename to a document before the computer can save it. Responding to a screen prompt for a filename, Felicia enters *Script27.* When Felicia *saves* a new document, the word processing software assigns a disk storage area to it. If a file by the same name already exists on disk, the software asks if the file should be replaced. Answering yes means the disk file will be overwritten with the text currently being edited. The long-term storage of documents is an important capability of word processing software, because stored documents can be edited and printed at a later time.

After saving Script27, Felicia can *open* this document, modify it, and save it as many times as she wishes. Each time she opens it, the word processing software copies the current version of the document back into the computer's memory for further editing. In this way Felicia's writing of the script is an ongoing process.

## Formatting

Though editing operations enable Felicia to revise the contents of her script, ***formatting*** operations allow her to manipulate the document's appearance (see Figure 8.5). With formatting operations Felicia can create a document that is single-spaced, double-spaced, or triple-spaced. Line lengths and tab spacing, as well as the number of lines per document page, are determined through formatting operations. Felicia uses another formatting operation—centering text on a line—to center the title of her script. Figure 8.6 outlines a number of other formatting operations found in word processing application packages. The following are some of the most common.

**Header and Footer**    A *header* is one or more lines of text that appear at the top of each page in a document. The header often holds a document title, date, or page number. The header is entered only once, usually through a software guide or dialog box when requested by the user. The computer instructs the printer to duplicate the header at the top of each page.

    *Footers* are similar to headers; they are lines of text repeated at the bottom of each page. Most headers and footers offer separate control of the first and last pages of a

**8.5**

A user has a lot of control over a document's final printed format.

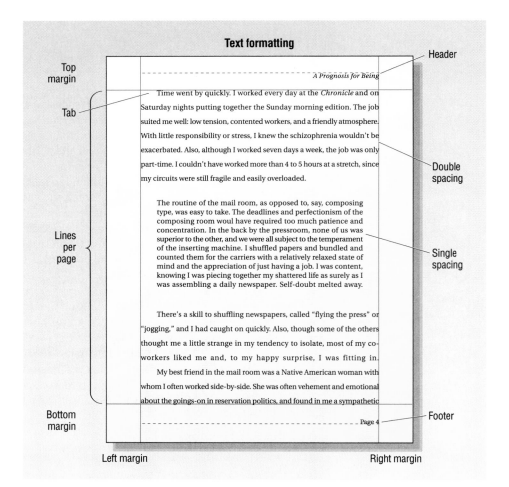

**8.6**

These formatting operations are common to most word processing packages.

## Common Formatting Operations

- Line spacing (single, double, triple)

- Left/right margins (characters per line)

- Top/bottom margins (lines per page)

- Tabulation (regular, decimal)

- Headers and footers

- Pagination

- Typeface

- Type style (bold, italic, underline)

- Character size

- Bullets and numbering

- Alignment and justification

document and the page numbering (Figure 8.5). This feature is called ***pagination***. For example, Felicia wishes to print a page number at the bottom-right corner of each page. A code is included in the footer, and the computer automatically tallies and prints the appropriate page numbers. Felicia also has the option of starting the page numbers at any value, omitting page numbers on the first page of each new scene, or eliminating them altogether.

**Text Alignment**   Users have many alignment options, as shown in Figure 8.7. When text is ***aligned***, it is flush, or even, along the margins or centered within the margins. With *full justification* there is alignment of the text at both the left and right margins. The computer justifies text by inserting ***soft spaces*** between words to bring all lines to one length. Like soft returns, soft spaces are added or deleted by the software as needed. Text with *left alignment* is flush to the left margin and no soft spaces are added, leaving a ragged right margin. *Right alignment* is just the opposite, with the text aligned along the right margin and a ragged left margin. Text centered between the two margins, like a title, is considered to have *center alignment*.

**Bullets, Numbering, and Tabulation**   Many documents contain lists of words or phrases that are presented in a column format. These could be a list of ingredients in a recipe, items in a sales order, or characters in a script. Word processing software offers two ways to arrange these lists. When a list has *bullets,* each item on the list is preceded by a symbol, usually a large dot or square, as shown in Figure 8.6. Bulleting calls attention to the items on the list without implying any sequence. An ordered list can automatically be

**8.7**

Word processing users select fonts and determine how the text is aligned.

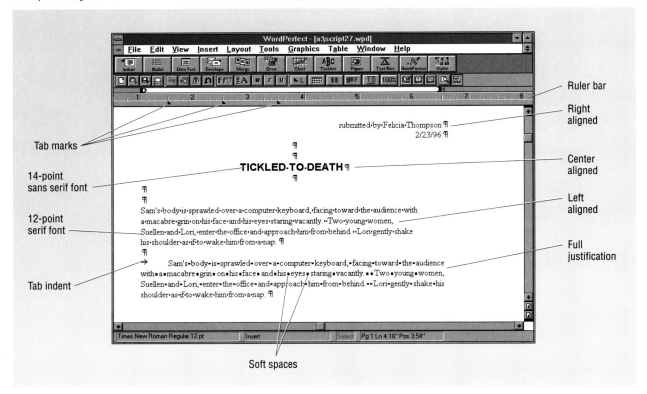

Ruler bar

Right aligned

Center aligned

Left aligned

Full justification

Tab marks

14-point sans serif font

12-point serif font

Tab indent

Soft spaces

numbered. In both cases, the list is highlighted and the appropriate menu option or icon is chosen. Some word processing packages provide the option to sort alphabetically any list the user highlights.

Anyone who has used a typewriter knows that tabs can be reset for a particular job. There are usually default tabs for the software set at common indentation points for paragraphs and columns. Left-, right-, center-, and decimal-align tabs can be set for various purposes. Word processing software allows the user to set tabs through a menu option or by moving markers on a *ruler bar* above the text (see Figure 8.7). Many software packages allow decimal tabs to be set to show where numbers of different sizes can be aligned on the decimal point. This is useful when a document contains a list of financial data.

**Orphans and Widows**    Besides controlling the number of lines on a page, many word processing packages can eliminate orphans and widows in a document. An *orphan* occurs when only the first line of a paragraph falls at the bottom of the page and the rest of the paragraph must be printed on the next page. When all but the last line of a paragraph fits on a page, the last line of the paragraph on the next page is called a *widow* (see Figure 8.8). Eliminating widows and orphans is really a matter of aesthetics. The user can choose the minimum number of lines that will be separated by pagination. For example, Felicia may choose to have at least two lines of any character's dialog at the top or bottom of a page for better continuity and thus easier reading.

**8.8**

Pagination of paragraphs can produce orphans and widows, which users can eliminate with word processing options.

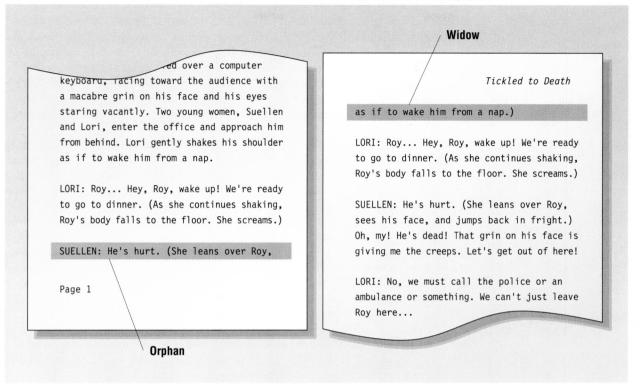

...ed over a computer keyboard, racing toward the audience with a macabre grin on his face and his eyes staring vacantly. Two young women, Suellen and Lori, enter the office and approach him from behind. Lori gently shakes his shoulder as if to wake him from a nap.

LORI: Roy... Hey, Roy, wake up! We're ready to go to dinner. (As she continues shaking, Roy's body falls to the floor. She screams.)

SUELLEN: He's hurt. (She leans over Roy,

Page 1

**Orphan**

**Widow**

*Tickled to Death*

as if to wake him from a nap.)

LORI: Roy... Hey, Roy, wake up! We're ready to go to dinner. (As she continues shaking, Roy's body falls to the floor. She screams.)

SUELLEN: He's hurt. (She leans over Roy, sees his face, and jumps back in fright.) Oh, my! He's dead! That grin on his face is giving me the creeps. Let's get out of here!

LORI: No, we must call the police or an ambulance or something. We can't just leave Roy here...

**Print Options**   The print options of a word processing package let users output selected pages of a document. Through these options the user can also control the size, style, spacing, and density of characters. For example, the software usually offers a variety of *font* options, which determine the typeface, size, and style of printed characters (see Figure 8.7). These options are explored in more detail in the section on desktop publishing later in this chapter.

Printing characters in boldface to make them darker is a common feature of word processing software. Word processors also enable the user to underline words or print them in italics. Felicia can produce these type styles in two ways. By the use of a toggle key or several keystrokes, the style option is turned on. Anything Felicia types will be in this font until she toggles the option off. She can also use the mouse to highlight text already typed and then apply the font option. The highlighted block will be changed to the chosen font. Printing options, of course, are limited to the capabilities of the output hardware.

## ■ Integrated Services

Many word processing packages have expanded their capabilities beyond the editing and formatting features just discussed. These packages are able to save commonly used formatting options or to import text created on other word processors. Other integrated services can create personalized form letters, check for spelling and grammatical errors, and provide a variety of useful features for many word processing users.

**Utilities**   With her script written, edited, and formatted, Felicia calls upon several software utilities that check the spelling, grammar, and writing style. Her word processing package allows Felicia to access these features without exiting the document being edited. As a result, these advanced editing procedures can be performed while the document is still on-screen. Word processing software frequently includes a dictionary and thesaurus. With a few keystrokes, these utilities are at Felicia's disposal. Looking up the spelling and meaning of words, or finding a suitable synonym, becomes an interactive procedure.

After proofreading her script, Felicia realizes that the word *macabre* does not sound right in the context. The *thesaurus,* shown in Figure 8.9, helps Felicia identify synonyms by displaying them in a window within the text. Felicia moves the cursor to the alternative of her choice, and the thesaurus automatically replaces the highlighted word with the selected synonym, *grotesque,* when she clicks the Replace button.

Related software is the *spelling checker,* offered with most word processing packages. Processing routines match each word in a document with words in an electronic dictionary. Any word not found in the dictionary is highlighted. The user then reviews the highlighted word, correcting errors or leaving the word as it is. Users can add unusual words and names to the dictionary to prevent the spelling checker from interpreting those words as errors. Spelling checkers may also include a word-count feature, which totals the number of words in the document or in a highlighted block of text.

Some word processors are even equipped with a **hyphenation help** utility. This software consults a dictionary to look up words that are too long to fit at the end of a line. The dictionary contains information about where a word may be broken. As an optional part of the word-wrapping operation, the computer breaks the word between syllables and inserts a hyphen.

**8.9**

This thesaurus suggests alternatives to the word *macabre*.

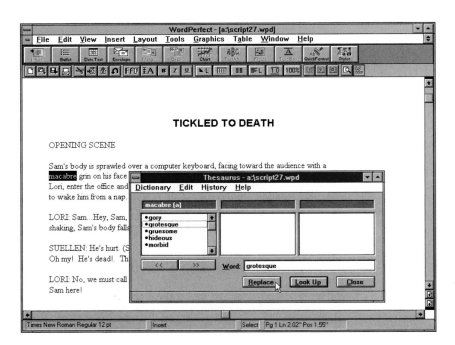

**8.10**

Writing analyzers help authors improve the quality and readability of their work.

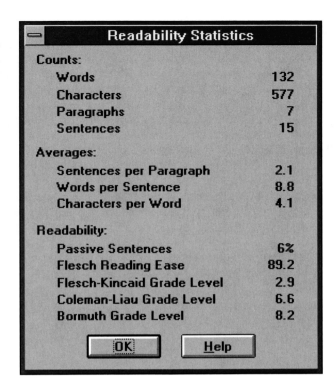

**Readability Statistics**

**Counts:**

| | |
|---|---|
| Words | 132 |
| Characters | 577 |
| Paragraphs | 7 |
| Sentences | 15 |

**Averages:**

| | |
|---|---|
| Sentences per Paragraph | 2.1 |
| Words per Sentence | 8.8 |
| Characters per Word | 4.1 |

**Readability:**

| | |
|---|---|
| Passive Sentences | 6% |
| Flesch Reading Ease | 89.2 |
| Flesch-Kincaid Grade Level | 2.9 |
| Coleman-Liau Grade Level | 6.6 |
| Bormuth Grade Level | 8.2 |

OK    Help

**Writing Analyzer**   Other support packages critique Felicia's writing style. The *writing analyzer* shown in Figure 8.10 works directly from Felicia's word processing software. When she starts this option, it computes a reading level and other statistics for Felicia's script. In other words, it indicates what grade level of education is assumed for the reader to understand the words. The writing analyzer also identifies the use of passive voice, flags long or complex sentences, highlights jargon, and provides a list of frequently used words. Both the writing analyzer and the spelling checker are developed for modern writing. Analyzing text written long ago or in a unique literary style would contain many words and phrases that today's software would interpret as incorrect.

**Style Sheets**   The ability to create documents with similar formatting options has led to the development of style sheets. *Style sheets* allow word processing users to save the formatting options they established for a particular report, letter, memo, or any text file. These options could include the following:

- ◆  Margin settings
- ◆  Tab locations
- ◆  Left or right alignment, full justification
- ◆  Line spacing
- ◆  Number of lines per page
- ◆  Headers or footers
- ◆  Fonts

When users need to create a similar document, they load the style sheet (also called a *template*), and the word processing software automatically uses the desired formatting options. For example, if the director of Felicia's script requires certain margins and indentation, she can save time by creating a style sheet that includes these specifications. This eliminates having to reset formatting options for each new script. Style sheets may also be available for printing forms, labels, or envelopes.

Many word processing packages contain software guides similar to those mentioned in chapter 6: A user can create a personal letterhead, memo form, or fax cover letter by answering the questions posed by the guide. The guide allows the user to choose among the most commonly used features to create a unique style sheet.

**Merging Files**   The use of style sheets also helps people standardize commonly prepared documents, such as a form letter. Many word processing packages support

**8.11**

A form letter can be merged with a data file containing names and addresses by using a word processor.

*file merge,* or mail merge, capabilities. The letter is combined with data files containing names and addresses of the people who will receive it. This letter consists of a *boilerplate*—standard or frequently used paragraphs and spaces or codes left for specific details. Figure 8.11 illustrates how codes can be added to a letter to merge a data file into the letter at specified locations.

**Who's Who**

## Bruce Bastian
(b. 1949)

As director of the Brigham Young University marching band and a graduate student in music, Bruce Bastian developed a highly successful computer graphics program to simulate band formations and print marching instructions. When BYU replaced Bastian, he was encouraged by Alan Ashton, a BYU professor, to pursue a master's degree in computer science, Ashton's field. Later Bastian and Ashton developed a word processor for the Data General minicomputer used by the city of Orem, Utah. By 1980 they made their program available to other users. Soon after the IBM PC came

## Alan Ashton
(b. 1943)

out in 1981, they rewrote the word processing package for it and named the software WordPerfect.

Since its public introduction in 1982, WordPerfect has become the most widely used word processing software. It is available in more than 15 languages, can import graphics and other objects, and contains symbols for science and mathematics. In the early days, Bastian or Ashton would stop work to help anyone who called into WordPerfect's telephone help service. Today, the WordPerfect help line alone involves 500 people and more than 10,000 calls per day.

**8.12**

Word processing add-ons can include access to an atlas, almanac, and quotations from within the word-processed document.

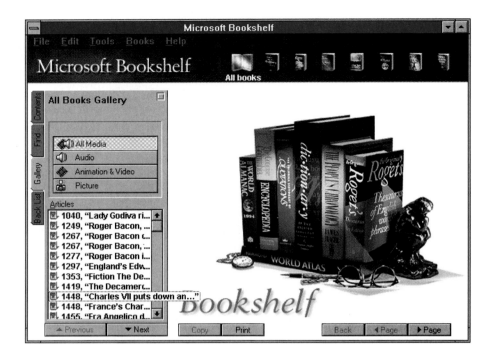

**Add-on Features**  Despite the many options offered by word processing software, it cannot manipulate a document in all ways that might be useful to a writer. For these users, there are separate software packages that can be used with a word-processed file. Software is available to easily create an outline that can later be expanded into text. For large documents, there exist packages that can analyze a document and produce an index and table of contents. With the indexing program, a list of keywords for the index are first entered by the user before the index is compiled.

Editors of documents can use a *redlining* program. Named after the red pencil marks found on a manually edited document, a redlining program allows the editor to suggest changes to the text without modifying the original document. Authors can then review both their document and the editor's changes.

Other add-on features include access to files of common quotations, atlases, and encyclopedias (see Figure 8.12). Detailed bibliographies can be formatted with specialized software. The enhancement of a word processing package with a dictionary and thesaurus in a foreign language can be a boon to a language student.

The quality of a word-processed document can be improved by using the word processing software to its fullest capacity and integrating add-on software. Desktop publishing software improves the appearance of the finished text to an even higher level.

## DESKTOP PUBLISHING

Many users of word processing packages need to go beyond the formatting features previously described. Some want to integrate graphics and other objects. Others must manipulate the text into columns, banners, and headlines like a newspaper. Still others

**8.13**

Desktop publishing software works on a personal computer with access to a scanner, mouse, high-quality screen, and laser printer.

require the quality found in professionally published material. People who want sophisticated document designs for advertisements, newsletters, brochures, and other customer-oriented documents no longer need to hire professional designers and typesetters. Now they can do this work on their personal computer with a desktop publishing package (see Figure 8.13).

The hardware components of a desktop publishing system are similar to those used in word processing, although a high-quality monitor and laser printer are a must. A scanner is also important because it can capture and save text, photographic images, and graphics on disk. A *full-page monitor* displays what would be printed on an entire page of a document. Typefaces, graphics, and formatting appear on-screen exactly as they will on the printed page. This feature is called **WYSIWYG** *(what you see is what you get)*. Laser printers, which print six or more pages a minute, can reproduce the WYSIWYG display on paper, even in color.

The dividing line between word processing and desktop publishing packages is no longer clear. Most word processors can import graphics, handle color output, and use a variety of fonts just like desktop publishers. The first desktop publishers had few editing features, so a correct and complete word-processed file was necessary before this software could be used. Current desktop publishing software has a complete editor as well as many of the features, such as a dictionary and thesaurus, found in word processing packages.

Many word processing packages now contain features to produce *camera-ready copy,* a printed document in final form. This version is printed using a high-resolution printer, often a laser printer, so it can be photographed for traditional plate printing or professionally copied. However, it is generally accepted that desktop publishing brings to the user three additional levels of control over a document's design and layout. These levels of control include: page composition, typography, and file integration.

## ■ Page Composition

The best printing technology in the world cannot make a poorly designed document look professional. On the other hand, a desktop publishing system can enhance a document put together by using basic design principles. For example, the "three easy pieces" principle employed by photographers, artists, architects, and other professional designers advocates breaking a page design into thirds. As shown in Figure 8.14, it does

**8.14**

Designers can lay out a document in thirds horizontally (landscape) or vertically (portrait) and need to balance the design elements on the page.

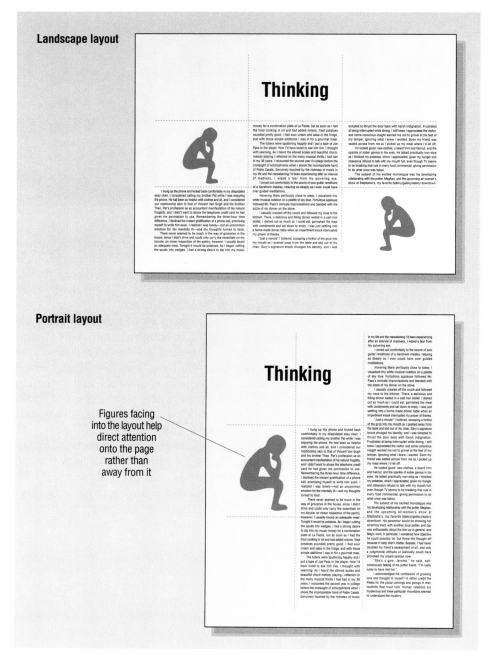

Landscape layout

Portrait layout

Figures facing into the layout help direct attention onto the page rather than away from it

not matter whether the document is sectioned off horizontally *(landscape)* or vertically *(portrait)*. By using the three easy pieces principle, designers avoid drawing the reader's eye to the middle of the page. If anything, they want to draw the eye to the top-left corner, because we read from left to right and top to bottom.

**White Space**   With the three easy pieces principle governing the basic page composition, the designer's objective is to fill the page with text, graphics, and objects without it appearing cluttered or unbalanced. Therefore, unused areas of the document, called *white space,* are very important. Good designs use a lot of white space. Usually designs with plenty of white space are more appealing than those that overpower the reader with too many design elements. Nothing intimidates readers more than turning the page and finding densely printed words to read or complex graphs to decipher.

**Adding Emphasis**   A document that catches our eye causes us to pay attention. Words such as *love, money, easy,* or *save* serve this purpose in advertisements. For added emphasis, designers change the weight of the font to **bold** or *italic*. Other options include underlining and using UPPERCASE LETTERS. Figure 8.15 uses the television show title *Tickled to Death* as a design element. Such graphic objects as boxes, bars, and icons also emphasize words and draw attention to specific areas of the document. The secret is to not overemphasize. A page filled with arrows or bold words is no longer effective. On the other hand, what separates a professional from an amateur is knowing when to use these principles and when to break the rules for additional impact.

**8.15**

Attention-grabbing words in unusual shapes catch the reader's eye.

**8.16**

General rules for effective document design.

## Design and Layout

■ Lay out document in thirds

■ Avoid centering text or images in the middle of the page

■ Balance graphs, illustrations, and text on the page

■ Position images to draw the eye into the page

■ Use plenty of white space

■ Do not overuse emphasized words in bold, italic, underlining, or all uppercase

When images and graphics are integrated into a document, they need to be balanced on the page with each other and the text. Balance includes maintaining even margins on all four sides of the page. In addition, designers place images so they draw the reader's eye into the page, not toward the margins. These basic design and layout rules, along with others, are listed in Figure 8.16.

## ■ Typography

Part of composing a page is selecting fonts for headings, captions, and other design elements in the document. For a commonly used application, such as a newsletter, a style sheet can determine which fonts and how many columns are used. In selecting a font, the designer decides on a style, size, and typeface. Text is usually printed in a roman (standard) style. As mentioned earlier, bold, italic, and underlining are used for emphasis.

Professional printers measure type size in *points*. One point equals $1/72$ inch. Figures 8.7 and 8.17 illustrate several sizes of type. Textbooks, reports, and most documents use 10- to 12-point type as a standard; 6-point type is considered fine print. Chapter headings and headlines range from 14 to 24 point.

As you would expect, type size affects the number of characters printed per inch. The smaller the type size, the more words fit on a line. Another way of increasing the number of characters on a line is through *kerning*—using the shapes of the characters themselves to fit them closer to each other (see Figure 8.17). By using tight *tracking*, more type can be fit into the same space than with loose tracking. Tracking, or letterspacing, affects not just single characters but an entire block of text. This feature may be important when the text must conform to an unusual shape.

*Proportional spacing* is a way of naturally fitting letters together. Letters and symbols are given different spacing depending on their widths, rather than equal space for each character as on a typewriter. For example, the letters *M* and *W* require more space than the letters *i* and *l*. When each letter in a font is given equal space, it is known as a *monospace font*.

**8.17**

Typography concerns the size, style, and spacing of characters in a document.

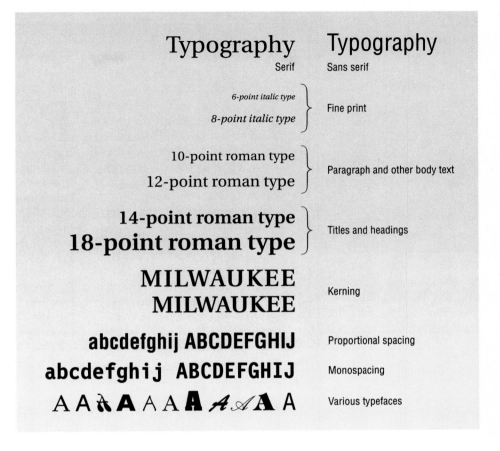

Professional printers were the first to use the terms *serif* and *sans serif* to describe typefaces. *Typeface* describes the design of the characters in a font. A typeface with *serifs* has short line segments or extensions projecting from upper or lower ends of the strokes of a character, for example, the leg of an uppercase *T* or *R*. As shown in Figure 8.17, *sans serif* (without serif) type does not include these short lines.

It is generally acknowledged that serif type is easier to read, that serifs draw the reader's eye across the printed line. These typefaces are also more traditional. Reports and books written in the United States often use serif type for standard text, reserving sans serif type for titles, headings, and captions. Europeans are more liberal in their application of sans serif typefaces, using them in a wider range of situations.

For special situations, such as the beginning of a book chapter, the first character of the text may be printed in a different font. An enlarged first letter, called a *drop cap*, is top-aligned with the first line of text and embedded in the first paragraph (see Figure 8.18).

The variety of fonts and other design features of a desktop publishing package need to be translated for accurate reproduction through a laser printer or even a traditional typesetting system. The **page definition language (PDL)** of a desktop publishing package codes document files for this purpose. Fortunately, this encoding is transparent to the user. Each output device used with a desktop publisher contains an embedded computer with instructions for understanding the PDL. PostScript is a popular PDL.

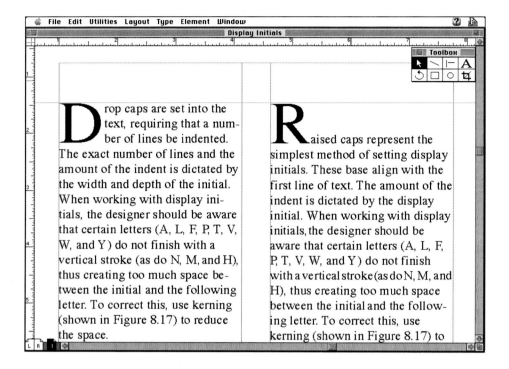

## File Integration

Pictures, graphs, illustrations, and photographs add interest and clarify written descriptions. This is one reason why desktop publishing software imports a wide variety of file formats, including those images captured by a scanner. These file formats generally fall into three categories: text, graphics, and objects. Because the popular word processing packages save text in different formats, a desktop publisher must be flexible enough to accept them all.

Distinguishing between images and graphics presents another reason. They are created or reproduced by different types of software packages and are stored in different file formats. An image is a photograph that has been scanned or captured with a digital camera. Basically, anything you can create with pencil on paper is a graphic. A graphic may be purchased or produced by the user with drawing software. The demand for ready-to-go art is so high that designers can purchase *clip art.* Figure 8.19 illustrates just a few of the thousands of graphics that are available in a clip-art set. Clip art is available on paper, which may be scanned, or on disk, which can be directly imported. Many word processing and desktop publishing packages include clip-art libraries.

If a camera or scanner is needed to capture an object, it is considered an image. Desktop publishing packages can accept scanned photographs, but the quality of reproduction depends on the scanner and printer. The grays found in the black-and-white photographs in newspapers are produced in *halftones.* The image is made up of various sizes and placement of black dots on a white background, which tricks the eye into seeing varying shades of gray. It requires a very high quality laser printer to produce halftone images of photographic quality. Multicolored images can be accurately reproduced after they are scanned by using *color separation,* available on some desktop publishing systems. As shown in Figure 8.20, each page is printed in four colors (yellow,

**8.19**

Clip art is packaged and sold to designers as ready-to-use graphics.

**8.20**

In color separation, a master copy of each color is produced to print four-color images.

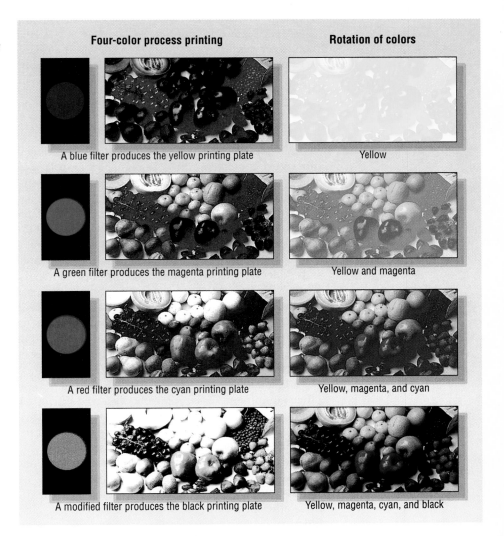

magenta, cyan, and black). When printed on top of one another, they produce the full-color images you see in this book.

Desktop publishing can never be a substitute for clear, concise, and imaginative writing. It can make a well-written document look better, but does little to hide incomplete sentences, misspellings, and overused words. In the final analysis, the words used when composing a document still come from you. Selection of the type size and style is your choice. Human hands and minds determine the final placement of graphs and pictures in the document.

## AUTOMATING THE OFFICE

Everyone has a place where he or she writes letters, pays bills, and keeps personal records. The work varies, but several activities are common: reading correspondence and reports, filing important data, and organizing ideas and data into words, graphics, and images. These places of work—our offices—are changing as computer hardware replaces such tools as typewriters and mimeograph machines. Desktop TSR (terminate stay resident) software reduces the need for address books, calculators, and calendars. Instead of on paper, letters, reports, and memos are created online and stored on disks.

### ▇ Electronic Offices

In businesses, computers have increased office efficiency when they are connected with other office equipment. This development, known as *office automation*, replaces manual office procedures and encompasses the following elements: word processing, desktop publishing, electronic mail, electronic filing, voice mail, and access to networks.

In automated offices, transactions are completed with increasing speed. As a result, automated office techniques have stimulated the very business demands they are helping to meet. By using word processing and desktop publishing in the automated office, attractive and correct documents are output at high speeds. The result is a rise in productivity. Accuracy and attractiveness are necessary for all formal documents, particularly in business. A letter, for example, represents the sender. In addition to conveying information, the letter forms an image. The appearance of the letter makes a statement about the sender just as clothes reveal a person's tastes and preferences. To promote a positive image, correspondence should be appealing to the eye, as well as accurate and easy to read. When an office sends out advertising or sales literature, the design is especially important.

In an automated office, personal computers are linked through a LAN to other office equipment. Geographically dispersed offices use telephones to interconnect equipment in a WAN. In a small office, the equipment is usually directly linked by cable. For example, a word processor might be connected to a nearby intelligent copier to reproduce a text document. A secretary using a word processor would issue a command to make 100 copies of a report. Without further intervention from the secretary, the word processor would retrieve the report from disk and send it to the copier. The copier would translate the commands, making the requested copies in collated order. This method is more efficient than producing 100 copies on a regular printer. The copier is a faster, quieter, and less expensive means of reproduction than the letter-quality printers normally attached to word processors. Furthermore, the file could be reproduced on copiers around the country as easily as in the same office.

Because it is possible for different users in a network to be working on different word processors and desktop publishers, several ways to produce compatible document files have been developed. By using *portable document software,* users can produce documents that can be read and printed by anyone, regardless of the original fonts and formatting. This software will not allow editing of the file, but can be most useful for producing online help files or files for use on the Internet. For files going onto the Internet's World Wide Web (see chapter 4), a specific marking language is used: *HTML (Hypertext Markup Language)* uses tags to describe a document's contents and how it relates to other documents. Other applications of hypertext are discussed in chapter 10.

Networks of personal computers in automated offices often use electronic mail (e-mail) to replace or enhance the traditional interoffice mail system. As mentioned in chapter 4, e-mail can be sent to one person, several people, or everyone connected to the network. Similarly, voice mail reduces paper output and can be sent to any combination of users.

*Electronic filing* methods replace the tedious and error-prone task of maintaining paper records in metal file cabinets. The computer keeps an index of the names of documents and the dates they are stored. To access a file, the user need only enter a name. The computer consults the index, then locates and retrieves the desired document. Automatic filing directed by the computer prevents carelessness and misfiling in handling documents.

Automated offices may evolve into *paperless offices.* In such an office, word processors, desktop publishing software, e-mail, voice mail, and electronic filing systems are combined. Documents exist only within the computer system; fewer paper copies are stored. Documents held on a network server can be accessed by users at any time. Further, files can be shared by users more readily. The original version of a document remains in storage, so that several users may request a copy at the same time. Documents are printed only when they need to be sent to someone outside the office. In the paperless office, paper is not altogether eliminated, but it is significantly decreased.

## Advertising

One of the fringe benefits of automating an office is that it promotes the exchange of ideas and information. An advertising agency serves as a good example of how increased communication supports creative thinking. Making people aware of the goods or services to be sold is crucial to an effective advertising campaign. In this age of multimedia television and four-color print, a great deal of effort goes into making a new (or old) product appear desirable to potential customers. An idea started as an e-mail memo could evolve through a barrage of follow-up memos into a new advertising campaign. The personnel in an automated office could then coordinate writing and publishing the proposal, scheduling meetings, printing contracts, and even creating the sales literature using computer technology and the groupware discussed in chapter 4.

Attractive sales literature can be personalized in another automated office by an informed salesperson. By using word processing software to merge data from customer data files, a salesperson can produce attractive personalized brochures for prospective customers. An attached individualized letter would also include the customer's name and address along with a reference to past purchases and specific information about an upcoming sale.

# 8.21

Electronic publishing supports the online development of each newspaper page.

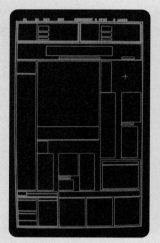

## ■ Journalism

Over the past 20 years, automated offices have dramatically changed journalism. The image of a reporter sweeping the last page out of the typewriter while shouting for the copyboy to pick up the work is no longer accurate. Now journalists use PCs linked through a network to the desk editor. With the press of a few keys, stories are transferred to the editor for online review and revision.

Increasingly smaller portable computers are even letting reporters take computers into the field. With a battery-operated portable computer, a reporter can write and store a story at the scene or while attending a sporting event. A nearby telephone links the portable to the newspaper's main computer for data transfer.

The factorylike atmosphere that once prevailed in the typesetting department before a newspaper went to press is also changing. Small foundries with molten lead used for setting type have become obsolete. Now newspapers employ sophisticated *electronic publishing* systems that run high-speed printing presses and control page composition, typography, and file integration just like desktop publishing software. The masthead, stories, headlines, and photos can be positioned on-screen as shown in Figure 8.21.

When each element of the page is in place, the computer produces a film on the page, which is used to make copies of the paper. As a result, news stories composed on a computer and stored on disk need not be retyped by a typesetter. The electronic

**8.22**

This reporter can enter up-to-the-minute sports news into a computer and send it via telephone to an electronic publishing system.

publishing system just incorporates the files with graphics and images to produce the final plates used by the printing presses. Electronic publishing also facilitates sending files over networks for producing overseas, regional, and local editions of national newspapers.

Most newspapers have communication links to large news-gathering services such as the Associated Press (AP). As these news services constantly update their databases, local newspapers receive instant notification on computers dedicated to receiving wire copy. Late-breaking news reports can be shared immediately with all subscribers to the news service. Similarly, syndicated columns and features are sent like electronic mail over communication lines.

The need for electronic offices is not confined to print journalism. Broadcasters also convey the news with the help of word processors. Although anchorpersons appear to stare directly into your living room as you watch the news, they are actually reading a script displayed on a TelePrompTer placed right over the lens of the camera. The script is prepared by word processing software and displayed via the TelePrompTer.

## Electronic Classrooms

As word processing, networks of PCs, and other features of the automated office gradually become part of education, an electronic classroom has evolved. Computers are found in grade schools, high schools, and colleges as computer literacy becomes a graduation requirement. Though computer use on campus encompasses many computer applications, one of the most widespread for schools is word processing.

A teacher can generate bulletins, written assignments, tests, and syllabi with a word processor. The documents can be stored and revised easily. Generating a make-up test, for example, is accomplished quickly with the aid of utilities and editing techniques. The teacher decides to retain or replace questions, then makes the changes quickly on-screen. The test can then be sent through a network to a student at home or in the hospital.

Students, of course, use word processing to complete written assignments. Using a manual typewriter, a student might retype several drafts of a report before the document is completed. With the help of a computer and word processing software, however, the student can move from first to final draft with little duplication of effort. Personal computers and word processing software are a boon to creative writers, especially those with poor typing skills.

Desktop publishing is also being used in schools to produce newsletters, posters, student newspapers, and yearbooks. Some high schools even have printing classes, where students use desktop publishing to learn the printing business.

Many elementary schools use *banner programs* to help produce displays and awards. These programs contain their own clip art with many designs useful in printing birthday banners, award certificates, or designs for a bulletin board. The designs in a banner program can be personalized and edited similarly to a word processing document.

Some college campuses have even incorporated electronic mail systems for students and faculty. The e-mail system helps the faculty distribute assignments and allows students to submit homework electronically. It even allows students and faculty to participate in questions and answers through the exchange of e-mail during "electronic" office hours.

# A Closer Look at Selecting a Word Processing Package

**As a prospective buyer** of a word processor, it would be wise to learn as much as possible about the vast selection of packages on the market. The first step in the selection process is identifying your needs and the nature of the applications that will meet those needs. Some users might need a word processor to create one-page business letters or brief reports. Others may wish to create technical documents that are several pages long and include graphics and equations.

Software preferences depend largely on individual tastes. Methods for creating, formatting, editing, and printing a document may differ slightly or substantially from package to package. Hands-on testing of several packages enables users to evaluate features. In the final analysis, the price of a package should be balanced against its overall performance to determine the real value of the software. Here are some questions you should consider when purchasing a word processing package.

**Q:** Do you have any special formatting or printing requirements?

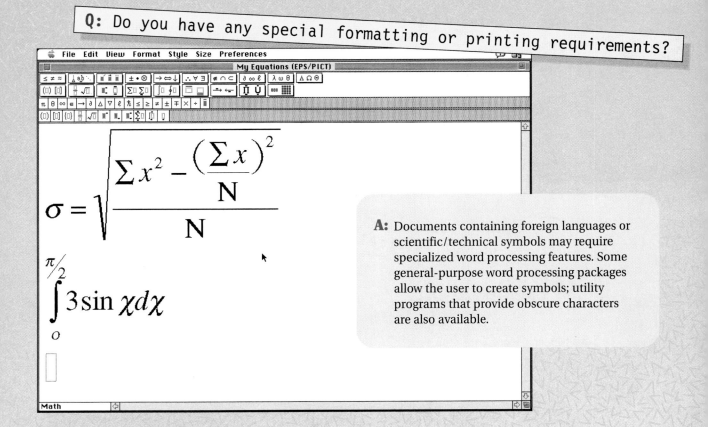

**A:** Documents containing foreign languages or scientific/technical symbols may require specialized word processing features. Some general-purpose word processing packages allow the user to create symbols; utility programs that provide obscure characters are also available.

**A:** Personal preference comes into play when evaluating spelling checkers, thesauruses, style sheet software guides, grammar checkers, or file-merging capabilities.

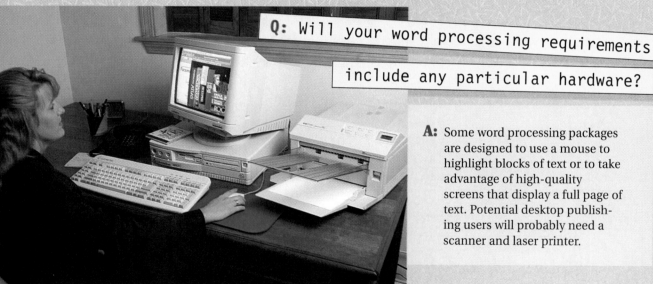

**A:** Some word processing packages are designed to use a mouse to highlight blocks of text or to take advantage of high-quality screens that display a full page of text. Potential desktop publishing users will probably need a scanner and laser printer.

**A:** Support materials such as tutorials are geared toward new users, whereas manuals, help screens, icons, and prompts serve everyone.

**Q:** Is the software compatible with the hardware available to you at work, school, or through friends?

**A:** People interested in sharing electronic documents with others need to know what the common file formats and formatting codes are. Professional users may want to obtain portable document software.

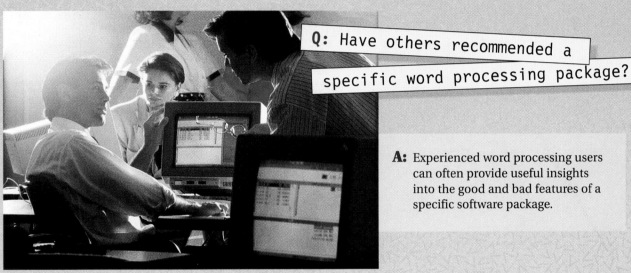

**Q:** Have others recommended a specific word processing package?

**A:** Experienced word processing users can often provide useful insights into the good and bad features of a specific software package.

**Q:** What do the software reviews in the computer magazines have to say about the packages you like?

**A:** Software reviews performed by computer magazines list features, give retail prices, and often provide information on several comparable packages.

## Summary of Features — Word Processors for Windows

■ = YES ☐ = NO
N/A = Not applicable:
The product does not have this feature

Products listed in alphabetical order

| | Ami Pro | Microsoft Word for Windows | WordPerfect for Windows |
|---|---|---|---|
| **TEXT-FORMATTING FEATURES** | | | |
| Broken underline | ■ | ■ | ■ |
| Double underline | ■ | ■ | ■ |
| Strikethrough | ■ | ■ | ■ |
| Small capitals | ■ | ■ | ■ |
| Variable page length within document | ■ | ■ | ■ |
| Automatic renumbering of pages after formatting | ■ | ■ | ■ |
| Vertical centering | ■ | ■ | ■ |
| Conditional page breaks | ■ | ■ | ■ |
| Paragraph linking | ■ | ■ | ■ |
| Sorting | ■ | ■ | ■ |
| Line numbering | ■ | ■ | ■ |
| Portrait and landscape pages within single document | ■ | ■ | ■ |
| **TEXT ENTRY AND EDITING FEATURES** | | | |
| User can adjust margins on ruler | ■ | ■ | ■ |
| User can adjust columns on ruler | ■ | ■ | ■ |
| Paragraph marker display option | ■ | ■ | ■ |
| Format code display option | ☐ | ☐ | ■ |
| Maximum number of undelete levels | 4 | 1 | 3 |
| Widow and orphan control | ■ | ■ | ■ |
| Zoom feature | ■ | ■ | ■ |
| User-adjustable zoom levels | 10-400% | 25-200% | Unlimited |
| Appends block to file on-disk | ☐ | ■ | ■ |
| Search-and-replace: | | | |
| Searches forward and backward | ■ | ■ | ■ |
| Searches within other files | ■ | ☐ | ■ |
| Performs case-sensitive searches | ■ | ■ | ☐ |

| | Ami Pro | Microsoft Word for Windows | WordPerfect for Windows |
|---|---|---|---|
| **FILE-HANDLING FEATURES** | | | |
| Maximum number of documents open simultaneously | 9 | 9 | 9 |
| Performs backup at user selected time intervals | ■ | ■ | ■ |
| Includes file management functions | ■ | ■ | ■ |
| Searches disk for filenames | ☐ | ■ | ■ |
| Searches disk for text within files | ■ | ■ | ■ |
| File import/export format: | | | |
| Ami Pro | ■/■ | ☐/☐ | ■/■ |
| Microsoft Word | ■/■ | ■/■ | ■/■ |
| Microsoft Word for Windows | ■/■ | ■/■ | ■/■ |
| MultiMate | ■/■ | ■/■ | ■/■ |
| WordPerfect | ■/■ | ■/■ | ■/■ |
| WordStar | ■/■ | ■/■ | ■/■ |
| **HYPHENATION AND GRAMMAR FEATURES** | | | |
| Hyphenation | ■ | ■ | ■ |
| Customizable hyphenation dictionary | ☐ | ■ | ■ |
| User can enter soft hyphens from keyboard | ■ | ■ | ■ |
| Hyphenation on a paragraph level | ■ | ■ | ■ |
| Limits number of consecutive hyphens at end of columns | ■ | ■ | ☐ |
| Spell-checker: | | | |
| Number of words in standard dictionary | 130,000 | 130,000 | 115,000 |
| Spell-checks defined block | ■ | ■ | ■ |
| Spell-checks document with one command | ■ | ■ | ■ |

## CHAPTER FACTS

- Word processing is the writing, editing, formatting, storing, and printing of documents.

- Editing is the creation, storage, and revision of text.

- Specific editing features include word wrap, cursor control, insertion, deletion, cut, copy, paste, undo, find, and replace.

- Formatting is the manipulation of a document's appearance.

- Specific formatting features include line space and length, margins, tabulation, headers and footers, bullets, numbering, orphan and widow control, pagination, print font, type styles, and alignment.

- Word processing packages can be integrated with other utilities to increase user productivity. These include a spelling checker, thesaurus, style sheet, writing analyzer, hyphenation help, and file merging.

- Software add-ons to word processing include outlining, redlining, index and table of contents production, and access to additional reference sources.

- Desktop publishing software controls page composition, typography, and the integration of files created by other application software. The result is camera-ready output.

- Hardware components of a desktop publishing system include personal computer, scanner, mouse, full-page monitor, laser printer, and software.

- To avoid centering the reader's eye in the middle of the page, subdivide a page into thirds when laying out text and graphics.

- Good designs use plenty of white space.

- Serif typefaces are most often used with blocks of text, whereas sans serif typefaces are used for headings and titles.

- Office automation, including word processing, desktop publishing, electronic mail, voice mail, network usage, and electronic filing, has increased office productivity.

- Electronic filing involves storing and retrieving documents on disk. When used with word processors and other online data processing systems, e-mail can replace an organization's internal mail service.

- Personalized advertising literature is created by merging data files of customer information with a word-processed form letter.

- Journalists work in automated offices for writing stories, accessing online news services, and electronically publishing books, newspapers, newsletters, and articles. TelePrompTers and word processing aid in television broadcasting.

- Teachers prepare tests, syllabi, and assignments in electronic classrooms, where students also write and edit assignments.

- Word processing software should be evaluated on how well it fits the user's needs, the features it contains, its aids to new users, and its integration with other software.

## TERMS TO REMEMBER

| | | |
|---|---|---|
| alignment | formatting | pagination |
| block | hard return | portrait |
| clip art | hyphenation help | soft return |
| editing | import | soft space |
| electronic filing | landscape | style sheet |
| electronic publishing | office automation | word wrap |
| external copy | page definition language | WYSIWYG |
| font | (PDL) | |

## MIX AND MATCH

*Complete the following definitions with the Terms to Remember.*

1. The _____ provides codes for output of text on a laser printer.

2. Printing technology that runs high-speed printing presses and controls page composition, typography, and file integration is known as _____.

3. _____ is the word processing feature that includes counting pages and printing page numbers.

4. The _____ comprises the style, weight, and size of a printed character.

5. The carriage return entered into the text when the user presses the Return or Enter key is known as a(n) _____.

6. _____ refers to graphics and images on paper or disk that are purchased for use by designers.

7. Many word processing programs can _____ graphics, images, or text created by other software into a single document.

8. Controlling the final appearance of a document is referred to as _____.

9. _____ orientation is the horizontal layout of a page.

10. The spaces added between words to fully justify text between the left and right margins are known as _____.

11. Selected text within a document that can be independently moved, copied, or deleted is referred to as a(n) _____.

12. When a document is entered without hard returns, the word processor senses the margins and moves words to the next line as needed; this is known as _____.

13. _____ is the feature of a word processing or desktop publishing package that shows on the monitor exactly how a document will look when printed.

## REVIEW QUESTIONS

1. Define the Terms to Remember.

2. How do the following editing operations work?

    | | | |
    |---|---|---|
    | insert | cut and paste | replace |
    | delete | copy | save |
    | undo | find | open |

3. What are eleven formatting operations common to most word processing software?

4. How is a left-aligned document different from one with full, center, or right alignment?

5. Identify and describe six services that can be integrated with word processing.

6. What formatting operations are controlled by style sheets?

7. How is a boilerplate used?

8. What are some examples of add-on features available for word processing?

9. When compared to word processing software, what additional levels of control are available with desktop publishing?

10. Explain six features of good document design and layout.

11. What sizes of type are associated with fine print, standard text, and headlines or titles?

12. Identify situations in which serif and sans serif type are used.

13. Briefly describe the three basic file types that desktop publishing software imports from other software packages.

14. Describe six operations of an automated office.

15. When is a paper copy necessary in a paperless office?

16. Explain how a business can use word processing software to create personalized advertising.

17. Describe six ways the electronic office has changed journalism.

18. How do teachers and students use an electronic classroom?

19. What seven steps should be a part of the evaluation process when purchasing a new word processing package?

## APPLYING WHAT YOU'VE LEARNED

1. All computer systems are made up of these five components: people, procedures, data, programs, and hardware. For each of the following systems, name or describe what makes up each component:
   a. desktop-publishing a brochure
   b. sending an e-mail message
   c. editing a report in a paperless office
   d. filing a letter using electronic filing
   e. writing a term paper on a word processor

2. Keep track of mail to your household for a week. What type of correspondence has been done (or could have been done) with a word processor? Do you think the use of a word processor enhances or detracts from the quality and "personalized" nature of the correspondence?

3. Make a list of the features you would require in a word processor, assuming that money is not a limiting factor. Include any character types, related software, and printing options. Also list the user aids (help screens, prompts, and the like), integrated services, and add-on features you would like to have now and in the future.

4. The text mentions the use of automated offices in journalism, education, business, law, and government. List the ways information technology might be useful in these occupations:
   a. manager for a professional sports team
   b. regional manager for a charitable organization such as the Red Cross or United Way
   c. director for a state lottery
   d. museum curator

5. Writers can use spelling checkers, writing analyzers, and a thesaurus to aid in creative or technical writing. Other available related software includes gender checkers (for nonsexist writing) and grammar checkers. Do you feel that such software helps to increase the writing skills of, or acts as a crutch for, writers lacking fundamental writing skills? Is using a word processor unfair to those who do not have one?

6. Investigate a desktop publishing package that could be useful to you in school, in an organization, or in a job situation. Use information from sales literature, retail store salespeople, or magazines to determine the following:
   a. What type of user interface does it use?
   b. What editing options does it offer?
   c. On what kinds of computers does it work?
   d. What kinds of printers does it support?
   e. Does it handle color graphics?
   f. Can it be used with other software packages?
   g. What input hardware is needed?
   h. What training manuals or tutorials are included?
   i. What are the memory and disk space requirements?
   j. How much does the package cost?

7. Designing an interesting page layout and desktop-publishing a document takes time. Identify three types of documents that should be—and three that should not be—desktop published.

# Electronic Spreadsheets

**I**f you work at
organizing and manipulating numbers,
you will want to know about electronic
spreadsheets. It does not matter if you are
handling the accounts of a large
multinational corporation, the grades for a
composition class, or the operating
expenses for your club. Electronic
spreadsheet packages help you total a
column of numbers in the blink of an eye.
Averages and other statistics are easily
performed on whole tables of numbers.
This personal productivity software will
get the job done faster and with
fewer errors and headaches.

## PRESENTING AND PROCESSING NUMBERS

Numbers are used to make decisions and evaluate performance. The results of many activities are expressed as numbers. The profit from the sale of a house is expressed numerically as money. Performance in school often is measured as a grade point average, which involves numbers to indicate academic success. Film and restaurant critics often convey their opinion by placing it on a scale of 1 to 4. Numbers are an inescapable part of modern living (Figure 9.1).

### Manual Worksheets

Controlling activities involving numbers often requires planning and processing. These activities can be performed on a worksheet like the one in Figure 9.2. A *worksheet* organizes related numbers and labels into rows and columns. This easy-to-read format allows users to compare numbers for different activities and for different periods of time. With this information you could analyze present conditions and use the analysis to influence future plans.

**9.1**

Computers input, process, output, and store the current price of stocks and commodities for traders worldwide.

For decades business managers created worksheets to evaluate performance and predict trends. Although used primarily in financial applications, this method of organizing data has expanded to encompass such areas as scoring sporting events, keeping class gradebooks, doing statistical analysis, and tracking cultural trends. In each case, people have used worksheets to support decision making with data.

Basically, worksheets are tables that organize data for easy comparison. Comprising horizontal rows and vertical columns, worksheets resemble a grid. In financial applications, rows typically are used to distinguish items to be evaluated, whereas columns represent different periods of time. A worksheet for figuring monthly income and expenses, for example, might include thirteen columns—one for each month of the year and an additional column for year-end totals.

Each unit, or *cell*, on the grid is the intersection of a column and a row. Cells contain items of data or instructions for processing the data. On manual worksheets the content of each cell is usually written in pencil. To change a cell value, the pencil marks are erased. This method produces somewhat sloppy worksheets, but it spares people from having to create an entirely new worksheet when data changes.

Another drawback to using manual worksheets is the time it takes to change data values. Quite often, changing one value requires recalculation of several other worksheet values. Recalculating totals and averages are examples. This task becomes frustrating and tiresome when using worksheets designed for "what if" speculations. What-if questions allow people to determine the probable results from a given set of conditions. For example, how would the budget in Figure 9.2 change if insurance rates went up starting in March?

Usually, several worksheets are required to assess all the alternatives in what-if situations. A store manager might wish to determine quarterly profits given a 5, 6, or 7 percent increase in sales. Three manual worksheets would be created, requiring three different sets of calculations. Producing complete what-if analyses can require a good deal of time and energy.

**9.2**

Manually prepared worksheets like this one have been around for hundreds of years. This work is now performed by electronic spreadsheets that help computer users quickly and accurately manipulate worksheet numbers.

## Electronic Spreadsheets

The late 1970s brought a breakthrough in worksheet analysis with the introduction of VisiCalc electronic spreadsheet software, which teamed worksheets with computers. (VisiCalc's inventors, Daniel Bricklin and Robert Frankston, are highlighted in Who's Who in this chapter.) An electronic spreadsheet program displays a worksheet on the computer's screen. Cells are filled with text, numbers, and formulas entered through the keyboard. Moving or copying data is accomplished with a few keystrokes or mouse clicks. With electronic spreadsheet software, people can edit a worksheet without making messy erasures.

One of the most valuable features of the electronic spreadsheet is its ability to perform calculations. Cells can contain arithmetic symbols that instruct the computer to add, subtract, multiply, or divide values from other cells. Upon entry of a single instruction, the computer performs these calculations with speed and accuracy. People can ask any number of what-if questions by changing numbers or formulas, and the spreadsheet then quickly recalculates new answers. Thus, armed with a computer and electronic spreadsheet software, people interested in forecasting no longer need to spend long hours with a calculator to develop a complete what-if analysis.

The primary value of electronic spreadsheets lies in the ease of making and processing changes. People can create large worksheets—a thousand rows by several hundred columns—with greater accuracy and in less time than with manual methods.

As a result, people can test data under many circumstances to build a broader base of information from which to make decisions.

## SPREADSHEET FUNDAMENTALS

Electronic spreadsheets are useful for all types of personal and business applications. Figure 9.3 shows a worksheet created by Tony LaFriend, the administrative assistant at City Bus Service. His supervisor and manager of the bus company helped him plan the worksheet organization.

**9.3**

The City Bus Service budget worksheet is designed to store financial data for an entire year and to identify accounts that are under or over budget.

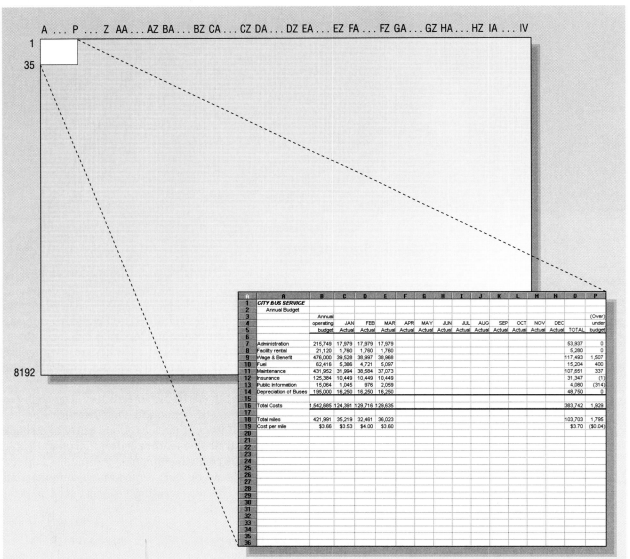

| | A | B | C | D | E | F | G | H | I | J | K | L | M | N | O | P |
|---|---|---|---|---|---|---|---|---|---|---|---|---|---|---|---|---|
| 1 | CITY BUS SERVICE | | | | | | | | | | | | | | | |
| 2 | Annual Budget | | | | | | | | | | | | | | | |
| 3 | | Annual | | | | | | | | | | | | | | (Over) |
| 4 | | operating | JAN | FEB | MAR | APR | MAY | JUN | JUL | AUG | SEP | OCT | NOV | DEC | | under |
| 5 | | budget | Actual | Actual | Actual | Actual | Actual | Actual | Actual | Actual | Actual | Actual | Actual | Actual | TOTAL | budget |
| 6 | | | | | | | | | | | | | | | | |
| 7 | Administration | 215,749 | 17,979 | 17,979 | 17,979 | | | | | | | | | | 53,937 | 0 |
| 8 | Facility rental | 21,120 | 1,760 | 1,760 | 1,760 | | | | | | | | | | 5,280 | 0 |
| 9 | Wage & Benefit | 476,000 | 39,528 | 38,997 | 38,968 | | | | | | | | | | 117,493 | 1,507 |
| 10 | Fuel | 62,416 | 5,386 | 4,721 | 5,097 | | | | | | | | | | 15,204 | 400 |
| 11 | Maintenance | 431,952 | 31,994 | 38,584 | 37,073 | | | | | | | | | | 107,651 | 337 |
| 12 | Insurance | 125,384 | 10,449 | 10,449 | 10,449 | | | | | | | | | | 31,347 | (1) |
| 13 | Public Information | 15,064 | 1,045 | 976 | 2,059 | | | | | | | | | | 4,080 | (314) |
| 14 | Depreciation of Buses | 195,000 | 16,250 | 16,250 | 16,250 | | | | | | | | | | 48,750 | 0 |
| 15 | | | | | | | | | | | | | | | | |
| 16 | Total Costs | 1,542,685 | 124,391 | 129,716 | 129,635 | | | | | | | | | | 383,742 | 1,929 |
| 17 | | | | | | | | | | | | | | | | |
| 18 | Total miles | 421,991 | 35,219 | 32,461 | 36,023 | | | | | | | | | | 103,703 | 1,795 |
| 19 | Cost per mile | $3.66 | $3.53 | $4.00 | $3.60 | | | | | | | | | | $3.70 | ($0.04) |
| 20 | | | | | | | | | | | | | | | | |
| 21 | | | | | | | | | | | | | | | | |
| 22 | | | | | | | | | | | | | | | | |
| 23 | | | | | | | | | | | | | | | | |
| 24 | | | | | | | | | | | | | | | | |
| 25 | | | | | | | | | | | | | | | | |
| 26 | | | | | | | | | | | | | | | | |
| 27 | | | | | | | | | | | | | | | | |
| 28 | | | | | | | | | | | | | | | | |
| 29 | | | | | | | | | | | | | | | | |
| 30 | | | | | | | | | | | | | | | | |
| 31 | | | | | | | | | | | | | | | | |
| 32 | | | | | | | | | | | | | | | | |
| 33 | | | | | | | | | | | | | | | | |
| 34 | | | | | | | | | | | | | | | | |
| 35 | | | | | | | | | | | | | | | | |
| 36 | | | | | | | | | | | | | | | | |

As shown in Figure 9.3, Tony included rows for eight expense items, along with two rows for tracking total miles driven and cost per mile. The first column contains identifying labels or text for each row; an additional row holds total costs. Tony's complete worksheet includes columns for actual monthly expenses as well as columns for the annual operating budget and actual yearly totals. The final column on the right contains the difference between actual and budgeted totals for the year.

Tony followed a number of steps to create this worksheet. First, he identified the purpose of the worksheet. In this case, he wanted to keep track of all expenses to help City Bus Service stay within a budget. By maintaining a worksheet, he could pinpoint areas in which the company was overspending.

Tony entered numbers and formulas into appropriate worksheet cells. Each cell is identified by its **cell address**, which is the associated column letter and row number. He instructed the computer to calculate the cost per mile shown in Figure 9.4 by entering

**9.4**

Electronic spreadsheets use the command menu or icon bar to initiate program operations, the status line to indicate display formats along with the current operating mode, and the data entry line for input.

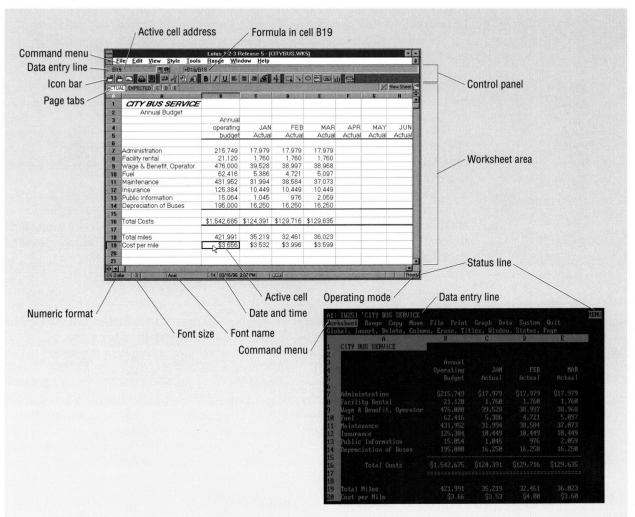

a formula in cell B19. Other computations help Tony see that City Bus Company was under budget in wages, fuel, maintenance, and public information. Also, insurance costs were only $1 over budget. These figures would help his boss decide if the company could afford to start additional bus routes.

The electronic spreadsheet software Tony uses creates row-and-column worksheets and relies on a popular user interface. As shown in Figure 9.4, the screen display is divided into three areas: the control panel, the worksheet area, and the status line.

## Control Panel

The *control panel* helps users with data entry, editing, formatting, and processing activities. Typically, a spreadsheet's control panel usually comprises three lines: the command menu, the icon bar, and the data entry line, as shown in Figure 9.4. The *command menu* is the row of spreadsheet menus and their associated commands. Selections included on the command menu enable the user to create and format worksheets, load them with data, and then process and print reports. Spreadsheets that employ a graphical user interface (GUI) use drop-down menus and an *icon bar,* also shown in Figure 9.4. Common menu options are represented by different icons on the bar.

Some spreadsheet packages enter data directly onto the worksheet as the user types on the keyboard. In other packages, numbers, labels, and formulas are displayed in the control panel's *data entry line* at the same time they are entered into the active cell. Users select the *active cell* by moving the screen pointer to a specific cell and clicking the mouse button. Cursor-control keys are also used to highlight the active cell. A dark or beaded box, called the *cell selector,* surrounds the active cell.

Pressing the Enter key or clicking on the Enter icon sets the data in the active cell. During data entry, the user can click on the Cancel icon or press the Esc (Escape) key to cancel the operation. Either action closes the data entry line and clears any data already entered. Pressing Esc also closes menu options and dialog boxes.

The data entry line is also used to edit data already on the worksheet. Data in the active cell is usually displayed in the data entry line. Pressing the F2 function key or clicking the mouse when the pointer is over the active cell copies the cell's contents to the data entry line. Users can then erase the current cell contents by using the Delete or Backspace key, or they can type in new data.

## Worksheet Area

A standard screen display usually holds about 20 rows of a worksheet, but worksheets with more rows may, of course, be built. The character style and size selected by the user determine the number of rows displayed on-screen. Scrolling the worksheet up and down enables the user to view different sections of it when a large number of rows are involved.

Similarly, the screen may not accommodate viewing all columns in a worksheet. Usually, fewer than 10 columns may be displayed at one time, depending on the column width and screen size. Cursor control can instruct the computer to scroll the display from side to side to permit viewing of different column sections. For example, since Tony wanted to include actual expenses for each month, the entire worksheet will not fit on-screen. To view different sections, he would use the cursor-control keys or mouse to scroll to the left and right.

Sometimes the user needs to freeze a row or column of labels on-screen. For example, Tony locks columns A and B in the budget worksheet to keep the row labels (Administration, Facility Rental, etc.) and budget amounts on-screen when he scrolls to the right. This feature is called ***title locking***. It allows the user to display nonadjacent, or noncontiguous, columns and rows on-screen as shown in Figure 9.9.

When a worksheet fills hundreds of columns and rows, it becomes difficult to manage. Many spreadsheet packages offer ***three-dimensional worksheets*** as an alternative to organizing data in a single worksheet. Think of a three-dimensional worksheet as an address book with multiple pages, each with its own tab (Figure 9.4). Each page contains a complete worksheet. The user organizes related data on different pages instead of in different locations on the same worksheet. Tony enters the operating budget approved by the board of directors on page A and changes the page tab to ACTUAL. He copies this information to page B for use in what-if budget scenarios and labels the page tab EXPECTED (Figure 9.4). With this multidimensional worksheet file, he can easily switch between the two pages to compare actual with expected costs.

## Status Line

The ***status line*** sometimes displays the active cell's default font and other formats, the current date and time, as well as the spreadsheet's active operating state, or *mode*. Other spreadsheet packages display messages to the user on the status line. These messages could warn users about error conditions or display helpful prompts. Every status line indicates the spreadsheet's current operating mode. Common modes of operation include the following:

- Ready mode: when the spreadsheet is waiting for a command
- Enter mode: for data entry of numbers (values) or text (labels)
- Menu mode: when a menu is open
- Edit mode: active when changes to data are in progress
- Wait mode: period of time when spreadsheet is not responding to mouse or keyboard input
- Error mode: when the spreadsheet software encounters a processing problem

Other operating modes are discussed in the user's manual. Status lines often are located on the first or last line of the spreadsheet display.

## Labels

In building his worksheet, Tony inputs three types of data in the cells: labels, values, and formulas. Initially, the labels were on rows and columns to help Tony know where to put numeric values and formulas. In many spreadsheet packages, any data that starts with a letter is considered a ***label***. Labels are not used in calculations. If a user wanted a label containing just numbers, a specific ***label prefix*** character would have to precede the numeric data; these prefix characters also determine the label's alignment within the cell:

| | |
|---|---|
| " | align left |
| ' | align right |
| ^ | center |

**9.5**

A spreadsheet allows the user a great deal of control over the look of the worksheet's labels and values.

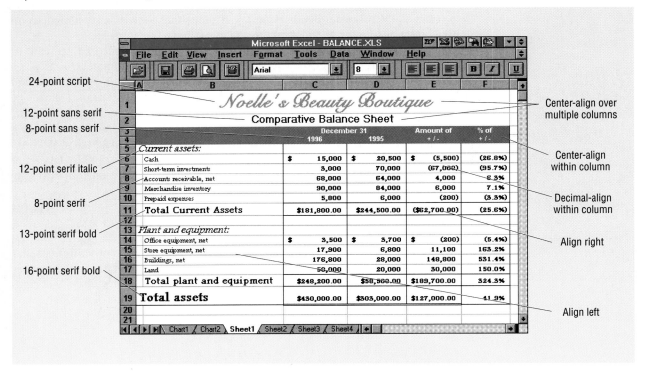

Menu options and icons are also available to align labels (see Figure 9.5) within the active cell.

### Values

Numeric data, or *values,* can be entered into any cell. As with numeric data, only minus signs and decimal points can be included with the numbers. Other symbols, such as dollar signs and commas, are controlled by the formatting feature explained later.

Dates and time are also treated as values. Each spreadsheet has assigned some date in the past the number 1 and sequentially numbers each day since then. January 1, 1900, is often day 1. In this case, 35124 is February 29, 1996 (a leap day), 35125 is March 1, 1996, and so on. The worksheet displays March 1, 1996, or 3/1/96, but internally the date is stored as 35125. As you can see, this technique allows the spreadsheet to easily account for leap years. Furthermore, it simplifies the situation in which the spreadsheet must determine a date for 30 days past some due date. Libraries and many businesses use dates in this way for their accounting and inventory control systems.

### Formulas

When Tony wanted to find the total cost of the 1996 budget, he entered a formula into cell B16. Typically, formulas allow the user to add, subtract, multiply, or divide any values found in the spreadsheet. Symbols that commonly are used to signify these arithmetic

# Daniel Bricklin

(b. 1951)

# Robert Frankston

(b. 19??)

Daniel Bricklin was in the Electrical Engineering/Computer Science Department at MIT when he met Robert Frankston in 1973. Together they worked on an early word processing program called WPS-8. While attending Harvard Graduate School of Business, Bricklin and Frankston were looking for a way to do accounting procedures on a computer. After a long search, they decided to arrange a grid of cells into rows and columns. Cells at the intersection of each row and column took on the column letter and row number as a reference. Their product, written in Frankston's attic, called VisiCalc, was not a popular program at first. The two joined with publisher Dan Fylstra of Personal Software to form Visicorp. The group was unsuccessful in trying to sell VisiCalc to large microcomputer manufacturers such as Apple and Altair. After placing an advertisement in the May 1979 issue of *BYTE* magazine, however, the software gained prominence. Although legal issues led to the splitup of Visicorp, the ideas VisiCalc represented became a standard for later spreadsheets like Lotus 1-2-3 or Excel. Bricklin later worked for a time at Lotus Corporation.

**9.6**

A range of cells is identified by the cell address of the first and last cell. Cell ranges can be moved, copied, added together, or averaged.

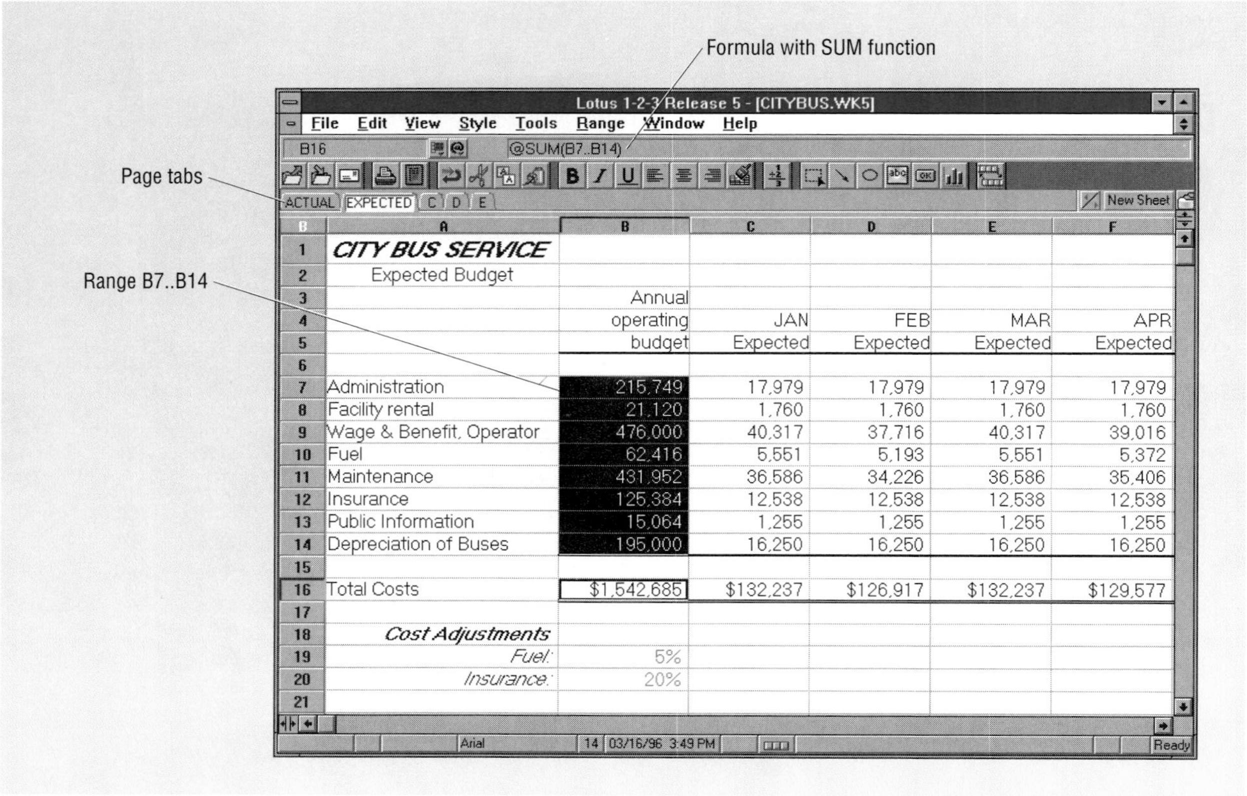

Formula with SUM function

Page tabs

Range B7..B14

operations include the plus sign (+) indicating addition, the minus sign (–) indicating subtraction, the asterisk (*) indicating multiplication, and the forward slash (/) indicating division. Formulas start with either an equal sign (=) or an arithmetic operator. One way to display the total annual operating budget would be to enter this formula into cell B16:

```
= B7 + B8 + B9 + B10 + B11 + B12 + B13 + B14
```

Once the formula is entered into the cell, the spreadsheet displays the result on the worksheet. Although the worksheet displays the numeric value $1,542,685, the content of the cell is still a formula. If Tony changes the value in B7, the displayed value in B16 is automatically recalculated because it is based on a formula that uses B7.

## Functions

Another symbol used by most spreadsheets is @. Depending on the particular software package, the @ symbol or equal sign (=) identifies a built-in *function* that performs a common operation such as summing or averaging a column of numbers. In Figure 9.6, Tony totals the expenses in column B by using this function:

```
@SUM(B7..B14)
```

**9.7**

Electronic spreadsheets have a variety of built-in formulas called functions that are available to users.

## Common Spreadsheet Functions

| Function | Description |
|----------|-------------|
| ABS | Absolute value |
| AVG | Average of a set of numbers |
| COS | Cosine of number |
| COUNT | Count the number of cells in range |
| EXP | Exponent of number |
| FV | Future value of loan |
| INT | Integer component of number |
| IRR | Internal rate of return |
| LOG | Base 10 log of number |
| MAX | Maximum value in a range of numbers |
| MIN | Minimum value in a range of numbers |
| RAND | Random number generator |
| NPV | Net present value |
| PMT | Monthly mortgage payment |
| PV | Present value |
| SIN | Sine of number |
| SQR | Square root of number |
| STD | Standard deviation in a range of numbers |
| TAN | Tangent of number |
| VAR | Variance within a range of numbers |

The SUM function is just one of many provided by the spreadsheet software. Most spreadsheets are equipped with functions that perform common statistical computations such as averages (AVG) or a count of the number of entries within a range of cells (COUNT). These packages also include advanced mathematical or statistical calculations such as finding trigonometric values, square roots, and standard deviations (see Figure 9.7). Other spreadsheet functions are used to identify maximum and minimum values or to generate random numbers. These functions fall into several categories: financial, engineering, mathematical, statistical, database, search, calendar, text-based, and logical.

### Cell Ranges

The SUM function used by Tony contains a common notation that identifies a *range* of cells in column B (B7..B14). A range, or *block,* of cells is defined by the first and last cells in the group. In this case, the range is defined by the first cell in the column to be used (Administration costs in cell B7) and the last cell in the group (Depreciation of Buses in cell B14). This range is highlighted in Figure 9.6. Depending on the spreadsheet package, one period, two periods, or a colon separates the cell addresses.

Using a range in a formula keeps it from becoming long and complicated. A range of cells in a worksheet can even be given its own unique *range name*. For example, Total-Costs for the range B7..B14 and Jan-Costs for the range C7..C14 would be acceptable range names. Range names help users identify common blocks of data and minimize mistakes created by leaving out cells when copying or moving data ranges.

## COMMON SPREADSHEET COMMANDS

The software Tony is using has many options available to help him build a worksheet. With these commands, he designs a worksheet format, puts values into the cells, makes changes, and prints the results.

### ■ Format

Most spreadsheet programs have default worksheet settings consisting of display formats for labels, values, column widths, and so on. The spreadsheet will use this standard format unless the user requests a change. Typically, the user selects options from a *Format* menu or related icons in the control panel to change these default values. For example, in Figure 9.3 Tony prepared his worksheet for a 12-month period, using 16 columns: one for row labels, one for each of the 12 months, two for totals, and one for the amount over/under budget. The size of each cell differs with the type of data it contains. Tony increased the default width for cells that contain labels. Because the default column width allows only nine characters, Tony increased the width in the first column. This lets him use longer labels such as *Administration* and *Depreciation of Buses.*

A new generation of spreadsheets now incorporates many of the text formatting features found in word processing and desktop publishing. The user can control the type size and style along with accenting important data with bold, italic, or underlining. In Tony's case, all of the worksheet columns contain numbers except the first, which contains labels. The numbers throughout this worksheet reflect money. Tony uses the spreadsheet's *global format* feature to override the default format to display all numbers rounded to the nearest dollar, that is, no decimal places. Global in this case means the format is changed for all worksheet cells. He also selectively changes how values are displayed in the Total cost row (row 16). By using the *range format* feature, he changes the display for row 16 to the currency format. As shown in Figure 9.6, this display format precedes each number with a dollar sign ($). A partial list of the display formats for labels and values is shown in Figure 9.5.

Many spreadsheet packages even offer an ***autoformatting*** feature to help users create professional-looking worksheets. You should consider your audience and application before choosing one of the predesigned formats. Some designs work best on paper; others lend themselves to overhead transparencies. Figure 9.8 shows some of the suggested autoformats for Tony's budget worksheet.

### ■ Cut and Copy

Flexibility is a key feature of spreadsheets. For this reason most spreadsheets provide commands that transfer data. The *Cut* and *Paste* commands, as the names indicate, allow the user to change the location of data or a formula to another spreadsheet cell. The Cut command temporarily removes selected cells from the worksheet. The user then

## 9.8

The autoformatting features let users select preset worksheet styles.

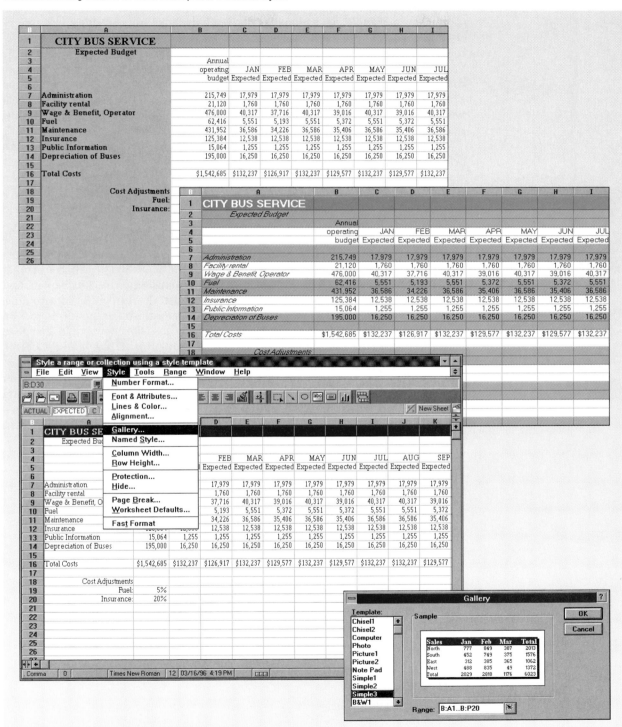

identifies where the data is to be moved by changing the active cell. The Paste command inserts the cut data into the active cell. When a range of data is pasted, the top-left cell in the range is placed in the active cell.

The Copy and Paste commands duplicate the contents of a single cell, row, or column at another position in the worksheet. Each of these operations spares the user the trouble—and the risk of error—involved in reentering data and formulas. Both the Cut and Copy commands can work with ranges of cells. For example, Tony wants to make a copy of the entire annual budget and rework it to reflect the expected budget. This range of cells, with all data, labels, and formulas, is then copied to the next worksheet page. The copy is now available for him to modify, and the original annual budget remains unchanged.

Copying a cell or range of cells creates a problem, however. When a formula with cell references is copied, should cell addresses stay the same or reflect the change in worksheet location? The solution has been to create two types of cell references. An *absolute cell reference* does not change when moved to a new cell address. But when a *relative cell reference* is used, the cell address changes to maintain the relationship represented in the original formula.

To clarify the distinction between absolute and relative cell references, take a close look at the City Bus Service worksheet in Figure 9.6. To compute the bus company's expected January costs, Tony entered the formula @SUM(C7..C14) into cell C16. In other words, all of the cells in column C associated with Administration, Facility Rentals, and so on, are added together and put into the row for Total Costs (row 16). To save time, Tony copies this formula to the other Total Costs cells for the other months in row 16. He uses the relative cell reference @SUM(C7..C14) because the copy should change to reflect the column in which it is located. Therefore, the copy in cell D16 is @SUM(D7..D14), which displays the Total Costs for February.

Absolute cell references are used when the same cell needs to be used no matter where a formula is copied. In Tony's software package, absolute cell addresses are indicated with a dollar sign ($). The formulas for expected costs all use the budgeted amount for annual operations in column B. To figure expected Administration costs, the annual budget in B7 is divided by 12. The formula +$B$7/12 is entered into cell C7 to reflect Administration costs for January. Tony saves time by copying this formula to the remaining cells for February to December. However, he does not want the reference to cell B7 to change, so he uses a dollar sign to identify the cell row ($B) and column ($7) as absolute. The formula Tony enters into cell C7 and copies to the range D7..N7 includes the absolute cell address $B$7.

### ▧ Insert, Delete, and Undo

As the uses for a worksheet expand, row-and-column requirements are likely to change. Like in word processing, Insert and Delete commands enable the user to modify a worksheet without reentering the entire file. The *Insert* command allows the user to place a blank row or column at any point in the worksheet. The *Delete* command removes rows or columns from an existing worksheet. For example, as Tony modifies the expected budget worksheet he recently copied from the annual budget, he may want to delete the last columns (Total and Over/Under Budget), which are no longer applicable (Figure 9.9).

Electronic spreadsheets also offer users an *Undo* command. This feature allows users to recall data that was erased when deleting a cell, row, column, or range. To

**9.9**

Users easily delete selected rows or columns by pressing the Delete key or selecting Delete from a menu. Nonadjacent columns are displayed on-screen using the spreadsheet's title-locking feature.

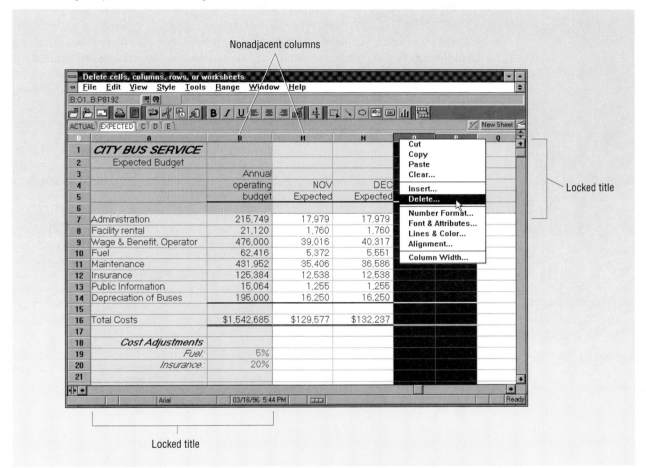

Nonadjacent columns

Locked title

Locked title

support this feature, the electronic spreadsheet temporarily stores deleted data in memory. The user can recall this data by selecting the appropriate menu option. This data is permanently lost, however, when other data is deleted and takes its place in temporary memory.

## ■ Find, Replace, and Go To

When large worksheets need to be modified, users can locate specific labels, values, or cell references with the *Find* command. The *Replace* command is used when data values or formula entries need to be changed. This feature offers *global* and *discretionary replaces*. Users are asked to confirm each replacement when a discretionary replace is activated. Global replaces automatically change values without further user involvement.

The *Go To* command lets the user jump to any cell on the worksheet. Once Go To is selected from a menu or activated using a function key, the user enters the desired cell address. If necessary, the spreadsheet changes the worksheet display and moves the cell selector to the indicated cell.

## Save and Open

Worksheets are stored on disk as part of an electronic spreadsheet's *Save* command. This feature is sometimes referred to as filing a worksheet. Stored spreadsheet files can be recalled at a later date for further use. This procedure—bringing a saved file to the screen for revision and processing—is accomplished with the *Open* command. A saved worksheet can be opened, changed, and saved under the original filename.

Sometimes a modified worksheet is saved under a new filename using the *Save As* command. Users then retain both the original and the changed versions of the worksheet file. This is one method for creating several what-if scenarios. A worksheet that is similar in format to an existing worksheet is modified to examine a specific what-if condition and saved under a new name. The new version can then be modified in different ways, leaving the original intact for comparisons.

Electronic spreadsheet users often become so involved with their work that they forget to save their worksheets. Forgetting to periodically save their work to disk leaves them vulnerable to losing their data if the system crashes or a power failure occurs. As a result, many spreadsheet packages offer a ***timed backup*** feature. This feature automatically saves the active worksheet to disk at specified time intervals. The user can turn this feature on and off and adjust the amount of time that elapses between saves.

## Print

Printouts can be useful in examining expansive worksheets that extend beyond the screen's limits. Instead of scrolling the worksheet from section to section, the City Bus Service manager can have a printed version of the entire worksheet to take home for late-night work.

A *hard copy* of the worksheet can be obtained by initiating the *Print* command. Tony LaFriend has two printing orientations to select from: *portrait* (vertical) and *landscape* (horizontal). He can request a printout of a spreadsheet file that has been saved to disk, or he can print the spreadsheet currently in main memory.

Users have the option of adding headers, footers, and repeating titles to a worksheet as it is printed. The report title, current date, page number, or worksheet filename could be added to a header or footer to help organize multiple-page reports. A ***print title*** is a row or column from the worksheet that needs to be printed on every page. Tony creates a print title by using columns A and B. The labels (*Administration, Facility rental,* etc.) in column A, budget allocations, and header (1996 Budget Year/page number) are then printed on each page of the budget, as shown in Figure 9.10. Horizontal and vertical gridlines can also be turned off if desired.

## Protect

To prevent accidental erasure of data, many spreadsheet packages include a *Protect* command. Data from protected worksheet cells can be accessed but not overwritten. A user-developer might protect specific labels and numeric constants, while leaving other cells unprotected. Fellow workers and friends can then use the worksheet, but are limited to entering data into the unprotected cells.

**9.10**

In this preview of the printed worksheet, the print titles (column A labels and column B budget allocations) and header (1996 Budget Year and page number) print on every page.

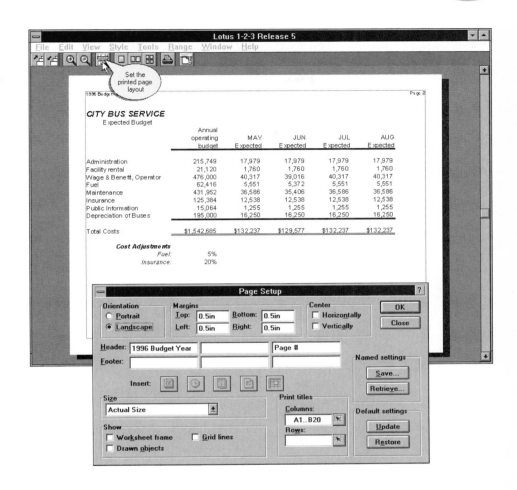

Users can also ***password-protect*** a worksheet file. When anyone tries to retrieve a password-protected file, the spreadsheet asks for the unique password. If the user cannot provide the password, the spreadsheet denies access to the worksheet file.

## Macros

The operations described previously can be combined to create extremely complex worksheets. Furthermore, in developing large spreadsheets, users often need to repeat the same combination of operations. As a result, many electronic spreadsheets allow users to create ***macros*** that recall a series of related operations by using a menu or through a few simple keystrokes. Macros are like small programs that users build into their worksheets. When the user presses the designated keys or selects the macro's name from a menu, the electronic spreadsheet activates *(runs)* the macro, executing the associated operations. Macros are not unique to spreadsheets; word processing users can also automate operations using macros.

Macros can be used for a wide variety of purposes. For example, users can create macros that add and average numbers in any given set of cells or print selected parts of the worksheet. Price lists from wholesale vendors are often distributed to retail stores as a worksheet. Rather than sending a new worksheet when prices change, some vendors

**9.11**

Data organized as a worksheet are universally recognizable and easily export to database and graphics software.

## Reasons for Organizing Data into a Worksheet

■ A worksheet's row-and-column layout is a widely recognized data format

■ Worksheet data easily converts to a database file structure

■ Worksheet values easily convert to graphs and charts

send customers a macro that automatically updates old prices in the original worksheet. To change this worksheet by hand would require a dozen or more operations. However, once installed as a macro, a few keystrokes or a menu selection calls these operations into action.

## ■ Exporting Data

Within an automated office, data organized into worksheets becomes a tremendous source of information, as outlined in Figure 9.11. Teamed with word processing, databases, graphics programs, and networks, spreadsheets give and receive a boost in processing power. With word processing, for example, Tony does not have to reenter the budget data, because he can easily insert part of the budget worksheet into the Quarterly Budget report.

Organizing data in a worksheet is often accomplished without having to manually enter the data. Users can instruct the computer to import or export data with a database program. When importing data into specified worksheet locations, the computer reads the database file, finds the selected data fields, and duplicates them into worksheet cells.

*Exporting* is the opposite of importing. It describes a situation in which worksheet data is shared with other application packages. Exporting worksheet data to a database program, for example, requires adding a row of field names in row 1. These names identify the data in the associated column (the use of field names in discussed in more detail in chapter 11). Sharing data in this way increases personal productivity and data integrity, because someone is spared the time-consuming task of reentering data, and new data entry errors are not introduced.

With connections to a network, worksheets can be built with data from remote files and databases. Additionally, completed worksheets can be transmitted over communication lines among users at multiple locations. For example, local branch offices of a bank would prepare their budgets on a PC-based spreadsheet program and send them electronically to the main office. The budget director would check them with a compatible mainframe-based spreadsheet and transmit the budget worksheets back to the branches with suggestions. One advantage is that all branch budgets are in the same format and can easily be compared to one another. When transmitted through electronic mail, budgets prepared in the morning can be in the director's hands before lunch.

Completed worksheets also can be used to generate graphics. Many spreadsheet programs provide software guides that help users present worksheet data graphically (see Figure 9.12). The worksheet data can also be exported to an independent graphics program. In either case, the user selects the option desired, then specifies which cells are to be reflected in the graphic. For example, the analysis of voters by age group shown in Figure 9.12 was produce by a multiscreen software guide. As pictured, the voters were broken into groups by age:

◆ 512 of the voters are between the ages of 18 and 30, inclusive

◆ 828 of the voters are between the ages of 31 and 45, inclusive

◆ 721 of the voters are between the ages of 46 and 60, inclusive

◆ 1,297 of the voters are over the age of 60

As Figure 9.12 illustrates, these numbers were translated into percentages and presented in graphic form. Each slice of the pie chart is in proportion to the percentage it represents. The graphics generated may even be more accurate than hand-produced charts.

**9.12**

Presentation graphics, such as this pie chart, add visual interest to worksheet data and often make data that is difficult to interpret more accessible.

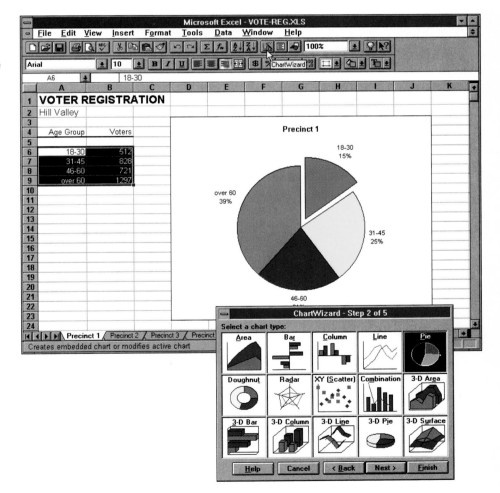

## Exit

To exit a spreadsheet program after a processing session, the *Exit* command is used. Exiting is sometimes referred to as quitting or closing an application. This spreadsheet operation removes all temporary files from disk and usually returns computer control back to the operating system. In integrated software, however, the Exit command may produce a Startup menu, listing all available programs in the package. From there the user may begin another processing task or return to the operating system.

## SPREADSHEETS AS A TOOL

Many uses exist for spreadsheets besides business applications. Any situation in which groups of numbers must be organized and analyzed would be a good candidate for a spreadsheet. A variety of electronic spreadsheet packages are available, most of which use either a shell or a graphical user interface. Figure 9.13 overviews software features you should look for when purchasing an electronic spreadsheet.

### Personal Applications

Budgets are not the only application in the home for spreadsheets. Financial planning—including mortgages, insurance, and purchase of stocks—can be assisted by worksheet manipulation. People interested in retirement or vacation planning can ask what-if questions on the computer. The results can help them to determine how present activities will affect their retirement income or vacation.

Another tool available to spreadsheets users involves creating templates. A ***template*** is a predefined worksheet format containing labels and formulas but without data. It can be reused many times to create worksheets for similar applications. For example, the loan amortization worksheet in Figure 9.14 was originally opened as a template with all the values set to zero. The results you see in the figure were generated by filling in the cells highlighted in the Inputs section (top right). In this case: 14,000 (loan), .06 (interest rate), 10 (loan period), 1996 (base year) and Jan (base month). This template is used to ask what-if questions about borrowing money for a new car or home. The template is retrieved and individualized for a specific loan. If the user wants to save a particular what-if scenario, the worksheet is saved under a different filename. As a result, the template remains unchanged and can be used again.

Electronic spreadsheets also can be used to itemize home inventories for insurance purposes. Hobbyists with large collections also can maintain current inventories of items and compute their collection's present and future values. People watching their weight can use a spreadsheet to count calories and help with menu planning.

### Volunteer Activities

Many of the spreadsheet applications in business also can apply to volunteer activities. Budgets, membership dues, and hours of volunteer time contributed by members can be tracked and analyzed on a worksheet. What was once one of the most difficult duties of a club secretary or treasurer can be streamlined with the help of a personal computer and electronic spreadsheet.

## 9.13

Hardware requirements and personal needs must both be considered when purchasing an electronic spreadsheet package.

### Evaluating Electronic Spreadsheet Software

#### USER NEEDS

**Expected size of largest worksheets**

_____ rows

_____ columns

**File integration**

☐ imports different file formats: _____

☐ exports different file formats: _____

☐ Three-dimensional (3D) worksheets

☐ Find and Replace operations

☐ Presentation graphics

    ☐ 2D and 3D

    ☐ allows special annotations

    ☐ drawing features

    ☐ others: _____

**Special formats**

☐ imports different file formats: _____

☐ foreign currency symbols: _____

☐ mathematics symbols: _____

☐ different date presentations: _____

☐ others: _____

**User interface**

☐ command-driven

☐ shell (menus)

☐ graphical

☐ Timed backups

☐ Worksheets with password protection

☐ Turn off/on automatic recalulation operation

#### TECHNICAL SUPPORT

☐ Local training available

    ☐ schools: _____

    _____

    ☐ computer stores: _____

    _____

    ☐ user groups: _____

    _____

    ☐ other: _____

    _____

☐ Context-sensitive help screens

☐ Easy-to-read manual

☐ Tutorials for beginners

☐ Telephone support

    ☐ toll-free

    ☐ at your expense

#### HARDWARE REQUIREMENTS

☐ Compatible with your computer

**Minimums**

_____ memory

_____ disk space

**Peripheral support**

☐ mouse

☐ printer

☐ color monitor

☐ CD-ROM

**9.14**

Electronic spreadsheets support personal applications such as financial planning.

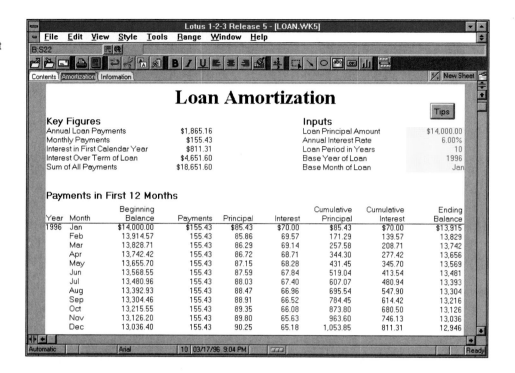

## Education

At schools, a large number of students must be enrolled, educated, and evaluated by relatively few teachers and administrators. Spreadsheets can be used to expedite these activities. Admissions personnel can use spreadsheets to keep track of the number of students in different majors or ethnic categories. This can aid in recruiting students. Financial aid available to a student can be calculated on a worksheet that contains the student's income and expenses, as well as money available from scholarships and loans.

Teachers can keep attendance records and grades by using a spreadsheet. The computation functions available on spreadsheets make weighting certain tests and dropping the lowest scores easy. They also aid in determining final grades.

## Athletics

Scoring any event from a pee-wee soccer game to professional baseball can be enhanced by using a spreadsheet. Professionals and amateurs alike can benefit from the analysis of personal and team statistics. If you are in a bowling league, a computer with the help of a spreadsheet can figure your handicap, record pin totals over the season, and even compute league standings. In other sports, knowing what an individual has done in the past helps a coach anticipate what the athlete can do today. Spreadsheets also can be used to analyze opponents' performances for potential weaknesses.

# A Closer Look at
# Designing a
# Better Worksheet

**R**ows and columns of numbers can boggle the mind if not laid out in an easy-to-read manner. Furthermore, information presented in a worksheet is only as good as the numbers entered by the user. Good worksheet design draws the reader's eye to critical numbers. It supports decisions by making it easy to change critical variables to answer what-if questions. Effective design also employs error checking for data entry mistakes. What follows are a few tips that will help you get the most from your electronic spreadsheet.

**Q: Are the headings and labels easy to understand?**

| | A | B | C | D | E | F | G |
|---|---|---|---|---|---|---|---|
| 1 | *C B SERVICE* | | | | | | |
| 2 | Expected | | | | | | |
| 3 | | | | | | | |
| 4 | | | Month | | | | |
| 5 | | ITEMS | 1 | 2 | 3 | 4 | 5 |
| 6 | | | | | | | |
| 7 | Adm. | 215749.00 | 17979.08 | 17979.08 | 17979.08 | 17979.08 | 17979.08 |
| 8 | Facil. rent | 21120.00 | 1760.00 | 1760.00 | 1760.00 | 1760.00 | 1760.00 |
| 9 | W & B - Drivers | 476000.00 | 40316.94 | 36415.30 | 40316.94 | 39016.39 | 40316.94 |
| 10 | Fuel | 62416.00 | 5286.60 | 4774.99 | 5286.60 | 5116.07 | 5286.60 |
| 11 | Main. | 431952.00 | 36586.10 | 33045.51 | 36586.10 | 35405.90 | 36586.10 |
| 12 | Insur. | 125384.00 | 10448.67 | 10448.67 | 10448.67 | 10448.67 | 10448.67 |
| 13 | P R | 15064.00 | 1255.33 | 1255.33 | 1255.33 | 1255.33 | 1255.33 |
| 14 | Bus Deprec. | 195000.00 | 16250.00 | 16250.00 | 16250.00 | 16250.00 | 16250.00 |
| 15 | | | | | | | |
| 16 | Total: | 1542685.00 | 129882.72 | 121928.89 | 129882.72 | 127231.44 | 129882.72 |
| 17 | | | | | | | |
| 18 | | | | | | | |
| 19 | | | | | | | |
| 20 | | | | | | | |
| 21 | | | | | | | |

**A:** Do not use abbreviations. Complete words used as labels are easier to read and help new users understand worksheet dynamics.

**Q: Would deleting a row or column accidentally delete other data?**

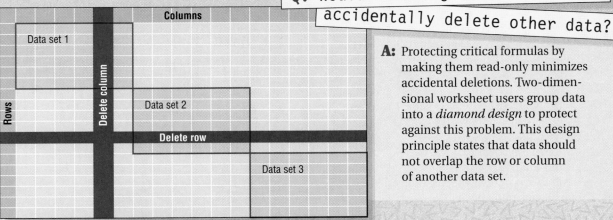

**A:** Protecting critical formulas by making them read-only minimizes accidental deletions. Two-dimensional worksheet users group data into a *diamond design* to protect against this problem. This design principle states that data should not overlap the row or column of another data set.

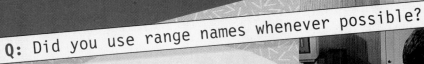

**Q:** Did you use range names whenever possible?

**A:** Range names help
end users identify related data and
minimizes copy or paste errors
involving large sets of data.

Range name: Jan-Costs

**Q:** Did you isolate
critical variables?

**A:** Values that periodically
change should be grouped
into a specific area of the
worksheet. This simplifies
changes, reduces errors, and
makes what-if questions
easier to answer.

| C16 | | @SUM(JAN-COSTS) | | | | |
|---|---|---|---|---|---|---|

ACTUAL | EXPECTED | C | D | E                                   New Sheet

| | A | B | C | D | E | F |
|---|---|---|---|---|---|---|
| 1 | *CITY BUS SERVICE* | | | | | |
| 2 | Expected Budget | | | | | |
| 3 | | Annual | | | | |
| 4 | | operating budget | JAN Expected | FEB Expected | MAR Expected | APR Expected |
| 7 | Administration | 215,749 | 17,979 | 17,979 | 17,979 | 17,979 |
| 8 | Facility rental | 21,120 | 1,760 | 1,760 | 1,760 | 1,760 |
| 9 | Wage & Benefit, Operator | 476,000 | 40,317 | 37,716 | 40,317 | 39,016 |
| 10 | Fuel | 62,416 | 5,551 | 5,193 | 5,551 | 5,372 |
| 11 | Maintenance | 431,952 | 36,586 | 34,226 | 36,586 | 35,406 |
| 12 | Insurance | 125,384 | 12,538 | 12,538 | 12,538 | 12,538 |
| 13 | Public Information | 15,064 | 1,255 | 1,255 | 1,255 | 1,255 |
| 14 | Depreciation of Buses | 195,000 | 16,250 | 16,250 | 16,250 | 16,250 |
| 15 | | | | | | |
| 16 | Total Costs | $1,542,685 | $132,237 | $126,917 | $132,237 | $129,577 |
| 17 | | | | | | |
| 18 | *Cost Adjustments* | | | | | |
| 19 | *Fuel:* | 5% | | | | |
| 20 | *Insurance:* | 20% | | | | |
| 21 | | | | | | |

Isolated variables critical to what-if questions

**Q:** Did you include error checks on input data?

**A:** Every spreadsheet program can
perform logical operations. In
this example, an error message
displays if data less than 0% or
greater than 100% is entered.
Error checks of this type help
reduce data entry errors.

@IF (B19>1#OR#B19<0"ERROR?"," ")

# Cost Adjustments
## Fuel: 600% Error?
## Insurance: 20%

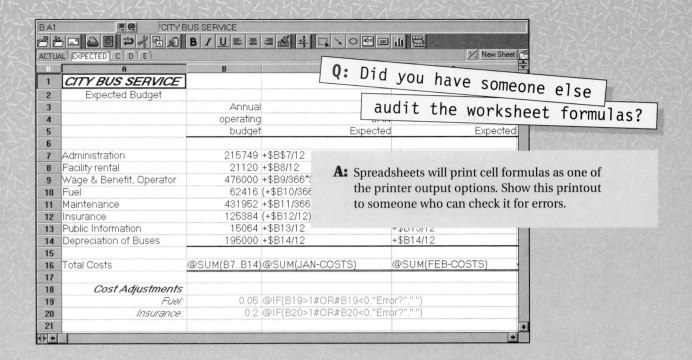

Spreadsheet screenshot (ACTUAL/EXPECTED sheet):

| B:A1 | | 'CITY BUS SERVICE | | |
|---|---|---|---|---|

| B | A | B | | |
|---|---|---|---|---|
| 1 | *CITY BUS SERVICE* | | | |
| 2 | Expected Budget | | | |
| 3 | | Annual | | |
| 4 | | operating | | |
| 5 | | budget | Expected | Expected |
| 6 | | | | |
| 7 | Administration | 215749 +$B$7/12 | | |
| 8 | Facility rental | 21120 +$B8/12 | | |
| 9 | Wage & Benefit, Operator | 476000 +$B9/366*3 | | |
| 10 | Fuel | 62416 (+$B10/366 | | |
| 11 | Maintenance | 431952 +$B11/366 | | |
| 12 | Insurance | 125384 (+$B12/12) | | |
| 13 | Public Information | 15064 +$B13/12 | +$B13/12 | |
| 14 | Depreciation of Buses | 195000 +$B14/12 | +$B14/12 | |
| 15 | | | | |
| 16 | Total Costs | @SUM(B7..B14) | @SUM(JAN-COSTS) | @SUM(FEB-COSTS) |
| 17 | | | | |
| 18 | *Cost Adjustments* | | | |
| 19 | *Fuel:* | 0.05 @IF(B19>1#OR#B19<0,"Error?"," ") | | |
| 20 | *Insurance:* | 0.2 @IF(B20>1#OR#B20<0,"Error?"," ") | | |
| 21 | | | | |

**Q:** Did you have someone else audit the worksheet formulas?

**A:** Spreadsheets will print cell formulas as one of the printer output options. Show this printout to someone who can check it for errors.

**Q:** Did you identify the author?

**A:** Giving yourself credit covers several bets. First, it never hurts to have your name associated with a useful tool. Second, other users might benefit from knowing who to contact for further clarification. Adding the current date whenever changes are made is also recommended.

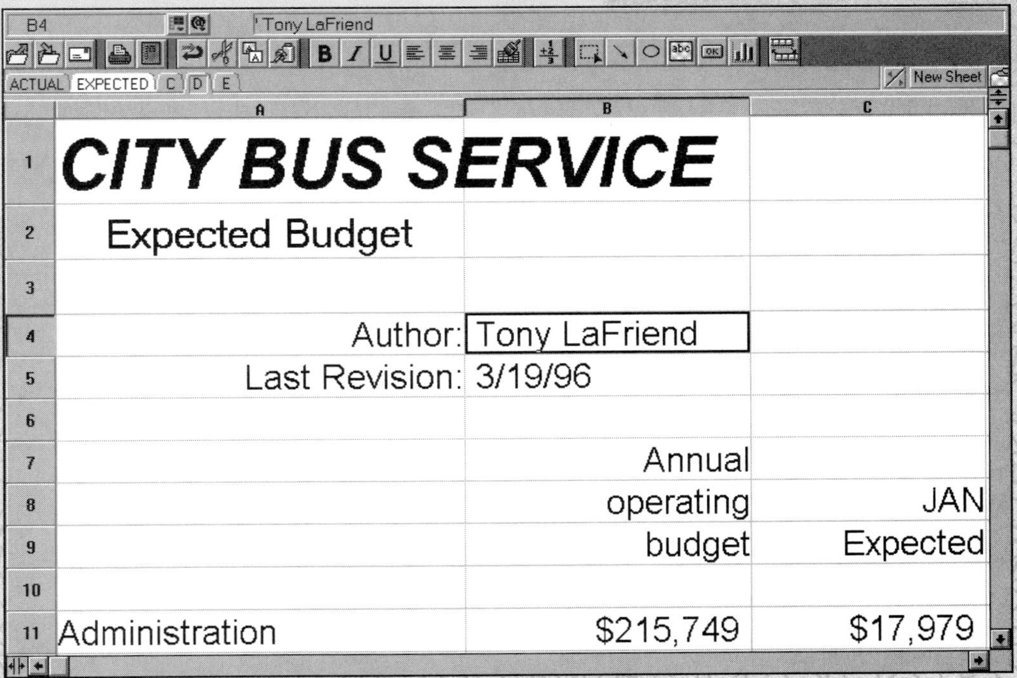

Second spreadsheet screenshot:

| B4 | | 'Tony LaFriend | | |
|---|---|---|---|---|

| | A | B | C |
|---|---|---|---|
| 1 | **CITY BUS SERVICE** | | |
| 2 | Expected Budget | | |
| 3 | | | |
| 4 | Author: | Tony LaFriend | |
| 5 | Last Revision: | 3/19/96 | |
| 6 | | | |
| 7 | | Annual | |
| 8 | | operating | JAN |
| 9 | | budget | Expected |
| 10 | | | |
| 11 | Administration | $215,749 | $17,979 |

## ▪ Science

Scientists working in a variety of areas use electronic spreadsheets as a tool to help organize and analyze research data. For example, botanists interested in the effects of acid rain on local forests can take portable computers running electronic spreadsheets into the field. Data from randomly selected trees is entered and analyzed, using the advanced mathematical functions provided by the spreadsheet. These completed worksheets can then be shared with researchers from around the country through a network.

Electronic spreadsheets can be of special benefit to large research projects because of the standard row-and-column format. Once scientists have decided on the data they wish to collect, spreadsheets provide a common means of organizing and sharing the results. For example, public health officials monitoring a measles outbreak can use identical forms throughout the country to report data. It would then be easy to assemble the data as three-dimensional worksheets and analyze it on a regional basis.

## ▪ Manufacturing

Spreadsheet programs will import data from almost any other application package so long as it is organized in a usable file format. Specialized design and manufacturing programs take advantage of a spreadsheet's versatility. An engineer may now use a graphics package to draw a three-dimensional part. The design program partitions the drawing into small areas and stores relevant measurements of size in a file. When this data is put into a worksheet along with the prices of materials, the engineer can calculate the cost of the part very accurately. If the price of a particular raw material increases, the spreadsheet program allows easy updating of total costs.

---

### CHAPTER FACTS

- ▪ An electronic spreadsheet is a tool for financial planning. For years managers have used worksheets in a paper-and-pencil form. The electronic spreadsheet allows easy alteration of data and uses the computer to perform calculations.

- ▪ An electronic worksheet is made up of horizontal rows and vertical columns, whose intersections are called cells. The contents of cells can be labels, numeric values, or formulas.

- ▪ Each spreadsheet displays command options in the control panel. The status line displays the current operating mode.

- ▪ A worksheet can display nonadjacent columns or rows by freezing labels on the screen with the title-locking feature.

- ▪ Three-dimensional worksheets are stacked on top of one another like pages in an address book.

- Worksheets can be manipulated by using the variety of operations available with the spreadsheet software. These operations include data entry, format, cut, copy, paste, insert, delete, undo, find, replace, save, open, print, protect, and exit.

- Built-in functions automatically compute a variety of financial, engineering, and mathematical operations such as loan payments, variances, and averages.

- Absolute cell references do not change when cut or copied. Relative references maintain the relationship represented in the original formula.

- Users create macros, which automatically initiate spreadsheet operations and functions.

- Data from many spreadsheets can be integrated with other software packages. It can be used with databases for easy data entry, with networks to send worksheets to remote users, and with graphics packages to display representations of the data in chart form.

- Applications for spreadsheets include uses in business, the home, schools, sports, volunteer activities, scientific research, manufacturing, and cost accounting.

- Good worksheet design includes descriptive labels, isolation of critical variables, use of range names, cross-checking of totals, protecting important cells, and incorporating error checking whenever possible.

## TERMS TO REMEMBER

| | | |
|---|---|---|
| absolute cell reference | icon bar | template |
| active cell | label | three-dimensional |
| autoformatting | label prefix | worksheet |
| cell | macro | timed backup |
| cell address | password-protect | title locking |
| cell selector | print title | value |
| control panel | range | worksheet |
| export | relative cell reference | |
| function | status line | |

## MIX AND MATCH

*Complete the following definitions with the Terms to Remember.*

1. A predefined operation that performs common mathematical and other processing routines is called a(n) _____.

2. The column letter and row number of a specific worksheet cell constitute the _____.

3. A worksheet with labels and formulas but no values is called a(n) _____.

4. A(n) _____ is a group of cells within a worksheet that are defined by the first and last cells.

5. The intersection of a single column and row on a worksheet is called a(n) _____.

6. Transferring data in a compatible format from one software application package to another is known as _____.

7. Text used to describe a worksheet or worksheet data is called a(n) _____.

8. A(n) _____ comprises a series of worksheets visually stacked on top of one another.

9. A worksheet row or column that is printed on every page is called a(n) _____.

10. A(n) _____ file can be opened only after the user enters a unique code.

11. A(n) _____ within a formula does not change when it is copied.

12. Related data organized into a row/column format constitute a(n) _____.

13. A(n) _____ is a stored series of software operations a user writes and activates upon command.

14. Numeric data within a worksheet are called _____.

15. A(n) _____ within a formula changes when it is copied.

## REVIEW QUESTIONS

1. Define the Terms to Remember.

2. What are two disadvantages of using paper-and-pencil worksheets?

3. What are two advantages of using electronic spreadsheets?

4. Identify three types of control panel lines and explain how they are used.

5. How does a user change the active cell?

6. Which keyboard key cancels the current spreadsheet operation, shuts an open menu, or closes a dialog box?

7. What type of information is displayed on the status line?

8. Identify three types of data used by an electronic spreadsheet.

9. How are dates and times stored by an electronic spreadsheet?

10. How are range names used within a worksheet?

11. Identify and briefly describe 14 common spreadsheet commands.

12. What is the difference between an electronic spreadsheet's global and range formatting features?

13. How is an absolute cell reference different from a relative cell reference?

14. How do the Save and Save As commands differ?

15. How are title locking and print titles used?

16. What are two ways a user can protect a worksheet?

17. How do you run a macro?

18. What are the advantages of organizing data in a worksheet?

19. What are the applications for electronic spreadsheets at home, with volunteer organizations, in school, in sports, as part of scientific analysis, and in manufacturing/design?

20. What are six features of good worksheet design?

## APPLYING WHAT YOU'VE LEARNED

1. Design a personal budget for a spreadsheet, using a template or graph paper. Include the number of rows and columns you will need, how each column will be labeled, and any formula required. List five what-if questions you would like to ask.

2. Use an actual spreadsheet to enter the budget you designed in project 1 above. Enter the proposed budget figures for the year and the actual figures for last month (or an estimate). Save and print the worksheet. Then answer one of the what-if questions you listed. Print the modified worksheet.

3. For the following spreadsheet applications, list the labels that would appear on the rows and columns. Name three what-if questions for each that could be useful to the user.
   a. attendance records for a grade school class
   b. budget for the school computer center
   c. scoring a Little League baseball game (or other sport)
   d. monitoring volunteers' hours at a local soup kitchen
   e. grades for your entire computer class

4. Examine a spreadsheet package in depth. Find the user's manual or description of one used in school, available in a retail store, or described in a magazine.
   a. Does it support three-dimensional worksheets? What is the maximum number of rows and columns allowed?
   b. What common file formats can it import and export?
   c. What functions can be used on the spreadsheet?
   d. How much memory and disk space does it require?
   e. With what kind of operating system does it work?
   f. What is its cost?

5. Applications for spreadsheets abound in many careers. Name five uses for a spreadsheet (not already mentioned in the text) that you would find useful now or in your future career.

6. Not all financial and numerical problems can be solved with a spreadsheet. Name three types of problems concerning numbers that would not be solved efficiently with a spreadsheet.

# Graphics and Multimedia

**W**hen presenting your ideas and information to others, you can increase the impact with audio or visual enhancements. In a competitive world, your work needs every advantage it can get. The charts and diagrams of presentation graphics and the artistic results of free-drawing graphics can make a fact or idea more interesting to an audience. Adding the powerful tools of sound, music, voice, animation, and video gives you a multimedia presentation. Multimedia has revolutionized graphic arts, business presentations, educational technology, and the media. New opportunities are available to those who know what graphics and multimedia tools are available and how to use them.

## GRAPHICAL TOOLS

Images provide a powerful source of information for many people and clearly communicate ideas that would be difficult or impossible to portray in words. For example:

- You can find your way far more easily with a road map than with written directions.
- An instant replay is more vivid and telling than thousands of words of narration by sportscasters.
- Children use images to learn through educational television.
- Art can be appreciated across generations and cultures.

Ever since prehistoric people created drawings on cave walls in southern France, people have used pictures for communication. Computers have become the tools of choice for graphic communication.

## Representing Graphics and Images

As mentioned in chapter 8, computer graphics are those drawings or charts that could be produced on paper with a pencil, eraser, and a lot of patience. Graphics can be developed internally by using a spreadsheet or other software, or input with hardware such as a mouse, joystick, keyboard, or scanner. The images that appear on a monitor consist of visual data that is converted from another media, for example, film or video. Two approaches are used to display these graphics and images.

By using **bit mapping**, also called *pixel graphics,* the computer treats a video screen, paper, or film as a pattern of tightly packed dots. Bit mapping means that each **pixel**, or picture element, has a separate memory position that is represented by a color or shade of gray. Figure 10.1 shows the bit mapping of a graphic from Figure 9.12. The total pattern of digitized pixels makes up a black-and-white or color illustration. The lines and curves in the bit-mapped graphic of Figure 10.1 are not very smooth, as seen when the figure is enlarged.

**Vector graphics** use a different type of software that allows continuous lines and smooth curves to be drawn between points on the screen, as in Figure 10.2. The graphics

### 10.1

Bit-mapped graphics use thousands of pixels of varying colors to create an image. The exploded pie chart highlights one artist's sales from the spreadsheet data in Figure 9.12.

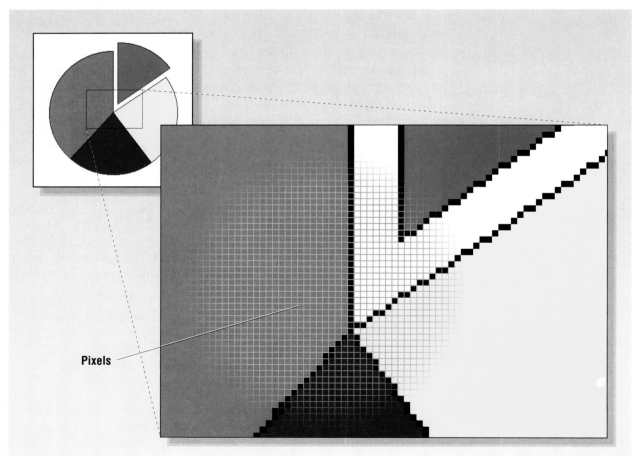

Pixels

**10.2**

Vector graphics are based on mathematically determined points, lines, and curves, rather than a grid of pixels. Shapes can easily be edited and assigned colors and textures, and can even depict three-dimensional objects.

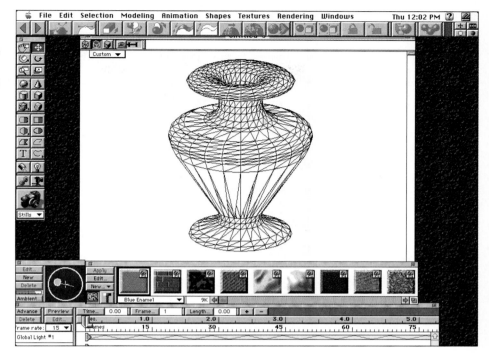

are stored as mathematical formulas, not pixel locations. Vector graphic output is made up of independent objects that are erased or moved as a unit. For example, a drawing of a table would consist of separate vector graphics: a top and four independent legs. Vector graphics can be found in some video games. Engineers, architects, draftspersons, scientists, and others use vector graphics to create precise designs.

Computers actually re-create graphics and images through techniques that *digitize* the data. Digitizing is converting an image into a binary code. Specialized input hardware, such as a scanner, digitizes an image by converting each pixel into a binary code that can be located on a row/column (XY) coordinate scale.

Computer-generated images are everywhere. When you play a video game, watch a scoreboard at a stadium, or view an animated TV commercial, you are a user of computer graphics. Blueprints, sales charts, and maps may be the result of computer-based processing. Computer graphics is a rapidly growing application area that will have a major impact on application and system software for some time to come.

## Types of Computer Graphics

Extensive use of *presentation graphics* is made in many organizations. These graphics techniques represent numeric data in standard formats, as seen in many business applications. Bar graphs, pie charts, and other examples of presentation graphics are shown in Figures 10.4 through 10.7, with the original data for these graphics shown in Figure 10.3.

Computer graphics can also be more artistic. Like an artist uses canvas or an architect uses a drafting table, the computer can be viewed as a tool for drawing or creating graphics. These applications require *free-drawing graphics*, where the shapes, colors, and patterns are under the control of the user.

**10.3**

Presentation graphics software often uses data originally stored in spreadsheets or databases. The following four figures use data from this spreadsheet.

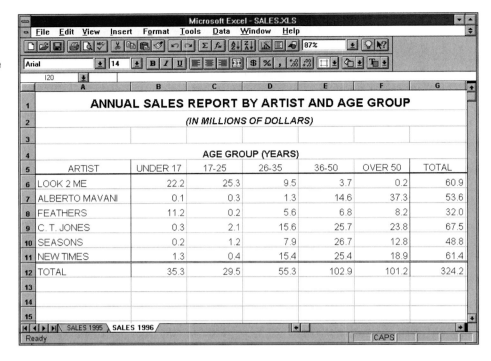

ANNUAL SALES REPORT BY ARTIST AND AGE GROUP

(IN MILLIONS OF DOLLARS)

AGE GROUP (YEARS)

| ARTIST | UNDER 17 | 17-25 | 26-35 | 36-50 | OVER 50 | TOTAL |
|---|---|---|---|---|---|---|
| LOOK 2 ME | 22.2 | 25.3 | 9.5 | 3.7 | 0.2 | 60.9 |
| ALBERTO MAVANI | 0.1 | 0.3 | 1.3 | 14.6 | 37.3 | 53.6 |
| FEATHERS | 11.2 | 0.2 | 5.6 | 6.8 | 8.2 | 32.0 |
| C. T. JONES | 0.3 | 2.1 | 15.6 | 25.7 | 23.8 | 67.5 |
| SEASONS | 0.2 | 1.2 | 7.9 | 26.7 | 12.8 | 48.8 |
| NEW TIMES | 1.3 | 0.4 | 15.4 | 25.4 | 18.9 | 61.4 |
| TOTAL | 35.3 | 29.5 | 55.3 | 102.9 | 101.2 | 324.2 |

## PRESENTATION GRAPHICS

Graphics can be used to produce visual support for written reports. In many cases, information contained in large reports, taking hours to read, can be charted or graphed for better comprehension. Although the full, textual reports are still needed, you can emphasize the important points of the report with computer-produced graphics. Research has shown that information presented through graphics is remembered better than written explanations.

Presentation graphics come in several forms. Increases in sales may be displayed with a manager's line graph, whereas a sociologist might show ethnic makeup of a city with a pie chart. Most presentation graphics fall under one of five categories: pie charts, bar graphs, line graphs, area graphs, and symbol charts.

Graphics provide a clear way of displaying both individual and grouped statistics. The Panorama Music Company records and distributes tapes and compact discs for just a few recording artists. The sales manager, Stephanie Reboy, uses presentation graphics to show how individual artists contributed to total sales last year. A further breakdown of sales by age of customer explains the sources of income. Although data is kept on a spreadsheet as in Figure 10.3, Stephanie uses the graphics features integrated into the spreadsheet software to create the charts she needs.

### Pie Charts

By using a *pie chart*, data can be presented as parts relative to a whole. Pie charts derive their name from their shape, circles divided into wedges, like slices of a pie. Pie charts show percentages, proportions, or ratios of a total. Each wedge of the pie represents a certain portion of the whole. The sum of all the wedges is 100 percent.

**10.4**

The annual sales spreadsheet in Figure 10.3 provided the basis for this pie chart.

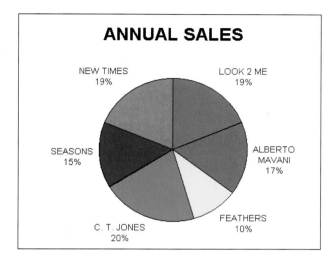

At the end of the fiscal year, Stephanie used a pie chart to show each artist's contribution to the company's total sales, as shown in Figure 10.4. Using another technique, slices of the pie can be separated from the main circle to create an *exploded pie chart* (see Figure 10.1). Stephanie highlighted the sales of Look 2 Me, a pop music group, by using the exploded pie chart.

### Bar Graphs

When her manager asked how sales were distributed over age groups, Stephanie presented the sales of each recording artist, as compared to customer age group, with a *bar graph*. Bar charts, as bar graphs are also known, display numeric data as lines or bars of representative length. Scales, or marked values, at the bottom or side of the graphic convey the meaning of the graph. For example, the bar graph in Figure 10.5a shows how all artists compared in record sales by age groups. This bar graph is based on the same

**10.5**

**(a)** Bar graphs provide a graphical comparison of values, such as annual sales for each artist in each consumer age group.

**(b)** Stacked-bar graphs show the composition of each bar's value.

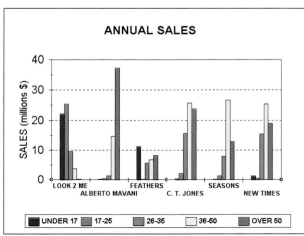

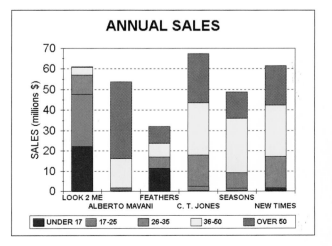

**10.6**

**(a)** Line graphs are used to trace performance over time or to chart statistical trends.

**(b)** An area graph emphasizes the region beneath the line in a line graph.

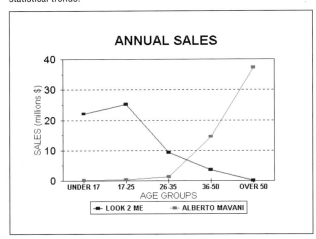

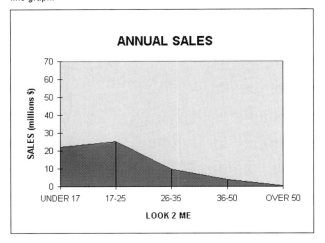

spreadsheet as the pie chart. From this graphic it is easy to see that Alberto Mavani is most popular with the over-50 age group whereas Look 2 Me had the majority of its sales in customers under age 25. The scale at the bottom of the chart is called the *legend;* it identifies the age groups. The scale at the left indicates the amount of sales in millions of dollars. Different colors or shading helps to distinguish age groups.

To show subcategories of a total within a single bar, a ***stacked-bar graph*** is used. This type of graph represents data by showing divided rather than individual bars. Figure 10.5b depicts a stacked-bar graph, displaying the breakdown of each recording artist's sales by age group of customer. Though the data is the same for both bar graphs, the stacked-bar graph clearly shows the accumulated sales for each artist whereas the regular bar graph does not.

## Line Graphs

Trends can be tracked by ***line graphs***. Like bar graphs, line graphs have two sets of scales, at the top or bottom and on one side. Traditionally, the horizontal scale reflects related categories or changes in time. A special type of line graph is known as an *xy graph,* in which both horizontal and vertical scales represent continuous measurements, such as weight or time, rather than distinct categories such as political party or ethnic background. Some xy graphs display points rather than lines to represent the relationship between the x and y scales.

Figure 10.6a illustrates the sales for two recording artists, Look 2 Me and Alberto Mavani, relative to different consumer age groups. The data for each artist is indicated by a separate line containing a unique symbol and/or color. The legend at the bottom of the graph explains which artist's sales a symbol represents. Because line graphs are used to show trends, the user must avoid showing too many lines on one graph—multiple lines make trends difficult to determine.

**10.7**

By using a software guide, a variety of formats are available for presenting data accurately and in an interesting manner.

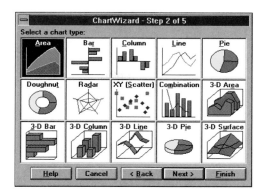

## Area Graphs

Volume can be shown in an ***area graph,*** where the space beneath a single-line graph is shaded. In some fields, such as economics and mathematics, the actual value of this area may be significant. At other times the area is shown just for emphasis. Figure 10.6b shows an area graph.

## Symbol Charts

Other types of presentation graphics (Figure 10.7) can help clarify data. *Symbol charts* use colors and symbols to highlight data values. Maps with color-coded areas or exploded regions display a geographical arrangement of information. Flowcharts, hierarchy charts, and scatter diagrams are graphics for such specialized audiences as management or systems analysts.

## Creating Presentation Graphics

Graphics software converts data values to shapes or points on a grid. Then it creates the digital patterns to produce output. Many application packages—such as word processors, spreadsheets, statistical packages, and database programs—contain features to produce graphic output or to import graphics produced by other software. Regardless of the software package and type of graphic, four levels of information are required to create presentation graphics.

**Identify Type of Graphic** The user selects the type of presentation graphic needed from a menu or by clicking on an icon. The five basic categories of presentation graphics can be presented in a variety of formats:

♦ Two-dimensional (2D)

♦ Three-dimensional (3D)

♦ Rotated

♦ Combined with other graphics

All of the graphic categories illustrated previously were in two dimensions, usually involving horizontal and vertical scales. Three-dimensional pie charts and bar graphs are available to summarize data on several levels, as shown in Figure 10.7. Bar graphs, traditionally presented as vertical columns, can be rotated into horizontal form. Many types of graphics can be combined to compare data in different formats.

Three-dimensional formats and combined graphics must be used with care. By including too much data or creating too complex a graphic, the viewer's understanding could be diminished. Also, it is possible when using 3D bar graphs to have values of a bar hidden behind higher bars in the figure. This unintentional but significant misrepresentation of the data relationships is also a potential problem with 3D line and area graphs.

**Identify Data**   After the type of graphic is chosen, the software prompts the user for data. When a pie chart is requested, for example, the software guide will ask the user for the filename and location of the data. So long as the data has been previously stored, the user does not need to reenter it. When only selected data from the file is needed, the user specifies which fields (cells) or records (rows) to be included. At this point a graphic can be output. However, as shown in Figure 10.8a, there is little information to identify what the graphic represents.

**Identify Labels**   To clarify the meaning of the graphic, labels and scales must be added. These labels can be taken from the data file or entered by the user. In Figure 10.8b, the bottom scale came from the first column of the spreadsheet (Figure 10.3), containing names of the artists. The side scale, SALES (millions $), was entered by the user. In both cases, the software sets scales based on the range of data values used. The user can manually reset these scales when necessary.

**Create Title and Legend**   To complete the graphic, a title and legend may be included (as shown in Figure 10.5). A title provides a general description of the output (such as *Annual Sales*). Legends explain the specific meaning of any symbols, colors, or shading. Titles and legends are usually prompted by the software guide and entered by the user via the keyboard. Figure 10.9 lists some tips for producing effective presentation graphics.

**10.8**

To be effective, graphics must be properly designed and labeled.
**(a)** This bar graph lacks labels and a meaningful scale.

**(b)** Even this graph is not useful without a legend or title.

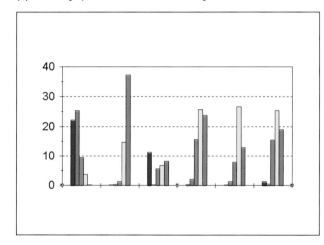

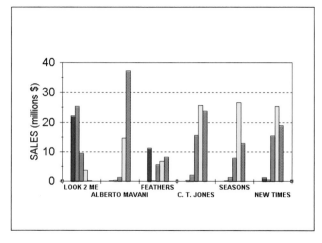

**10.9**

Well-designed presentation graphics will catch viewers' attention and inform them of important data and trends.

## Tips for Good Presentation Graphics

- Choose an appropriate type of graphic to represent the data
- Avoid showing too much information on one graph
- Be sure that lower values are not hidden behind higher values in 3D graphs
- Have clear labels and legends for all graphs
- Use color or shading to distinguish among elements in a graph

# Douglas Englebart

(b. 1925)

The name Douglas Engelbart is hardly a household word, yet this man is responsible for developing the mouse, creating windows, and is one of the originators of hypertext. The reason? Engelbart has striven to find ways to make the computer friendly and available to ordinary people, but without fame or wealth as a life goal. Stanford Research International (now SRI) was the site of Engelbart's research, starting in the 1950s. Under his direction, the mouse and other aspects of graphical user interfaces were developed. His research continues as he heads the Bootstrap Institute in California. There the theme is CSCW (Computer Supported Cooperative Work)—multiuser and multiorganizational efforts to improve the connection between people and technology.

In the 1960s Engelbart with his colleagues Ted Nelson and Andries van Dam devised hypertext (see A Closer Look, chapter 11) as a method of organizing information similar to human thinking. Until recently, this concept of nonlinear thought and programming was not widely appre-

ciated. Now there is a boom in hypertext-based products, and its webbing logic forms the basis for Internet home pages. Engelbart thinks that hypertext, its applications, and associated hardware are just in their infancy. Hypertext is a natural vehicle for textbooks and multimedia work, with multiuser projects and hyperlinks to great databases like the Library of Congress. The hardware need not be as primitive as a laptop or notebook computer. Any human sensing aid, even eyeglasses, could be an access point to this vast world.

Who's Who

## FREE-DRAWING GRAPHICS

By using free-drawing graphics software, a creative artist or engineer can produce high-quality, complex drawings. Although each free-drawing graphics package has unique capabilities to help the user, most have some features in common. After the free-drawing software is loaded, the user opens a file that acts like a canvas. This is done with an icon button or menu selection. Initial designs and menu selections are input with a mouse or a specialized drawing board called a tablet. Sometimes the design is imported from an external file or scanned from a design on paper. For larger designs, scrolling may be necessary to move the screen display from position to position.

A variety of features are available for the large number of free-drawing bit-mapped graphics programs. Drawing options are displayed as icons in the palette and toolbox (see Figure 10.10). Utility options are activated from drop-down menus.

Panorama Music Company was pleased to hear that one of its clients, Look 2 Me, was selected to write and perform the theme song for a big-budget animated film, *Underground.* A graphic artist was immediately subcontracted to create a design to be used in posters, advertisements, and the cover of the CD and tape releasing the song.

Rob Merrill is a graphic artist who uses free-drawing graphics for much of his work. By using a graphics package, Rob can easily change his design and store it in a file. After Rob has made some initial sketches, he starts up a graphics package on his personal computer.

### ■ The Palette

The *palette* provides an opportunity for Rob to choose the colors, patterns, and shading needed in the design. Palettes contain boxes showing the available color and pattern options. Sophisticated graphics packages can provide thousands of color choices. The

**10.10**

A graphic artist uses the palette and toolbox when drawing and selecting program options.

Toolbox

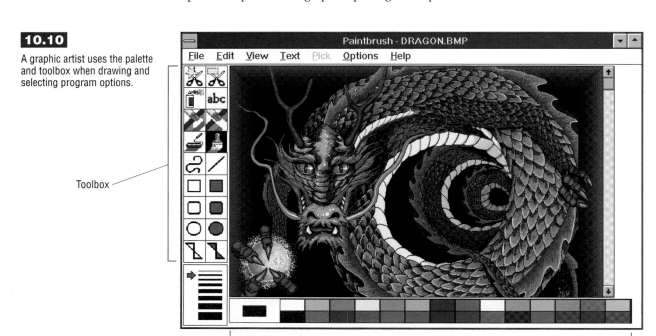

Palette

palette may include patterns of dots, stripes, or lattices. The palette can also provide a variety of simulated textures (brush strokes, paint-roller marks, gritty, smooth) from which Rob can choose. These textures give the design an almost three-dimensional quality. Users can also mix their own colors and design original patterns with some free-drawing software.

## The Toolbox

The icon menu of a *toolbox* provides Rob with options for brush strokes, shapes, and text formatting, along with other editing features. He selects the desired tools by moving the pointer over the icon button and clicking. Most free-drawing software contains these common tools: Shapes, Fill Bucket, Brush, Spraycan, Scissors, Fatbits, Eraser, and Text tool.

**Shapes**　By using the *Shape* tools, Rob can easily draw standard shapes such as circles, squares, and polygons. The shapes may be filled solid or left as an outline. As Rob rolls the mouse across the desktop, the movement is echoed on the screen, drawing the figures. Depending on the software package, this tool produces either a bit-mapped or vector graphic. Rob uses vector graphic Shape tools to create the subway car (see Figure 10.11) because it gives him the flexibility to move the graphic. If bit mapping is to be used with this graphic, he will export the graphics file to another free-drawing graphics package.

　　The *Stretch* option, as its name implies, widens and distorts these geometric figures. For example, Rob clicks on the rectangle icon in the toolbox and then somewhere in the drawing area to draw a window for the subway car. If he decides the windows aren't wide enough, he can stretch them to a larger size. The car is actually a collection of vector graphics that Rob stretches and distorts to bend into perspective so the lines converge to a vanishing point.

**Fill Bucket**　Using bit-mapped graphics, any enclosed shape can be filled by using the *Fill Bucket* tool. Rob clicks on the fill bucket icon, then on the desired pattern or color, and finally within any enclosed area in the design. The pattern or color selected from the palette automatically fills the entire area, such as the back wall or the subway station platform in Figure 10.11.

**Brush**　The *Brush* tool enables Rob to create visual patterns using different line widths and shapes. Brushes can be large or small, round or flat, straight or tapered, acting like either a paintbrush or a pencil. Rob can select from the palette the color of "paint" or "lead" to be used. To color the bat shown in Figure 10.11, Rob uses various brushes, some with opaque paint, some with translucent paint that allows the underlying sketch lines to show through. Rob's artistic eye coordinates the hand movements that draw the bat pixel-by-pixel, just as it would if he were painting with conventional media.

**Spraycan**　The effect of using an actual can of spraypaint or an airbrush is reproduced by the *Spraycan* tool. As Rob moves the spraycan across the screen very quickly, a light spattering of the selected pattern creates the subtle shading and the graffiti on the subway car. Rob can select certain areas to paint, leaving other areas untouched. He can also control the size and density of the spray. This allows Rob to achieve the delicate shading commonly seen in airbrushed pictures. Some free-drawing graphics packages also include *special-effects filters*. Different combinations of filters are used to blur, sharpen, and add textures to parts of the image.

**10.11**

Free-drawing software helped to create this CD cover. **(a)** Starting in a vector-based graphics application, the artist draws geometric shapes to build a subway car. **(b)** The finished car is duplicated twice more and aligned. **(c)** The three cars are rotated into perspective. **(d)** Moving to an application with bit-mapped graphics tools, the artist fills areas with color. **(e)** The Spraycan tool is used to add shading and graffiti. **(f)** A sketch of a cartoon bat by a member of the group is scanned and added to the foreground. **(g)** Various brushes and painting styles are used to color the bat, and filters add motion-blur, glow, and texture effects to the background. **(h)** Type is added in a vector graphics application. **(i)** The final cover.

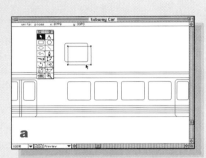
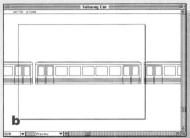
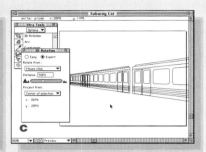
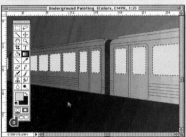
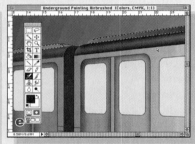

**Scissors**   The *Scissors* tool enables Rob to indicate a part of the graphic for special handling. This area can be copied to other areas, filled with textures, or modified with various filters. For example, Rob can select just the windows of the subway to add a glow effect, or select just the background to add the stalactite shapes without affecting the rest of the drawing. With the figure of the bat selected in another file, he can copy and paste it into the foreground, then move it about until he finds just the right place to position it.

**Fatbits**   Rob can magnify a specific section of a bit-mapped graphic to view a pixel-by-pixel enlargement by using the *Fatbits* tool. For example, he can refine the drawing of the bat by inspecting the magnified portion, turning pixels on or off to change lines and patterns. Figure 10.1 at the beginning of the chapter shows a fatbits representation of a pie chart.

**Eraser**   The *Eraser* tool works much like a chalkboard eraser. As Rob moves the eraser across the screen with the mouse, the areas touched by the eraser are cleared of colors and patterns. Rob can control the width of the eraser just like that of the brush.

**Text Tool**   To type text onto the screen, Rob uses a keyboard. He can select fonts and type size, just like in a desktop publishing package. Rob uses the Text tool to add the group's name and the title of the album to the design (Figure 10.11). Another menu gives Rob the options of bold, italic, outlined, shadowed, or justified text.

## ■ Free-Drawing Utilities

Other menus contain standard utilities, some as simple as clearing the screen or printing the graphic. Utilities are also available for saving a graphics file and for opening a file from disk. A special utility is used to undo the last request made by a user in creating a graphic. Rob can experiment with different visual effects, then use this utility to remove the last change. These utilities make it easy to try to save different designs.

Graphics produced by inputting dimensions and mathematical relationships into the computer also make use of specialized utilities. With this information the computer draws a three-dimensional view of an object. The object can be tilted, rotated, and viewed from all sides with use of these utilities (see Figure 10.12).

Many free-drawing packages let the user layer different design elements. For example, an architect designing a floor plan could draw electrical wiring as one layer and plumbing as another. The layers can be printed or viewed as part of the total design or one layer at a time. The plumber, for instance, would be given the complete design and a copy of the layer containing water lines and drainpipes.

## ■ Bit-mapped Versus Vector Graphics Tools

Some of the tools available in free-drawing bit-mapped graphics programs are also common to vector graphics drawing programs. Both have features like the Brush, Shapes, and Fill Bucket tools. In a vector graphics program, however, each shape produced is considered a separate object, for example, the squares and rectangles that make up the subway car. The object is contained in its own layer, which can be copied, deleted, stretched, or moved. Because the Fatbits tool is unavailable, changes to a drawing are made by modifying objects within the drawing. An object can be grouped with other

**10.12**

Free-drawn, three-dimensional images can be tilted, rotated, and viewed from all sides.

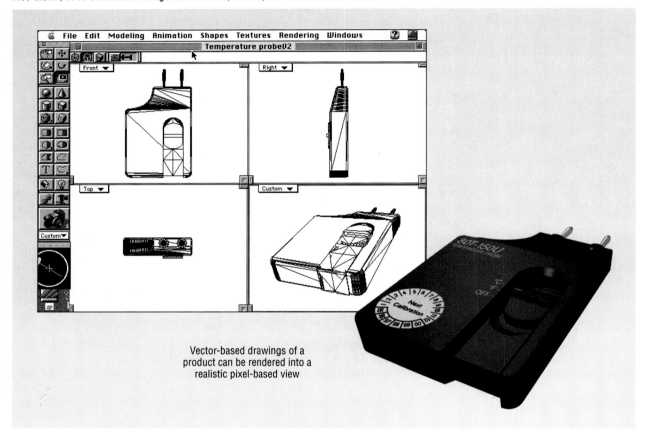

Vector-based drawings of a
product can be rendered into a
realistic pixel-based view

objects into a single, larger object which can then be modified as a unit. The subway car is such a grouped object. Vector graphics programs allow objects to overlap, and the user can control which object is on top of the others, features not available with bit-mapped graphics.

## MULTIMEDIA

Advances in both hardware and software allow a developer to go beyond static presentation and free-drawing graphics. Text and graphics can be enhanced with audio, video, and animation by using the techniques of *multimedia* production.

As the poster/CD jacket design is being developed for the theme song from *Underground,* an independent video firm hired by Panorama Music creates the music video accompanying the release of the song and movie. To be competitive, the video company relies heavily on multimedia hardware and software.

The multimedia hardware required depends on the sophistication of its users. Professional production studios may use complex audio- and video-capture equipment along with having film processing and editing capabilities. This hardware may come

**10.13**

A toolbox and frame selection tools allow imported visual images to be edited frame by frame.

from different vendors and thus create compatibility problems. Even for the novice multimedia user, equipment standards are of concern. In 1990 Microsoft, Tandy, AT&T, and eight other computer hardware and software manufacturers agreed upon an *MPC (multimedia PC)* standard. A computer system considered meeting MPC standards has, at a minimum, a CD-ROM drive, sound board, and multimedia extensions to Microsoft's Windows graphical interface. Upgrading kits exist to bring many older computers up to MPC standards. Qualifying new computers will carry an MPC label.

## Visual Data

Data used in a presentation or free-drawing graphics package is already digitized for storage and processing by a computer. Similar techniques are used when other sources of visual data are available. When the video firm wishes to use a photograph in the music video, it can be input by using a scanner or from the disk of a digital camera. More likely, film clips, perhaps of the band playing the song, will be included in the video. These images, as well as visual data from television and videotape, is converted into a series of *frames* to be stored on disk in one of several standard video formats.

Although each frame is a still picture or image, a series of frames shown in quick succession give the impression of moving pictures. Thirty frames per second is a common standard. Expansion cards can connect a video recorder or television directly to a computer. As the visual data is input, each frame is numbered automatically by the software.

A toolbox in multimedia software allows a developer at the video firm to examine and edit, frame by frame, a video of the band (see Figure 10.13). All of the tools available in free-drawing software are also available in the multimedia toolbox. The following section introduces some of the additional tools that are included.

**Frame Selection**    The *frame selection* tools available in a multimedia toolbox are quite similar to those on a video recorder/player. They include forward, fast forward, reverse, stop, play, and pause. These options are activated when the developer moves a mouse pointer over a small button on the screen, like that of a VCR player. A search tool allows a user to find a specific frame number. Sections of the video can be cut, pasted, or copied, similar to parts of a graphic. Image-editing software may also include the capability to build storyboards or to lay out selected frames, as shown at the top of Figure 10.13.

**Speed Control**    While icons control basic movement through the visual data, its display speed is measured in *frames per second (fps)*. Some multimedia packages allow the developer to use *speed control* to change the fps value. This feature can be used to help synchronize audio data with visual data, such as the music with the movements of the band. Also, unique effects can be produced by slowing down or speeding up a video sequence.

**Color and Contrast Control**    The video developer can use *color and contrast control* within a single frame to add color or change emphasis. Specialized software is required to realistically colorize a black-and-white video sequence (Figure 10.14). This software not only controls color quality but aids the user in the subtleties of shading, feathering, blurring, and other techniques to improve realism. At the other extreme, unusual colors and contrasts could be used to grab the viewers' attention.

**Object Integration**    By using frame reference numbers, the *object integration* feature allows a new video or audio sequence to be overlaid or inserted anywhere into the music video. This ability to integrate data from different sources could result in a scene where the human band is interacting with an animated character from the movie.

**Morphing**    By using *morphing* techniques, a developer can seamlessly blend one image into another. Mathematical and graphics routines use key locations on the starting and ending frames to create a transition between them, as shown at the bottom of Figure 10.15. The complexity of this technique may require a long time and much disk storage area

**10.14**

Specialized software is used to realistically colorize a black-and-white video.

**10.15**

Morphing software facilitates smooth video transition between images.

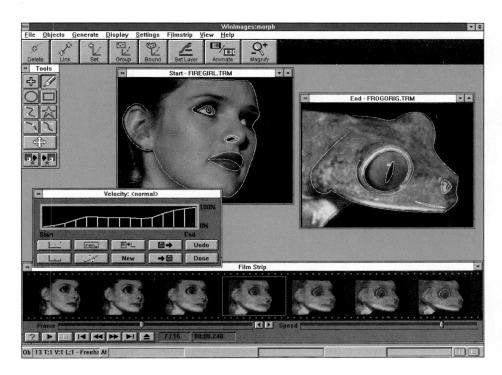

for sophisticated morphs. Advertisements often involve morphing to create unrealistic but eye-catching images.

**Image Exporting**   Once completed, the video can be exported to other software or stored in several ways. The visual images can be stored as a series of files, each containing one or more frames. The files themselves can be output frame by frame onto paper, slides, videotape, or film. Also, images can be saved for later importation into other types of software, like free-drawing or desktop publishing applications. Because the images are digitized, related files can require a lot of computer memory and disk storage space.

## ■ Audio Data

A movie soundtrack and a recording of the band's music can be integrated on the video by using multimedia tools that manipulate audio data. Audio data also includes voices and sound effects. Particular multimedia features are needed to allow maximum control by the developer of audio data.

**Measure Selection**   One way multimedia software helps the developer control audio data is by breaking the recording into measures, based on timing. By using the *measure selection* option, a developer can edit the sounds within each measure. Editing can include adding, deleting, or changing the timing and pitch of sounds within a measure.

**Channel Separation**   When editing music or voice, it is possible to create harmonies by simultaneously playing sounds that were recorded separately. Each individual source of sound is recorded on a separate *audio channel*. The channels can then be individually

**10.16**

Each separate channel of an audio file can be analyzed and edited. Many of the buttons are similar to those found on a tape recorder/player.

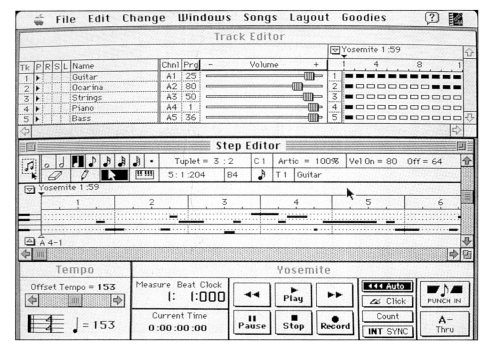

controlled for volume and playback speed. For example, each band member can be recorded on different days and mixed into the final version at a later date.

**Playback Control**   With the *playback control* feature of a multimedia package, the developer can not only control the volume of audio data on each separate channel, as shown in Figure 10.16, but can include fade in and fade out, echoing, and other effects. Several of these techniques are used to refine the music video.

The ability to control the quality of audio data on individual channels would be incomplete without the power to integrate those channels. Multimedia software contains features to *synchronize* the sounds on different channels as well as to import other forms of audio data. By using synchronization features, the developer of the music video can integrate the band's performance of the title song for *Underground* with the video of the band's performance and clips from the movie itself.

## ■ Animation

By combining output from free-drawing software with multimedia production techniques, graphic artists can develop animated films and cartoons, as shown in Figure 10.17. *Animation* is the sequencing of single drawings as frames, resulting in motion. Traditional animation was costly and complex. In the first animated productions, each second of an animated film used 36 hand-drawn graphics. Today television requires only 30 frames per second for broadcast, and animators employ computers both to create the drawings and to sequence their movement.

Computer-animated graphics require sophisticated application generators. Once a drawing is completed, instructions have to be input as to the type of movement required. Once the instructions have been entered, however, creating motion of animated

**10.17**

This frame of a feature film uses the shading features of an animation system to give it a near photo quality.

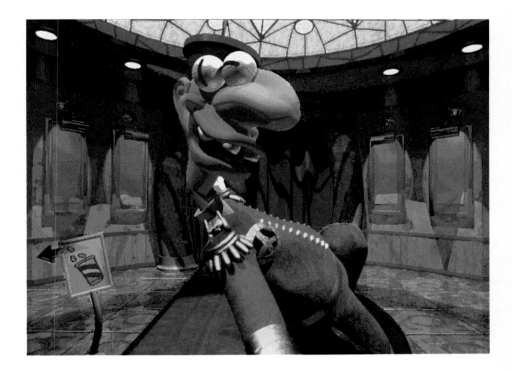

characters and objects is relatively quick and easy. Animators use free-drawing software to manipulate motion sequences. As video images are created one frame at a time (see Figure 10.17), a video or motion picture camera records the sequence of images. These techniques are used not only in producing commercials and cartoons, but for a variety of applications in other areas as well.

## GRAPHICS AND MULTIMEDIA APPLICATIONS

Some graphics and multimedia applications are purely art. At times, the computer is used only in the design phase. An artist might produce the initial design for a weaving pattern, sculpture, or still life on the computer but create the piece by hand. In other cases, the computer graphic, enhanced with audio, is the finished product. Television commercials often use images produced with computer graphics. Computer-constructed images also become the background shots in motion pictures, as in a futuristic film for which a set may be difficult to build. Engineers and architects use graphics applications to design machines and buildings. Multimedia software can be used to present the design in a format that includes movement and sound. Graphics and multimedia software are powerful tools in the hands of creative and informed users.

### Business and Scientific Presentations

Businesspeople and scientists turn to graphics and multimedia to present their information with a flair. Reports with a lot of detailed information can be clearly summarized by a pie chart or other form of presentation graphic. An analysis of data can be enlivened

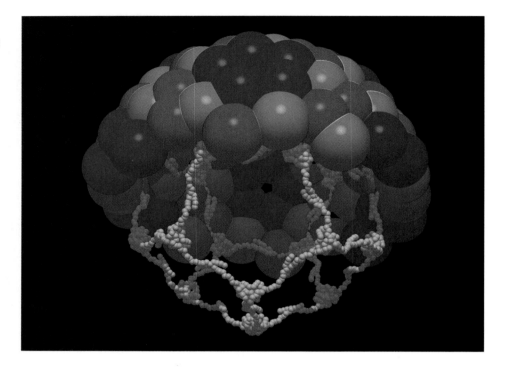

with colorful slides or animation. A University of Minnesota/3M study concluded that presentations including visual aids were 43 percent more persuasive than those without. Furthermore, research at the Wharton School of Business found that business meetings involving graphics were shorter with consensus being reached more quickly. As shown in Figure 10.18, scientific information can be shared in an interesting manner. In short, graphics and multimedia help businesspeople and scientists present important information while keeping people awake during long or otherwise dry meetings.

## Computer-Aided Design

Developing a major new product, such as an aircraft or automobile, formerly involved a cycle of activities that lasted five to nine years. Well over half of this time was spent in research and design. Before actual construction of the new product could start, designers had to figure out how the new product would look and how it would meet performance and safety goals. The same was true for development of a major building or architectural feature; skilled architects had to draw and redraw many sets of pictures and detailed plans. Once the drawing was finalized, cameras mounted on stands photographed the image to produce color slides.

The design, analysis, and simulation of new products with computers is known collectively as *computer-aided design (CAD)*. A designer inputs data by using a keyboard, mouse, touch-sensitive screen, or scanner using software containing many of the features of free-drawing packages. The computer forms images by digitizing entered data. These images can be rotated on the screen for close evaluation of appearance and prospective performance before prototypes are built. Some software will graphically simulate the effects of wind, earthquakes, or other environmental factors upon the design. Simulations involve complex computations used to predict how the design will react under different

**10.19**

With a computer-aided design (CAD) system, engineers can design new products as well as test to see if safety standards are met.

situations. Mathematical equations representing environmental stresses are accessed by the software. The computer then runs the design through the equations, sometimes showing the effects with animation, as in Figure 10.19. This process enables a designer to observe weaknesses in the design before the actual product is made. Computer simulations, in effect, drive cars or cross bridges long before the designs become reality.

## ■ Computer Imaging

When a computer combines data, mathematics, and graphics to see what is normally difficult or impossible for a person to observe, this process is called *computer imaging*. Medical researchers use computer imaging to graphically display the expected results of a specific procedure. As shown in Figure 10.20, doctors can combine data and images into a three-dimensional graphic. This can aid them in simulating the best procedures to use in a delicate surgery.

Computer imaging is used to reconstruct what no longer exists or simulate what might be. Pictures of long-missing children are computer aged to suggest what they might look like now. Archaeologists can plot the layout of an ancient city using data from a dig site. Lawyer/artist teams use graphics software to reconstruct an accident or scene of a crime for a trial. Prospective cosmetic surgery patients can see what they will look like after the work is done. Some hair salons can even show you how a new hair color or style will affect your looks.

## ■ Athletics and the Performing Arts

Using applicable graphics software, coaches can analyze an athlete's performance. For example, a computer might record the motion of a runner as input through a specialized scanner. Or the computer might digitize films of the athlete in action. The body movements are reproduced graphically, as in Figure 10.21, then compared with computer

**10.20**

Actual slices of a human body were enhanced by computer imaging to create this 3D visualization.

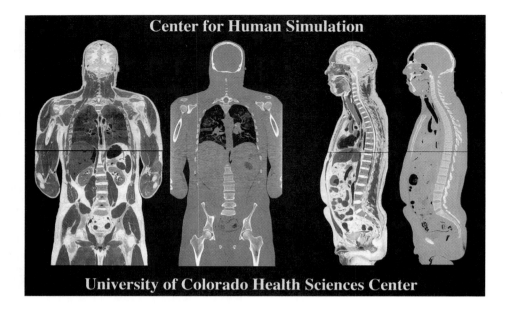

models representing desired form. Sometimes the computer can identify subtle variations in an athlete's form that could hurt his or her performance. Coaches and athletes work together to use computer graphics to improve form and performance.

Like a coach, a choreographer can use computer graphics to analyze a dancer's movement. Dance notation has become a common application for choreographers as well. Because a film or video record of a dance cannot show all of the dancers' movements

**10.21**

Medical researchers at the Olympic training center in Colorado use computer-generated graphics to analyze a runner's form and performance.

in detail, dance notators are using the computer to create a graphic record of a performance. In one notation system, an animated stick figure is used to represent each dancer, and movements are stored as data. Multimedia software can integrate the musical score with the dancers' movements. Choreographers and play directors are also using graphics software to design character movement, sets, and lighting. Multimedia software was used to choreograph the Look 2 Me video with the *Underground* theme song. Like engineers using CAD, these designers can experiment with different effects and see the total picture before having to work with the actual production.

### MIDI

For more than two decades, musicians have been using electronics to enhance and distort the sounds created by traditional musical instruments. Electric guitars, pianos, wind, brass, and percussion instruments have been enhanced to create new sounds. A standard has been developed within the music industry for connecting electric instruments to each other and to computers. The standard is called *MIDI*, which stands for *Musical Instrument Digital Interface*. As the name suggests, MIDI provides a standard set of binary codes that represent musical sounds, called *events* (Figure 10.22).

The actual sound or music is not sent in a MIDI file. Instead, a series of binary codes are transmitted by the instrument to the computer. These codes represent three characteristics: whether a note is to be switched on or off, the code for the note (such as 3C for middle C), and a velocity code for volume control.

The MIDI codes can be generated by a pianolike keyboard and sent through a cable to a synthesizer that plays (or stops playing) the note at a certain volume. By using a combination of voices (or sounds) controlled by a program, MIDI allows a musician to use a piano keyboard or joystick to generate the sounds of many different instruments.

**10.22**

MIDI standards allow a musician to create and synchronize sound volume and speed for each channel in a musical composition.

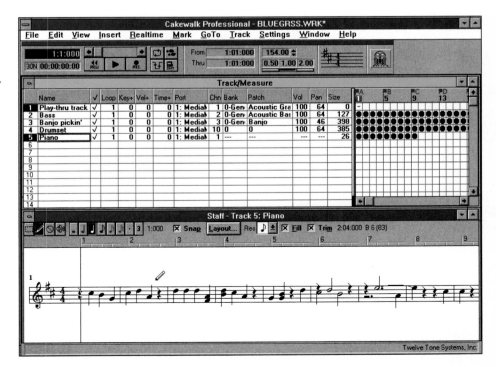

# A Closer Look at Computer Art

**W**hat is art? The use of technology in creative art has brought us no closer to answering this ancient question. It has, however, broadened the canvas for artists and opened avenues of creativity and artistic expression for everyone. If you have the opportunity to experiment with a graphic arts system—even a simple paint program—you may discover a creative side you never knew you had!

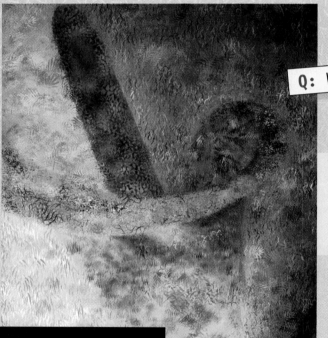

**Q: What can computer technology bring to the world of art?**

**A:** Technology brings to an artist's toolbox light, colors, and precision. Pixels on a screen can be as captivating as pencil on paper and brush on canvas.

**Q: How is computer art different?**

**A:** In the past, artists played with light through stained and etched glass. Images are now illuminated by RGB monitors.

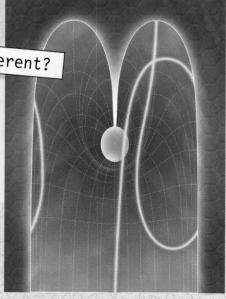

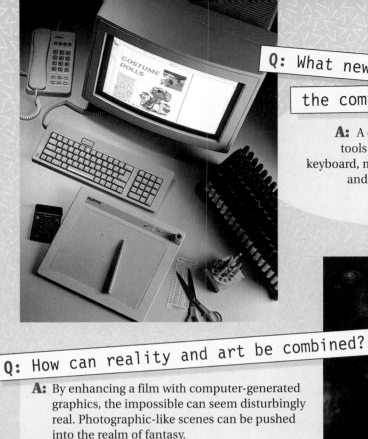

**Q:** What new tools does the computer artist use?

**A:** A computer artist's tools could include a keyboard, mouse, scanner, tablet, and video camera.

**Q:** How can reality and art be combined?

**A:** By enhancing a film with computer-generated graphics, the impossible can seem disturbingly real. Photographic-like scenes can be pushed into the realm of fantasy.

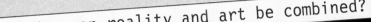

**Q:** What is the future of computer art?

**A:** We can only wait and see.

Music composition software can edit the MIDI codes to allow mixing of these sounds onto different channels, as shown in Figure 10.22. When played simultaneously, the result can sound like a small group of musicians or an entire orchestra. An additional advantage is that the developer need not know how to play all the instruments he or she can generate in a MIDI file. Because the data is stored in a recognizable binary code, it can be used by a variety of equipment. As MIDI technology is perfected, it gets more difficult to distinguish synthesized output from a recording of a live performance.

## ■ Space Exploration

Graphics applications extend beyond earthly uses. Computer-controlled space probes record images of Mars, Venus, the Moon, and other galactic bodies as streams of digital data. The images are sent back to an Earth base and converted into graphics. Specialists analyze the graphics, then use image enhancement techniques to adjust the pictures to indicate surface conditions (Figure 10.23).

These image enhancement techniques can fill in missing data by checking surrounding pixels and estimating the likely content of an unknown pixel value. The contrast in images is improved by using temperatures, particle densities, and other conditions on the celestial body as data. These image enhancement techniques change the pictures from shades of gray to various intensities of color.

**10.23**

NASA uses computers to enhance digitized pictures from space probes and telescopes.

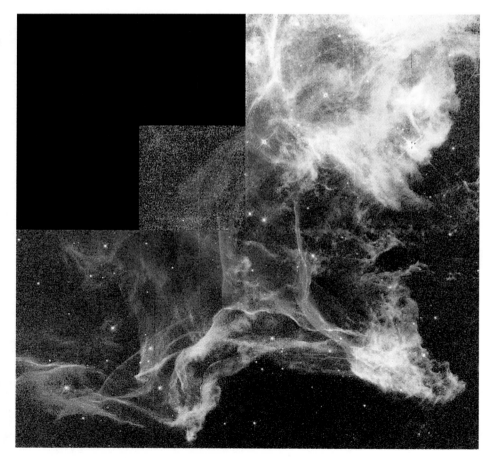

## CHAPTER FACTS

- Graphic images can be produced through bit mapping (also called pixel graphics) or vector graphics.

- Presentation graphics can be pie charts, exploded pie charts, bar graphs, stacked-bar graphs, line graphs, area graphs, or symbol charts.

- Pie charts show how components proportionally make up a whole. Each slice represents a single component.

- Bar graphs display data as varying lengths of bars, each showing the relative quantity or measurement of a value.

- Line graphs show the trends found in a group of data over time.

- Area charts contain a shaded area below the line in a single-line graph.

- Symbol charts use colors and symbols to accentuate data values.

- Enhancements to presentation graphics include two- and three-dimensional graphs, rotation, and combination graphs.

- Presentation graphics are created by identifying the type of graphic, the data to be included, and labels for the graphic, and by stating the graphic title and legends.

- Free-drawing graphics software includes a palette, toolbox, and drop-down menus to aid the user.

- The palette allows the user to choose colors and shading for the graphic.

- The toolbox includes tools for creating the graphic. These include Shapes, Fill Bucket, Brush, Spraycan, Scissors, Fatbits, Eraser, and Text tools.

- Each shape drawn using vector graphics is an object that can be moved, copied, deleted, or combined with other objects.

- Multimedia is the coordination of text, visual images, and audio data into a single presentation.

- Visual data is stored and edited in frames that can be edited by using frame selection, speed control, color and contrast control, integration, and image exporting.

- The measures in audio data can be selectively edited for volume, channel separation, and synchronization.

- Graphics applications include animation for film and videotape, business and scientific presentations, computer-aided design (CAD), computer imaging, analysis of body movement for athletics and performing arts, and space exploration.

- MIDI (Musical Instrument Digital Interface) standards for digitized musical events allows a musician to synthesize audio signals and control the volume, duration, and type of instrument they represent.

## TERMS TO REMEMBER

| | | |
|---|---|---|
| animation | computer imaging | multimedia |
| area graph | digitize | pie chart |
| audio channel | exploded pie chart | pixel |
| bar graph | frame | presentation graphics |
| bit mapping | free-drawing graphics | stacked-bar graph |
| computer-aided design (CAD) | line graph | vector graphics |

## MIX AND MATCH

*Complete the following definitions with the Terms to Remember.*

1. A(n) _____ is a graphic showing data as different lengths of bars.

2. A graphic showing trends in data with a continuous line is called a(n) _____.

3. _____ is visual images of motions produced by rapid presentation of drawn or computer-generated graphics.

4. To convert a point on a drawing into mathematical coordinates, it must be _____.

5. _____ are images based on solid lines and curves, rather than the points of bit-mapped graphics.

6. _____ comprises patterns of pixels that make up a graphic image.

7. Visual data such as film or video is divided into _____.

8. A(n) _____ is one component of an array or matrix of dots that makes up a visual image.

9. A(n) _____ is a division of audio data, representing a single voice or instrument.

10. The combination of textual, audio, and visual data under software control for importing, editing, and exporting is known as _____.

11. _____ are created using the computer much as an artist uses a canvas.

12. A circle graphic divided into slices, each representing the proportion one component has when related to the whole is called a(n) _____.

13. A bar graph in which each bar is broken down to show its components is called a(n) _____.

14. The information technology application wherein computers are used to create two- or three-dimensional drawings is known as _____.

15. _____ include graphs and symbol charts, often from a worksheet, used in business and other applications.

## REVIEW QUESTIONS

1. Define the Terms to Remember.

2. What types of information are associated with each pixel in bit mapping?

3. Describe two ways to create a graphic image.

4. What are the four levels of information needed by graphics software to produce presentation graphics?

5. What options do the palette, toolbox, and drop-down menus provide for free-drawing graphics software?

6. Identify five tips to good presentation graphics design.

7. How do the Brush, Spraycan, Shapes, Stretch, Fill Bucket, Scissors, Fatbits, Eraser, and Text tools work?

8. Briefly explain how these multimedia options work: frame selection, speed control, color and contrast control, object integration, and image exporting.

9. How is morphing used?

10. What are four ways audio data can be controlled and edited?

11. How do animators use computers in their work?

12. How are computer-generated graphics or multimedia used in business or scientific presentations, computer-aided design, computer imaging, athletics and performing arts, and space exploration?

13. What is MIDI and how is it used?

## APPLYING WHAT YOU'VE LEARNED

1. Applications for both presentation and free-drawing graphics exist in most career areas. Name three uses for graphics software in your chosen field (other than those mentioned in the text). Will the graphics be presentation or free-drawn?

2. Explain how graphics software can enhance user understanding in these situations:
   a. presentation of the ethnic groups that make up the faculty of your school
   b. advertising the opening of a new video rental store
   c. showing how to assemble a bicycle from a kit
   d. demonstrating how renovation of a historical building may change its appearance

3. Use a graphics package to produce and print a presentation graphic reflecting a simple collection of data. This could be your personal budget, grade point average over time, or another application. Be sure that the graphic is clearly labeled and contains a legend.

4. Use a graphics package to produce a simple freehand drawing such as a map to your house, a greeting card, or a self-portrait. Make use of the palette and toolbox to show a variety of shapes and patterns. Save and print the graphic.

5. Use a multimedia package to learn about a new subject or review an old one. What features of multimedia learning do you like the best? Which ones do you like the least?

**C**omputer information systems allow you access to vast amounts of information. You might wonder why anyone would need to work with so much data. However, you probably now have files or different lists, perhaps in overcrowded file cabinets, that could be arranged into personal databases. You need to know how to organize this data, thereby reducing clutter and promoting better access to important information.

Not only is there a place for personal information systems in your future, but you already have access to a wide variety of public data. Airline schedules, library card catalogs, and sports statistics are organized into databases available to the knowledgeable consumer. Understanding how data management software organizes and retrieves information can increase your productivity when electronically accessing consumer and public data.

## DATA PROCESSING

Stored data is an extremely valuable asset for any person or organization using a computer system. Individuals, schools, businesses, and other users rely on data to conduct their daily activities (Figure 11.1). Everyone organizes data for storage and use; computers just make it easier. For instance, let's look at the different collections of data used by your local video store.

**11.1**

Every business transaction creates valuable data. Computer information systems maintained by a local video rental store track hundreds of tapes and thousands of rental transactions.

As a customer, your name, address, and telephone number are collected into a *record*. The records are organized by a unique customer number given to each customer. Together, these records become the Customer *file*. Data from your record is on a plastic ID card like the one shown in Figure 11.2. Your customer number might appear as a bar code on this card. The store also maintains an Inventory file of every videotape the store rents. Each tape has a unique number bar-coded on it.

Sometimes data files are processed independently. The store manager can access the videotape Inventory file to see if a specific tape is rented. When data is integrated with other data files, even more information is available. For example, combining data from the Customer file with the Inventory file allows the manager to find which customer rented a specific tape. By relating files within a database, it is possible to allow easy access to a variety of data items.

If the video store's data is properly organized, customers and employees can get different types of information. For instance, one customer might want a list of all the available adventure movies that run over two hours. Also, the store manager could list overdue tapes or compute the store's weekly income.

However, stored data must be organized according to its intended use. Different file and database schemes exist for different applications, and different access methods fit varying data processing requirements. In turn, these access methods determine the physical arrangement of data on storage media. Two basic types of file access methods are available: sequential and direct.

## ■ Sequential Access

Finding a specific record by using *sequential access* means starting with the first record and looking at each consecutive record in the file until the specific record is found. Sequential access methods work equally well with tape or disk storage. Records are retrieved in the sequence in which they were originally stored. As an example, songs on

**11.2**

Integrating data from the Customer and Inventory data files provides complete access to information related to videotape rentals.

Nick Harris
734 Mercury Drive
Hackley, MI 49442
(616) 555-0034

Expires 2/21/98

**BOOMTOWN**
VIDEO RENTALS

0 00008 81464 7

Customer identification card

Videotape

Inventory
Rentals
Movies
Customers

a commercially produced music tape are organized for sequential access. When you play a tape, the songs are heard in a predetermined order. Once the songs are stored on the tape, they cannot easily be rearranged.

If you wish to hear the sixth song on a prerecorded tape, you must listen to the first five or fast-forward past them. In either case, the first five songs must be run through the tape player in sequence. Similarly, a computer that uses sequential access methods reads one record at a time to locate the desired record. To retrieve the fifty-fifth record in a data file, the first 54 must be read by the tape or disk drive.

Each record in a file should have at least one key field, or *key*, that makes the record unique. Keys serve to identify and organize records in a file. Locating a specific record by using sequential access methods means the key from each record is examined until a match is found or the last record is processed. For instance, in the video store's Inventory file, the key field is the unique number the store assigns to every videotape. When the file is initially stored on disk, the records are placed in order by tape number. This arrangement establishes a logical organization of the data in the file. Thus, for sequential access, records are arranged in order by a key field prior to being saved on tape or disk, as shown in Figure 11.3.

Sequential access methods are best for situations in which every record must be read and processed. Printing weekly paychecks is a good example of using sequential

11.3

The videotape Inventory file is
organized for sequential access
by tape number.

| Videotape Inventory File | | | | |
| --- | --- | --- | --- | --- |
| Tape Number | Movie ID | Available | Purchase Date | Purchase Price |
| 16827 | 101 | Y | 1/5/93 | $39.75 |
| 16828 | 101 | Y | 1/5/93 | $39.75 |
| 23184 | 113 | Y | 3/5/93 | $42.85 |
| 23185 | 113 | Y | 3/5/93 | $42.85 |
| 23186 | 113 | Y | 3/5/93 | $42.85 |
| 23187 | 113 | Y | 10/5/93 | $42.85 |
| 37611 | 114 | N | 3/17/93 | $35.60 |
| 37612 | 114 | Y | 3/17/93 | $35.60 |
| 39955 | 111 | Y | 4/2/93 | $29.95 |
| 39956 | 111 | Y | 4/2/93 | $29.95 |
| 40012 | 102 | Y | 3/27/88 | $39.75 |
| 40013 | 102 | Y | 3/27/88 | $39.75 |
| 40014 | 102 | Y | 3/27/88 | $39.75 |
| 42137 | 109 | Y | 7/9/93 | $35.60 |
| 42138 | 109 | Y | 7/9/93 | $35.60 |
| 42139 | 109 | Y | 7/9/93 | $35.60 |
| 43765 | 115 | N | 11/12/89 | $29.95 |
| 43766 | 115 | Y | 6/22/90 | $29.95 |
| 44331 | 116 | Y | 11/12/89 | $29.95 |
| 44332 | 116 | N | 11/12/89 | $29.95 |
| 48130 | 103 | Y | 3/5/88 | $42.85 |
| 48131 | 103 | Y | 3/5/88 | $42.85 |

Record: 21   of 65376

access for *batch processing.* When results are not needed on an immediate basis, records can be collected into groups (batches) and processed all at once.

Payroll programs batch-process records in the Employee file to print paychecks and change *(update)* federal and state tax records. Updating involves adding or deleting records to or from a file or modifying existing records. During payroll processing, every employee's record is updated in some way: Either wages and taxes are added to yearly totals, or time is subtracted from sick leave or vacation time. This approach affords a greater level of security, because all the paychecks are printed at one time.

Sequential access is impractical when users cannot predict the order in which records need to be accessed. For instance, video store employees must be able to process videotape rental requests one at a time, in any order. If the store employees sequentially accessed videotape and customer records, it could take an unacceptably long time to find records near the end of the file.

## ■ Direct Access

*Direct access,* also called random access, is possible when data is stored on disk. The computer system uses an index or other technique to identify a record's location within a file. Once the disk location is known, the computer can directly access an individual record without processing other records. This access method uses a key field to identify the record. Disk storage provides fast access to individual records, especially when the order of retrieval cannot be predicted.

To support direct access, an *index,* or index file, is created. The index is based on a specific key field and contains a separate directory that identifies where each record is physically located (see Figure 11.4). To find any record, the computer consults the index, looks up the disk location, then performs a direct access operation.

## 11.4

Indexes allow a record to be directly accessed from a file on disk.

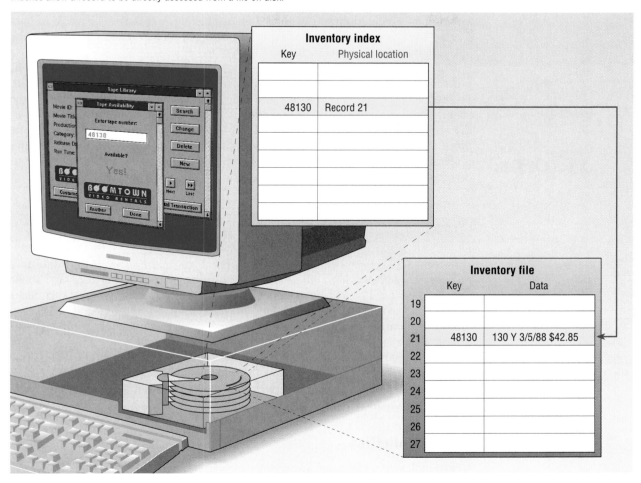

Using an index to access data cuts down on the number of records that are read when searching for a record. It is similar to using the index at the back of this book. When you look up the definition to a "term to remember," the index sends you to a specific page within the book. This allows you to skip over the other pages. Once you get to the page in question, a quick scan of the page reveals the definition. Sequentially searching one page at a time from the beginning of the book would be a lot slower in most cases.

Creating an index does not eliminate sequential access to data, but provides users with the option of directly accessing data when necessary. This versatility is the primary advantage of creating an index. The method of accessing data can be altered according to a user's needs. For example, the video Inventory file would be a prime candidate for an index. Direct access by tape number would expedite individual customer rentals as they occur. But sequential access by tape number would be preferred in preparing monthly inventory reports for the store manager. Thus, indexed files provide the flexibility to meet a wide range of accessing and processing needs.

Another direct access technique employs *linked lists*. When using linked lists, the *disk addresses* of related data become part of a data set. This disk address is the link that identifies where other data is stored on disk. As a result, the data can be widely distributed throughout a high-capacity disk or across disks in a network. Consider a multimedia presentation with related text and images on the history of the Academy Awards. The text describing the winner of the Best Picture award each year would include a linked list to a video clip from the movie. A listing of each Best Soundtrack would be linked to the related musical score.

Direct access supports real-time processing. As the name implies, ***real-time processing*** means the computer system processes a user request as soon as it is input. The user waits only as long as it takes the computer to process the input and output the results. The time between the user's request and the computer's output is referred to as the *response time*. Research has shown that users become impatient with real-time processing when the response time is longer than three seconds. Therefore, computer professionals use direct access techniques when designing systems that require real-time processing.

## DATA MANAGEMENT

Different data processing abilities distinguish file management and database management software. ***File management software*** helps maximize user access to a single data file. Files used by a file management system are often called *flat files*. A flat file is not designed to integrate (combine data) with other data files. File integration is left to ***database management software***. These software packages interconnect the contents of several files for flexible storage and retrieval.

Both database and file management systems have many common features. These data management systems allow users to define field types, validate input data, keep data up-to-date, maintain data security, create reports, and handle individual inquiries about data contained in the database or file.

### ▨ Data Definition

A data management program oversees the physical organization of files on disk, as well as input and output operations. Well-designed software enables users to define, add, delete, and change records efficiently. Normally, users start by using *data definition commands* to identify fields and organize related records.

Teresa Romero is responsible for Boomtown Video's rental data. In some organizations she would be called a ***data administrator***. Her duties include designing files and databases, setting up the rights and responsibilities for accessing data, training employees in proper backup procedures, and evaluating the performance of the store's data management systems.

Teresa uses the *Create* command to identify the fields associated with the Customer file shown in Figure 11.5. In doing so, each field is given a *field name*, sometimes called an attribute name, such as *Customer Number, First Name, Last Name, Address,* or *Photo ID*. The field name refers to the data, but is not data itself. It identifies specific data and is useful when designing data entry forms or report formats. The expected size (number of characters or digits), type of data, and field name for each field become a description of the ***file structure***. At this time Teresa can also establish error checks and identify key fields as part of the file structure.

## 11.5

Field (attribute) names, data types, and data sizes associated with customer records are all identified as part of the file structure.

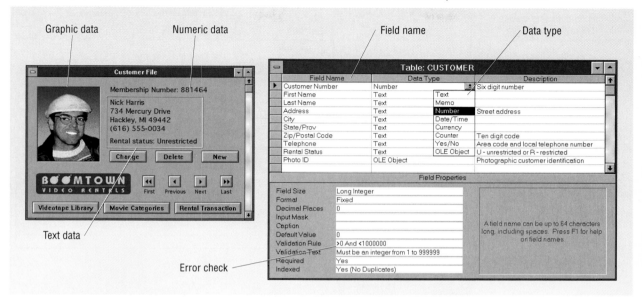

Figure 11.5 shows how common data types could be used within a customer record. The customer number is numeric, with name and address data typed as text. A photograph of the customer is identified as an OLE (object linking and embedding) graphic. Teresa followed these basic design rules when creating the file structure:

♦ Include unique key field. *Example:* Student identification, Social Security number, or customer code.

♦ Don't combine data into one field. *Example:* Name should be divided into several fields, that is, prefix, first name, and last name.

♦ Don't create a field when data can be derived from other data. *Example:* A person's age can be determined using a birthdate field.

♦ Make field length large enough to hold longest data item. *Example:* Set aside 20 characters for the last-name field.

♦ Change field's default format to one that is compatible with the most frequently entered data. *Example:* Financial data formatted with two decimal places.

### ■ Data Manipulation

Teresa is also supervising the training of new store managers in using Boomtown's data. They are learning a command syntax known as the *data manipulation commands.* By training store managers to use the data manipulation commands, Teresa is placing a great deal of control back into the end users' hands. In addition, she is relieving the store's computer professionals of the day-to-day responsibility for maintaining the data. During the training session, Teresa explains how each command performs a critical role in data entry, security, and maintenance.

## 11.6

A filter allows users to display records that meet specific conditions. In this case, movies with a PG13 rating are viewed in a table format.

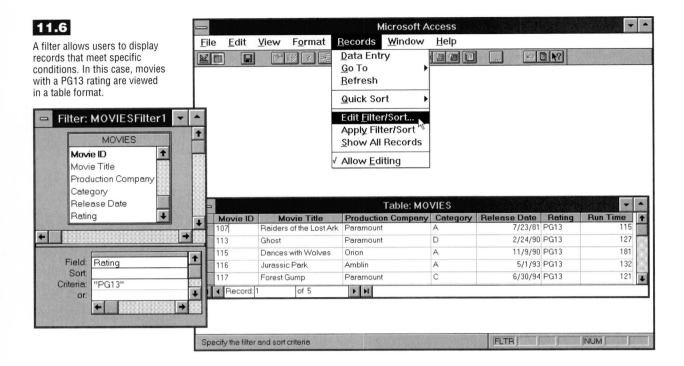

**View** There are a variety of ways to display the contents of a data file. Each is said to be a different *view* of the data. One popular view is in a row-and-column format similar to a worksheet; this *table view* organizes records in rows and lines up common fields in the same column (see Figure 11.6). Usually, the field names are displayed in column headers. In a *record view*, records are displayed one after another with each row containing the contents of a single field and the associated field name, as shown in Figure 11.7. When changes to the field size or type need to be made, the *file structure view* is used. This view is similar to the original screen used with the Create command (see right side of Figure 11.5).

**Find and Go To** The data management program can display records that fit certain logical conditions by using the *Find* command. The store manager might want to look up the current rental status of tape 23184. Given this tape number, the data management software searches the Inventory file and displays the first record that matches. The *Go To* command is used when the user wants to display a record based on its relative location in the file. The user might want to display the first or last record in a file or look at the previous or next record as they occur sequentially in the file.

A store customer might want a list of all the PG13-rated movies currently available (see Figure 11.6). By looking for the characters *PG13* in the Rating field of the Movies file, the data management program could *filter* the display to show only those records that fit the criterion. In this case, only those records in which the Rating field equals "PG13" are displayed. Filtering data is usually limited to records within the same file.

**Append** The *Append* command allows the user to add new records to a file. Most data management packages will provide a data entry screen like the one shown in Figure 11.7, which shows the designated fields. These screens can be customized as necessary. Store

**11.7**

New data is often shown to users using a record view. Data entry screens like these are automatically generated by the data management program or created by a user-developer.

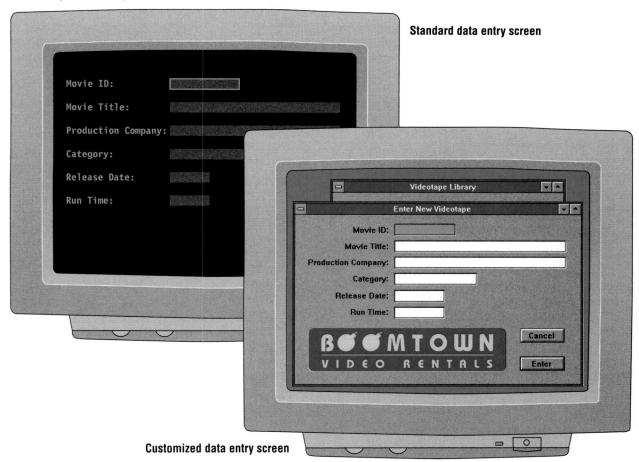

**Standard data entry screen**

Movie ID:

Movie Title:

Production Company:

Category:

Release Date:

Run Time:

Videotape Library

Enter New Videotape

Movie ID:

Movie Title:

Production Company:

Category:

Release Date:

Run Time:

**B
MTOWN**

**V I D E O   R E N T A L S**

Cancel

Enter

**Customized data entry screen**

managers will instruct their staff on the procedures for entering new data into the appropriate fields as new movies are purchased for the store.

**Update**   The staff will change data entries in records with the *Update* command. This operation, for instance, is needed to keep customer data current. Staff members update the Customer file records with new addresses and telephone numbers of customers who have recently moved. Often the data entry screen used for appending new records is also used to update records, because both situations require the display of all the associated fields.

**Sort**   The *Sort* command physically reorders the records in a file by placing data into a sequence defined by the user. The operation is conducted through use of a sort field. This sort field is part of the record and serves as the basis for the sort. For example, movie titles would be a suitable sort field for creating a viewing guide. The sorted file could be used for printing a complete list of movies in alphabetical order by title.

**Index**   The *Index* operation allows users to access records in different key order while maintaining a file's original record sequencing. This task is accomplished by creating an index file that uses the key field to identify a disk address for each record. For example, the Customer file might be maintained in customer number order and indexed by last name and zip code. Because the postal service requires bulk mail to be organized by postal code (zip code), this index is used when printing personalized advertisements. As a result, customer records are processed and mailing labels output in postal code order.

Generally, the difference between sorting and indexing comes down to whether you want to physically reorganize records in the file. If you do, then sort the file using the desired key field to reorder the records. Indexes allow you to keep the current record order, while viewing or printing records in a different order.

**Protect**   Access to data maintained by data management software needs to be controlled. Teresa uses the *Protect* command to assign a password to the Customer file. Once the password is assigned, the user must enter it before the data management software will open the file. In other situations, Teresa can protect a file by designating it as read-only. For instance, one terminal in the store might allow customers access to a read-only Movies file. The customers could see all the movies carried by the store, but they could not change the contents of the file.

## Queries and Application Generators

After the data administrator has defined and created critical files, a customized user interface is developed. Software packages called *application generators* are purchased or provided with the data management system to support this development. Through various menus and graphical tools, a user-developer can design data entry screens, informational screens, and printed reports.

Teresa uses an application generator to develop a user-friendly interface for answering customer questions about movies carried by the video store. The application generator helps her create the icons and data entry prompts the data management system uses to access desired information. Customers will use a touch-sensitive screen to select movies by name, category, run time, or release date.

These requests for movie information are known as queries. A *query* is a user request to a data management system for information. Queries allow users to access, but not change, data. Each screen option created by the video store's application generator activates different predefined queries. Like other user interfaces, queries come in many formats.

**Structured Query Language**   *Structured query language*, or *SQL*, is a popular command-driven interface. It is a set of data manipulation commands consisting of designated keywords. For example, an informed user who wanted to print all adventure movie titles and related categories from records with a run time greater than 120 minutes created this SQL query:

```
SELECT  MovieTitle, Category, Rating, RunTime
FROM    Movies
WHERE   RunTime > 120 and Category = "A"
```

These commands would direct the data management system to search the Movies file for records with a value greater than 120 in the Run Time field and a value in the

**11.8**

Queries by example employ a graphical interface that lets users identify specific fields and conditions. This query lists all movie titles in the adventure category (A) that have run times of more than 120 minutes.

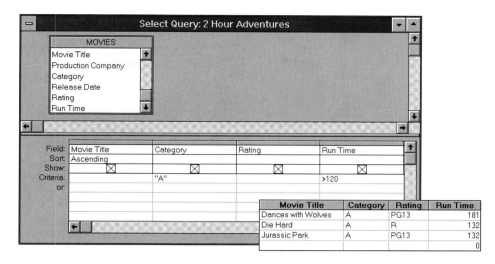

Category field of A. The data management system then displays the movie title, category, rating, and run time held in those selected records. Many programming languages recognize SQL commands, which allows them to be included as program instructions.

**Natural Language Queries**　Some packages enable the user to enter a query in ordinary English. The data management program deciphers the request to initiate processing through use of a *natural language interface.* For example, a video store manager might make the following natural language (English) request:

```
Find all customers who have a tape overdue by more than 5 days.

Print customer names and telephone numbers in sorted order based on
    the telephone number.

Display all the adventure movie titles and ratings that run for more
    than 2 hours.
```

The data management system would translate these requests into computer-executable actions.

**Query by Example**　Data management software with a graphical user interface often employs *query by example (QBE),* as illustrated in Figure 11.8. In this case, the user is requesting a list of all adventure movies with a run time of more than 120 minutes. This is essentially the same request made earlier using SQL. An x in the checkbox marks fields the user wants displayed. Conditions under the field name stipulate search conditions, for example, run times more than 120 minutes and movie category equal to A (adventure).

## ▨ Report Generators

Every data management package and associated application generator should be equipped with capabilities to create hard-copy output. These interfaces are called *report generators.* A report generator interface lets the user modify and design printed documents. Typically, report generators allow users to establish headers, footers, margin widths, pagination, page lengths, and line spacing. Additional report-writing capabilities include printing mailing labels, arranging fields, and making calculations used for report subtotals, totals, and averages.

## DATABASE MANAGEMENT

Many processing activities in an organization are integrated. Data processed in one application might well affect several other applications. Instead of building a file to meet the requirements of a single application, databases are organized for use in multiple applications. A database consists of several related files. Data held in databases appears only once. Key fields are repeated in multiple locations as references to related data items. For each processing job, the data fields needed are identified and accessed through these key field references. This is accomplished with database management software.

Users define data needed for a processing job, and the database program manipulates and controls access to the needed data. The database software also maintains an extensive set of indexes or incorporates linked lists that reflect the interrelationships among data fields.

Duplication of data is avoided in databases, except for keys that tie data fields together. If the video store uses a database program, a movie's title, category, run time, and release date would not be repeated for every copy of the movie maintained by the video store. Instead, each movie would have its own ID and every copy would have a unique tape number. As shown in Figure 11.9, a database management system would integrate the data from two files (Inventory and Movies) in order to avoid data redundancy.

**11.9**

The video store created two files (Inventory and Movies) to promote data integrity within the videotape data. There is a unique tape number for each tape, and movie ID for each movie. Movie information appears only once in the Movies file. Copies of the same movie each have a different tape number and refer to movie data by using the movie ID.

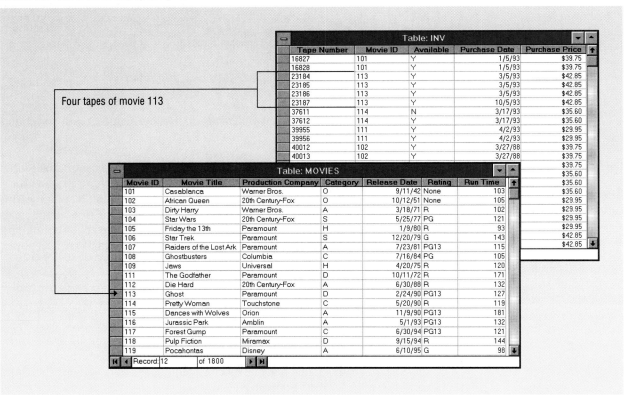

# Dr. Edgar F. Codd

(b. 1923)

The interrelated nature of data had been recognized from the beginning of computing. Before 1970 the most advanced data organizations were hierarchies. Through a series of articles in the 1970s, Dr. Edgar F. Codd presented a new organization—the relational database. Codd's theories had a basis in mathematics, but were so radical for the time that they were met with skepticism. The simplicity of the relational model won over software designers, and relational database management systems (RDBMSs) were made available. In 1985 Codd wrote the guidelines for RDBMSs in the form of 12 rules. They are, in simplified terms, as follows:

1. Data should be presented to the user in table form.

2. Every data element should be accessible without ambiguity.

3. A field should be allowed to remain empty for future use.

4. The description of a database should be accessible to the user.

5. A database must support a clearly defined language to define the database, view the definition, manipulate the data, and restrict some data values to maintain integrity.

6. Data should be able to be changed through any view available to the user.

7. All records in a file must be able to be added, deleted, or changed with a single command.

8. Changes in how data is stored or retrieved should not affect how the user accesses the data.

9. The user's view of the data should be unaffected by its actual form in files.

10. Constraints on user input should exist to maintain data integrity.

11. A database design should allow for distribution of data over several computer sites.

12. Data fields that affect the organization of the database cannot be changed.

This would not be the case for stores using a file management system. Without file integration, every tape record would have to include the movie title and other information, even if the store had four copies (records) of the same movie.

The same is true for rental records within a file management system. Any customer renting several videotapes would have basic information, such as name and telephone number, repeated for each rental. This redundancy of data means that the updating of records is error prone. If a customer moves, the telephone number could be incorrect in several records.

*Data integrity* is critical and it is in jeopardy when redundant data must be updated. A data management system loses its data integrity when one field in one record is updated while related fields in other records remain unchanged. Maintaining data integrity is just one of several problems associated with file processing. Another problem centers on the difficulty in cross-referencing information among the files. Special requests for information residing across several files require the development of new programs or depend on manual processing. As a result, people have come to appreciate the potential knowledge they can gain from integrated data and have begun to demand more sophisticated data management software (see Figure 11.10).

## Database Designs

As people became more experienced in using computer systems, they recognized that relationships existed among all data files connected to the operation of an organization. In all types of organizations—businesses, governments, schools, churches, and volunteer agencies—a global view of the value of data and its many relationships began to take shape. It was seen that each data file represented a small part of an organization's operating cycle. Combined, the data and the relationships among the data items presented a model of the organization, its operations, its status, and its potential.

An integrated set of data files—a database—allows easy cross-referencing of related data items, promotes data integrity, and minimizes data redundancy. Databases are formed, in simple terms, by creating links between files. Sometimes these links are provided by indexes that locate related data in other files. Linked lists and other techniques are also used to integrate data files into a single database.

A database is seen as a useful, interrelated set of files within which individual records and fields are identified and located through the use of data manipulation commands and queries. Each database is built upon a *data model*, or a plan the computer uses for storing and accessing data items. Data models used in building databases fall within four main categories: hierarchical, network, hypermedia, and relational.

These data models handle the relationship between records in files differently. Data relationships, or *cardinality*, are either one-to-one, one-to-many, or many-to-many. In other words, cardinality refers to how a record in a database relates to records in other files. Database models usually incorporate either one-to-many relationships (one videotape rented many times) or many-to-many relationships (many videotapes rented many times).

## Hierarchical Model

A hierarchy is an organization that follows a top-down (or parent/child) structure which represents a series of one-to-many relationships. A typical organization chart for a company presents a hierarchical structure. The highest-ranking executives are

## 11.10

User needs, technical support, and hardware requirements must be considered when purchasing data management software.

### Evaluating Data Management Software

#### USER NEEDS

- ☐ Need to integrate files into a database

**Expected maximums in most sophisticated application**

- _____ fields/record
- _____ records/file
- _____ files/database

**File formats**

- ☐ imports different file formats: _____
- ☐ exports different file formats: _____

**Preferred user interface**

- ☐ command-driven
- ☐ shell (menus)
- ☐ graphical
- ☐ natural language

**Data formats**

- ☐ text: _____
- ☐ numbers: _____
- ☐ graphics: _____
- ☐ images: _____
- ☐ sounds: _____
- ☐ others: _____

**Special utilities**

- ☐ application generator: _____
- ☐ queries: _____
- ☐ report generator: _____
- ☐ Option to save queries and report formats
- ☐ Error correction
  - ☐ checks data integrity of designated fields
  - ☐ customized error checks
- ☐ Data security and password protection
- ☐ Works within network operating environments: 

_____

#### TECHNICAL SUPPORT

- ☐ Local training available
  - ☐ schools: _____

    _____
  - ☐ computer stores: _____

    _____
  - ☐ user groups: _____

    _____
  - ☐ other: _____

    _____
- ☐ Context-sensitive help screens
- ☐ Easy-to-read manual
- ☐ Tutorials for beginners
- ☐ Telephone support
  - ☐ toll-free
  - ☐ at your expense

#### HARDWARE REQUIREMENTS

- ☐ Compatible with your computer

**Minimums**

- _____ memory
- _____ disk space

**Peripheral support**

- ☐ mouse
- ☐ printer
- ☐ color monitor
- ☐ CD-ROM

## 11.11

Hierarchical database models are characterized by a top-down design and structured access paths representing one-to-many data relationships.

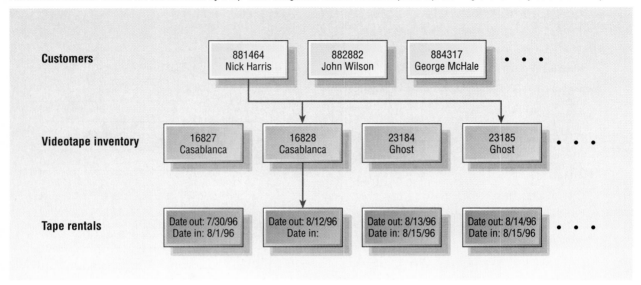

placed at the top of the chart, and relationships with subordinates are shown on a top-down basis.

A *hierarchical model* for a database follows the same principle. Data items and references to those items are related in a top-down structure. For example, the video store might structure a database as shown in Figure 11.11. At the top of this hierarchical model are the customers, at the next level are videotapes rented by the store, followed by tape rentals that connect a customer to specific tapes. One customer can rent many videotapes. In turn, one videotape can be rented many times.

In this instance a hierarchical model makes possible orderly navigation of paths to the desired information through a series of related items. A potential disadvantage is that the same path must be followed for each access operation. Data access operations always begin, in this instance, with the customer. This design is useful if you want to know which tapes a customer has rented. It is less useful if someone wants to find out how many times a specific tape has been rented.

### Network Model

A *network model* resembles a hierarchy in that both contain structured access paths. With a network, however, it is not necessary to follow a top-down order for each access of the database, and multiple access paths are possible between records. As a result, network models usually use linked lists to support these many-to-many relationships. Networks can be entered at different points, with access routes leading in many directions. In the video store example, a network model makes it possible to access rental data by either customer number or tape number, as shown in Figure 11.12. Unlike a hierarchical data model, a network model supports a situation wherein the store can find out which customer rented a specific tape, along with how many times that tape has been rented.

## 11.12

Network database models can access data in a variety of ways using preset access paths representing many-to-many data relationships.

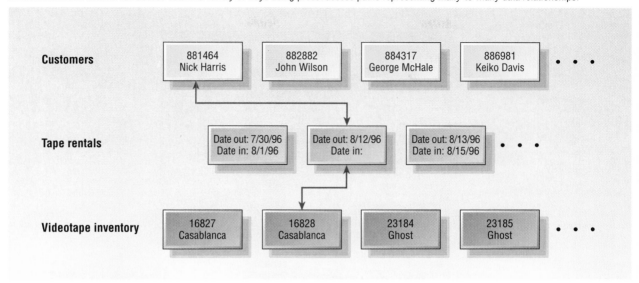

### Hypermedia Model

The Internet's World Wide Web uses a *hypermedia* database model to link related data across interconnected computers. Like a network model, hypermedia supports many-to-many relationships. Object-oriented databases often use a hypermedia model. Multimedia applications are created using hypermedia application generators. Associated data is organized into screen displays called *pages* (records), which incorporate any mix of text, numbers, sound, or graphics. Related pages are grouped together into files, sometimes called *stacks*. When the database is limited to text, it is called ***hypertext***. The Closer Look at the end of this chapter examines hypermedia applications.

Hypermedia users navigate through a file, moving one page at a time. Each page has a unique combination of text, graphics, and/or images that convey information to the user. Hot words or icons identify links to additional information. At any point in the session, users can click on button icons to skip to different pages within the active file or in other files. For example, Figure 11.13 illustrates how hypermedia software can help people select a movie to rent. After selecting a movie, in this case *Gone With the Wind*, information related to actors and awards, as well as video clips or sound samples, are available by activating related hot words or buttons.

### Relational Model

The success of the ***relational database*** model has revolutionized the design and development of database management systems, because it can handle one-to-many and many-to-many relationships. As mentioned in this chapter's Who's Who, Dr. Edgar F. Codd's model employs a series of files organized as data tables. A ***table*** consists of a matrix of columns *(attributes)* and rows *(tuples)* into which data can be placed. The

**11.13**

Hypermedia users navigate through stacks one page at a time or jump to additional information by clicking on hot words, icons, or list box options.

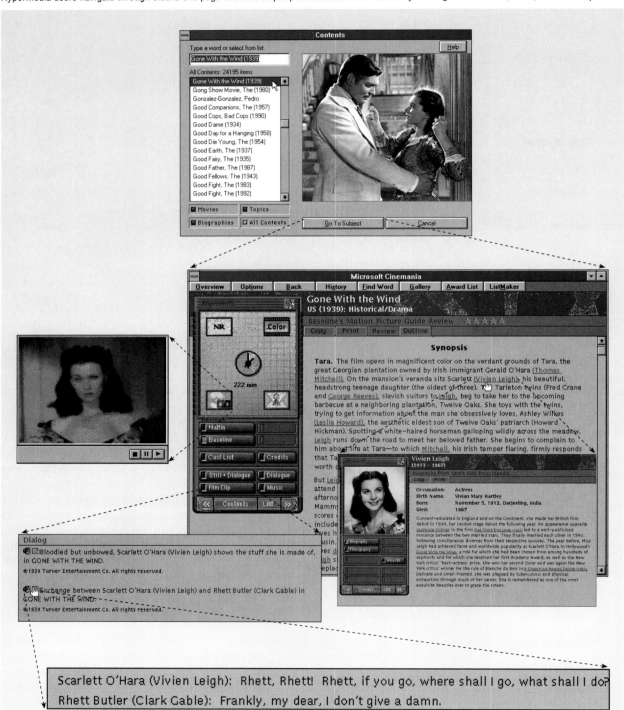

**11.14**

Relational database models allow flexible access to data by integrating data tables (files) using common data fields. In this model the Customer Number field links data from the Customer and Rentals tables. The Tape Number field links the Rentals and Inventory tables, and the Movie ID field links the Inventory and Movies tables.

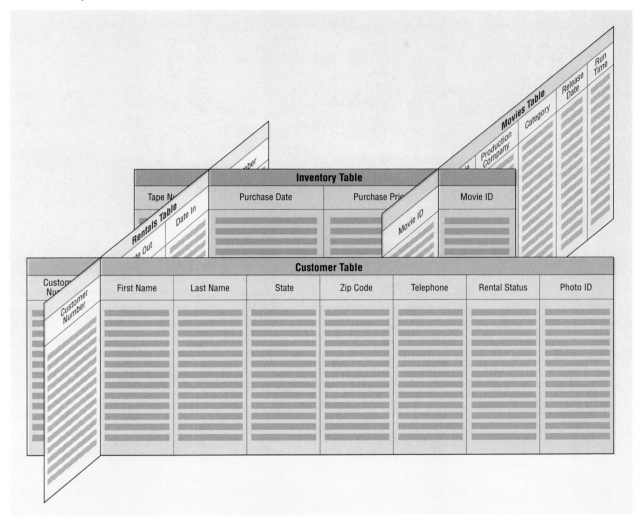

example in Figure 11.14 contains the tables used by Boomtown Video Rentals. Each table is divided into a series of columns that represent data fields and rows that represent records.

To implement a relational model, a series of relationships or tables would be established for each of two or more sets of data. Common fields establish relations between two tables. To support videotape rentals, for example, there would be relations for each movie, tape, customer, and rental. These tables would interconnect, using the Movie ID, Tape Number, and Customer Number fields to form multiple relations, as illustrated in Figure 11.14.

To support the queries that access data from different tables, users of relational database management software utilize some variation of the Select command.

## ...ABOUT BACKUP TIPS

- Keep multiple copies—redundancy is key to a good backup strategy

- Test backups frequently

- Store backups in a secure off-site location

- Replace tapes regularly with fresh ones

- Perform incremental backups of critical data throughout the day

**Select**    The *relational database management system (RDBMS)* retrieves records that fit certain logical conditions under the *Select* command. For example, the video store manager might want a list of the dates that the currently rented tapes left the store. Furthermore, the list is to include the customer's name and telephone number.

```
SELECT  DateOut from Rentals,
        FirstName from Customer using CustomerNumber,
        LastName from Customer using CustomerNumber,
        Telephone from Customer using CustomerNumber
WHERE
        DateIn is blank
```

The RDBMS needs to display data from the Rentals and Customer tables with the Customer Number field serving as the link between the two. If the Date In field in the Rentals table is blank (tape is still out), the RDBMS displays the associated Date Out. The customer's name and telephone number are also displayed by using the related fields from the Customer table.

A RDBMS and related application generators have other capabilities beyond those available to file management packages. These commands create new relationships by combining data into new tables.

**Project**    The *Project* (pronounced "pra-'jekt") command is used to create an abbreviated version of an existing database table. In a relational database, certain columns of a data table are copied, or projected, into a new table. For example, data related to movies within the adventure category could be projected into a new Adventure Movies table.

It should be pointed out here that the difference between the Select and Project commands centers on the creation of a new table. The Select command usually displays data from different tables but does not create a new table. The Project command creates a new table.

**11.15**

The Join command links data from different tables to create a new table of common elements.

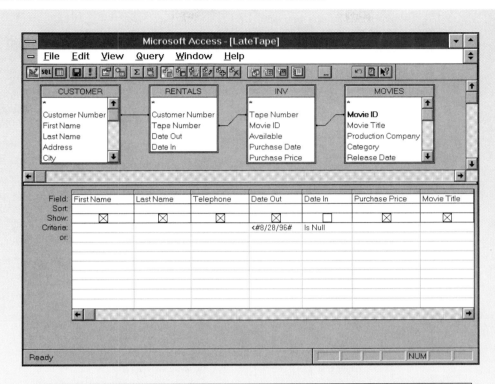

**Join** Portions of multiple files can be brought together into a single file through use of the *Join* command. In Figure 11.15 the Late Tape table is created by joining elements from the Customer, Rentals, Inventory, and Movie tables. The Date Out field comes from the Rentals table; the customer name and telephone number are supplied by the Customer table. When the Date In field in the Rentals table is empty (null), the tape is still out, and the Movie Title field from the Movies table is joined to the Late Tape table. The Purchase Price field from the Inventory table is used to compute the replacement cost.

**Subtract** Relational database programs have a *Subtract* command that compares two tables and creates a third table containing the uncommon elements. If the Rentals table is subtracted from the Customer table, the resulting table contains a list of customers that do not have a match in the Rentals table. Any customer names isolated by the use of the Subtract command identify customers who have not recently rented videotapes. If the Rentals table includes videotape rentals for the past year, the store manager might want to follow up on the status of these customers.

**11.16**

When properly designed, databases expand as users' needs grow while providing them with easy access to a wide range of related information.

## Pros and Cons of Database Processing

### Pros

- Allows users easy cross-referencing of related data items

- Promotes data integrity by eliminating data redundancy

- Once a database is in place, application generators help reduce the cost of new user interfaces

- Application generators also reduce time to develop new user interfaces

### Cons

- It takes time to develop integrated database files

- Users need expertise with application and database design

- Multiuser systems need security procedures and precautions

## Pros and Cons of Database Processing

A database can be difficult and expensive to create. The time it takes to customize software, the need for database design expertise, and the cost to set up and maintain a database are its main drawbacks. Before anyone undertakes the job of building a database, the potential advantages should be weighed against the costs (Figure 11.16).

Database systems working on a network with multiple users need established precautions and security measures. Access to confidential data should be password-protected, and care must be taken to ensure the data integrity of key fields. Procedures must exist that eliminate problems associated with *concurrent updates*. A concurrent update occurs when two users try to make changes to the same record at the same time. Problems like this result in two customers both being promised the same inventory item. This problem is avoided by having the database management software lock out (prevent access to) other users while a record is being updated.

The main advantage offered by a database is, perhaps, reduction in the cost of developing new applications. Once the database is in place, application generators make it easy to generate queries or reports. Procedures for creating new computer applications are covered in chapter 13. At this point the important factors are, first, to recognize that application development can be time-consuming and costly. The second factor is that most of the cost of application development lies in writing special programs to build, maintain, and access those files. If database management software and a workable application generator are in place, most of the costs of file design and data access programs are eliminated.

Another important advantage of a database lies in reduction of data redundancy. When each application is supported by its own files, it is inevitable that some data content will be duplicated. This means procedures must be established so that all occurrences of a data item are updated with each transaction that affects the item. As mentioned earlier, when a video store customer moves, the address must be updated in several files when a file management system is used. This adds cost and complexity to computer operations. Any failure to update a data item reduces the reliability of an organization's computer resources. However, if the video store uses a database, the address needs to be changed only once.

In the days when most databases had to be assembled entirely from scratch, costs could be difficult to justify. Today there are literally scores of user-friendly application generators that work with reliable database management software. Such software reduces costs and efforts, making databases practical for most computer users.

## APPLICATIONS FOR DATA MANAGEMENT SOFTWARE

You will find that data management systems are the heart and soul of any information system application. Some of these applications can be managed by using personal computer systems. A small business might use a personal computer to maintain inventory and customer records similar to Boomtown Video's system. In other situations, more complex multiuser applications, often related to organizational or public databases, work within computer networks. Airline flight schedules or census statistics fall into this category.

Keep in mind that data management is an important part of modern society. The following sections review some of the most prominent uses for file and database management systems.

### Education

Data management systems work behind the scenes to help teachers and administrators keep student records up-to-date. Schools, from elementary to college level, maintain files and databases to keep track of business functions as well as academic records. Data files for inventory and payroll keep these institutions functioning efficiently.

Teachers can use file management programs on PCs to store student grades and test questions. Test-generating software can select problems and assignments at random from a test bank, or teachers can pick specific questions. Along with the test, the software can develop matching answer keys. Thus, a teacher equipped with a file management system is able to vary test materials with ease. In addition, database software allows teachers to track individual student progress through course materials. By integrating test results with course objectives, database software can create individualized feedback sheets for students. These sheets would identify study materials to review, based on test results.

Counselors use computers to help students determine occupational and academic preferences. Large databases hold volumes of information about educational and experience requirements for a variety of jobs. By tying into these databases, counselors can direct students to careers that match their skills and goals. If a student decides to pursue a further educational degree, another database can help locate scholarship and loan programs.

## Public Health

At many hospitals and clinics, computers decrease the time doctors and other professionals often spend in recording patient information and health histories. Patients provide information at computer terminals under prompting from the computer. These entries are incorporated into a patient history file that enables a medical professional to spend more time with patients and less time writing information into files. When these history files are incorporated into the hospital's database management system, they support medical diagnosis (see Figure 11.17), laboratory analysis, and even patient billing.

Pharmacies use computers to keep track of drug-dispensing activities. Prescription records entered into computers can be found quickly for responses to inquiries or for refilling prescriptions. In addition, some databases contain information that helps pharmacists spot potential problems with interactions between newly prescribed drugs and medications that a patient may already be taking.

Public health officials use databases to store and analyze data concerning new diseases and to monitor potential epidemics. Researchers at the Centers for Disease Control, for example, collect data from medical specialists around the country. With the help of database programs, the researchers can keep current on health dangers and suggested treatments.

Another use for databases in public health is the nationwide Poison Control Center. The center keeps a database containing information on poisons and their antidotes. Most household products, such as cleaners and medicines, are found in this database. A database program's ability to cross-reference information allows it to access antidotes, based on the brand name or contents of a product. Using data communication software, an emergency center in any state can call the Poison Control Center.

**11.17**

During an emergency, health professionals can access a hospital's database to help relate patient symptoms to similar cases and medical histories.

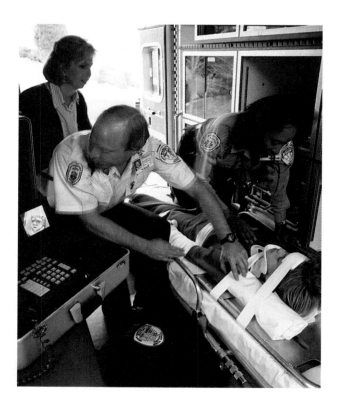

## Law Enforcement

Police officers, FBI agents, attorneys, and judges all use databases in performing their jobs. Some databases store a vast amount of data about criminal, civil, and contract law. One of the largest law enforcement databases is run by the FBI's National Crime Information Center (NCIC). The NCIC database stores data on crimes, criminals, victims, and stolen property. State law enforcement agencies can query the NCIC system whenever they need information. They also can add data to the system. This and other information, such as fingerprint images, can be shared by officers and court officials across the country.

Some police officers access databases from their patrol cars. A license plate number, for example, is a key field. The officer enters queries that determine if the car and/or its owner are listed in databases that keep track of stolen cars or "wants and warrants." Responses to the queries let an officer know whether to expect danger in connection with an arrest or when approaching a suspect (see Figure 11.18).

Courts use databases to help judges, legal secretaries, and clerks perform their jobs. The text of a state and/or municipal legal code can be stored in a database and searched for legal precedents or references. Case information and court decisions also are retained in online databases. Other data management systems organize and track information related to court scheduling and inventory evidence.

**11.18**

Access to databases by on-duty law enforcement officers provides immediate access to "wants and warrants," which helps them prepare and protect themselves.

**11.19**

As a car is developed, part specifications are entered into a database that production and servicepeople can access for the life of the product.

## Automotive Repair

In some cases, file and database management systems are replacing small libraries of reference materials. When you take your car for a tune-up, your mechanic could be using a computer-based reference search to check part numbers and engine specifications (see Figure 11.19). Easy access to information on many models of cars makes these systems ideal for mechanics who service a wide variety of vehicles. In addition, these electronic manuals are easily updated by the manufacturer and require less storage space than printed manuals. The U.S. Navy claims it has made some of its warships more than 2,000 pounds lighter by replacing paper copies of manuals with the electronic equivalent.

## Libraries

Databases have found their way into libraries with reference searches (see Figure 11.20). Here computers can search through large databases composed of titles, authors, and subject descriptions by looking for keywords. For example, several library services allow students to search a database for any book or article containing the words *computer-based training* in the title.

**11.20**

Library services are supported by database programs that control patron records and lending activities and perform reference searches.

Hundreds of hours in research time can be saved by having the computer do the initial search through the literature. Although this service is expensive with specialized databases, it can be cost beneficial if the right keywords are used. On the other hand, someone doing a report on computer literacy who uses just the keyword *computer* will be no better off than before. The books and articles containing that keyword would fill a small library.

## ■ Agriculture

Farmers use data management systems to keep livestock records. Original costs, identification, maintenance costs, births, losses due to death, and selling prices are data fields contained in a record assigned to each animal. The data management system maintains individual records of animals and organizes this information for many uses. For example, a farmer might wish to compare original costs with selling prices for all livestock during a specified period. By identifying a few key fields, the farmer can instruct the data management program to locate and display the desired information quickly and easily.

Farmers also keep records on livestock and poultry breeding, which contain genealogies over multiple generations. This data, in turn, helps scientists and farmers to breed desirable traits into herds or flocks. Examples include milk yield from dairy cows, rapid growth in chickens, large breast in turkeys, and other characteristics.

Some breeding cooperatives have data management programs to track selected breeds of livestock. Data files on thoroughbred horses, beef and dairy cattle, and other livestock make up different databases.

# A Closer Look at Hypermedia

**Many of the advantages** of marrying computer and communication technologies are incorporated into new applications being developed for software that uses a hypermedia database model. To illustrate a practical use for hypermedia, let's surf the Internet's World Wide Web (WWW) and plan a trip to Paris, France.

**Q: Who uses hypermedia?**

**A:** Anyone with a need to explore options or learn more about a subject is a potential user of hypermedia. This would include businesspeople, students, travel agents, and workers learning about new equipment. People using "the Web" are hypermedia users.

**Q: What kind of information can you get?**

**A:** Information found in a hypermedia file (stack) is limited only by the imagination of the designer. Our trip to Paris starts with a map of network servers in Europe. This page provides links to maps of major cities, points of interest, lodging, and restaurants. The hypermedia software indexes each file on a starting screen, or *home page,* the user initially sees.

**Q: How do you navigate through all the stacks of information?**

**A:** Users navigate through the hypermedia pages by highlighting buttons, using the keyboard or a mouse. When available, arrows buttons usually take the user sequentially through the active file, one page at a time. Different-colored *hot words* directly access related information found on different pages or in other files.

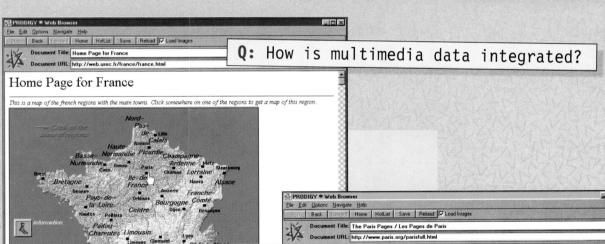

**Q: How is multimedia data integrated?**

**A:** Items from list boxes, buttons, and hot words all serve as links to different types of data. For example, clicking on the information button could link the user with an annotated map of the city, marking different places of interest.

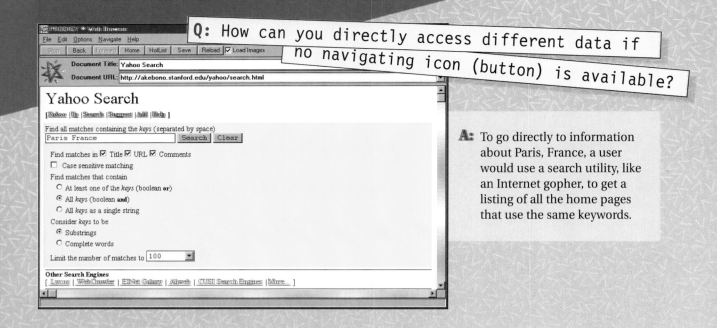

**A:** To go directly to information about Paris, France, a user would use a search utility, like an Internet gopher, to get a listing of all the home pages that use the same keywords.

Q: How do you acquire hypermedia files?

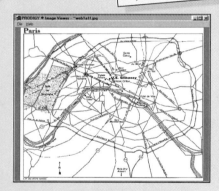

**A:** Although hypermedia files are available for purchase to users with enough disk space and money, many of the best files are open to the public. Public access to the Internet's World Wide Web provides a wide array of data to informed users.

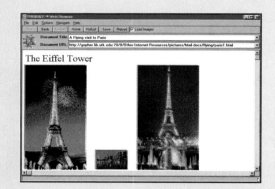

Q: Can people develop their own pages and files?

**A:** Interested user-developers can change text, create new line art, and link new pages to a file using the Hypertext Markup Language (HTML) discussed in chapter 8. Word processing software that supports HTML is used to create new files.

## CHAPTER FACTS

■ Data can be retrieved from both disks and tapes by using sequential access, but only from disks when using direct access.

■ Indexes and linked lists allow users to directly access data from disk.

■ Batch processing supports sequential access, whereas real-time processing relies on direct access techniques.

■ File management systems access one file at a time, which makes requests for information residing in multiple files more difficult to obtain. Duplicate data across files can also create problems of loss of data integrity.

■ In databases, files are linked by common key fields. This eliminates data redundancy and allows access by multiple application programs.

■ Data management software creates a file's structure through data definition commands, organizes data through data manipulation commands, and allows queries to be made through different user interfaces.

■ Data manipulation commands allow the user to control files through View, Find, Go To, Append, Update, Sort, Index, and Protect operations.

■ Application and report generators help users create data entry screens, queries, and printed documents.

■ A data model reflects the cardinality a computer system uses when storing and accessing data items.

■ Databases can be organized into one of four models: hierarchical, network, hypermedia, or relational.

■ Multimedia applications combined with data management techniques are incorporated into hypermedia application generators.

■ Relational database programs can create new tables by using Project, Join, and Subtract operations.

■ Databases reduce time and costs for developing new applications while eliminating data redundancy. They can be expensive and difficult to set up.

■ Data integrity is critical when data management systems are accessed by multiple users.

■ Database programs are useful in many areas including education, medicine and public health, law, agriculture, and reference systems.

## TERMS TO REMEMBER

| | | |
|---|---|---|
| application generator | file management software | query by example (QBE) |
| batch processing | file structure | real-time processing |
| data administrator | filter | relational database |
| data integrity | hypertext | report generator |
| data model | index | sequential access |
| database management | key | table |
|    software | query | update |
| direct access | | |

## MIX AND MATCH

*Complete the following definitions with the Terms to Remember.*

1. The field used to identify a record in a file is called the _____.

2. The _____ is a description of a data file (or table) that includes for each field an attribute name, data type, error checks, and expected size.

3. A user request for information is called a(n) _____.

4. _____ refers to processing data in groups.

5. A characteristic of a data file whereby every data field is accurate and properly identified is referred to as _____.

6. A(n) _____ is an independent file within a relational database.

7. _____ creates, stores, and accesses integrated data files.

8. To _____ is to add, change, or delete data in a file.

9. _____ means finding one record without processing other records.

10. _____ maximizes access to a flat file.

11. The individual responsible for an organization's data is the _____.

12. A(n) _____ is a separate file based on a key field, which identifies the location of a record within a data file.

13. The interface for designing and modifying printed documents is a(n) _____.

14. _____ means finding an individual record by looking at one record at a time.

15. Data organized into tables and integrated by joining the tables constitutes a(n) _____.

## REVIEW QUESTIONS

1. Define the Terms to Remember.

2. What types of storage media are used with sequential and direct access methods?

3. How is the key field used when sequentially accessing a record and when directly accessing a record?

4. What type of access methods are used with batch processing and real-time processing?

5. Why are flat files associated with file management software?

6. What features do file management and database management systems have in common?

7. What are four responsibilities of a data administrator?

8. Explain the function of the Create, View, Find, Go To, Append, Update, Sort, Index, Protect, Select, Project, Join, and Subtract commands.

9. What type of user interfaces are represented by the structured query language and query by example?

10. Identify five document design features a report generator handles.

11. How can a database lose its data integrity?

12. What are two disadvantages of file processing?

13. Identify the cardinality of the hierarchical, network, hypermedia, and relational database models.

14. What are four advantages of using a database and three potential disadvantages?

15. How do school administrators, teachers, and counselors use file and database management?

16. In what ways can access to a database help doctors, pharmacists, and public health officials?

17. Explain how police officers, FBI agents, and judges utilize file and database management programs to perform their jobs.

18. How can a data management system help an automotive repair technician?

19. How could the use of a reference search help you in school?

20. How does a hypermedia user navigate through the cards in a stack?

## APPLYING WHAT YOU'VE LEARNED

1. Describe two applications (not in the text) for each type of access method: sequential and direct. Include the fields in a typical record and identify an appropriate key field.

2. Use one of the database models described in the text to organize the data that would be needed in one of these applications. Make a general diagram of the data relationships as shown in the text.
   a. recording flights in and out of a local airport
   b. accessing a student database by student number, name, or major
   c. sending advertising to credit card customers based on the types of purchases they make
   d. setting up a reference search system in a library
   e. creating a reference manual for a new motorcycle

3. Several database programs exist for use on microcomputers. Information about them can be obtained from computer magazines and retail stores. Investigate one of these programs. Report on the commands it includes, type of model (if known) it uses, its memory requirements, how much data it can hold, and its cost. Find out if classes or tutorials are available to train users.

4. Write a natural language command that would produce the following data:
   a. list of drivers with expired licenses
   b. list of voters who voted in the last local election
   c. list of library patrons with overdue books
   d. names of salespeople who earned more than $1,000 in commissions last month
   e. list of employees within a year of retirement

5. Multimedia applications using hypermedia have incredible potential. Describe an application for hypermedia. What type of graphics, images, and sounds would be integrated with text and numbers? How would the stacks be organized? Draw a sample home page and identify the different types of data used on-screen.

# Information Systems

**W**hen the components of a computer system are thoughtfully combined, they facilitate the sharing of information and support decision making. Chapter 12 discusses how managers in any organization can sharpen their decision-making skills by using knowledge derived from computer systems. Applications for management information systems and decision support systems are examined from a user's perspective.

Careful planning must accompany the design of any computer system. In chapter 13, different approaches to developing and upgrading computer systems are overviewed. This chapter emphasizes that users should be involved in the identification and evaluation of system requirements, as well as provided adequate training. In addition, chapter 13 stresses the responsibilities of the computer professionals who design system components and organize implementation strategies.

An important part of system design and implementation revolves around the creation of computer programs. Chapter 14 examines the choices computer programmers make between writing new software and modifying existing programs. Design techniques for creating new programs and several of the most common programming languages are discussed. Maintenance is presented as an ongoing operation necessary for the long life of any program and associated computer system.

# Management and Decision Support Systems

**M**anagement, its theories, and its tools are found not only in the world of business; any organization, from a large corporation or government agency to a school, church, or volunteer service, requires information to control resources and achieve goals.
Information technology can help you plan, organize, direct, and control activities when you are in a position to manage people. Although computers do not provide the answer to every problem, information technology is a powerful tool for effective decision making.
By accessing complete, correct, and timely data, you can integrate past performance with today's solutions and plans for the future.

## MANAGEMENT INFORMATION SYSTEMS

The success of any organization is strongly dependent on information. Management's role is to use this information to plan events, solve problems, and supervise people. Daily activities provide much of the data from which useful information is derived—for example, the number of meals served (restaurant), types of sales made (auto parts store), or location of emergency calls (fire station). A *management information system (MIS)* is the collection of both computerized and manual systems which provides information about ongoing activities to an organization's decision makers. Whether they know it or not, all organizations have an MIS, although the level of sophistication can vary widely. The billing information of a self-employed accountant is part of an MIS. So is the employee database of a multinational corporation. A business's annual report, a school's student list, or the telephone tree for a volunteer agency are all important parts of an MIS for their respective organizations.

**12.1**

An MIS does not require a computer—only the collection, organization, and dissemination of information.

Look again at the definition of MIS. Although it is a collection of systems, it does not necessarily include a computer. An MIS can be composed entirely of data, procedures, and personnel. Computer hardware and programs need not be involved (Figure 12.1).

Records kept by hand constituted the early MISs. Important data was stored in ledger books, spreadsheets, and card files. The expansion of large government programs such as Social Security and Medicaid increased demand over the years for information by the government and decision makers. The advent of computers allowed people to solve such burgeoning information problems by organizing data into files and databases on tape and disk.

File processing systems, discussed in chapter 11, were a partial solution to this organization problem, but using separate files made it difficult for managers to obtain related data and keep it updated. Many organizations now use database programs to integrate their data files and plot data relationships, making information more accessible.

The extent of computer involvement in an MIS varies with the size and purpose of an organization. Some use database programs exclusively whereas others still keep data by hand. This chapter focuses on the role of computers in a management information system.

## People Using Management Information

The management of many business areas needs information to operate effectively. Administration, counseling, engineering, accounting, manufacturing, marketing, education, personnel, public health, and sales are all information-intensive activities, requiring management decisions.

## 12.2

Management decision making addresses different goals and concerns as problems are solved at different management levels.

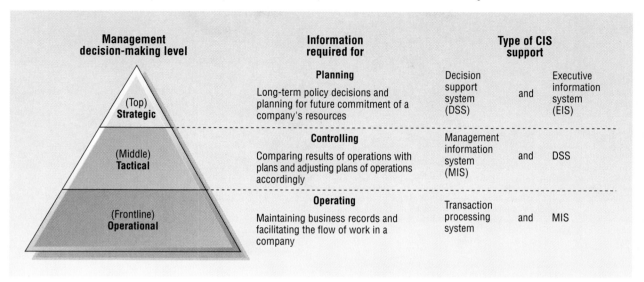

| Management decision-making level | Information required for | Type of CIS support |
|---|---|---|
| **(Top) Strategic** | **Planning** Long-term policy decisions and planning for future commitment of a company's resources | Decision support system (DSS) and Executive information system (EIS) |
| **(Middle) Tactical** | **Controlling** Comparing results of operations with plans and adjusting plans of operations accordingly | Management information system (MIS) and DSS |
| **(Frontline) Operational** | **Operating** Maintaining business records and facilitating the flow of work in a company | Transaction processing system and MIS |

The amount of detail required in computer-generated information varies with the scope of decision making to be supported. Some management decisions demand immediate attention, yet are short-term in nature, requiring highly detailed information. Large-scale decisions having long-term effects on the organization usually are supported by less-detailed information covering a broader range of interest.

For example, a retail store supervisor responsible for the sporting goods department may receive and use detailed computer output showing every sale of equipment sorted by model and size. A store manager working at the next management level might want to know only the total sales figure for a single department compared to other departments and total sales for the entire store. At this level the information is used to determine how much space to allocate for an individual department and to decide upon the size of its staff and the value of its stock.

At the main office of a store chain, upper-level management may require only summaries of storewide figures. The job of top managers is to monitor overall profitability, so an executive may not need to know what is happening in individual departments. In this sense, the content of the information is far less detailed. The scope of the information, however, is far greater and may involve hundreds of stores.

This comparison highlights the value of information as a management tool. Problem-solving tools, including computers, should be used to match information with the responsibilities of the individual and the decisions to be made. The example of management requirements in the department store situation identifies three levels at which management occurs and decisions are made (see Figure 12.2):

**Frontline Management**   The department supervisor has responsibility for the day-to-day support of transactions in a single department. In this *frontline management* position, all of the person's attention is focused on a single organizational unit. The manager has time to digest and react to highly detailed information.

**12.3**

Operational decisions about daily
activities are made by frontline
management.

**Middle Management**   The manager of the entire store would be considered *middle management*. The middle manager is responsible for evaluating the performance of each supervisor, meeting store sales goals, and keeping inventories at reasonable levels. Intermediate levels of detail are required by middle management. For example, a store manager receives information on departmental sales levels but would not need detailed listings of each sales transaction.

**Top Management**   The president and other high-level decision makers of the store chain are part of the organization's *top management*, or *executives*. These people make few short-term decisions on daily operations. Instead, decisions by top management have far greater consequences. Executives decide where and when to open new stores or to close existing outlets, and what kinds of products and services are to be offered by the chain as a whole. For example, is it profitable for the department store chain to operate garden shops, automotive service centers, or travel agencies? The people at the top management level are charged, broadly, with determining the mission and strategy of the organization.

The three managerial levels require different types and amounts of management information as depicted by the pyramid in Figure 12.2. The frontline managers, at the base of the pyramid, make *operational decisions*, which involve the high-volume, detailed data of everyday transactions and weekly trends. Current and accurate data is required for a supervisor to make daily operational decisions (see Figure 12.3).

Middle managers make *tactical decisions*. The activities and operational decisions of frontline management are summarized to provide a broader scope of information with less detail. This information is used by middle management to make short-term tactical decisions that impact how, when, and where an organization's resources are used (see Figure 12.4).

*Strategic decisions* are made by those managers at the top of the organizational pyramid. Information resulting from lower-level decisions is summarized and interpreted

**12.4**

Middle management makes tactical decisions about short-term problems.

before it reaches this strategic level. Executives, then, use information that is low in volume yet broad in scope to make long-term strategic decisions with wide-ranging effects. Decisions that make an impact on the whole organization—such as relocating stores, shifting the marketing focus to a new audience, and modifying personnel requirements—are matters left to top management (see Figure 12.5).

   Decisions made and information generated by a level of management affects other managers in the organization. The main job of strategic managers is to plan what is to become of the organization. Lower levels of management implement these

**12.5**

Top management makes long-term decisions causing wide-ranging effects.

strategic decisions. Operational frontline managers deal with today's problems, while middle managers make tactical decisions about this month's stock levels or next season's products. Data generated by all management levels is used to help evaluate previous decisions.

This examination of management levels used the example of a department store, but similar levels exist in most organizations. Decision makers in a manufacturing plant would include a shift supervisor (frontline management), plant manager (middle management), and company president or CEO (top management). A university has faculty, department chairpeople, and deans to represent the three management levels. Each management level may include a variety of decision makers. In a factory, frontline management would involve foremen as well as shift supervisors. Top management of a university is made up of deans, the board of trustees, and a president. Management information systems must be designed to support all levels of decision making.

It is becoming more common to find a new position at the top of an organization's management—the *chief information officer (CIO)*. This executive is responsible not only for the computing facilities in an organization, but for all the data collection and organization, along with all information dissemination in the MIS. The CIO would make strategic decisions about large-scale information use such as establishing organization-wide networks, setting information security policy, or deciding if a client/server network design is needed. Just like other top managers, the CIO bases decisions on summaries of information generated by other management levels.

## Data for Management Information

Management information systems involve more than just management; of equal importance is the information. Information is gathered during different parts of a transaction cycle. The *transaction cycle* is the input, processing, output, and storage of a single transaction in an organization. A system that oversees this process is known as a ***transaction processing system***. Whether completing a single customer order, manufacturing one car, or registering a single student, processing each of these transactions generates data for the MIS. The transaction processing system collects and organizes the day-to-day activities of an organization and it is the foundation of any MIS.

To aid in organizing information gathered by the MIS, an organization can divide data into four general areas: financial, personnel, research, and production/sales. As shown in Figure 12.6, each type of data can be subdivided even further, depending on the organization.

*Financial data* includes information on how the organization's resources translate into money. Reports on an organization's profit and loss, assets and liabilities, and other resources of value would result from use of financial data.

Management of human resources would provide *personnel data*. Not only a list of employees, but figures on their productivity, absenteeism, and retirement may be important to all levels of decision makers.

*Research data* includes analysis of past performance and plans for future projects. For example, stores research customer satisfaction, volunteer agencies investigate sources of future funding, and colleges review student recruitment plans and how to improve them.

*Production/sales data* involves information about the actual products made, products sold, or services provided. Manufacturing plants would maintain data on inventory levels and raw material orders. Organizations that are service oriented—such

**12.6**

Data incorporated into an organization's MIS covers finances, personnel, research, and productivity.

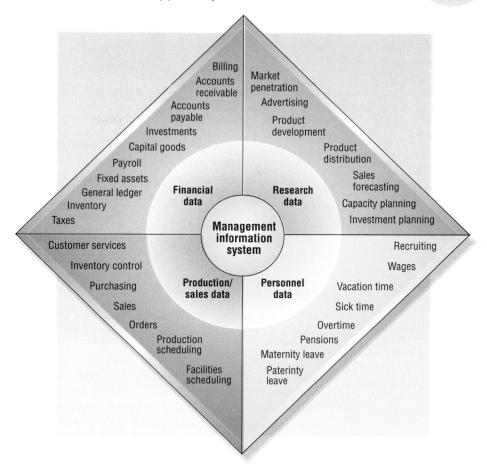

Billing
Accounts receivable
Accounts payable
Investments
Capital goods
Payroll
Fixed assets
General ledger
Inventory
Taxes

Market penetration
Advertising
Product development
Product distribution
Sales forecasting
Capacity planning
Investment planning

**Financial data**

**Research data**

**Management information system**

Customer services
Inventory control
Purchasing
Sales
Orders
Production scheduling
Facilities scheduling

**Production/ sales data**

**Personnel data**

Recruiting
Wages
Vacation time
Sick time
Overtime
Pensions
Maternity leave
Paterinty leave

as schools, churches, volunteer agencies, or travel agencies—would have production/ sales data measuring the number of people served and how they were helped.

## Organizing Data into Reports

A successful MIS must not only collect and organize the data but provide the variety of reports critical to each management level. Effective reports are designed to reflect the types of data needed for each type of decision made. Reports can be either scheduled for routine production or available on demand. The presentation of information in reports differs with the types of problems at management levels. Report formats generally fall into one of three categories: detailed, summary, and exception reports.

**Detailed Reports**   Frontline management uses *detailed reports* to examine day-to-day operations. A detailed report that lists students enrolled in a class may be used daily by a teacher. Each student's name and number are displayed on a separate line of the report.

Detailed reports usually contain one printed line for each item or record in the database or file. By using a detailed report, the department store supervisor can examine the status of each item sold in the department. The report in Figure 12.7 contains the description of items, stock on hand, stock on order, and sales. With this information, the supervisor can make operational decisions about what stock to reorder or which merchandise to discontinue.

**12.7**

Detailed reports provide frontline managers with specific data needed for day-to-day decisions.

page 2

**BEST BARGAIN STORES, INC.**
**Detailed Inventory Report**
**(5/16/96)**
**Department: Sports Equipment (32)**

| Number | Product Description | Stock On Hand | Stock On Order | Stock Below Reorder Point |
|--------|---------------------|---------------|----------------|---------------------------|
| 1101 | Leather Basketball | 12 | 0 | |
| 1102 | Leather Football | 3 | 5 | * |
| 1103 | 8 ft. Jump Rope | 21 | 0 | |
| 1104 | 12 ft. Jump Rope | 15 | 0 | |
| 1105 | Tennis Balls (3/pkg.) | 35 | 50 | * |
| . | . | . | . | . |
| . | . | . | . | . |
| . | . | . | . | . |

**Summary Reports**   When large amounts of data need to be analyzed, it is not usually necessary to see all of it at one time. A *summary report* is useful in such situations because it condenses day-to-day operational data into totals and averages.

By comparing trends in summarized data, some tactical and strategic decisions can be made. Summary reports that show total store sales over several years help department store executives decide when to close or expand certain stores. A university department chairperson can prepare a request for additional facilities by looking at summaries of classroom and lab use (see Figure 12.8).

**Exception Reports**   *Exception reports,* like summary reports, result from analysis of data. Comparisons are used to produce exception reports, which identify departures from normal operations or contain only the data that meets specified conditions.

**12.8**

This summary report encapsulates data related to the utilization of dozens of rooms over an entire day.

**WHATSAMATTA UNIVERSITY**
**Summary of Facility Daytime Utilization Report**
**Date: November 8, 1996**
**Building: Haworth Hall**

| Hours | Classroom Utilization | Laboratory Utilization |
|-------|----------------------|------------------------|
| 7-8 | 5% | 45% |
| 8-9 | 60% | 95% |
| 9-10 | 100% | 100% |
| 11-12 | 100% | 100% |
| 12-1 | 100% | 100% |
| 1-2 | 90% | 95% |
| 2-3 | 73% | 100% |
| 3-4 | 25% | 100% |
| 4-5 | 7% | 72% |
| Average | 62% | 90% |

**WHATSAMATTA UNIVERSITY**
Gold Star Contributors
(Contributions over $1,000 as of 6/30/96)

| Name | Contribution | Alumni (year) |
|------|-------------|---------------|
| Ms. Elaine Anderson | $1,050 | 71 |
| Mr. and Mrs. Baker | $2,100 | 67/69 |
| Mr. Stanley Borkenstein | $1,700 | 76 |
| Dr. Emma Nielson | $2,500 | 83 |
| Ted and Alice Baker | $5,000 | 80/80 |
| . | . | . |
| . | . | . |
| . | . | . |

Exception reports can show the early-warning signs of an impending problem. The vice-president of finance for a department store chain may notice increased numbers of unpaid customer charge accounts going to collection agencies. An exception report that lists overdue accounts would aid executives in reviewing the company's charge policy.

Both negative and positive trends can be highlighted by exception reports. A university may produce an exception report listing the names of alumni who have contributed more than $1,000 (see Figure 12.9). The university president would be delighted to see that this exception report contains more large contributions than reports from previous years.

Information and reports generated by the MIS are important for the successful operation of any organization. For strategic planning, however, managers must also anticipate what is going to happen. Future problems and anticipated needs can be examined with the help of decision support systems.

## DECISION SUPPORT SYSTEMS

An MIS may not be able to provide all the information needed to make important decisions in an organization. Managers are expected to make intelligent guesses on how today's conditions will affect tomorrow's productivity. They can get help with this problem in several ways. As mentioned in chapter 9, managers can use electronic spreadsheets to try out different financial scenarios—the what-if questions. Also, database queries, discussed in chapter 11, can access relevant data from an MIS. To provide additional information, computer professionals can help managers create a *model*, or mathematical representation, of a problem to be studied. When these last two elements are brought together to aid in long-range planning, they become the foundation of a decision support system. A *decision support system (DSS)* is a real-time computer system that aids managers in solving problems through queries and modeling (Figure 12.10). Decision support systems designed specifically for strategic decisions by top-level managers are called *executive information systems (EISs)*.

A user of a DSS inputs queries and variables for the model through a natural language interface and a GUI. Pull-down menus, icon buttons, online help screens, and other features are also included in a DSS to increase user-friendliness and assist with data entry.

**12.10**

Decision support systems assist managers by providing a variety of models and other organized information for effective decision making.

## Modeling

Any organizational decision involves forces that work against each other. Increased costs for labor and maintenance face a department store that wishes to maximize profits by expanding services. Price increases may help, but managers know that when prices are raised too high, customers will shop elsewhere. How can managers account for all of the interactions, examine all possible alternatives, and still arrive at the best solution? Modeling on a DSS may provide the necessary information.

An executive considering adding automotive centers to a chain of department stores, for example, must look at many factors that will affect the profitability of these centers:

♦ Does each store already own the land needed to support an automotive center?

♦ What additional building considerations must be made (parking, lighting, access from busy streets)?

♦ On a typical visit to an automotive service center, how much does the average customer spend?

♦ Which services should be offered at the centers: self- or full-service gasoline, brake and muffler service, 24-hour towing?

♦ How many customers must be served each month for a service center to break even?

♦ What should be the investment in equipment and inventory for each center?

♦ Are there enough trained technicians in the area to staff the centers?

♦ What is the density and use of other automotive centers in the area?

It is obvious that there is too much information for one person to process mentally. Detailed records could be manually accumulated and organized, but this requires a lot of work and time. As a result, computer models are used to assist with this type of complex problem solving.

One type of modeling that evaluates a variety of complex factors is called *linear programming*. Linear programming is a technique for finding an optimum solution for

**12.11**

This linear program is used to model the costs associated with opening an automotive service center.

## Linear Programming Model

### Profitability of Auto Service Centers

**Goal:** To maximize service center profits, given realistic expectations of revenue and cost constraints for capital outlay, labor, inventory, etc.

**Question:** Which individual services will contribute most to profitability?

**Some model variables:** $x_i$ = activities associated with service center
($x_1$ = gas, $x_2$ = auto parts, $x_3$ = brakes, $x_4$ = mufflers, etc.)
$p_i$ = profits associated with activity $x_i$
$c_i$ = capital outlay required for $x_i$
$l_i$ = first-year labor costs for $x_i$
$n_i$ = start-up inventory costs for $x_i$
$r_i$ = expected revenues for $x_i$
$a_i$ = advertising budget for $x_i$
⋮
⋮

**Model:** maximize $\sum p_i$      (profit for all services)

**Given:** $\sum a_i x_i \leq 33000$      (total advertising budget is \$33,000)

**Constraints:** $l_1 x_1 > 16500$      (estimated labor for gas service is
(showing                                        more than \$16,500)
estimates of
costs for $l_3 x_3 = 0.81 l_4 x_4$      (labor costs for brake department is 81% of
each item)                                          muffler department costs)

$30000 \leq n_2 x_2 \leq 350000$      (auto parts inventory is
\$300,000 to \$350,000)

$c_3 x_3 + c_4 x_4 > 95000$      (brake and muffler shops' set-up
costs are over \$95,000)
⋮
⋮

**Equations:** $p_2 = r_2 x_2 - 0.10 c_2 x_2 - l_2 x_2 - a_2 x_2 - 0.63 n_2 x_2 \ldots$
(show actual                    ↑                     ↑
make-up of           depreciation    auto part inventory turnaround
profit for each
service) $p_3 = r_3 x_3 - 0.81 l_4 x_4 - a_3 x_3 - \ldots$
                   ↑
labor costs related to those of muffler shop

a problem in which each condition or constraint is represented by a mathematical equation (see Figure 12.11). Because complex equations are involved, computers are used for accuracy and to speed up processing in linear programming. Sometimes opposing goals must be met. For example, any automotive service center would like to maximize profit, but this can be done only under the constraints of meeting payroll obligations, licensing fees, maintenance costs, and so forth. A DSS that uses linear programming would maximize goals while minimizing constraints. Such calculations often are far too complex to do manually, so computer models are used. A disadvantage, however, is that each goal and constraint must be described in precise mathematical terms to realistically model the actual situation.

By using a DSS, an executive can create models that reflect alternative decisions. In the service center example, one decision might involve whether to sell gasoline at service centers. A model can help pull together costs of installing the necessary equipment and storage tanks. The costs of land, buildings, entrances, and other requirements are included in the model. When all start-up costs are accumulated, they are processed by a DSS to produce forecasts on depreciation of these costs over a number of years. Then operating costs such as payroll and purchasing gasoline could be estimated.

A decision support system could be used to project different levels of expected income for the gasoline retailing operation. The output of this model is a reliable estimate of the volume of gasoline each center would have to sell per month to cover expenses and produce a profit. It might take many weeks to develop the sophisticated level of this information if the work is done manually; but with a computer, the effort can be completed in hours once the raw data has been gathered and the model created.

A DSS can take both guesswork and detailed drudgery out of major decisions. In the preceding example, a model is used to aid in deciding whether gas should be sold at an automotive center. Each element of an automotive center's operation (brake shop, engine repair, etc.) could be examined through a DSS. Once a model of this type is created, executives can "exercise" it to test results under varying conditions. The result would be a projection of the business volume required to reach a break-even point for each area and for the service center as a whole. Similar models could be developed for company mergers, organizational downsizing, and efficiency analysis in many areas of business.

## ■ Data Analysis Using Queries

Modeling presents an overall view of a problem and tests various solutions, whereas a query, which involves a data manipulation language, can be used to formulate specific what-if questions. As discussed in chapter 11, a query uses a command language and/ or examples to retrieve information from a database. Figure 12.12 shows how a request

**12.12**

By using structured query language, this query requests a list of customers with a restricted code in their database record.

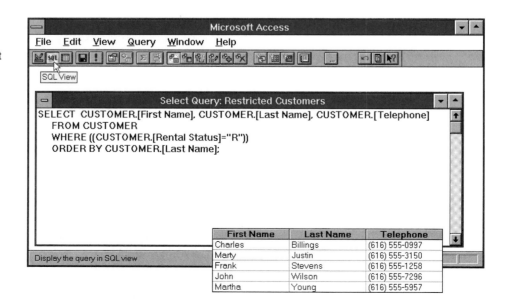

## ...ABOUT THE ADVANTAGES OF EDI (ELECTRONIC DATA INTERCHANGE)

- Minimizes delivery time by eliminating the day's wait required for documents sent by mail
- Reduces clerical errors by eliminating human intervention
- Saves employee hours by eliminating the need for time-consuming order entry
- Allows staff to work more productively
- Accelerates information flow and order processing time
- Greatly improves supplier service levels

SOURCE: *Office Automation*, November 1993, page 58.

for a list of video store customers with a restricted rental status is implemented in structured query language (SQL).

One advantage of a query is that a manager can use this aspect of a DSS without the help of a computer professional. While sitting at a network node and querying a financial database, a university administrator receives immediate feedback on such questions as: If we raise tuition by 5% and maintain current enrollment levels, how much additional revenue will be generated? or, How will keeping the library open 2 hours longer affect security costs? These answers are solicited merely by typing the questions, using a few keywords.

Although a query language is easier to use than modeling software for nonprofessionals, it is limited to a series of single, relatively straightforward questions. The predictive value, however, of both modeling and data analysis with queries easily surpasses the quality of manual forecasting.

## ACTIVITIES AND TOOLS TO ENHANCE DECISION MAKING

By using computer-based management and decision support tools, managers can make intelligent choices that improve the service and profitability of an organization. The decision makers can respond effectively to increased competition and unexpected opportunities or emergencies by examining important data and modeling different alternatives. All of these good things do not automatically happen just because an organization purchases a few computers. All levels of management must make a commitment to use the technology to increase personal, departmental, and corporate productivity.

An organization's mix of MISs and DSSs depends upon the transaction processing systems currently being used, the organizational structure (centralized versus distributed decision making), current resources, corporate culture, and the technological literacy of decision makers. Manufacturers build products, so they need to analyze inventories, operating expenses, mean time between equipment failures, and so on. Travel agencies, hospitals, law firms, and other service-oriented industries track the number of clients served, billable hours, and the like. Although these organizations have much in common—such as payroll—specialized decision-making tools have evolved to meet the diversity in organizational needs. Personal productivity tools like electronic spreadsheets and presentation graphics software serve unique MIS and DSS applications within every organization. Other tools and activities can increase management's effectiveness.

## ■ Materials Requirement Planning

*Materials requirement planning (MRP)* has been successfully used in industry for some time. In this activity, production schedules and current inventory for associated parts and materials become the data a computer system uses to schedule the purchase and delivery of additional supplies. These MRP systems help management minimize money invested in inventory, which frees an organization's finances for other purposes such as advertising or research and development (Figure 12.13).

Some advanced MRP systems support recent manufacturing trends toward just-in-time inventory. *Just-in-time inventory* means that materials or parts arrive shortly before they are needed. Deliveries are scheduled by managers using information supplied by an MRP system. This activity minimizes the money tied up in inventory and reduces inventory storage costs. Japanese industry first used MRP systems for just-in-time inventory in the late 1950s. Both the American and Japanese automotive industries have now gone to this type of inventory system, and other manufacturers are starting to follow their lead.

MRP systems facilitate the development of *flexible manufacturing*. By using computer-controlled machining tools and assembly lines with just-in-time inventory, a company could quickly change specifications of the product being manufactured, or even change to a different product. Of course, there are disadvantages. Some standardized parts or procedures may be required, and flexible manufacturing requires much long-range planning in factory setup. In these times of rapid change, however, the potential benefits are immense.

**12.13**

Materials requirement planning software helps managers track inventory levels and production schedules in order to deliver materials just in time.

THINK

# Thomas John Watson Sr.

(1874-1956)

As a young man, Thomas Watson sold pianos, organs, and caskets. He joined National Cash Register (NCR) as a salesman. By age 33, he was the third most powerful man at NCR, leaving it to become president of Computing Tabulating Recording Company in 1913 and president of IBM in 1924. From his earliest days as a manager, Watson favored the sales force over technical workers. Although he established research and development groups, he felt that the salespeople, being closest to customers, should generate the ideas for new products and services. He funded the MARK I, an early computer, and then used IBM to surpass it with the IBM SECC in 1947. The SECC could do 21,000 calculations per second.

Watson believed that through consistent quality service and respect for customers, one could build a thriving business.

As IBM grew, it produced one of the first general-purpose computers using integrated circuit technology, the System/360, in 1964. It was really a family of computers that allowed customers to choose among nine different processors and several types of input/output hardware to customize their system. Watson was much admired by President Roosevelt and was offered the Secretary of Commerce position and an ambassador-ship, both of which he declined. He ruled IBM with an iron fist. When his son, Thomas Watson Jr., took over IBM in 1956, the senior Watson lived only another two months.

## ■ Self-Directed Work Teams and Virtual Corporations

With fast and reliable communications between people being critical to any organization, it should come as little surprise that networks and groupware are becoming popular. The move toward *self-directed work teams* has motivated many organizations to design computer systems that support group decision making. This type of employee work team is empowered to make management decisions that solve specific problems. For instance, an office furniture company might form a team to design, at a reasonable cost, an ergonomic desk chair. Team members would include a designer, cost accountant, structural engineer, manufacturing engineer, office manager, and representatives from suppliers. This team would have the freedom to tap into the organization's other resources if necessary.

As illustrated in chapter 4, groupware supports team communication through e-mail and teleconferencing when members are geographically distributed. Electronic mail also helps people easily disseminate data without the necessity of time-consuming meetings, personal telephone calls, or mass mailings. The chair designer could e-mail rough sketches of new chair designs to other team members. The same groupware system can schedule and coordinate a team teleconference to discuss the designs. Daily updates of the design database would keep all members current.

Even when team members work in the same building, they can use groupware to support decision making. This groupware application is known as a *group decision support system (GDSS)*. A GDSS uses groupware operating on a network as the means by which team members can define a problem, discuss possible solutions, and delegate responsibilities. Many GDSS users feel more comfortable using the system instead of attending a group meeting, because it allows the anonymous submission of ideas and suggestions. As a result, everyone's ideas are given equal weight when considered by the group.

On a larger scale, the *virtual corporation* facilitates the design of a tailor-made organization. This legal entity unites a group of independent companies that provide products and services as would a single organization (Figure 12.14). Each company, or partner, specializes in some aspect of production or service. For example, different companies may handle the financial, marketing, personnel, legal, and research requirements of a single product or service, such as a notebook computer or specialized medical equipment. Every film produced, for example, is a unified effort of financiers, a design team, set construction crew, special effects company, and caterers, to name

**12.14**

In a virtual corporation, independent companies temporarily unite to provide specialized products and services.

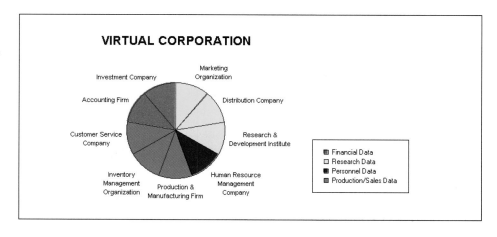

but a few. The life span of a virtual corporation may be as short as the time needed to produce one product or as long as many years. During this time, the virtual corporation can use a computer system to track financial data and facilitate telecommunication, as the need for communication and global decision sharing is obviously very important. Management information systems, GDSSs, and networking tools must work effectively not only within the independent partners but in sharing information such as product design and manufacturing/marketing strategies within the entire corporation. Information acquired may also go with the partners when the virtual corporation ends.

## Quality Control

The routine checking of a product or process to make sure it meets a predefined standard is *quality control*. Inferior training or raw materials, worn tools, improper equipment setup, or human errors create quality control problems. Quality control is the key to the long-term success of a product, service, and organization. If a good design or idea falls victim to poor production or service quality, consumers will discontinue buying it. Increased competition in the global marketplace has forced many organizations to reexamine their quality control procedures.

By using *statistical process control (SPC)* procedures, a manager can eliminate quality control problems before they start. The idea behind SPC is to continuously improve a process until every defect is found and eliminated. Manufacturers use SPC procedures because they realize it is cheaper to find a defective part before it is installed and fails. If a defective 50-cent part is found before it is installed, the organization loses 50 cents. If it is installed in a $100,000 machine that is returned or needs service, the expense to the organization is considerably more.

In SPC, workers and/or computers monitor production by statistically selecting certain pieces for detailed inspection. Control charts, like the one shown in Figure 12.15, document whether each piece sampled is within acceptable limits of quality. Statistical packages then analyze this production data to identify current production trends. When SPC reports indicate that quality is declining, changes to the production process are made. For example, in machining new auto parts, a worn cutting tool or drill bit is replaced. Unexpected quality changes are immediately flagged, which prompts managers to reexamine the quality of the materials being used or equipment operation and setup.

**12.15**

Statistical process control (SPC) procedures chart the results of a specific process, looking for trends that indicate potential quality control problems.

Statistical process control procedures are also applied to sales and customer service data. An organization can identify problems by analyzing data collected directly or indirectly from customers. If the statistical trends indicate a decline in service quality, changes must be made. This may require retraining people or reevaluating how the services are delivered. For example, an increase in patient complaints about long waits may require a hospital to reevaluate admission procedures.

## Total Quality Management

*Total quality management* is not limited to the manufacturing industry. It is an organization-wide management philosophy focusing on customer satisfaction through quality control of every service and product. Total quality management can be a goal of service-oriented agencies like hospitals, volunteer organizations like a blood bank, or any government agency. Furthermore, a computer-based MIS and DSS can rely on popular personal productivity software to achieve the goals of total quality management.

As mentioned in chapter 9, the rows and columns in an electronic spreadsheet contain numbers and formulas that can help people project results and choose among alternatives. Applications that require the summarization of data, or the clear presentation of important data, can best be done on a spreadsheet. Summaries of financial, personnel, research, and production/sales data can be arranged on a spreadsheet in an easy-to-use and familiar format. Other advantages to using an electronic spreadsheet for decision support are listed in Figure 12.16.

After critical data is analyzed, it is necessary to communicate clearly the ideas behind plans or decisions. Information is often communicated most easily through use of graphics, images, and sound. As a result, many spreadsheet and database packages automatically link data with multimedia and presentation graphics packages. When such integration is available, graphic output is easily created by using existing data from worksheet or database files.

Spreadsheets can be one of the building blocks of an organization's MIS. For example, all departments in a hospital could use the same budget template when planning annual budgets, but each department head would enter data unique to that department. Top management could analyze the budgets for all departments with a global

**12.16**

Electronic spreadsheets can help managers achieve total quality management goals by presenting data in a clear, easy-to-read format that can be standardized across an organization.

### Decision Support Using Electronic Spreadsheets

- Gives a clear, organized presentation of important data

- Provides a standard format for exchanging data with other software and across a network

- Can be used to create instructive graphics to summarize data

- Is an inexpensive alternative to some expensive DSS capabilities

- Allows users to manipulate data to answer what-if questions

view and then make strategic decisions based on the entire hospital's financial situation. These decisions could include increasing outpatient services such as a sports medicine clinic, or extending pharmacy hours for walk-in orders. Each department head can adjust his or her spreadsheet budget to quickly and easily reflect strategic plans.

In addition, not every organization can afford the power of a customized MIS or DSS. Although the blood bank in a resort community needs the data analysis and what-if capabilities available on a DSS, an electronic spreadsheet can provide an inexpensive alternative. The agency's director can use the spreadsheet program to get answers to questions like the following:

- If tourism increases 10% next summer and traffic accidents increase proportionately, how much blood will be needed?
- How many new donors must be acquired to fill this need?
- How effective have public service announcements been in increasing walk-in blood donors?
- How much more advertising will be needed next summer?

As you can see, electronic spreadsheets and graphics support total quality management at several levels. They organize data in familiar ways and also allow the manipulation of data to obtain answers for some of the what-if questions asked of the larger, more expensive DSS. Electronic spreadsheets can play a role in both enhancing existing decision-making functions and serving as a focal point for a small organization's MIS.

## Expert Systems

Some of the first practical applications of work in artificial intelligence were powerful problem-solving software for decision makers, called expert systems. *Artificial intelligence* is the application of computer technology to simulate human thought and judgment. *Expert systems* contain logic patterns for decision making and probabilities of expected outcomes based on information available from experts. Creating an expert system requires more than retrieval of data from large databases. Experts in a specific field *(domain)* are interviewed to record their knowledge and the rules by which they make decisions. Expert systems have three components: knowledge base, inference engine, and user interface (see Figure 12.17).

The *knowledge base* used by an expert system goes far beyond the capabilities of databases. It contains facts, objects, data relationships, and assumptions that the computer professional, working with domain experts, combines to form the rules used for decision making in a specific field. The knowledge base for a domain, combined with the powerful retrieval and decision-making *inference engine*, drives an expert system. When presented with a problem, the inference engine software can draw new conclusions and add this information to its knowledge base. The vast knowledge base and numerous decision-making rules are made easily accessible to users through the user interface.

One expert system, called Caduceus, contains information about human diseases, related symptoms, and diagnostic tests in its knowledge base. Doctors then enter queries based on symptoms of their patients (see Figure 12.18). This expert system responds with a list of possible diagnoses and the probability of their occurrence. It also suggests the least expensive and least painful tests to be administered first. The expert system will defer on a diagnosis if not enough information is available.

An expert system's interface provides user access to the inference engine, which works with a knowledge base to draw conclusions and make recommendations.

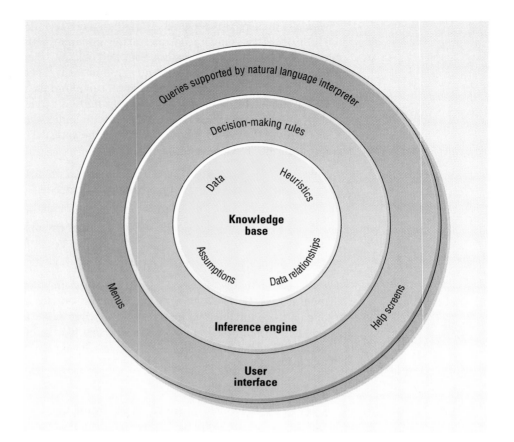

Expert systems, like people, approach a given problem from different directions. With a *forward chaining* approach, symptoms or situations are provided, and the expert system attempts to identify the problem. With *backward chaining* the problem is described, and the system looks for solutions by identifying possible causes.

Backward chaining is considered goal-driven, because the expert system starts with an explanation of the results, and its goal is to find evidence supporting these results. Expert systems in market research could use a backward-chaining approach to identify target markets. For example, the system could examine demographic data and recommend to a beverage company that it target young adults for cola ads because of their high consumption of the product. An expert system can suggest an investment strategy consistent with a person's resources and goals.

*Forward chaining* is data-driven because the system starts with all the available data and tries to draw a conclusion from it. Medical diagnosis systems, like Caduceus, can use a forward-chaining approach. A patient's symptoms are input, and the expert system uses its knowledge base and inference engine to match the symptoms with a successful treatment strategy. Similar expert systems diagnose automobile malfunctions.

Expert systems are built to *assist* decision makers, not replace them. They can support solutions suggested by experienced personnel and present alternative courses of action. In addition, an expert system can increase the knowledge normally acquired by people through experience. For example, a new intern working in a free clinic

## 12.18

This is a sample session between an expert system and a medical professional.

```
PATIENT 1
(1) Patient's name:(first-last)
**FRED SMITH

(2) Sex:
**MALE

(3) Age:
**55

(4) Have you been able to obtain positive cultures from a site at which Fred
Smith has an infection?
**YES

        ------------------------------INFECTION-1-----------------------------
        (5) What is the infection?
        **PRIMARY-BACTEREMIA

        (6) Please give the date and approximate time when signs or symptoms of
        the primary-bacteremia (INFECTION-1) first appeared (mo/da/yr)
        **MAY 5, 1975

        The most recent positive culture associated with the primary-bacteremia
        (INFECTION-1) will be referred to as:

        ------------------------------CULTURE-1-------------------------------
        (7) From what site was the specimen for CULTURE-1 taken?
        **BLOOD

My therapy recommendation will be based on the following probable infection(s)
and potential causative organism(s):

INFECTION-1 is PRIMARY-BACTEREMIA
                                                        {Possible identities}
<Item 1> The identity of ORGANISM-1 may be PSEUDOMONAS-AERUGINOSA
<Item 2> The identity of ORGANISM-1 may be KLEBSIELLA-PNEUMONIAE
<Item 3> The identity of ORGANISM-1 may be E. COLI
<Item 4> The identity of ORGANISM-1 may be BACTEROIDES-FRAGILIS
<Item 5> The identity of ORGANISM-1 may be ENTEROBACTER
<Item 6> The identity of ORGANISM-1 may be PROTEUS-NON-MIRABILIS

(46) On a scale of 0 to 4, where higher numbers indicate increasing severity,
how would you rate Fred Smith's degree of sickness?
**3

(47) Does Fred Smith have a clinically significant allergic reaction to any
antimicrobal agent?
**NO

(48) Fred Smith's weight in kilograms (or <number> POUNDS):
**70
                                {note that 2 drugs cover for 6 potential organisms}
[REC 1] My preferred therapy recommendation is as follows:
In order to cover for Items <1 2 3 5 6>:
    Give: GENTAMICIN
    Dose: 119 mg (1.7 mg/kg) q8h IV [or IM] for 10 days
    Comments: Modify dose in renal failure
In order to cover from Item <4>:
    Give: CLINDAMYCIN
    Dose: 595 mg (8.5 mg/kg) q6h IV [or IM] for 14 days
    Comments: If diarrhea or other GI symptoms develop, patient should be
    evaluated for possible pseudomembranous colitis.

Do you wish to see the next choice therapy?
                                        {alternative choices are available}
**Y
```

# A Closer Look at Presentation Software

**If you have ever given a presentation,** you know the importance of getting and maintaining the audience's interest. Presentation packages—a combination of word processing, graphics, and multimedia software—help the speaker make a professional presentation with coordinated electronic slide shows, transparencies, outlines, and handouts. For example, a businessperson could use presentation software in preparing for a meeting at which opening an auto service franchise is discussed. Salespeople, teachers, ministers, businesspeople—in fact, anyone who gives presentations or lectures in front of an audience—can use the features of this software.

**Q:** What is presentation software?

**A:** Presentation software is an integrated package that allows a user to input an outline for a presentation. The outline may be edited and enhanced with imported visual data, such as a scanned image, a drawing, or clip art. The text and pictures can be output in a variety of forms.

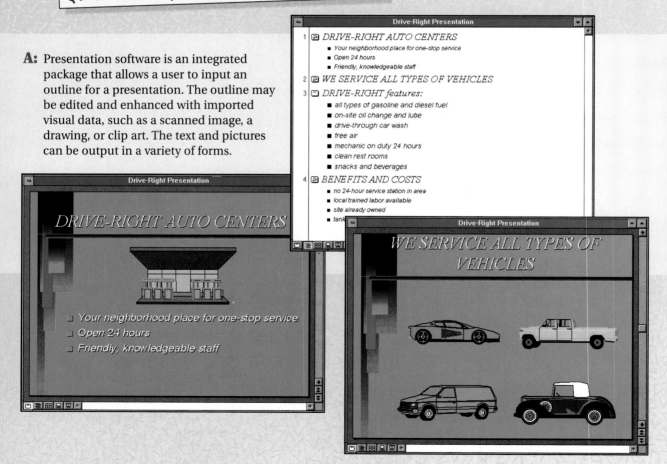

**Q:** Why use presentation software?

**A:** There are a number of advantages. The major points of a lecture or presentation can be covered without using a chalkboard or overhead projector. If a computer is used in the presentation, important points in the talk can be reviewed or topics skipped at will. The speaker has increased control over the presentation speed and organization.

**Q:** What kinds of images can be incorporated into a presentation?

**A:** Most software packages contain collections of clip art that can be freely used. Photographs can be scanned and graphics imported from spreadsheet and drawing packages. Additional libraries of photos and clip art can be purchased.

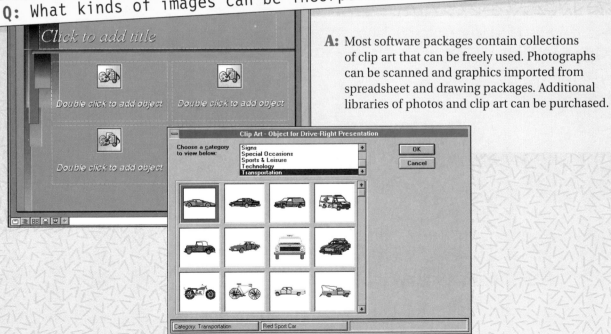

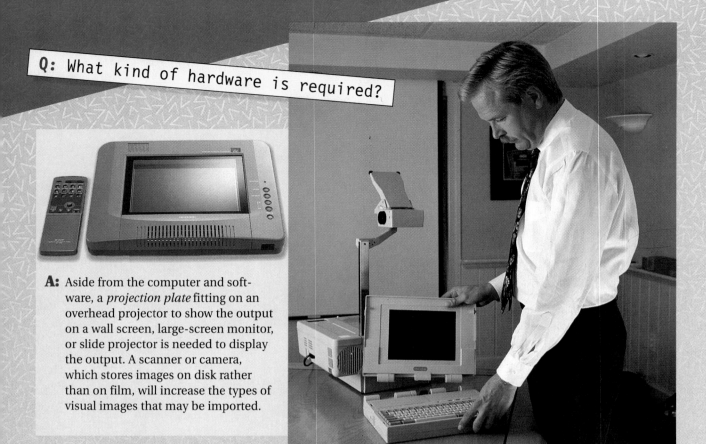

**A:** Aside from the computer and software, a *projection plate* fitting on an overhead projector to show the output on a wall screen, large-screen monitor, or slide projector is needed to display the output. A scanner or camera, which stores images on disk rather than on film, will increase the types of visual images that may be imported.

**Q:** Is the presentation difficult to lay out and edit?

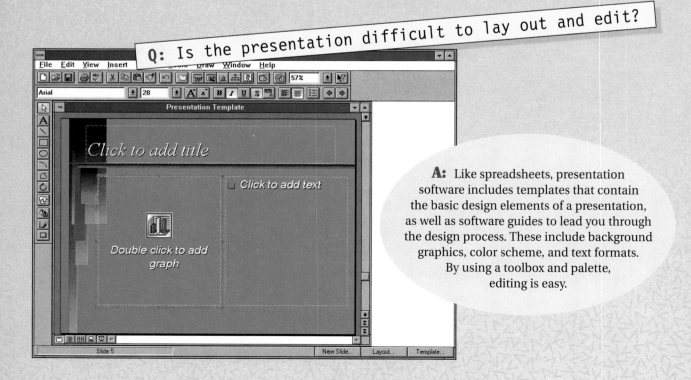

**A:** Like spreadsheets, presentation software includes templates that contain the basic design elements of a presentation, as well as software guides to lead you through the design process. These include background graphics, color scheme, and text formats. By using a toolbox and palette, editing is easy.

**A:** If the presenter has a computer available, the outline and accompanying images can be shown directly on a screen, one frame at a time. Presentations can be coordinated with background music or sound effects. Paper copies or transparencies of an outline can be generated on a laser printer. The outline can also be transmitted over a phone line to a professional service which will convert it to color slides.

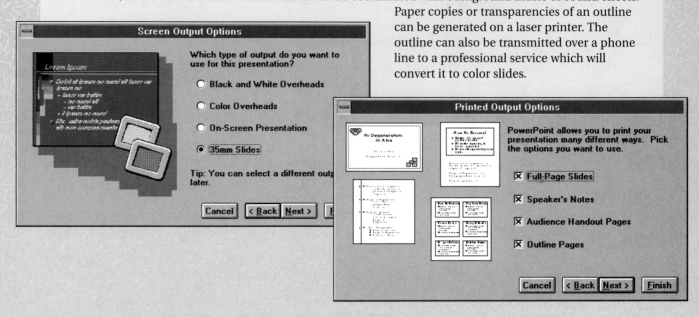

**Q:** How can I compare the features of presentation software packages?

**A:** Magazines and computer journals contain comparison lists and reviews of the newest software. Of course, it is best to talk to current users and try the software yourself before you buy.

### Summary of Features — Presentation Software Packages

| | asion 3.0 indows | Freelance Graphics 2.1 for Windows | PowerPoint 4.0 for Windows | Harvard Graphics 3.0 for Windows | Presentations 3.0 for Windows |
|---|---|---|---|---|---|
| **PRESENTATION CREATION** | | | | | |
| ...formance | Good | Excellent | Good | Good | Good |
| Slide creation | Good | Good | Good | Good | Good |
| Text handling | Good | Good | Good | Fair | Excellent |
| Multimedia capabilities | Excellent | Good | Good | Good | Good |
| **EASE OF USE** | | | | | |
| User interface | Good | Good | Excellent | Good | Excellent |
| Interapplication communication | Good | Good | Excellent | Good | Excellent |
| Task automation | NA | NA | NA | NA | Excellent |
| **EASE OF LEARNING** | | | | | |
| Tutorial | Good | Excellent | Good | Excellent | Excellent |
| Documentation | Good | Fair | Fair | Fair | Fair |
| Online help | Good | Good | Good | Excellent | Excellent |
| **WORKGROUP CAPABILITIES** | | | | | |
| Presentation management | Excellent | Excellent | Excellent | Excellent | Excellent |
| Support for multiple users | Good | Good | Good | Good | Good |
| Data-sharing capabilities | Fair | Good | Good | Good | Excellent |
| **PRESENTATION OUTPUT** | | | | | |
| On-screen viewing | Good | Good | Good | Good | Good |
| Notes and handouts | Good | Good | Good | Good | Good |
| Printed output | Good | Good | Good | Good | Good |
| **CROSS-PLATFORM CAPABILITIES** | | | | | |
| Support for multiple platforms | Good | Fair | Good | NA | NA |
| Consistency of user interface | Good | Good | Good | NA | NA |
| File-format compatibility | Good | Good | Good | Fair | Good |
| **EASE OF INSTALLATION** | | | | | |

would not have the resources or experts found in a hospital. An expert system would expand the intern's own knowledge base by identifying rare illnesses and suggesting possible treatments.

Like expert systems, decision support systems do not make final decisions; they only provide logical alternatives. The actual decision making is left to people. The system is designed to draw from a wide variety of specialized data. Users simply need to ask the right questions.

---

### CHAPTER FACTS

- The collection of manual and computerized systems used in assembling and retrieving an organization's data for decision making is called its management information system (MIS).

- In any organization, management's role is to solve problems, plan events, and supervise people. Management has three levels: frontline management, middle management, and top management or executives.

- Frontline managers make operational decisions about daily transactions. They use detailed reports to show information about each transaction.

- Middle management makes tactical decisions about short-range problems, using summary and exception reports about the organization.

- Top management makes strategic long-range decisions that have far-reaching effects. They use summary and exception reports to show organizational trends.

- Managerial data can be organized into financial, personnel, research, and production/sales groups.

- A decision support system (DSS) is a real-time computer system that includes modeling software and queries for data retrieval. It is used for long-term decision making.

- Modeling is the mathematical representation of a problem. One way of finding an optimum solution is through linear programming, which uses precise definitions of problem goals and constraints.

- Queries retrieve data to answer what-if questions posed by decision makers.

- Materials requirement planning (MRP) applications allow management to schedule the purchase and delivery of supplies in a way that minimizes the money invested in inventory. MRP supports just-in-time inventory systems.

- Management-level decisions are made by self-directed work teams that use group decision support systems to coordinate the flow of ideas and information among team members.

- Virtual corporations rely on electronic communications for organization and support.

- Statistical process control (SPC) procedures help organizations maintain high levels of quality control by using statistical analysis of production/sales data to identify potential problems.

- An organization-wide commitment to customer satisfaction through quality control of services and products is known as total quality management.

- Expert systems combine a knowledge base with retrieval and decision-making software. They concentrate on one specific area of knowledge and "learn" by storing the conclusions they draw.

## TERMS TO REMEMBER

decision support system (DSS)
executive information system (EIS)
expert system
frontline management
inference engine
knowledge base
management information system (MIS)

materials requirement planning (MPR)
middle management
model
operational decision
quality control
self-directed work team
statistical process control (SPC)

strategic decision
tactical decision
top management
total quality management
transaction processing system
virtual corporation

## MIX AND MATCH

*Complete the following definitions with the Terms to Remember.*

1. A mathematical representation of a problem or organizational situation is called a(n) _____.

2. A(n) _____ is short term and made by middle managers.

3. People who make operational decisions about daily activities in an organization are referred to as _____.

4. _____ is a philosophy that focuses on customer satisfaction through quality control of every service and product.

5. A real-time computer system that aids managers in solving problems through data retrieval and modeling is called a(n) _____.

6. _____ consists of the routine checking of a product or process to make sure it meets a predefined standard.

7. A user interface, inference engine, and knowledge base that contain decision-making rules and probabilities for expected outcomes constitute a(n) _____.

8. A(n) _____ is a collection of independent companies legally forming a temporary corporation to produce specific goods or services.

9. _____ comprises procedures used to eliminate quality control problems by statistically selecting certain parts or activities for detailed inspection.

10. A(n) _____ oversees the input, processing, output, and storage of an organization's transaction data.

11. A(n) _____ provides information, based on transaction processing data, to an organization's decision makers.

12. A group of people empowered to make management decisions to solve a specific problem are known as a(n) _____.

13. Software that uses existing inventory and production schedules to order and ship raw materials is called _____.

14. A(n) _____ is made daily by frontline managers.

15. A(n) _____ is long-term and made by top management.

## REVIEW QUESTIONS

1. What is the role of management in an organization?

2. What types of decisions and problems do the three levels of management handle?

3. What are the duties of a chief information officer?

4. What are the four types of data gathered by an MIS?

5. What types of reports do the different levels of management need to perform their jobs?

6. What is an advantage and a disadvantage of using linear programming models?

7. How are models and queries used as part of decision support systems?

8. What determines an organization's mix of management and decision support software?

9. How does materials requirement planning support just-in-time inventory?

10. How can self-directed work teams use a group decision support system?

11. Why would some people prefer to use a group decision support system over physically attending a meeting?

12. How does a virtual corporation rely on computer technology?

13. Why is quality control important?

14. Identify the three components of an expert system and explain how each works.

15. How can expert systems assist experienced and inexperienced people?

## APPLYING WHAT YOU'VE LEARNED

1. Computers are involved in almost every aspect of an organization's decision making. What type of organization may not need a computer at the present time? If this organization continues to grow, will it be possible for it to exist without a computer in the future? Explain.

2. Pick an organization with which you are familiar. It can be a business, school, or volunteer agency. Name three examples for each type of data available from an MIS. Describe what might be contained on typical detailed, exception, and summary reports for that organization.

3. Currently under discussion are innovative tools and activities in business and manufacturing that involve computer technology. Examples are virtual corporations, downsizing, interenterprise, reengineering, and soft versus hard manufacturing. Find an article on one of these concepts or another you have heard about. Summarize the article and list any new terminology used. How do the concepts presented in the article apply to school, your workplace, or other familiar organizations?

4. With each level of management come different responsibilities and rewards. Interview or read about a person at one of the three management levels. What are the benefits? What kinds of stress and deadlines exist? How far-reaching are the decisions he or she makes, and how much responsibility must the manager take if the decision is wrong? What tools does this manager use to help him or her make decisions?

5. A decision support system or expert system provides assistance to decision makers but does not actually make the decision. In your chosen career field, what types of decisions may be aided by the large base of data available in a DSS or expert system? Are there any decisions that should rely solely on human efforts?

6. Imagine you are an "expert" being interviewed to provide information for a knowledge base. After picking an area of interest to you, list ten different types of data that would have to be included in the knowledge base. For each type of data, name a possible source of that information. Also, list five different types of decisions an expert system in that field should be able to analyze.

7. Statistical process control is being used with a variety of processes. Make a list of five places where SPC could be employed. What production/sales data is used by the system? How would the data be collected?

CHAPTER

# 13

# System Design and Implementation

**T**he chances are good that one day you will need to purchase a small computer system. You will find that many of the rules computer professionals apply when designing computer systems for businesses can also be applied to purchasing personal computer systems. In fact, the steps in system development are basically the same for the design of any system: a new house, baseball team, formal garden, or personal computer system.

## HANDLING INFORMATION PROBLEMS

Computers can introduce valuable but expensive technology to organizations. Managers may have to learn to think differently before their organizations can realize the potential value of computers. When we look at early developments in system design, we can appreciate the extent of change required to harness the power of computers.

### Designing New Systems

When the first production computers were introduced in the 1950s, they represented a substantial investment in an unproven albeit promising technology. Computer hardware at this time cost millions of dollars. Developing the software needed to operate the computers required a large investment of time, money, and personnel, but there was really no choice. Large organizations were finding it impossible to keep up with the information processing and paperwork requirements of the post–World War II economic expansion.

The computer obviously held the potential solution, but computer technology was too formidable for most managers. As a result, the technology could be utilized only through a new breed of technicians who spoke the language of computers. These computer professionals, for their part, had virtually no understanding of organizational problems or needs. A communication gap formed, hindering the match of computer applications with their prospective users.

Developing information systems for computer processing was a major undertaking. The amounts of data involved and the complexity of programs proved overwhelming. Experienced project managers found some similarities between the activities required to develop a computer system and those associated with the creation and implementation of new products and services. Comparatively few organizations had experience with projects of this scope, however.

Because of communication and technological obstacles, many early attempts to develop large computer systems resulted in disaster. One common problem centered around the development of advanced systems that failed to solve the initial business problems. This was a major result of the lack of communication between managers and technicians.

Another type of unpleasant surprise came in the form of costs for these *systems development projects*. The steps taken to define and create new system solutions to existing problems demanded time and money. A major airline reservation system developed during the 1950s, for example, was reported to have overrun its original budget by some $40 million. Initial systems for processing checks and deposit slips in banks experienced even greater cost overruns.

## System Life Cycle

Once the obstacles in system development were identified, methods for bridging the communication gap were not far behind. A number of organizations devised project development techniques similar to those successful in the defense and aerospace industries. Also, at about this time, these methods were being used to manage a project aimed at putting an American astronaut on the moon (Figure 13.1).

**13.1**

The life-cycle approach to systems development was applied to coordinate complex tasks like landing people on the moon.

The method is simple and proven. Any major systems project will involve solving problems that cannot be known or understood completely in advance. There are just too many details associated with a major project. To make projects of this type manageable, the overall job is broken into a series of small activities. These subsets of the problem are small enough to be understood and planned. In the case of space exploration, a different scientific team was assigned to each major area of research: space vehicle structures, life-support systems, radiation shielding, navigation, propulsion systems, and so forth.

Similar thinking led computer specialists to devise a project design structure, also known as a *life cycle*, that partitions the job of developing a system into a series of parts, or steps. Management then can understand and monitor projects on a step-by-step basis, taking care to avoid situations in which designs fail to solve problems or major cost overruns occur. As a fundamental precaution, the life-cycle methodology requires users and organizational managers to be involved in the development process.

Users contribute to the process by specifying their needs, reviewing proposed solutions, and finally testing the results. Top managers review progress at each step in the project. Reports to top managers make it possible to approve the project for further development, to cancel the commitment, or to amend the mission of the project at several junctures along the way. The establishment of control, in turn, provides a framework that promotes effective communication and understanding.

Project control methods are standard within most organizations that develop computer information systems. However, the standards tend to be individualized. That is, each organization generally establishes project structures and reporting requirements to solve the problems defined by its management. The life-cycle or project structure in each organization differs from that of every other organization. This is dictated by the size of the organization, the scope of the problem, and the type of equipment used. Small organizations and individuals that use PCs have different needs than larger organizations, with interconnected networks of PCs, minicomputers, and mainframes. Nonetheless, there are common requirements for all systems development projects (see Figure 13.2). The description of the life cycle presented in the remainder of this chapter is based on those common factors.

**13.2**

Systems development conforms to a four-step life cycle that involves defining requirements, evaluating alternatives, design, and implementation.

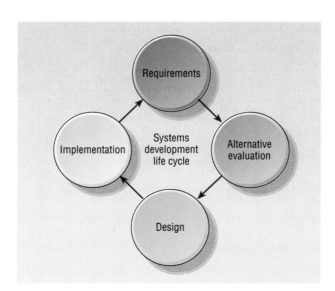

A typical life-cycle structure used to guide the development of a computer information-tion system can be organized into four steps: requirements, alternative evaluation, design, and implementation. Each major step can be broken into a series of phases that are more specific in nature.

## LIFE-CYCLE STEP 1: REQUIREMENTS

To avoid developing systems that fail to solve the identified problem(s), virtually all life cycles begin by defining system requirements. This initial phase tends to be relatively informal and often short in duration. It includes both an initial review of the project goals and a study of the feasibility of reaching those goals (see Figure 13.3).

### Initial Review

Systems development should begin with a user request, or at least with close user involvement. Ideally, users who have gained some sophistication with computer capabilities are the first to identify a problem. One or more users develop a formal request (in writing), which is reviewed by the organization's systems development group. Ideas for improving an existing system or information about new computer software are put forward as solutions for a problem. In an organization that does not have systems

**13.3**

The requirements step focuses on clearly identifying the problem to be solved.

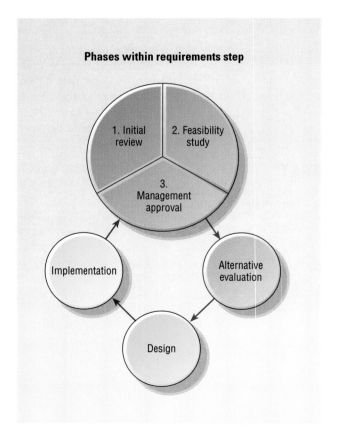

# Charles Babbage

(1791-1871)

Some time prior to 1822, Charles Babbage and his friend, John Herschel, were checking data calculated manually for the Astronomical Society, when the pair found many errors. In frustration, Babbage remarked to Herschel, "I wish to God these calculations had been executed by steam!" Steam engines were a common source of power in Babbage's day. He began work on a solution. The outcome of the scientist's efforts was a blueprint for the "difference engine." Composed of gears and wheels, the difference engine would compute functions in the form

$$y = a + bx + cx^2 + \ldots + gx^6$$

His work was funded by the British government, but Babbage was never able to complete the difference engine. While he was working on that project, he designed a new device, the "analytical engine." This machine was designed to compute any mathematical function, in any form. While trying to spread word of his inventions, he met the Countess of Lovelace.

Babbage's design for the analytical engine used many ideas now found in modern computers. The "engine" contained a "store" for numeric data, which had room for 1,000 variables of 50 digits each. Arithmetic operations were done in the "mill." Programs for the mill were to be written on punched cards. The "engine" would perform logical operations by ringing a bell when a variable went below 0 or above capacity. The machine also was intended to drive a typesetter for output. All operations were to work mechanically. Unfortunately, Babbage did not finish any of his inventions. He was always flitting between projects and changing specifications—an example of classic errors in the systems design process. Just recently, working models of several of his inventions were finally built.

development professionals, a user-developer or an outside consultant may investigate a problem and its possible solutions.

The problem or idea is discussed, and a systems analyst—a specialist in computer systems development—is assigned to perform an *initial review.* During this review the analyst interviews users to identify the source of a problem, trying to determine if the problem has a computer-based solution. Sometimes the problem involves lack of procedures or poor management and can be corrected without a new computer solution. If the issue involves looking at new software, the analyst reviews what the software should do and its role in the existing system.

Regardless of the starting point, the initial review is devoted primarily to the analysis of user operations and responsibilities in the specific area being studied. Users are responsible for helping the systems analyst understand the basic operations involved in how the system presently works. Users must also identify the problems, opportunities, and benefits resulting from application of a computer to the issue under study.

Once the user has done this, the systems analyst can make a preliminary estimate of the time and cost involved in implementing the initial idea. The user-identified benefits are quantified and compared to the costs estimated by the analyst. The analyst's findings are written into the initial review and presented to management. At this time MIS managers or other tactical decision makers decide whether the idea has enough merit to pursue an in-depth feasibility study.

## Feasibility Study

In the second requirements phase, a **feasibility study** is conducted. This study determines whether the project is realistic in terms of time, costs, and resources. Additional users and analysts become involved as part of an **application development team**. This team is responsible for carrying out the systems development project, including the design and implementation of the new system. They gather enough information to define and describe user operations in terms of volumes of transactions, number of people involved, turnaround or deadline requirements, uses for accumulated data, methods of data storage, current problems, and opportunities for improvement.

**13.4**

One way of collecting data for a feasibility study is to have members of the application development team observe and interview users.

The main techniques for data gathering are questionnaires, interviews, observations, data flow diagrams, and collecting sample documents. Questionnaires are employed when a large number of users must be involved with a feasibility study. When managers or other key people are involved, personal interviews are conducted (see Figure 13.4). Observations and sample documents help team members identify where data originates and where it is used in an organization. The resulting **data flow diagram** (see Figure 13.5) provides a visual representation of how the data and people interact.

At this point the team concentrates on the main applications and work assignments. Experienced analysts follow a well-known guideline: the rule of 80–20. This means that in any system, 20 percent of the documents or tasks will represent 80 percent of the work. An important skill for analysts, therefore, lies in recognizing and concentrating on the 20 percent of the activities and processes that are the key to any system.

## 13.5

Data flow diagrams show the movement and processing of data throughout an application. Circles show processes, and boxes show entities, such as people, who are involved with the process. Lines and arrows identify how data flows within the application; open-ended rectangles indicate data storage.

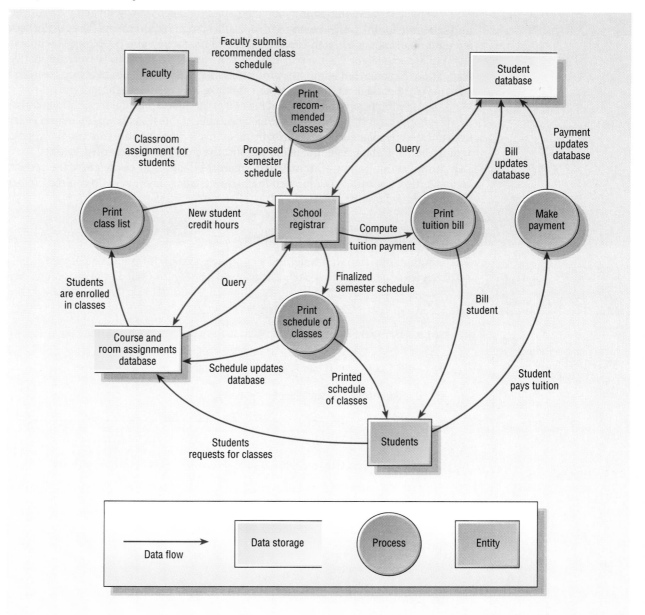

The team gains enough knowledge of operations so that it can develop initial plans about the computer equipment to be used, the storage space required, the number of people who will be involved, the overall design or specifications for required programs, and any procedures or training required.

A result of a feasibility study should be a preliminary cost/benefit analysis, budget, and schedule for the project along with specific system requirements. The *cost/benefit analysis* quantifies associated costs in terms of time, money, and people and compares them to expected benefits. These estimates will be refined as part of step 2: alternative evaluation. Experienced computer professionals should be able to estimate costs and benefits close enough so that managers can make informed decisions.

The feasibility report delivered at the end of this phase provides a recommendation on whether systems development should continue. At this time, key people from every area affected by the new system formally meet to ask questions and discuss the system requirements. If the decision makers support the project, management is asked for a substantial commitment of money and organizational resources to carry the project forward. Also, a schedule is approved that requests assignment of people to the project for an extended time.

## ■ Requirements for a PC System

The requirements step in developing a computer system for home or personal use is relatively short because fewer users are involved (see Figure 13.6). Initial review involves

**13.6**

Purchasing a personal computer requires examining finances, needs, and potential locations for using the system once it is set up.

### Requirements for a Personal Computer System

▨ Identify needs and review finances

▨ Decide who will be using the new system
All the time: _____
Sometimes: _____

▨ List types of personal productivity software and specialized software you want
Personal finance: _____
General business: _____
Education: _____
Entertainment: _____
Telecommunications: _____

▨ Determine the location of the equipment
Electrical outlets: _____
Work space: _____
Security: _____
Glare from windows or lights: _____

balancing finances against short- and long-term computer needs. The primary question is: What do you want to do with a computer system?

Business, entertainment, education, graphics, or telecommunications are all reasonable needs. Examine each need to see if it requires specialized software or if it can be accomplished with personal productivity software like word processing, spreadsheets, and so forth. Furthermore, identify each application as a current or future need, since you may be purchasing the system in stages. The general rule at this point is to dream a little. You will quickly become practical as your budget limits the scope of your initial purchase.

Most of the time, a personal computer system will not be used by just one individual. List everyone who will have access to the new computer system and see if their needs are included in the initial review. Finally, think about where the computer system will be located. Is there sufficient work space in this area? Are there enough grounded electrical outlets to power a computer, monitor, and printer? Is the location secure and out of a high-traffic area? By carefully thinking through these concerns, you ensure that all of your requirements for the new computer system are included.

## LIFE-CYCLE STEP 2: ALTERNATIVE EVALUATION

The initial step that defines requirements covers the entire scope of the proposed project, including all problems and benefits that can be foreseen. Each succeeding step does the same, but in greater depth. That is, users and computer professionals review the same application repeatedly, in more detail each time. At each step the development team gains a more detailed, clearer view of the problems and methods of solution. The second step involves identifying alternatives and then selecting the best alternative for fulfilling the system requirements (see Figure 13.7).

**13.7**

During the alternative evaluation, every reasonable solution to the problem is examined before a recommendation is made to management.

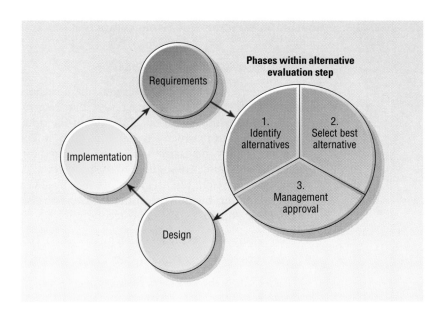

## ■ Identifying Alternatives

A new systems development project affects all five components of a computer system in some way. Even if some components are not directly changed, the systems analyst must examine each to see how it influences the other system components. The basic system requirements established as a result of the initial review identify what the system is suppose to accomplish. Next, alternative ways of achieving these requirements need consideration.

When examining available solutions for solving the problem, the application development team should include a wide range of alternatives. Each alternative must specifically address all five components of a computer system. The alternatives will differ by how system components are acquired or modified. This does not necessarily mean that new computer hardware or software will be purchased. Many times, changes in existing procedures or personnel will solve the problem. The systems development process is iterative (repeats); as each component is examined, requirements for the others may change.

For example, a hospital that establishes a new outpatient clinic at a remote location can consider several alternatives. The new clinic can be connected to the hospital's network by adding data communication capabilities, can retain its own client/server network, or can hire a *service bureau*, or outside agency, to handle its data processing needs. As shown in Figure 13.8, each of these alternatives, in turn, would require a different mix of personnel, peripherals, software, data organization, and procedures.

Not all systems development projects require new hardware or network connections. Sometimes it is just a matter of deciding which personal productivity software to use to solve the problem. A large law firm may decide to standardize the word processing packages used by its offices across the country. In this case, the computer hardware already exists, and the consulting systems analyst would need to poll the legal secretaries and paraprofessionals to define software requirements. Although the data and hardware would not be affected by the new software, participating personnel must be trained and new procedures written for them. The alternatives would be selected from off-the-shelf word processing software.

## ■ Selecting the Best Alternative

Once the alternatives have been selected, the next phase is to pick the one that best meets the system requirements. In a report to management, alternatives are described in detail along with related cost/benefit projections. The team also justifies its recommendation as to which alternative is the best. This alternative is not always the least expensive nor the easiest to implement. The best alternative must be one that provides the most effective solution to the problem.

When the system requirements are met by several alternatives, cost and time requirements then become deciding factors. In this situation, the following cost considerations should be taken into account:

- ◆ Development costs are less than maintenance costs
- ◆ Purchase costs are often less than implementation costs

Both relate to the long-term costs associated with many computer-based solutions. For example, many organizations will spend more than $30,000 on training and support costs for a PC system costing under $5,000.

# Augusta Ada Byron
(Countess of Lovelace)

(1815-1852)

A woman considered to be the world's first programmer came from an elite background. Augusta Ada Byron was the daughter of Lord Byron, the poet. She was educated well and showed an early aptitude for mathematics. Marriage gave her the title Countess of Lovelace. When Charles Babbage brought his invention, the difference engine, to her mother's home, Ada was intrigued by its potential. Babbage and the countess kept up a correspondence for years. A technical account of Babbage's invention was made public through the writings of General Luigi Menabrea. Countess Lovelace translated the paper and added copious notes. She also included detailed operating instructions—a precursor of computer programs. However, Babbage was never able to get the difference engine to work. She and Babbage attempted to use the difference engine to develop a winning system for the horse races. The invention was no more successful here, as she had to pawn her family's jewels twice to pay gambling debts. The countess died of cancer at age 37, at the same age and of the same cause as her famous father. Ada, a major programming language adopted in the early 1980s by the U.S. Department of Defense, is named in her honor.

**13.8**

Identification of alternative solutions to meet the needs of a new system is an important part of the systems development process. Three alternatives are illustrated here.

## Alternatives for a New Outpatient Clinic

### System Component—Alternative 1: Client/server network

Hardware: Server, personal computers, printers, network cabling

Programs: Network programs and new application programs

Data: Create new file/databases

Procedures: Operating, maintenance, backup, data collection, emergency/troubleshooting

People: Train existing staff as users; hire and train network/database administrator

### System Component—Alternative 2: Connect to hospital's network

Hardware: Purchase workstations and multiplexers; lease ISDN and other equipment from telephone company

Programs: Use network operating system and application programs currently maintained by hospital

Data: Use hospital's database

Procedures: Data collection, emergency/troubleshooting

People: Train existing staff as users

### System Component—Alternative 3: Hire service bureau

Hardware: Service bureau provides hardware

Programs: Service bureau provides software

Data: Create new files for every application or create a database

Procedures: Data collection

People: Train existing staff as users

*Note:* Cost/benefit analysis and list of intangibles not included

Providing alternative solutions to a problem supports good management decision making (see Figure 13.9). If managers are presented with alternatives ranging from the easiest and least expensive to more complex and expensive solutions, they will probably support the team's decision, since they know what alternatives have been rejected. Also, management must consider the hidden or intangible costs and benefits for alternatives. Employee satisfaction or stress, increased availability of management information, and improved customer service are intangible costs and benefits. These may not be classified in dollar terms but are still important to consider. For example, the installation of a new computer system in a department store during the Christmas rush may be most effective in solving a processing problem, but such a solution could be stressful to already harried employees.

The final action in this step is to obtain management approval of the alternative selected by the development team. Projections of costs and benefits will be considered reliable if they are supported by both users and computer professionals. At this time, schedules and budget projections are reaffirmed as management approves the start of

**13.9**

The alternatives along with their comparative costs and benefits are presented to management for approval.

the design step. It is possible for management to reject the proposal at this point, however. They may request that another alternative be investigated more thoroughly or dismiss the project altogether if conditions within the organization have changed.

## Alternatives for a PC System

When examining alternatives for your personal computer system, remember that software drives hardware: The software you select determines your hardware requirements. For instance, minimum internal memory requirements and choice of operating system are dictated by software selection. Some alternatives are just a matter of personal choice—the keyboard layout, for instance. On the other hand, most computer professionals agree that a minimum of two disk drives should be available to simplify copying and backup procedures (see Figure 13.10).

At this juncture you must weigh the costs of software and hardware against the benefits. High-speed computers with multitasking capabilities will cost more than slower machines and may not suit your needs. Can you afford a high-capacity hard disk at this time? How important are portability, sound, and data communication? Do you need a high-speed laser printer, or can you get by with an ink-jet printer? Is color printing important? Internal expansion slots on a PC's motherboard provide an opportunity to later add system components you cannot afford at this time. Make sure you have enough expansion slots to accommodate future peripheral purchases.

Personal computer systems do include intangible costs and benefits. Although your system may eventually increase your productivity, you will need time to familiarize yourself with new software and hardware. New equipment may require new office furniture or perhaps some remodeling work. Hidden ongoing costs include purchasing disks, paper, printer supplies, service, and software revisions. You must realize that you may spend as much on software and incidentals as you will on hardware. The result of the alternative evaluation step is to complete a list of hardware and software features, without specifying particular brand names.

**13.10**

Before purchasing a personal computer system, hardware and software performance must be weighed against price.

## Alternatives for a Personal Computer System

■ Software drives hardware: identify the software packages you need to start

Word processing: _____

Spreadsheet: _____

Graphics: _____

Database: _____

Network browser: _____

Electronic mail or telecommunications: _____

■ Identify necessary system components

Minimum memory: _____

Operating system: _____

Minimum monitor size: _____

Keyboard layout: _____

Minimum storage capacity of two disk drives: _____

Modem or network expansion card: _____

Specialized input hardware (scanner, voice, etc.): _____

Specialized output hardware (sound, color printer, etc.): _____

Open expansion slots: _____

■ Performance versus price considerations for system components

Storage capacity of hard disk: _____

Access speed of hard disk: _____

Processor speed and external data bus: _____

Monitor size and resolution: _____

CD-ROM drive speed: _____

Modem speed: _____

Ergonomic keyboard and chair: _____

■ Cost and benefits

● Cost: time spent learning to operate new software and hardware

● Cost: miscellaneous expenses for floppy disks, paper, print cartridges, etc.

● Cost: monthly costs of information services

● Benefit: time saved through increased personal productivity

● Benefit: reduced postage costs

● Benefit: a competitive edge

## LIFE-CYCLE STEP 3: DESIGN

The purpose of the design step is explained best by the end product that marks its completion. Typically, this step concludes with the acceptance of a document called *system specifications*, a description that covers, in enough detail to satisfy both management and users, all of the requirements and procedures to be incorporated in the new system.

Included in the system specifications will be designs and samples of all of the transaction forms, input screens, and output documents to be produced. Also included will be descriptions of the procedures to be followed by all involved personnel, as well as related functions and services to be provided by computer professionals. Equipment to be installed is described in general without specific makes and model numbers of devices (see Figure 13.11).

Experienced computer professionals know that this is a critical point in the systems development life cycle. Failures are often traced back to this time and may relate to one of the following mistakes:

♦ Inadequate user involvement. *Failure:* New system does not meet users' needs.

♦ Not canceling bad or unproductive projects when the systems development process goes astray. *Failure:* Unnecessary software or hardware purchased.

**13.11**

Each component of a new computer system must be examined as part of the design step.

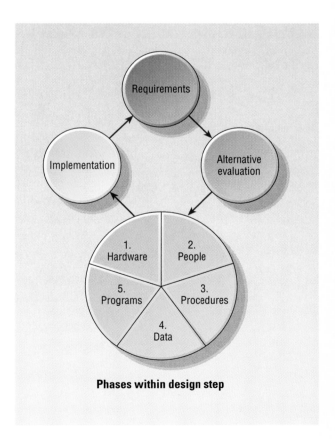

**Phases within design step**

◆ Poor communication within system among computer professionals and users. *Failure:* Critical system requirements get overlooked.

◆ Inadequate testing of solution before implementing it. *Failure:* Commit to deadline before checking to see if new software and hardware is working.

## ■ Prototyping and CASE Tools

To aid in creating and managing the different aspects of an involved systems design, many design tools have been developed, two of the more important being prototyping and project management software. These software tools differ in scope, but their usefulness has made them necessary additions to the repertoire of the systems analyst. Project management software is examined in detail as part of the Closer Look at the end of this chapter.

In the design process, models of screens for data input and reports for output need to be mocked up for user and management approval. Since program support of

## ...ABOUT IMPROVING INTERVIEWING SKILLS

Although the methods of obtaining useful information from the user vary greatly, if conducted properly the personal interview will bring the best results and best understanding.

An important key to excellent interviewing skills is the ability of the analyst to deal with the different personalities and attitudes of the interviewees. If the analyst can modify personal style to complement the personality, a channel of communication will be established that will allow ideas to be effectively communicated and the needed information to be obtained.

Studies indicate that verbal messages convey 7 percent, intonations convey 38 percent, and body language conveys 55 percent of the total message. Body language is the key factor, and the alert and well-informed analyst and interviewer should take advantage of this fact during the interview.

In listening to the interviewee as an employee, the interviewer has specific goals:

● To raise the level of employee motivation

● To increase the readiness of subordinates to accept change

● To improve the quality of all managerial decisions

● To develop teamwork and morale

Active listening is characterized by a nonjudgmental attempt on one person's part to allow the other person to explore a problem. Use of body language that encourages openness and acceptance should motivate the employee to participate in the interview more fully, and this should be the interviewer's goal in obtaining information. As with other attitudes, openness encourages similar feelings.

**13.12**

This prototyping tool gives designers a choice of dialog boxes to create. The generic About dialog box generated here could be modified to look like the box shown at the top of Figure 13.14.

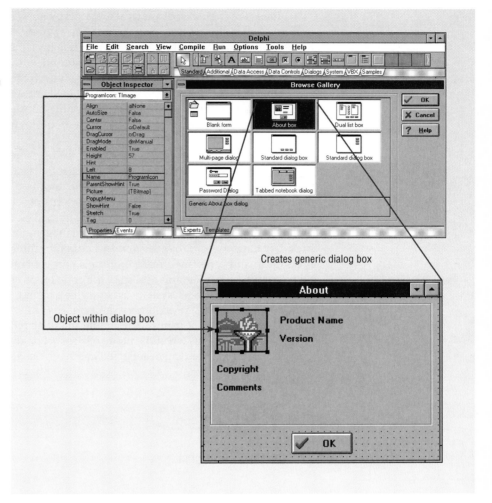

Creates generic dialog box

Object within dialog box

input and output is not necessary at this stage, systems analysts have used pencil sketches or typed samples. Recently, software packages have been developed that specialize in ***prototyping***, the modeling or simulation of user interfaces. Prototyping tools give systems analysts the ability to mock up an input screen, complete with menus, windows, help screens, and highlighting, as shown in Figure 13.12. Users then input sample data into the prototype and evaluate the interface. Although the data would not be processed, trying the model gives users a realistic idea of what data input would involve. Any changes users suggest to the screen format can be easily implemented with the prototype software. Sample reports, output screens, and other forms of user interaction with the system can be simulated. With prototyping tools, a systems analyst can model all or just part of a proposed system.

The advantages of prototyping are obvious. It enables users to see exactly what to expect and invites them to become involved with the design of the system. The ease of using prototyping allows fine-tuning of user interfaces until they please everyone involved. This eliminates costly changes later in the development process.

There are some disadvantages of prototyping, especially when users are not well informed. First, the prototype of a report, for example, is just a model and should not be interpreted as a signal that the new report is ready to use. Second, the ease with which changes can be made to a prototype does not reflect the work involved in producing the actual screen or report. Any changes to user interfaces need to be made at this design stage, not when the new system is being installed or tested. Third, what users may find desirable in a prototype may be too costly or time-consuming to include in the system. Systems analysts and managers must be aware of the pitfalls in using prototyping as well as its benefits to the users.

Whereas prototyping aids in designing the user interfaces, *CASE (computer-aided software engineering) tools* are software packages that facilitate management of the entire systems development process. Each CASE tool is a program used by computer professionals for a different aspect of the systems development project. For example, CASE tools exist to assist in conducting feasibility studies, developing project descriptions for alternative evaluations, and generating management reports. Many CASE tools use a resident database, or *project dictionary,* containing information about the new system's IPOS cycle and other features. CASE tools can generate data flow diagrams for the requirements step, diagrams and software code for programmers, and screen designs. By combining these tools, systems analysts have a powerful CASE toolkit that supports each step in a systems development project (see Figure 13.13).

The advantage of using CASE is that many activities can be automated and/or integrated. That means when the name of a report or activity is changed in one part of the system, the changes will be reflected in the project dictionary and other parts of the

**13.13**

A variety of software is sold under the name of CASE tools. You will find a mixed bag of packages that support different combinations of the software tools listed here.

## CASE Tools

**Chart and diagram managers**
- Flowcharts
- Data flow diagrams
- Structure charts
- Questionnaires and surveys
- PERT charts
- Gantt charts

**Report and documentation managers**
- User's manuals and guidelines
- System specifications
- Program specifications
- Evaluations
- Electronic mail

**Queries**
- SQL
- QBE

**Prototypes**

**Programming support**
- Object and program libraries
- Compilers and interpreters

**Tracking implementation schedule**
- People's time
- Interim completion dates

**Tracking project costs**
- People
- Materials

system. Also, some CASE packages will find inconsistencies in requirements within the system design. This technology improves productivity of the systems analyst and the development team.

Cost is one disadvantage of using CASE tools. Because of the complexity of these tools, only organizations with large systems development projects can maximize their use. Also, there are few standards from package to package. This means that a system developed with one CASE toolkit cannot be easily maintained with another. As this technology evolves, expect to see some standardization in software development tools as well as an effort to make them available to PC users and smaller organizations.

Regardless of the design tools used, it is important that all five components of the new system be studied. This is essential whether the system is for a large organization or a personal computer user. Any change to an existing system, no matter how small, will probably have some effect on hardware, programs, data, procedures, and people.

## Hardware

If new computer equipment is required, working parameters for selecting it are determined in the design step of the system life cycle. Secondary storage and memory requirements for computers are chosen. Peripheral equipment, such as printers, must have detailed specifications concerning speed, method of printing, and print style. The keyboard's layout, the screen size, and the screen resolution must be chosen. Specifications for data communication hardware and software need to be listed. The office facilities to be affected are studied to see where and how any new equipment, wiring, and/or furniture will be accommodated.

When speed is important, a **benchmark test** compares software and hardware performance against a minimum standard agreed upon by management and the application development team. For instance, a benchmark of three seconds might be set for the response time of a new order entry system. Systems with slower response times during testing are disqualified.

An implementation and installation plan must be developed. If new computer and/or data communication equipment is required, a **request for proposal (RFP)** describes hardware specifications, including benchmarks, and requests vendors to propose solutions. The proposals sent by vendors in response to the RFP include descriptions of desired hardware and software, training, and service with associated costs. The RFP is the first step in securing bids and placing orders for new equipment. When a person is buying a new personal computer system for home, comparison shopping at several local computer stores substitutes for a formal RFP. The acquisition of large computers and network hardware, however, can require long periods of advanced planning and installation. In many situations the equipment delivery schedule determines when a system can be implemented.

## Programs

Existing software can be modified or new programs acquired. If changes must be made to programs, they can be done by the internal programming staff or hired out to *contract programmers,* who become temporary consultants to the organization. When existing programs do not solve the problem, new programs must be obtained. Sources for new programs include buying them from a third party or writing them from scratch. Buying software "off the shelf" is usually cheaper than writing it, even when a competent staff of computer professionals is available! Even if you can't find exactly what you want, programs purchased from software vendors can often be customized. In any case, detailed program specifications must be written and reviewed by users. The development of program specifications is covered in more detail in chapter 14.

Computer professionals use software tools to help users understand what will be involved in the new or changed application. *Report generators* like the one shown at the bottom of Figure 13.14 have replaced preprinted *print charts* that analysts once used to indicate exactly how printed output will look. CASE tools and application generators also provide form or *screen generation* capabilities that work in the same way. These screen and report mock-ups show users exactly how data entry screens or informational

**13.14**

The report generator screen at the bottom of this figure creates a mock-up of a Customer Details report users can see and print out. A prototyped dialog box mimics the user interface that will access this and other reports.

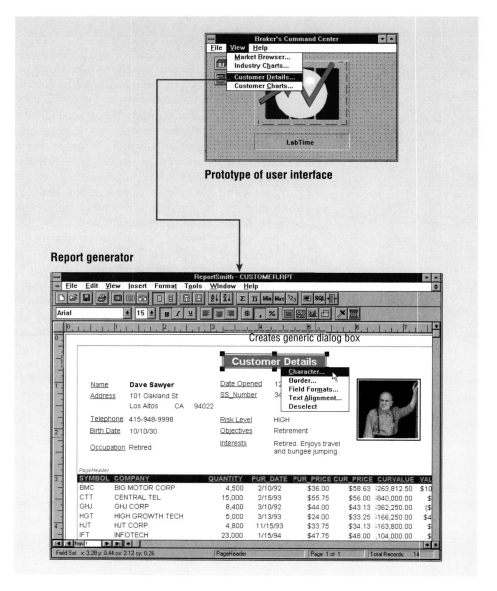

Prototype of user interface

Report generator

reports will look. By showing users screens and sample reports and asking them to approve each design, analysts increase the chances that the reports and displays will later be used effectively. As illustrated in Figure 13.14, when prototyping is available, it can be used to show active models of the report and screen designs.

## ■ Data and Procedures

At this time, decisions are made concerning the organization and layout of data. Decisions are also made about whether to use a database or file management system (see chapter 11). Usually, because they rarely involve the users directly, computer professionals make these decisions. Identifying the field attributes for a data file is most often accomplished using the Create command of a CASE tool or data management system. This command (a sample screen for which is shown in Figure 11.5), helps the professionals organize the locations of fields within records. CASE tools may help by suggesting data designs for the existing system specifications.

A change in any of the other four computer system components is usually accompanied by a review of present procedures or a change in policy. Operating procedures must be updated or created whenever new hardware or software is purchased. Users and systems analysts will often visit sites that have implemented similar projects to see what procedures they use. Implementation planning begins at this time. Training strategies and document distribution plans start and carry through to the end of the project.

## ■ People

The success of the next phase, implementation, depends on how involved users are with the design of the system. When users are involved, they have a stake in seeing that the new system succeeds. Sometimes people have to be hired to operate new equipment. At other times new people are temporarily involved with consulting and training. It is critical that the application development team identifies the personnel required to implement the new system as well as those needed to maintain it.

The culmination of the design step of a project comes when users agree in writing that the specifications will solve the identified problems and produce the projected benefits. At this point the users have "signed off" on the system specifications, and the computer professionals have accepted the specifications they will meet. For their part, computer professionals commit to an implementation schedule for this final step.

It would be nice to think that the system specifications are now locked, never to be changed, but large-scale projects that span many months need more flexibility. Modern organizations for the most part are in a constant state of fluctuation as they compete for resources. Therefore, one job of the systems analyst and other computer professionals is to know when to allow changes to the system specifications after the users have signed off. No hard-and-fast rules for this type of decision exist.

The *Gantt chart* in Figure 13.15 is often used to track the implementation schedule. Project management software and CASE tools use Gantt charts to identify when different phases begin, estimate their duration, and provide an overview of which activities occur concurrently during implementation. Because a major development project may take several years to finish, coordination of personnel and facilities is essential to maintaining productivity.

### 13.15

Gantt charts track multiple tasks associated with a systems development project and flag situations in which there are resource conflicts in terms of time, equipment, or people.

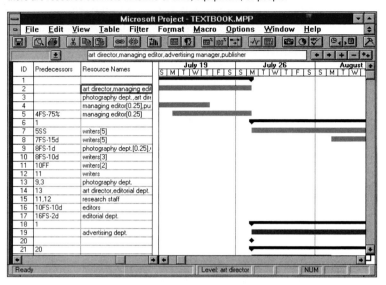

## Designing a PC System

In a home-based systems development project, you may agree informally upon a design solution with other users involved. In any case, the list of system features evolves into the system specifications, which identify particular brand names and model numbers (see Figure 13.16). Make sure the application packages that you need are easy to use, have readable documentation, and integrate with other software. Your software choices will, to a great degree, dictate hardware manufacturers and models.

Now is the time to get price estimates on hardware and software from local retailers and catalogs. Compare warranties and delivery dates as well as prices. Be aware that retail prices will generally be higher but may include training or local repair services. In either case, check that complete systems documentation is available as part of the purchase price. A purchase price may not include necessary cables or paper, additional disks or tapes, or extra ribbons for printers. A personalized Gantt chart can help you coordinate the purchase and setup of equipment. In addition, it can aid you in planning future acquisitions, such as adding a modem, expanding memory, or upgrading to a laser printer.

## LIFE-CYCLE STEP 4: IMPLEMENTATION

Within the context of a systems development project, implementation involves the activities that put a new system into operation and those that maintain its successful use. The actual changeover to operational status occurs during the latter part of this step. Gantt charts, like the one in Figure 13.15, identify the initial phases and their

**13.16**

These system specifications are used when purchasing a new personal computer system.

## Designing a Personal Computer System

■ **Convert system requirements into system specifications**

- For each software package
  - ☐ Software manufacturer: _____
  - ☐ Best price: _____
  - ☐ Where to buy: _____

  *Features to look for:*
  - ☐ Easy-to-use
  - ☐ Readable documentation
  - ☐ Telephone support
  - ☐ Integrates with other software

- Hardware
  - ☐ Processor: _____
  - ☐ Processor speed: _____
  - ☐ Expansion bus: _____
  - ☐ Memory: _____
  - ☐ Monitor size: _____
  - ☐ Floppy disk storage capacity: _____
  - ☐ Hard disk storage capacity: _____
  - ☐ Modem speed: _____
  - ☐ Multimedia capabilities: _____
  - ☐ Open expansion slots: _____

■ **Where to get price estimates**

- Retail stores
- Catalogs
- Advertisements in computer magazines
- Online shopping services
- Electronic bulletin boards

■ **What is included in the price besides hardware and software?**

- ☐ Training
- ☐ Service
- ☐ Toll-free support
- ☐ On-site warranty repair
- ☐ Ancillaries: _____

■ **Create timeline for purchase**

■ **Purchase system components**

**13.17**

During the implementation step, all of the components of the new computer system are brought together for installation.

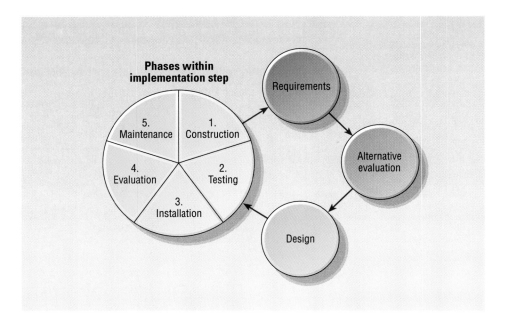

**Phases within implementation step**

5. Maintenance
1. Construction
4. Evaluation
2. Testing
3. Installation

Requirements

Alternative evaluation

Design

expected duration. This last step of the life cycle includes coding and testing, installation, evaluation, and maintenance phases (see Figure 13.17).

## Coding and Testing

The activities within this phase are technical in nature. This usually is the point in the project at which users play only minimal roles until testing begins. Users on the application development team are replaced by technical support specialists, senior programmers, computer operations personnel, network specialists, and database administrators. The job is to establish all of the computer-related requirements that will have to be in place before the new system becomes operational.

The main activity of the coding phase is the preparation and testing of programs for the new system. If new programs are to be written or if purchased programs need to be customized, the coding of program sections or modules is assigned to one or more programmers. Each module is tested as it is written. As connecting modules are completed, testing extends to sets of modules, then to entire programs. Testing is a constantly repeated process that examines all phases of the program's IPOS cycle. In some instances test data may be applied to test multiple programs, or systems of programs (see chapter 14). Preliminary testing by the systems development staff is referred to as *alpha-testing*.

When traditional programming techniques are used, coding and testing can account for up to 50 percent of the cost of systems development. As a result, computer professionals write their own programs from scratch only as a last resort. This cost factor has motivated attempts to automate or shortcut the programming process. Some of these streamlined methods are described briefly in chapter 14.

Other implementation activities include the installation of new equipment and, after the programs are available, the performance of complete system tests. A *system test* is the actual operation of the new system, carried out by users with real application data. Usually, this data has been processed previously under existing systems. Thus, the expected results are known from previous processing. A system test then serves to exercise a new system to make sure users understand and are satisfied with the results that will be delivered. Usually, before a new program is officially installed, a small set of users test it as part of *beta-testing*.

Because users perform the system test, it is necessary to complete at least some of the training for the new system. Training efforts must encompass both a core group of users and the computer center personnel who will provide support. To achieve a realistic system test, at least some files that will interact with the new application must be created.

At the conclusion of the testing phase, the new system has been developed in its entirety and is ready for use. Separation of testing from installation serves to reassure users and management. The new system, now fully tested, can be put to work with confidence.

## Installation

No matter how extensive preparations might be, stress and some confusion are inevitable when a new system is to be installed. The act of starting up a new computer system is referred to as either **installation** or *conversion*. Emotions can be involved as well as changes in procedures.

Before installation can start, all the system documentation must be complete. Installing a new system means the use of the old tools and methods ceases. The experience can be like parting with an old friend. Individual employees, for example, may have used the previous methods and equipment for 5, 10, or even 15 years. The old ways worked for them; people were familiar with and comfortable in the routines they followed. If conversion is to be successful, training programs should assure employees that the new ways are for their good and for the good of the organization.

Computer professionals participate in the installation phase primarily as consultants. Analysts and programmers should be available to answer questions and resolve problems, but computer operators should take over the operation of the system. Users should start working with the output they need in their everyday job responsibilities.

Problems will inevitably arise. Any problems that affect the ability of the system to function or the reliability of results should be fixed immediately. Any other problems should be considered part of system maintenance, which is covered later in this chapter. The goal of installation is an operational system.

One of the major jobs of a system conversion often lies in setting up files or a database to support the new system. Difficulties generally center around the need to tie file conversion to day-to-day operations. For example, major operating crunches were experienced in the days when banks changed from manual bookkeeping methods to online computer systems. Typically, a branch or operating unit of the bank closed out its manual files on a Friday. Immediately, a team of temporary employees would enter the offices on Friday evening and work all weekend to transfer thousands of records into a computer file, and also to establish balance controls between computer files and their predecessors.

Because of the extent and importance of the work involved, systems professionals have devised a number of methods that can be used to complete an installation (see Figure 13.18). These include the following four: parallel operation, phased transition, pilot operation, and direct cutover ("the plunge").

**13.18**

This chart illustrates different approaches for converting from one system to another.

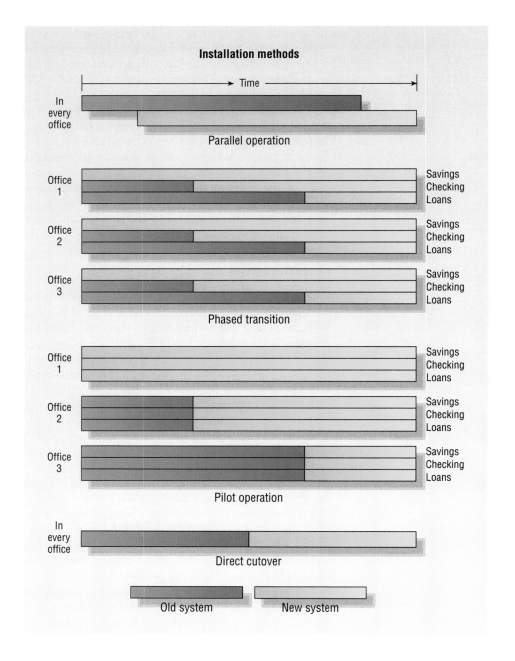

**Installation methods**

Time

In every office

Parallel operation

Office 1 — Savings / Checking / Loans

Office 2 — Savings / Checking / Loans

Office 3 — Savings / Checking / Loans

Phased transition

Office 1 — Savings / Checking / Loans

Office 2 — Savings / Checking / Loans

Office 3 — Savings / Checking / Loans

Pilot operation

In every office

Direct cutover

Old system        New system

**Parallel Operation**    Under a *parallel operation*, both the existing and the new systems are run, side-by-side, for some time. Results of the two systems are compared to provide both protection and control. The length of time for parallel operation can vary. Usually, the old system is retained through one or two processing cycles with the new system. A system that produced month-end accounting reports would be operated in parallel for one or two months.

Parallel operation can provide users a chance to become comfortable with change before old methods disappear. This method also provides an opportunity to establish the improvements the new system implements. Most important of all, the parallel approach involves the least risk and the most protection for the organization. The disadvantage of parallel operations is that the organization must pay the additional cost in time and labor of running both systems, as well as provide facilities for both the new and old systems.

**Phased Transition**   A *phased transition* provides the same basic advantages as parallel operation. The difference is that under this method the overlap is piecemeal. In a phased transition, part of the system is put into operation throughout the organization. Once it is working, another part or piece is installed. This phased transition continues until the whole system is in operation across the organization. Figure 13.18 illustrates how a new bank system might start with computerizing only savings accounts in all its branches, then go on to checking accounts, loans, club plans, and others. The idea is that the new system impacts only one portion or function of the organization at a time.

**Pilot Operation**   A *pilot operation* takes a different approach than is used in a phased transition. Rather than scheduling installation for the entire organization, a small pilot operation is set up. This pilot runs the complete new system in only part of the organization until the system has proven itself. For example, a bank using a pilot operation would install the entire system in one branch office. When it is working properly, the system would be gradually installed in other branch offices one at a time.

**Direct Cutover**   Under *direct cutover*, sometimes called the plunge, an existing system is terminated, and the new one takes over immediately. This method generally is used when gradual techniques are impractical. The situation of a bank branch installing online service is a good example. The equipment used by tellers to serve customers is changed. There is no opportunity to use both systems concurrently or to handle part of the customers one way and the others differently. The conversion is complete and immediate.

## Evaluation

Accountability is part of the process of management. Accountability is also part of the reason that the life-cycle approach to systems development works. Recall that, at the onset, users and computer professionals are asked to join in identifying both projected benefits and costs for systems development. These forecasts and commitments do little good if management does not make the necessary effort to follow up by comparing actual results with forecasts.

Accordingly, it is customary to perform a review of results shortly after each new system is installed and running. At this point the memories of people on the project team about activities and results are fresh and reliable. They are in an ideal position to pinpoint problems and to benefit from mistakes that can be identified. Also, this is a good time to list the opportunities that already have been uncovered for system enhancement. These potential improvements can be used in the early portions of the maintenance phase, which runs through the entire useful life of a system.

In addition to the review that takes place shortly after installation, many organizations try to hold another review session about four to six months after a system becomes operational (see Figure 13.19). This second review is based upon the perspective of experience. The organization has had enough service from the new system so that findings about benefits and savings are well known. This represents an ideal time to compare actual results with projections, and to learn from the successes and difficulties that are identified.

**13.19**

Evaluation of a new system begins just after it is installed. Another major evaluation of the system often occurs several months later to compare expectations with actual results.

## Maintenance

Maintenance begins as soon as a system becomes operational and lasts as long as it is in use. In this sense, *maintenance* encompasses product support and oversees any modification to the operational system.

**Product Support**   Once the system is operational, new users still need to be trained and experienced users helped with day-to-day problems. Training and help with operational problems are types of *product support*. Help desks with telephone hotlines and online help through network connections are common ways of delivering product support.

**Change Control**   Every computer system goes though changes. Computer professionals implement *change control* procedures to oversee modifications as they are made. For example, change control procedures are needed when laws or regulations mandate that computer programs comply to new changes by a specified date. If a tax rate changes, a corresponding modification is needed in related programs after a designated date.

Enhancements are recognized opportunities for improvement. These typically are uncovered by users who notice that adding a capability to an existing system may increase its value. As an illustration, a payroll system may be expandable to provide labor cost information for the manufacturing department. The revision to accomplish this may seem minor; however, if this request occurs after the system design has been completed, most computer professionals will avoid changing the design. Too much can go wrong. Schedules and budgets can be destroyed. Instead, a list of enhancement opportunities usually is started during the late stages of a development project. These opportunities are carried forward into the ongoing maintenance phase of the life cycle. Figure 13.20 diagrams all the phases of a complete life cycle.

**13.20**

By following each phase in the systems development life cycle, a new computer system can be created in a cost-effective manner.

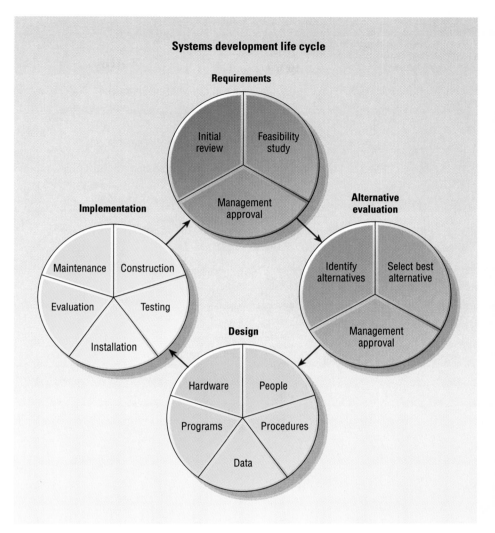

Systems development life cycle

The need for early enhancements is commonplace. Even a brand-new system can start its useful life with a backlog of maintenance requests. In the course of use, new opportunities will be identified for each application. As these are uncovered, they are reviewed for feasibility, and work is scheduled on maintenance projects, which tend to be miniature versions of systems development projects.

**Retirement**   Many life cycles include *retirement*. The point in time when a computer program or an entire system is taken offline can be planned or fall victim to newer versions or more sophisticated technology. Many Intel-based PC systems are retiring command-driven MS-DOS and PC-DOS in favor of more graphical alternatives. Mainframe computer systems are retired and replaced by client/server networks.

**13.21**

Proper setup and maintenance of a personal computer ensures that users can put it to good use.

## Setup and Maintenance of a PC System

■ **Setup**

- Clean and dry work environment

- Plenty of work space

- Storage for floppy disks and manuals

- Proper lighting and seating

- Surge protector

- Screen glare shield

- Antistatic pad

- Fill out warranty cards

■ **Maintenance**

- Backup (data files and software masters)

- Clean mouse and printer

- Cover keyboard

- Defragment hard disk periodically

- Clean and align disk drive heads

## ■ Setup and Maintenance of a PC System

Your implementation of a new computer system at home may be no more involved than removing components from their boxes and making sure the operating system boots properly (see Figure 13.21). Don't forget to keep any warranty or service information that comes with the equipment. Placement of the equipment in a work area may be one of the most critical decisions you make. Look for a clean, dry work environment with plenty of room for materials around the computer. Proper lighting and seating is necessary for user comfort and health. If improper lighting causes screen glare, screen shields can be purchased to eliminate it. Computer professionals often recommend using a surge protector and antistatic pads for long equipment life.

Personal computer users can avoid problems by practicing regular maintenance. This includes covering the keyboard when not in use, cleaning disk drive heads and printer, and backing up important data and software.

# A Closer Look at Project Management Software

**S**pecialized software, such as CASE tools, exists to help computer professionals develop new systems and incorporates many features associated with *project management software*. This type of personal productivity software helps people track, plan, and schedule many concurrent projects, whether they involve computers or not. Let's look at a landscaping firm and how its owner uses project management software to assist in organizing the personnel, materials, and equipment needed for several landscaping projects.

**Q:** How can project management software help organize projects?

**A:** Project management software helps users identify dependencies, that is, situations in which one task depends on other resources. A landscaper uses this software to spot critical resources, flag deadlines, and identify a logical order for completing each task. For example, earth is moved and plants are ordered before planting is done. Priorities must be input along with costs, time each worker can spend on the project, and necessary machinery to complete the job.

```
                    PROJECT MANAGEMENT REPORT

  PROJECT: Harrington                        START DATE: 4/25
                                             DEADLINE: 6/29
  - - - - - - - - - - - - - - - - - - - - - - - - - - - - - - - -
  TASK: order plants                         PRIORITY: 1
      START DATE:  4/26
      DEADLINE:    5/12
      PERSONNEL:
          NAME: Johnson      WAGE: 14.00     % TIME: 25

      EQUIPMENT: none
  - - - - - - - - - - - - - - - - - - - - - - - - - - - - - - - -
  TASK: level plant bed
      START DATE:  5/1
      DEADLINE:    5/7
      PERSONNEL:                             TOT EST HOURS: 60
          NAME: Wilson       WAGE: 12.50     % TIME: 50
          NAME: Nettle       WAGE:  7.25     % TIME: 75

      EQUIPMENT:
          NAME: backhoe      COST: 23.00     EST TIME: 16 hr
          NAME: bulldozer    COST: 19.00     EST TIME: 12.5 hr
  - - - - - - - - - - - - - - - - - - - - - - - - - - - - - - - -
  TASK: back retaining wall
      START DATE:  5/1
      DEADLINE:    5/11
      PERSONNEL:                             TOT EST HOURS: 75
          NAME: Abrams       WAGE:  9.25     % TIME: 75
          NAME: Nettle       WAGE:  7.25     % TIME: 25
          NAME: Quentin      WAGE:  6.25     % TIME: 100

      EQUIPMENT:
          NAME: bulldozer    COST: 19.00     EST TIME: 3.5 hr
          NAME: dump truck   COST: 12.00     EST TIME: 5 hr
```

**Q:** What kinds of information are available from the package?

**A:** Project management software provides time management, job scheduling, resource (personnel and material) management, and cost estimation. A Gantt chart, as in Figure 13.15, and some of the CASE tools discussed in the text are commonly available with this software.

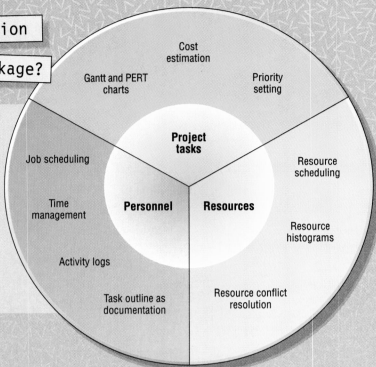

**Q:** How does the software handle resource conflicts?

```
              PERSONNEL SCHEDULE

PROJECT: Harrington


                WORKER      HOURS      TASK
- - - - - - - - - - - - - - - - - - - - - - - - - - -

WEEK: 4/26
                Johnson     10         order plants

WEEK: 5/1
                Wilson      15         level plant beds

                Nettle      40         level plant beds


WEEK: 5/8
   ***          Nettle      5          level plant beds

                Abrams      10         back retaining wall

   ***          Nettle      40         back retaining wall

                Quentin     15         back retaining wall



*** denotes personnel time conflict
```

**A:** Resource conflicts occur when the personnel, equipment, or materials for a job are not available when needed. This could be due to workers' vacations, a dump truck being used on another job, broken equipment, or late orders. Project management software flags potential conflicts within a single project or between projects and resolves them when possible. For example, worker Nettle is incorrectly scheduled for 45 hours during one week.

**A:** *PERT (program evaluation and review technique)* is a key element in project management software. PERT charts show the order and time requirements for each task in a project as boxes connected by lines. The *critical path*, highlighted in the figure, shows the combination of events requiring the most time.

Often several tasks are independent of the others. In landscaping, retaining walls in the backyard can be built while sod is being laid in the front.

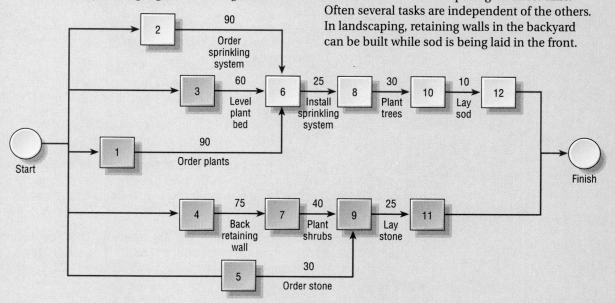

| | | | |
|---|---|---|---|
| 2 | 90 | | |
| | Order sprinkling system | | |

| 3 | 60 | 6 | 25 | 8 | 30 | 10 | 10 | 12 |
|---|---|---|---|---|---|---|---|---|
| | Level plant bed | | Install sprinkling system | | Plant trees | | Lay sod | |

Start

| 1 | 90 |
|---|---|
| | Order plants |

Finish

| 4 | 75 | 7 | 40 | 9 | 25 | 11 |
|---|---|---|---|---|---|---|
| | Back retaining wall | | Plant shrubs | | Lay stone | |

| 5 | 30 |
|---|---|
| | Order stone |

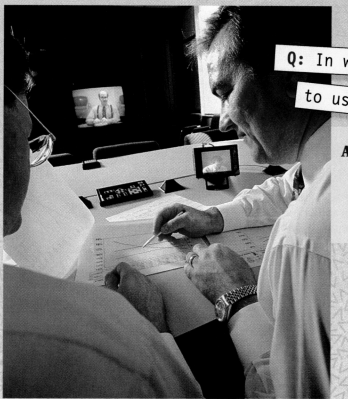

**A:** This software is best used in complex projects that involve many steps, projects taking place in many locations simultaneously, and projects with new managers who need the help of experienced managers not on-site.

---

### CHAPTER FACTS

- A systems development project is more easily managed by breaking it down into four life-cycle steps: requirements, alternative evaluation, design, and implementation.

- The requirements step involves three phases: initial review, feasibility study, and management approval.

- In the initial review, a systems analyst makes a preliminary estimate of time and costs, deciding whether the project has a computer solution.

- Data flow diagrams provide a picture of how an existing or proposed system works.

- The feasibility study involves other computer professionals and users. They gather relevant data and interview participating users, producing a report of budget, schedule, and system requirements. Management approval is required in order to proceed.

- During the alternative evaluation step, options are researched by the analysts for comparison through a cost/benefit study. The alternatives, the top choice, and rationale are presented to management for approval.

- The design step involves developing specifications for each of the five system components. Hardware requirements are listed; special forms showing input/output arrangements are approved by users; data file organization is determined; new procedures for operations and training are written; and personnel requirements are listed.

- Prototyping allows the systems analyst to create working models of screens, reports, and other user interfaces.

- A CASE toolkit contains software (CASE tools) and a project dictionary that help systems analysts manage the systems development process using diagrams and charts.

- The implementation step consists of five phases: coding, testing, installation, evaluation, and maintenance.

- During the coding phase, hardware is ordered and software is obtained or written. Programs, hardware, and procedures are then tested—both separately and with a system test.

- System implementation can happen as a parallel operation, phased transition, pilot operation, or direct cutover. Maintenance is an ongoing procedure to make necessary changes to software.

- Project management software contains programs to help managers schedule, plan, and track projects. Features include time management, job scheduling, contract tracking, resource (personnel and material) management, and cost estimation programs.

## TERMS TO REMEMBER

application development
    team
benchmark test
CASE (computer-aided
    software engineering)
    tools
cost/benefit analysis
critical path
data flow diagram
direct cutover
feasibility study

Gantt chart
installation
life cycle
maintenance
parallel operation
PERT (program evaluation
    and review technique)
phased transition
pilot operation

project management
    software
prototyping
request for proposal (RFP)
retirement
service bureau
system specifications
system test
systems development
    project

## MIX AND MATCH

*Complete the following definitions with the Terms to Remember.*

1.  _____ is the point in time when a computer program or an entire computer system is no longer used.

2.  A(n) _____ comprises the steps taken to define and create new system solutions to existing problems.

3.  Keeping one or more of a computer system's components up-to-date and related people trained constitutes system _____.

4.  Modeling user interfaces (screens and reports) by users as part of the initial system design is known as _____.

5.  A(n) _____ shows starting dates and duration for different activities in the systems development process.

6.  The method of conversion wherein the old system is removed and the new system is immediately installed is called a(n) _____.

7.  The document detailing requirements and procedures to be incorporated into a new computer system is referred to as the _____.

8.  A(n) _____ is the type of installation whereby the entire new system is tried in just a small part of the organization.

9.  A group of people responsible for defining system specifications and performing feasibility studies is known as a(n) _____.

10. A(n) _____ determines if a systems development project is realistic.

11. A(n) _____ compares software and hardware performance against an agreed-upon standard.

12. A visual representation of how data and people interact is called a(n) _____.

13. A(n) _____ is an outside agency that handles data processing needs for an organization.

14. The combination of events that requires the most time to complete is known as the _____.

15. _____ are software that uses a project dictionary with charting tools to help computer professionals manage a systems development project.

## REVIEW QUESTIONS

1. Define the Terms to Remember.

2. How are systems development projects made more manageable?

3. What special precautions should be added to the systems development process to help ensure success?

4. Who performs an initial review, and what are their responsibilities?

5. Who determines if a new computer system has merit and initiates the feasibility study?

6. What data-gathering techniques are part of the feasibility study?

7. Describe how the requirements step applies to the purchase of a personal computer system.

8. How does providing management with a list of alternative system solutions promote good management decision making?

9. What are three intangible costs and benefits managers must consider when evaluating system alternatives?

10. What decisions are made in the final phase of the alternative evaluation step?

11. What decisions are made when evaluating alternatives for a personal computer system?

12. Name two advantages and two disadvantages of prototyping.

13. Identify an advantage and three disadvantages of using CASE tools.

14. Use the five components of a computer system to describe the activities and requirements that make up a set of system specifications.

15. What happens at the end of the design step?

16. What activities are involved in designing a personal computer system?

17. What happens during the coding and testing phase?

18. Who needs to be trained before the system test can occur?

19. What must be completed before installation starts?

20. What is the purpose of the immediate and six-month follow-up reviews of a completed systems development project?

21. Explain the difference between product support and change control during the maintenance phase.

22. Describe the steps in the life cycle of a systems development process. Be sure to identify the phases associated with each step.

23. What steps are included in the setup and maintenance of a new personal computer system?

24. Explain the features common to project management software.

## APPLYING WHAT YOU'VE LEARNED

1. The systems development life cycle can be applied when any major decisions or purchases are made, even those not involving computer systems. Choose an area in which you will have to make a decision in the near future. It could involve school, finding a job or a new place to live, buying a car, or some other decision. Organize your decision making by using the four steps and associated phases in the life cycle. For each step, outline what is involved relating to your decision. Include any ideas on alternatives, feasibility, benchmarks, and so on.

2. The type of installation method used depends upon the specific application, the experience of the users, and how involved the change will be. For each installation method (parallel operation, phased transition, pilot operation, and direct cutover), list a situation not mentioned in the text in which this method seems to be the best approach. Briefly explain why you feel the method is appropriate.

3. It is sometimes difficult to list all of the costs and benefits resulting from a systems development project. List two each of tangible costs, tangible benefits, intangible costs, and intangible benefits that may arise from installing a new computer system in a retail store. Use examples different from the text.

4. For each of the following situations, list three examples of cyclic, legal, or company policy changes that could result in maintenance for the computer system.
   a. a local branch of a large bank
   b. a college or university
   c. a tax accountant
   d. a public utility such as electric or gas
   e. a local drugstore

5. An application development team involves a variety of people. List the qualifications and personality traits each of these people should have to be an effective team member: systems analyst, user, network administrator, programmer.

6. Should any exceptions to the rule "documentation must be complete before a new system is installed" be allowed? Explain your position.

# CHAPTER 14

# Software Development

**P**rograms are the instructions for a computer. Although you no longer must learn programming to be an informed user, it is important to understand the concepts and languages involved in creating programs. Developing macros for word processing or electronic spreadsheet applications is a form of programming in which many informed users participate.

Acquiring software to solve an application problem, either through purchase or programming, makes you a part of a systems design project. When you learn about the program development process, you can better communicate the application requirements to a computer professional. If we spark your interest in programming, a class in one of the languages described or an advanced class in macro development or database programming may be a logical next step for you.

## PEOPLE AND PROGRAMMING

Programs control the data retrieval, processing, and storage functions within a computer system to create problem-solving applications. The exact requirements for the program must be determined by people who understand the details of the problem itself. How involved a person gets in the program development process depends upon his or her level of knowledge and the type of program required.

## Levels of User Involvement

Most end users have little need to get very involved in developing a program from scratch. End users and user-developers customize application software, such as spreadsheets and word processors, by programming macros to automate software operations. As explained in chapter 9, a macro allows a series of program operations, such as printing or file merging, to be started with a few keystrokes. Commands and logic for writing macros depend upon the individual software package.

Programming opportunities are available for user-developers willing to invest the time and effort. Complex multimedia applications can be programmed through application generators, also known as *authoring systems*. These software packages allow creation of a customized user interface and provide access to data management programs. In addition, many database management systems have their own programming languages that can be used to enhance the objects created by screen and report generators.

Application programs, such as a payroll package, inventory system, word processor, or database management system, are created by professional application programmers. Developing efficient, accurate, and user-friendly programs from scratch requires organized efforts by trained personnel. For a specific application such as payroll, programmers must be made aware by users and managers of every problem and how it affects the organization. General-purpose applications, like a word processor, require flexibility and user-friendliness, which must be included by the programmers. Application programmers should have in-depth knowledge of the principles of computer processing, supplemented by total fluency in one or more programming languages, as discussed later in this chapter.

People who write systems programs (operating systems and programming language translators) must efficiently use the computer's storage and I/O capabilities. These systems programmers concentrate on details that may be machine-specific (Intel versus Motorola) and hardware-oriented (such as saving files on disks). Although high-level tools make it easier to produce individual modules or entire programs, proper design and effective resource planning remain essential to successful development and implementation of computer software.

## Misconceptions About Programming

When a new application program is written from scratch, programming can take as much as 50 percent of the overall systems development budget. Even if application packages exist that can be adapted to the needs of a new system, programming is still important. Programming skills are required to design, develop, and apply computers to solve information problems. The job postings in Figure 14.1 are typical for people seeking careers in computer programming.

To people inexperienced with software development, programming may seem to be simply writing program instructions, or *code*, that causes computers to execute a specific IPOS cycle. This is far from the truth. Developing a program is an extensive process that involves problem definition, functional and technical design, coding, testing, and documentation. The program must be specified and designed in all detail necessary for implementation before the writing of code even begins.

## 14.1

A variety of opportunities are available for programmers and related professionals.

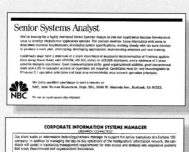

### The Four-Step Programming Process

The implementation step of the four-step system life cycle, described in chapter 13, is where the program development process fits. Development of software occurs parallel to the purchase, testing, and installation of hardware.

The programming process follows a four-step structure of its own to organize the production of application programs for a computer system. Like the system life cycle,

**14.2**

Program development takes place within the systems development process as part of the implementation step.

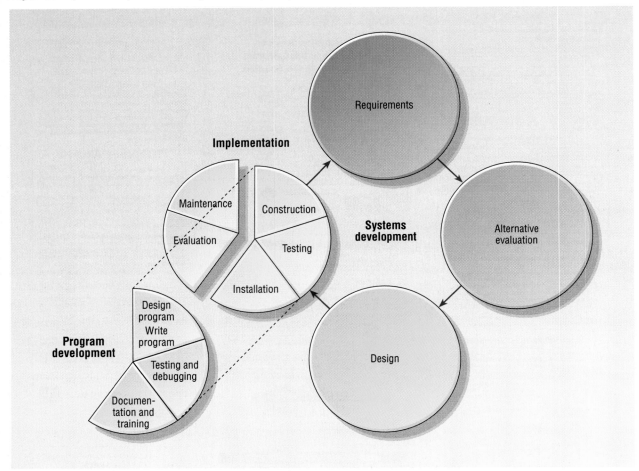

program development projects vary in scope with the professionals and organizations involved and what level of programming will be required. However, the overall picture (see Figure 14.2) can be illustrated through four steps in the programming process: designing the program, writing program code, testing and debugging the program, and documentation and training.

## DESIGNING THE PROGRAM

*Program specifications* form the basis for the program design. They are part of the system specifications, including what the users expect from the system as well as the technical interpretations of processing requirements prepared by the systems analyst. If the software to be designed is stand-alone and is not part of a larger systems development project, program requirements need to be obtained, similar to the requirements step of the system life cycle. As discussed in chapter 13, the designs of printed output, prepared by report generators, and input screen prototypes are considered part of the program specifications. Also included is a set of test data to be processed by the program. Complete testing helps to ensure quality, accuracy, and acceptance of programs for use within a system.

## Defining the Problem

Since computer programs are written to solve problems, the programmer must look at the problem from the user's perspective (see Figure 14.3). Data entry methods and forms of output to be generated appear as prototypes which are approved by the users. Although transparent to most users, one of the important considerations is the long-term storage requirements for data files. Almost any file created within or maintained by a program will require expansion over time. A programmer who understands both the present and future needs for data storage and retrieval will create a program with a long, useful life.

The same is true for any type of computer program. An expert system for doctors must anticipate the kinds of queries that will be presented and have capacity for expansion. Scientific programmers must anticipate researchers' present and future needs. Such multimedia presentations as an almanac may not be written for longevity but are programmed with a specific audience in mind. Application software is customized to personal standards. Even a macro written for an electronic spreadsheet should be written for long-term, practical use, keeping in mind that it may be modified later.

## Unstructured Programs

In the early years of computer programming, programmers had no standard techniques or design methods to follow. Programs were written mostly to solve current problems,

Problem definition is the starting point for program development.

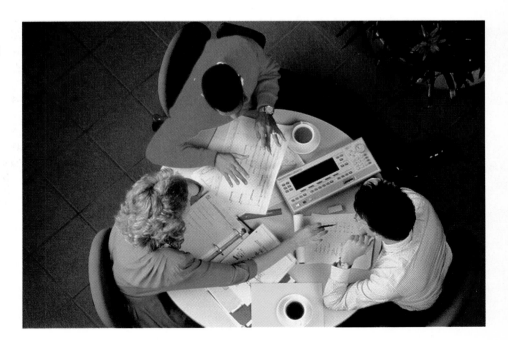

## ...ABOUT WARRANTIES

Whatever the warranty for your computer hardware or software states, follow these rules:

- Keep the original boxes so you can safely ship the product back to the manufacturer or to a repair facility if necessary

- Check the parts (or disks) immediately upon receiving them to see if they work properly

- Keep all paperwork, such as receipts, warranties, and contracts

- Make sure you have all claims from the manufacturer or store representative in writing

- Pay by credit card, because the credit card companies will hold payment and investigate claims

- Deal with established companies who will be around long enough to honor their warranties to the letter

*Source: Compute,* February 1993, page 90.

without much consideration of future needs like expanding file space or adding program options. As a result, many programs met users' immediate needs but were difficult to modify or expand later.

Sometimes major modifications must be made to a program during its life span. Like a family who wants to winterize a summer cottage, a maintenance programmer is sometimes asked to modify a program's structure in a way that it was not originally designed to handle. A cottage would need major renovation, including a new furnace, insulation, energy-efficient windows, updated kitchen and baths, along with other changes for year-round living. Sometimes, confronted with these problems, it is easier and more cost-efficient to just tear down the cottage and build a new home from scratch.

When a program needed major changes, a programmer had similar problems in making structural changes. First, the original programmer was not always the one who was making the modifications. Sometimes the program was accompanied by little or no documentation. Like the summer cottage, the program was often designed to handle specific applications with little flexibility. For example, there would be limits on file sizes, new types of fields could not be input, or a program using batch data could not be adapted to interactive use. Many times programmers found it best to just rewrite the programs from scratch.

The reason for the difficulty was not the competence of the programmer, but the method with which the program was written. Modifying a program was easier if the code was not written in an unstructured manner. **Unstructured programs** were written using a linear, or top-down, approach to problem solving. One instruction sequentially followed another until a particular condition was reached. At this point the program

**14.4**

Unstructured programs are executed in a linear fashion, whereas structured programs execute modules of code.

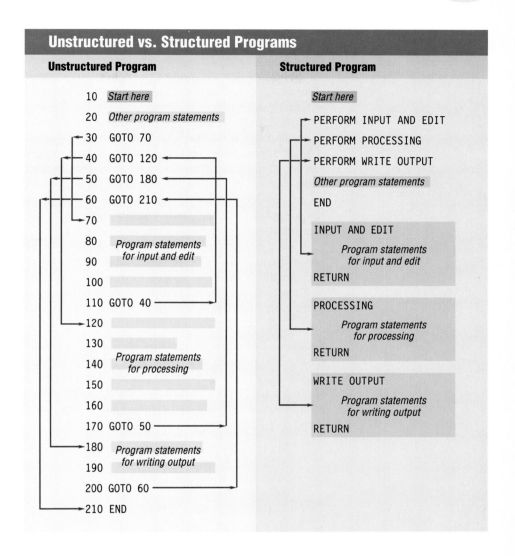

## Unstructured vs. Structured Programs

logic branched to another part of the program and continued sequentially from there. The more complex the program, the more the branching overlapped.

The logic of these early unstructured programs was difficult enough for a maintenance programmer to follow, let alone modify. One could not predict how new or modified code would affect the logic for the rest of the program. Changes to programs were often made in a patchwork fashion, with branches to these patches scattered throughout the program. If someone were to trace the logical flow of the program with lines, there would be much overlapping. Figure 14.4 illustrates why unstructured programs were said to contain "spaghetti" logic.

During this time, programming was considered more of an art than a science. The people trained to program were, for the most part, computer professionals and not users. By the beginning of the 1970s, more than 85 percent of an organization's programming costs were going for program maintenance. Computer scientists started searching for ways to reduce these costs and make programs easier to modify.

## ■ Structured Programs

The development of system software made computer scientists realize that most computer programs, regardless of application, processed data through arrangements of similar processing code. This observation altered program development in two important ways.

First, utility software, provided by computer manufacturers, contains common processing functions that were used by many programs. These utilities, discussed in chapter 3, performed such operations as data compression, disk optimization, and hardware emulation. Other utilities made merging files and managing large data files easier. Instead of rewriting the code for these frequently used processing functions, programmers could call up and use these utilities. Scientific programmers also shared the program code for mathematical routines to save time and ensure accurate computations.

Even more influential was the second change in program development, *structured programs*. In a structured program, all aspects of the IPOS cycle can be broken down and coded into three simple structures: sequence, selection, and iteration. This design technique affected the way programmers approached the programming process itself. Every program could be written with these three structures.

**Sequence Structure**   In a *sequence*, instructions are followed one after another in the same preset order in which they appear within the program, unless told to branch to another statement. The following segment of a payroll program would be one example of a sequence. Hours worked and hourly pay rate are entered as data, multiplied to produce the gross pay, and then gross pay is displayed.

```
PRINT "ENTER THE HOURS WORKED THIS WEEK"
INPUT HOURS
PRINT "ENTER HOURLY PAY RATE"
INPUT RATE
PAY = HOURS * RATE
PRINT "GROSS PAY: "; PAY
```

**Selection Structure**   *Selection* means that one of two alternative sequences of instructions is chosen, based on a logical condition. For example, in the following segment of a payroll program, hours worked by an employee are compared to 40 hours, the typical workweek. When hours worked are greater than 40, both the overtime (time and one-half) and regular pay calculations are done. Otherwise, just the regular pay calculations are performed with overtime set to 0. Regardless of which calculations are selected, regular and overtime pay are added to equal total pay.

```
IF HOURS > 40 THEN
    OVERTIME = (HOURS - 40) * (RATE * 1.5)
    REGULAR = RATE * 40
ELSE
    OVERTIME = 0.00
    REGULAR = HOURS * RATE
ENDIF
PAY = REGULAR + OVERTIME
```

**Iteration Structure**　When a sequence of instructions is repeated for as long as a programmer dictates or until some processing condition changes, *iteration* has occurred. In the following example, data is entered, regular and overtime pay are calculated, and total pay is displayed so long as the user enters "YES" to a query to continue. This process is repeated until the logical condition—RESPONSE$ = "YES"—is no longer true.

```
RESPONSE$ = "YES"
WHILE RESPONSE$ = "YES"
      PRINT "ENTER THE HOURS WORKED THIS WEEK"
      INPUT HOURS
      PRINT "ENTER HOURLY PAY RATE"
      INPUT RATE
      IF HOURS > 40 THEN
            OVERTIME = (HOURS - 40) * (RATE * 1.5)
            REGULAR = RATE * 40
      ELSE
            OVERTIME = 0.00
            REGULAR = HOURS * RATE
      ENDIF
      PAY = REGULAR + OVERTIME
      PRINT "GROSS PAY: "; PAY
      INPUT "DO YOU WISH TO CONTINUE? (YES/NO)"; RESPONSE$
WEND
END
```

The structured approach permits some flexibility. The same program may be designed differently by different programmers. In each case, however, the designer establishes segments of code that can be linked to form a workable, modifiable program.

The key to using the three structures effectively is to organize them into modules. A *module* is a set of instructions that performs one specific function or action within a program. For example, most structured application programs contain separate modules for data entry, error checking, processing, and screen or printer output (see Figure 14.4). A typical module contains no more than a page (about 50 lines) of code and usually can be written in a short period of time by a single programmer. A structured program may consists of any number of modules, each called upon as needed.

Modules and structured programming give a programmer several advantages over using unstructured design techniques. Since each module is small and considered independent of the other modules in a program, modules in the same program can be written by different programmers and tested separately before being combined into the final program. Modules from one program can also be used in another program. Modules can be purchased or shared among organizations, which is especially important to systems and scientific programmers. When a program needs to be modified, only those modules affected have to be changed. This reduces programming effort and costs, along with facilitating testing of the modified program.

For users working with a macro language, producing structured programs is made easy. A macro itself is a self-contained module, and the limited macro commands available are already similar to those of structured code. When using a more complex authoring system, a user-developer may find that the language lends itself to producing structured modules. With the advent of multimedia and more-visual orientation of users, object-oriented program design is an important design alternative.

## Object-Oriented Programs

Structured methodology greatly changed how people logically design programs. The current popularity of object-oriented programming is asking programmers and users to radically rethink how they view program design and coding. ***Object-oriented programming (OOP)*** bases program logic on objects rather than modules. An *object* is a self-contained collection of programming code and data descriptions that complete a single task or program function. Like a module, objects can be put together to form a single program. Each object can be tested separately and used by other programs. Unlike a module, an object contains more than code to perform some aspect of the IPOS cycle. An object has three components:

♦ A name that identifies its function

♦ Related data names and descriptions

♦ Methods that can be used to process the data

A collection of objects used to solve a problem is considered an object-oriented program. This *encapsulation* of both the descriptions of the data required for the task and the instructions (methods) to perform requested actions into an object makes OOP a unique way to look at program design.

An object may contain a document, graphic, audio sequence, worksheet, or window as well as any related methods for processing and manipulating these data items. For example, a graphics program may contain an object called CIRCLE. Data includes location of the center of the circle, its radius, and color. The instructions to draw, fill, or erase the circle would be included in the object methods. Additional methods might include calculations to determine diameter, area, and circumference. Other objects like LINE, CURVE, RECTANGLE, and POLYGON would contain similar information and may make up a *class,* or set of similar objects, called SHAPES.

When a program references an object, it sends a message containing required data (that is, center location, radius, and color) and what result is required (draw circle). The object performs the necessary processing using the methods contained within itself. Therefore, each object is completely independent of other objects. However, the processing an object performs (fill) may be common to several applications. It is not unusual for the same object to be used in several programs, reducing coding time.

A payroll system could be written using object-oriented programming methods. As shown in Figure 14.5, several classes would be involved, each with unique objects. The class DEDUCTIONS, for example, would contain three types of taxes, insurance premiums, and voluntary credit union deductions, all affecting a paycheck in the same general way. Figure 14.5 also shows the components of several individual objects. Obviously, these few objects would not constitute an entire payroll program. A more complete diagram is shown in Figure 14.6.

Object-oriented programming is obviously a more complex process than structured programming. This is an initial disadvantage to programmers; however, once an object is written, it can be used in other programs or as a model for other objects in a class. Managing graphic output was one of the first uses for OOP. For example, an object that moves a graphic image to a specified screen location could be used in the free-drawing feature of a graphics package, to define borders in desktop publishing, or for the movement of a missile toward a target in a video game. It is this reliance on previously developed objects that makes object-oriented programming a factor in decreasing the time spent in program development.

**14.5**

An object contains an identifying name, data fields, and methods for processing the data. Objects of similar functions are collected into classes.

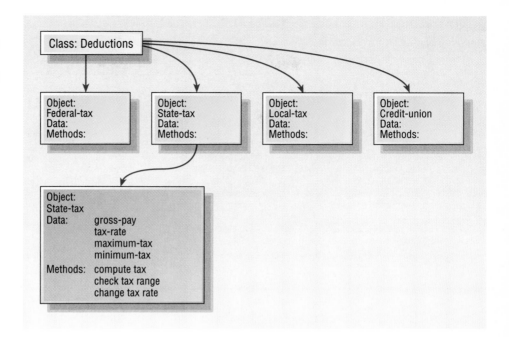

For the user-developer creating an application with an authoring system, object-oriented programming is a natural. As humans, we see most things as objects. If an authoring system contains predefined objects such as windows, icons, buttons, and menus, they can be customized and arranged easily. A user-developer requiring a dialog box as part of a program can copy the dialog box object and change some data fields or size and shape, but the essential function of the dialog box to accept input remains intact.

## ■ Tools for Program Design

Modules and objects become the elements of program design. Programmers have several tools to help them organize and show the relationships of these elements before coding a program. Each tool differs in how the modules and objects are presented.

**Structure Charts**   Figure 14.6 shows an overview of the general structure for a payroll program. This type of graphic representation is called a ***structure chart***. As shown, a structure chart organizes a program into a series of levels. Modules or objects are identified by rectangles and are normally executed in order from the top downward and from left to right at each level. This kind of top-down arrangement is known as a hierarchy and is commonly seen in organizational charts. Therefore, a structure chart is also known as a *hierarchy chart.*

The structure chart provides a standard framework within which many programs can be designed. By organizing the top levels of the chart, the programmer creates an outline for the general processing functions of the program. The specific steps involved in lower levels of the chart are developed as additional program modules are created or as objects inherit characteristics from higher-level objects. This "top-down" refinement of the program design occurs as the programmer uses design tools to break each module or object into specific program instructions.

## 14.6

Structure charts identify the program modules or objects needed to solve a particular problem.

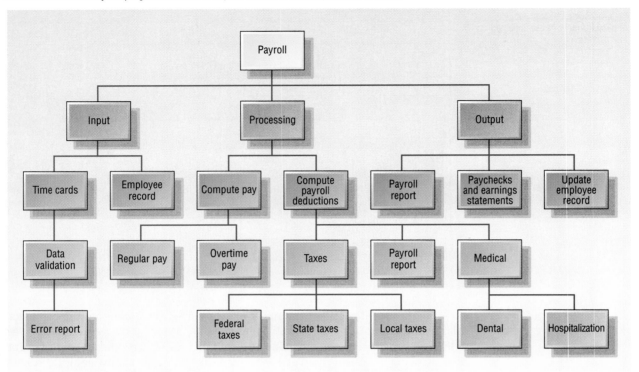

**Flowcharts**   A program *flowchart* is a common method for defining the logical steps of flow within a program, by using a series of symbols to identify the basic IPOS functions within programs. These symbols are positioned and linked to form a graphic representation of a program's logic. For example, Figure 14.7 shows a flowchart for the payroll program example. A flowchart is a graphic method for showing the sequences, selections, and iterations within a program or module. Software is now available for creating a printable flowchart from program code or user design.

**Pseudocode**   Some programmers prefer to use actual words, or *pseudocode*, to represent program steps rather than flowcharting with symbols. Pseudocode became popular because it lent itself to the design of structured programs. Figure 14.8 illustrates the pseudocode version of the payroll program. Many programmers prefer pseudocode because it is similar to the actual language of coding.

Flexibility is one advantage of designing through the use of structure charts, pseudocode, or flowcharting. These tools can be translated into program code for any high-level programming language, independent of specific language rules. The choice between structure charts, pseudocode, and flowcharting is a matter of personal preference and company standards. Other design tools, providing various charts and program logic diagrams, are also available. Another advantage is that these tools provide a basis for reviewing program design among all members of an application development team, including users and technicians. Their nontechnical nature makes these tools reasonable choices for end users and user-developers creating their own programs.

**14.7**

This flowchart uses symbols and arrows to outline the program logic for a simple payroll processing program.

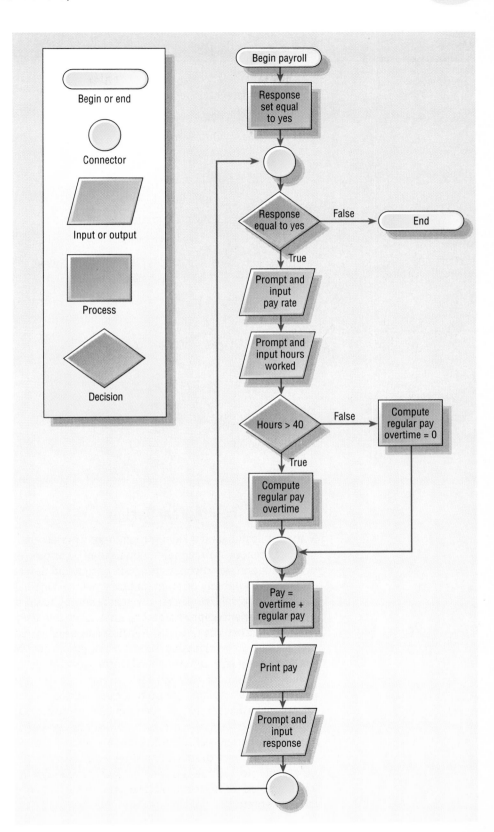

**14.8**

Pseudocode uses words to outline the logic needed for a simple payroll program.

---

## Pseudocode

Begin Payroll Program

    Set Response = Yes

    Do while Response = Yes

        Display "Enter Hours Worked"

        Accept Hours

        Display "Enter Hourly Payrate"

        Accept Rate

        If Hours are greater than 40

            then Overtime Pay = (Hours − 40) * (Rate * 1.5)

                Regular Pay = Rate * 40

            else Overtime Pay = 0

                Regular Pay = Rate * Hours

        End if

        Pay = Regular Pay + Overtime Pay

        Display Pay

        Display "Do you wish to continue?"

        Accept Response

    End do while

End Payroll Program

---

## ▪ Testing the Program Design

Many application and systems programming projects require the effort of an entire team of programmers. Although individuals may be responsible for coding a particular area of the program, teamwork in program design and development can help to ensure the quality and reliability of program performance. One initial quality control measure is the detailed review of designs by programming team members before actual coding begins. Experienced programmers, knowledgeable users, and/or managers review all design documents in a step-by-step procedure known as a ***structured walkthrough*** (see Figure 14.9). By working together, a small group of computer professionals can track the processing of data through the entire program design sequence. The purpose of a walkthrough is to identify any design weaknesses or logic errors before actual program code writing takes place. The more errors that can be uncovered at this stage, the greater the program quality is likely to be. Even non-professional programmers can benefit from explaining the logic of a program to another user. Someone else can provide a fresh look at a design, possibly finding inconsistencies that were missed.

    Complete program design should also include a set of test data used to validate programs from the module or object level up through the complete system. ***Test data*** is an assembled set of data that makes use of all the processing features and controls in the new program.

**14.9**

Structured walkthroughs promote the review and discussion of program design and code with other programming team members.

For each program function to be tested, test data must include both valid and invalid items. For example, a payroll program might limit the value of checks that can be printed to a minimum of $20 and a maximum of $5,000. To test this program function, the values $19, $20, $5,000, and $5,001 might be included in the test data. These data items would test the full range of acceptable values and ensure that the program can adequately handle unacceptable data outside both ends of the range.

Extensive sets of test data should be designed to test all operational functions of every module and object, as well as the entire program. It is important that preparation of test data be completed during the design stage of program development, before coding begins. The idea of test data is to validate the actual program. Quality assurance is greater if development of test data precedes and is separate from the coding operation so a programmer would not be tempted to adjust the data to the coded program. This applies to user-developers as well.

## WRITING PROGRAM CODE

Coding should be a routine, relatively straightforward process if sufficient care is taken with program design. For some high-level programming languages, one instruction or line of code is written for each line of pseudocode or each flowcharting symbol. Other languages require several lines of code to implement a pseudocode line or flowchart symbol. To understand the differences in programming languages, we must first examine what the computer does with a high-level computer program.

### Language Translators

Before high-level programming languages, computers were complicated to program. Each instruction had to be written directly in the computer's own machine language, which represents internal switch settings as l's and 0's, binary code. The complexity of writing these machine language programs was reduced when assembly languages were developed in the 1950s. Programmers using assembly languages relied on translating programs, called *assemblers,* to relieve the burden of coding computer programs in highly detailed machine language. Instead of using binary code, programs were written in symbolic assembly languages. Then assembler software translated these programs into binary code that the computer could understand. One line of assembly code is usually required for each machine language instruction to be generated. By today's standards, this method of program translation is simple but inefficient, because higher-level languages do not maintain this one-to-one relationship. Still, the development of assemblers is considered a turning point in the history of programming and a forerunner of high-level languages.

Although assembler languages are still used for some types of systems programming, they have been replaced by more sophisticated, user-friendly, high-level programming languages and *fourth-generation languages (4GLs).* Because code must still be translated to bit patterns, these languages rely on one of two sophisticated language translators called compilers and interpreters. For each high-level program statement translated, a compiler or interpreter generates several machine language statements. Compared with assemblers, these language translators allow programmers to write larger, more complex, error-free programs in less time.

**Compilers**    *Compilers* are available for most high-level languages. Figure 14.10 shows how a compiler translates a program into machine code. First, the application program

**14.10**

Compilers translate programs written in a high-level language into a complete machine language program, or list each instruction that could not be converted. Only when completely translated can the program be executed.

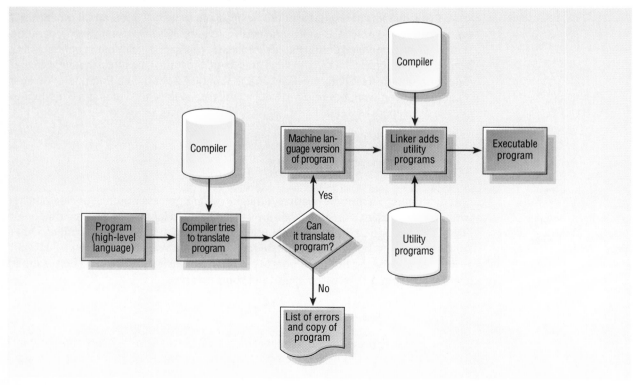

written in a high-level programming language is loaded into memory along with a translator program for that language. The compiler checks the program for errors in translating the code into machine language.

Syntax errors may prevent the translation from being completed. A *syntax error* is a spelling error or mistake in the grammar of the high-level language that the computer

## John G. Kemeny

(b. 1926)

## Thomas E. Kurtz

(b. 1928)

Despite the existence of many computers and programming languages like FORTRAN and COBOL, programming a computer was complicated in the 1960s. A person needed to have a strong working knowledge of the computer equipment, and the languages lent themselves best to scientific and engineering applications. John Kemeny was Mathematics Department chairman at Dartmouth College in the early 1960s. He had worked on the H-bomb project in Los Alamos and had been an assistant to Albert Einstein. Dartmouth's computer center manager, Thomas Kurtz, convinced Kemeny that the university computer should be time-shared. Together they urged their peers to consider that computer literacy was as important as reading, writing, and arithmetic.

To increase student access, Kemeny and Kurtz developed BASIC in 1964, consisting of 14 different statements. The ease of using BASIC became apparent. Students could program after only two hours of instruction. Many were not science or engineering majors. By placing BASIC in the public domain, its use spread. Bill Gates wrote a version of BASIC to use on the Altair, an early micro-processor; it later became a standard language packaged with all micro-computers. Kemeny and Kurtz tried to set standards for BASIC to unify the many existing versions. In 1985 they released TRUE BASIC, which they saw as a powerful version that could help make programs portable—usable on different types of computers. Although BASIC is no longer the predominant language for college students, many children are taught it in elementary school and high school.

## 14.11

Interpreters translate high-level language programs into machine code one line at a time, executing each instruction before translating the next. The translation is not saved.

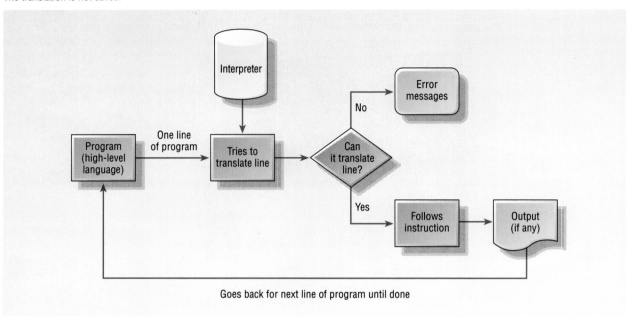

Goes back for next line of program until done

cannot translate. For example, the COBOL instruction MULTIPLE PAY-RATE BY HOURS GIVING REGULAR-PAY cannot be translated. To the COBOL compiler, this line is untranslatable because MULTIPLE is not a valid instruction. When the programmer corrects the syntax error by replacing MULTIPLE with MULTIPLY, this COBOL instruction can be translated into machine code.

Unfortunately, a program can contain other errors besides those of syntax. A compiler is not able to find *logic errors*. This type of error is syntactically correct and translatable but produces the wrong results. If the programmer accidentally wrote MULTIPLY PAY-RATE BY EMPLOYEE-NUMBER GIVING REGULAR-PAY, the instruction would be translated into machine code. However, the results would be incorrect because hours worked, not employee number, is used in calculating pay. Another example of a logic error would be using a plus sign when a minus sign is needed.

When the program translation is error-free, the operating system activates a linker. The *linker* program embeds utilities needed for input, output, or processing within the translated program. For example, a program that writes to disk may require data compression routines to be included. When linking is complete, the program is ready for use.

At this point the original COBOL program or other high-level language program is saved for future updates or modifications. The complete translation, including utilities, is either stored on disk for later use or *executed,* followed one step at a time, by the processing unit. To use a compiler, a computer system must have enough memory to store the application program in both high-level and machine language forms as well as the compiler itself.

**Interpreters**   Using an *interpreter* involves translating a high-level language program in a different way. Interpreters translate and execute one high-level program instruction at a time. Each instruction is acted upon directly after it is translated. Then the translation is discarded. If the program's logic dictates that instructions are repeated, each instruction must be translated again. As shown in Figure 14.11, this translation/execution process is repeated until the program comes to its logical conclusion or the interpreter finds a syntax error. The advantage of using an interpreter is that it requires a minimum amount of memory. Just the interpreter and the single instruction it is translating must be stored. However, because the translated version of the program is not saved, the original program must be translated each time it is used, slowing down processing.

## ■ Finding Program Errors

It is difficult to find logic errors in a program no matter what kind of language translator is used. A finished program, for example, may have 10,000 or more lines of code. Programmers must observe results and apply logical reasoning to identify where errors occur. Each time a correction is made, it may be necessary to retranslate the program and retest the object or module of the program that has been modified. Errors within coded programs are called *bugs;* the process of finding and correcting these errors is known as ***debugging*** a program (see Figure 14.12). Some high-level language compilers and interpreters contain debugging features that allow the programmer to trace the program step by step, displaying what data is being processed and stored along the way.

## ■ Programming Languages

Deciding which programming language to use depends on the specific needs of an application and its users as well as standards followed in the organization. Through the years, more than 200 programming languages have been developed, some of which are quite specialized. Figure 14.13 contains a summary of the major strengths and weaknesses of the most popular high-level languages along with six examples of program code.

**14.12**

Debugging a program requires intense detailed effort by experienced computer programmers.

```
       Integer Num1, Num2, Sum
       Read (5,10) Num1, Num2
  10   Format (2I4)
       Sum = Num1 + Num2
       Write (6,20) Num1, Num2 Sum
  20   Format (10X, 'The Sum of ', I4, ' + ', I4, ' is ', I5)
       Stop
       End
```

**FORTRAN**

### 14.13

A sampling of the variety of programming languages (see table on the facing page).

```
Program Add_it;
Var Num1, Num2, Sum: Integer;


Begin
 Readln (Num1, Num2);
    Num1 + Num2;
    ln('The sum of ', Num1:4, ' + ', Num2:4, ' is ', Sum:5);
```

**PASCAL**

```
Identification Division.
 Program-ID. Addition.

Environment Division.
 Input-Output Section.
       .
       .
       .
Data Division.
 File Section.
 FD Data-in
  Label records are standard.
 01 Numbers-to-be-processed.
    05  Number-1-In     PIC 999.
    05  Number-2-In     PIC 999.

 FD Answer-out
  Label records are omitted.
 01 Sum-to-be-printed   PIC X(27).

 Working-Storage Section.
 01 Temporary-work-area.
    05  Filler          PIC X(10)   Value "The Sum of ".
    05  Number-1-Out    PIC 999.
    05  Filler          PIC XXX     Value " + ".
    05  Number-2-Out    PIC 999.
    05  Filler          PIC X(4)    Value " is ".
    05  Sum-Out         PIC 9(4).

Procedure Division.
 Processing-Routine.
  Open input Data-in
  output Answer-out.
 Read Data-in.
 Add Number-1-In, Number-2-In giving Sum-Out.
 Move Number-1-In to Number-1-Out
 Move Numb
 Write Sum
 Close Dat
  Answer-o
 Stop run.
```

**COBOL**

```
              FILE DESCRIPTION SPECIFICATIONS

Numbin    IP   F    80      Disk     5
Numbout   O    F    182  OF Printer

              INPUT FORMAT SPECIFICATIONS

Filein    NS   01
                                1    30Num1
                                4    60Num2

              CALCULATION SPECIFICATIONS

01        Num1      Add  Num2 Sum  42

              OUTPUT FORMAT SPECIFICATIONS

Numout    H    207  1P
          OR        OF
                                     34 'The sum of 2 numbers'
          D    1    01
                                     20 'The sum of '
                            Num1 3   24
                                     26 ' + '
                            Num2 3   30
                                     33 ' is '
                            Sum  3   38
```

**RPG**

```
BUTTERF.FRM
Object: [general]        Proc: [declarations]
Sub Timer1_Timer ()
Static PickBmp As Integer
   Main.Move Main.Left + 20, Main.Top - 5
   If PickBmp Then
       Main.Picture = OpenWings.Picture    ' Load open butterfly.
   Else
       Main.Picture = CloseWings.Picture   ' Load closed butterfly.
   End If
   PickBmp = Not PickBmp                    ' Toggle the value.
End Sub
```

Butterfly

**Visual BASIC**

How many customers do we have in the Big Apple?

I don't know what you mean by the Big Apple.

New York City

The XYZ Company has 201 customers with addresses in New York City

How many purchased guitars this year?

34

**Natural Language**

**14.13** *(Continued)*

Because computer languages were designed to handle applications in different fields of work, each has its own strengths and weaknesses.

## Comparision of Computer Programming Languages

| Language | Applications | Strengths | Weaknesses |
|---|---|---|---|
| Ada | Scientific, Department of Defense | Easy to structure programs | Complex, takes time to master |
| BASIC | Educational, simple scientific and business | Easy to learn, widely used with PCs | Difficult to structure; weak I/O capabilities |
| C | Systems and graphics | Portable, easy to structure programs | Complex, takes time to master |
| C++ | Systems and graphics | Portable, object-oriented | Complex, takes time to master |
| COBOL | Business | Self-documenting, easy to structure, widely used | Verbose, complex computations are awkward |
| FORTRAN | Scientific and graphics | Handles complex computations for science and graphics | Difficult to structure, weak I/O capabilities |
| Fourth-generation | Databases, application generators, graphics | Simplifies program development, easy commands | Limited to advanced applications |
| LOGO | Educational | Easy to learn, allows simple graphics and geometry | Few applications outside of education |
| Natural language | Decision support systems, expert systems | Uses human language | Limited applications at present |
| Pascal | Education | Easy to structure, can be object-oriented | Weak I/O capabilities |
| RPG | Business | Easy to generate reports, nonprocedural | Difficult to structure, complex calculations awkward |
| Visual BASIC | Systems programs, GUIs | Object-oriented, BASIC-like code | May be difficult for beginners to learn |

## TESTING AND DEBUGGING

Prior to release of the new system to users, a complete system test is done on the newly written program. A system test, described in chapter 13, involves two major sets of activities: testing all modules, objects, and complete programs, and testing the system under realistic operating conditions.

### Program Testing

When programs are written in modules or objects, they are put through a series of top-down test procedures. The bottom level of a program is an individual module or object. Every programmer is responsible for testing program sections as they are written.

Part of a system test involves checking the interconnections among modules and objects. To check program modules, stub testing techniques often are employed. *Stub testing* is the execution of selected program modules to see if they interact correctly. Quite often the stub is an incomplete module designed to stand in for other, more complex modules. It may do no more than display that the stub has (or has not) been executed in the proper sequence. In some instances standard stub modules are used that input data to or receive output from the module being tested. Although objects are not interconnected in OOP, stub testing is still done to check logical flow through the object. In every new program, each section must be tested and debugged before it is included in the overall system.

Strenuous testing is done even if the program is only being maintained or updated. If the program was designed by using structured or object-oriented techniques, just one or two sections can be modified without having to recode the other modules. Each changed module or object is tested separately and then joined with the rest of the program.

At the next level of testing, groups of modules or hierarchies of objects are tested. This process builds until complete portions of structured programs are tested as integrated units. Ultimately, the entire set of programs that forms an application is processed with a complete set of test data. When all debugging and recompilation of programs is complete, a full test can be performed.

This procedure is iterative, being repeated many times until the entire program is tested and is ready for integration into the overall system. The testing ensures that the programs produce reliable and complete output as well as being able to handle a variety of data and detect input errors. Then the program can become part of the system test.

### System Test

A *system test,* as described in chapter 13, involves operation of the complete system, including new equipment and documented procedures by users or by an independent team of employees. System tests usually are performed with realistic data input. Output from the new system is manually compared to hand-kept records or previously processed data. All of the documentation needed to operate and maintain programs and application procedures is required for the test situation to be realistic.

During a system test, program bugs or shortcomings often are discovered. It may be necessary to modify programs before final acceptance of the system. For these reasons

# Grace Murray Hopper

(1906-1992)

Without a doubt, Admiral Grace Hopper, U.S. Navy, retired, was the grande dame of computing. From an early age, she had an interest in how things worked. She earned a Ph.D. in mathematics from Yale and became a professor at Vassar, her alma mater. During World War II, Hopper enlisted in the WAVES, following the family tradition of Navy service. In 1944 she was assigned to work on programming MARK I, the first digital computing machine. She and her programming team provided the Navy with important calculations for artillery, supply schedules, and even computing for the atomic bomb project. The MARK II followed, becoming the site of a famous computing moment. One day the MARK II stopped working. Hopper found a moth caught in an electrical relay to be the cause. She taped the moth to an activity logbook and wrote, "First actual case of bug being found." Although *bug* had been a term for

mechanical defect since the 1880s, Hopper was the first to apply the word to computers—and the term became popular.

After the war she joined the Naval Reserves while she worked as senior mathematician for the UNIVAC, the first completely electronic computer. Hopper worked with computers until her mandatory retirement from the Navy in 1966 at age 60. Less than a year later, the Navy recalled her to help get its computers to work together. This project developed into the COBOL programming language, the most popular business-oriented language. She was promoted to captain in 1973, commodore in 1983, and rear admiral in 1985, the first woman to do so. She retired again in 1986 at age 80.

After her retirement, Grace Hopper became a teacher, talking about computers all over the country up to 300 days a year. When she died in 1992, she was buried with full military honors. The Navy has named its large computing center in San Diego and a new guided-missile destroyer in her honor.

it is important to keep a log of all findings during a system test and to use this log to be sure that programming and system documentation is modified to reflect all changes.

After an internal system test is complete, many commercial software developers run two more types of tests on the software. Prerelease copies of the software, with documentation, are sent to a selected group of users outside the company. These people field-test the software in real-life situations. This step of system testing, called *beta-testing*, may help to find additional bugs in the software.

Some commercial developers even have on-site usability testing labs. People using the new software in the lab are monitored as to how they use the software. Recording actual keystrokes or mistakes made by the users can help developers make improvements in future software versions.

## DOCUMENTATION AND TRAINING

Constant enhancement of programs is a requirement built into the very nature of computer systems. As soon as a new system becomes operational, it is a candidate for modification. Computer applications are modified throughout their useful lives, either to meet regulations or to capitalize on newly discovered opportunities.

From a programming standpoint, this means that the documentation prepared by any programmer must be readable and usable by any other programmer. In this way, any programmer can be assigned to modify both programs and supporting documentation as enhancement is required.

Careful documentation also is important because, in most instances today, commercial programming is a team effort. Many computer systems require programs large enough to warrant assignment of at least two and possibly more than 50 programmers to the same project. To promote better communication among programmers, it is imperative that professionals within any organization follow the same standards for design and documentation. This helps to ensure that the modules and objects will interact smoothly during program execution. This is especially true when developing software for public use—perhaps a new application package. Uniform methods must be followed in preparation of structure charts, flowcharts, pseudocode, and other documentation.

For individual user-developers, documentation is also necessary (see Figure 14.14). Although a program may not be modified by anyone else, the original programmer needs

**14.14**

Complete documentation includes user's manuals, sample reports, and screen displays. It is necessary for correct use of the program.

**14.15**

User training must be completed before programs are put into regular use.

to keep a complete set of documentation to help in making future changes. Even as small a project as a spreadsheet macro should involve notes, either within the program or on paper, on the capabilities and limitations of the instructions. This is especially true when the program is not being constantly used. Time makes us forget how even simple programs we have written work.

## User Training

Although programming is a major part of the implementation step of a systems development project, user training must also be an integral part (see Figure 14.15). Users, managers of users, computer operators, and other personnel require training on the new program. At these levels everyone needs extensive documentation. Manuals must be prepared both for training sessions and for reference during ongoing operation of the system. Complete documentation of program design and coding must be included in the data library, along with copies of the disks or tapes that hold the backup of the new programs. Users writing their own programs often find they wish to share those that others may find useful. If you are sharing or selling a program that you have written, clear user's instructions are important as well. Good documentation and training will reduce those late-night calls from friends having trouble with a program you wrote.

In short, a lot of loose ends and technical details must be tied together before a system is operational. This final step of a programming project is set up, in large part, to ensure that all the necessary details are covered. At the end of the project is a meeting at which the project manager, the director of computer operations, and the data librarian review all documentation in detail, request any additions, and ultimately accept the documents and the storage media. This review evaluates the efficiency and the quality of the programming effort, providing a learning experience and a basis for improvement of future projects.

## Program Maintenance

As is discussed in the following chapter, programs can become a basis for use of the computer in security breaches and theft. Therefore, once programs are turned over to operations personnel, procedures must be put into place that guard against both misuse and obsolescence of programs and their supporting documents.

# A Closer Look at Programming Languages

**A**s with human languages, programming languages differ in vocabulary and the structure of statements. The following examples represent a simple IPOS cycle with a selection and an iteration. To emphasize language differences, the same functions are shown in COBOL, BASIC, C++, and dBASE code. Each program allows input of two numbers from a disk file, computes their sum, finds the larger number, and stores the numbers, larger value, and sum in a different disk file. The same idea can be expressed in several ways within the same language, so a programmer can develop a style—not unlike a novelist.

**Q:** How are fields, records, and files set up for the data?

**A:** In all four examples, the input file A:DATAFILE.IN is located on the disk in drive A and made ready for access. An output file called B:RESULTS.OUT is also set up on the disk in drive B for later use.

## C++

```cpp
#include <fstream.h>
enum {failure, success};

int main(void)
{
    int Number1, Number2, Sum, Maximum;
    ifstream f_in("A:Datafile.in");
 if (!f_in) {
    cerr << "Unable to open the input file." << endl;
    return failure;
}
 ofstream f_out("B:Results.out");
 if (!f_out) {
    cerr << "Unable to open the output file." << endl;
    return failure;
}
```

## BASIC

```
OPEN "A:DATAFILE.IN" FOR INPUT AS FILE#1
OPEN "B:RESULTS.OUT" FOR OUTPUT AS FILE#2
```

## COBOL

```
FILE-CONTROL.
    SELECT DATA-IN
        ASSIGN TO DISK.
    SELECT DATA-OUT
        ASSIGN TO DISK.

FD  DATA-IN
    VALUE OF DATA-IN IS "A:DATAFILE.IN".
    01  NUMBERS-TO-BE-PROCESSED.
        05  NUMBER-1-IN          PIC 999.
        05  NUMBER-2-IN          PIC 999.

FD  DATA-OUT
    VALUE OF DATA-OUT IS "B:RESULTS.OUT".
    01  OUTPUT-LINE-1.
        05  FILLER  PIC X(11)    VALUE "THE SUM OF ".
        05  NUMBER-1-OUT         PIC ZZ9.
        05  FILLER  PIC X(5)     VALUE " AND ".
        05  NUMBER-2-OUT         PIC ZZ9.
        05  FILLER  PIC X(4)     VALUE " IS ".
        05  SUM-OUT PIC ZZZ9.
    01  OUTPUT-LINE-2
        05  FILLER  PIC X(17)    VALUE "LARGER NUMBER IS".
        05  MAXIMUM-OUT          PIC ZZ9.

WORKING-STORAGE SECTION.
    01  END-OF-FILE PIC X.
```

## dBASE

```
select 1
use DATAFILE     (data already stored in database)

select 2
use RESULTS      (report file already formatted in database)

report form RESULTS to file B:RESULTS.DBF
```

## COBOL

```
OPEN INPUT DATA-IN.
READ DATA-IN AT END MOVE 'Y' TO END-OF-FILE.
```

**Q:** What code is required to read the two numbers from the file on disk?

**A:** Each data value is read from the disk and assigned a variable name (NUMBER1 and NUMBER2), storage areas whose names remain constant but whose contents change with the data. The number of variable names and the order in which they are read must be specified in the program.

## BASIC

```
INPUT#1, NUMBER1, NUMBER2
```

## C++

```
f_in >> Number1 >> Number2;
```

## dBASE

```
get NUMBER1, NUMBER2
skip (goes to next record)
```

## COBOL

```
ADD NUMBER-1-IN, NUMBER-2-IN GIVING SUM.
```

**Q:** Can we just use a plus sign and equal sign to get the sum?

**A:** No, each programming language uses a slightly different method to do an arithmetic operation such as addition. Most languages still require the mathematical signs to which we are accustomed, but the form of the computation may look different. The answer is assigned its own variable name. In this example, the variable name SUM is used.

## BASIC

```
SUM = NUMBER1 + NUMBER2
```

## C++

```
Sum = Number1 + Number2;
```

## dBASE

```
store NUMBER1 + NUMBER2 to SUM
```

**A:** Most languages include a selection statement of the following form:

*IF a comparison is true THEN*
*perform an action*
*ELSE (if comparison is not true)*
*perform a different action*

### COBOL

```
IF NUMBER-1-IN > NUMBER-2-IN
    MOVE NUMBER-1-IN TO MAXIMUM
ELSE
    MOVE NUMBER-2-IN TO MAXIMUM.
```

### C++

```
if (Number1 > Number2)
    Maximum = Number1;
else
    Maximum = Number2;
```

### BASIC

```
IF (NUMBER1 > NUMBER2) THEN
    MAXIMUM = NUMBER1
ELSE
    MAXIMUM = NUMBER2
```

### dBASE

```
if NUMBER1 > NUMBER2
    store NUMBER1 to MAXIMUM
else
    store NUMBER2 to MAXIMUM
```

## Q: Is output to a disk similar to input?

### COBOL

```
MOVE NUMBER-1-IN TO NUMBER-1-OUT.
MOVE NUMBER-2-IN TO NUMBER-2-OUT.

WRITE OUTPUT-LINE-1.
WRITE OUTPUT-LINE-2.
```

### BASIC

```
PRINT#2 "THE SUM OF "; NUMBER1; " AND "; NUMBER2; " IS "; NUM
PRINT#2 "LARGER NUMBER IS "; MAXIMUM
```

### C++

```
f_out << Number1 << " + " << Number2 << " = " << Sum << endl;
f_out "Larger number is " << Maximum
```

**A:** Usually there are different program statements for input and output. Both, however, must show which drive contains the referenced disk, the name of the file on the disk, how many variables there are, and the order in which the data is stored.

### dBASE

```
@MLINE,    1 say "THE SUM OF "
@MLINE,   12 say NUMBER1 picture "999"
@MLINE,   15 say " AND "
@MLINE,   20 say NUMBER2 picture "999"
@MLINE,   23 say " IS "
@MLINE,   27 say SUM picture "9999"

@MLINE+1,  1 say "LARGER NUMBER IS "
@MLINE+1, 18 say MAXIMUM picture "999"
```

A: For any iteration, the program must contain the code to be repeated and the number of times to cycle through the code. In this example, the IPOS cycle will be looped through over and over until all the data in the input file has been processed. *EOF* stands for end of file.

## COBOL

```
PERFORM PROCESSING-LOOP UNTIL END-OF-FILE = "Y"
PROCESSING LOOP.
    READ DATA-IN AT END MOVE 'Y' TO END-OF-FILE.
    ...
    WRITE OUTPUT-LINE-1.
    WRITE OUTPUT-LINE-2.
```

## BASIC

```
DO WHILE NOT EOF(1)

    INPUT#1, NUMBER1, NUMBER2
       ...
    PRINT#2 "THE SUM OF "; NUMBER1; " AND "; NUMBER2; " IS "; SUM
       ...
LOOP

END
```

## C++

```
while (!f_in.eof()) {
    f_in >> Number1 >> Number2;
       ...
    f_out << Number1 << " + " << Number2 << " = " << Sum << endl;
 }
f_in.close();
f_out.close();
return success;
```

## dBASE

```
do while .not. eof()
    get NUMBER1, NUMBER2
    skip (goes to next record)
       ...

enddo
```

For every disk or tape kept within a data library, records of its use should be established and maintained. The original code is checked out only to authorized people, who must account for everything they do to the programs. Any changes must lead to amendment of the master and distributed copies of code, documentation, and manuals. Different edition, or *version*, numbers should be assigned to each modified edition of documents and storage media. Responsible people must not lose sight of the fact that program documentation and storage media are major assets of their organization. These assets must be guarded and handled with the same level of care accorded to money and securities.

## CHAPTER FACTS

- Programming is more than just writing code. Properly designed programs require a four-step process: designing the program, writing the program code, testing and debugging, and documentation and training.

- Good design methods for programs include structured programming. In a structured program, code is organized into three structures: sequence, selection, and iteration.

- Programs can be organized by modules, each handling a specific function. Single modules can be modified without affecting the logic of the entire program.

- Object-oriented programming (OOP) is another program organization method in which an object contains a relevant name, descriptions of the data, and the processing methods needed to generate a specified result.

- Program design is done through a structure chart in a top-down manner. Flowcharts and pseudocode show step-by-step programming logic. Before code is written, logic is reviewed in a structured walkthrough. Test data examines all conditions of the program.

- Language translators convert high-level languages into machine language.

- Assemblers convert assembly language programs into machine language, each instruction representing one machine instruction.

- Compilers translate entire programs line by line. If errors are found, they are listed. If the translation is error-free, a linker program embeds needed utilities. The translation is then executed.

- Interpreters translate, then execute, the program one line at a time. This continues until the program is completed or an error is found. The translation is not saved.

- A programming language is chosen that best fits the particular application. A variety of languages are available, including FORTRAN,

COBOL, BASIC, Visual BASIC, Pascal, Ada, C, C++, and RPG. Other languages allow easier access to databases and reports (fourth-generation languages) and for queries in human languages (natural languages).

▪ Bugs in the program code and logic are detected through another structured walkthrough. Each module is tested independently through stub testing. Finally, the entire program is tried out on the test data.

▪ Documentation is important when maintaining programs and in team programming. The latest versions of programs and documentation should be carefully stored.

▪ Program maintenance is an ongoing procedure involving modifications for cyclic operations, new laws, and changes in company policy.

## TERMS TO REMEMBER

| | | |
|---|---|---|
| authoring system | logic error | structure chart |
| code | module | structured program |
| compiler | object-oriented | structured walkthrough |
| debugging | programming (OOP) | syntax error |
| execute | program specifications | test data |
| flowchart | pseudocode | unstructured program |
| interpreter | selection | version |
| iteration | sequence | |

## MIX AND MATCH

*Complete the following definitions with the Terms to Remember.*

1. A(n) _____ is a high-level language translator that checks the entire program for errors; translations are saved.

2. A program error that is translatable but does not produce correct results is called a(n) _____.

3. _____ is a method of representing program logic by using English (or other natural language) phrases in an outline form.

4. A program error that is not translatable is called a(n) _____.

5. In _____, a program is organized into units, each containing both descriptions of the data and methods of processing necessary to perform a task.

6. A graphic representation of the relationships among modules or objects in a program is called a(n) _____.

7. When a computer is _____ a program, it follows instructions one at a time.

8. Each new edition of software and documentation is called a(n) _____.

9. _____ is the process of finding and correcting program errors.

10. A subset of a computer program containing code that performs only a single function is called a(n) _____.

11. A(n) _____ is organized to contain only three logical structures: sequence, selection, and iteration.

12. _____ are sets of data that represent all extremes and normal conditions the program would experience.

13. A program that translates and executes one high-level language instruction at a time, and translations are not saved, is called a(n) _____.

14. _____ is another term for a program instruction.

15. A method of representing program logic by using different symbols and arrows is known as _____.

## REVIEW QUESTIONS

1. Define the Terms to Remember.

2. What types of programming are done by end users, user-developers, application programmers, and systems programmers?

3. Identify the four steps in the programming process.

4. Identify the three structures found in a structured program.

5. How is a program module different from an object?

6. What are two advantages of using structure charts, flowcharts, or pseudocode to design a program?

7. How does a line of pseudocode or a flowcharting symbol relate to program code?

8. Describe two activities that help programmers check the reliability of their programs.

9. How are assemblers different from high-level language translators?

10. Explain the differences between an interpreter and a compiler. Give an advantage and disadvantage of using each.

11. Identify the types of applications associated with these programming languages: FORTRAN, COBOL, BASIC, Visual BASIC, LOGO, Pascal, Ada, C, C++, RPG, fourth-generation languages, and natural languages.

12. What activities are associated with a system test?

13. How can the design of structured programs help in program maintenance?

14. What is one requirement for a realistic system test?

15. Identify two reasons why program documentation is important.

16. What happens during a documentation review?

17. What is program maintenance?

## APPLYING WHAT YOU'VE LEARNED

1. Designing tools, such as structure charts, pseudocode, and flowcharts, are used for more than just programming projects; they are similar to term paper outlines, assembly instructions, recipes, and wiring diagrams. Use both flowcharting and pseudocode to give a step-by-step analysis of how to solve one of the following:
   a. drive to some remote or hard-to-get-to place
   b. start up a computer and load a program
   c. solve a long-division problem in math

2. Several hundred computer programming languages have been developed over the years. Some are now obsolete, whereas others are used only in specialized applications. Report on a programming language not mentioned in the text. Find out about its main use, when and where it was developed, and some advantages or disadvantages of the language. SNOBOL, FORTH, APL, PL/1, LISP, Modula-2, Smalltalk, and ALGOL are some languages. Other language names can be found in ads for programmers, computer dictionaries, or guides to published books.

3. It takes a particular type of person to be a programmer. What professional skills do you think would be most beneficial? What personality traits could make a programmer effective? What traits might hamper a programmer on the job?

4. It is important that test data be developed that tries out all options and extreme conditions in a program. It should also include invalid or incorrect data to make sure that it is picked up by the program. For each application, describe a set of test data.
   a. checking to see that a valid date is input into a program in the form mm/dd/yy, such as 06/24/96
   b. keeping reservations for a hotel
   c. scheduling classes and rooms for a small college
   d. computing telephone bills

# Technological Trends

**C**hapter 15 discusses the potential abuses to personal privacy by organizations using computer systems. Ethical issues related to using technology are examined. The chapter also enumerates warning signs for computer crimes and helps people identify ways to protect their computer systems from viruses and other destructive programs. Every computer user needs to be aware and informed about protecting systems from electronic invasions, natural disasters, and fraudulent schemes.

Finally, chapter 16 takes a close look at future trends in technology. As career options related to these trends are explored in detail, the need for continuing education is emphasized. New career paths related to technological development will open up for people with the prerequisite skills or the willingness to acquire them. Many of these skills center on the ability to operate and maintain a computer system.

# Privacy, Ethics, Crime, and Security

# FROM THE USER'S POINT OF VIEW

**I**nformation has become a valuable asset for both individuals and organizations. As you become comfortable working with technology, you will naturally explore new methods for gathering, storing, and exchanging data. With this power, there is also potential for abuse. Used with malice or neglect, computer technology can become a tool for committing crimes or infringing upon your individual rights to privacy. In this chapter we explore these rights, discuss related ethical issues, identify some of the warning signs of computer abuses, and describe how to maintain the security of computer systems.

## PRIVACY

Computers can store personal information about every aspect of your life. The information held about you in a computer file can be used for beneficial purposes. A nation understands the make-up of its citizens by maintaining census data on individuals. Your financial records can be exchanged electronically between banks and credit offices, perhaps to expedite processing of a loan application. The positive uses for personal data files abound. However, computer-based data files also are prime targets of abuse. Consider the following hypothetical case.

The first of the month has arrived and your rent payment is due. However, you feel your landlord has neglected his maintenance duties. You notify the landlord that you have decided to hold your rent payment in escrow as allowed by city ordinance until the dispute is settled. Eventually, you reach an agreement and pay your rent. Life seems to have returned to normal—until you discover that your landlord has adversely affected your credit and credibility.

When you apply for a car loan, your application is denied because you are listed as a poor credit risk. You ask why, but the car agency doesn't know. After looking into the matter, you find that your landlord reported you to a credit agency for nonpayment when you legally held back your rent. In addition, when looking for another place to rent, you are constantly turned down. Later, you find your name on a list of "troublemakers" shared among local landlords in the area.

♦ Have you been treated unfairly for asserting your legal rights as a tenant?

♦ Has your privacy been violated when information about you was reported to the other landlords?

♦ Is your landlord guilty of violating your constitutional rights by reporting false or incomplete information to the credit agency?

♦ Were the credit agency and car dealer too willing to accept unverified information about your creditworthiness?

In this case, you may be the victim of misused computer technology. Your privacy may have been invaded; a crime may have been committed. Certainly, your landlord has behaved in an unethical manner by not providing completely accurate information. The credit agency may be guilty of negligence for not verifying the information. Computer technology was used to your disadvantage.

## ■ Invasions of Privacy

Computers don't invade anybody's privacy—people do. And because computer systems are designed to be user-friendly, it may not be difficult for unauthorized people to get access to personal data. People must be able to protect their computer files and limit file access only to authorized users.

The protection procedures used depend on individual situations. For example, consider what happens when you ask for credit. The prospective creditor asks you to provide information about yourself, your financial situation, and any loans you have made in the past. Almost every loan application has a provision under which you give the prospective lender permission to check on your credit status. Lenders need to know an individual's financial history to protect their investments. This means that lenders can contact computer credit services, banks, retailers, or others with whom you have done business.

Once you give permission to have your credit checked, you have given up some of your rights to privacy (Figure 15.1). You should carefully read anything you sign, especially papers related to borrowing money. Before you sign, be sure you understand what rights you are surrendering. You also should come to an understanding with the party that asks for permission to investigate you. For example, you can ask what happens if negative information is reported. Make it clear that you feel you have a right to see and explain any negative reports that might be issued. On the other hand, if you know of past problems with credit or other personal information, it is better to explain the problem in advance. If the information will disqualify you, save the embarrassment of authorizing an information search. Don't apply for credit until you are fairly sure you will qualify. Computer files may contain information on almost any business transaction in which you have been involved.

If you learn of any negative information reported about you, be aware that you have the right to correct any errors. There have been instances in which bad credit information has been entered into the wrong records. Also, businesspeople can make unjustified or incomplete reports about your actions, as in the example of the rent dispute.

**15.1**

When authorizing a personal credit check, you surrender some of your rights to privacy.

## ▥ The Right to Privacy

The right to privacy—to various extents—is guaranteed by law. The best-known legal basis for claims to privacy are contained in the Fourth Amendment of the U.S. Constitution. The Fourth Amendment protects U.S. citizens from "unreasonable searches and seizures . . . of person, house, papers and effects." This language is general and has been subject to considerable debate and many lawsuits. To clarify the meaning of the Fourth Amendment, Congress has passed a number of laws related to privacy, some of which are briefly described in Figure 15.2.

In 1977 a committee representing the U.S. Department of Health, Education, and Welfare proposed the following Code of Fair Information Practice:

1. No secret databases:  There must be no secret record-keeping systems containing personal data.

2. Right of individual access:  Individuals must be able to find out what information about them is stored and how it is used.

3. Right of consent:  Information about individuals obtained for one purpose cannot be used for other purposes without their consent.

## 15.2

These federal laws in the United States of America are related to privacy.

# Privacy Laws

▨ **Freedom of Information Act (1970)**

Personal data maintained by the federal government became accessible to any citizen who wanted it through this act. Unless release of the data threatens national security or infringes upon someone else's privacy, information must be furnished in response to requests.

▨ **Fair Credit Reporting Act (1970)**

This law gives individuals the right to examine and, if desired, challenge information held in their credit files. It also prohibits the exchange of credit information with unauthorized users.

▨ **Privacy Act (1974)**

This act aims at reducing the amount of irrelevant information collected by federal agencies and maintained in government computer files. These agencies are required to reveal how they intend to use the information they keep. In addition, permission must be obtained from affected individuals before the information is used for other than the stated purposes. The effectiveness of this act is dampened by the difficulty in establishing the relevance of an item of data. As another shortcoming, the law applies only to government agencies.

▨ **Education Privacy Act (1974)**

This law restricts access to grades, evaluations, and other computer-based data maintained by private and public schools. It also establishes a student's right to examine and challenge personal data maintained by these systems.

▨ **Right to Financial Privacy Act (1978)**

This act sets strict guidelines for federal agencies wishing to review bank accounts, but does not regulate state agencies or bank employees.

▨ **Electronic Communications Privacy Act (1986)**

This law provides privacy protection to communications involving new forms of technology. In particular, this legislation clearly identifies electronic mail and makes it a federal crime to intercept these computer-based transmissions.

▨ **Computer Fraud and Abuse Act (1986)**

This act allows for the prosecution of people who gain unauthorized access to computers or databases.

▨ **Video Privacy Protection Act (1988)**

This law specifically bars retailers from selling or disclosing video-rental data without a court order or the consumer's consent. This legislation was enacted after a list of videotapes rented by U.S. Supreme Court nominee Robert Bork was printed by a Washington newspaper at the time of his confirmation hearings.

▨ **Computer Matching and Privacy Act (1988)**

Federal agencies are regulated in the types of government computer files they can match to verify personal information. Matches are made to determine if a person may be ineligible for federal benefits or defaulting on government loans. A person can challenge the information if incorrect.

4. Right to correct: Individuals must be able to correct or amend records of information about them.

5. Assurance of reliability and proper use: Organizations creating, maintaining, using, or disseminating records of identifiably personal data must make sure the data is reliable. They must take precautions to prevent such data from being misused.

Although this code has not been enacted into law, it serves as a common-sense guideline for handling personal information.

## ETHICS

Privacy and the use of computer-based data are at the heart of a broader issue—ethical standards. Ethical standards usually are not established by government legislation, although ignoring ethical issues could mean engaging in illegal activities. Instead, *ethical standards* are a set of principles a person uses when considering the rights, privileges, and anticipated responses of all persons and groups likely to be affected by an individual's or organization's actions.

### Ethical Issues

Many ethical issues are outside specific legal precedents or fall into gray areas within the law. Therefore, a personal ethical standard must supply the principles for specific courses of action. These standards come into play every day. Do you eavesdrop on a cellular phone conversation you accidentally pick up (Figure 15.3)? Is it unethical to sell

**15.3**

Personal privacy can be invaded in many ways—for example, eavesdropping on cellular telephone conversations.

the car "as is" without mentioning the bad brakes and the crack in the engine block? Consider these technology-based ethical issues:

♦ Not registering or paying the registration fee for a shareware package you commonly use

♦ Reading someone's e-mail without permission

♦ Using your company's computer system for personal business activities

♦ Purchasing a software package with a limited license agreement for your personal computer and installing a copy of the package on the computer at work

♦ Publishing a research paper, which uses data from a database collected by others, without their permission

♦ Misrepresenting environmental or performance statistics by rounding off data values before the final analysis is performed

♦ Using, without permission, a colleague's worksheet template or expert system to help you put together a bid for a competing project

♦ Monitoring, without their knowledge, employees' data entry rates and number of breaks, using their own computer systems

♦ Firing an employee based on data that was obtained by unapproved work monitoring or from unverified sources (Figure 15.4)

Quite often, ethical blunders arise from miscommunications and the mishandling of people. These errors take place when one person does not take the rights of others into consideration before engaging in an activity or when two sides have conflicting viewpoints.

**15.4**

Managers using computers to monitor employees without their knowledge is one of many ethical issues facing people working with information technology.

## ■ Ethical Guidelines

Many organizations are establishing ethical guidelines for members and employees (see Figure 15.5). These organizations feel that high ethical standards equate to good employee performance, healthy customer relations, and fewer legal problems.

**15.5**

Many organizations ask their members or employees to subscribe to a code of conduct and ethics.

## The ACM Code of Ethics and Professional Conduct

### PREAMBLE

*Commitment to professional conduct is expected of every member (voting members, associate members, and student members) of the Association for Computing Machinery (ACM). This code identifies several issues professionals are likely to face, and provdes guidelines for dealing with them. Section 1 presents fundamental ethical considerations, while Section 2 addresses additional considerations of professional conduct. Statements in Section 3 pertain more specifically to individuals who have a leadership role, whether in the workplace or in a professional organization such as ACM. Guidelines for encouraging compliance with this Code are given in Section 4.*

### 1. General Moral Imperatives

As an ACM member, I will . . .

1.1   Contirbute to society and human well-being,

1.2   Avoid harm to others,

1.3   Be honest and trustworthy,

1.4   Be fair and take action not to discriminate,

1.5   Honor property rights including copyrights and patents,

1.6   Give proper credit for intellectual property,

1.7   Access computing and communication resources only when authorized to do so,

1.8   Respect the privacy of others,

1.9   Honor confidentiality.

### 2. More Specific Professional Responsibilities

As an ACM computing professional, I will . . .

2.1   Strive to achieve the highest quality in both the process and products of professional work,

2.2   Acquire and maintain professional competence,

2.3   Know and respect existing laws pertaining to professional work,

2.4   Accept and provide appropriate professional review,

2.5   Give comprehensive and thorough evaluations of computer systems and their impacts, with special emphasis on possible risks,

2.6   Honor contracts, agreements, and assigned responsibilities,

2.7   Improve public understanding of computing and its consequences.

### 3. Organizational Leadership Imperatives

As an ACM member and organizational leader, I will . . .

3.1   Articulate social responsibilities of members of an organizational unit and encourage full acceptance of those responsibilities,

3.2   Manage personnel and resources to design and build information systems that enhance the quality of working life,

3.3   Acknowledge and support proper and authorized uses of an organization's computing and communication resources,

3.4   Ensure that users and those who will be affected by a system have their needs clearly articulated during the assessment and design of requirements, and that later the system must be validated to meet requirements,

3.5   Articulate and support policies that protect the dignity of users and others affected by a computing system,

3.6   Create opportunities for members of the organization to learn the principles and limitations of computer systems.

### 4. Compliance with the Code

As an ACM member, I will . . .

4.1   Uphold and promote the principles of this Code,

4.2   Agree to take appropriate action leading to a remedy if the Code is violated,

4.3   Treat violations of this Code as inconsistent with membership in the ACM.

*Draft revision, February 12, 1992,* Communications of the ACM, *May 1992, pp. 94–95. Copyright © 1993 McGraw-Hill, Inc. All rights reserved.*

Consultant Darlene Orlov (cited by Cole, 1991*) has clients ask 12 questions when considering potentially unethical actions.

♦ Is the situation legal?

♦ How do you feel about the situation? Are you feeling unusually anxious? Are you feeling fearful?

♦ Does your conscience bother you?

♦ Will any rules, policies, or regulations be violated?

♦ Is the proposed action consistent with past practice?

♦ How would you feel if the details of this situation appeared on the front page of the local newspaper?

♦ Does this situation require that you lie about the process or the results?

♦ Do you consider this to be an "extraordinary" situation that demands an unusual response?

♦ Are you acting fairly? Would you want to be treated this way?

♦ Would you be able to discuss the proposed situation with your immediate supervisor? The president of the organization? Your family? The organization's clients?

♦ If a close friend of yours took this action, how would you feel?

♦ Will you have to hide or keep your actions secret? Has someone warned you not to disclose your actions to anyone?

When in doubt, ask for advice. Another person's point of view is often missing when unethical actions occur. By getting another perspective before acting, you can shed new light on the situation.

## Our Responsibilities and Opportunities

Privacy and ethical issues often arise from a volatile mixture of our personal point of view and the use of information. Some type of computer-recorded information is maintained for nearly every person in the United States. It starts when we are born—most birth certificates now are computer-generated; computer-maintained records about us continue to be created and accessed throughout our lives. If misuse of this information is to be avoided, preventive measures have to come from us.

Knowledge and legislation are the tools we use to control the impact technology has on society. As citizens, we have the responsibility to make our voices heard when abuses occur. We can do this through consumer power and by knowing and insisting on our rights. If you become involved with the design or operation of computer systems, you will have the opportunity to ensure that the system is responsibly designed and made secure to reduce the potential of misuse.

---

* Cole, Diane. "Companies Crack Down on Dishonesty," *Managing Your Career*, published by the *Wall Street Journal*, Spring 1991, pp. 8-11.

## CRIME

Information is power. Constructive use of information opens great potential for improvements and benefits. The fact that millions of computers exist establishes that they are wanted and that they are serving the needs of people and organizations. Used properly, computers are powerful and valuable tools.

Computers can be and have been misused, however. In the hands of a dishonest person with knowledge about sensitive systems, the computer can become a powerful, hard-to-detect tool for the criminal.

### Examples of Computer Crime

The news media have detailed hundreds of crimes that involved computers. To make matters worse, experts fear that reported cases make up only a small portion of overall computer crime because many such crimes go undetected, and many that are detected are not reported. Banks and other financial institutions are particularly negligent in reporting computer crimes because they don't want to undermine public confidence in them. The five situations described below provide examples of the dangers involved.

**Michigan State University**   In the 1980s Michigan State University employed a large time-sharing computer system to support research and academic applications needed by faculty and several thousand students. At that time two students developed and implemented a plan to steal passwords and computer time from other users.

The plan was simple. Many students went to the computer lab to complete assignments on personal computers linked to the larger system. Knowing this, the thieves wrote a program that mimicked the larger computer's login procedures. Unsuspecting students would enter their passwords into a personal computer running with the thieves' fake program. The program stored the passwords, then displayed an error message. Thinking the PC had problems, students would move to another machine. They never knew their passwords had been stolen. The thieves would collect the passwords and use the accounts later.

An alert university programmer eventually caught the thieves. The programmer was unaware that his password had been stolen until he noticed activity reported on his account at 2 A.M. His suspicions that someone was tampering with his account were confirmed when subsequent reports of activity at odd hours led to the capture of the culprits. Computer-based record keeping contributed to their downfall.

**Pacific Telephone Company**   Jerry Schneider was a whiz kid who built his own computer system when he was 10. By the time he was in high school, he had started his own electronics company. Schneider started out as a *hacker,* a self-taught computer hobbyist. He also used his knowledge to gain unauthorized access to computers. While he was a part-time college student, Schneider discovered a way to steal electronic equipment from Pacific Telephone Company. He retrieved old computer printouts and other documentation from a Pacific Telephone trash container to acquire correct account numbers, passwords, and procedures. Then, using a computer in his home, he ordered parts without being billed for them.

Schneider had expensive telephone components delivered to his home and to other locations. Once, he used his computer to order delivery of a $25,000 switchboard to a

**15.6**

Although most computer crimes are committed by employees of an organization, outsiders are responsible for many crimes as well.

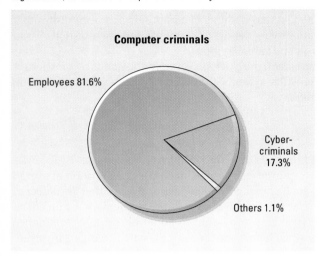

**Computer criminals**

Employees 81.6%

Cyber-criminals 17.3%

Others 1.1%

manhole cover at the intersection of two streets. He picked up the switchboard in a Pacific Telephone truck he bought at a company surplus auction.

Much of the equipment Schneider stole in this way was resold to Pacific Telephone. In fact, he used the company's own computer system to determine which stock levels were low, so he would know what items to steal. Schneider's crime spree ended when one of his own employees turned him in after a dispute over pay. Jerry's story and others like it has given hackers a bad name. Now the term is often associated with unauthorized computer activities. Hackers like to refer to their criminal counterparts as crackers, cyber-terrorists, or cyber-criminals (Figure 15.6).

**Penn Central Railroad**　　The case of Penn Central Railroad revolved around missing boxcars. The computer criminals in this case tampered with a computerized freight flow system, and boxcars were routed to a small railroad company outside of Chicago. There the boxcars seemed to have disappeared. The computer system was modified so that the missing boxcars would not be reported.

Investigation indicated that the boxcars had been repainted and used by other railroad companies. According to some estimates, about 400 boxcars were stolen in this manner. But Penn Central wished to minimize attention to the crime and chose not to prosecute.

**Equity Funding Corporation**　　Equity Funding Corporation was a group of companies that handled investments and insurance. Top-level managers from some of these companies lied about company profits to attract investors. In addition, they created volumes of fake insurance policies, then sold them, packaged with valid policies, to other insurance companies. The system was programmed to report only valid policies for auditing purposes. Once the scam was uncovered, more than 20 people were convicted of federal charges. Estimates of losses were as high as $2 billion.

**Your Hometown**　　Computers are used for the same types of criminal activity every day in schools, homes, and businesses. A computer user shares a new program with a friend or associate by making an illegal copy of the software (see Figure 15.7). This type of criminal activity seems quite small by comparison to the Equity Funding or Pacific Telephone cases, but when many small crimes are added together, the sum represents the theft of millions of dollars in software each year.

Software houses have started to take legal measures to fight back. The Lotus Development Corporation collected a sizable out-of-court settlement from the Heath Group, whose employees allegedly made illegal copies of the Lotus 1-2-3 spreadsheet software. Recently, colleges have been convicted of breaking a copyright law and putting too many copies of a software package on a network, resulting in a large fine. Such actions illustrate the software houses' view that transferring programs without permission is stealing. Copying software is no different from walking out of a store without paying for merchandise.

## 15.7

Copying software for a friend is a computer crime if you do so with copyrighted programs.

COPY SOFTWARE ILLEGALLY AND YOU COULD GET THIS HARDWARE ABSOLUTELY FREE.

Software piracy isn't just a crime. It's a shame. Because most people who do it aren't even aware that it's illegal. If you copy software that's protected by copyright, you could lose your job, face a civil suit, pay a $250,000 fine and possibly be imprisoned.

So get the facts now. For more information about the legal use of software, contact the Software Publishers Association Piracy Hotline at 1-800-388-7478. Because in a court of law, ignorance is one thing you won't be able to plead.

1-800-388-7478

Don't Copy That Floppy

## Types of Computer Crime

Each of the examples presented involves a fraud in which the perpetrator uses deceit or misrepresentation for unlawful gain. When the value of the item is greater than $500, the act becomes a felony, or a major crime, under the laws of most states. Although the potential for fraud was present in each case, different types of crimes were committed. The following section distinguishes five categories of computer crime.

**Stealing Computer Time**   The Michigan State students robbed their fellow computer users first of their passwords, then of their time allocations. Computer time is money.

**Stealing Data**   Financial data, customer information, or original designs or plans can be stolen from computer files. In the Pacific Telephone case, data was stolen from a trash bin to support the computer-aided theft of expensive equipment. With the use of paper shredders, illegal access could have been reduced.

**Manipulating Data**   The Penn Central case showed that data could be manipulated to direct events and people's actions—in this case, the rerouting of boxcars.

**Changing Programs**   This method was used to cover up the crimes committed by Equity Funding executives. Usually, this type of computer crime is committed by computer professionals.

**Stealing Computer Programs**   Software buyers often do not realize they have purchased merely the right to use software, not the software itself. In most cases, users are restricted to making a single copy of original diskettes which may be used only for backup. This means that the software is not legally theirs to give to others.

Software copyright laws essentially mean you are bound by the copyright agreement you entered into with the software manufacturer. This is important because the right to make copies may vary among manufacturers. You must read the copyright license for every package, as these may even vary from package to package of the same manufacturer.

One of the most widespread crimes involves the illegal copying of software. Because theft of computer data and software often involves making copies, the original remains intact. As a result, this type of computer crime often is difficult to detect.

## Signals of Potential Computer Crime

In places where computer crimes have occurred, a number of warning signals have been noted. Most of the signs indicate poor control of the computer system or a lack of education on the part of users.

The most common signs include some that you may have observed:

♦ The computer system seems to run people instead of people running the system.

♦ People expect computers to solve major problems that already exist, when these problems really indicate other underlying difficulties.

♦ Users cannot communicate with the computer professionals.

♦ Users are not asked to contribute ideas during the planning stages of systems development; instead, they are told how the system will be designed.

♦ No clear-cut procedures are established for who may use equipment and when it may be used.

♦ Documentation of system design and use is incomplete.

♦ Decision makers participate in programming and troubleshooting activities.

♦ Computer professionals are given no guidelines within which to work.

♦ Access to data and software facilities is easy and uncontrolled.

♦ Errors in processing occur frequently, but without adequate investigation.

♦ People are not held specifically accountable for the system operations.

As you can see, all five components of a computer system must be protected from computer crime. Access to hardware and software must be limited to qualified people. Data must be complete, accurate, and monitored for illegal changes. Procedures must be developed to help people operate and control the system properly.

## ■ Viruses and Other Destructive Software

In the cases described earlier, computer systems are used as tools to support fraudulent activities. In the mid-1980s, a new problem arose wherein computer hardware, software, and data were the target of malicious damage. The cause of the damage is a computer program called a *virus*. The virus invades a computer system by attaching itself to other commonly used programs (hosts). After the host program is loaded into the computer memory, the virus permanently installs itself on the new computer system. Once installed, the virus can display unwanted messages, erase data, or even promote activities that damage hardware (see Figure 15.8). Viruses and other destructive programs have several modes of operation. What follows are brief descriptions of some of the most troublesome.

**Worms**    Whereas a virus attaches itself to other programs, another type of parasitic program, called a *worm,* is self-contained. Worms cause problems by continually duplicating themselves in every available memory address. As a result, the worms fill a computer's memory and bring all other processing activities to a halt.

**Trojan Horses**    The Trojan horse from ancient Greek history was used to conquer the city of Troy, as soldiers were hidden inside this "victory" gift. The same devious plan is used with a *Trojan horse* virus. In this case, the Trojan horse program hides inside another program and erases data while the user examines the other software. Game demonstrations can potentially hide Trojan horse programs and, as unsuspecting users shoot down alien invaders, the Trojan horse program erases their hard disk. A Trojan horse program is technically not considered a virus because it is not self-replicating.

**Bombs**    *Time bombs* are similar to Trojan horse programs. Both hide within innocent-looking software packages and do not duplicate themselves. The difference is that time bombs are time dependent. They often are introduced to a computer system as an "inside" job. Disgruntled, fired employees leave their employers a time bomb as a going-away present. The time bomb is hidden within software commonly used by the organization and activates at a preset time to delete critical files. *Logic bombs* are basically the same, but are triggered by a specific action. Removing a specific employee name from the employee file or the five thousandth time you typed *WIN* might launch a logic bomb.

**Virus and Worm Protection**   Common sense goes a long way in protecting your computer system from destructive programs. Your first line of protection is to limit software acquisition to packages purchased from reliable vendors or shareware distributors. Software copied from a "friend" could prove to be harmful to your computer system. Following are a few facts about how these destructive programs spread.

## Peter Norton

(b. 1943)

Although his name and picture appear on millions of books and software packages worldwide, Peter Norton is a very private person. His Norton Utilities are a group of very useful programs for all PC users, including software to restore deleted files and optimize hard disk space. Norton's first experience with computers was using an IBM 1620 mainframe as part of a summer accounting job in 1964. When the computer crashed, there was no way to easily find out what was wrong. Norton wrote a program that tracked down the error and then he distributed this program for free—a precursor of the Utilities.

Before starting his company, Peter Norton Computing, Inc., in the early 1980s, Norton was a junior engineer at Boeing, then served two years in the Army as a conscientious objector/ medical corpsman, spent four years in a Buddhist monastery in California, and traveled Europe for a year. In 1981 Norton purchased one of the original IBM PCs. Over the years, his company has developed antivirus software, graphical user interfaces, and system utilities. Norton also wrote several user-friendly guides about the IBM PC. His company's success skyrocketed. In 1990 he sold his company to Symantec for stock worth more than $300 million.

Peter Norton still dabbles in writing, but his main interest is contemporary American art. In fact, the Nortons are routinely listed as one of the top 200 art collectors in the world. Unfazed by wealth and success, he lives with his family in a modest home and stays out of the limelight.

**Who's Who**

**15.8**

A computer system infected with a virus copies the virus to other disks, erases important files, and displays unwanted messages.

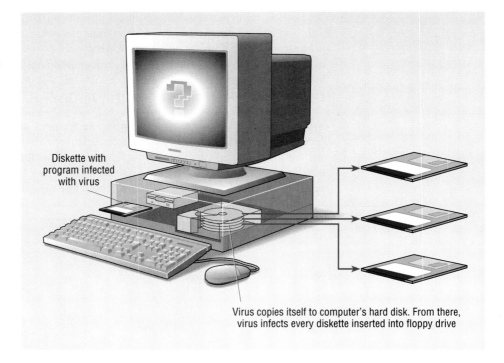

Diskette with program infected with virus

Virus copies itself to computer's hard disk. From there, virus infects every diskette inserted into floppy drive

- A virus cannot infect a computer unless an infected program is run or the computer is booted from an infected disk
- A virus cannot infect a write-protected disk (this may change)
- A virus cannot attach to a data file (computer systems are not infected by data files)
- A virus cannot spread on its own from one type of computer to another (that is, an Intel-based virus cannot spread to a Motorola-based computer like the Apple Macintosh)
- A virus cannot spontaneously generate—they are written by people just like other computer programs are

Commercial *antivirus software*, also called a *vaccine*, can detect common viruses, worms, and the like, as shown in Figure 15.9. Some operating systems have built-in antivirus features. This software should be used to scan every disk before you use it. If you suspect that your system has been invaded, look for telltale warning signs:

- Changes in the size of data files or operating system utility programs
- Unexplained loss of data
- Changes to icons, menus, or windows
- Increase in disk activity during booting
- Strange messages appearing on the screen or printer
- Decrease in available memory

If you suspect that your system has been infected, turn off the computer immediately. This means turning the power off, not resetting the machine. Some viruses

**15.9**

Antivirus software is designed to locate and remove destructive programs like viruses from a computer's memory or disks.

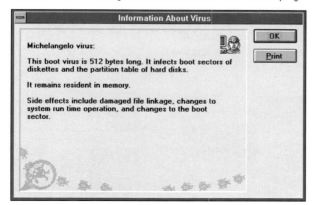

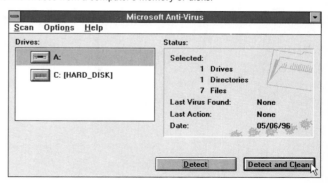

can survive a reset. Boot the computer from a clean operating system disk, often on a diskette. Next use antivirus software to scan your disks, starting with the operating system disk that boots the computer or the system's hard disk. Many of the antivirus programs not only spot unwanted programs, but can delete them and repair the damage done to files.

In some cases, files cannot be recovered and you must rely on your backup copies. If clean backup copies exist, this option presents few problems. If your backup is infected, the antivirus software must be used. Some antivirus software can even read compressed data files that are commonly used during backup.

## SECURITY

Preventing computer crime and the invasion of viruses or privacy is a matter of security. In this sense the term *security* applies to all procedures designed to protect computers and information resources against unauthorized activities (Figure 15.10). Even with an extensive security system in place, there is no such thing as complete protection for a computer system and its information assets.

With many computer systems, demands for immediate processing overshadow security concerns. People are so involved with getting their work done that the monitoring of operations is slack. Input is not as controlled as it should be, and output is not always checked for accuracy and completeness. Often, security components are left out of the programs as programmers concern themselves only with the processing tasks to be completed.

The cost of security is another consideration. Building a secure system takes time and resources. Once security measures are in place, the system may be more expensive to operate. If a user spends half of each workday verifying output, half of his salary is spent on security, or, figuring it another way, the cost of completing work assignments is doubled. Built-in security features in programs require the processing of more instructions. The result is a slowdown in processing as well as a demand for more computer power.

**15.10**

Building a secure computer system takes time and additional resources.

People must strike a balance between no security and nearly complete security. The cost of security should be weighed against the price of potential losses. Security needs should be defined according to the data and the equipment they protect. The bottom line is that computer equipment is expensive and time-consuming to replace. Furthermore, the data stored on every computer system is invaluable and almost impossible to replace without methodical backup.

Personal computers systems are especially vulnerable. To protect data and equipment, the user must decide who has access, then enforce this decision. Effective enforcement depends on two factors: physical controls and data security measures.

### ■ Physical Controls

The physical protection of equipment can be a difficult task. Often computer equipment is located in locked, windowless rooms to deter unauthorized individuals from entering. The pieces of equipment themselves are chained down (Figure 15.11) In addition, each piece might have a unique serial number. This expedites inventory and allows for easy identification of misplaced or stolen items. Special care needs to be taken with portable computing equipment. Locks are available for some laptop computers when not in use.

Physical security requires more than control over unauthorized access to computer equipment and programs (Figure 15.10). Disasters such as fires, floods, earthquakes, or even terrorist bombings are major threats that occur unpredictably but require preparation and readiness. Protective and recovery measures must be in place, ready for instant activation. This means storing hardware serial numbers and master copies

**15.11**

Computer systems of all sizes can be protected by these common-sense controls.

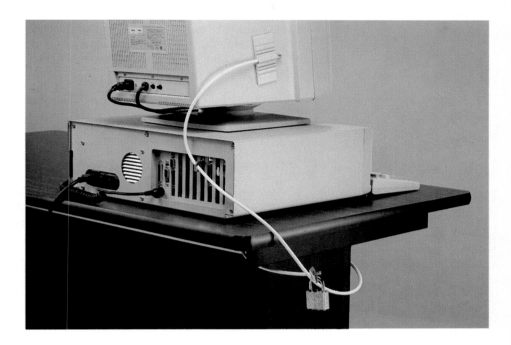

## Physical Controls for Computer System Security

- Outside access to computer hardware is limited

- Equipment is physically secured to tables and floor

- Identification numbers are on all equipment, manuals, and software

- Physical access is limited to authorized people

- Computer centers are built to withstand natural disasters

- Smoke detection and fire-extinguishing systems are installed that do not harm electronic equipment

- Unused storage media is placed in a secure library

- Access to hardware is password-protected

of software in a local bank's safe-deposit box or a small, personal, fireproof safe. In addition, smoke detectors and waterless fire extinguishers are a must for every office or home with a personal computer system.

## ■ Data Security

After physical security measures have been established, data security takes over to ensure that sensitive data is kept confidential. Physical security is external; access to the computer itself is controlled. Data security takes place as part of storing data or when accessing a computer system or integrated network. There are several ways you can protect data:

◆ Physically lock up tapes and disks

◆ Physically take data with you

◆ Password-protect data

◆ Encrypt data

Locked away in a drawer or safe-deposit box, disks are relatively safe from unauthorized access. Copying important files to a floppy disk and taking the data with you also ensures a great deal of data security, so long as copies are removed from fixed disk drives and backup is provided.

**Password Protection**   Passwords and unique accounts can separate and secure the work of individual users on networks. *Passwords* are a combination of letters, numbers, or symbols known only to the user. This secret code limits access or the ability to alter information. A password may be required to access an individual computer, software, bulletin board, information service, or e-mail system. Figure 15.12 shows how a password is set up within a screen saver utility. Only users who know the password can turn off the screen saver and use this system.

A bank customer who has been issued an ATM (automatic-teller machine) personal identification number can access his or her bank account from anywhere around town. If someone is foolish enough to leave this password in a wallet, and the

**15.12**

Passwords work only if they are kept confidential.

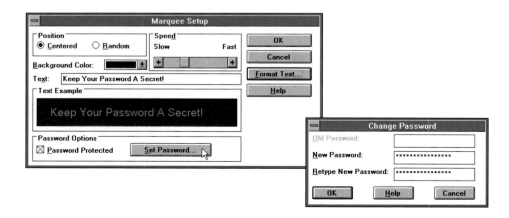

wallet is stolen, an unauthorized person can gain access to the account. The system has no control over this security break. Users would be wise to protect their passwords and change them periodically.

Varying degrees of security clearance can be indicated by an individual's password. Bulletin board users might be issued a password permitting them to read and leave messages. A bulletin board operator (sysop) has a special password enabling him or her to assign passwords to new users, deny access to system abusers, remove messages, and even modify the bulletin board program. But passwords are effective only if they are kept secret. The possibility that confidential information will be leaked is ever present.

**Data Encryption**   Data encryption programs keep data and software from prying eyes. *Data encryption* is the act of scrambling data and programs so that the encrypted version is unintelligible without a decoding (decryption) program. Encryption programs are especially useful to encode data sent over public communication lines. For example, the *Data Encryption Standard (DES)* is an data encryption method commonly used by banks, insurance companies, and U.S. government agencies. It is based on a 56-bit binary code that serves as the key for converting text and other data into numbers and then scrambles the original data. Scrambling the data involves substituting one number for another and reordering the numeric sequence. The DES actually scrambles the original data 16 times to create the encrypted version. The key determines the replacement and reordering sequences for each scrambling. The only way to convert the document back into its original form is to use the original DES key to unscramble the encrypted version in reverse order.

Since a dedicated supercomputer is fast enough to break the DES encryption scheme by checking all 72 quadrillion DES key combinations, computer professionals are currently designing more-sophisticated schemes. One solution is to use additional encryption techniques on the DES key. The encrypted DES key is then protected from supercomputer intervention as it is sent to the recipient who needs it to decode the encrypted DES data. As a result, the recipient uses one encryption method to decode the DES key, then uses the DES key to decode the encrypted data.

**Digital Signatures**   Electronic mail and other computer-based transactions need to be more secure if they are going to be used as legal documents and for financial negotiations. But how does the recipient verify that an e-mail contract or fund transfer came from the person whose name is on the document? In a paper-and-ink world, a signature validates a contract or check. The electronic answer is to incorporate a *digital signature*, which creates an encrypted document only the recipient can read.

The *Digital Signature Standard (DSS)* proposed by the National Institute of Standards uses a data encryption technique that relies on a private and public key. The private key is actually two very large prime numbers your computer system uses to decode electronic documents sent to you. A prime number cannot be evenly divided by any whole numbers but itself and 1. Like the DES, this key is used to unscramble the contents of the document. The public key is published, like telephone numbers in a phone book, and is available to everyone's computer through networks or information services to scramble messages. For instance, your lawyer can look up your public key and use it to encrypt a letter only your private key can unlock. If your public code was used, you can feel confident that you are the only one who can read the letter (see Figure 15.13).

**15.13**

When using a digital signature, the private key contains two huge prime numbers which are multiplied together to create the related public key. Because the public key is so large, it is nearly impossible to figure out the numbers used as the private key.

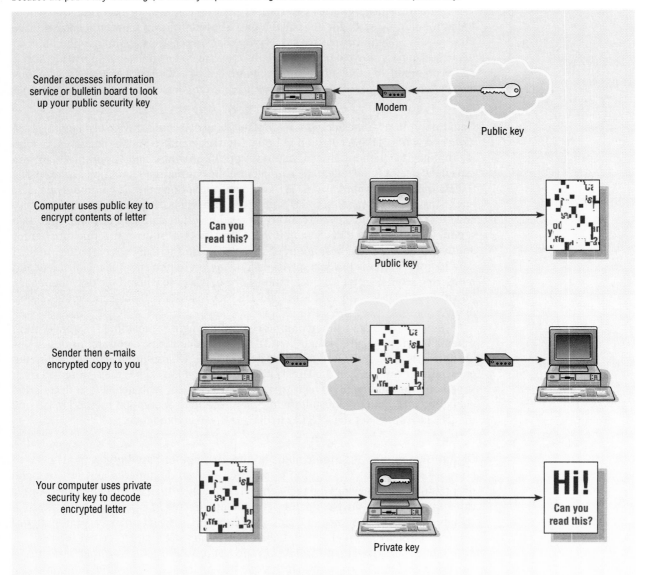

Sender accesses information service or bulletin board to look up your public security key

Modem

Public key

Computer uses public key to encrypt contents of letter

**Hi!** Can you read this?

Public key

Sender then e-mails encrypted copy to you

Your computer uses private security key to decode encrypted letter

Private key

**Hi!** Can you read this?

## ▨ Organizational Security

Computer professionals know that a computer system is only as secure as its weakest link. To meet this challenge, security is everyone's responsibility. Organization-wide security procedures, known as *electronic data processing (EDP) controls*, work with all five components of the computer system. The basic categories of EDP controls are: management controls, computer resource controls, and input, processing, and output controls.

**15.14**

By taking an active role in overseeing computer operations, management plays an important part in the system's security.

### Summary of Management Controls

■ Management demonstrates knowledge and support of security measures for organization's computer resources

■ Management sets direction for computer-related activities

**Management Controls**   Over the years, professionals have learned that management must be closely involved with data processing decisions. When decision makers do not take an active part in the control of data processing, they invite trouble. The idea behind *management controls* is that the mere awareness by top managers of the processing activities taking place can increase the security of a computer system considerably. Though managers need not participate in the physical tasks required to process data, they should set the direction of processing activities (Figure 15.14).

**Computer Resource Controls**   With *computer resource controls*, a close watch is kept on computer center and network resources. In many situations the use of equipment, such as network servers or mainframe computers, must be restricted to authorized personnel. In other situations office security may require people to use a magnetically encoded plastic card or a key combination applied to an electronic lock to enter a computer room. Closed-circuit television cameras may monitor and record the entrance

### ...ABOUT RULES OF PC ETIQUETTE

● Never reorganize a coworker's hard disk

● Never kill a file you didn't create

● Don't pick up a phone while the modem is transmitting

● Keep your fingers off other people's monitors

● Don't abscond with another's software

● Don't redefine another's keyboard

● Never rub your feet on nylon carpet and then touch floppies

● Never advise: "Try reformatting your hard disk"

● Don't open a multiuser file and go to lunch

● Don't dillydally on a bulletin board

*Source: Personal Computing*, October 1986, page 124.

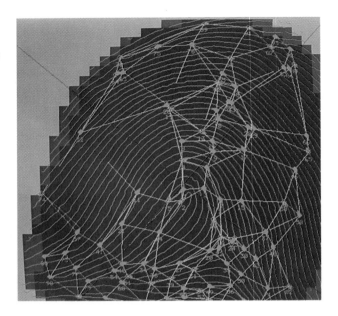

**15.15**

Biometric security devices use physical characteristics to identify an individual before allowing him or her access to secure computer environments. Here a fingerprint is analyzed to determine if it matches unique identifying information for this person.

to the computer center. *Biometric security devices* use biological information, such as fingerprints, voice patterns, retina patterns, and signatures, to identify authorized users (Figure 15.15). Limiting access to computer hardware reduces traffic, helps eliminate errors, and promotes security.

Another type of computer resource control involves separating the responsibilities of computer professionals. To prevent any one employee from gaining unlimited access to the entire system, at least two categories of computer center employees should be created: operations personnel and developmental personnel. The operations group controls the equipment and application programs in use, whereas the developmental group creates new systems. These divisions complement each other and provide security checks and balances.

Computer resource control also relies on scrupulous record keeping. Procedures and job schedules need to be documented and verified. All processing jobs within a computer center should be accommodated within a precise schedule. Supervisors must examine operations to verify that the procedures are followed, and records of computer activity need to be reviewed regularly. In addition, schedules and procedures must be stable—that is, operators should not be able to change them easily and frequently (Figure 15.16).

In addition to protecting computing resources during normal operations, equipment in a computer center should be arranged to withstand the earth's rumblings and other natural disasters. Every organization needs a ***disaster recovery plan*** containing procedures that specify measures to be applied if computer or data resources are damaged or destroyed (Figure 15.17). A disaster recovery plan actually addresses procedures in four different areas:

- ◆ Emergency procedures
- ◆ Backup procedures
- ◆ Recovery procedures
- ◆ Test procedures

**15.16**

Computer center controls help ensure the security of information processed and stored by computers.

## Summary of Computer Resource Controls

▧ Access to computer resources is controlled

▧ Responsibilities of computer professionals are separated into operations and development

▧ Activities are scheduled and schedules are kept

▧ Operations personnel are supervised and not allowed to change schedules

▧ Operating procedures are documented

**15.17**

Organizations dependent on their computer systems must have disaster recovery plans in place in case of man-made or natural disasters.

## Disaster Recovery Planning

▧ **Emergency procedures**
  - Evacuation plan
  - Call list
  - List of people with on-site responsibilities
  - Uninterruptable power supply
  - System shutdown procedures

▧ **Backup procedures**
  - When to back up files
  - Where to store backup
  - Cold versus hot site readiness
  - Reciprocal backup relationships with another organization

▧ **Recovery procedures**
  - Identify disaster scenarios
  - Train people to handle different scenarios

▧ **Test procedures**
  - Check to see if plan works

Emergency procedures try to prepare people for problems that occur during the disaster and immediately afterward. Evacuation plans for the building need to be developed along with a list of people to notify and list of people to let back in to assess the damage. Some computer centers plan for power failures by acquiring an *uninterruptable power supply (UPS).* This equipment contains surge-protection circuitry and a battery that can maintain system resources long enough for the orderly shutdown of the system.

Backup procedures can include use of a *hot site,* which is a complete backup computer center available for immediate use, or a *cold site,* an empty facility ready to accept an organization's computing equipment at a moment's notice. Use of backup files, staff training in recovery procedures, and plans to notify clients and customers must also be in place. Part of this planning might include making backup arrangements with another organization which agrees to temporarily share equipment and facilities when a disaster strikes.

The steps for getting computer resources operational again become the recovery procedures. This will usually involve documenting different disaster scenarios, then training users and professionals to get the system and data back online. Procedures for testing the recovery plan identify how the organization practices and prepares for different disasters. Mock drills often highlight weaknesses in the disaster recovery plan.

## Input, Processing, and Output Controls

Management has the responsibility of organizing *input, processing, and output controls* (Figure 15.18). Input controls affect data before it is entered into the computer. Managers need to establish a standard form for input data. Users and data entry personnel must be instructed to reject input presented in improper form.

**15.18**

Input, processing, and output controls that contribute to the security of computer-maintained information are summarized in this checklist.

### Summary of Input, Processing, and Output Controls

■ **Input**
- Established standards for input data
- Verification of control totals
- Use of passwords

■ **Processing**
- Clearly stated procedures and schedules
- Review of activity logs
- Documentation

■ **Output**
- Documented procedures for distributing output
- Use of control totals to double-check accuracy of output
- Limit access to output to authorized personnel

# A Closer Look at
# Privacy—
# Is It Still Possible?

**A**t one time or another everyone gets sent junk mail, answers an unsolicited telephone call during dinner, or has a salesperson invade their personal space without permission. As these frustrating situations occur, several questions immediately come to mind. What follows are answers to some of these questions.

**Q:** How do organizations get my name, and how do I stop them?

**A:** Answering surveys, filling out warranty cards, and public documents like birth certificates and deeds all generate personal data that organizations buy and sell. You cannot stop all of it, but when given the option of including personal information, *just say no!*

**Personal Data**

| First name: | Last/surname: |
| --- | --- |
| Waterbury | Farthington |

OK

Company:

New Old Lompoc House

Cancel

Street address:

687 Bluff Road

| City/town: | State/province: |
| --- | --- |
| Lompoc | CA |

| Zip/postal code: | Country: |
| --- | --- |
| 90752 | United States of America |

| Area code: | Home phone: | Marital Status |
| --- | --- | --- |

| Date of Birth | Ethnic Origin | Years of Education |
| --- | --- | --- |

**Please provide the followi**

| Serial Number | 02-181-12859 | |
| --- | --- | --- |
| First Name | Mahatma | M.I. D |
| Company | Tofu Hut | |
| Street Address | 8743 N. Ravenswood | |
| City | Chicago | |
| Zip/Postal Code | 60640-1199 | |
| Phone | (312)555-9832 | |

◉ Yes, I want a free *Adobe* Magazine subscription.
Birthday (month/day only) 02/21 (in order to validate your subscription)
○ No, I don't want a free *Adobe* Magazine subscription.

☐ Occasionally we make our mailing list available to companies that offer related services. If you do not want your name included, click here.

**Previous**

**Cancel**

**Continue**

**Q:** Why do organizations want all this personal data?

**A:** Organizations call it demographic data and use it as part of decision support systems. These systems in turn help government agencies plan growth, and businesses target customers for advertisements and, in some cases, product development.

**Q:** Can I remove my name and information from a database?

**A:** Usually not, but you do have the right to verify the accuracy of credit information or records maintained by the government. In some cases, such as catalog mailings, you can write to the organization and ask them not to send information. The federal government has forms for requesting a copy of your records. Credit information is available, but you may have to pay to see it.

---

Form Approved
OMB No. 0960-0466                              SP

## Request for Earnings and Benefit Estimate Statement

☐ Please check this box if you want to get your statement in Spanish instead of English.

Please print or type your answers. When you have completed the form, fold it and mail it to us.

1. Name shown on your Social Security card:

_____ _____
First Name                        Middle Initial

_____
Last Name Only

2. Your Social Security number as shown on your card:

☐☐☐-☐☐-☐☐☐☐

3. Your date of birth

_____ _____ _____
Month    Day     Year

4. Other Social Security numbers you have used:

☐☐☐-☐☐-☐☐☐☐
☐☐☐-☐☐-☐☐☐☐

5. Your sex: ☐ Male    ☐ Female

6. Other names you have used
   *(including a maiden name):*

_____

_____

For items 7 and 9 show only earnings covered by **Social Security.** Do NOT include wages from State, local or Federal Government employment that are NOT covered for Social Security or that are covered ONLY by Medicare.

7. Show your actual earnings (wages and/or net self-employment income) for last year and your estimated earnings for this year.

   A. Last year's actual earnings: *(Dollars Only)*

   $ ☐☐☐,☐☐☐.☐☐

   B. This year's estimated earnings: *(Dollars Only)*

   $ ☐☐☐,☐☐☐.☐☐

8. Show the age at which you plan to stop working.

   ☐☐ *(Show only one age)*

9. Below, show the average yearly amount (not your total future lifetime earnings) that you think you will earn between now and when you plan to stop working. Include cost-of-living, performance or scheduled pay increases or bonuses.

   If you expect to earn significantly more or less in the future due to promotions, job changes, part-time work, or an absence from the work force, enter the amount that most closely reflects your future average yearly earnings.

   If you don't expect any significant changes, show the same amount you are earning now (the amount in 7B).

   Future average yearly earnings: *(Dollars Only)*

   $ ☐☐☐,☐☐☐.☐☐

10. Address where you want us to send the statement.

    Name
    _____

    Street Address (Include Apt. No., P.O. Box, or Rural Route)
    _____

    _____
    City            State        Zip Code

    **Notice:**
    I am asking for information about my own Social Security record or the record of a person I am authorized to represent. I understand that when requesting information on a deceased person, I must include proof of death and relationship or appointment. I further understand that if I deliberately request information under false pretenses , I may be guilty of a Federal crime and could be fined and/or imprisoned. I authorize you to use a contractor to send the statement of earnings and benefit estimates to the person named in item 10.

    ▶

    **Please sign your name (Do Not Print)**
    _____

    _____
    Date         (Area Code) Daytime Telephone No.

Form **SSA-7004-SM** (4-95) Destroy prior editions        ♻ Printed on recycled paper

**Q: Are there any situations in which it is desirable to provide personal information?**

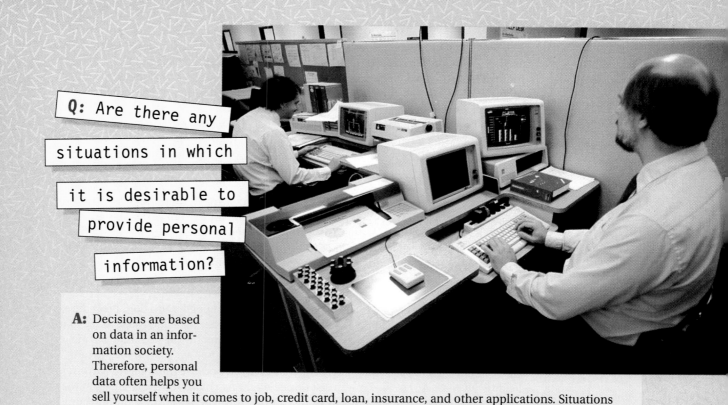

**A:** Decisions are based on data in an information society. Therefore, personal data often helps you sell yourself when it comes to job, credit card, loan, insurance, and other applications. Situations like census tabulations and income taxes require you to provide complete and correct data by law.

**Q: How can I protect my name and other personal data and keep it from people who misuse it?**

**A:** First and foremost, do not provide personal data unless it is required. If the data is being misused, ask to have it removed. Your next step is to seek a restraining order or court injunction. Because many of the federal laws involve only public databases, you could also become involved in advocacy work on new privacy legislation for privately maintained databases.

When appropriate, output should be compared against *control totals* made independently of the computer system. People use control totals to double-check the accuracy of figures produced by the computer system. Typically used as part of batch input, the transactions to be processed are counted manually, and the total is recorded. A control total is determined by making manual calculations independent of the computer system to check input operations.

In financial applications, the control total does not necessarily deal with money. Before processing a batch of payroll time sheets, the hour amounts on all time sheets could be added and recorded as the control total. Once processing is completed, computer-generated totals are compared with the control total. Any discrepancies indicate a possible error in data entry.

Input into network applications is harder to control. System programs can use passwords and account numbers to accept only certain input from designated users or locations. One way to protect networks from unauthorized remote access is through *call-back security*. Users who work at home or known locations away from the office provide the remote telephone number to the network administrator. When users want to log in from a remote location, they call the computer system and then hang up. The computer then calls them back at the prearranged number.

Controls over the processing of data rely mainly on documentation. Procedures and schedules must be clearly stated and strictly followed for effective security of a computer system. Supervisors have the responsibility of monitoring operations to make sure these conditions are being met.

Online systems pose different security challenges, because transactions can often be difficult to trace. For example, a sales price might be changed several times online, without producing a written record of the transaction. The absence of these records presents a major security risk. As a result, online programs often instruct the computer to record each change on an **activity log**. An activity log, or summary of online activity, is used to correct errors or assist auditors in reviewing records.

Management should keep records of all processing errors and system failures. Each correction requires documentation. Data processing supervisors can review these records to trace unauthorized activity or other problems. The records also help supervisors evaluate employee performance.

Finally, people need to control the output from all data processing activities. Procedures for distributing output must be documented and followed. Only authorized users should have access to output. These users need to examine returned output for completeness and accuracy. Checking control totals, as previously noted, raises the level of security in output.

## CHAPTER FACTS

- Computer abuse and its prevention involve four issues: individual privacy, ethical standards, computer crime, and computer system security.

- An individual's rights to privacy are covered legally by the Fourth Amendment to the U.S. Constitution and numerous privacy acts.

- Ethical standards take the rights of others into consideration.

- The impact of computers can best be controlled through legislation and the education of consumers.

- Stealing computer time, programs, and data and changing data or programs are the major types of computer crime.

- Eleven warning signals often identify organizations that are vulnerable to computer crime.

- Viruses, worms, Trojan horses, and bombs can infect unprotected computer systems, erasing programs and data, as well as damage equipment.

- All computer systems can benefit from physical controls and data security. Precautions should be taken against natural disasters and fires. Data encryption and other protections against illegal copying also are useful.

- Security is everyone's concern, and organizations use EDP (electronic data processing) controls for management, computer resources, data input, processing, and output.

- The best way to protect personal privacy is to not give other people or organizations personal data unless it is absolutely necessary.

## TERMS TO REMEMBER

| | | |
|---|---|---|
| activity log | electronic data processing | management controls |
| antivirus software | (EDP) controls | password |
| computer resource control | ethical standards | virus |
| data encryption | input, processing, and | |
| digital signature | output controls | |
| disaster recovery plan | | |

## MIX AND MATCH

*Complete the following definitions with the Terms to Remember.*

1. Scrambling data before sending or saving it is known as _____.

2. A(n) _____ is a destructive program that invades a computer system by attaching itself to other commonly used programs.

3. Procedures for accepting data and keeping control totals are referred to as _____.

4. _____ is a computer program that identifies disk files that have been infected by a virus or worm.

5. Procedures to be followed if an organization's computer systems are disabled or destroyed constitute a(n) _____.

6. _____ are a set of rules a person or organization uses when considering the rights of others.

7. One type of _____ involves separating computer professionals into operations and developmental groups.

8. A summary of online activities kept for security purposes is called a(n) _____.

9. A(n) _____ uses a private and public key to create an encrypted document.

10. A(n) _____ is a unique combination of letters, numbers, or symbols known only to the user.

## R E V I E W   Q U E S T I O N S

1. Define the Terms to Remember.

2. When can a creditor legally invade a person's privacy?

3. What is the best-known legal basis for individual claims to privacy in the United States? What does it say?

4. What are the five guidelines of the Code of Fair Information Practice?

5. Why would an organization establish ethical guidelines?

6. Identify 12 questions you should consider before taking potentially unethical actions.

7. What are two means of controlling computer impact?

8. Identify five types of computer crime.

9. What are 11 warning signals of computer crime?

10. How do computer-oriented viruses, worms, Trojan horses, and bombs differ?

11. What are five ways a virus *cannot* spread?

12. What are six warning signs of an infected computer system?

13. What are eight types of physical controls that can be used to secure a computer system?

14. How can data be protected?

15. Describe three EDP controls that are oriented toward protecting an organization's computer system(s).

16. What is the best way to protect your personal privacy?

## APPLYING WHAT YOU'VE LEARNED

1.  Some people say, "The best way to catch a criminal is to think like a criminal." Using the warning signs and physical controls mentioned in the text, make a list of five ways security could be improved in your school computer lab or a room containing a home computer. Describe any new procedures or people that would have to be involved.

2.  It is part of our legal system to make the punishment fit the crime. Some computer criminals are teenagers or younger. Do you think it is fair to try them as adults? Are prison and/or fines reasonable punishments for them? What would be other ways they could make restitution for their computer crimes? Write a short paper explaining your views.

3.  Some people have suggested that all telecommunication hardware (telephones, computers, fax machines) contain integrated circuits with voice and data encryption firmware. All conversations and data would automatically be encrypted when sent. This hardware solution could allow government agencies to read encrypted data when it was deemed necessary. Do you think this proposal should be adopted? Why or why not?

4.  Research one of the biometric security devices mentioned in the text or one you have seen elsewhere. What biological characteristic does it detect and how? What is the cost? Where do you think such a device could best be used? Where would the device be inappropriate?

5.  Most programs on diskette can be easily copied despite any regulations or copyrights. If you produced a program to be sold and wished to protect it from being copied, what would you do? Write what you think is a reasonable software copyright agreement.

6.  Computer technology allows managers to monitor the work of employees electronically. Computers can track errors, count keystrokes, and even monitor breaks. Do you think employees have a right to know when their work is being monitored? Should this data be used to determine raises and promotions? What limits, if any, should be placed on the use of electronic work monitoring? Would you have any problem working for an organization that electronically monitored employees?

# Keeping Up with Change

# FROM THE USER'S POINT OF VIEW

The very fabric of our society is being altered by the fast-paced development of technology. Computers are helping to connect homes, schools, and businesses, linking consumers and workers to an endless variety of news, information, and entertainment. The speed at which innovations take place reflects how fast career skills and requirements change. Most people will change jobs several times in their life. If you view your work as part of a career path, instead of just performing a specific job, education becomes a lifelong, continuing process. Keeping up with changes means you understand how technology impacts your life and are willing to learn how to take advantage of it.

## AN INFORMATION SOCIETY

The computer has always been a tool with great problem-solving potential. The challenge is to identify problems and develop appropriate computer solutions. Today, computers have brought us to the threshold of what has been called an information society. An *information society* consists of a large group of people within a country or region wherein most workers generate or depend upon information for performance of their jobs. Today, information is one of the largest exports of the United States. News services, banks, insurance companies, and television stations are just a few of the organizations that collect data, process it into information, distribute it, and store it as a major part of their business (Figure 16.1). As consumers, we buy some of this information as newspapers and cable television.

The use of technological tools requires an understanding of how the tools work and what they can be expected to do. The day of simply pressing a button or turning

**16.1**

In an information society, workers generate and depend upon information to perform their jobs.

a crank in performance of a job is nearly over. People preparing themselves for tomorrow's workforce must realize that well-paying manual-labor jobs will be harder to find. Fewer jobs will require people to move or assemble parts. Those currently performing such jobs must seriously consider retraining in skills compatible with developments in technology.

## Consumer Electronics

Microprocessors and memory chips are being embedded into many consumer goods. This makes the items more "intelligent" and has certainly made our life easier and more interesting. Consumers are finding it important to understand basic computer concepts so they can maximize the usefulness of the products we use each day. Technology is taking us far beyond the video telephones, at-home shopping, and personal digital assistants that were, until recently, futuristic applications of computer technology.

**Smart Homes**    As Andrea is leaving for work she has a last-minute conversation with her house:

> "Computer, close all windows and lock the doors after I leave."
>
> *"Do you want any windows left open for ventilation?"*
>
> "What would you recommend?"
>
> *"Best cross-ventilation today will be achieved by opening the kitchen and southwest master bedroom windows."*
>
> "OK. And record tonight's local and national news, stock market closing, and weather."

*"Do you still want a search of the news media for downhill-ski sales?"*

"Yes. Also, scan for any news on the expected buyout of Technocorp. Contact me immediately if there are any large sales of its stock on the Exchange."

*"Your curling iron is on."*

"Oops! Turn it off and also run a diagnostic on the high-definition television/video camera in the den. Find the probability of a breakdown in the next six months. Schedule the appointment for the next recommended preventive maintenance check."

*"Acknowledged."*

Science fiction? Yes, but not for long. The smart house and technology to support it exists now. The smart house is a good example of a small local area network. Every appliance, smoke detector, and sensor has its own processor and memory (Figure 16.2).

### 16.2

Security, utility, and maintenance systems are networked in a smart house to provide its owners with optimum control.

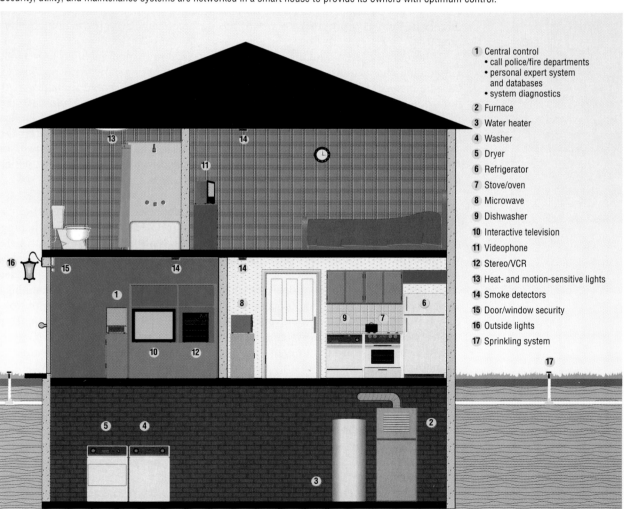

1 Central control
 • call police/fire departments
 • personal expert system and databases
 • system diagnostics
2 Furnace
3 Water heater
4 Washer
5 Dryer
6 Refrigerator
7 Stove/oven
8 Microwave
9 Dishwasher
10 Interactive television
11 Videophone
12 Stereo/VCR
13 Heat- and motion-sensitive lights
14 Smoke detectors
15 Door/window security
16 Outside lights
17 Sprinkling system

Each device is self-sufficient and communicates with a personal computer. Homeowners can use voice recognition or a central console to activate the desired combination of equipment anywhere in the house. Furthermore, the voice-recognition system replaces the need for security keys, because the system unlocks doors on command using unique biometric data—the homeowner's voice.

Smart homes provide increased safety and energy efficiency. Lights automatically turn on and off when people enter or leave a room. Heating and air conditioning is based on programmed consumer daily schedules as well as sensors for both inside and outside temperatures. Lawn and garden watering is determined by sensors in the lawn that know enough to turn themselves off in the rain. Sensors near a pool can sound an alarm when a child gets too close. Even simple actions, like turning down the stereo volume when the telephone or doorbell rings, can be under computer control.

The dangers of gas leaks, appliance fires, or accidental electric shocks are greatly reduced in these automated homes. Electric and gas systems are kept inactive until the appropriate appliance is connected to the system. The appliance's built-in processor identifies itself, and only then is gas or electricity supplied. This feature, and constant power usage monitoring, prevents children from getting shocked when poking fingers into open electrical outlets or adults from overloading circuits. If a fire does start, the telephone system can notify the authorities automatically, even if the homeowners are there.

Recent agreements among major consumer electronics manufacturers have made automating a home much easier and less expensive. A new wiring standard for appliances, called *Consumer Electronics Bus (CEBus),* will allow common household appliances with embedded CEBus circuitry to communicate with each other regardless of manufacturer. Although smart houses used to require special wiring and outlets, with CEBus homeowners can plug these appliances into existing wiring. By using a CEBus controller, the appliance can be turned off and on via a computer program, remote control, or telephone call. Much of this technology will be used in larger buildings in which environmental control, security, and even elevators will be smart.

**Smart Transportation**     Computer technology has impacted all aspects of our transportation system as well. For years trains have used computers to direct track switching, and airports have relied on traffic control systems to assist human traffic controllers. We know that technology has been indispensable in the development of manned space vehicles, submarines, airplanes, and even racing cars. But many of us are using embedded computers every day in our personal cars and trucks. As shown in Figure 16.3, automobiles presently use embedded microprocessors in antilock breaks, air bags, climate controls, transmissions, carburetors, instrument panel controls, power steering, suspension control, security, and sound systems. New cars are being manufactured with I/O ports into which diagnostic equipment is plugged. Mechanics use software to analyze automotive functions and identify the parts that need servicing. Increased reliability and serviceability for cars has resulted from the harnessing of computers.

Computers are already helping drivers to locate their destinations (see Figure 16.4). CD-ROMs containing detailed road maps can be displayed on a screen near the driver. Telecommunication hardware and software links the car with global positioning satellites pinpointing the car's location. The driver can change the display to the traffic or weather report by using a touch-sensitive screen or voice input. This technology is also available with navigation maps for boaters. A similar device already exists on international airplane flights. Overhead screens display the plane's location, along with such information as miles/kilometers and time to destination.

**16.3**

Automobiles use embedded computers in a variety of ways.

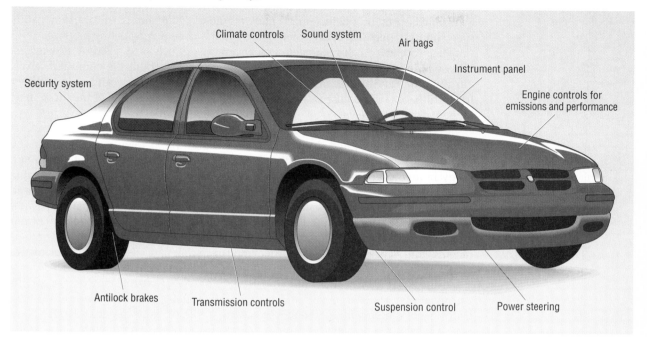

Climate controls · Sound system · Air bags · Instrument panel · Security system · Engine controls for emissions and performance · Antilock brakes · Transmission controls · Suspension control · Power steering

**16.4**

Through the use of CD-ROM and telecommunication technology, drivers can see maps of their current location.

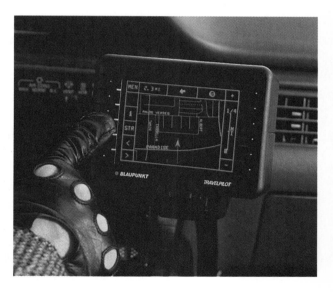

Car radios take on a new look through a nationwide Radio Broadcast Data System. More than 500 stations will not only transmit music but also display the song's title and artist on a small screen near the radio. A listener can also program the radio to find only stations of a certain format, such as rock and roll or classical, and automatically tune in while traveling cross-country. Broadcasts would be interrupted for important weather and traffic information.

It is becoming more common to see automated speed detection lanes on the nation's highways and streets. A laser, similar to those used by traffic police, detects the speed of passing cars and displays it, warning motorists if they are going too fast. Sensors can presently detect speed and volume of traffic and close lanes or modify speed limits as needed. An extension of this is automated driving on the proposed IVHS (Intelligent Vehicle/Highway System). When a problem such as a stalled car is detected, IVHS will lower surrounding cars' speed through receivers in the cars themselves. Turning our cars over to autopilot will increase fuel efficiency and reduce driver frustration, but will require us to change how we view driving. Cars of the future may literally drive themselves.

**Home Entertainment and Communications**    From the first computer games in the 1970s, people have been interested in how they can use technology for entertainment. Many homeowners are plugging a variety of equipment into telephone and cable television services. One of the benefits of living in an information society is the increased availability of leisure activities. Information services help by letting people play or preview games at home through their PCs and the service's computer network. People from around the world can play together through these communication networks, with options ranging from a chess challenge to participating in complex adventure games that involve many players.

These same networks will allow users to preview first-run movies, see an off-Broadway play, watch a concert in Europe, or even watch a TV show they missed. When a movie looks interesting, you rent it by having the information service download it to your television. Anticipating this trend toward customized entertainment, some video rental stores have expanded into the music CD market. You can go to a store and record exactly the pieces of music you wish on a CD, picking from thousands of selections.

Another way people can spend their leisure time is talking to their television sets by using *interactive television*, as shown in Figure 16.5. Some cable television users now

**16.5**

A variety of consumer services will be available through interactive television.

have control boxes that are linked to the cable company's computer. The control box becomes input hardware that lets the viewer respond to the televised program. Polls can be taken as viewers punch the appropriate button on their control boxes to respond to posed questions. It is anticipated that voting for national and local elections via television will become a reality. Currently, viewers can respond online to game shows and advertisements. Commercials will be tailored to the consumers in a particular household. Students can even return answers to questions a teacher poses as they watch educational television.

Technology has also changed the way we shop. At present, consumers can peruse classified ads on the Internet and use e-mail to contact the sellers. Online catalogs are available from a variety of retail companies who work with information services to showcase their products. Once connected to the system, users identify what they want, and the computer searches through the product line to find the requested information and prices. With interactive television, customers can request a video demonstration of a product or see clothing modeled before making a purchase. Billing and payment is done electronically, and users can request their bank balance to see if they are within their budget.

**Virtual Reality**   Through the use of complex programs and specialized hardware, we can now take computerized entertainment one dimension further. Imagine walking on the moon, fighting dragons, or swimming near a volcano two miles under the ocean. A virtual reality can put you there. In a ***virtual reality***, the user is immersed in a computer-generated environment.

The hardware required for virtual reality looks like something from science fiction. Earphones, goggles, gloves, and bodysuits containing sensors to help interact with the virtual reality. The goggles, shown in Figure 16.6, enable the wearer to experience three-dimensional views of a computer simulation. As the user moves his or her head, the view changes. Movements of the hands or body act as input that takes the user through

**16.6**

Virtual realities can allow a person to experience, through sight and touch, situations simulated by computers. Here a woman bikes through a fantasy landscape.

the virtual reality scenario. Sensors in the gloves allow the user to move and pick up virtual objects. The actions of the user are responded to by the virtual reality program.

Due to the expense of equipment and software, many of the best virtual realities are still in research labs. Flight simulators and other training environments have been made more realistic with virtual reality. However, some firms offer a pay-to-play opportunity, where a virtual reality game can be rented by the minute. Software exists for less evasive and less expensive virtual realities; for example, a person can design a new home and then use a mouse to travel through the 3D images of the rooms displayed on-screen. A landscape design can be aged to show plant growth over many years with the user walking through the property.

It is the potential of virtual reality that most excites computer scientists and users. Education would drastically change as a student could learn anatomy from the inside of the human body or a fireman could train on equipment in a virtual reality of a burning house. Manipulating objects in a virtual reality is already being used to help victims of spinal cord injuries relearn complex motor skills. With virtual reality you are *in* a movie or video game, not just watching it.

## ■ Computer-Integrated Workplaces

Many of our jobs have been directly or indirectly affected by changes in technology. If the changes take place at our desktop or worksite, we notice them immediately. However, many new technological ideas are showing up behind the scenes as well.

We have come a long way since Henry Ford offered people a car in any color they wanted, so long as it was black. Today, any automotive salesperson can deliver a car to you that has the exact options and colors you want. By entering customer specifications into an integrated manufacturing system, a matching car can be found or built. The trend toward "customized" mass-produced goods continues to increase. Rather than produce an item and hope the customer will like it as is, such products as trucks, cars, modular housing, furniture, and clothing are made to order at mass-production prices.

To facilitate the speed of designing and producing new and customized products, engineers can quickly create prototypes with computers. One way this is accomplished is by having a computer control an ultraviolet light source aimed at the surface of a vat filled with photocurable polymers—plastic that hardens when exposed to light. Wherever the light hits, the liquid turns solid, forming a thin layer of hard plastic. The floor of the vat is lowered and the liquid surface is again exposed to light. This creates a second layer of plastic on top of the first. By repeating this process, called *stereolithography,* customized parts, both hollow and solid, can be quickly built up (see Figure 16.7). This part can be used directly or serve as a model for casting in another material. Use of stereolithography includes not only machine parts but identical copies of priceless, fragile sculptures that would not survive handling in museums.

Stereolithography is one of several computer applications that speed up the manufacturing process. Combined together these processes are known as **computer-integrated manufacturing. CIM,** as it is called, is a combination of computer-aided design (CAD), computer-aided machining (CAM), numerical control (NC), robotics, and materials requirement planning, which are unified by common data communication protocols.

When an order comes in for a custom product, such as a car, the specifications are input into a database. When necessary, CAD systems manipulate these data into useful designs and identify materials. These materials specifications become part of just-in-time inventory. Resource planning software schedules when the actual production begins. As the car is being built, the specification data will affect both humans and

**16.7**

By exposing liquid plastic to ultraviolet light, a 3D model can be built with more precision and in less time than with traditional milling methods.

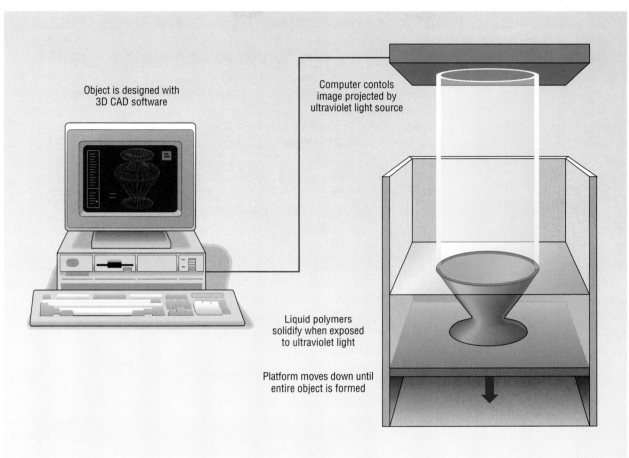

Object is designed with
3D CAD software

Computer contols
image projected by
ultraviolet light source

Liquid polymers
solidify when exposed
to ultraviolet light

Platform moves down until
entire object is formed

machines. People will know what color upholstery to install, and the path a welding robot takes will be unique to the model and options ordered.

In the field of health science, technology has vastly improved the research and practice of medicine. Embedded computers have allowed many devices common in hospitals, such as medical lasers, to be miniaturized for use in field hospitals or remote sites. Simulations of surgery via a computer monitor and mouse have been in existence for several years, as have computer-monitored pacemakers. Current research, however, centers around the use of robots for surgery. A robot is programmed to perform surgical procedures under control of a human surgeon. With a robot, the cutting with scalpel and laser required for brain, eye, and ear surgery would be more precise.

## ■ Global Economy and the Cashless Society

The information society has transformed the global economy. Data is electronically exchanged among financial markets around the world, affecting the price of wheat in the Ukraine, the value of the yen in Japan, and the unemployment rate in Mexico. Our

## ...TIPS FOR WORD PROCESSING A RÉSUMÉ

Many large companies receive hundreds of résumés a year. They use scanners to input the résumés and tracking software to search for potential employees. A jazzy résumé meant to catch a recruiter's eye will only confuse a computer. According to Resumix Inc., a maker of résumé tracking software, here are the new rules of résumé writing:

- Exotic typefaces, underlining, and decorative graphics don't scan well.

- Send originals, not copies, and don't use a dot-matrix printer.

- Too-small print may confuse the scanner; don't go below 12-point type.

- Use standard 8.5 by 11-inch paper and do not fold. Words in a crease can't be read easily.

- Use white or light-beige paper. Blues and grays minimize the contrast between the letters and background.

- Avoid double columns. The scanner reads from left to right.

- Technical jargon is a good idea. A computer search will target keywords specific to your profession.

Source: *U.S. News & World Report*, 26 October 1992, page 93.

ability to immediately exchange ideas, transactions, and funds through international networks allows businesspeople from around the world to compete in a global economy.

To support this global economy, the banking industry has developed an interconnected *electronic funds transfer (EFT)* system, which minimizes the work involved in transferring money between banks. Through the use of electronic passwords and credit cards, computer literate end users can advise their banks to pay their rent and other bills electronically. The bank completes the transaction by automatically moving the money from their account to the landlord's and other designated accounts. This system facilitates the payment for goods ordered via Internet or interactive television.

The success of EFT, EDI, and other computer-based networks has some people even talking about a *cashless society*. Instead of using coins, paper money, or checks, we would make all of our purchases via electronic transactions. Individuals and businesses would have universal account numbers. When workers are paid, their employers make electronic deposits to employee accounts; at the same time, the employer's account would be reduced. A cashless society may be far in the future, but we can see its beginning with the smart cards, telephone cards, and debit cards becoming popular.

## Emerging Technologies

Although no one can accurately predict the future, we can do a good job of guessing by looking at recent technological trends. What could be found only in a research laboratory a few years ago, like a personal digital assistant or virtual reality, now is commercially available. Another trend is that products originally developed for research or commercial purposes are redesigned for individual consumers. From research labs, animation studios, and users of large databases come requests for more powerful and more efficient computers with faster and larger storage capabilities. This continuous drive for increases in performance has led to major developments in processing hardware, storage hardware, and software design. These trends on the technological horizon let us glimpse into the future.

**Superconductor Materials**   To speed up the transfer of data and programs within computer hardware, researchers have sought to reduce the resistance of the materials conducting the electricity. The late 1980s brought a materials science breakthrough: *superconductors*. Superconductors lose all resistance to the flow of electricity at a given temperature. These materials provide the fastest possible means of electronically transmitting data within and among computer components (see Who's Who in this chapter). Superconductors are helping computers break processing-speed barriers.

**Optical Computers**   Other hardware improvements are being developed that do not even use electricity to operate; instead, light is used for both data transmittal and its processing. Fiber-optic cables are currently used as a communication channel to transmit data as light pulses. Currently, research centers around development of a processing unit containing very fast light-activated switches (see Figure 16.8). An *optical computer* would use these switches and fiber optics to increase processing and data transmission speeds. Additional advantages are that optical computers generate less component-degrading heat and are less vulnerable to electrical and other interference than those completely dependent on electricity.

**16.8**

Light, rather than electricity, is the power behind the circuitry of optical computers.

**DNA Computers**   If you can imagine each of the cells in your body as a tiny processor connected by your nervous system, you can see that computers and communication technologies really imitate the complexity already found in natural systems. In combining biology and computer science, a handful of researchers have been able to use synthetic DNA as a computer itself. DNA is a biological system's alternative to binary codes. Although currently, *DNA computers* are much slower and far less sophisticated than even a personal computer, the potential is tremendous. Such computers use the ability of the DNA in cells to work efficiently at many small tasks that need to be done in parallel. With so many different kinds of cells, many types of tasks can be accomplished. Such computers would cost very little and have almost no energy output. With the "intelligence" that a cell has to distinguish between its own kind and invaders such as viruses, DNA computers could be used for decoding encrypted data.

**Genetic Algorithms and Fuzzy Logic**   In the field of software, two innovations are influencing new computer applications. Despite the name, *genetic algorithms* have nothing to do with actual genetics. The name comes from the fact that this problem-solving software contains code that acts like living and evolving organisms. Through chance, different objects (areas of code) are combined, producing new programs that are tested as a possible solution. Just like in life, programs can improve or go extinct. Current applications include finding an optimum production for a tractor manufacturer, designs for a miniaturized computer chip, map of a potential fiber-optic network, and the proper mix of stocks and bond investments for a financial firm.

    *Fuzzy logic* seems to be an oxymoron. Although we view logic as precise, fuzzy logic tries to impart a logical structure to imprecise measurements, numbers, and theories by setting up relationships among existing information. In many situations, there are continuously changing conditions that could affect an output. The automatic focus for a video camera could use a fuzzy logic controller to keep the picture clear as the user aims at various scenery. Fuzzy logic could detect an individual's handwriting despite day-to-day inconsistencies. Although no one anticipates fuzzy logic to completely replace the digital logic of today's computers, it is being widely used in home appliances, video equipment, computers, and other areas in which the variations in physical input need to be recognized and acted upon.

**Artificial Intelligence**   In the growing area of *artificial intelligence (AI)*, computers are simulating human thought and judgment. Artificial intelligence synthesizes computer science, psychology, linguistics, and other specialized fields to perform tasks with humanlike logic. Expert systems, discussed in chapter 12, are one application of artificial intelligence.

    Among the AI developments expected are heuristic problem-solving techniques. The term *heuristic* describes a method by which problems are solved through application of general rules and information based on experience. Instead of following sequences of instructions to devise solutions, heuristic software applies rules proven to be effective in the past. As an example, heuristic techniques are being used to develop programs that can sort and grade produce, efficiently pack a truck or boxcar with different sizes of containers, and control complex air and ground traffic. Recently, an AI chess program learned enough to beat a human grand chessmaster for the first time. When people are in these situations, they evaluate a constantly changing environment but act according to preset rules, acquiring experience as they go; AI systems use the rules given to them as well, learning from experience and applying this information to new experiences.

With the aid of personal expert systems, education can be individualized and on a need-to-know basis. For example, as you get ready to build a new deck in the backyard, the list of building materials is put together with the help of an expert deck construction system you have downloaded from an information utility. The materials are ordered from the local lumberyard through the same network. As you start cutting lumber and pounding nails, the expert system helps you figure out how to construct the deck in the easiest, safest, and most efficient way. Similar home tutors will be available for interior design, landscaping, electrical wiring, plumbing, and a variety of do-it-yourself projects. A personal expert system could even help you diagnose problems with your tropical fish, as illustrated in Figure 16.9.

**16.9**

Personal expert systems use artificial intelligence techniques to help you solve common problems in your home or workplace.

## PERSONAL EXPERT SYSTEM

?     This fish has white bubbles growing around its fins and gills.
     What's wrong?
☞     You have identified a swordtail fish.
     This fish is susceptible to a fish virus known as Ich.

?     Can I cure it?
☞     All the fish in your tank need to be treated.

?     What should I do?
☞     α Ich Treatment for freshwater fish:

     1. add I tsp. Malashite Green for each 10 gallons of water
     2. raise water temperature to 83 degrees.

## SKILLS UPDATING

The changes computers bring to society happen rather quickly, a matter of months rather than years. When changes occur that rapidly, obsolescence of hardware and software, as well as of our knowledge and skills, is bound to be a major problem. *Obsolescence*, present in any technology-driven field, describes the rate at which equipment and the skills and knowledge associated with it become outdated and, eventually, useless.

In the past, new generations of hardware and software were introduced about every 10 years. However, it is not uncommon to presently see a new version of software less than a year after its predecessor. The maximum storage capacity of a memory chip has doubled yearly within the past 10 years, while cost has correspondingly decreased. Computer equipment purchased today will probably have to be replaced, along with its accompanying software, within a few years.

This technological obsolescence has both good and bad effects on computer professionals and users. On the positive side, the rapid rate of change means that new jobs and entirely new career opportunities are becoming available each year. For qualified people, this change represents the opportunity to upgrade or alter their careers. However, to remain current and competitive, users must constantly keep their knowledge and skills updated. Education does not stop with a diploma, certificate, or degree.

### On-the-job Training

Many people in the workforce recognize that knowledge and skills about computers and their applications can improve their chances of career growth. Since computers are general-purpose tools, they can be configured with almost infinite combinations of hardware and software to meet the needs of specific users and applications. This means that each computer-using organization must train its employees on the unique features of its own computer systems (Figure 16.10).

**16.10**

Basic knowledge of computers is an integral part of many careers.

On-the-job training sessions tend to be brief and highly focused. Typically, an organization prepares manuals to be used for training, which can be used to look up solutions to problems after a new employee is trained or a computer system is operational. Most on-the-job training programs deal with specific applications. Sessions may run from a half-day to as long as a week. Employees are expected to leave these sessions and move right into regular use of equipment and procedures as part of job performance.

General or administrative skills as well as proficiency of specific computer applications may be covered in on-the-job training. For example, many organizations run in-house seminars on such management topics as supervisory skills, stress management, financial operations, and decision making.

# J. Georg Bednorz

(b. 1950)

# Karl Alex Müller

(b. 1927)

Since its discovery in 1911, super-conductivity has intrigued engineers and physicists. A superconductor is a material that loses all resistance to the flow of electricity when cooled to a low temperature. Despite many years of research, it was impossible to predict which material could be used as superconductors. Scientists saw great potential for super-conductors as a means to transport electricity efficiently and inex-pensively. But expensive equipment was needed to bring the materials down to very low temperatures.

In the early 1980s, two research-ers at IBM's research laboratories in Zurich, J. Georg Bednorz and Karl A. Müller, tried a variety of compounds that they could easily make. For a while they had to share lab equipment with others and almost lost their funding. After reading an article about French research in an unrelated area, Bednorz decided to add copper to a mixture of lanthanum, barium, nickel, and oxygen. In early 1986 Bednorz and Müller were able to show that superconductivity started in their material at a temperature of 35 degrees Kelvin (-397°F or -283°C). This was 12 degrees Kelvin higher than any previous studies and was a big step on the road to supercon-ductor practicality. Their research was painstakingly done but greeted with skepticism. As scientists were able to replicate their results, other research in the area prolifer-ated. Bednorz and Müller were awarded the 1987 Nobel Prize for Physics.

**Who's Who**

In addition, organizations often sponsor attendance by employees at colleges or technical institutes. The company may reimburse an employee all or part of the tuition for a job-related college course. Or an organization may make a degree a condition of retaining or upgrading a job. If enough employees need the same training, a class may be offered at the job site taught by either in-house trainers or professional educators.

## ■ Workshops and Conferences

Workshops and conferences provide opportunities for improving skills beyond on-the-job training programs. A **workshop** or *seminar* concentrates on a single topic and can last from a few hours to several days. In many ways, workshops are like formal schooling; there are lectures, demonstrations, and materials to read. However, the participants are usually not tested or graded. These opportunities occur away from the working environment and may involve expertise not found locally.

*Conferences* focus on larger, more encompassing themes, such as robotics, CAD, or multimedia. Many conference speakers give presentations about different aspects of a subject. These presentations are usually one to two hours long, with several presentations occurring simultaneously. There is often a display area, as shown in Figure 16.11, where vendors and publishers can demonstrate related products.

Workshops and conferences both provide a means for people to share ideas and information with others who have common interests. These activities, along with on-the-job training, are often are referred to as *continuing education*. To avoid technological obsolescence of their knowledge and skills, people who work with computers typically are required to spend a quarter to a third of their time (personal and working) in continuing education. Other sources for continuing the learning process, distinct from schools and job-related training, are also available.

**16.11**

Conferences provide opportunities for users with common interests to meet each other and view new technology.

## Recreational and Professional Publications

People who perform similar jobs or who work in a specific industry share common professional interests. Computer programmers, for example, are interested in new software and coding techniques. In the medical field, interests center around innovative medications or treatments. Manufacturing engineers may wish to share information about new types of production techniques or tools. Businesspeople need to know what products and services their competition provides.

A major branch of the publishing industry has evolved to meet these continuing-education needs. Special-interest newspapers, journals, newsletters, and magazines are published to supply information to specific interest groups (see Figure 16.12). Tens of thousands of professional publications are produced regularly. More than 750 of these cover specific computer-related topics, and many more cover applications of computers in particular industries or professions.

Reading one or more special-interest publications should be a part of the continuing-education effort for every computer professional and serious end user. You will encounter a number of these publications at school and in the workplace. Make it a practice to review the contents of such publications carefully and regularly by subscribing to or arranging to read some of these publications, perhaps in the public or company libraries.

It is easy for a busy professional to get behind on his or her professional reading. A good way to keep current is to review a publication's table of contents, then read those articles that spark your interest. Advertisements may offer opportunities for trying new hardware or software. At the very least, be aware that professional publications will establish an information lifeline that you will need to keep your knowledge base from becoming obsolete.

**16.12**

Reading recreational and professional publications provides an easy way to keep your knowledge current.

**16.13**

Computer technology has had an impact on almost every college curriculum.

## CAREER PATHS

A career is not just a single job. Very few people retire from the same job or organization at which they started working. Those of us with an eye toward the future can make the most of our working lives by realizing that our careers will probably be a series of related jobs, or a *career path*.

If we identify long-term career goals, we can make intelligent decisions supporting a career path that will lead us toward those goals. Otherwise, we could aimlessly jump from one job to another, dissatisfied with our accomplishments at each step. Or, worse yet, we could stay in the same job because we have nothing better to do or are too lazy to change.

Career goals are never easy to choose and are certainly subject to change. You need to have a career goal in mind when writing a résumé, applying for a new job, or selecting new fields to study. The computer-related fields offer opportunities to people with varied ranges of knowledge and skills. A few jobs are open to persons with only a high-school education. Far greater opportunities, with higher earning and growth potential, are open to those who go on to college.

Almost every college curriculum has been affected by recent developments in computers, microelectronics, and networks (see Figure 16.13). As a result, many students are trained as end users as part of their degree requirements. They may have taken a computer literacy course or studied computers as part of another class. Those students interested in working as computer professionals can find several college-level courses to qualify them for technical careers. Computer-related career areas include: end-user computing, information systems, computer science, and computer engineering.

### ■ End-user Computing

Just as computer technology has affected every facet of working experience, so has it become an integral part of virtually every college department. When computers were new, colleges and universities tended to have a single, comparatively large computer center serving all academic departments. Students from various departments did their computing through this central facility.

Now PCs can be found in most academic departments, as well as in libraries and dormitories. After a general introductory class or appropriate experience, specific field-related applications are taught within the appropriate departments. To illustrate, medical and nursing schools use computers to train students in patient monitoring, medical diagnosis, and even administration of hospitals and medical offices. Similarly, departments in science, engineering, business, education, liberal arts, fine arts, social science, and other specialties tend to have equipment, software, and courses designed to meet specific needs of their present students and future computer users.

Each new technological advance brings with it the opportunity for new careers in end-user computing (see Figure 16.14). For those with an interest in graphics and

**16.14**

Many career goals and interests can be met in jobs related to computer information systems.

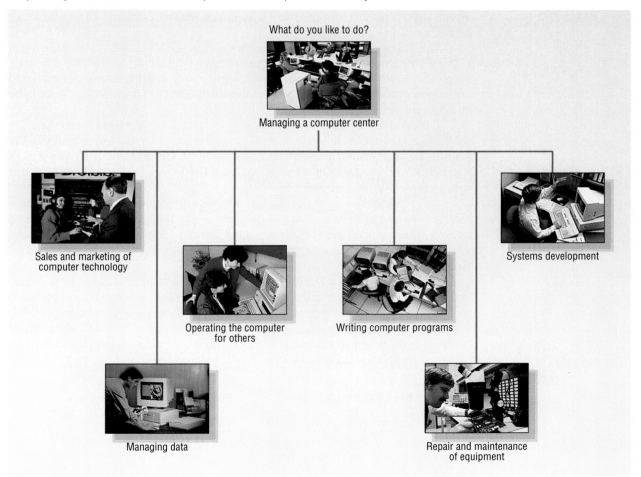

What do you like to do?

Managing a computer center

Sales and marketing of computer technology

Operating the computer for others

Writing computer programs

Systems development

Managing data

Repair and maintenance of equipment

the arts, career choices are available in the fields of animation, graphic design, and advertising. In all career fields, information specialists are needed to help others with the complexity of using information services and online references searches. Educators can be found in many organizations, training people to use new software and hardware. Regardless of your combination of talents and academic interests, rewarding careers involving computers and technology abound.

## ■ Information Systems

There are a number of career opportunities in delivering the services necessary to keep networks and computer systems working. Some of the specific job descriptions were covered in earlier chapters. Specialties within this career area include end-user support, computer operations, data entry and control, database management, network engineering, systems analysis, computer programming, and project management (Figure 16.15).

As computer systems became more sophisticated, great shortages of qualified people developed. There has been a continuous demand since the 1950s for people with the skills to design and successfully implement new computer-based systems. Recently, the need is for a new category of specialist—people trained to create and install information systems in business, scientific, manufacturing, and educational organizations. This specialty, *computer information systems (CIS)*, is now a popular major on many college campuses.

The CIS curriculum stresses a sequence of courses in business and management, along with classes in computer programming, application generators, networks, telecommunications, systems development, and decision making. Individuals interested in computers and applications-oriented problem solving will find a CIS program to be both interesting and profitable.

Professionals in CIS can attain certification with a *Certificate in Data Processing (CDP)*. To receive a CDP, individuals must pass a five-part examination prepared by the Institute for Certification of Computer Professionals (ICCP) and have five years of work experience with computer information systems. Two years of college course work can substitute for two years of work experience.

A CDP candidate must pass all five sections within three years. Once a section has been passed, it does not have to be taken again. If a section is failed, it can be retaken. The five sections of the exam are: hardware, computer programming and software, principles of management, quantitative methods and accounting, and systems analysis and design.

Individuals who have received a CDP may place these initials following their name to show others their professional certification. The CDP is only one of several certifications available to computer professionals. A *Certificate in Computer Programming (CCP)* is also available through the ICCP by specialized tests covering business, scientific, or systems programming. Proper certification can help professionals advance along their chosen career path (see Figure 16.15).

## ■ Computer Science

Mathematics and engineering departments of educational institutions have been involved with computers since the earliest days, because early computers were designed and programmed by mathematicians and engineers. Through the years the study of the mathematical and logical aspects of computing evolved into a specialty covering the

**16.15**

There are many career paths available for computer professionals working in information systems.

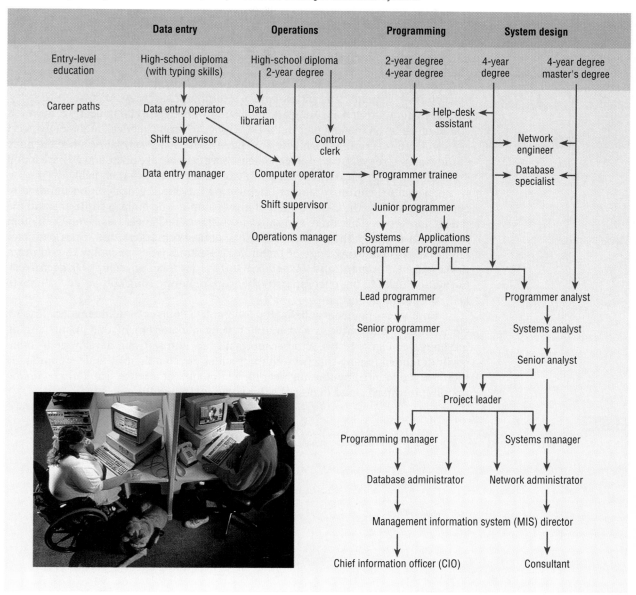

| | Data entry | Operations | Programming | System design |
|---|---|---|---|---|
| Entry-level education | High-school diploma (with typing skills) | High-school diploma / 2-year degree | 2-year degree / 4-year degree | 4-year degree / 4-year degree master's degree |

Career paths:

Data entry: Data entry operator → Shift supervisor → Data entry manager

Data librarian

Operations: Control clerk; Computer operator → Shift supervisor → Operations manager

Computer operator → Programmer trainee

Programming: Help-desk assistant; Programmer trainee → Junior programmer → Systems programmer / Applications programmer → Lead programmer → Senior programmer

System design: Network engineer; Database specialist; Programmer analyst → Systems analyst → Senior analyst

Project leader → Programming manager / Systems manager

Programming manager → Database administrator → Management information system (MIS) director → Chief information officer (CIO)

Systems manager → Network administrator → Consultant

control of computers' data manipulation capabilities. Today people who specialize in techniques for designing system software and apply these techniques to the handling of data and programs are known as ***computer scientists***.

As the demand for more-advanced software increases, so does the demand for qualified computer scientists. Since system software controls computer operation, it is not unusual for a large computer installation to have more money tied up in system software than in computer equipment. Personal computing also requires user-friendly system software. Computer scientists are responsible for developing and maintaining system software. They take classes in computer programming, data structures, and the design of such system software as operating systems and compilers. People with this experience work for hardware manufacturers and software developers and as technical specialists responsible for software maintenance within organizations.

## ■ Computer Engineering

Persons who complete course work in *computer engineering* specialize in the development, manufacture, and assembly of computer hardware. At most universities, studies in computer engineering are associated with electrical engineering; however, computers play an integral part in the job of mechanical, chemical, and bioengineers as well. Persons entering this highly diversified field usually specialize, since the body of knowledge is so great. Computer engineers have become like doctors, who have found it impossible to keep up with all the knowledge associated with their field.

Specialties within computer engineering include the design and building of computer circuitry; the development of input, output, and storage hardware; and the interaction between hardware and software. Computer engineers also work with other researchers to design the parallel processors, optical computers, and superconductor circuitry on the cutting edge of technology. Persons who specialize in computer processing equipment and associated software are called *computer architects*. Computer architecture encompasses the work of configuring computer systems to achieve specific performance.

Computer engineers and architects complete courses in mathematics, physics, electronics, system software, circuit design, project management, and manufacturing methods (see Figure 16.16). And because hardware and software developments often occur in tandem, many colleges and universities are coordinating and/or combining their programs in computer engineering and computer science. The term *computer architecture* often is used to describe this combined specialty.

**16.16**

Electrical and computer engineers can follow career paths in computer manufacturing and systems maintenance.

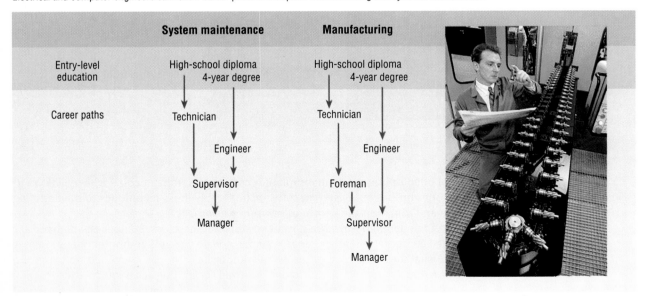

## Professional Organizations

Many professional organizations have evolved to support different computer-oriented career paths. Members of these groups enjoy establishing peer contacts to exchange ideas and information. Thousands of professional, trade, and business associations serve millions of members in specialized industries or jobs. Members are attracted by common, shared interests (Figure 16.17). As examples, each of the four major computer disciplines has at least one association serving its particular needs:

♦ The *Association for System Management (ASM)* has a membership consisting largely of systems analysts for various organizations.

♦ The *Data Processing Management Association (DPMA)* appeals to a wide variety of computer professionals from operators and programmers to computer center managers.

♦ The *Association for Computing Machinery (ACM)* serves computer scientists and others involved in computer architecture.

♦ The *Institute of Electrical and Electronic Engineers (IEEE)* has its own special-interest group representing the interests of hardware and circuitry specialists, the people who design and build computer equipment.

Each of these organizations has been around for more than 20 years with membership rosters that run into the tens of thousands. They have local chapters throughout the country as well as student chapters on many college campuses. By joining a student chapter of a professional organization, future computer professionals can begin to build working relationships with their peers.

Many other professional associations and societies have subgroups that specialize in computer applications. Examples include associations serving the health, education, banking, insurance, and petroleum fields. In each case, managers, scientists, and others can exchange ideas and views with computer professionals who have chosen to specialize in the needs of specific fields.

**16.17**

Membership in a professional organization promotes new ideas and personal growth.

### How Professional Organizations Support Personal Development

■ Provide personal and professional contacts

■ Support student members with on-campus chapters

■ Hold local meetings and presentations

■ Publish newsletters and magazines

■ Sponsor seminars, training sessions, conferences, conventions, and trade shows

■ Offer hardware and software discounts due to large buying power

■ Provide certification of professional skills

# A Closer Look at
# Emerging Technologies

**S**ome future trends are easy to predict. You can anticipate the advent of smaller, faster, and less expensive personal computers. We have discussed in this chapter the potential impact of recent developments in processing hardware and software. Other technological trends will have a tremendous impact on narrow groups of users—for example, computer-aided prosthetics for the physically challenged, or computer-based trading by financial arbitrageurs.

A few new technologies just emerging from research and development laboratories have the potential to change everyone's life. What follows are some questions you probably never thought to ask about emerging technologies.

**Q: What is a neural network?**

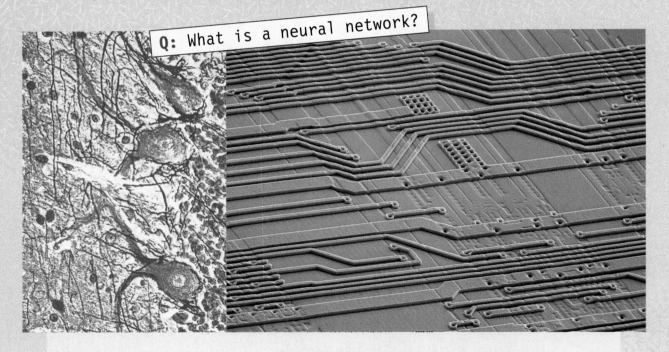

**A:** Computer scientists want to simulate a person's ability to recognize patterns. To do so, they integrate thousands of specialized processors, a kind of silicon neuron, onto chips. Neurological connections in the human brain are modeled by the movement of electrons through the circuitry model. These *neural networks* are taught basic discriminations through a set of learning trials. For instance, the difference between your voice and a friend's is taught by providing different examples. The system tries to guess after each example and learns to discriminate the difference through trial and error.

**Q: What types of work do nanomachines perform?**

**A:** *Nanomachines* incorporate gears, levers, lenses, ball bearings, and sensors that are smaller than the period at the end of this sentence. These microscopic machines could clear a person's clogged arteries, clean up pollutants, continuously sense air pressure in your tires, or intravenously manufacture and administer life-supporting drugs. Like a tiny bulldozer, a nanomachine can move atoms across a surface, creating man-made molecules.

**Q: What is a memory cube?**

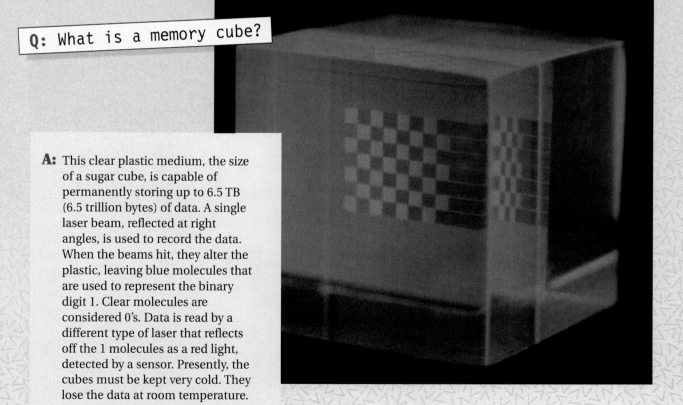

**A:** This clear plastic medium, the size of a sugar cube, is capable of permanently storing up to 6.5 TB (6.5 trillion bytes) of data. A single laser beam, reflected at right angles, is used to record the data. When the beams hit, they alter the plastic, leaving blue molecules that are used to represent the binary digit 1. Clear molecules are considered 0's. Data is read by a different type of laser that reflects off the 1 molecules as a red light, detected by a sensor. Presently, the cubes must be kept very cold. They lose the data at room temperature.

**Q:** What comes next after portable computers?

**A:** Engineers and fashion designers are collaborating on wearable computers. Their goal is to create hardware that is comfortable and enhances job performance. For example, a computer used to take inventory would include an optical scanner on the hand or arm, with a voice-activated database system worn around the neck. An emergency medical technician uses a sensor on his hand to read vital signs, which are displayed on goggles and sent ahead to the hospital.

**Q:** What's in the future for holograms?

**A:** A hologram is a 3D image that seems to float in space and changes as you move around it. Holographic images can now be seen on credit cards, magazine covers, and posters. Creating them requires hours of precisely filming an object from many angles. Researchers are using supercomputers to take a computer-generated object, rotate it, and store the images for later projection. Although only simple shapes can now be created, graphic workstations of the future will allow a user to create a hologram interactively, as he or she draws it on a screen.

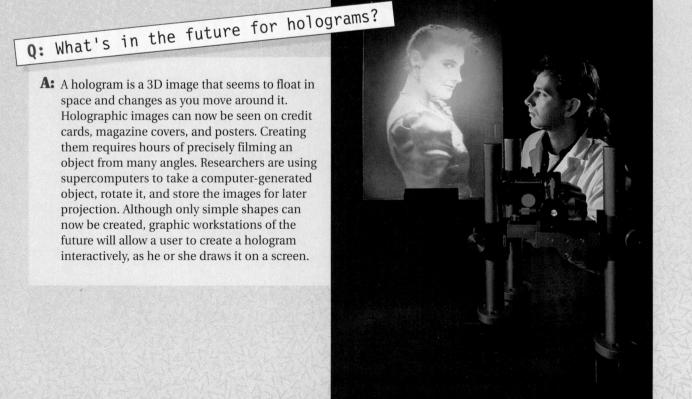

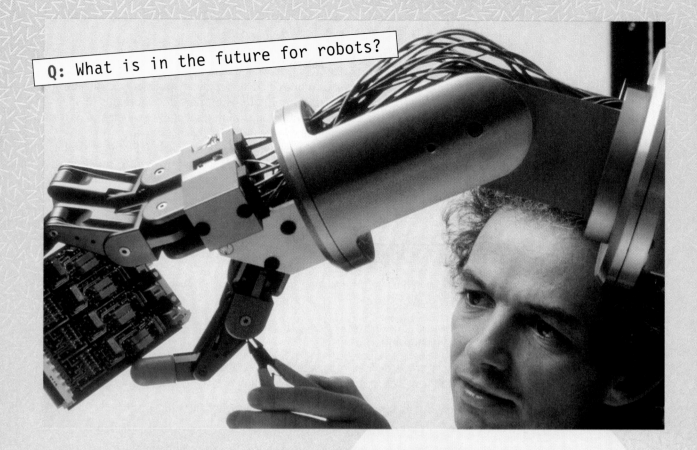

**Q:** What is in the future for robots?

**A:** By combining artificial intelligence and robotics, researchers are creating robots that learn from their movements. One scientist is using the behavior of insects to build multilegged robots that detect and avoid obstacles for exploring the planet Mars. A robotic arm that learns a precise, complex movement such as buttering bread, holds promise for the advancement of user-controlled artificial limbs.

Typical participation in a professional organization begins with regular meetings of the local chapter, usually once a month. Officers of the chapters are responsible for planning meetings, discussions, and presentations on new developments of special interest to members. Often the national organization has a staff that helps to provide speakers or materials for local meetings.

Most associations or societies publish newsletters or magazines for their members. In addition, organizations sponsor and conduct workshops, training sessions, conferences, conventions, or trade shows. These activities can play important roles in the continuing education of end users and professionals.

## CHAPTER FACTS

- We now live in an information society wherein many people's work generates or depends on information.

- Computer-literate workers are critical to an organization's success within the global economy.

- Smart homes contain appliances with embedded computers, which make them safer and more energy efficient.

- Automobiles employ embedded computers to control operations, passenger comfort, and security.

- Information services could offer a wide range of entertainment options, including the ability to preview and rent the latest video games and first-run movies.

- Interactive television enables customers to give direct feedback to the television station.

- Virtual reality allows people to experience a 3D computer simulation by using special gloves, goggles, and body suits.

- Robotics, CAD, CAM, materials requirement planning, and a communication standard work together as part of computer-integrated manufacturing (CIM).

- International electronic funds transfer (EFT) systems use computer networks to handle financial transactions that support a global economy.

- A possible extension of EFT would involve a cashless society wherein checks and money would become obsolete.

- By using superconducting materials in computers, processing speed and efficiency can be greatly improved.

- Optical computers use light-activated switches and fiber optics to operate the processing hardware.

■ By using a DNA computer, technology taps into the ability of DNA to contain program instructions.

■ Genetic algorithms use chance to combine program code to create and improve solutions to problems.

■ Infinite variations of input used to control output can be processed using software and controllers with fuzzy logic.

■ Artificial intelligence uses heuristic rules to make decisions like a person would.

■ Technological obsolescence has created new opportunities for qualified people but necessitates continuous updating of skills.

■ Workers can keep their skills up-to-date by participating in on-the-job training, workshops, and conferences.

■ Professional publications provide a way for specialists to keep up with the newest research in their field.

■ Career opportunities as computer professionals exist in computer information systems, computer science, and engineering, each requiring different skills and formal education. Some groom people for promotion to higher-level positions.

■ Professional organizations foster communication among peers, offer chances for continuing education, hold local meetings, publish journals, and sponsor student chapters.

## TERMS TO REMEMBER

career path
cashless society
computer architect
computer engineering
computer information
   systems (CIS)

computer-integrated
   manufacturing (CIM)
computer scientist
conference
information society
interactive television

nanomachine
neural network
optical computer
superconductor
virtual reality
workshop

## MIX AND MATCH

*Complete the following definitions with the Terms to Remember.*

1. A(n) _____ is experimental processing hardware using light-activated switches for processing and optical fibers to transmit data.

2. _____ is an area of specialization that concerns the creation of systems in business, science, education, and manufacturing.

3. The technology featuring computer-generated images displayed in goggles as 3D output and controlled by the physical movements of the user is known as _____.

4. A(n) _____ is an extremely small machine with gears, levers, and other working features.

5. A person who specializes in designing system software is known as a(n) _____.

6. _____ lose all electrical resistance at a set temperature.

7. A(n) _____ system utilizes the features of CAD/CAM, robotics, and numerical control, linked together by a communications standard.

8. A(n) _____ contains a large group of people whose work generates or depends upon information.

9. A(n) _____ is an array of processors integrated into a communication network that mimics connections in the human brain.

10. A(n) _____ specializes in developing processing equipment and associated electronics.

11. A series of related jobs is called a(n) _____.

12. A(n) _____ is a professional meeting covering a broad subject area and includes concurrent presentations and product displays.

13. An educational meeting concentrating on a single topic is a(n) _____.

14. _____ is a concentration in the development, manufacturing, and assembly of hardware.

15. _____ lets users communicate through the control box to the television station.

## REVIEW QUESTIONS

1. Define the Terms to Remember.

2. What implications does an information society have on well-paying manual-labor jobs?

3. How do smart homes increase the homeowner's safety and the home's energy efficiency?

4. What are 10 applications for embedded computers in cars?

5. Identify three trends for cars of the future.

6. How could information services compete with cable television and video rental stores?

7. Describe four applications for interactive television.

8. How does stereolithography work? Name two applications for it.

9. What are six emerging technologies?

10. What are five uses for personal expert systems at home?

11. Identify a good and a bad effect of obsolescence for computer professionals and users.

12. Describe the focus of on-the-job training, workshops, and conferences.

13. What is a good way to review professional publications?

14. Describe the skills associated with people graduating from college programs in computer information systems, computer science, and computer engineering. Identify classes associated with each area of study.

15. How can a computer professional earn a CDP or CCP?

16. How do professional organizations support personal development?

17. Relate the orientation of the Data Processing Management Association (DPMA), Association for System Management (ASM), Association for Computing Machinery (ACM), and Institute of Electrical and Electronic Engineers (IEEE) with college programs discussed earlier.

## APPLYING WHAT YOU'VE LEARNED

1. Some people look forward to a cashless society whereas others would find it undesirable. What are some positive aspects of living in a cashless society? Some negative aspects? How could a cashless society be abused? Would you foresee a decrease in money-related crime? Would a cashless society improve social conditions?

2. Smart cars promote improved security, comfort, fuel efficiency, and environmental safety. What is a disadvantage of using many embedded computers in cars?

3. Find five job ads in the newspaper for computer professionals. What additional qualifications and educational requirements are listed besides those mentioned in the text? What salaries and other benefits are stated? How much experience is required? Do any sound like jobs you would like to have someday? Why or why not?

4. Check your public and/or school library for professional publications related in some way to computers. Make a list of them, including what type of professionals they are written for, how often they are published, and whether they are sponsored by a professional organization. Be sure to include noncomputer-industry publications, such as those in medicine, business, and manufacturing.

5. It is becoming more common for people to make "midlife career changes." That means a middle-aged person will completely change the type and area of work he or she is doing. This often involves going back to school or starting out at a low-paying job in a new field.
   a. What are the advantages and disadvantages of this?
   b. Why do you think a person would want to make such a change?
   c. Do you think employers would want to hire a person like this?
   d. Could you see yourself making a change like this? Why or why not?

6. Although computers are constantly increasing in power and speed, there are still some things they cannot do. Describe three problems that are too big for computers to solve.

7. Do a short report on one of the emerging technologies mentioned in the text or another one you have read about. Find out the origins of the technology and its current state of research. Have any consumer products yet been developed from this technology?

# APPENDIX

# A

# Buying a Personal Computer System

# FROM THE USER'S POINT OF VIEW

**B**uying a personal computer is like ordering from a large menu. There is a lot from which to choose but you don't necessarily want (or need) everything listed. The price of the item may also influence your decision. Despite the vast and sometimes confusing array of hardware and software available for a PC, the decisions you make should be based on two things: your present and anticipated computing needs. Your current needs are the top priority, tempered by an eye on your budget.

You will discover that purchasing a personal computer is not much different from making any other major purchase. This appendix is designed to help you organize your thoughts, structure your decision, and ultimately define the personal computer system that will best satisfy your needs and budget.

## NEEDS ANALYSIS AND SOFTWARE

As discussed in chapter 13, the first steps in acquiring a new computer system are defining system requirements and evaluating alternatives. Deciding on how you want to use a computer sets in motion a search for suitable application packages. Once selected, related software requirements determine minimum hardware specifications. To start, ask yourself some simple questions:

♦ Do I work primarily with words, numbers, sound, and/or images?

♦ Will the computer be used at home? School? Work?

♦ Will others be using this system besides myself?

♦ Who will be using the output from this computer system and what form should the output take?

◆ What things will a computer system let me do that I cannot do now?

◆ How much can I reasonably afford to pay for a PC system including software and supplies?

Personal computer systems can be easily customized to your individual needs with just a little time and effort. What follows is a close examination of how to purchase a new computer system when software is not automatically bundled with the hardware.

**A.1**

Many software packages exist to make you more productive. Choosing the appropriate software is the first step in buying a personal computer system.

## Common Productivity Software and Their Uses

### Word Processing Package

- Writing letters, reports, articles, homework, and the like
- Editing written work
- Creating brochures and advertisements
- Small-business and club correspondence
- Mailing lists
- Training and self-improvement
- Research
- E-mail and fax
- Hobbies, like writing or genealogy

### Electronic Spreadsheet

- Financial planning
- Personal record keeping, such as inventories
- Small-business and club bookkeeping
- Data analysis
- Business graphics

### Database Management Program

- Research
- Personal planning, like an address book and calendars
- Personal record keeping
- Small-business and club record keeping
- Mailing lists
- Hobbies

### Graphics Package

- Creating brochures and advertisements
- Art creation
- Craft design
- Personal designs such as for letterheads and business cards
- Designs for home improvement, landscaping, and so on

### Other Common Packages

- Presentation software
- Computer-aided design (CAD)
- Video editor
- Project management
- Games
- Clip art and video
- Multimedia tutorials and reference material
- Data communication
- Disk optimization and compression

When establishing your budget, you should set aside as much money for software and initial supplies as you do for hardware.

## Application Packages

Software drives hardware. This basic tenet of computer system purchasing means that computer equipment needs to be picked based on what software will be used. Throughout the text, many types of software have been discussed. Chapters 8 through 11 examined the most common personal productivity software. In Figure A.1, some specific uses of these packages are summarized. Use this list to prioritize how you and other users will work with the new system.

After deciding how you would use a new computer system, you can take a closer look at the computer programs that handle these tasks. To keep things manageable, select the five most important applications and focus on evaluating software that supports those applications. As mentioned in chapter 3, the best way to get started is by asking friends about how they use their computer systems and by reading software reviews in magazines. Compatibility with software used at school or work is another consideration. Finally, try different programs at stores, in a class, or using a friend's PC. Personal experience is the best way to decide on which software packages you like.

In turn, each of these application packages may dictate a specific operating system and hardware. Most commonly, the choice is between an Intel-based (IBM and compatibles) or a Motorola-based (Apple Macintosh) processor. Once you select a personal mix of application packages, the search becomes a little easier because you can now identify a specific operating system and the hardware manufacturers among which to compare prices.

## User Interface

Conventional wisdom (see Figure A.2) supports the premise that new users are best served by a graphical user interface (GUI). As a result, your selection of application packages will probably have you working with one of two operating environments: either a Macintosh using Mac-OS, or an IBM/compatible running some version of Microsoft Windows. If compatibility with computers at work is a priority, another user interface might be your choice.

**A.2**

No matter what hardware and software people use, most personal computer users would agree with these basic assumptions.

### Conventional Wisdom

#### When Purchasing a Personal Computer System

- Never underbuy. It is usually more expensive and always more aggravating to upgrade your computer system.

- Graphical user interfaces such as Windows and Mac-OS are easier for new users to learn than command-driven interfaces like MS-DOS.

- Memory and hard disk requirements never go down. Always buy more than is strictly necessary. Disk storage will fill up fast.

- Buy the largest, highest-quality color monitor and most comfortable keyboard and mouse you can afford. This hardware will be in constant use, so its design and comfort to you are important.

- Slow disk access makes you wait just as much as a slow processor does.

- Buy reputable brands from a reputable source. A one-year on-site warranty is worthless if the company is quickly out of business.

- Buy the best you can afford and don't look back! Sooner or later (probably sooner), your system will sell for less than you paid for it.

- Don't wait until the prices are at their lowest. By the time the price goes down, new and better equipment is available. At that rate, you will never buy a computer!

**A.3**

The operating environment or GUI used determines minimum and recommended requirements in the computer system's processor and memory.

## Requirements for Common Operating Environments

| Operating Environment | Processor | Memory |
|---|---|---|
| DOS | 8088 or higher | 512 K (min.) |
| Windows 3.1 | 80386X or higher | 4 MB (min.) <br> 8 MB (rec.) |
| Windows 95 | 80386DX or higher | 8 MB (min.) <br> 16 MB (rec.) |
| Macintosh | 68030 or higher | 8 MB (min.) |
| PowerPC | PowerPC 603 or higher | 16 MB (rec.) |

## PROCESSING-HARDWARE REQUIREMENTS

Many processing-hardware options are available regardless of the operating environment you use. However, there are some minimum requirements for efficient and complete implementation. The table in Figure A.3 provides both the minimum and recommended specifications for a computer system's processor and memory needed for common operating environments.

### Processor

When asked what kind of computer they own, many people respond with a processor name rather than a brand. For example, "I've got a 486" or "We use a Pentium at work." It is the speed (in megahertz), not the name, that is really important. The speeds of various processors are shown in Figure 5.7. Use these as general guidelines only. Microprocessor specifications, for instance, are constantly changing. Your future software needs, using multitasking requiring several packages, and the ability to connect to a network may change processing and storage requirements. A more detailed description of processors and memory is in chapter 5.

### Memory

Random access memory (RAM) requirements must also be chosen by a computer system buyer. It wasn't long ago that 4 MB was considered sufficient for most PC users. Today, commonly used productivity suites and even some games require 4 MB at a minimum. A smart approach would be to purchase a computer containing at least 8 MB with openings for additional memory. Adding more RAM later can increase the long-term usability of a machine.

Additional memory in the form of cache memory is commonly available for PCs. As described in chapter 5, cache supports faster processing by making readily available the data most likely to be processed next. It is not uncommon to find computer systems bundled with 256 K cache memory.

Graphics capability places an additional burden on memory requirements. At a minimum, 1 megabyte of graphics memory on the video board is recommended.

## PERIPHERAL HARDWARE CONSIDERATIONS

When it comes to input, output, and storage hardware, it is hardly a case of "one size fits all." For many applications a keyboard, mouse, monitor, and printer will suffice as the input/output hardware. Hard disk capacity is determined by present and anticipated storage needs for both data and programs. However, there are choices to be made for every peripheral you buy.

### ■ Input

Figure 6.13 lists input hardware available to the PC user. In some cases, you have a choice of which device to purchase. For example, using a mouse versus a trackball for doing graphics or working with a GUI is a matter of personal preference. Some keyboards are designed to "click" as each key is pressed. Others are designed to be as quiet as possible. Certain software packages, some games for example, also require specific types of peripherals.

Many of these peripherals have ergonomic considerations as well, as mentioned in chapter 6. If you are a good touch typist or will be doing a lot of work with a mouse, it would be worth the extra money to consider upgrading the keyboard or mouse found with many prepackaged, or bundled, computer systems to a more ergonomically sound design. Finding the proper fit takes time and patience. The best approach would be to borrow such a peripheral from a friend or other source for a few days of intensive work. Like a pair of new shoes, the keyboard or mouse may feel good in the store but be uncomfortable after a few hours of use.

### ■ Output

When choosing a monitor, you may think the first decision is whether to buy one with a monochrome or color display. Many computer users agree, however, that monochrome monitors should be considered an option only when on a very tight budget or when purchasing a portable computer. Obviously, games and graphics packages require the use of color, but most other types of software, including GUIs, word processing, and spreadsheets use color to make editing and finding commands easier. Conventional wisdom says buy the highest-quality and largest color monitor you can afford, because color screens are easier on the eyes. A 14-inch diagonal screen is considered a minimum size for a nonportable machine. Also, if you will be working with detailed graphics or have vision problems, consider buying a larger monitor (17-inch diagonal or more).

Picking a printer depends upon several factors. In Figure A.4, suggestions as to printer type are based on cost, printing speed, and quality of print. Ink-jet color printers are also available at a reasonable price. When looking at an ink-jet color printer, it is desirable to have a printer cartridge that lets you fill or replace each color separately. If you will use a color printer only occasionally, you may find local printshops or computer stores that charge for rental of a color printer on a per-page basis.

Although most personal computers have built-in speakers and limited sound capabilities, these speakers are often inadequate for music or multimedia applications.

**A.4**

Print quality, speed, and cost are all factored into the purchase of a new printer. The fastest printers with the highest-quality output cost the most. Slower printers with draft-quality output are the least expensive.

| Printer Comparisons | | | |
|---|---|---|---|
| | **Dot-matrix** | **Ink-jet** | **Laser** |
| **Cost** | inexpensive | moderate | expensive |
| **Speed** | slower than 4 pages per minute | slower than 4 pages per minute | 4 pages per minute or more |
| **Print quality** | draft quality | letter quality | letter quality |

If high-fidelity sound and multimedia are important, you should seriously consider adding a sound card (16-bit FM minimum) and two small but powerful speakers to the system specifications. An inexpensive alternative is to use headphones. A headphone jack is usually available on the front panel of the CD-ROM drive or at the back of the sound card.

## Storage

Decisions on storage hardware relate to the size, storage capacity, access speed, and number of disk drives your system will have. For all practical purposes, the current generation of application software requires access to a hard disk. At least one diskette (floppy disk) drive is also needed to transfer data and programs to the hard disk and for backup. Access time is important when comparing disk drives of similar size and capacity. As you might expect, faster is better and usually more expensive. Figure 7.13 shows a comparison of the speeds, transfer rates, and capacities for common storage media. Because most software packages require a minimum of 10 to 15 MB just for storage, it is recommended that a computer system have a hard disk capacity of at least 720 MB. This may seem like a lot of "extra room," but with the operating system, other software, and data, the hard disk can fill up quickly. A large disk capacity is especially important if the system will have several users or you plan on storing a lot of graphics on it.

Most software packages for Intel-compatible systems have diskettes available in both 5.25-inch and 3.5-inch sizes. The smaller diskette is emerging as a standard, however. Macintosh computers already routinely use 3.5-inch diskettes. Unless you use other computers with disks of varying sizes, most users need only one diskette drive. If you will be transferring data to other Intel-compatible computer systems with different disk drive sizes, consider one drive of each size (see Figure A.5). Review chapter 7 if you have questions about diskettes and floppy disk drives.

Tape drives can provide a fast and an inexpensive way to back up data and program files stored on a hard disk. This type of storage hardware easily fits under the disk drives of most desktop systems and is very useful when the hard disk capacity is large. The alternative is a slow backup on many diskettes.

Even a user who does not plan on playing computer games should seriously consider including a CD-ROM drive in the system specifications. The increased use of multimedia for educational, reference, and other software makes a CD-ROM almost a must for a current system. Remember, if you see a PC with multimedia PC (MPC) specifications, a CD-ROM drive is included. The comparative speeds of CD-ROM drives are shown in Figure 7.13. Recommended is the quad-speed CD-ROM drive, with double-speed a minimum.

**A.5**

Every PC system needs at least one diskette (floppy disk) drive for transferring data and programs between systems. Users look at compatibility and storage issues to decide on the number of drives, along with the disk size and storage capacity.

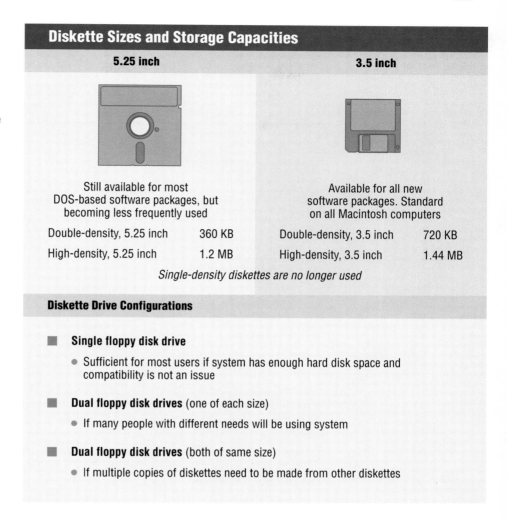

## Diskette Sizes and Storage Capacities

| 5.25 inch | | 3.5 inch | |
|---|---|---|---|
| Still available for most DOS-based software packages, but becoming less frequently used | | Available for all new software packages. Standard on all Macintosh computers | |
| Double-density, 5.25 inch | 360 KB | Double-density, 3.5 inch | 720 KB |
| High-density, 5.25 inch | 1.2 MB | High-density, 3.5 inch | 1.44 MB |

*Single-density diskettes are no longer used*

### Diskette Drive Configurations

- **Single floppy disk drive**
  - Sufficient for most users if system has enough hard disk space and compatibility is not an issue

- **Dual floppy disk drives** (one of each size)
  - If many people with different needs will be using system

- **Dual floppy disk drives** (both of same size)
  - If multiple copies of diskettes need to be made from other diskettes

## ▓ Expansion Slots and I/O Ports

Conventional wisdom says never underbuy, because it is more expensive and aggravating to upgrade later (see Figure A.2). Make sure you have enough expansion slots to add that sound board, fax/modem, or CD-ROM drive when you need it. Your best bet is to have several open expansion slots when you purchase your new system. In other words, after you have accounted for all your current and foreseeable needs, you should still have room to add a few more expansion boards.

The number of expansion slots is not the only thing to consider when buying a system. If you will be sending data over communication lines, you will want to have at least one serial port; a mouse will also require a serial port. A printer next to the system would use a parallel port. If you will be connecting external devices such as tape backup, a plotter, or additional input device, check on which type of port is required. Even an entry-level system should include both PCI and ISA expansion buses, as described in chapter 5.

**A.6**

Computers are set up in three basic configurations: those you take with you, those you place on top of your desk, and those you fit under the desk.

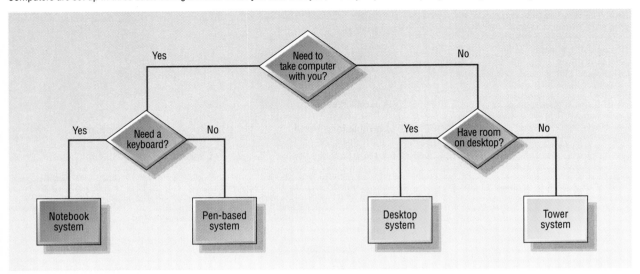

### Configuration

The configuration, or arrangement, of the computer system depends on your need for portability and available work space. The flowchart in Figure A.6 can help you determine which size and arrangement of the processing hardware will work best for you. Remember, portable computers are more expensive, easier to steal, and rely on batteries that need recharging after a few hours of operation. They also have smaller keyboards, screens, and hard disk capacities. Though these keyboard and screen limitations are acceptable when traveling, long-term usage can place a physical strain on the user.

Consider purchasing a full-sized keyboard and monitor for use when the portable computer is not "on the road." You will need to make sure the portable computer has additional ports to handle an extra keyboard and monitor. Some systems are designed to facilitate having full-sized computer system with portability. These machines are essentially portables with small keyboards and flat screens. They fit into a "docking station" which consists of a full-sized monitor, keyboard, and protective housing.

Computer housing can take several forms. If you have a large table or desk area, the horizontal arrangement or desktop configuration may be useful, with the monitor over the computer. Many people find a tower, or vertical, configuration better because the computer can slide beneath the desk yet still be accessible. For cramped work areas, minitower configurations are available as well.

## COMPLETE SYSTEM REQUIREMENTS

Regardless of the type of system you are acquiring, some additional decisions must be made at the time of purchase. As mentioned in chapter 2, training and service provided by full-service computer stores must be weighed against the lower costs offered by discount stores and mail-order houses. Compare computer warranties. How long is the

**A.7**

This list is designed to remind you of the odds and ends you should include when purchasing your first computer system.

## Computer System Shopping List

### Miscellaneous Items

☐ Mouse pad

☐ Diskettes, extra for backup

☐ Diskette holder or organizer

☐ CD-ROM organizer

☐ Tape, if tape backup available

☐ Surge protector

☐ UPS (uninterruptable power supply)

☐ Extra batteries for a portable computer

☐ Paper and forms for printer

☐ Extra ribbon or cartridge for printer

☐ Necessary cables for monitor, keyboard, printer

☐ Covers for keyboard and computer

☐ Ergonomic desk and chair

☐ Document stand

☐ Swivel arm to support monitor

☐ Screen glare protector

☐ Antistatic pad

☐ Lock for portable computer

☐ On-site service warranty

☐ Increased insurance coverage for equipment

☐ Additional phone line if using a modem

☐ Monthly information service fees

warranty and does it include on-site repair? If on-site repair is not available, where is the closest service center?

Other items should be considered for safe and efficient computing. The miscellaneous shopping list, as shown in Figure A.7, can help you complete your purchases.

## ▨ Where to Buy a Computer

As with any major purchase, most people comparison-shop before buying a personal computer system. With list of specifications in hand (see Figure A.8), make the rounds of the local computer stores. Ask the salespersons about what hardware, software, training, and warranty is included in the price. Also check several catalogs and computer magazines to see how these features compare. Libraries and bookstores will have several computer magazines full of advertisements for computer systems available by mail. Remember, mail-order may be less expensive, but training and warranties are probably more limited.

## ▨ Used Computers

Your budget plays a critical role in this process. To be realistic, the process of purchasing a personal computer changes drastically if your budget for a basic system is under $1,000. In this situation, consider purchasing a used computer system. Local newspapers and bulletin boards often advertise used personal computer systems.

**Advantages to purchasing a used computer:**

♦ best possible price

♦ software usually is included in the purchase

♦ you can thoroughly test the system and try the software before purchasing

**Disadvantages to purchasing a used computer:**

♦ older technology may not support new application packages

♦ older technology may not support new peripheral hardware

♦ increased chance of system failure because of previous usage

♦ no warranty

♦ not all of your needs may be met with the system

Much of the decision making discussed in this appendix is reduced when buying a used system. Software and peripheral hardware usually come with it, so you are purchasing a complete package. Computer stores often bundle application packages and system software with a new computer system for the same reason. It makes purchasing a new computer system less intimidating because many of the decisions are already made.

To help you organize your hardware and software priorities, Figure A.8 acts as a final worksheet. Use this summary when comparing systems at stores or as you investigate mail-order prices and used computers.

---

### *SUMMARY*

▨ Users should identify individual needs and applications for a personal computer before buying one.

▨ Friends, family, magazines, and computer classes help people learn about and use different application packages.

▨ Half of the budget for a new PC system should be for software and accessories such as paper, disks, and print cartridges. The other half is for the computer and peripherals.

▨ A user's personal mix of application packages determines the operating system, user interface, and basic hardware specifications.

▨ Microprocessor speeds, memory, and hard disk capacity are determined by the number of applications and related resource requirements.

**A.8**

When you get serious about purchasing a new computer system, fill out this worksheet and have it handy when evaluating different systems.

## Personal Computer System Needs Analysis

**Software required for desired applications**

_____
_____
_____
_____

| **Software used most often** | **Memory required** | **Disk space required** |
|---|---|---|
| 1. _____ | _____ | _____ |
| 2. _____ | _____ | _____ |
| 3. _____ | _____ | _____ |
| 4. _____ | _____ | _____ |
| 5. _____ | _____ | _____ |

Minimum total memory _____

Minimum disk storage _____ (add together all software requirements)

**Computer type and operating system** (check one)

☐ Intel-based (IBM or compatible)     ☐ Intel-based     ☐ Apple Macintosh
   with Windows/DOS                       with Windows 95      with Mac-OS

**Processor required** _____ running at _____ megahertz

**Configuration:**  ☐ tower  ☐ desktop  ☐ notebook  ☐ pen-based

**Number/type of I/O ports needed:**  _____ serial  _____ parallel

**Number of expansion slots needed:** _____

**Keyboard:**  ☐ standard  ☐ ergonomic

**GUI input device:**  ☐ mouse  ☐ trackball  ☐ joystick

**Monitor size (diagonal):**  ☐ 14"  ☐ 15"  ☐ 17"  ☐ 21"

**Monitor type:**  ☐ monochrome  ☐ color (SVGA, XGA)  graphics memory: _____

**Printer type:**  ☐ dot-matrix  ☐ ink-jet  ☐ laser

**Color printer:**  ☐ yes  ☐ no

**Other features:**

| | | | |
|---|---|---|---|
| sound card | ☐ yes | ☐ no | _____ bit capacity |
| tape backup | ☐ yes | ☐ no | _____ storage capacity |
| CD-ROM | ☐ yes | ☐ no | _____ speed |
| cache memory | ☐ yes | ☐ no | _____ size |
| fax/modem | ☐ yes | ☐ no | _____ speed |

**Notes on:**

Warranty: _____
_____
_____

Training: _____
_____
_____

Miscellaneous items to purchase: _____
_____
_____
_____

- Every system should have a keyboard, monitor, printer, hard disk, and at least one diskette drive.

- Potential buyers should not scrimp on machine/user interfaces. Comfortable keyboards and pointing devices, along with high-resolution color monitors, make computers easier to use.

- Printers are evaluated by their speed, print quality, and cost.

- Access speeds are a means of comparing disk drives of similar size and storage capacity.

- Disk drives using 3.5-inch diskettes are becoming the PC standard. Include two diskette drives with a new system if you use both 3.5- and 5.25-inch disks or if you often make duplicate copies of different diskette sizes.

- Peripherals will dictate the number and types of I/O ports to be included.

- Personal needs and interests may dictate whether to include a sound card, fax/modem, CD-ROM drive, or tape drive in your hardware specifications.

- A new computer should have open expansion slots on the motherboard after the minimum hardware specifications have been met.

- When considering portable versus desktop or tower configurations, the additional expense and vulnerability of a portable must be weighed against the convenience of always having access to your computer.

- Used computers offer affordable prices but lack a warranty and may not handle newer software specifications.

- Training and service provided by full-service computer stores must be weighed against lower costs offered by discount and mail-order sources.

- Compare warranty length and arrangements for repairing problems before buying a new computer system.

## REVIEW QUESTIONS

1. How would you use a personal computer? (*Hint:* See Figure A.1.)

2. What three software packages do you think you would use most often?

3. Would you purchase an Intel-compatible, Apple Macintosh, or another make of personal computer? How did you make this decision? (*Hint:* See Applying What You've Learned, project 2.)

4.  How much memory and what hard disk capacity would you include in a new personal computer system?

5.  What are your requirements for a printer? What type of printer would you get?

6.  What applications require that you use a color monitor?

7.  How many diskette drives would you need and at what storage capacity?

8.  What peripherals do you need beyond a keyboard, monitor, printer, hard disk drive, and diskette drive?

9.  What type of configuration (portable, desktop, or tower) best serves your needs?

10. What items besides hardware and software would you need to purchase to make a new computer system operational? (*Hint:* See Figure A.7.)

11. Where would you go to purchase a new computer?

12. Would you purchase a used computer system instead of a new one? Explain your rationale.

## APPLYING WHAT YOU'VE LEARNED

1.  Talk to three friends who have personal computers. Ask them how they use their systems. What software packages do they use the most? What features do they like the best? Would they recommend any specific application packages? What would they do differently if they were purchasing their computers again?

2.  For each of your three software priorities, evaluate at least two competing packages. For each package, list the computer it requires (Intel-compatible or Macintosh), its minimum memory requirements, and how much hard disk storage is needed.

3.  Compare two of these three types of pointing devices: mouse, trackball, or pen with tablet. Use a free-drawing package or similar graphics software when working with each device. Which input device do you prefer? What are the characteristics that make this device most desirable for your circumstances?

4.  Use three different printers. Print the same document, using each printer's highest-quality print mode. Rank the hard-copy output from best to worst. How many pages per minute does each printer output? How much does each cost? Which one, if any, would you purchase? Explain your reasoning.

5.  Examine 15-, 17-, and 21-inch color monitors of similar video quality. How much do they weigh? What is the difference in cost? Which monitor best meets your needs? Why?

6.  Research the cost of hard disks. Compare equipment produced by three manufacturers in terms of access speeds and cost per megabyte of storage capacity.

7.  Compare the prices and capabilities of two competitive peripherals of your choice; modems, sound boards, CD-ROM drives, or other peripherals that attach to a personal computer are acceptable. Identify the alternatives and explain why you would purchase one over the other.

# Operating a Personal Computer Using Windows 3.1

# FROM THE USER'S POINT OF VIEW

**B**efore you start to use personal productivity software or learn to program, you need to review operating procedures for IBM and Intel-based personal computers. The following Windows tutorial provides a brief overview of some of the more important procedures associated with Microsoft Windows 3.1. These procedures help you learn how to locate files and programs on disk, and print files, and they provide a convenient means of copying important disk resources.

You need access to an IBM or Intel-based compatible computer using Microsoft Windows 3.1 and a floppy disk to complete the tutorial. Because Windows 3.1 requires lots of internal memory and makes extensive use of disk storage, we assume you are using a personal computer with a hard disk or have access to a local area network. Instructions or data you should enter into the computer using the keyboard are preceded by a ▶.

## PERSONAL COMPUTER START-UP PROCEDURES

IBM and other Intel-based personal computers use a *disk operating system (DOS)* developed by the Microsoft Corporation. Called **MS-DOS**, it is the most commonly used operating system in the world. It is licensed from Microsoft and distributed by IBM Corporation as **PC-DOS**. Microsoft has enhanced DOS's user-friendliness by creating a compatible graphical user interface (GUI) called **Windows 3.1**. New versions of Windows—Windows NT and Windows 95—are themselves operating systems and do not need DOS to operate. This appendix covers a widely used version of the GUI, Windows 3.1. Appendix C explains how to use the next release, Windows 95.

## ▨ System Orientation

*Booting* describes the procedure for starting up a computer system. As part of the booting process, IBM and Intel-based computers automatically look for and load a command program, named COMMAND.COM, from the operating system into memory.

Because a disk with DOS must be in a designated disk drive when booting a microcomputer, associated procedures will vary. If this is your first time, consult the user's manual or ask the teacher or lab assistant for help. To complete this tutorial, carefully follow the actions associated with each ▷ symbol below. What appears on-screen is preceded by the ▨ symbol.

▷ **Turn on your computer, monitor, and printer if necessary.**

    ▨ *Displays capital letter and > symbol.*

If your computer system follows the standard booting steps, the computer displays the current date and time and gives you a chance to change them. Many computer systems are customized to display menus, launch a GUI such as Windows, or describe procedures or copyright infringement policies. You will need to familiarize yourself with the procedures used by your personal computer.

## ▨ Loading Windows

After entering the date and time, you have completed the booting process. Windows can now be loaded into memory from disk. We use the abbreviation *WIN* to load Windows. If your screen currently looks like Figure B.1, you can skip the following step.

**B.1**

The Program Manager window provides an area from which DOS operations and other application programs are executed.

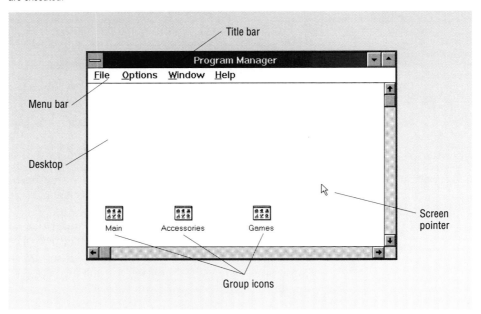

▶ Type **win** and press Enter.

░ *Loads Windows and displays the Program Manager window, as shown in Figure B.1.*

Windows is a user-friendly GUI that reduces the time required to understand basic computer operations and learn new applications. Currently on-screen is the desktop, your window into the computer. The ***desktop*** is aptly named, since you work with images on-screen in the same way that you work with papers, folders, and office tools and supplies laid out on an actual desktop. This desktop metaphor is the basis for all screen displays and processing activities under the control of Windows.

## PROGRAM MANAGER

The opening window is usually the ***Program Manager***. It contains ***group icons*** that organize the programs and data files available to the system. Users open a group icon displayed in the Program Manager window by ***double-clicking*** the mouse (pressing the left mouse button twice in rapid succession) with the pointer on the desired icon. The desktop in Figure B.1 contains three group icons, which identify games, main system controls, and accessories such as a calendar and calculator. When opened, each group icon displays a collection of program icons associated with application packages and other programs the user has installed.

Across the top of the screen, under the words *Program Manager*, is the ***menu bar***. The menu bar permits access to several drop-down menus, each containing processing commands. The File, Options, Window, and Help menu names are shown in Figure B.1. These menu names are standard whenever you view the Program Manager but can be different for other software packages.

All choices from the menu bar, as well as icon manipulations, are controlled primarily with the mouse. Keyboard alternatives are available, but will not be discussed in detail as a part of this brief introduction. As you grasp and move the mouse across a flat surface, a *screen pointer* moves in a corresponding fashion around the screen. When you work within the desktop, the pointer is shaped like an arrow (see Figure B.1); however, it changes into other shapes depending on which activity is in progress.

### ░ Using a Mouse

You can lift the mouse and set it back down again without changing the location of the pointer on-screen. This action may be necessary if you do not have enough room to move the pointer across the screen in one continuous movement of the mouse.

At first, using a mouse may seem awkward. However, this device's operation will soon become second nature. The speed and ease with which you can do things using a mouse will increase your productivity many times over.

A basic technique for working with Windows is to select an icon and either activate it or move it around the screen. You select an icon by pointing to it with the arrow pointer and ***clicking*** (pressing and releasing) the left mouse button once. You must select an object before you can use it. In this tutorial, *clicking* will always mean pressing and releasing the left mouse button.

▷ **Move the arrow pointer so that it rests on the Main icon.**

> **NOTE:** *If the Main window is already open, as shown in Figure B.4, close the window and any other open windows by skipping forward to the section on the control box on page 543.*

▷ **Click the left mouse button.**

> ▦ *The icon name, Main, is highlighted and a control menu is displayed, as shown in Figure B.2.*

The control menu is closed by clicking on any open area of the desktop or Program Manager window.

▷ **Move the pointer off the Main icon and into an open area.**

▷ **Click the mouse button.**

> ▦ *Closes the control menu.*

You can reposition an object on the desktop by pointing to it and then holding down the left mouse button while moving, or ***dragging***, the mouse.

▷ **Select the Accessories icon and press and hold down the left mouse button.**

> ▦ *Highlights the Accessories icon.*

▷ **While holding down the button, move the mouse up and to the left to reposition the icon on-screen.**

> ▦ *The icon's label disappears as it is dragged.*

▷ **Release the mouse button.**

> ▦ *The icon is repositioned to its new location.*

These clicking and dragging techniques are used for other mouse operations besides selecting and moving icons. They are basic techniques for controlling many activities you perform while using Windows and other programs on the computer.

**B.2**

Pointing and clicking on a group icon activates a control menu and highlights the icon name.

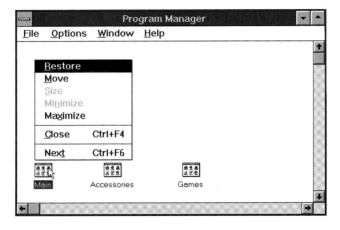

## ■ Selecting Options from Drop-Down Menus

We need to explore how options are executed by using the mouse to access drop-down menus. The menu bar contains the names of all available menus (see Figure B.1). You select one of the drop-down menus by clicking on the menu name, for instance, <u>H</u>elp. Drop-down menu options stay hidden in the menu bar until the user selects that name; when the menu is selected, it opens to list program options. Once an option is selected, the menu rolls back up into the menu bar.

▶ **Click on the <u>H</u>elp menu in the menu bar.**

■ *The menu options are displayed, as shown in Figure B.3.*

This Help menu can be of great assistance as you learn how to use Windows and related programs. It is designed to answer questions about specific problems because it is *context-sensitive help*. This means the information displayed when Help is activated relates to the screen display currently being used. In other words, if you are playing a game and ask for help, the help screen provides information about the game.

▶ **Click on <u>W</u>indows Tutorial.**

■ *Displays opening screen of Windows Tutorial.*

This interactive tutorial introduces basic mouse and Windows skills. If you have time, walk through one or both of these tutorials. If you do not wish to use the tutorials at this time, you can escape them.

▶ **Press Esc.**

■ *Asks you to verify that you want to exit the tutorial.*

▶ **Press y.**

■ *Returns to the Program Manager window.*

If you decide not to choose a menu item after you have opened a menu, simply move the pointer outside the menu so that no item is selected and click the mouse button. The menu disappears and you are back to the desktop.

**B.3**

Drop-down menus, such as Help, are activated by clicking on the menu name.

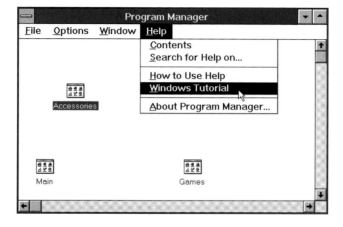

You can easily scan the menus to see all of the options available on the menu bar.

▷ **Click and hold on File in the menu bar.**

    ▨ *The menu options are listed.*

▷ **Without releasing the mouse button, slowly drag the pointer along the menu bar horizontally from left to right.**

    ▨ *As each menu name is highlighted, its drop-down menu is shown.*

▷ **Release the mouse button.**

    ▨ *All highlighting of menus is turned off. If not, move the pointer anywhere outside the menu and click.*

    *NOTE: Some of the names of the menu items may appear dimmed, or shown in gray rather than black. These are menu options that are not available at this time. You cannot select a dimmed option. These items will become available at different times and under other processing circumstances.*

## ▨ Executing Program Options

Applications are activated by double-clicking on the associated icon. This action overlays another window on top of the Program Manager and makes additional icons available to users.

▷ **Double-click on the Main icon.**

    ▨ *Displays a window similar to Figure B.4.*

**B.4**

Double-clicking on the Main icon results in overlaying the Program Manager window with the Main window.

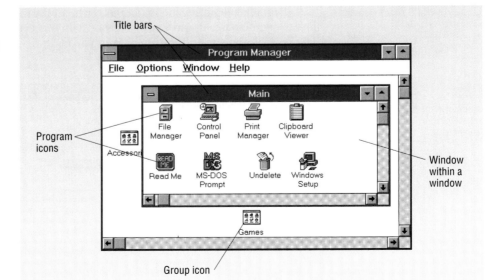

*NOTE: There are two other ways to open a window besides double-clicking on the icon. First click on the icon; then you can highlight the Restore option of the control menu shown in Figure B.2, or use the File menu to select the Open option.*

## COMMON WINDOW FEATURES

Your screen now shows the Main window overlaid on the Program Manager window (Figure B.4). Each window has common descriptive and functional parts that need exploring.

### ▨ Title Bar

The window's name, such as *Program Manager* or *Main* in Figure B.4, appears in the ***title bar*** across the top of the window. At both ends of the title bar are small boxes that will be discussed later. Below the title bar of application windows is the menu bar, which lists names of various drop-down menus. Windows associated with group icons, such as Main, do not have menu bars.

Windows can be moved anywhere on-screen by clicking within the title bar and dragging to reposition the window. You may need to do this if you have several overlapping windows on-screen at the same time.

▶ **If the screen does not presently show a small Main window within the Program Manager window (like Figure B.5) click on the ⬍ button on the menu bar.**

**B.5**

Users change a window's size by dragging one corner to a new screen location or by clicking on the maximize or minimize buttons in the top-right corner of each window.

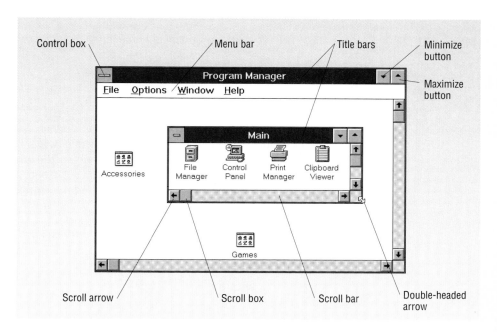

Control box — Menu bar — Title bars — Minimize button — Maximize button

Scroll arrow — Scroll box — Scroll bar — Double-headed arrow

▶ **Move the pointer within the Main title bar.**

▶ **Hold down the mouse button and drag the pointer somewhere else on-screen.**

▪ *The outline of the window is dragged with the pointer.*

▶ **Release the mouse button.**

▪ *The window snaps to its new position.*

▶ **Use the mouse to center the Main window in the space available.**

## ▪ Sizing a Window

You have complete control over the location and size of each window. Not only can you drag a window around the screen, you can grab the line around the window, called the *window frame*, and drag it to a new location or change the window's dimensions.

▶ **Position the pointer at the bottom-right corner of the Main window.**

▪ *The pointer changes to a double-headed arrow, as shown in Figure B.5.*

▶ **Hold down the mouse button.**

▪ *Lines in the window dim.*

▶ **Drag the window's corner toward the upper-left corner of the screen until at least one icon disappears from within the window.**

▪ *The window outline follows the pointer.*

▶ **Release the mouse button.**

▪ *The window contracts to reach the pointer location. Any icon outside that area of the desktop will be hidden.*

## ▪ Scroll Bars

When a window is reduced in size, *scroll bars* appear along the right and bottom edges of the window (see Figure B.5). A *scroll box* within each scroll bar identifies which portion of the window is currently being viewed. Dragging the scroll box or clicking on the *scroll arrows* brings hidden icons into view. You can tell if there are hidden icons in the window because of the presence of a scroll bar. When the complete contents of a window are displayed, no scroll bars are present.

▶ **Click once on the scroll arrow that points right (or down).**

▪ *Icons in the window move off toward the left (or up).*

▶ **Click within the scroll bar.**

▪ *Icons in the window move in the opposite direction.*

**B.6**

Clicking on the minimize button
(down arrow) on the title bar
converts windows into an icon.

Program
Manager

## Maximize and Minimize Window Size

In Figure B.5, the maximize and minimize buttons appear in the upper-right corner of the window. The *maximize button* is on the right, appearing as an up arrow. When it is clicked, the window expands to fill the screen and the double-arrow *restore button* takes its place. When the restore button is clicked, the window returns to its previous size. Double-clicking on the title bar also maximizes the associated window.

▶ **Click once on the Main window maximize button.**

   ▪ *The Main window expands to fill the Program Manager window.*

▶ **Click on the restore button to the right of the title bar.**

   ▪ *The Main window returns to its previous size.*

The *minimize button* appears as a down arrow and is located to the left of the maximize button. It is used to convert a window to an icon, as shown in Figure B.6. Double-clicking on the icon restores the window.

▶ **Click on the minimize button in the Program Manager title bar.**

   ▪ *The window is replaced by an icon.*

▶ **Double-click on the Program Manager icon.**

   ▪ *The Program Manager window returns to its original size.*

## Control Box

When you are finished using a window, you close it by double-clicking on the *control box* in the upper-left corner (see Figure B.5). A single click on the control box activates the window's control menu (Figure B.2). Selecting Close from the control menu removes the related window from the screen. Before closing the Main window, you should resize it so that it includes all the available icons.

▶ **Drag the window frame of the Main window to include the File Manager, Control Panel, and other icons.**

▶ **Double-click on the Main window control box.**

   ▪ *The window is reduced to the Main icon in the Program Manager window.*

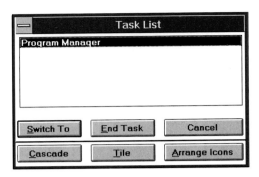

**B.7**

The Task List provides a roster of open programs and the capabilities to arrange, close, and activate them.

## Task List

One of the strengths of Windows 3.1 is its ability to clearly show multitasking—more than one program open and running at the same time. To help arrange, close, or change tasks, the *Task List* is used. It shows the programs currently open.

▶ **Hold down** Ctrl **and press** Esc **.**

> ▨ *The Task List appears, with Program Manager listed.*
>
> **NOTE:** *If the Task List does not appear immediately, release* Ctrl, *press* Esc *once, then repeat the above action. This technique is useful whenever the Task List seems unavailable.*

The Task List, as shown in Figure B.7, shows a single window open, Program Manager. Opening other windows involves double-clicking on their respective icons. The currently active window will appear at the top of the Task List.

▶ **Click on the Cancel button in the Task List.**

> ▨ *The Task List closes.*

▶ **Double-click on the Main icon.**

> ▨ *The Main window opens.*

▶ **Double-click on the Print Manager icon.**

> ▨ *The Print Manager window overlays the Main window.*

▶ **If necessary, move the Print Manager window so that the title bar of the Main window and the File Manager icon can be seen.**

## Checking for a Formatted Disk

Before continuing, let's check to see if your floppy disk is formatted. As described in chapter 7, a disk needs tracks, sectors, and a disk directory before storing data or programs. The easiest way to check for an unformatted disk is to use the File Manager.

▶ **If there is another disk in drive A, remove it from the disk drive.**

▶ **Put your data disk in drive A. If necessary, close the drive door or latch.**

▶ **Double-click on the File Manager icon.**

▧ *The File Manager window opens.*

▶ **Click on the drive A icon (shown in Figure B.14).**

One of two things happens at this point. If your data disk is formatted, the File Manager displays the disk directory. If the disk is unformatted, the File Manager displays the message "The disk in drive A is not formatted. Do you want to format it now?" You should click on the Yes button. As a result, the Format Disk dialog box appears. To format the disk, click on the OK button. Then click on Yes when asked to confirm formatting the disk. It will take several minutes to format the disk. In either case, your screen should be displaying the drive A directory.

▧ *The File Manager displays active drive A disk directory.*

▶ **Double-click on the control box of the File Manager window.**

▧ *The File Manager window closes and the Print Manager disappears from the screen.*

▶ **Double-click on the control box of the Main window.**

▧ *The Main window closes.*

Because Main is a group icon, closing it down does not mean the programs within it, such as Print Manager, are also closed. We will use the Task List shortly to check on which programs are open.

▶ **Double-click on the Accessories icon.**

▧ *The Accessories window opens.*

▶ **Maximize the Accessories window.**

▧ *The Accessories window expands to fill the screen.*

▶ **Double-click on the Clock icon.**

▧ *The Clock window opens within the Accessories window.*

▶ **If necessary, move the Clock window so that the Paintbrush icon can be seen.**

▶ **Double-click on the Paintbrush icon.**

▧ *The Paintbrush window overlays the Accessories window; the Clock window disappears.*

▶ **Hold down** Ctrl **and press** Esc **to open the Task List.**

▧ *The Task List opens on top of the Paintbrush window, showing four programs listed: Paintbrush, Program Manager, Clock, and Print Manager.*

### ■ Cascading and Tiling Windows

The Task List not only lists the open programs but allows you to control how their windows are displayed. Two arrangements are available: cascade and tile. The *cascade* arrangement places all the windows in a stack in the order they appear in the Task List, with the menu bars visible. Clicking on a title bar brings that window to the top of the stack. Only the active window can be used at this time.

▷ **Click on C̲ascade.**

■ *The Task List disappears, and the open windows are arranged as a stack with Paintbrush on top, as shown in Figure B.8.*

▷ **Click on the Print Manager title bar.**

■ *The Print Manager window is brought to the top with its title bar darkened, indicating that it is the active window.*

The *tile* arrangement shows all the windows in reduced size, side by side. The window of the program at the top of the Task List will appear in the upper left. With tiling, you can work in any of the visible windows at any time by clicking anywhere within the window to make it active.

▷ **Hold down Ctrl and press Esc to open the Task List.**

■ *The Task List opens with Print Manager at the top.*

▷ **Click on T̲ile.**

■ *The Task List disappears, and the windows are arranged in tiles, as shown in Figure B.9.*

**B.8**

When program windows are cascaded, a program may be activated by clicking on its title bar.

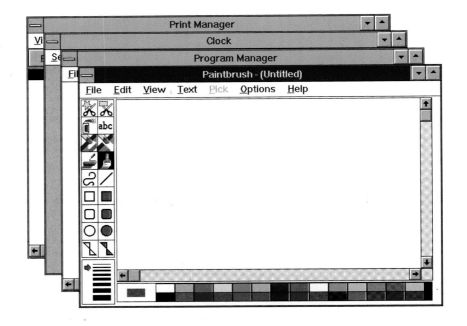

**B.9**

Tiling windows reduces the size of all open windows to display them simultaneously.

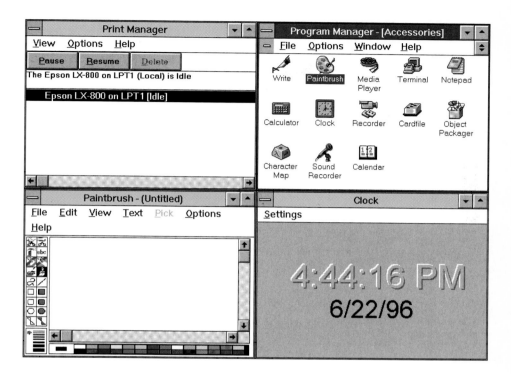

▶ **Click anywhere in the Clock window.**

░ *The Clock window is made active, as indicated by the darkened title bar.*

The Task List also provides a way to close a window, thereby ending program execution. Recall that a window can also be closed by double-clicking on its control box.

▶ **Open the Task List ( Ctrl + Esc ).**

░ *The Task List appears.*

▶ **If Clock is not already highlighted, click on it.**

▶ **Click on End Task.**

░ *The Task List and Clock window disappear. The other three windows remain on-screen.*

## PRINT MANAGER

Although personal computers manage an individual mix of programs for each user, every computer using Windows 3.1 has available some programs in common. You have seen in the previous section that desktop programs, like the clock, provide helpful information or utilities for everyone. Two other Windows programs can help control the output and storage of programs and data. This section explores the Print Manager; the File Manager is discussed later in this appendix.

Most application software contain a menu option to print a previously saved file or what appears in the program window. So long as Windows 3.1 itself was installed with the proper drivers, printing is a simple process. When working in a network environment, with many printers or several users sharing a single printer, you may want more control over the printing process. The *Print Manager* program makes this possible.

At this point you have three programs open: the Print Manager, Program Manager, and Paintbrush. To see how the Print Manager works, you will create a simple graphic in Paintbrush, save it as a file, and print it out.

▶ **Click on the maximize button of the Paintbrush window.**

▨ *The Paintbrush window fills the screen, as shown in Figure B.10.*

The Paintbrush window contains several features for creating color graphics. Aside from the menu bar at the top, there are also a palette at the bottom and a toolbox at the left side. As explained in chapter 10, the *palette* contains the colors available for drawing and filling areas of the screen. The *toolbox* displays the variety of options used to create the graphic. Figure B.11 identifies the tools in the toolbox. Graphics are made by clicking on a tool and a color, then locating a starting point with the screen pointer. Most tools work as long as the left mouse button is held down.

**B.10**

Paintbrush is a free-drawing graphics package available to all users of Windows 3.1.

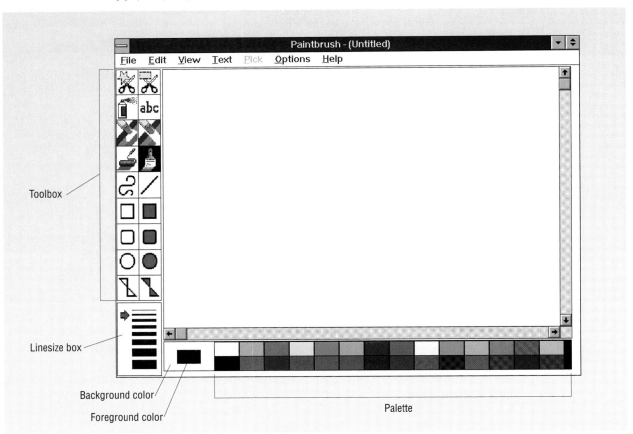

**B.11**

The Paintbrush toolbox provides a variety of ways to create drawings.

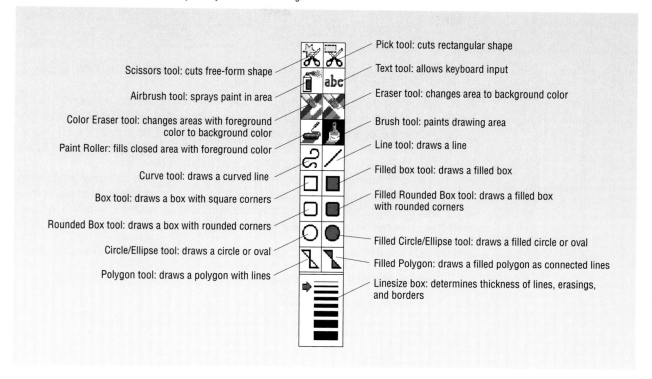

Scissors tool: cuts free-form shape

Airbrush tool: sprays paint in area

Color Eraser tool: changes areas with foreground color to background color

Paint Roller: fills closed area with foreground color

Curve tool: draws a curved line

Box tool: draws a box with square corners

Rounded Box tool: draws a box with rounded corners

Circle/Ellipse tool: draws a circle or oval

Polygon tool: draws a polygon with lines

Pick tool: cuts rectangular shape

Text tool: allows keyboard input

Eraser tool: changes area to background color

Brush tool: paints drawing area

Line tool: draws a line

Filled box tool: draws a filled box

Filled Rounded Box tool: draws a filled box with rounded corners

Filled Circle/Ellipse tool: draws a filled circle or oval

Filled Polygon: draws a filled polygon as connected lines

Linesize box: determines thickness of lines, erasings, and borders

▶ **Click on the Text tool in the toolbox.**

▪ *The screen pointer changes to an I-beam.*

▶ **Click near the upper-left corner of the blank window.**

▪ *A blinking insertion point appears.*

▶ **Type your full name and press** [Enter]. **The** [Backspace] **key will erase any characters just typed.**

▪ *Your name appears in the window, and the insertion point is at the beginning of the next line.*

▶ **Type your computer course number and today's date, each on a different line.**

▶ **Use the palette and different tools in the toolbox to produce a simple graphic like a drawing or your signature. Remember that some printers will not print colors.**

▪ *The graphic appears in the Paintbrush window.*

▶ **When the graphic is complete, click on the restore button of the Paintbrush window.**

     ▓ *The Paintbrush window returns to its original place among the tiles. Only part of the graphic may be shown in the reduced window.*

## ▓ Saving a Program

Most application programs have a menu option to save window's contents or other information to a file on disk. This tutorial assumes you will be putting your disk in drive A, usually the top or leftmost disk drive. Your drawing will be saved in a file named EXAMPLE.BMP. The .BMP extension is automatically given to the filename by the Paintbrush program, representing a bit-mapped graphics file.

    Acceptable filenames use any combination of letters or numbers up to eight characters. Filenames cannot include spaces. If necessary, use a hyphen or underscore character instead of a space. The DOS user's manual lists acceptable characters. A three-character extension is permissible if it follows a period—for instance, EXAMPLE.BMP.

▶ **Insert your diskette into drive A and close the drive door if necessary.**

▶ **Click on the File menu in the Paintbrush window.**

     ▓ *The File menu drops down.*

▶ **Click on the Save option.**

     ▓ *The Save As dialog box opens, with the File Name text box highlighted, as shown in Figure B.12.*

Although you clicked on the Save option in the File menu, Paintbrush uses the Save As command. This happens only the first time a new file is saved. Routinely, Save

**B.12**

When a file is saved for the first time or under a new name, the Save As dialog box appears, allowing you to change the filename or disk location where it is stored.

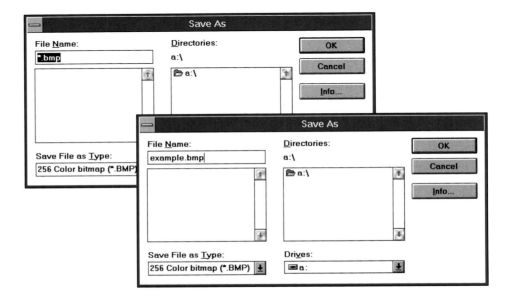

is used for updating files already saved, whereas Save As gives the information in memory a new filename or disk location.

▶ **If a: is not displayed in the list box under Dri̲ves, click on the list box under Dri̲ves, then click on a:.**

　▨ *The Drives list box should now contain a: highlighted.*

▶ **Click in the File N̲ame text box.**

　▨ *The insertion point is at the end of the highlighted filename.*

▶ **Delete the old filename by pressing ⌷Backspace⌷.**

▶ **Type example.bmp and press ⌷Enter⌷. It does not matter if you use upper- or lowercase letters.**

　▨ *The Save As dialog box disappears, and the filename EXAMPLE.BMP appears in the Paintbrush title bar. When the hourglass icon disappears, the file is saved on disk.*

## ▨ Printing a File

To print a file requires actions similar to saving it. Make sure you are connected to a printer and that it is turned on.

▶ **Click on the F̲ile menu in the Paintbrush window.**

　▨ *The File menu drops down.*

▶ **Click on the P̲rint option.**

　▨ *The Print dialog box opens, as shown in Figure B.13.*

▶ **Click on the OK button.**

　▨ *A message box appears, reporting that the file is being printed. After a short delay, the name of the file will appear in the Print Manager window, under the name of the printer. The drawing is output on the printer, and the filename disappears from the Print Manager window.*

▶ **Click on the F̲ile menu in the Paintbrush window.**

　▨ *The File menu appears.*

**B.13**

The Print dialog box allows you to control how a file will be printed.

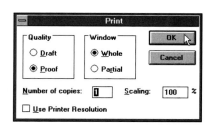

▶ **Click on the <u>N</u>ew option.**

  ▪ *The File menu disappears, and the Paintbrush window is cleared. However, your drawing is saved.*

  **NOTE:** *If the printer is unavailable or not working properly, it is possible that a printer error has occurred. At this point you will find Print Manager named twice in the Task List. One of these is the original listing and the other represents a Print Manager window with an error message. Opening the window with the message will allow you to resume printing once the printer error is fixed.*

Normally, it not required that the Print Manager window be opened in order to print a file. Using the Print Manager allows you to see how printouts are controlled through another program and to fix printer errors. You can close the Print Manager without affecting future printing. You can also close the Accessories window without closing Paintbrush, whose icon is in the Accessories group. This is possible because Accessories is a window containing several program icons but is not a program itself.

▶ **Bring up the Task List by holding down Ctrl and pressing Esc.**

  ▪ *The Task List appears.*

▶ **Click on Print Manager if it is not already highlighted.**

▶ **Click on <u>E</u>nd Task.**

  ▪ *The Task List disappears.*

▶ **Bring up the Task List again by holding down Ctrl and pressing Esc.**

  ▪ *The Task List appears.*

▶ **Click on Program Manager.**

▶ **Click on the <u>S</u>witch To button.**

  ▪ *The Program Manager window appears.*

▶ **Click on the maximize button of the Program Manager window.**

  ▪ *The Program Manager window is maximized, and the Accessories window appears.*

▶ **Double-click on the control box for the Accessories window.**

  ▪ *The Accessories window closes.*

## FILE MANAGER

Whereas the Task List allows you to arrange and close program windows, the *File Manager* expands the control you have over disk files, including those on the hard disk. With the File Manager you can rename, copy, move, and delete files of all types. To start, the File Manager icon in the Main group needs to be activated.

**B.14**

Programs and data files are organized into folders (subdirectories), which are added to the disk's root directory.

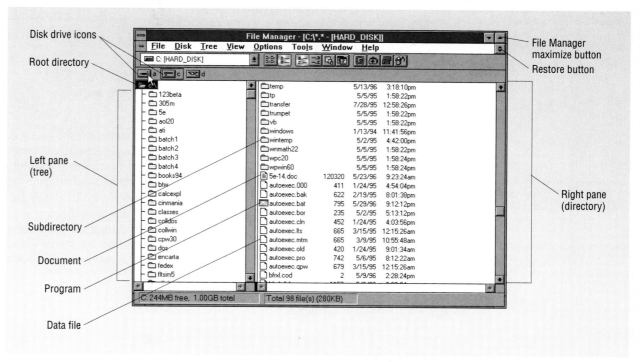

▷ **Double-click on the Main icon.**

▨ *Overlays the Main window on the Program Manager window.*

▷ **Double-click on the File Manager icon.**

▨ *Displays the File Manager window, similar to Figure B.14.*

▷ **Maximize the File Manager window if it is not already maximized.**

▨ *The File Manager window fills the screen.*

The File Manager window in Figure B.14 contains a directory window that is split into two panes: tree and directory. Normally, applications and documents are organized within disk directories in some systematic fashion. When graphically displayed, this hierarchy of disk directories looks like a tree. A disk directory appears in the tree pane as a *file folder* icon 🗀. A folder can be found within another folder or may itself contain other folders. These folders are actually DOS subdirectories (see Appendix D). How applications and documents are organized within folders and subdirectories is up to the user. There should be some logic to the grouping scheme, however, to make it easy to locate related applications and documents.

When a folder/directory is highlighted in the tree pane, the directory pane displays a list of filenames. These are the data files and programs stored in the highlighted directory.

▶ **Click on the View menu and select Tree and Directory.**

▦ *Splits the File Manager window into two panes, if it wasn't already.*

▶ **Click on the Tree menu and select Expand All.**

▦ *Displays the complete directory tree for your disk, if not already displayed.*

> **NOTE:** *If you used a new disk for this tutorial, you will have only one file saved, EXAMPLE.BMP. You will see no differences before and after selecting Expand All.*

When a disk is formatted, a ***root directory*** is created to catalog the filenames of data and programs stored on the disk. The notation A:\ is used to identify the root directory of the disk in drive A. As you can see in Figure B.14, the root and any subdirectories appear as file folders. They work like electronic file folders in organizing programs and data according to common attributes. A well-organized hard disk has DOS and Windows subdirectories for storing utility programs, other subdirectories for application packages, and separate subdirectories for related data. Every computer system has a unique mix of file folders, programs, and data files. In the tree and directory panes, programs will appear with the icon �–¡ and documents will have a ▤ icon.

## ▦ Creating Copies of Files

The File Manager helps you copy important files by duplicating them onto another disk, within another directory, or in the same directory with another name. Copying files is a simple task using the Copy command in the File menu. You are going to make a copy of the EXAMPLE.BMP file and save it as NEWCOPY.BMP. Both files will be in the root directory.

▶ **Click on the file EXAMPLE.BMP or on its icon in the directory pane.**

▦ *EXAMPLE.BMP is highlighted.*

▶ **Click on the File menu and select the Copy option.**

▦ *The Copy dialog box appears, as shown in Figure B.15. The cursor is in the To text box.*

▶ **Type newcopy.bmp and press ⌴Enter .**

▦ *The Copy dialog box disappears, and the file NEWCOPY.BMP is in the root directory.*

> **NOTE:** *Pressing ⌴Enter initiates action just like clicking on the OK button. Anytime a button is highlighted as the OK button is in Figure B.15, pressing ⌴Enter is the keyboard alternative.*

**B.15**

Changing filenames when copying files uses the Copy option of the File menu, the current directory designation, and a new filename for the duplicate.

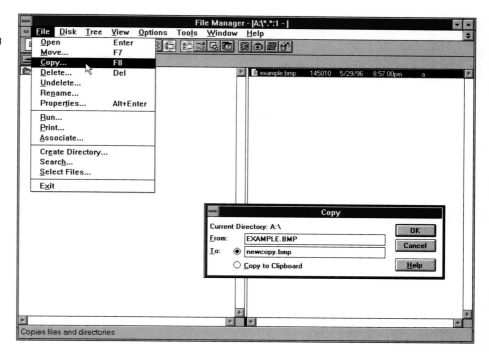

## Renaming Files

What if a filename needs to be changed? The File Manager performs this operation through the Rename option of the File menu. As illustrated in Figure B.16, you are going to change NEWCOPY.BMP to NEXTNAME.BMP in the root directory.

▶ **Click on NEWCOPY.BMP.**

▧ *Highlights NEWCOPY.BMP and its icon.*

▶ **Click on the File menu and select Rename.**

▧ *Displays the Rename dialog box.*

▶ **Type nextname.bmp, as shown in Figure B.16, and press Enter.**

▧ *The filename changes to NEXTNAME.BMP.*

**B.16**

Filenames are changed by using the Rename option of the File menu.

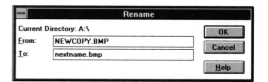

**B.17**

The Delete dialog box asks you to confirm a file deletion before removing the file from the disk directory.

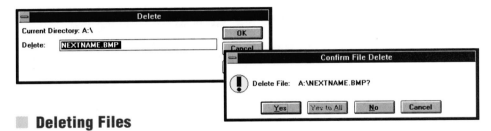

## Deleting Files

At some time you will want to delete an unwanted file or files from disk. This task is easily accomplished by highlighting the files and pressing Delete or selecting the Delete option from the File menu. You will now delete the newly renamed file NEXTNAME.BMP.

▶ **Click on NEXTNAME.BMP if it is not already highlighted.**

　▦ *Highlights NEXTNAME.BMP.*

▶ **Press ⌊Delete⌋.**

　▦ *Displays the Delete dialog box, as shown in Figure B.17.*

▶ **Click on OK.**

　▦ *Displays the Confirm File Delete dialog box (Figure B.17).*

▶ **Click on <u>Y</u>es after visually confirming that the correct file is being deleted.**

　▦ *Only EXAMPLE.BMP is left in the disk directory.*

## Making Subdirectories

As you begin working with the computer, you will create documents using a variety of application software. Over time, these documents will need to be organized in some fashion—by subject, type of application package used, and so on. You will need to establish a filing system wherein related documents are placed within folders *(subdirectories)* on your disk.

　　To create new folders for organizing software and documents, you must make sure that you open the folder within which you want to put the new folder. With the root directory of the disk in drive A active, you are going to create a new directory called PROJECTS. When naming a new subdirectory, you must follow the DOS rules for filenames—that is, up to eight characters in the filename and three characters in the optional extension.

▶ **Make sure the a:\ folder is highlighted in the tree pane. If not, click on it.**

▶ **Click on the <u>F</u>ile menu and select Cr<u>e</u>ate Directory.**

　▦ *Displays the Create Directory dialog box.*

▶ **Type projects, as shown in Figure B.18, and click on OK.**

　▦ *Adds a file folder labeled PROJECTS to the tree and root directory, as shown in Figure B.18.*

**B.18**

A file folder icon identifies a disk directory which is used to organize programs and data on the disk.

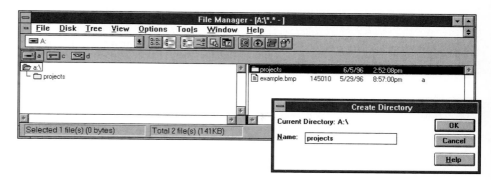

## Displaying Two Directories

It is often helpful to display two disk directories at the same time. Checking the dates on backup files or copying files to your backup disk are both situations in which displaying the source and target drives or directories is useful. Two terms, *source* and *target,* are often used to differentiate between a file's current location and where you want it to go. *Source* identifies a specific filename and its disk or directory; *target* refers to the file's new location. You are going to create a new window in the File Manager and display the contents of the PROJECTS subdirectory in it.

▶ **Click on the Window menu and select New Window.**

  ▦ *Opens window with A:\\\*.\*:2 in the title bar.*

▶ **Click on the Window menu again and select Tile.**

  ▦ *The two windows, named A:\\\*.\*:2 and A:\\\*.\*:1 are tiled horizontally, as shown in Figure B.19.*

**B.19**

Dragging a program or data file icon from one directory window to another while holding down the Ctrl key copies the related disk file to another disk.

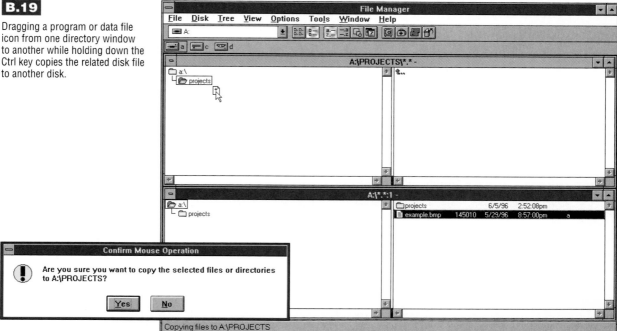

▶ **Click on PROJECTS in the tree pane of the top window.**

▨ *Highlights PROJECTS, displaying no files on the right.*

## ▨ Copying and Moving Files

When windows are tiled, files can be moved between folders or from one disk to another by dragging the file from one window to another. Files are copied if you hold down the Ctrl key while dragging the filename. While you are dragging the file, you will see the screen pointer change to include a document icon ▤ with a plus sign (+) in it. This indicates that the file is being copied, not moved. Here you will copy EXAMPLE.BMP as found in the root directory to the PROJECTS subdirectory. The newly copied file should appear in the subdirectory listing.

▶ **Click on EXAMPLE.BMP in the bottom window.**

▨ *Highlights EXAMPLE.BMP.*

▶ **While holding down Ctrl, drag the highlighted filename and icon to the PROJECTS icon in the top window, as shown in Figure B.19.**

▨ *Displays the Confirm Mouse Operation dialog box shown in Figure B.19.*

▶ **Click on the Yes button.**

▨ *Displays the Copying dialog box and copies EXAMPLE.BMP to the PROJECTS subdirectory.*

This drag-and-drop approach to copying a file is quick and easy, and ensures that both files have the same name. To change the name of the copy, you can use the Rename option in the File menu as described previously.

You just copied a file from one directory to a subdirectory using the drag-and-drop technique. To move a file instead of copying it, hold down the Alt key rather than Ctrl while dragging the icons between directories or disks.

## ▨ Removing Subdirectories from Disk

Proper disk management dictates the constant addition and removal of file folders as projects and software come into use or become inactive. Although the root directory cannot be removed, all other folders (subdirectories) are fair game. A file folder must be empty except for ▟.. before removing it. This icon represents an internal index linking the file folder to the root directory or another file folder. If you try to delete a directory with files in it, Windows will systematically ask if you want to delete each file.

File folders, like files, can be deleted by highlighting the associated icon and pressing Delete. An alternative is to highlight the folder name and select the Delete option from the File menu. As with many Windows features, there are several ways to accomplish the same action.

▶ **Click on the PROJECTS icon in the tree pane of the top window.**

▶ **Click on the File menu and select Delete.**

▨ *Displays the Delete dialog box, as shown in Figure B.20.*

**B.20**

Files, programs, and other folders must be removed from a subdirectory before it is deleted.

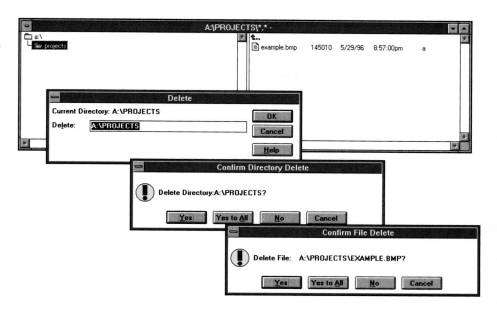

▷ **Click on OK.**

    *Displays the Confirm Directory Delete dialog box.*

▷ **Click on Yes.**

    *Displays the Confirm File Delete dialog box.*

▷ **Click on Yes.**

    *Removes the PROJECTS folder from the drive A directory tree in both windows.*

## SYSTEM SHUTDOWN

When you are through for the day, the computer system needs to be shut down. One good rule of thumb is to never turn off a computer while an application program is still running. Furthermore, always exit the Program Manager and return to the DOS prompt before turning off the equipment. Ask your instructor what procedure is preferred at your school.

▷ **Bring up the Task List by holding down** Ctrl **and pressing** Esc**.**

    *The Task List appears, showing File Manager, Program Manager, and Paintbrush.*

▷ **Click on Paintbrush and then on End Task.**

    *The Task List disappears, leaving the File Manager on-screen.*

**B.21**

Always exit a program to the Program Manager and return to the DOS prompt before turning off your computer system.

▶ **Double-click on the File Manager control box at the top-left corner of the screen.**

　▪ *Returns to the Program Manager window.*

　**NOTE:** *If you do not double-click fast enough, Windows displays the control menu. Click on Close to exit the File Manager.*

▶ **Close any open windows.**

▶ **Double-click on the Program Manager control box.**

　▪ *Displays the Exit Windows dialog box shown in Figure B.21.*

▶ **Click on OK.**

　▪ *Displays the DOS prompt.*

▶ **Remove the disk from drive A, return it to a protective cover or case, and store it in a safe place.**

▶ **Turn off the computer.**

▶ **Turn off the monitor and printer, if necessary.**

## S U M M A R Y

▪ Windows is a graphical user interface that uses a desktop metaphor to represent different computer operations as icons. File folders, calendars, and calculators are icons found on the desktop.

▪ Pull-down menus are found in the menu bar.

▪ Icons and menus are selected on the desktop by moving the mouse to locate the screen pointer over the item. Clicking the mouse button activates the menu or associated application program.

▪ Icons and windows are repositioned on the desktop by using the mouse to drag them to a new location.

▪ Windows are identified by the name in the title bar.

▪ The dimensions of a window are altered by dragging the window frame or by clicking on the maximize and restore buttons.

- Clicking on the scroll arrows and dragging the scroll box changes a window's view.

- Double-clicking on the control box closes a window.

- The Task List provides a way to arrange, change, and close open program windows.

- Windows can be put into cascade or tile formation with the Task List.

- The Print Manager enables you to have close control over the printers used for output.

- Paintbrush is a free-drawing program provided with Windows that includes a palette and toolbox.

- The File Manager provides menus that help you create new folders, rename files, delete files, and remove folders.

- Application programs, data files, and documents are organized into different file folders (subdirectories).

- New file folders can be created, renamed, and deleted at any time.

- More than one directory pane can be open at the same time.

- Files are copied from one file folder to another by dragging the associated icon over the other folder while holding down Ctrl. Files are moved from one disk to another in the same way while holding down Alt.

- A file folder must be empty before it is removed from the disk directory.

- Exiting Windows returns the user back to a DOS prompt.

## TERMS TO REMEMBER

| | | |
|---|---|---|
| cascade | maximize button | scroll arrow |
| click | menu bar | scroll bar |
| control box | minimize button | scroll box |
| desktop | MS-DOS | Task List |
| double-click | PC-DOS | tile |
| drag | Print Manager | title bar |
| file folder | Program Manager | window frame |
| File Manager | restore button | Windows 3.1 |
| group icon | root directory | |

## MIX AND MATCH

*Complete the following definitions with the Terms to Remember.*

1. The screen layout associated with a graphical user interface that uses icons which represent documents, file folders, calculators, and other office tools is called the

   _____.

2. When open program windows are arranged in a stack, or in _____ formation, only title bars are visible behind the top window.

3. The _____ is an icon with double arrows at the top-right corner of the title bar next to the minimize button.

4. The _____ is the horizontal area across the top of a window that displays the window's name.

5. A(n) _____ found in the Program Manager organizes related programs and data files.

6. Clicking on the _____ opens a menu that allows you to close, open, or move the associated window; double-clicking closes the associated window.

7. A(n) _____ appears on the right or bottom edge of a window or list box when only a partial view is available.

8. Repositioning an icon or window by pointing to it and holding down the mouse button while moving the pointer is called _____.

9. _____ is using the Task List to arrange open program windows by reducing them so that all windows may be seen side by side.

10. Clicking on the _____ expands the related window to fill the screen.

11. Pressing the mouse button once to initiate action or to select a program option is called

    _____.

12. The _____ allows you to create and delete subdirectories, as well as move, copy, rename, and delete files.

13. The _____ displays the group icons and program icons that may be opened.

14. The _____ shows all open programs and allows them to be arranged and closed.

15. The _____ icon in the File Manager represents a specific subdirectory.

## REVIEW QUESTIONS

1. Define the Terms to Remember.

2. How do you load and run Windows?

3. How do you move an icon around the desktop?

4. Describe how an option is selected from a drop-down menu.

5. Why are some menu options dimmed?

6. What are three ways to open a window?

7. Describe four ways to alter the size of a window.

8. How do you close a window?

9. How do you open the Task List?

10. How do you use the Task List to close a program?

11. Identify the rules for acceptable DOS/Windows filenames.

12. What are two different procedures for copying a file from one disk to another, keeping the same name? How do you change the name of the duplicate when copying?

13. How do you rename an existing disk file using Windows?

14. What are two different ways to use Windows to delete files from disk?

15. How are new file folders or subdirectories added to a disk?

16. Explain how you would use Windows to display two disk directories at the same time.

17. How can you move a file from one disk to another?

18. What conditions must exist before a subdirectory can be removed from a disk?

19. How do you use Windows to remove an existing subdirectory folder from a disk?

20. How do you exit Windows and return to the DOS prompt?

## APPLYING WHAT YOU'VE LEARNED

1. Use a Windows user's manual or online help to find the File Manager feature that allows you to protect a file from accidental erasure. (*Hint:* These files are said to be read-only.)

2. Use the File Manager to display filenames in order by creation date. How would you display files in order by their size? Which presentation format do you prefer? Explain your answer.

3. A general rule for file management is to make one file folder for related documents and another file folder for each application package. For example, users are encouraged to create one folder for their word processing program and other folders for letters, reports, and so forth. Graphically illustrate how you would organize file folders on a hard disk. Assume you are using at least three different application packages.

4. If your computer system uses a color monitor, how would you change the color of the desktop? How would you change the title bar color? What colors should not be used for the desktop? Explain your answer.

# Operating a Personal Computer Using Windows 95

**B**efore you start to use personal productivity software or learn to program, you need to review operating procedures for Windows and Intel-based personal computers. The following Windows tutorial provides a brief overview of some of the more important procedures associated with Microsoft Windows 95. These procedures help you learn how to locate files and programs on disk, and print files, and they provide a convenient means of copying important disk resources.

You need access to an IBM or Intel-based compatible computer using Microsoft Windows 95 and a new floppy disk to complete this tutorial. Because Windows 95 requires lots of internal memory and makes extensive use of disk storage, we assume you are using a personal computer with a hard disk or have access to a local area network. Instructions or data you should enter into the computer using the keyboard are preceded by a ▶.

## WINDOWS 95 START-UP

IBM and other Intel-based personal computers can use several operating systems developed by the Microsoft Corporation. Early systems used *MS-DOS (Microsoft disk operating system)*. The **Windows 95** operating system is Microsoft's replacement for DOS and the DOS-compatible graphical user interface (GUI) called *Windows 3.1*. Windows 95 is a stand-alone operating system and does not need MS-DOS to operate. This appendix covers Windows 95. Appendix B explains how to use Windows 3.1.

**C.1**

Windows 95 uses a desktop metaphor with My Computer and Recycle Bin icons representing program options.

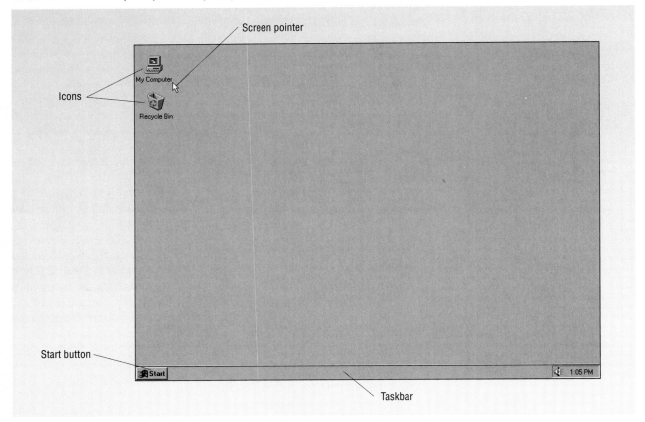

## ▨ System Orientation

*Booting* describes the procedure for starting up a computer system. IBM and Intel-based computers automatically look for and load several system programs from the operating system into memory as a part of the booting process.

Because a disk or CD-ROM with Windows 95 must be in a designated drive when booting a microcomputer, associated procedures will vary. If this is your first time, consult the user's manual or ask the teacher or lab assistant for help. To complete this tutorial, carefully follow the actions associated with each ▷ symbol below. What appears on-screen is preceded by the ▨ symbol.

> ▷ **Turn on your computer, monitor, and printer if necessary.**

> > ▨ *Displays Windows 95 desktop, as shown in Figure C.1.*

## ▨ Windows Desktop

If your computer system follows the standard Windows 95 booting steps, the computer shows you the Windows 95 copyright screen before displaying a screen similar to

Figure C.1. Windows is a user-friendly GUI that reduces the time required to understand basic computer operations and learn new applications. Currently on-screen is the desktop, your window into the computer. The ***desktop*** is aptly named, since you work with images on the screen in the same way that you work with papers, folders, and office tools and supplies laid out on an actual desktop. This desktop metaphor is the basis for all screen displays and processing activities under the control of Windows.

The desktop in Figure C.1 contains the items commonly found on the Windows 95 desktop: icons, taskbar, and Start button. Small graphics, or *icons,* identify commonly used programs and files. The ***taskbar*** along the bottom of the window displays the names of active programs currently running on the computer. You use the ***Start button*** to run different programs.

## ▨ Using a Mouse

As you grasp and move the mouse across a flat surface, a screen pointer moves in a corresponding fashion around the screen. When you work within the desktop, the pointer is shaped like an arrow (see Figure C.1); however, it changes into other shapes, depending on which activity is in progress.

You can lift the mouse and set it back down again without changing the location of the pointer on-screen. This action may be necessary if you do not have enough room to move the pointer across the screen in one continuous movement of the mouse.

At first, using a mouse may seem awkward. However, this device's operation will soon become second nature. The speed and ease with which you can do things using a mouse will increase your productivity many times over.

A basic technique for working with Windows is to select an icon and either activate it or move it around the screen. You select an icon by pointing to it with the arrow pointer and ***clicking*** (pressing) and releasing the left mouse button once. You must select an object before you can use it. In this tutorial, *clicking* means pressing and releasing the left mouse button. Clicking on the ***My Computer*** icon opens a window that lists computer resources, such as number and types of disk drives, and allows you to manage files.

▷ **Move the arrow pointer so that it rests on the My Computer  icon.**

> **NOTE:** *If the My Computer window is already open, as shown in Figure C.3, close the window and any other open windows by skipping forward to the section on the close button on page 574.*

▷ **Click the left mouse button.**

> ▨ *The My Computer icon is highlighted, as shown in Figure C.2.*

▷ **Move the pointer to an open area of the desktop.**

▷ **Click the mouse button.**

> ▨ *Deselects the My Computer icon.*

You can reposition an object on the desktop by pointing to it and then holding down the left mouse button while moving, or ***dragging***, the mouse.

Pointing and clicking on a icon
highlights it.

▷ **Click on the Recycle Bin 🗑 icon and press and hold down the left mouse button.**

▫ *Highlights Recycle Bin icon.*

▷ **While holding down the button, move the mouse down and to the right to reposition the icon on-screen.**

▫ *An outline of the icon and label move as the screen pointer is dragged across the screen.*

▷ **Release the mouse button.**

▫ *The icon is repositioned to its new location.*

These clicking and dragging techniques are used for other mouse operations besides selecting and moving icons. They are basic techniques for controlling many activities you perform while using Windows and other programs on the computer. For example, dragging a program or file icon into the Recycle Bin removes the associated file from disk.

## COMMON WINDOW FEATURES

Windows 95 draws its name from that fact that programs and files are displayed in a screen area called a *window.* Windows are opened by ***double-clicking*** (pressing the left mouse button twice in rapid succession) on a program icon or using the Start button to display menu options containing programs and files.

▷ **Double-click on the My Computer icon.**

▫ *Opens the My Computer window and adds My Computer to the taskbar, as shown in Figure C.3.*

*  *NOTE: If you cannot get the My Computer window open by double-clicking on the icon, click on the icon once to highlight it, then press Enter.*

▫ **Title Bar**

The My Computer window displays icons for each disk drive attached to your computer system along with folders for the Control Panel and printers. The window's name, such as *My Computer,* appears in the ***title bar*** across the top of the window. At the right side of the title bar are three buttons that will be discussed later.

## C.3

The My Computer window contains icons representing current computer resources.

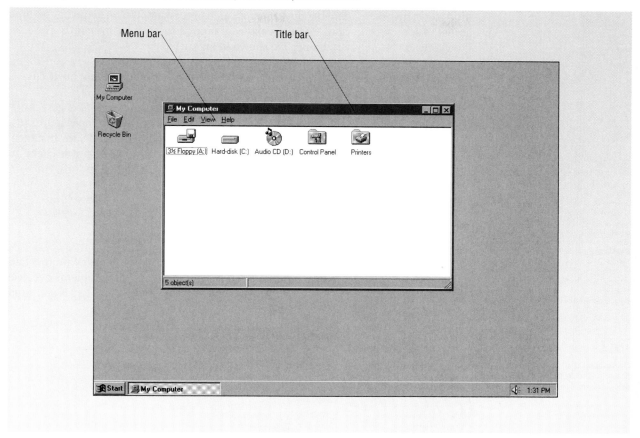

Windows can be moved anywhere on-screen by clicking within the title bar and dragging to reposition the window. You may need to do this if you have several overlapping windows on-screen at the same time.

▶ **If the My Computer window completely covers the desktop, make it smaller by clicking on the 🗗 button, displayed in the middle on the right side of the My Computer title bar.**

▶ **Move the pointer within the My Computer title bar.**

▶ **Hold down the mouse button and drag the pointer somewhere else on-screen.**

   ▫ *The outline of the window is dragged with the pointer.*

▶ **Release the mouse button.**

   ▫ *The window snaps into its new position.*

▶ **Use the mouse to center the My Computer window in the space available.**

## ■ Menu Bar

Below the title bar of the application window is the ***menu bar***, which lists names of various drop-down menus. A menu bar does not appear in every window. The menu bar permits access to several drop-down menus, each containing processing commands. The File, Edit, View, and Help menu names are shown in Figure C.3.

All choices from the menu bar, as well as icon manipulations, are controlled primarily with the mouse. Keyboard alternatives are available, but will not be discussed in detail as a part of this brief introduction.

We need to explore how options are executed by using the mouse to access drop-down menus. The menu bar contains the names of all available menus (see Figure C.3). You select one of the drop-down menus by clicking on the menu name, for instance, Help. Drop-down menu options stay hidden in the menu bar until the user clicks on the menu name. When the menu is selected, it opens to list program options. Once an option is selected, the menu rolls back up into the menu bar.

▶ **Click on the Help menu in the menu bar.**

■ *The menu options are displayed, as shown in Figure C.4.*

This Help menu can be of great assistance as you learn how to use Windows and related programs. It is designed to answer questions about specific problems because it is *context-sensitive help.* This means the information displayed when Help is activated

**C.4**

Drop-down menus, such as Help, are activated by clicking on the menu name.

Drop-down menu

Help Topics dialog box

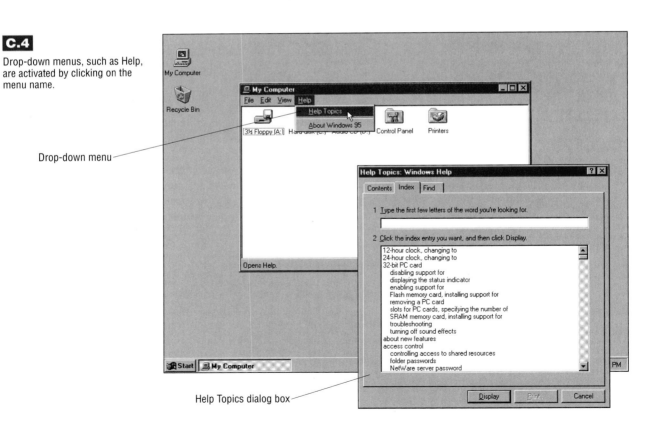

relates to the screen display currently being used. In other words, if you are playing a game and ask for help, the help screen provides information about the game.

▶ **Click on Help Topics.**

▪ *Displays the Help Topics dialog box.*

This dialog box provides three approaches to help though the use of tabs: Contents, Index, and Find. Clicking on the tab displays the associated dialog box. If you have time, walk through one or more of these help features. If you do not wish to use the help at this time, you can return to the My Computer window by pressing the Esc key or clicking on the Cancel button.

▶ **Press [Esc].**

▪ *The Help Topics dialog box closes, and My Computer becomes the active window.*

If you decide not to choose a menu item after you have opened a menu, simply move the pointer outside the menu so that no item is selected, and click the mouse button; the menu disappears.

You can easily scan the menus to see all of the options available on the menu bar.

▶ **Click and hold on File in the menu bar.**

▪ *The menu options are listed.*

▶ **Slowly drag the pointer along the menu bar horizontally from left to right.**

▪ *As each menu name is highlighted, the related drop-down menu is shown.*

▶ **Click on an empty area of the window.**

▪ *Closes the open menu.*

> *NOTE: Some of the names of the menu items may appear dimmed. These are menu options that are not available at this time. You cannot select a dimmed option. These items will become available at different times and under other processing circumstances.*

## ▪ Sizing a Window

You have complete control over the location and size of each window. Not only can you drag a window around the screen, you can grab the line around the window, called the *window frame*, and drag it to a new location or change the window's dimensions.

▶ **Position the pointer at the bottom-right corner of the My Computer window.**

▪ *The pointer changes to a double-headed arrow, as shown in Figure C.5.*

▶ **Hold down the mouse button.**

**C.5**

You change a window's size by dragging one corner to a new location or by clicking on the enlarge button in the top-right corner of each window.

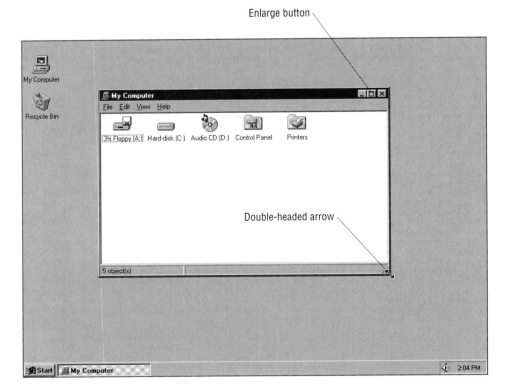

Drag the window's corner toward the upper-left corner of the screen until at least one icon falls outside the window.

*The window outline gets smaller as it follows the pointer.*

Release the mouse button.

*The window contracts as it moves with the pointer. Any icon outside that area of the desktop will be hidden.*

## Scroll Bars

When a window is reduced in size, *scroll bars* appear along the right or bottom edges of the window (see Figure C.6). A *scroll box* within each scroll bar identifies which portion of the window is currently being viewed. Dragging the scroll box or clicking on the *scroll arrows* brings hidden icons into view. You can tell if there are hidden icons in the window because of the presence of a scroll bar. When the complete contents of a window are displayed, no scroll bars are present.

Click once on the scroll arrow that points right (or down).

*Icons in the window move off toward the left (or up).*

**C.6**

Dragging the scroll box or clicking on either scroll arrow changes the view within the related window.

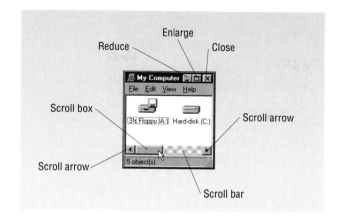

> **Click within the scroll bar, but not on the scroll box.**

> *Icons in the window move in the opposite direction.*

## Enlarge and Reduce Window Size

In Figure C.6, the reduce ▬, enlarge ▢, and close ✕ buttons appear in the upper-right corner of the window. The *enlarge button,* or *maximize button,* is in the middle, appearing as a small window with a title bar. When it is clicked, the window expands to fill the screen, and the *restore button* ⬒ takes its place. When the restore button is clicked, the window returns to its previous size. Double-clicking on the title bar also maximizes and restores the associated window.

> **Click once on the My Computer enlarge button.**

> *The My Computer window expands to fill the desktop.*

> **Click on the restore button.**

> *The window returns to its previous size.*

The *reduce button,* or *minimize button,* appears as a horizontal line and is located to the left of the maximize button. Clicking on this button returns a window to the taskbar, as shown in Figure C.7. Clicking on the window name or associated icon on the taskbar restores the window.

> **Click on the My Computer minimize button.**

> *The My Computer window disappears, and My Computer is added to the taskbar, as shown in Figure C.7.*

> **Click on My Computer on the taskbar.**

> *The My Computer window returns to its original size.*

**C.7**

Clicking on the reduce button closes window but keeps program name on the taskbar. Clicking on the program name opens the window again.

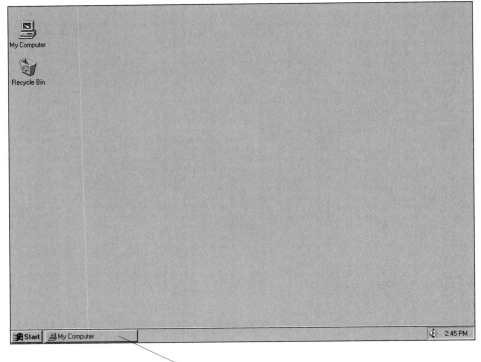

Reduced window on taskbar

### ▨ Close Button

When you are finished using a window, you close it by clicking on the ***close button*** at the left side of the title bar (see Figure C.6). Before closing the My Computer window, you should resize the window so it includes all the available icons.

▷ **Drag the My Computer window frame to include the Control Panel, Printers, and other icons.**

▷ **Click on the My Computer close button.**

   ▨ *The My Computer window disappears from the desktop and taskbar.*

### LAUNCHING PROGRAMS

Application programs are run *(launched)* by double-clicking on the associated icon or by using the Start button. To show you how this operation works, let's run the WordPad program that comes with Windows 95. The ***WordPad*** program is a word processing package you can use to write letters and reports.

▷ **Click on the Start button.**

   ▨ *Opens the Start menu.*

**C.8**

The Start button is used to run programs and open documents.

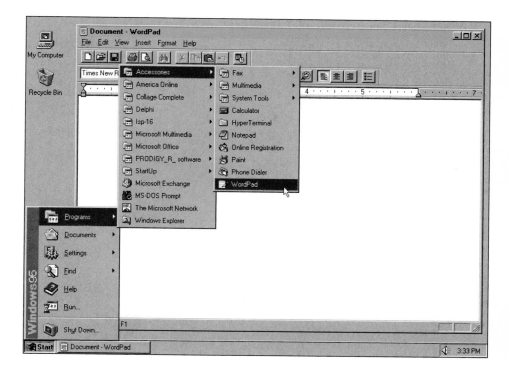

▶ **Move the screen pointer over the Programs option.**

░ *Opens the Programs menu.*

▶ **Move pointer to the Accessories option.**

░ *Opens the Accessories menu, as shown in Figure C.8.*

▶ **Click on WordPad.**

░ *Opens a WordPad document window (see background of Figure C.8).*

▶ **Maximize the window if necessary.**

░ *The WordPad window covers the desktop.*

▶ **Type your full name and press Enter.**

░ *Your name appears in the window, and the insertion point is at the beginning of the next line.*

▶ **Type your computer course number and today's date, each on a different line.**

░ *Three lines of text (your name, course number, and date) appear in the WordPad window.*

### ▨ Saving a File

Most application programs have a menu option to save window contents or other information to a file on disk. This tutorial assumes you will be putting your disk in drive A, usually the top or leftmost diskette drive. Your document will be saved in a file named example.doc. The .doc extension is automatically given to the filename by the WordPad program.

▶ **Insert your diskette into drive A and, if necessary, close the drive door.**

▶ **Click on the File menu.**

   ▨ *The File menu drops down.*

▶ **Click on the Save option.**

   ▨ *The Save As dialog box opens, with the File name text box highlighted, as shown in Figure C.9.*

Although you clicked on the Save option in the File menu, WordPad uses the Save As command. This happens only the first time a new file is saved. Routinely, Save is used for updating files already on disk, whereas Save As gives the information in memory a new filename. Windows 95 allows filenames up to 250 characters long, including spaces. If there is room, WordPad adds the three-character filename extension .doc to the end

**C.9**

The Save As dialog box allows you to designate a file's name and where it is stored.

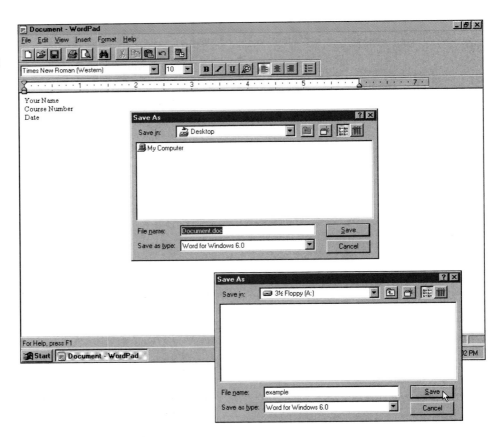

of the filename. Files that need to be compatible with MS-DOS/Windows 3.1 should be limited to eight characters (no spaces) and three characters in the optional extension.

▷ **Look at the Save in list box: 3½ Floppy [A:] or 5¼ Floppy [A:] should be displayed. If not, click on the down arrow to the right of the list box and select drive A.**

    ▨ *Drive A: appears in the Save in list box.*

    **NOTE:** *If a Save As message box appears that says, "The disk in drive A is not formatted. Do you want to format it now?" click on Yes. Files can be saved only on formatted disks. Most disks are sold already formatted; however, it is possible to format your disk now.*

▷ **Delete Document.doc from File name text box by clicking in the box and using either** ⌷Delete⌷ **or** ⌷Backspace⌷ **to remove the default filename.**

▷ **Type example**

    ▨ *Your Save As dialog box should look like Figure C.9.*

▷ **Click on Save.**

    ▨ *The Save As dialog box disappears, and the filename "example.doc" appears in the WordPad title bar. The file is saved on disk.*

## ▨ Printing a File

To print a file requires actions similar to saving it. Make sure you are connected to a printer and that it is turned on.

▷ **Click on the File menu.**

    ▨ *The File menu drops down.*

▷ **Click on the Print option.**

    ▨ *The Print dialog box opens, as shown in Figure C.10.*

▷ **Click on the OK button.**

    ▨ *A box appears (often very quickly), reporting that the file is being printed.*

    **NOTE:** *If the printer is unavailable or not working properly, it is possible that a printer error has occurred. At this point Windows 95 will display an error message, and Printers Folder appears on the taskbar. After you have figured out the problem, click on Retry.*

We are through using WordPad and need to close this application.

▷ **Click on the close button of the WordPad window.**

    ▨ *The WordPad window closes, and WordPad is removed from the taskbar.*

**C.10**

The Print dialog box identifies which printer is currently being used and how many copies of a document will be printed.

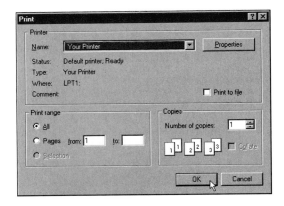

## WINDOWS EXPLORER

As you spend more time working with Windows 95, you need to perform some basic housekeeping, that is, copying files to backup disks, deleting old files, creating new file folders, and so on. These tasks can be accomplished using the My Computer or *Windows Explorer* windows. Since you have already opened My Computer, let's take a look at Windows Explorer. To start Windows Explorer, click on the Start button and use the Programs option.

▶ **Click on the Start button.**

▓ *Opens the Start menu.*

▶ **Click on the Programs option.**

▓ *Opens the Programs menu.*

▶ **Click on the Windows Explorer option.**

▓ *Opens the Exploring window.*

▶ **Look at the list box under the menu bar: 3½ Floppy [A:] or 5¼ Floppy [A:] should be displayed. If not, click on the down arrow to the right of the list box and select drive A.**

▓ *The contents of drive A appear in the list box, as shown in Figure C.11.*

▶ **Maximize the Exploring window if necessary.**

▓ *The Exploring window fills screen.*

The Exploring window in Figure C.11 is split into two panes. Normally, the computer's resources (desktop, hardware, applications, and documents) are organized in the left pane. The contents of the highlighted resource are shown in the right pane. For example, in Figure C.11 the drive A icon is highlighted in the left pane. At the same time, example.doc and other files stored on the disk in drive A are shown in the right pane. It is possible that your Exploring window is different from the one in Figure C.11. The following actions will make them the same if they are not already so.

The Windows Explorer allows you to examine computer resources, open file folders, and copy, rename, and delete files.

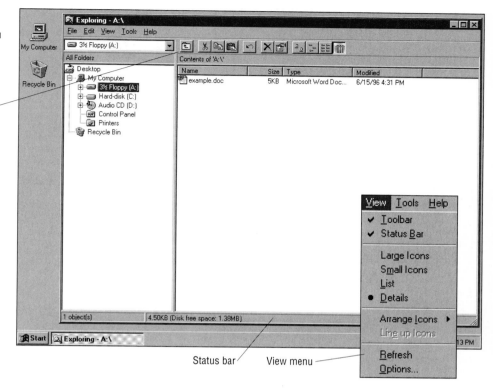

Toolbar

Status bar      View menu

▷ **Click on the View menu. A check mark should appear in front of Toolbar, as shown in the menu in Figure C.11; if not, click on the Toolbar option.**

■ *Adds the toolbar to the window, if it wasn't already there, and closes the menu.*

▷ **Click on the View menu. A check mark should appear in front of Status Bar, as shown in Figure C.11; if not, click on the Status Bar option.**

■ *Adds the status bar to the window, if it wasn't already there, and closes the menu.*

▷ **Click on the View menu. A bullet should appear in front of Details, as shown in Figure C.11; if not, click on the Details option.**

■ *Adds the files' size, type, creation date, and other information about files and programs, if it wasn't already there.*

**NOTE:** *If you used a new disk for this tutorial, you will have only one file, example.doc, saved.*

### ■ Creating Copies of Files

The Explorer helps you copy important files by duplicating them onto another disk, within another file folder, or in the same folder with another name. Copying files is a simple task involving the Copy and Paste options of the Edit menu. You are going to make a copy of the example.doc file. Windows 95 automatically names the new file "Copy of example.doc".

▶ **Click on the file example.doc or on its icon in the Exploring window.**

░ *Example.doc is highlighted.*

▶ **Click on the Edit menu and select the Copy option.**

░ *The document is temporarily stored in memory.*

▶ **Click on the Edit menu and select the Paste option.**

░ *The Copying message box appears (see Figure C.12), and the file is copied to the same file folder with the name "Copy of example.doc".*

## ▐ Renaming Files

What if a filename needs to be changed? The Explorer performs this operation through the Rename option of the File menu. You are going to change the Copy of example.doc filename to nextname.doc.

▶ **Click on Copy of example.doc if it is not already highlighted.**

░ *Highlights Copy of example.doc and its icon.*

**C.12**

Files can be copied from one disk to another, from one file folder to another, or within the same file folder.

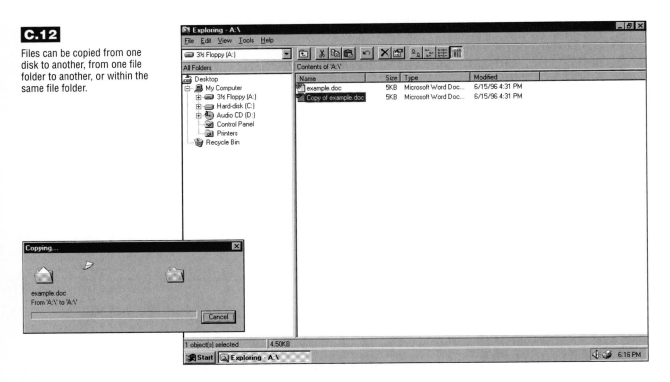

**C.13**

When renaming a file using the File menu Rename option, you just type over the old filename with the new name. Windows 95 allows filenames up to 250 characters, including spaces.

Cursor

▶ **Click on the File menu and select Rename.**

▓ *Places a box around Copy of example.doc with a flashing cursor on the right, as shown in Figure C.13.*

▶ **Type nextname.doc and press Enter.**

▓ *The filename changes to nextname.doc.*

## ▓ Deleting Files

At some time you will want to delete an unwanted file or files from disk. This task is easily accomplished by highlighting the files and pressing Delete or selecting the Delete option from the File menu. You will now delete the newly renamed file nextname.doc.

▶ **Click on nextname.doc if it is not already highlighted.**

▓ *Highlights nextname.doc.*

▶ **Press Delete.**

▓ *Displays the Confirm File Delete dialog box, as shown in Figure C.14.*

**C.14**

Before deleting a file, Windows 95 asks you to confirm that you want the file removed from disk.

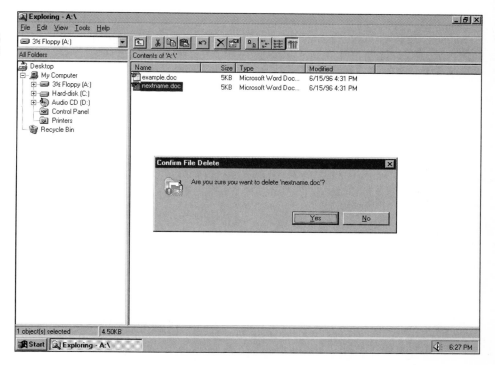

▶ **Click on Yes.**

▒ *Removes file.*

## ▒ Making File Folders

As you begin working with the computer, you will create documents using a variety of application software. Over time, these documents will need to be organized in some fashion—by subject, type of application package used, and so on. You will need to establish a filing system wherein related documents are placed within a designated disk directory on your disk.

A disk directory appears in the window as a ***file folder*** icon ▢. A folder can be found within another folder or may itself contain folders. When working with Windows 3.1 (Appendix B) or DOS (Appendix D) these file folders are called *subdirectories*. How applications and documents are organized within file folders is up to the user. There should be some logic to the grouping scheme, however, to make it easy to locate related applications and documents.

When a file folder is highlighted in the left pane of the Exploring window, the right pane displays a list of filenames, such as example.doc. These are the data files and programs stored in the highlighted file folder. To create new folders for organizing software and documents, you must make sure that you open the file folder or drive icon within which you want to put the new folder. You are going to create a new file folder called Projects. When naming a new file folder, you must follow the Windows 95 rules for filenames—that is, up to 250 characters in the filename.

▶ **Click on the drive A icon in the left pane of the Exploring window.**

▒ *The title bar and taskbar display "Exploring - A:\".*

When a disk is formatted, a *root directory* is created to catalog the filenames of data and programs stored on the disk. The notation A:\ is used to identify the root directory of the disk in drive A.

▶ **Click on the File menu and select New.**

▒ *Displays the New menu, as shown in Figure C.15.*

▶ **Click on the Folder option.**

▒ *Adds a new file folder to the Exploring window's right pane, as shown in Figure C.15.*

▶ **Type Projects and press Enter.**

▒ *Changes the file folder's name to Projects.*

## ▒ Displaying Two Directories

It is often helpful to display the contents of two file folders at the same time. Checking the dates on backup files or copying files to your backup disk are both situations in which displaying the original and backup is useful. Two terms, *source* and *target,* are often used to differentiate between a file's current location and where you want it to go.

**C.15**

File folders are added to a disk using the File menu New option and selecting Folder.

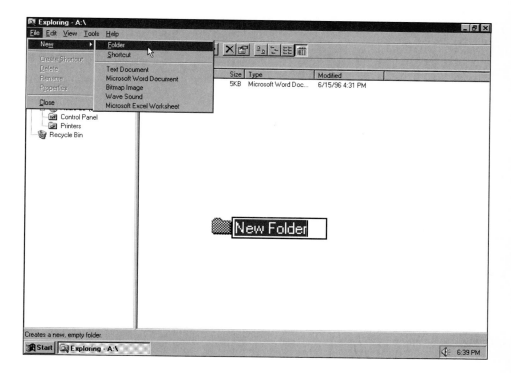

*Source* identifies a specific disk drive, filename, and its folder, whereas the *target* or *destination* refers to the file's new location. You are going to open another Exploring window and display the contents of the Projects subdirectory in it.

▶ **Click on the Start button, select the P̲rograms option, and choose Windows Explorer.**

       *Opens another Exploring window.*

▶ **Scroll the left pane up in the new Exploring window until you see the drive A icon.**

▶ **Click on the drive A icon.**

       *Displays the contents of the root directory, including example.doc and the Projects folder in the right pane.*

▶ **If a + appears in front of the drive A icon, click on it.**

       *Changes the + to a – and displays the Projects folder under the drive A icon, as shown in Figure C.16.*

The + next to a disk drive icon or file folder means that additional file folders and other icons are stored inside. Clicking on the + displays these options; clicking on the – removes them from the left pane display.

▶ **Click on the Projects folder in the left pane.**

       *Opens the Projects file folder. The right pane is empty because nothing has been saved or copied to Projects.*

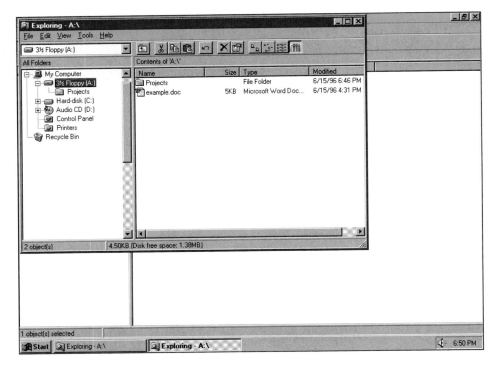

## Using the Right Mouse Button

Up until now, you have exclusively used the left mouse button to select options. However, clicking on the right mouse button displays a *shortcut menu*. The shortcut menu options will vary depending on the location of the screen pointer. Figure C.17 shows the shortcut menus associated with the taskbar, title bar, left pane, and right pane of the Exploring window.

The shortcut menu for the taskbar allows you to control how the open windows are displayed on-screen. Three arrangements are available: *Cascade*, *Tile Horizontally*, and *Tile Vertically*. The Cascade arrangement places all the windows in a stack in the order they appear on the taskbar. Clicking on a title bar brings that window on top of the stack. Only the active window can be used at this time.

▶ **Move the screen pointer over the taskbar (outside of any tasks, such as Exploring) and click the right mouse button.**

▓ *The shortcut menu opens.*

▶ **Click on Cascade.**

▓ *The open windows are arranged as a stack with Exploring - A:\Projects on top, as shown in Figure C.18.*

The Tile Vertically arrangement shows all the windows in reduced size, side by side. If Tile Horizontally is chosen, one window is on top of the other, as shown in Figure C.19. With tiling you can work in any of the visible windows at any time by clicking anywhere within the window to make it active.

**C.17**

Clicking the right mouse button opens a shortcut menu. The options available are determined by the location of the pointer.

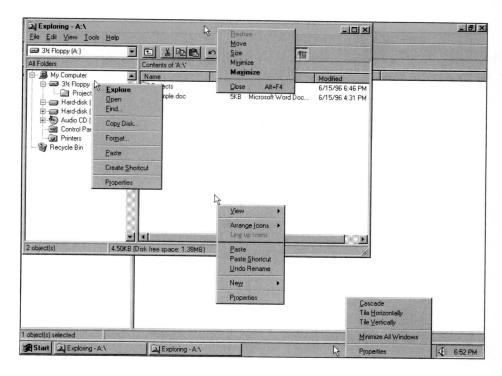

**C.18**

Cascaded windows are on top of each other with the active window in front. In this arrangement only the contents of the top window are visible.

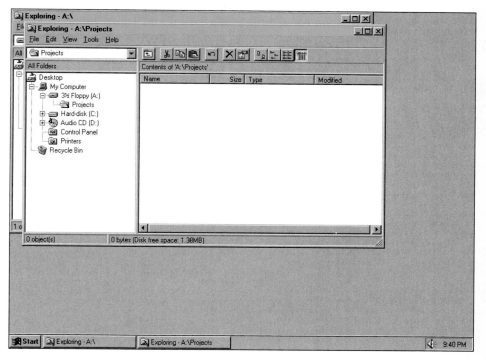

**C.19**

These windows are tiled horizontally.

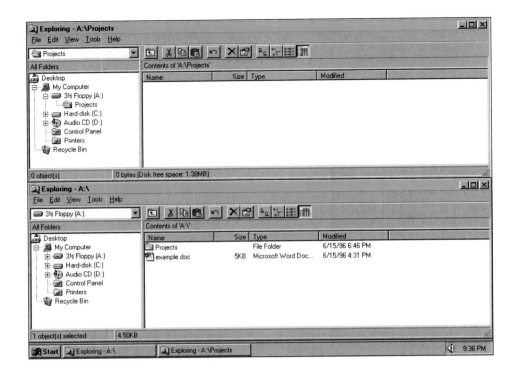

▶ **Move the screen pointer over the taskbar and click the right mouse button.**

▦ *The shortcut menu opens.*

▶ **Click on Tile Horizontal.**

▦ *The windows are arranged in tiles, one above the other, as shown in Figure C.19.*

▶ **Click on the example.doc file in the Exploring - A:\ window.**

▦ *The Exploring - A:\ window is made active, as indicated by the darkened menu bar, and example.doc highlighted.*

## ▦ Copying and Moving Files

When windows are tiled, files can be moved between folders or from one disk to another by dragging the file from one area to another. Files are copied if you hold down Ctrl while dragging the filename. When copying files, you will see the screen pointer change to include a plus sign (+), as shown in Figure C.20. This indicates that the file is being copied, not moved. Here you will copy example.doc from the root directory to the Projects folder. The newly copied file should appear in the contents area of the A:\Projects window.

▶ **While holding down ⌨Ctrl, drag example.doc to the empty right pane of the A:\Projects window.**

▦ *Displays the Copying message box while copying the file.*

**C.20**

Files can be copied (hold down Ctrl) or moved (hold down Alt) by dragging the filename from one window to another. The + next to the screen pointer in this figure means the file is being copied.

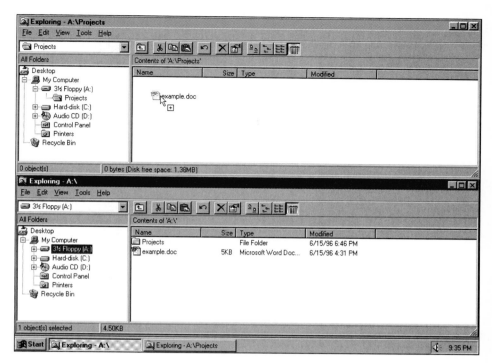

**NOTE:** *The pointer turns into a circle with a line through it ⊘ when dragged over areas in which files cannot be copied.*

This drag-and-drop approach to copying a file is quick and easy, and ensures you that both files have the same name. To change the name of the copy, you can use the Rename option in the File menu as described previously.

You just copied a file into the Projects file folder using the drag-and-drop technique. If the Alt key is used instead of the Ctrl key, Windows moves the file instead of copies it.

## ▇ Removing Folders from Disk

Proper disk management dictates the constant addition and removal of file folders as projects and software come into use or become inactive. Although the root directory cannot be removed, all other folders are fair game. Deleting a file folder deletes all the files and other file folders within it as well. File folders, like files, can be deleted by highlighting the associated icon and pressing Delete. An alternative is to highlight the icon and select the Delete option from the File menu. As with many Windows features, there are several ways to accomplish the same action.

▶ **Close the A:\Projects window.**

▇ *Only the Exploring - A:\ window remains open.*

▶ **Click on the Projects folder.**

▇ *Highlights folder.*

**C.21**

Deleting a file folder also deletes any files and file folders stored in it.

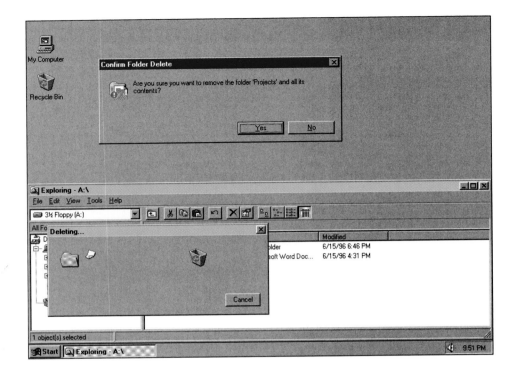

▶ **Click on the File menu and select Delete.**

  ▪ *Displays the Confirm Folder Delete dialog box, as shown in Figure C.21.*

▶ **Click on Yes.**

  ▪ *Displays the Deleting message box as it removes the Projects folder from drive A.*

## SYSTEM SHUTDOWN

When you are through for the day, the computer system needs to be shut down. One good rule of thumb is to never turn off a computer while an application program is still running. And always use the Start button's Shut Down option before turning off the computer and associated peripherals.

▶ **Click on the Start button and select Shut Down.**

  ▪ *Displays the Shut Down Windows dialog box, as shown in Figure C.22.*

▶ **Make sure the Shut down the computer? radio button is selected.**

▶ **Click on Yes.**

  ▪ *Displays the Windows 95 logo for a few seconds, then clears the screen and displays: "You can now safely turn off your computer".*

**C.22**

Always use the Start button menu's Shut Down option before turning off your computer.

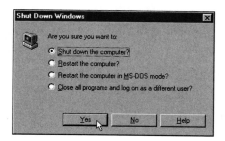

▶ **Remove the disk from drive A, return it to a protective cover, and store it in a safe place.**

▶ **Turn off the computer.**

▶ **Turn off the monitor if necessary.**

## SUMMARY

▪ Windows 95 is a graphical user interface that uses a desktop metaphor to represent different computer operations as icons.

▪ The Start button's Programs options list all the programs that are available to run on your computer.

▪ Drop-down menus are found in the menu bar.

▪ Icons and menus are selected on the desktop by moving the mouse to locate the screen pointer over the item. Clicking the mouse button activates the menu or associated program option.

▪ Icons and windows are repositioned on the desktop by using the mouse to drag them to a new location.

▪ New unformatted diskettes are automatically formatted the first time they are used by Windows 95.

▪ Windows are identified by the name in the title bar.

▪ The dimensions of a window are altered by dragging the window frame or by clicking on the enlarge (maximize) and reduce (minimize) buttons.

▪ Clicking on the scroll arrows and dragging the scroll box changes a window's view.

▪ Clicking on the close button removes a window from the screen and taskbar.

▪ Application programs, data files, and documents are organized into different file folders.

- New file folders can be created, renamed, and deleted at any time.

- Files are moved from one file folder to another by dragging the associated icon over the other folder. Files are copied from one disk to another in the same way.

- The Windows Explorer provides menus that help the user create new folders, rename files, delete files, and remove folders.

- The contents of more than one file folder can be shown at the same time by displaying each folder in a different Exploring window.

- All the programs and files in a file folder are deleted when the file folder they are in is deleted.

- Always use the Start button's Shut Down option before turning off your computer.

## TERMS TO REMEMBER

| | | |
|---|---|---|
| cascade | menu bar | Start button |
| click | My Computer | taskbar |
| close button | reduce button | tile horizontally |
| desktop | restore button | tile vertically |
| double-click | scroll arrow | title bar |
| drag | scroll bar | Windows 95 |
| enlarge button | scroll box | Windows Explorer |
| file folder | shortcut menu | WordPad |

## MIX AND MATCH

*Complete the following definition with the Terms to Remember.*

1. A(n) _____ is found at either end of a scroll bar.

2. Stacking windows on top of each other in order of appearance on the taskbar is known as _____ .

3. The _____ runs across the top of a window and displays menu names.

4. The _____ runs across the top of a window and displays the window's name.

5. Clicking on the _____ provides a menu of programs that can be run.

6. Clicking on the _____ removes a window from screen.

7. Clicking on the _____ returns an enlarged window to its original dimensions.

8. Pressing the mouse button twice in rapid succession is called _____.

9. Clicking on the _____ expands the related window to fill the screen.

10. Repositioning an icon or window on-screen using the mouse is called _____.

11. The square within a scroll bar is called a(n) _____.

## REVIEW QUESTIONS

1. Define the Terms to Remember.

2. What is the first screen you use when running Windows 95?

3. How do you move an icon around the desktop?

4. Describe how an option is selected from a drop-down menu.

5. Why are some menu options dimmed?

6. Describe three ways to alter the size of a window.

7. How do you close a window?

8. Identify two ways a run a computer program using Windows 95.

9. What is the difference between using the File menu Save and Save As options?

10. Identify the rules for acceptable Windows 95 filenames.

11. What happens when you try to use an unformatted disk?

12. What happens when you click the right mouse button?

13. Explain how you would use Windows to display the contents of two different file folders at the same time.

14. What are two different procedures for copying a file?

15. How do you rename a file using Windows 95?

16. How are new file folders added to a disk?

17. How are Ctrl and Alt used when dragging a file from one window to another?

18. What are two different ways to use Windows to delete files from disk?

19. What happens when you delete a file folder?

20. How do you exit Windows 95?

## APPLYING WHAT YOU'VE LEARNED

1. A file can also be deleted from disk by dragging it over the Recycle Bin. Use the Windows 95 Help menu to find out how you can "undelete" files deleted in this way.

2. Use the Windows 95 Help menu to find the Windows Explorer feature that allows you to protect a file from accidental erasure. (*Hint:* These files are said to be read-only.)

3. Use Windows Explorer to display filenames in order by creation date. How would you display files in order by their size? Which presentation format do you prefer? Explain your answer.

4. A general rule for file management is to make one file folder for related documents and another file folder for each application package. For example, users are encouraged to create one folder for their word processing program and other folders for letters, reports, and so forth. Graphically illustrate how you would organize file folders on a hard disk. Assume you are using at least three different application packages.

5. If your computer system uses a color monitor, how would you change the color of the desktop? How would you change the title bar color? What colors should not be used for the desktop? Explain your answer.

# Introduction to MS-DOS/PC-DOS

**B**efore you start to use personal productivity software or learn to program, you need to review operating procedures for IBM and other Intel-based personal computers. The following DOS tutorial provides a brief overview of some important PC operating system commands. You use these instructions to prepare new disks to store data, to locate files and programs on disk, and to back up important disk resources. A data diskette and access to a personal computer are required to complete this tutorial. Pay close attention to instructions or data you should enter into the computer using the keyboard. They are preceded by a ▶.

## PERSONAL COMPUTER START-UP PROCEDURES

IBM and other Intel-based personal computers use a *disk operating system (DOS)* developed by the Microsoft Corporation. Called **MS-DOS**, it is the most commonly used operating system in the world. Licensed and distributed by IBM Corporation as **PC-DOS**, this operating system has evolved through many revisions up to version 6.0 and beyond.

### ■ System Orientation

*Booting* describes the procedure for starting up a computer system. IBM and Intel-based computers automatically look for and load a command program, named COMMAND.COM, from the system disk with the operating system; COMMAND.COM is placed into memory as a part of the booting process and remains there until the computer is turned off.

Because a disk with DOS must be in a designated disk drive when booting a microcomputer, associated procedures will vary. If this is your first time, consult the user's manual or ask the teacher or lab assistant for help. To complete this tutorial, carefully follow the actions associated with each ▷ symbol below.

▷ **Turn on your computer, screen, and printer if necessary.**

▨ *Displays capital letter, colon, and > symbol.*

If your computer system follows the standard booting steps, the computer displays the current date and time and gives you a chance to change them. Many computer systems are customized to display menus, launch a GUI, or describe procedures or copyright infringement policies. You will need to familiarize yourself with the procedures used by your personal computer.

## ▨ DOS Prompt

After the booting process is complete, the system usually displays the letter associated with the default disk drive, followed by a > symbol. The *default disk drive* is the drive DOS assumes the user wants to use. For example, microcomputers using drive A (see Figure D.1) as the default drive display A> or A:\>. Hard disk systems defaulting to drive C (see Figure D.1) display C> or C:\>. This display is known as the *DOS prompt*. It tells the user that DOS is ready for instructions. In addition, the DOS prompt identifies the default drive.

**D.1**

Depending on the location of the DOS on disk, different procedures are used to start up (boot) a personal computer. The appearance of the DOS prompt means the computer system is ready to accept DOS commands.

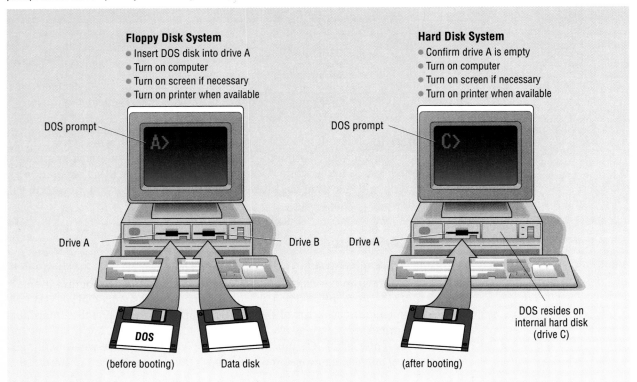

**Floppy Disk System**
- Insert DOS disk into drive A
- Turn on computer
- Turn on screen if necessary
- Turn on printer when available

**Hard Disk System**
- Confirm drive A is empty
- Turn on computer
- Turn on screen if necessary
- Turn on printer when available

DOS prompt — A>

Drive A    Drive B    Drive A

DOS prompt — C>

DOS resides on internal hard disk (drive C)

DOS (before booting)    Data disk    (after booting)

## DOS COMMANDS AND UTILITY PROGRAMS

What follows is an introduction to some of the most important instructions DOS uses. Each DOS instruction, such as COPY or FORMAT, is entered after the DOS prompt, using a similar word order, or syntax: first the DOS instruction, a space, and then a list of the file or program names and the disk drive on which they are found. The designated drive and filename become one word, for example, A:\EXAMPLE.TXT. A colon always follows the drive letter, A: in this example. The \ (backslash) indicates that the file is located on the primary or root disk directory. A period separates the filename, EXAMPLE, from the filename extension, TXT.

Lists of filenames are separated by a space. Acceptable file or program names use any combination of letters or numbers up to eight characters. You can type in either upper- or lowercase letters. Filenames cannot include spaces. If necessary, use a hyphen instead of a space, as in LAB-1. The DOS user's manual lists other acceptable characters. A three-character filename extension is permissible if it follows a period, for instance, ANNUAL.RPT would be allowed.

DOS instructions are either internal commands or external utility programs. Internal *commands* are performed by the COMMAND.COM program that is loaded into memory during booting. These operations can be performed at any time. External *utility programs* must be loaded from disk before being executed. These utility programs are found on one or two DOS disks that are purchased with the computer hardware.

Floppy disk users must be sure the appropriate DOS disk is in the default drive before executing a DOS instruction that relies on an external utility program. When DOS cannot find a utility program, it displays "Bad command or filename". Hard disk systems and computers within a LAN should be configured to access utility programs at any time.

### Formatting a New (or Old) Disk

Only new disks need to be formatted, and many new disks are preformatted when purchased. If you have a preformatted data disk, you can skip this section and continue with the next section on changing the default drive.

Formatting a new disk requires the *FORMAT* utility program. Systems without hard disks that boot using a floppy disk must have the DOS disk in drive A, as shown in Figure D.1. Your computer can't load and execute the external FORMAT utility program if it can't find it. If your computer has both a hard disk drive and dual floppy disk drives of the same size, follow instructions for single-floppy-disk systems.

▶ *Single floppy disk drive:* **Place new floppy disk in drive A.**

▶ *Dual floppy disk drives:* **Place the DOS disk in drive A and a new floppy disk in drive B.**

▶ **If necessary, close the drive door(s) to secure the floppy disk(s).**

To format a new disk, enter FORMAT after the DOS prompt, press the spacebar, and type the drive designation for the target drive, followed immediately by a colon. Press the spacebar again and enter /V. Now press the Enter key. The computer will walk you through formatting a new disk by displaying a series of prompts. If the following prompts do not appear, check the Error Correction Checklist in Figure D.2 and try again.

**D.2**

Things to check when a DOS instruction does not work.

## Error Correction Checklist

If a DOS message indicates that an instruction has not been executed properly, check the following:

- Disk(s) is (are) properly positioned in the drive, not upside down or backward.
- Disk drive door(s) is (are) closed.
- The DOS instruction and all filenames are followed by a space.
- There are no spaces between the drive letter, colons, search path, and filenames in the DOS instruction; for example,

  **A:\PROJECTS\EXAMPLE.TXT**

  is correct.

Note that although uppercase characters are shown here, you can input DOS commands in both upper- and lowercase characters.

▶ ***Drive A users:*** Type **FORMAT A: /V** [Enter].

***Drive B users:*** Type **FORMAT B: /V** [Enter].

```
Insert new diskette for drive ?: and strike ENTER when ready
```

***NOTE:*** *If the error message "Bad command or filename" appears instead, enter* ***cd****, press* [Enter]*, and try again. If the error message persists, ask your instructor for help.*

▶ **Press** [Enter].

```
Percent formatted                          Different displays are possible.
Formatting . . . Format Complete           This message may vary.
Volume label (11 characters, Enter for none)?
```

▶ **Type *your last name*** [Enter].

```
1,457,664 bytes total disk space           These numbers will vary,
1,457,664 bytes available on disk          depending on the type of disk used.
Format another(Y/N)?
```

▶ **Type N and press** [Enter]**. If you have another disk to format, type Y and press** [Enter]**.**

The critical information is displayed by DOS after you have entered your name. The number of bytes (characters) of total disk space should equal the bytes available on disk, as shown in Figure D.3. If not, the system displays a third line, which lists the number of bytes in bad sectors.

**D.3**

DOS display when formatting a high-capacity 3.5-inch diskette.

```
C>format a: /v
Insert new diskette for drive A:
and press ENTER when ready...

Checking existing disk format.
Verifying 1.44M
Format complete.

Volume label (11 characters, ENTER for none)? yourname

    1,457,664 bytes total disk space
    1,457,664 bytes available on disk

        512 bytes in each allocation unit.
      2,847 allocation units available on disk.

Volume Serial Number is 2317-14D8

Format another (Y/N)?n


C>
```

> **NOTE:** *When bad sectors appear, don't panic. Take the disk out of the drive and put it back in. Then try to format the disk again. Most often the disk will format without problems on a second or third try. If the bad sectors persist after three attempts, return the disk to the store from which it was purchased and exchange it for another disk.*

DOS provides PC users alternatives within each instruction. The /V that was part of the FORMAT instruction you just entered is an example of an optional parameter *(switch)*. Use of these switches is not mandatory; they do, however, allow the user a greater level of control over DOS activities.

When used with the FORMAT instruction, the /V, or "volume" switch, prompts DOS to ask for an 11-character *volume label* (an internal label), which is stored as part of the disk directory. You entered your last name as the volume label. DOS versions 4.0 and higher automatically ask for a volume label, which eliminates the need to use this switch.

Several switches are available and described in detail in the DOS user's manual. Later we will outline two switches used by the directory (DIR) command. These optional parameters are identified by a slash (/) and follow the DOS instruction after the drive designations. We have found that DOS provides more descriptive error messages when you include a blank space in front of each switch. Do not confuse the slash (/) that designates a switch and the backslash (\) that identifies the root directory.

### ■ Changing the Default Drive

The default disk drive is the drive DOS uses when no disk drive letter is included in an instruction. To change the default drive, enter the letter of the drive you wish to become the new default drive, and immediately follow it with a colon (:). Then press Enter (see Figure D.4). Many computer systems require that a formatted disk be in the new default drive before you change to it.

**D.4**

Changing the system's default disk drive.

```
C>a:

A>
```

▷ **Data disk in drive A:** Type **A:**[Enter].

　▨ *DOS prompt changes to A>.*

▷ **Data disk in drive B:** Type **B:**[Enter].

　▨ *DOS prompt changes to B>.*

> **NOTE:** *If you do not have the data disk in the drive, DOS displays the message: "Not ready error reading drive ?" No harm is done. Insert a disk and press **R** for retry. When the disk drive is unavailable, DOS displays: "Invalid drive specification". This message informs the user that DOS was unable to accomplish a task as instructed. DOS messages usually occur with spelling errors or incomplete instructions. When an error occurs, review the message, identify the mistake, and try again.*

## ▨ Creating Copies of Files

The internal *COPY* command is one of the most versatile DOS instructions. It lets you create new data files or back up important files by transferring a duplicate to another disk. You create a new file by copying data from the keyboard to a disk location. DOS recognizes the reserved word *CON* (for console) as input from the keyboard, as shown in Figure D.5. A *reserved word* is a special combination of characters that reference designated hardware or system attributes. Besides CON, *PRN* (printer), *LPT1* (parallel port 1), and *COM1* (serial port 1) are examples of DOS reserved words. Reserved words cannot be used as filenames.

**D.5**

This COPY command uses the reserved word *CON* to create a new file using keyboard input.

```
A>copy con example.txt
your name
computer course number
today's date

^Z
        1 file(s) copied

A>
```

▶ Type **COPY CON EXAMPLE.TXT** Enter.

▧ *The cursor moves to the beginning of the next line.*

▶ Type *your name* Enter.

*computer course number* Enter.

*today's date* Enter.

▧ *Displays data on-screen.*

▶ Hold down Ctrl and press **Z**.

▧ *Displays ^Z.*

▶ Press Enter.

▧ `1 file(s) copied`

> *NOTE: If a file with the same name already exists on the disk, DOS will ask if the new file should overwrite the old file. Type **Y** to replace the old copy with the new and **N** to do nothing.*

You have just created the file EXAMPLE.TXT on the default disk. The COPY command can also make a duplicate of this file. What follows is the COPY command that gives the duplicate the filename NEWCOPY.LAB. A new name is necessary because every file in the same directory must have a unique name.

Two terms, *source* and *target,* are often used to differentiate between a file's current location and where you want it to go. The *source* identifies a specific filename and the drive containing the storage media on which it is stored. The *target* refers to the file's new location and, if specified, new filename. Reserved words, such as *CON,* can also be a source whereas others, like *PRN,* can serve as a target. The COPY command shown in Figure D.6 uses the file EXAMPLE.TXT as the source and the file NEWCOPY.LAB on the default drive as the target.

▧ *Displays DOS prompt.*

▶ Type **COPY EXAMPLE.TXT NEWCOPY.LAB** Enter.

▧ `1 file(s) copied`

**D.6**

Copying EXAMPLE.TXT and changing the name of the duplicate file to NEWCOPY.LAB.

```
A>copy example.txt newcopy.lab
        1 file(s) copied

A>
```

DOS allows several alternatives when using the COPY command. For example, changing NEWCOPY.LAB to C:\NEWCOPY.LAB copies the file to the root directory in drive C. If the filename is not included after the target drive when copying to another disk, DOS will use the original filename for the duplicate. Therefore, the command COPY EXAMPLE.TXT C:\ will create a duplicate file called EXAMPLE.TXT on the root directory of the disk in drive C.

## Displaying the Disk Directory

A disk's **root directory** is created during formatting. The directory, along with a *file allocation table (FAT)*, is used by DOS to locate data files and programs on a specific disk. The *DIR* instruction, an internal command, lists these files and programs on the screen. If a disk drive is not specified after DIR, DOS will display the directory of the disk in the default drive.

▶ **Type DIR** [Enter].

   ▪ *Displays the disk directory in the default drive.*

   *NOTE: If you forget to close the drive door, DOS will display this message:*
   ```
   Not ready error reading drive ?
   Abort, Retry, Fail?
   ```

   *Older versions of DOS display:*
   ```
   Not ready error reading drive ?
   Abort, Retry, Ignore?
   ```

These messages will also appear if the disk is unformatted or when no disk is present in the disk drive. In any case, make sure a formatted disk is in the drive, close the door, and press **R** for retry. If the message persists, press **A** for abort. Remove the disk and try another disk in its place.

To look at the directory of another disk, follow DIR with a space, the disk drive letter, and a colon. For example, DIR C: displays the disk directory in drive C. Because the list of files in a directory can be rather long, there are two switches that will help you keep the contents of the directory from scrolling off the screen.

**/P** The "page" switch forces DOS to stop when the directory listing fills the screen. The message, "Strike any key when ready . . ." allows you to continue displaying the remaining portions of the directory.

**/W** The "wide" switch forces DOS to eliminate the size, date, and time from the directory display. Five filenames and extensions appear on each line to compress the directory listing.

These switches can be used in combination when a directory in the wide mode scrolls off-screen.

▶ **Type DIR /W** [Enter].

   ▪ *Displays the files currently on disk in a wide format (see Figure D.7).*

**D.7**

DOS display of drive A directory using "wide" switch before renaming NEWCOPY.LAB to NEXTNAME.LAB.

```
A>dir /w

 Volume in drive A is YOURNAME
 Volume Serial Number is 2317-14D8
 Directory of A:\

EXAMPLE.TXT     NEWCOPY.LAB
        2 file(s)                126 bytes
        0 dir(s)          1,456,640 bytes free

A>ren newcopy.lab nextname.lab

A>dir

 Volume in drive A is YOURNAME
 Volume Serial Number is 2317-14D8
 Directory of A:\

EXAMPLE  TXT         63  05-19-96   1:23p
NEXTNAME LAB         63  05-19-96   1:23p
        2 file(s)                126 bytes
        0 dir(s)          1,456,640 bytes free

A>
```

## Renaming Files

What if a filename needs to be changed? The *RENAME* command performs this operation simply by entering the command and old filename, followed by the new filename. You have the option of using the abbreviation *REN* instead of RENAME. The drive designation, if used, precedes only the old filename. In other words, it is incorrect to use a drive designation before the new filename.

▶ Type **REN NEWCOPY.LAB NEXTNAME.LAB** (Enter).

    ▫ *Displays the DOS prompt.*

▶ Type **DIR** (Enter).

    ▫ *Displays every filename on the disk.*

Take a look at the disk directory displayed on-screen and in Figure D.7. The filename NEXTNAME.LAB should have replaced NEWCOPY.LAB in the display.

## Deleting Files

The *DEL* and *ERASE* instructions perform the same function. Both instructions are used to remove files from the disk directory. When doing so, you must identify a file by its name, extension, and disk location (if it is not in the default disk drive).

▶ Type **DEL NEXTNAME.LAB** (Enter).

    ▫ *Displays the DOS prompt.*

**D.8**

Deleting NEXTNAME.LAB from the root directory in drive A. DOS versions 5.0 or higher also allow users to undelete files erased from disk using the DEL or ERASE commands.

```
A>del nextname.lab

A>ver

MS-DOS 6.22

A>undelete nextname.lab
```

```
UNDELETE - A delete protection facility
Copyright (C) 1987-1993 Central Point Software, Inc.
All rights reserved.

Directory: A:\
File Specifications: NEXTNAME.LAB

    Delete Sentry control file not found.

    Deletion-tracking file not found.

    MS-DOS directory contains    1 deleted files.
    Of those,    1 files may be recovered.

Using the MS-DOS directory method.

    ?EXTNAME LAB        63  5-19-96  1:23p  ...A  Undelete (Y/N)?y
    Please type the first character for ?EXTNAME.LAB: n

File successfully undeleted.


A>
```

The file NEXTNAME.LAB is deleted from the disk directory (see Figure D.8). Unlike with the COPY command, DOS does not provide a message that reports the file is deleted. As shown in Figure D.13, DOS just displays another prompt after deleting the designated file. Once it is erased, it cannot be recovered by any DOS version before 5.0. However, commercial software is available that can restore deleted files if the problem is identified before any new files are added to the disk.

### Undeleting Files

If you are using DOS version 5.0 or higher, you can use the *UNDELETE* command to recover files deleted with DEL or ERASE. These commands do not actually remove the file from disk. Instead, a ? symbol replaces the first character in the filename stored in the disk directory. When DOS sees this symbol in the filename, it is programmed to use the related disk space as needed.

To determine whether you can use the UNDELETE command, you need to know what version of DOS the computer is using. The *VER* command displays the DOS version number currently running on the computer.

▶ **Type VER** [Enter].

▪ **MS-DOS version 5.00**       *DOS name and version number will vary.*

If you are not using version 5.0 or higher, skip to the next section on making subdirectories.

When using the UNDELETE command, you restore the file by replacing the ? symbol in the filename with the original character, as shown in Figure D.8.

▶ **Type UNDELETE NEXTNAME.LAB** [Enter].

▪ ```
Directory: ?:\
File Specifications: NEXTNAME.LAB
Delete Sentry control file not found.      May not appear.
Deletion-tracking file not found           May not appear.
MS-DOS directory contains 1 deleted files.
Of those, 1 files may be recovered.
Using the MS-DOS directory method.
?EXTNAME LAB   63   5-19-96   3:52p  ...A Undelete (Y/N)?
```

▶ **Type Y.**

▪ **Please type the first character for ?EXTNAME.LAB:**

▶ **Type N.**

▪ **File successfully undeleted.**

## ▪ Making Subdirectories

When a disk is formatted, a root directory is created to catalog the filenames of data and programs stored on the disk. The DOS *MKDIR* command, or its abbreviation *MD*, makes new directories, called **subdirectories**. New subdirectories are attached to the root directory or other subdirectories, as shown in Figure D.9. The root directory and subdirectories appear as file folders when graphical user interfaces are used with DOS (see Appendix B and Appendix C).

Subdirectories work like electronic file folders in organizing programs and data according to common attributes. As illustrated in Figure D.9, a well-organized hard disk has a DOS subdirectory for storing DOS utility programs, other subdirectories for application packages, and separate subdirectories for related data.

Each subdirectory is given its own name when created. Names given to subdirectories must follow the DOS rules for naming files and programs. When making a new subdirectory, the user must identify to DOS how the subdirectory relates to the root directory. This description is called the **search path**. In Figure D.9 the GARDEN subdirectory is subordinate to the PROJECTS subdirectory. In turn, PROJECTS is subordinate to the root directory. The notation A:\ identifies a search path to drive A's root directory. The notation A:\ PROJECTS identifies a search path to the PROJECTS
```

**D.9**

New subdirectories are appended to the root directory. Additional subdirectories can be subordinate to those attached to the root.

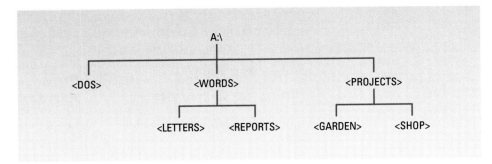

subdirectory. DIR A:\PROJECTS\GARDEN displays the contents of the GARDEN subdirectory found in PROJECTS.

Now create a new subdirectory, called PROJECTS, on the default disk, using the MD command.

▶ Type **MD PROJECTS** Enter.

▨ *Displays another DOS prompt.*

To verify that the PROJECTS subdirectory has been appended to the default directory, display the root directory in the default drive.

▶ Type **DIR** Enter.

▨ *Displays the disk's root directory.*

Somewhere within the directory you should find PROJECTS <DIR> . As you can see on your screen and in Figure D.10, subdirectories are listed in the disk directory to

**D.10**

Making the new subdirectory, PROJECTS, subordinate to the default disk's root directory.

```
A>md \projects

A>dir

 Volume in drive A is YOURNAME
 Volume Serial Number is 2317-14D8
 Directory of A:\

EXAMPLE  TXT          63  05-19-96   1:23p
NEXTNAME LAB          63  05-19-96   1:23p
PROJECTS      <DIR>       05-19-96   1:32p
        2 file(s)         126 bytes
        1 dir(s)     1,456,128 bytes free

A>
```

which they are subordinate (appended). A <DIR> indicator appears to the right of the subdirectory name to identify the entry as a subdirectory.

> **NOTE:** *If you are using an older version of DOS and were unable to undelete NEXTNAME.LAB, this file will be absent from the list of filenames.*

### ■ Changing from One Subdirectory to Another

The *CHDIR* or *CD* command activates different directories. This adds a new wrinkle to the status of the default drive. Until now the root directory has always been the ***active directory***. When DOS defaulted to a disk drive, the root directory was used. The change directory command now lets users change the active directory. To activate another directory, such as the PROJECTS subdirectory, precede the desired subdirectory name with CD, a space, and the search path.

▶ Type **CD \PROJECTS** Enter.

　▨ *Displays another DOS prompt.*

▶ Type **DIR** Enter.

　▨ *Displays the PROJECTS subdirectory.*

A new subdirectory contains a least two file references. They are shown in the directory on your screen as .<DIR> and ..<DIR> (see Figure D.11). These entries reference the current subdirectory (.) and the directory to which it is appended (..), in this case, the root directory. These references can be used with DOS commands. For example, DEL. erases all files in the active directory. CD.. is a valid reference to the root directory when PROJECTS is the active directory. CD \ always returns the user to the root directory on the default disk.

### ■ Customizing the DOS Prompt

The DOS prompt displays the active directory when you customize it using the *PROMPT* command. Special codes like $P (path), $D (date), $T (time), and $G (> symbol) indicate which data is included in the prompt. Entering the PROMPT command by itself returns the screen prompt back to its original format, as shown in Figure D.11.

▶ Type **PROMPT TODAY IS $D$G** Enter.

　▨ *Displays the DOS prompt with today's date.*

▶ Type **PROMPT** Enter.

　▨ *Returns the DOS prompt back to its original format.*

▶ Type **PROMPT $P$G** Enter.

　▨ *Displays the DOS prompt with the path to the active directory.*

Changing the directory to PROJECTS makes it the active directory in the default drive. You can customize the DOS prompt to include the active path and subdirectory name as well as the default disk drive by using the PROMPT command.

```
A>cd \projects

A>dir

 Volume in drive A is YOURNAME
 Volume Serial Number is 2317-14D8
 Directory of A:\PROJECTS

 .            <DIR>         05-19-96   1:32p
 ..           <DIR>         05-19-96   1:32p
        0 file(s)                  0 bytes
        2 dir(s)          1,456,128 bytes free

A>prompt Today is $d$g

Today is Sun 05-19-1996>prompt

A>prompt $p$g

A:\PROJECTS>
```

## Copying Files to a Subdirectory

You do not have to change to a subdirectory to copy or delete files from it. In this case, you will copy the file EXAMPLE.TXT from the root directory to the PROJECTS subdirectory and change its name to UPDATE.LAB (see Figure D.12).

The COPY command can duplicate designated files on any disk or subdirectory so long as a path to the target drive and directory precedes the filename.

```
A:\PROJECTS>copy \example.txt \projects\update.lab
        1 file(s) copied

A:\PROJECTS>dir

 Volume in drive A is YOURNAME
 Volume Serial Number is 2317-14D8
 Directory of A:\PROJECTS

 .            <DIR>         05-19-96   1:32p
 ..           <DIR>         05-19-96   1:32p
 UPDATE   LAB          63  05-19-96   1:23p
        1 file(s)                 63 bytes
        2 dir(s)          1,455,616 bytes free

A:\PROJECTS>
```

▶ Type **COPY \EXAMPLE.TXT \PROJECTS\UPDATE.LAB** `Enter`.

▦ `1 file(s) copied`

▶ Type **DIR** `Enter`.

▦ *Displays the PROJECTS subdirectory with UPDATE.LAB.*

## ▦ Removing Subdirectories from Disk

Proper disk management dictates the constant addition and removal of subdirectories as projects and software come into use or become inactive. The *RMDIR* or *RD* command removes a subdirectory from the disk's hierarchy of directories. You enter either command and follow it with the search path and subdirectory name. Although the root directory cannot be removed, all other directories are fair game.

A subdirectory must be empty except for the . and .. entries before removing it. This means all files and subordinate subdirectories must first be deleted or removed. Therefore, UPDATE.LAB must be deleted before the PROJECTS subdirectory is removed. Furthermore, you cannot remove an active subdirectory. As a result, you must delete UPDATE.LAB from the PROJECTS subdirectory and use the CD command to change back to the root directory.

▶ Type **DEL UPDATE.LAB** `Enter`.

▦ *Displays another DOS prompt.*

▶ Type **CD \** `Enter`.

▦ *Displays the DOS prompt with the root directory backslash.*

▶ Type **DIR** `Enter`.

▦ *Displays the root directory (note the reference to the PROJECTS subdirectory in Figure D.13).*

▶ Type **RD \PROJECTS** `Enter`.

▦ *Displays another DOS prompt.*

▶ Type **DIR** `Enter`.

▦ *Displays the root directory (note removal of the PROJECTS subdirectory, as shown in Figure D.13).*

**NOTE:** *If you cannot remove a subdirectory that appears to be empty and devoid of subordinate directories, check to make sure the subdirectory you are removing is not the active directory. When this is not the problem, there is a possibility that hidden files created by some software packages may exist in the subdirectory.* **Hidden files** *are not displayed with the DIR command. If hidden files exist on a subdirectory, your best alternative is to use commercially available utility programs that are designed to delete this type of file.*

**D.13**

The RD command removed PROJECTS from the hierarchy of drive A subdirectories.

```
A:\PROJECTS>del update.lab

A:\PROJECTS>cd \

A:\>dir

 Volume in drive A is YOURNAME
 Volume Serial Number is 2317-14D8
 Directory of A:\

EXAMPLE  TXT           63  05-19-96  1:23p
NEXTNAME LAB           63  05-19-96  1:23p
PROJECTS      <DIR>        05-19-96  1:32p
         2 file(s)           126 bytes
         1 dir(s)     1,456,128 bytes free
```

```
A:\>rd \projects

A:\>dir

 Volume in drive A is YOURNAME
 Volume Serial Number is 2317-14D8
 Directory of A:\

EXAMPLE  TXT           63  05-19-96  1:23p
NEXTNAME LAB           63  05-19-96  1:23p
         2 file(s)           126 bytes
         0 dir(s)     1,456,640 bytes free

A:\>
```

## Displaying Text Files

The DOS *TYPE* command displays the contents of a file on-screen. You will find it is practical to use the internal TYPE command only when displaying text files stored in an ASCII (American Standard Code of Information Interchange) format. Figure D.14 illustrates how the contents of EXAMPLE.TXT can be displayed using the TYPE command. However, programs and data files not stored in an ASCII format will appear as gibberish.

▶ Type **TYPE EXAMPLE.TXT** Enter.

  *Displays your name, computer course number, date, and time.*

**D.14**

Files saved on disk using ASCII format can be displayed using the DOS TYPE command.

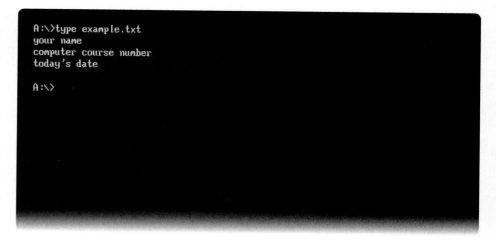

```
A:\>type example.txt
your name
computer course number
today's date

A:\>
```

### ▨ Printing the Screen

If a printer is connected directly to your computer, you can use the Print Screen or PrcSc key to print the screen's contents. If you are not connected to a printer, skip to the next section on system shutdown.

Printing the screen can be helpful in documenting computer errors. When you encounter an error message or situation you cannot handle, turn on the printer and press the Print Screen (PrtSc) key. The resulting output can be useful when describing the problem to others.

▷ **Make sure the printer is ready.**

▷ **Press** Print Screen **(or** Prt Sc**).**

▨ *The screen's contents are output to the printer.*

## SYSTEM SHUTDOWN

When you are through for the day, the computer system needs to be shut down. People with their own computers at work usually leave them on during the day and turn them off before going home. Those sharing a computer with others usually shut down the computer when they have completed an assignment. As a result, others know the computer is not being used when they find it turned off.

▷ **Remove any floppy disks from their drives, return them to their protective covers, and store them in a safe place.**

▷ **Turn off the computer.**

▷ **Turn off the printer if necessary.**

▷ **Turn off the monitor if necessary.**

## SUMMARY

- IBM and other Intel-based personal computers use MS-DOS or PC-DOS to control internal operations and manage system resources.

- A DOS disk must be available to the computer system before it is booted.

- DOS commands are stored in the computer's memory while it's running and can be executed from the DOS prompt at any time.

- DOS utilities are stored on disk and must be available before the utility is run. FORMAT is an example of a disk utility.

- Formatting a disk prepares it for use on a computer system by creating tracks, sectors, and a root directory.

- Entering a disk drive letter, a colon, and pressing Enter makes the designated drive the new default drive.

- The COPY command duplicates the contents of a data file or program on a new disk or subdirectory. A new filename can be assigned to the duplicate.

- A list of data files and programs stored on a disk is displayed using the DIR command.

- Filenames are changed using the RENAME command; REN is an acceptable abbreviation.

- The ERASE and DEL commands remove a data or program file from the disk directory. In some cases, the UNDELETE command can restore the file.

- Users can determine which version of DOS their computer is using by issuing the VER command.

- New directories are placed on a disk with the MD or MKDIR command. These subdirectories can be placed in the root directory or other subdirectories.

- The CD or CHDIR command changes the active disk directory used by DOS.

- Users customize the DOS prompt with the PROMPT command by adding the date, time, or active directory.

- Before a subdirectory is removed from a disk with the RD or RMDIR command, all files and subordinate directories currently stored within it must be removed.

- Pressing either Print Screen or Shift + PrtSc prints a copy of the screen display on the attached printer.

## TERMS TO REMEMBER

active directory
command
default disk drive
DOS prompt
hidden file

MS-DOS
PC-DOS
reserved word
root directory
search path

subdirectory
switch
utility program
volume label

## MIX AND MATCH

*Complete the following definitions with the Terms to Remember.*

1. The disk operating system developed by the Microsoft Corporation for personal computer systems is called _____.

2. The _____ is created when the disk is formatted.

3. One of the system programs stored on a DOS disk is a(n) _____.

4. The _____ is the screen display of the greater-than sign and the letter associated with the default disk drive.

5. A DOS instruction that can be executed at any time is called a(n) _____.

6. The command-driven operating system IBM used to distribute with its line of personal computers is called _____.

7. The _____ is a description of a subdirectory or file location on disk with respect to the disk's root directory.

8. The directory that DOS uses as a default is the _____.

9. A directory added to the root directory is called a(n) _____.

10. When no disk drive designation is included in an instruction, DOS uses the _____.

## REVIEW QUESTIONS

1. Define the Terms to Remember.

2. How do you boot an IBM or compatible personal computer?

3. Identify the rules for acceptable DOS filenames.

4. What situation must exist before a DOS utility program can be used?

5. How do you format a new disk?

6. What procedure is used to change the system's default disk drive?

7. What is the DOS syntax for copying a file from one disk to another, keeping the same name? How do you change the name of the duplicate when copying?

8. Explain how you would display the disk directory of any disk in any disk drive.

9. How do you rename existing disk files?

10. Which DOS instructions delete files from disk? How would you recover a deleted file?

11. How are new subdirectories created on a disk?

12. Explain how you use DOS to change the active disk directory.

13. How would you customize the DOS prompt to include the search path to the active directory?

14. What is the DOS syntax for removing an existing subdirectory from a disk?

15. Identify the conditions that must exist before a subdirectory can be removed from a disk.

16. What are the common steps for shutting down a microcomputer system?

17. What key(s) are used to output a screen display to the printer?

## APPLYING WHAT YOU'VE LEARNED

1. A volume label can be added to the disk directory when a disk is formatted. Use a DOS user's manual to find out what DOS instruction allows you to change the volume label.

2. DOS recognizes many more DIR switches than were discussed in Appendix D. Use a DOS user's manual for version 5.0 (or higher) to find the switch that prompts the DIR command to display filenames in order by their creation date. How would you display files in order by their size?

3. How could you use the COPY command to duplicate all the files in one disk directory to another disk? Could you do it using a single command? (*Hint:* Look up wildcard characters in the DOS user's manual.

4. Describe a situation in which the UNDELETE command would not work. Assume the command has been entered properly.

5. Customize the DOS prompt to display the time. When does the time in the display change?

6. Use a DOS user's manual to find a DOS instruction that identifies the presence of a hidden file on disk.

7. A general rule for file management is to make separate subdirectories for data files and application packages. For example, users are encouraged to create one subdirectory for their word processing program and other subdirectories for letters, reports, and so on. Graphically illustrate how you would organize subdirectories on a hard disk. Assume you are using at least three different application packages. Do not forget to account for DOS utility programs.

# Answers to Mix and Match

## CHAPTER 1

1. icon
2. binary code
3. transaction
4. information
5. simulation
6. numeric data
7. network
8. computer
9. user-friendly
10. offline
11. process control
12. artificial intelligence
13. printer
14. keyboard
15. hardware

## CHAPTER 2

1. record
2. monitor
3. word processing program
4. file
5. minicomputer
6. computer center
7. memory
8. procedure
9. graphics package
10. peripheral
11. processor
12. database program
13. mainframe
14. system software
15. electronic spreadsheet

## CHAPTER 3

1. public domain software
2. graphical user interface (GUI)
3. operating system
4. dialog box
5. filename
6. screen pointer
7. supervisor
8. command-driven interface
9. utility software
10. window
11. default
12. root directory
13. linking
14. machine language
15. cursor

## CHAPTER 4

1. voice mail
2. facsimile (fax) machine
3. teleconferencing
4. download
5. network administrator
6. information service
7. network topology
8. data communication
9. electronic data interchange (EDI)
10. bulletin board system (BBS)
11. uploading
12. server
13. modem
14. electronic mail (e-mail)
15. local area network (LAN)

## CHAPTER 5

1. personal digital assistant (PDA)
2. supercomputer
3. integrated circuit (IC)
4. fault-tolerant computer
5. byte
6. laptop computers
7. microprocessor
8. multiprocessing
9. expansion card
10. address
11. serial
12. motherboard
13. transistor
14. parallel
15. expansion slots

## CHAPTER 6

1. buffer
2. plotter
3. function keys
4. ergonomics
5. bar code
6. plug-n-play
7. robotics
8. scanner
9. laser printer
10. RGB monitor
11. computer output microfilm (COM)
12. software guide
13. touch-sensitive screen
14. NC (numerical control) machines
15. screen saver

## CHAPTER 7

1. disk cartridge
2. soft-sectored diskette
3. tape cartridge
4. communication channel
5. data compression
6. access time
7. cylinder
8. transfer rate
9. formatting
10. multiplexing
11. parking
12. write-protect window
13. optical disk
14. parity checking
15. disk track

## CHAPTER 8

1. page definition language (PDL)
2. electronic publishing
3. pagination
4. font
5. hard return
6. clip art
7. importing
8. formatting
9. landscape
10. soft spaces
11. block
12. word wrap
13. WYSIWYG

## CHAPTER 9

1. function
2. cell address
3. template
4. range
5. cell
6. exporting
7. label
8. three-dimensional worksheet
9. print title
10. password-protected
11. absolute cell reference
12. worksheet
13. macro
14. values
15. relative cell reference

## CHAPTER 10

1. bar graph
2. line graph
3. animation
4. digitized
5. vector graphics
6. bit mapping
7. frames
8. pixel
9. audio channel
10. multimedia
11. free-drawing graphics
12. pie chart
13. stacked-bar graph
14. computer-aided design (CAD)
15. presentation graphics

## CHAPTER 11

1. key
2. file structure
3. query
4. batch processing
5. data integrity
6. table
7. database management software
8. update
9. direct access
10. file management software
11. data administrator
12. index
13. report generator
14. sequential access
15. relational database

## CHAPTER 12

1. model
2. tactical decision
3. frontline management
4. total quality management
5. decision support system (DSS)
6. quality control
7. expert system
8. virtual corporation
9. statistical process control
10. transaction processing system
11. management information system (MIS)
12. self-directed work team
13. materials requirement planning (MRP)
14. operational decision
15. strategic decision

## CHAPTER 13

1. retirement
2. systems development project
3. maintenance
4. prototyping
5. Gantt chart
6. direct cutover
7. system specifications
8. pilot operation
9. application development team
10. feasibility study
11. benchmark test
12. data flow diagram
13. service bureau
14. critical path
15. CASE tools

## CHAPTER 14

1. compiler
2. logic error
3. pseudocode
4. syntax error
5. object-oriented programming (OOP)
6. structure chart
7. executing
8. version
9. debugging
10. module
11. structured program
12. test data
13. interpreter
14. code
15. flowcharting

## CHAPTER 15

1. data encryption
2. virus
3. input, processing, and output controls
4. antivirus software
5. disaster recovery plan
6. ethical standards
7. computer resource control
8. activity log
9. digital signature
10. password

## CHAPTER 16

1. optical computer
2. computer information systems (CIS)
3. virtual reality
4. nanomachine
5. computer scientist
6. superconductors
7. computer integrated manufacturing (CIM)
8. information society
9. neural network
10. computer engineer
11. career path
12. conference
13. workshop
14. computer architecture
15. interactive television

## APPENDIX B

1. desktop
2. cascade
3. restore button
4. title bar
5. group icon
6. control box
7. scroll bar
8. dragging
9. tiling
10. maximize button
11. clicking
12. File Manager
13. Program Manager
14. Task List
15. file folder

## APPENDIX C

1. scroll arrow
2. cascading
3. menu bar
4. title bar
5. Start button
6. close button
7. restore button
8. double-clicking
9. enlarge button
10. dragging
11. scroll box

## APPENDIX D

1. MS-DOS
2. root directory
3. utility program
4. DOS prompt
5. command
6. PC-DOS
7. search path
8. active directory
9. subdirectory
10. default disk drive

# Glossary

**4GL** *See* fourth-generation language.

**absolute cell reference** (spreadsheet) Reference to a specific cell address that does not change when it is moved or copied to another worksheet location.

**access** Retrieve data from storage media such as tape or disk.

**access mechanism** Machinery containing access arms and read/write heads in a disk drive.

**access time** The time it takes the read/write head to find requested data on storage media.

**ACM** *See* Association for Computing Machinery.

**active cell** (spreadsheet) Cell identified by cell selector which receives data or formula entered or pasted by user.

**active directory** Current directory or directory DOS uses as a default.

**activity log** A summary of online activities kept for security purposes.

**Ada** Named after Ada Lovelace; high-level programming language used in scientific applications, especially by the Department of Defense. It is self-structuring but complex, thus difficult to learn.

**address** Unique number assigned to each memory location within a computer's processing hardware.

**AI** *See* artificial intelligence.

**algorithm** Statement of the steps to be followed in solving a problem or performing a process.

**alignment** Making text flush along a margin.

**alphanumeric data** *See* textual data.

**alpha-testing** Preliminary system test performed by systems development staff.

**analog signal** Data expressed as continuous sound frequencies, such as the voice.

**animation** Visual images of motions produced by rapid presentation of drawn or computer-generated graphics.

**antivirus software** Computer program that identifies disk files which have been infected with a virus, worm, or other destructive program.

**Append** Database command that allows input of data into fields described by the Create command.

**application development team** Group of people responsible for defining specifications, performing feasibility studies, and overseeing a systems development project.

**application generator** Computer program with which users work to design data entry screens, user prompts, and printed reports.

**application package** Software designed for user-oriented problems that is packaged with a user's manual and legal contract.

**application software** Class of programs that solve specific user-oriented processing problems such as word processing, spreadsheet, database, and so on.

**apps** *See* computer application.

**archie** (Internet) Utility software used to locate files stored on FTP servers.

**area graph** Line graph with the area below the line shaded.

**arithmetic operation** Ability of a computer to do mathematical functions, such as addition and subtraction, with numerical data.

**artificial intelligence (AI)** Software applications that simulate human thought and judgment by the use of heuristic problem-solving techniques.

**ASCII (American Standard Code for Information Interchange)** Code for storing data that uses 7 bits to 1 byte and is commonly used in microcomputers; an extended version of ASCII uses 8 bits per byte.

**Ashton, Alan (b. 1943)** Creator, with Bruce Bastian, of WordPerfect word processing software in the early 1980s.

**ASM** *See* Association for System Management.

**assembler** Language-translating program for converting assembly language into machine language.

**assembly language** Second-generation programming language that uses abbreviations for machine language instructions.

**Association for Computing Machinery (ACM)**   Professional organization whose members consist of computer scientists and others involved in computer architecture.

**Association for System Management (ASM)**   Professional organization whose members consist of systems personnel, especially systems analysts.

**asymmetrical multiprocessing**   Each program is assigned a different processor in a parallel processing environment.

**asynchronous transmission**   Communication protocol wherein data is sent a single character at a time.

**attribute**   One field or column in a database table. For example, first name would be one attribute in a customer database table.

**attribute name**   Generic label that identifies each field in a database file.

**audio channel**   Division of audio data, representing a single voice or instrument.

**audiovisual data**   Data that people can hear or see—like voice, music, drawings, photographs, and video sequences.

**authoring system**   Software package that helps computer professionals create a customized user interface and associated data management system.

**autoformatting**   Preset worksheet styles the user selects to override current display options.

**Babbage, Charles (1791–1871)**   Designed the analytical engine in the 1820s. It contained a store for data and punched-card programs on a mill. These ideas were later used in designing computers.

**backup**   A current copy of an important data file or program, available in case original is lost or damaged.

**backup procedure**   Making a copy of important files and programs on another tape or disk.

**backward chaining**   Goal-driven problem-solving approach used by expert systems; a problem (goal) is given, and the expert system works backward to identify possible causes.

**banner program**   Software allowing users to create and print a variety of banners and awards that may be personalized.

**bar code**   Machine-readable collection of stripes of varying width used to identify items.

**bar graph**   Graphic showing data as different lengths of bars.

**Bardeen, John (b. 1908)**   Coinventor, with William Shockley and Walter Brattain, of the transistor and cowinner of the 1956 Nobel Prize for Physics.

**BASIC (Beginner's All-purpose Symbolic Instruction Code)**   High-level programming language used in education and on personal computers. It is easy to learn and is widely used.

**Bastian, Bruce (b. 1949)**   Creator, with Alan Ashton, of WordPerfect word processing software in the early 1980s.

**batch processing**   Processing data in groups.

**baud rate**   Rate at which data is transmitted through a modem or other communication hardware. It is measured as the speed at which a signal changes over a period of time and is often incorrectly equated with bits per second.

**BBS**   *See* bulletin board system.

**Bednorz, J. Georg (b. 1950)**   Cowinner, with Karl A. Müller, of the 1987 Nobel Prize for Physics for work done on superconductivity.

**benchmark test**   Comparing software and hardware performance against an agreed-upon standard.

**Bernoulli disk drive**   Drive using Daniel Bernoulli's law relating the actions of air or liquid over a surface. These cartridge disk drives safeguard against head crashes.

**beta-testing**   Prerelease testing of commercial software by potential outside users.

**binary code**   Pattern of on/off bits used to represent data in computer memory.

**binary digit**   The on or off state of a single computer circuit, represented as 1 and 0, respectively. Also known as a bit.

**biometrics security device**   Hardware that uses a biological characteristic, such as fingerprint or retina pattern, to determine security clearance.

**BIOS (basic input/output system)**   Firmware that describes the hardware used by a computer system.

**bit**   *See* binary digit.

**bit mapping**   Pattern of pixels making up a graphic image; also known as pixel graphics.

**bits per second (bps)**   A measurement of data transmission speeds by which the number of 0 and 1 digits per second are counted.

**block**   (disk or tape) Group of records on disk or tape.

**block**   (spreadsheet) *See* range.

**block**   (word processing) Selected text within a document that can be independently moved, copied, or deleted.

**boilerplate**   Partially completed document with spaces or codes for specific fields that are added later.

**bookmark**   User-determined points in a document that can be accessed at any time with the Go To feature.

**Boole, George (1815–1864)**   Developed the two-state (true/false) logic theory for mathematical expressions during the nineteenth century. His theories later became the basis for binary code.

**boot**   To start up a computer system, automatically copying system software into memory.

**bps**   *See* bits per second.

**Brattain, Walter (1902–1987)**   Coinventor, with John Bardeen and William Shockley, of the transistor and cowinner of the 1956 Nobel Prize for Physics.

**Bricklin, Daniel (b. 1951)**   Creator, with Robert Frankston, of VisiCalc, the first spreadsheet program.

**browser**   User interface for jumping from topic to topic when accessing network data.

**Brush tool**   Graphics tool that creates lines of different widths, shapes, and colors.

**buffer**   Small temporary storage area of data in memory or I/O hardware.

**bug**   An error within a computer program.

**bullet**   The symbol that precedes each item in a document's list.

**bulletin board system (BBS)**   Public access message system that allows users to leave or read messages.

**bus**   Circuitry path that connects the CPU with internal and external hardware.

**bus topology**   Network wherein all nodes are interconnected to each other through a single communication channel.

**button**   Labeled icon which initializes or cancels a program option.

**Byron, Augusta Ada (Countess of Lovelace) (1815–1852)**   Annotater and publisher of Charles Babbage's work in the 1840s. Her detailed instructions for operation are considered a precursor to modern programming.

**byte**   A group of bits representing a single character.

**C**   High-level programming language used in system programming and graphics. It is portable and easy to structure but is a complex language to learn.

**C++**   Object-oriented high-level programming language based on C, used in system programming and graphics. It is portable but quite complex.

**cache memory**   A part of memory that holds data for access by the processor. It is faster than disk access.

**CAD**   *See* computer-aided design.

**CAD/CAM**   *See* computer-aided design/computer-aided manufacturing.

**call-back security**   Type of network security wherein a remote user calls in and then hangs up. The computer then dials a preset number to call-back user, who then logs in to the system.

**CAM**   *See* computer-aided machining.

**camera-ready copy**   Printed document ready to be photographed for a traditional printing plate. Its current meaning is a document ready to be copied.

**card**   Hypertext data associated with a hypermedia screen display, similar to a data record.

**cardinality**   How a record in a database relates to records in other files. Database design could incorporate one-to-one, one-to-many, and many-to-many relationships.

**card punch**   Machine that punches holes, representing data, into punched cards.

**card reader**   Device that reads and translates the holes on a punched card for use as processing data.

**career path**   Series of related jobs.

**cascade**   (Windows) Stacking windows on top of each other in order of appearance in taskbar or Task List. Only the contents of the top screen, which is also the active screen, are shown.

**CASE tools**   *See* computer-aided software engineering tools.

**cashless society**   A society in which all financial transactions are done electronically, based upon an individual's universal account number.

**cathode ray tube (CRT)**   An output peripheral on which a visual display is shown on a screen; also known as monitor or VDT.

**CD**   (DOS) *See* CHDIR.

**CD-R (compact disc—recordable)**   CD-ROM–compatible optical disk that can accept data for permanent storage. Once the data is recorded on the disk, it cannot be erased but can be read as many times as needed.

**CD-ROM (compact disc with read-only memory)**   Removable disk that permanently stores data and cannot be changed; also known as CD or compact disc.

**cell**   Intersection of a single column and row on a worksheet.

**cell address**   The column letter and row number of a specific worksheet cell.

**cell selector**   Dark or beaded box that surrounds the active cell.

**central processing unit (CPU)**   The circuitry within the computer that performs arithmetic, logical, and communication/control operations.

**Certificate in Computer Programming (CCP)**   Awarded by the Institute for Certification of Computer Professionals (ICCP) to people who pass tests covering business, scientific, and system programming.

**Certificate in Data Processing (CDP)**   Awarded by the Institute for Certification of Computer Professionals (ICCP) to people who pass tests covering data processing hardware, computer programming and software, principles of management, quantitative methods and accounting, and systems analysis and design.

**CGA (color graphics adapter)**   Color monitor standard that displays 640 by 200 pixels in 16 colors.

**change control**   Procedures to oversee the modification of operational computer systems.

**character**   Smallest unit of data as a single digit, letter, or symbol.

**CHDIR (CD)**   Internal DOS command to change active directory.

**chief information officer (CIO)**   Executive responsible for the computing facilities and the collection, organization, and dissemination of all information. She/he also makes strategic decisions about information and security policy.

**chip**   A silicon wafer on which reside integrated circuits and other processing circuitry.

**CIM**   *See* computer-integrated manufacturing.

**CIO** *See* chief information officer.

**CIS** *See* computer information systems.

**class** A collection of objects with similar characteristics in data and methods.

**click** Pressing the mouse button once to initiate action or to select a program option.

**client/server** Network design wherein the end user's computer takes on processing tasks traditionally handled by a network server.

**clip art** A collection of graphics, images, or text created by other software which may be added to a document or design.

**Close** *See* Exit command.

**Close button** (Windows 95) Removes window from screen.

**CNC machine** *See* computer numerical control machine.

**coaxial cable** Communication channel commonly used for cable television that can handle 80 simultaneous data transmissions at speeds exceeding 10 million bps.

**COBOL (COmmon Business-Oriented Language)** High-level programming language used for business applications. It is self-documenting, easy to structure, and enjoys widespread use.

**Codd, Dr. Edgar F.** Wrote 12 rules on relational database design in the 1970s which still influence the field today.

**code** Program instruction.

**coding** The writing of computer software.

**cold site** Backup facilities, ready for use, available if an organization's original computer center cannot be used because of an emergency.

**collision** Simultaneous data transmissions from two different computers on the same communication channel, or concurrent attempts to access the same record from a database.

**color/contrast control** Multimedia editing feature that allows the user to change the colors or brightness of a visual image.

**color separation** Features of a desktop publishing system to produce a master in each of the colors needed for four-color printing of an image.

**COM** *See* computer output microfilm.

**COM1** (DOS) Reserved word that references serial port 1.

**command** DOS instruction that can be executed at any time.

**command-driven interface** Interface that uses keywords and syntax to initiate program options.

**command menu** Lists available electronic spreadsheet menus and their commands.

**communication channel** The medium by which data communication takes place. Common communication channels include twisted-pair wires, coaxial cable, microwave signals, and optical fibers.

**communication procedure** Actions people take to ensure accurate and fast sharing of data between computers.

**communication software** System software that transfers data from one computer system to another.

**compact disc (CD)** Removable disk that permanently stores data and cannot be changed; also known as CD-ROM.

**compatibility** The ability of software or peripherals to work on a variety of systems.

**compiler** High-level language translator that checks the entire program for errors. Translations are saved.

**computer** Machine that allows input of facts and figures, processes them, and outputs useful information.

**computer-aided design (CAD)** Application wherein people use computers to create two- or three-dimensional drawings, usually for industrial designs.

**computer-aided design/computer-aided maufacturing (CAD/CAM)** Communication between CAD and CAM programs that connects design and manufacturing equipment.

**computer-aided machining (CAM)** Use of programmable machines to control the manufacturing of products.

**computer-aided software engineering (CASE) tools** Software that uses a project dictionary with charting tools to help computer professionals manage a systems development project.

**computer applications (apps)** Any use for a computer.

**computer architect** Person who specializes in the development, manufacturing, and assembly of hardware.

**computer architecture** An academic program combining computer engineering and computer science.

**computer center** Centralized location for computer hardware and related professionals.

**computer engineer** Person who specializes in developing processing equipment and associated systems software.

**Computer Fraud and Abuse Act (1986)** Allows for the prosecution of people who gain unauthorized access to computers or databases.

**computer imaging** Using data, graphics, and mathematics to display complex images.

**computer information systems (CIS)** An area of specialization concerning the creation of systems in business, science, education, and manufacturing.

**computer-integrated manufacturing (CIM)** Manufacturing system that utilizes the features of CAD/CAM, robotics, and numerical control, linked together by a communications standard.

**Computer Matching and Privacy Act (1988)** Federal agencies are regulated in the types of government files they can match to verify personal information. A person can challenge the accuracy of the information.

**computer numerical control (CNC) machine**   Machines that use programs representing numeric specifications to produce precise machine parts.

**computer operator**   Person who ensures that computer hardware is functioning properly and runs different computer programs based on a preset schedule.

**computer output microfilm (COM)**   Output onto microfilm or microfiche of computer-generated data.

**computer professional**   Person who works directly with the development and operation of computer technology.

**computer program**   The set of instructions a computer follows in sequence to control the input, processing, output, and storage it is to perform; also known as program.

**computer resource control**   Computer professionals are divided into operations and development groups to maintain security.

**computer salesperson**   Person who sells computer hardware and/or software.

**computer scientist**   Person who specializes in developing techniques for designing system software and their applications in managing data and programs.

**computer system**   Collection of people, procedures, data, software, and hardware that work together to solve specific problems.

**CON**   Reserved word in DOS that references keyboard for input and screen for output. CON stands for the *console*, the place where computer operators enter commands on a large computer system.

**concurrent update**   Situation that occurs in updating data wherein different users make changes to the same record at the same time. The result is incorrect data in the updated record.

**conference**   A professional meeting covering a broad group of people whose work depends upon information.

**Consumer Electronics Bus (CEBus)**   Standard for internal wiring of consumer products enabling them to communicate in a smart house.

**contention**   Two computers trying to use a common communication channel at the same time.

**context-sensitive help**   Information displayed when a help screen is activated that relates to the program operation currently being used.

**continuing education**   Participation in on-the-job training, workshops, conferences, or other activities associated with the continuous improvement of job skills.

**contract programmer**   Computer programmer temporarily employed by an organization to work on a systems development project.

**control box**   (Windows) Icon found in the top-left corner of the title bar. Clicking on it opens the control menu, allowing you to close, open, or move the associated window. Double-clicking on the control box closes the associated window.

**control character**   Instructions (carriage return, cursor movement, and so on) available from the keyboard.

**control clerk**   Person who schedules when operators load and run computer programs in a computer center and delivers the information to the appropriate users.

**control panel**   Spreadsheet area that contains command, icon, and data entry lines.

**control total**   Security procedure in which errors are detected by comparing an independently computed total with the computer-generated equivalent.

**conversion**   Changing from an old system to a new system; also known as installation.

**COPY**   (DOS) Internal command that creates a duplicate of the designated program or data file.

**Copy**   (object linking and embedding) Duplicate an object in another application program so that neither the original nor the duplicate can be modified by the user.

**Copy and Paste**   (spreadsheet) Duplicates contents of selected cells into other worksheet columns or rows.

**Copy command**   (word processing) Duplicating a block of text somewhere else within the same document (internal copy) or another document (external copy).

**copy protection**   A method of storing software on a disk that prevents illegal copying by system utilities.

**cost/benefit analysis**   Report presenting both tangible and intangible costs and benefits of a systems project.

**CPU**   *See* central processing unit.

**crash**   Computer failure.

**Create**   Database command used to set up the file or database structure by forming new files and describing fields in records.

**critical path**   Combination of events within a project PERT chart that requires the most time to complete.

**CRT**   *See* cathode ray tube.

**cursor**   Blinking line or box showing where computer will display next keyboard entry.

**cursor control**   Use of keys on keyboard to move the cursor up, down, left, or right through a document.

**Cut and Paste**   (word processing, spreadsheet, graphics) Change location of text, data, or an object within a document or drawing by highlighting it, deleting it, and placing it elsewhere.

**cylinder**   Collection of tracks on a disk pack that can be read at one position of the access arm.

**DAT**   *See* digital audiotape.

**data**   Facts, figures, and images.

**data administrator**   Individual responsible for an organization's data.

**database**   Organized collections of data that can be retrieved and cross-referenced by a computer.

**database management software (DBMS)**   Computer program that creates, stores, and accesses integrated data files.

**database program**   Computer program that organizes and maintains related data files.

**data communication**   Sending data electronically from one location to another.

**data compression**   Reduces storage space that data takes up by replacing data redundancies with notations.

**data definition commands**   User interface that identifies fields and field characteristics (type and size) for records within a file.

**data encryption**   Scrambling or encoding data before sending or saving it.

**Data Encryption Standard (DES)**   Popular encryption method that uses a 56-bit key to encode data 16 times to create encrypted file.

**data entry**   Entering numbers and text into a computer for processing.

**data entry line**   Area of a spreadsheet control panel where data and formulas are input.

**data entry operator**   Person who inputs data into a computer, usually using a keyboard.

**data entry procedure**   Preparation and input of data into a computer system.

**data flow diagram**   Visual representation of how data and people interact.

**data integrity**   Characteristic of a data file whereby every data field is accurate and properly identified.

**data librarian**   Person who catalogs and stores tapes and disks in fireproof tape/disk library.

**data manipulation commands**   User interface that controls the access, updating, and manipulation of data within a file or database.

**data model**   Plan computer uses for storing and accessing data.

**data processing**   Using a computer to convert facts, figures, and images into useful information.

**Data Processing Management Association (DPMA)**   Organization whose members consist of computer information systems professionals.

**data storage and retrieval**   Capability of computers to store vast amounts of data and later search the data for related information.

**DBMS**   *See* database management software.

**debugging**   The process of finding and correcting program errors.

**decision support system (DSS)**   Real-time computer system that aids managers in solving problems through data retrieval and modeling.

**default**   Standard assumptions a computer system uses unless otherwise instructed.

**default disk drive**   Drive DOS uses when no drive designation is included in an instruction.

**defragmentation utility program**   Software that rewrites files on a disk so they use continuous sectors, thereby allowing faster reading and writing.

**DEL**   Internal DOS command to erase a filename from the designated disk directory.

**delete**   (word processing) Removes text from document. The Delete key or other combination of keys is used to remove the highlighted text.

**Delete command**   (spreadsheet) Removes row or column along with associated data and formulas.

**density**   Measure of storage media capacity.

**DES**   *See* Data Encryption Standard.

**desktop**   Screen layout associated with graphical user interface that uses icons that represent documents, file folders, calculators, and other office tools.

**desktop configuration**   Arrangement of personal computer hardware in which the computer is in horizontal housing and usually set on a desk or table. The monitor can be put on top of the computer or nearby.

**desktop publishing**   Software package that integrates text, graphics, and images created by other software packages. It allows users precise control over page layout as well as a wide selection of different fonts and design elements.

**detailed report**   A report showing one output line for each item in a file or database.

**device driver**   File used by operating system to identify operating characteristics of peripherals such as a mouse, printer, or scanner.

**diagnostic software**   Computer program that detects problems in hardware and software.

**dialog box**   Window that prompts the user to enter text, select names, or click on an icon to initiate or cancel a program option.

**diamond design**   Two-dimensional worksheet design wherein data is laid out in blocks so that data in one row or column does not overlap data on other blocks.

**digital audiotape (DAT)**   High-capacity tape cartridge format.

**digital camera**   Camera that stores images on disk rather than film for direct input into a computer.

**digital computer**   Computer that accepts programs and data converted to binary digits.

**digital signal**   Representing bit patterns as on or off electrical voltages.

**digital signature**   Use of a private and public key to create an encrypted document only the recipient can read.

**Digital Signature Standard (DSS)**   Data encryption technique for electronic documents proposed by National Institute of Standards; when sender uses recipient's published public key to encrypt a document, the receiver's private key is the only known means of decoding the document.

**digitize**   Conversion of a point on a drawing into XY coordinates. This is done by using a scanner or stylus on a tablet.

**DIR**   Internal DOS command to display the contents of a disk directory on-screen.

**direct access**   Finding one record without reading other records.

**direct cutover**   Method of conversion wherein the old system is removed and the new system is immediately installed.

**disaster recovery plan**   Procedures to be followed if an organization's computer systems are disabled or destroyed.

**discretionary replace**   As each designated word is found in a document in a Find operation, the user decides whether to replace it or not.

**disk**   Circular platter with concentric tracks that is used as a machine-readable storage medium.

**disk address**   Location of data on disk.

**disk cartridge**   Hard disk designed to be inserted and removed from the disk drive.

**disk controller**   Electronic circuitry, often found on an expansion board, that controls disk operations and the flow of data to and from the computer to one or more disk drives.

**disk directory**   Disk area that contains the filename, size, and date and time of creation of each data file or program saved to the disk; also known as a file folder in Windows.

**disk drive**   Storage hardware that reads and writes data using a disk.

**diskette**   Removable flexible disk, used to store computer-readable data; also known as a floppy disk.

**diskless workstation**   Personal computer system without a floppy disk drive. A diskless workstation is always connected to another computer, which handles data and program storage, but has a hard disk drive for booting.

**disk operating system (DOS)**   Collection of system software designed to control a computer system using disks for storage.

**disk pack**   Collection of hard disks stacked on top of each other to allow access and storage of large amounts of data.

**disk track**   One of the concentric circles on a disk surface where data is stored.

**distributed processing**   Putting data processing hardware where data originates.

**DNA computer**   Experimental computer that uses DNA to perform processing.

**documentation**   Written instructions, design diagrams, and support materials for a computer program.

**domain**   A specific area of influence or expertise.

**DOS**   *See* disk operating system.

**DOS prompt**   Screen display of letter associated with default disk drive and the greater-than sign.

**dot-matrix character**   A type of character made up of dots patterned within a matrix.

**double-click**   Pressing a mouse button twice in quick succession to run a program or activate a program operation.

**download**   Receiving data or programs directly from another computer.

**DPMA**   *See* Data Processing Management Association.

**drag**   Repositioning an icon or a window on-screen by pointing to it and holding down the mouse button while moving the mouse.

**drop cap**   Enlarged first letter of a paragraph in a document, top-aligning with the first line of text and dropping below to be embedded in the paragraph.

**drop-down menu**   Menu options that stay hidden in a menu bar at the top of the screen until the user selects it. When the menu is selected, the menu opens to list program options.

**DSS**   (data security) S*ee* digital signature standard.

**DSS**   (management information systems) *See* decision support system.

**dye sublimation printer**   Printer that fuses a gaseous form of colored inks onto special paper to produce photograph-quality output.

**EBCDIC (Extending Binary Coded Decimal Interchange Code)**   Binary code for storing data that includes 8 bits in 1 byte and is used in minicomputers and mainframes.

**Eckert, J. Presper (1919–1995)**   Built the electronic computer ENIAC with John Mauchly in 1946.

**EDI**   *See* electronic data interchange.

**editing**   Revising text in a document.

**EDP**   *See* electronic data processing.

**Education Privacy Act (1974)**   Restricts access to grades, evaluations, and other computer-based data maintained by schools. A student may examine and challenge the accuracy of the data.

**EFT**   *See* electronic funds transfer.

**EGA (extended graphics adapter)**   Color monitor standard that displays 640 by 350 pixels in 16 colors.

**Electronic Communications Privacy Act (1986)**   Provides privacy protection to communications involving new forms of technology. Electronic mail is identified, and intercepting e-mail becomes a crime.

**electronic data interchange (EDI)**   Organizations exchanging orders, bills, and banking information using data communication technology.

**electronic data processing (EDP) controls**   Security procedures for all computer system components.

**electronic filing**   Storing documents on disk instead of a file cabinet.

**electronic funds transfer (EFT)**   Computer network that allows financial transactions without the actual exchange of money or checks.

**electronic mail (e-mail)**   Sending and receiving memos, reports, and personal messages through a computer network.

**electronic mail address**   Identifies user name and user address for e-mail messages.

**electronic mailbox**   Personal disk file for storing the correspondence of an electronic mail system.

**electronic publishing**   Printing technology that runs high-speed printing presses and controls page composition, typography, and file integration.

**electronic spreadsheet**   Computer program that organizes numbers and associated text into rows and columns.

**electronic whiteboard**   Groupware feature that posts drawings, ideas, or questions on users' computer screens and allows answers or ideas from others to be physically displayed next to related information.

**electrostatic printer**   Printer that uses electrical impulses to put characters on electrostatic paper.

**ellipsis**   Series of three periods. When following a menu option, an ellipsis indicates that additional user input is necessary.

**e-mail**   *See* electronic mail.

**embed**   Duplicating an original object in another application package such that modifying the original will not affect the duplicate, but the duplicate can be changed using the original.

**embedded computer**   Computer built inside a tool or appliance.

**emergency procedure**   Actions people take to recover important data after a computer crash.

**emulation**   Utility program that mimics the operation of different computer hardware.

**encapsulation**   The capability of an object to contain both the data and methods for processing that data.

**end user**   Person who can use computer technology to organize data, stimulate new ideas, solve problems, and communicate the results to others.

**end-user computing**   End user is responsible for data entry, computer operations, and application of the resulting output.

**Englebart, Douglas (b. 1925)**   Inventor of the mouse, windows, and one of the originators of hypertext.

**enlarge button**   (Windows 95) Icon with a small window found as the middle button of three in the top-right corner of the title bar next to the reduce button. Clicking on the enlarge button expands the related window to fill the screen.

**Enter key**   Key on keyboard that transmits a carriage return.

**ERASE**   Internal DOS command to delete a filename from the designated disk directory.

**Eraser tool**   Graphics tool that clears the work area as it is moved around.

**ergonomics**   The study of how tools, furniture, and equipment can be designed to fit the human body.

**error detection**   Computer program that checks for data entry errors.

**error messages**   Listing of program errors or errors in running an application package. Suggested corrections may be given.

**error recovery procedure**   Actions people take to find and eliminate processing mistakes made by people or equipment failures.

**ethical standards**   Set of rules a person or organization uses when considering the rights of others.

**event**   A standard set of binary code representing a musical sound.

**event-driven programming**   Programming logic based on an event taking place, such as clicking on a button or icon, rather than the value of data.

**exception report**   A report that lists only those records fulfilling predefined specifications.

**execute**   Having the computer follow the instructions in a program; also known as run or launch.

**execution phase**   Part of the processing cycle in which the arithmetic or logical operation is performed by the processor or results are sent from the processor to memory.

**executive**   Another name of a person at the top management level.

**executive information system (EIS)**   Decision support system designed to aid in the strategic decisions made by top-level management.

**Exit command**   Deletes all temporary files and returns software control to the operating system. Also found in menus as Quit or Close.

**expansion bus**   Computer circuitry that connects processor with peripheral hardware.

**expansion card**   Circuit board designed to fit into an expansion slot of a microcomputer's motherboard to add memory or connect external hardware.

**expansion slot**   Place where expansion cards can be plugged into the motherboard's extension bus.

**expert system**   System that contains decision-making rules and probabilities for expected outcomes, based on information in a knowledge base.

**exploded pie chart**   A pie chart in which one slice is emphasized by separating it from the rest.

**export**   Transfer data in a compatible format from one software application package to another.

**external copy**   Copying a block of text from a document to an outside file.

**external disk drive**   Disk drive outside of the computer case that is connected to the computer through a parallel port.

**external modem**   Stand-alone modem that directly connects a computer to a communication channel.

**facsimile (fax) machine**   Machine that scans, transmits, and receives paper-based images over communication lines.

**Fair Credit Reporting Act (1970)**   Individuals have the right to examine and challenge information held in credit files. This information is also available only to authorized users.

**FAT**   *See* file allocation table.

**Fatbits tool**   Graphics tool that enlarges an image to allow editing of individual pixels.

**fault-tolerant computer**   A computer with duplicate processing components that is designed to switch to one set of components when the other set has problems.

**fax**   *See* facsimile machine.

**fax board**   Expansion card that connects computer to standard telephone jack and supports the sending and receiving of facsimile data.

**fax-modem**   Communication hardware with both data communication (modem) and image handling (fax) capabilities.

**feasibility study**   Study that determines if a systems development project is realistic.

**fiber-optic cable**   High-speed communication channel made from spun-glass filaments which handles more than 2,000 simultaneous data transmissions at speeds up to 1 billion bps.

**field**   Related group of letters, numbers, and symbols.

**field name**   Generic name given to each field in a file.

**fifth-generation computer**   Computer system containing natural language interfaces and expert system software, along with using parallel processors, fiber optics, or superconductors.

**file**   Group of related records.

**file allocation table (FAT)**   Index which identifies by sector number where a file is found on a disk. The file allocation table is stored along with the disk directory on a designated disk track.

**file folder**   Icon found in the Windows File Manager that represents a specific disk directory; also known as disk directory.

**file fragmentation**   When a file is stored in noncontinuous disk sectors.

**file management software**   Computer program that maximizes access to a flat file.

**File Manager**   Windows program that allows the user to create and delete subdirectories, as well as move, copy, rename, and delete files.

**file merging**   Feature of a word processing program that merges a letter with a file of names and addresses, resulting in personalized correspondence.

**filename**   Unique set of letters, numbers, and symbols that identifies a data file or program.

**filename extension**   A combination of three characters that are added to the end of a filename, preceded by a period, to identify a file or object.

**file structure**   Description of a data file (or table) that includes for each field an attribute name, data type, error checks, and expected size.

**file structure view**   Displays the attribute name, data type, error checks, a maximum field size for each field in a file.

**file transfer protocols (FTP)**   Standard data format for downloading files from the Internet to your personal computer.

**Fill Bucket tool**   Graphics tool that, when moved to an outlined shape, fills that shape with a color or pattern.

**filter**   Limiting display to records that meet a specific criterion.

**financial data**   Facts and figures about resources that relate to money, such as profit and loss, assets and liabilities, and cash flow.

**Find command**   (database) Displays only record and related fields fulfilling user-dictated criteria.

**Find command**   (word processing) Locates first occurrence of an indicated symbol or phase in a document. Subsequent occurrences can also be located when the operation is repeated.

**firmware**   Permanent software programmed onto a memory chip when it is manufactured.

**first-generation computer**   Computer manufactured in the late 1940s and early 1950s containing vacuum tubes, having no memory, and using magnetic drums as storage devices.

**fixed disk**   Disk permanently installed within the disk drive.

**flash memory**   Uses programmable read-only memory chips to store data. Flash memory is inserted in a PCMCIA slot with portable computers and in other situations where power consumption must be kept to a minimum.

**flat file**   Independent data file used by file management software. Flat files are not designed to integrate with other data files.

**flexible manufacturing**   Ability of a manufacturing company to quickly change computer-controlled production lines and machines to make a different product.

**floppy disk**   *See* diskette.

**flowchart**   A method of representing program logic by using different symbols and arrows.

**font**   Style, weight, and size of a printed character.

**footer**   Line that appears at the bottom of each document page.

**form feed**   Button on a continuous-feed printer that moves paper to the top of the next page.

**formatting**   (disk) Preparing a new disk by creating a disk directory and file allocation table.

**formatting**   (spreadsheet) Change column widths, fonts, and other worksheet display features.

**formatting**   (word processing) Controlling the final appearance of a document.

**FORTRAN (FORmula TRANslator)**   High-level programming language used for scientific and mathematical applications. It handles calculations easily but is difficult to structure.

**forum**   Network service that supports interactive input from network users concerning different topics of choice. It is an open-ended electronic whiteboard.

**forward chaining**   Data-driven problem-solving approach used by expert systems, which starts with all the known situations or symptoms of a problem and works forward by identifying common parameters that are characteristics of a specific problem.

**fourth-generation computer**   Computer with processing hardware characterized by very large-scale integrated circuits such as a microprocessor.

**fourth-generation language (4GL)**   Nonprocedural programming language wherein users indicate IPOS specifications with simple commands.

**fps**   *See* frames per second.

**frame**   Division of visual data like film or video. Each frame can be edited independently. Rapid runthrough of the frames creates animated movement.

**Frame Selection**   Multimedia feature that gives users the ability to find selected frames by using commands or button icons similar to a tape player.

**frames per second (fps)**   Display speed of visual data in multimedia software.

**Frankston, Robert**   Creator, with Daniel Bricklin, of VisiCalc, one of the first spreadsheet programs.

**free-drawing graphics**   Using the computer to create drawings of a screen much as an artist uses a canvas.

**Freedom of Information Act (1970)**   Personal data maintained by the federal government is accessible to any citizen who requests it unless the data's release threatens national security or infringes upon another person's privacy.

**frontline management**   People who make operational decisions about daily activities.

**FTP**   *See* file transfer protocols.

**full character**   Solid-print character similar to those of a typewriter, producing a high-quality print.

**full justification**   *See* justification.

**full-page monitor**   Screen display that shows an entire page of a word processing or desktop publishing document.

**full-duplex transmission**   Communication protocol that allows two-way simultaneous data transmissions between two computers.

**function**   Predefined operation that performs common mathematical, financial, and logical processing routine.

**function keys**   Keys that activate software features.

**fuzzy logic**   Logic based on decisions made when input can have infinitely many conditions.

**Gantt chart**   Chart showing starting dates and duration of different activities in the systems development process.

**Gates, William (b. 1955)**   Wrote BASIC interpreter for Altair microcomputer and founded Microsoft Corporation, the originator of MS-DOS and Windows.

**gateway**   Hardware that connects different network topologies.

**GDSS**   *See* group decision support system.

**genetic algorithm**   Program code that combines randomly and is tested as a possible solution to a problem.

**gigabyte**   1 billion bytes of memory.

**GIGO (garbage in, garbage out)**   Errors in data produce useless information.

**global format**   Change the default display options for all the cells in a worksheet.

**global replace**   Automatic replacement of all occurrences of a word or phrase without user involvement.

**gopher**   Used to search Internet host computers to locate filenames of interest.

**Go To command**   (database) Displays a record and related fields based on its relative location in a file. For example, the tenth, first, last, previous, or next record.

**Go To command**   (word processing) Takes screen pointer to user-defined bookmarks within a document.

**graphical user interface (GUI)**   Interface that relies on mouse or keyboard input to select menus or icons.

**graphics package**   Computer program that generates drawings and diagrams.

**green computing**   Use of computers and peripherals meeting EPA standards of low energy use when in sleep mode.

**group decision support system (GDSS)**   Groupware application whereby people connected to the same network define problems, discuss solutions, and delegate responsibilities.

**group icon**   Icon in the Windows Program Manager that organizes related programs and data files.

**groupware**   Software package that supports users connected through a network with integrated software and compatible data. Groupware applications include: common calendars, electronic mail, interactive conference calls, document sharing, and editing sessions with several users.

**GUI**   *See* graphical user interface.

**hacker**   Self-taught computer hobbyist. Hackers are often incorrectly associated by the popular press with unauthorized computer activities.

**half-duplex transmission**   Communication protocol that allows two-way data transmissions between two computers, but only in one direction at a time.

**halftone**   Arrangement of different sizes of black dots on white paper to simulate the gray tones of black-and-white photographs.

**hard card**   Expansion card with a built-in fixed disk.

**hard copy**   Paper copy of output.

**hard disk**   Nonremovable disk built into disk drive.

**hard disk drive**   Hardware used to read and write information on a hard disk. The drive accesses hard disks through access arms containing read/write heads.

**hard return**   A carriage return entered into the text when the user presses the Return or Enter key.

**hardware**   Computer and other associated equipment.

**hardwired**   Physically connected by wire or cable.

**head crash**   Hard disk drive's read/write mechanism touches disk surface, resulting in damage to disk and disk drive.

**header**   Line that appears at the top of each document page.

**help desk**   Group of computer professionals that answer questions related to computer operations.

**help screen**   Screen description of software features and explanation of error messages.

**heuristic**   The system of applying general rules and experiential information to solve problems by artificial intelligence.

**hidden file**   Filename that is not displayed as part of the disk directory.

**hierarchical model**   Data items and their references are organized in a parent/child fashion representing a one-to-many relationship among data. Access to data is made only from the top down.

**hierarchy chart**   *See* structure chart.

**high-level language**   Programming language that resembles human language.

**highlight**   Changing the intensity of certain characters on-screen for emphasis or to define a block.

**Hoff, Marcian (b. 1937)**   One of the first inventors of the microprocessor in the 1960s.

**Hollerith, Herman (1860–1929)**   Inventor of the punched card and associated hardware in the 1880s.

**home page**   First screen in a hypermedia application that serves as a table of contents.

**Hopper, Grace Murray (1906–1992)**   One of the original COBOL developers and programmer of early computers.

**host**   The central computer in a star network.

**hot site**   Backup facilities, containing ready-to-use hardware, available if an organization's original computer center cannot be used because of an emergency.

**hot word**   Area of a screen display that, when clicked on, initiates a program action; also known as jump term.

**HTML**   *See* Hypertext Markup Language.

**Hyatt, George (Gilbert) (b. 1938)**   One of the first inventors of the microprocessor in the 1960s.

**hybrid topology**   A network that uses gateways to incorporate two or more network topologies.

**hypermedia**   Object-oriented database model that supports many-to-many data relationships by organizing data into cards and stacks.

**hypertext**   Text-oriented database in which users jump from one screen display to another by using a mouse to select menu options or hot words. Hypertext applications use a hypermedia database model.

**Hypertext Markup Language (HTML)**   Editing language used on World Wide Web files that uses tags to describe the document's design and how it relates to other documents.

**hyphenation help**   Word processing software that consults a dictionary to inform user of possible places in a word for correct hyphenation.

**IC**   *See* integrated circuit.

**icon**   Picture of item, action, or computer operation.

**icon bar**   Selection of icons that represent different program operations.

**IEEE**   *See* Institute of Electrical and Electronic Engineers.

**import**   Incorporating a block of text or a graphic into a document from another application.

**index**   (database) Separate file based on a key field, which identifies location of a record within a data file.

**Index command**   Creates a separate database file based on a key field, which identifies the location of a record within a data file.

**inference engine**   Software component of an expert system.

**information**   Data that is processed into a format useful to people.

**information service**   A commercial service wherein users pay for access to a centralized computer system and its resources, which include e-mail, specialized databases, games, catalogs, and airline schedules.

**information society**   An area containing a large group of people whose work generates or depends upon information.

**information systems manager**   Person responsible for the effective and efficient use of an organization's computer resources by ensuring computer professionals complete scheduled jobs on time and within budget.

**informed user**   Person who understands how the components of a computer system work together to perform a task, who knows its limits, and who uses it for personal benefit and for the benefit of others.

**initial review**   A study done by a systems analyst to identify a problem and see if it has a computer-based solution.

**ink-jet printer**   Printer that sprays drops of ink on paper in patterns to form characters.

**input, processing, and output controls**   Procedures for accepting data and keeping control totals.

**Insert command**   (spreadsheet) Add new rows or columns.

**insertion point**   The cursor in a document where typed characters will be inserted.

**insert operation**   (word processing) Adding text to a document. The insertion point is placed where text must be inserted. The Insert key is pressed (if not already on), and the new text is typed.

**installation**   *See* conversion.

**Institute of Electrical and Electronic Engineers (IEEE)**   Professional organization whose members consist of computer and electrical engineers who design and build computer equipment.

**instruction phase**   Part of the processing cycle where a processor receives a machine language instruction from memory.

**integrated circuit (IC)**   A small, solid-state circuit placed with other electronic components on a silicon wafer.

**Integrated Services Digital Network (ISDN)**   Digital signal format that allows data to be sent digitally through standard telephone lines.

**integrated software**   Software package that provides user interfaces for several applications and a common data format for sharing data among those applications.

**interactive**   Direct communication with a computer wherein every request is immediately acted upon.

**interactive television**   A television containing a cable control box that lets users communicate through the control box to the television station.

**internal modem**   Modem on an expansion card that directly connects the computer to a communication channel.

**Internet**   Wide area network using a hybrid network topology that spans the globe, linking together a variety of schools, research centers, government offices, and businesses.

**interpreter**   Program that translates and executes one high-level language instruction at a time. Translations are not saved.

**I/O**   Input and output.

**IPOS (input, processing, output, storage) cycle**   A four-step computer-related process consisting of the input of data, processing of the data by the computer, output of information in some usable form, and storage of the results for later use.

**ISDN**   *See* Integrated Services Digital Network.

**iteration**   Basic structure of a computer program wherein a sequence of instructions is repeated until some processing condition is changed.

**Jacquard, Joseph Marie (1752–1834)**   Developer in 1801 of mechanized looms using punched cards for patterns.

**Jobs, Steve (b. 1955)**   Built the Apple I microcomputer in 1976 with Steve Wozniak and later formed Apple Computer Corporation.

**Join command**   (database) Allows users to merge portions of different database tables together into a new table.

**joystick**   A lever manipulated like an automobile stick shift, its action moving a cursor or object on-screen.

**jump term**   Area of screen display that, when clicked, initiates a program action; also known as a hot word.

**just-in-time inventory**   Inventory control method that schedules the shipment of parts and raw materials just before they are needed, in order to minimize storage costs and reduce spoilage of time-dependent products.

**justification**   Alignment of a document along both margins; also called full justification.

**K**   *See* kilobyte.

**Kapor, Mitch (b. 1951)**   Cofounder of the Electronic Frontier Foundation which defends the civil liberties of hackers and network users.

**Kemeny, John G. (b. 1926)**   Cocreator, with Thomas Kurtz, of BASIC in 1964.

**kerning**   Using the shapes of printed characters themselves to fit them closer to each other.

**key**   Field used to identify a record in a file.

**keyboard**   Input hardware containing typewriter-like keys which the user presses.

**keyboard overlay**   Paper or plastic sheet cut to fit around a keyboard, containing a brief description of keyboard commands.

**keypunch**  Input hardware, similar to a typewriter, where each keystroke represents a character.

**Kilby, Jack (b. 1923)**  Coinventor of the first working integrated circuit in 1959. Given joint credit with Robert Noyce.

**kilobyte (K)**  1,000 bytes of memory.

**knowledge base**  Contains the facts, data relationships, and probabilities of occurrences used by an expert system.

**Kurtz, Thomas E. (b. 1928)**  Cocreator, with John Kemeny, of BASIC in 1964.

**label**  Text that is used to describe a worksheet or worksheet data.

**label prefix**  (spreadsheet) Special character (', ", or ^) that determines label's placement within a cell.

**LAN**  *See* local area network.

**landscape**  Horizontal layout of document page.

**language translator**  Systems program that converts program instructions written in a high-level language into the computer's machine language.

**laptop computer**  Name given to a small portable computers containing keyboards.

**laser printer**  Printer that uses a laser to form characters on a drum. The image on the drum is developed, as in a copy machine, and the characters are printed on paper.

**launch**  *See* execute.

**left alignment**  Feature of a document whereby all lines of text are flush to the left margin.

**legend**  Key to symbols or colors on a presentation graphic.

**life cycle**  Problem-solving approach to systems design that divides a large job into a series of smaller steps.

**light pen**  Input device that is moved or touches the screen at certain points to select from a menu or make drawings.

**linear programming**  Type of modeling wherein an optimum solution for a problem is found for a given set of requirements and constraints.

**line feed**  Button on a continuous-feed printer that moves paper one line at a time through the printer when it is activated.

**line graph**  Graphic showing trends in data with a continuous line.

**line printer**  Impact printer producing one line at a time with speeds up to 2,000 lines per minute.

**linked list**  Reference to data at a different disk address that is incorporated into a data set.

**linker**  System software that embeds utility programs within a translated version of a high-level language program.

**linking**  Duplicating an original object in another application package and creating an active link so that the user can choose to update the duplicate when the original is changed.

**list box**  Displays a list of names or options. When the list is too long to fit in the box, scroll arrows move the list up and down to display different items within the list box.

**local area network (LAN)**  Interconnected computers within a confined service area.

**logical operation**  Ability of a computer to compare two values to see which is larger or if they are equal.

**logic bomb**  Destructive computer program that erases program and data files when triggered by a specific event. This type of troublemaking program is event-activated, hides inside another program, and cannot self-replicate.

**logic error**  Program error that is translatable but does not produce correct results.

**login script**  Set of commands to identify and link one computer into a computer network. User is usually asked to enter a user name and password before gaining access to the network.

**LOGO**  (from Greek *logos*) High-level programming language used in education. It is easy to learn and allows simple graphics but has few applications outside of education.

**LPT1**  (DOS) Reserved word that references parallel port 1.

**machine code**  *See* machine language.

**machine language**  Operating language unique to each computer that is made up of bits (0 or 1) representing electronic switches (off or on).

**macro**  A stored series of software operations a user can activate by using a menu or by pressing a few keys.

**magnetic-ink character recognition (MICR)**  Machine-readable input that uses a scanner to read magnetized characters at the bottom of checks.

**magneto-optical disk**  Erasable optical disk that uses lasers to read magnetically aligned bit patterns.

**mainframe**  Large computer which houses several processors and large amounts of memory.

**maintenance**  Keeping one or more of a computer system's components up-to-date and related people trained.

**maintenance programmer**  A person who modifies programs already in use in order to reflect a change in law or company policy.

**management controls**  Security procedures by which managers take control of data processing and set the computer center's direction, but not through direct participation in processing activities.

**management information system (MIS)**  System that provides information, based on transaction processing data, to an organization's decision makers.

**many-to-many data relationships**  Characteristic of a network or hypermedia database design wherein records contain multiple links to other records.

**map**  Identification of network resources available to specific users when they log in.

**materials requirement planning (MRP)**   Software that uses existing inventory and production schedules to order and ship raw materials.

**math coprocessor**   Microprocessor used by the CPU to speed up statistical processing.

**Mauchly, John W. (1907–1980)**   Built the electronic computer ENIAC with J. Presper Eckert in 1946.

**maximize button**   (Windows) Icon with an up arrow found in the top-right corner of the title bar next to the minimize button. Clicking on the maximize button expands the related window to fill the screen.

**MB**   *See* megabyte.

**MD**   *See* MKDIR.

**Measure Selection**   Multimedia feature allowing a user to find a particular measure of audio data.

**megabyte (MB)**   1 million bytes of memory.

**megahertz (MHz)**   1 million clock cycles per second; a measure of a microprocessor's processing speed.

**memory**   Computer circuitry inside a computer that temporarily stores data and programs.

**menu**   List of program options that allows a user to activate an option by highlighting it or by entering a single letter or number.

**menu bar**   Horizontal area that runs across the top of a window and displays menu names.

**message filtering**   E-mail feature that lets user sort incoming mail into selected mailboxes based on keywords.

**MHz**   *See* megahertz.

**MICR**   *See* magnetic-ink character recognition.

**microcomputer**   Small computer with a single processor for use by one person at a time.

**microfiche**   4- by 6-inch pages of film each holding information equivalent to a 200-page report.

**microfilm**   Pages of data stored on a reel of film.

**microprocessor**   A single chip containing input/output control, processing, and some memory circuitry.

**microsecond**   One millionth of a second; used to measure the speed of a computer's processor.

**microwave**   Wireless communication channel that handles more than 670 simultaneous data transmissions at speeds up to 300 million bps.

**middle management**   People who make tactical decisions about short-term problems.

**MIDI (Musical Instrument Digital Interface)**   Interface that allows musicians to connect instruments and computers for sound synthesizing.

**millisecond**   One thousandth of a second; used to measure the access speed of a computer's disk drive.

**minicomputer**   Processing hardware that handles limited number of users and programs at the same time using a single processor.

**minimize button**   (Windows) Icon with a down arrow found in the top-right corner of the title bar next to the maximize/restore button. Clicking on the minimize button converts window back into an icon.

**MIPS (million instructions per second)**   Used to measure the speed of a computer's processor.

**MIS**   *See* management information system.

**MKDIR (MD)**   Internal DOS command to add a subdirectory to a designated disk directory.

**mode**   Type of electronic spreadsheet operation.

**model**   Mathematical representation of a problem or organizational situation enabling the testing of various solutions.

**modem**   Device that converts a single data transmission from analog to digital signals or vice versa.

**module**   A subset of a computer program containing code that performs only a single function.

**monitor**   Screen as output hardware; also known as CRT or VDT.

**monochrome**   A single color, referring to a monitor with one color on a background.

**monospace font**   Font in which each character is given equal spacing.

**morphing**   Feature of multimedia production software that seamlessly blends one image into another based on mathematical and graphical routines.

**motherboard**   The primary circuit board in a microcomputer, containing the RAM and ROM chips and microprocessor.

**mouse**   Input device the user rolls on a flat service to control a pointer on-screen.

**MPC**   *See* multimedia PC.

**MRP**   *See* materials requirement planning.

**MS-DOS**   Disk operating system developed by the Microsoft Corporation for personal computer systems.

**Müller, Karl Alex (b. 1927)**   Cowinner, with J. Georg Bednorz, of the 1987 Nobel Prize for Physics for work done on superconductivity.

**multimedia**   The combination of textual, audio, and visual data under software control for importing, editing, and exporting.

**multimedia PC (MPC)**   Standard for personal computers using multimedia software that includes a CD-ROM, sound board, and multimedia extensions to Microsoft Windows graphical interface.

**multiplexer**   A device that combines signals from several incoming transmissions to be sent to the same computer. It can also separate signals from the computer to be sent to several terminals or workstations.

**multiplexing**   Process of routing data transmissions from several sources through the same communication channel to a common destination.

**multiprocessing**   Simultaneous processing of the same program through the use of several processors.

**multitasking**   One computer running two independent programs concurrently.

**My Computer**   (Windows 95) Icon and window that display computer resources and let user manage files.

**nanomachine**   An extremely small machine with gears, levers, and other working features.

**nanosecond**   One billionth of a second; used to measure the speed of a computer's processor.

**native format**   The file format normally used by application software.

**natural language**   Programming language used for decision support and expert systems. Commands closely reflect human languages.

**natural language interface**   Interface that relies on spoken words or typed instruction to initiate program options.

**network**   A system of computers and hardware sharing data and software over communication lines.

**network administrator**   Computer professional responsible for setting up user names and passwords as well as overseeing network operations and security.

**network card**   Expansion card that connects the computer to the communication cable used by a network.

**network engineer**   Operations person who maintains the hardware and software in a network.

**network model**   Multiple access paths to related data allowing data items to be accessed from different starting points.

**network operating system**   Operating system for a network that controls shared I/O hardware and memory resources.

**network topology**   Description of how computers are interconnected within a network.

**neural network**   Array of processors integrated into a communication network that mimics connections in the human brain.

**node**   One computer system within a network.

**non-procedural programming**   High-level language in which required tasks are defined in terms of operational parameters rather than listing sequential logical steps.

**nonvolatile memory**   Permanent computer memory that cannot be changed.

**Norton, Peter (b. 1943)**   Developer of Norton Utilities, antivirus programs, and user-friendly guides to DOS and PCs.

**notepad computer**   Very small portable computer with pen input capable of processing handwritten data.

**Noyce, Robert (1927–1990)**   Coinventor of the first working integrated circuit in 1959. Given joint credit with Jack Kilby.

**numeric data**   Data containing only numerals (0–9), decimal point, and plus (+) and negative (–) signs.

**object**   Self-contained data item that has meaning by itself, like a photograph or music.

**object**   (OOP) Section of program code in object-oriented programming that contains both the processing code and descriptions of related data to perform a single task.

**Object Integration**   Multimedia feature allowing insertion of a video, audio, graphic, or still image clip anywhere within an existing multimedia file.

**object-oriented programming (OOP)**   Programming methodology whereby a program is organized into units, each containing both descriptions of the data and methods of processing necessary to perform a task.

**obsolescence**   The rate at which equipment and its associated knowledge become outdated.

**OCR**   *See* optical character recognition.

**office automation**   Networking document-processing equipment together in an office.

**offline**   State of hardware when it is not communicating with the computer.

**OMR**   *See* optical mark recognition.

**one-to-many data relationship**   Characteristic of a top-down (parent/child) database design in which one record provides a link to data in other records.

**online**   State of hardware when it is in direct communication with a computer.

**Open command**   (spreadsheet) Copies the designated worksheet from disk into computer's memory.

**Open command**   (word processing) Copies a file or document into the computer's memory for further editing or printing.

**operating procedure**   Actions people take when using computer hardware and software correctly.

**operating system (OS)**   Group of system programs that help in the operation of a computer regardless of the application program being used.

**operational decision**   Day-to-day decision made by a frontline manager.

**operations personnel**   Persons concerned with the daily IPOS cycle. For example, they may be responsible for data entry, computer operations, or computer center equipment.

**optical character recognition (OCR)**   System of machine-readable input that allows direct entry of printed or typewritten characters with a scanner.

**optical computer**   Experimental processing hardware using light-activated switches for processing and optical fibers to transmit data.

**optical disk** High-capacity disk that is read using a low-power laser.

**optical mark recognition (OMR)** System of machine-readable input that allows scanners to read pencil marks, used on standardized tests and surveys.

**orphan** A single line of a paragraph appearing at the bottom of a document page with the rest of the paragraph on the next page.

**output** Results of computer processing.

**overwrite** Adding text to a document by typing over existing text.

**page** (hypermedia) Data associated with a hypermedia screen display, similar to a data record.

**page** Section of a running program that is stored on disk when not in use by a computer system with virtual memory.

**page definition language (PDL)** Coding of graphics, images, and text for use by laser printers.

**page printer** Printer that produces one page of output at a time with speeds of more than 300 pages per minute.

**pagination** Word processing feature that includes counting pages and printing page numbers.

**palette** Graphics software feature that displays the color and pattern options available.

**paperless office** Automated offices involving networked technology such as word processors, e-mail, and electronic filing systems. Only those documents going outside the office are on paper.

**parallel operation** Conversion method whereby both new and old systems are run side-by-side and results are compared.

**parallel port** I/O port that sends or receives 1 byte at a time.

**parallel processing** Computer with access to more than one processor.

**parity bit** Single bit added to the end of each byte, used to check if data has been correctly read or written.

**parity checking** Error detection technique that looks for either an even or odd number of 1 bits in each byte.

**park** Locking disk drive access arm in place.

**Pascal** (named after Blaise Pascal) High-level programming language used in education and for scientific purposes. It is self-structuring.

**Pascal, Blaise (1623–1662)** Created the first mechanical adding machine, the Pascaline, in the 1640s.

**password** Unique combination of letters, numbers, or symbols known only to the user and used to limit access to computer hardware and software.

**password-protected** File that is opened only after the user enters unique code.

**PC (personal computer)** *See* microcomputer.

**PC-DOS** Operating system IBM licensed from the Microsoft Corporation and distributed with its line of personal computers.

**PDA** *See* personal digital assistant.

**PDL** *See* page definition language.

**peer-to-peer network operating system** Evenly distributes network tasks involving communication protocols between all the computers in a network. This is practical only with 25 or fewer computers.

**pen-based computing** Using a PC that has a pen as the main or only input hardware.

**peripheral** Equipment attached to processing hardware for input and output.

**personal computer (PC)** *See* microcomputer.

**personal digital assistant (PDA)** Portable computer that uses pen-based input instead of a keyboard.

**personal productivity software** General-purpose programs that help people with personal applications, including word processing, spreadsheets, databases, and graphics.

**personnel data** Facts and figures about employees and their productivity, including address, Social Security number, date-of-hire, absenteeism, and so on.

**PERT (program evaluation and review technique)** Documenting order and time requirements for each task in a project as boxes connected by lines.

**phased transition** Piecemeal approach to conversion wherein part of the new system is put into operation throughout the entire organization.

**physical data** Data from the environment—for example, light, sound, humidity, and pressure.

**picosecond** One trillionth of a second; used to measure the speed of a computer's processor.

**pie chart** A circle divided into slices, each representing the proportion one component has when related to the whole. Each slice is labeled with the component name and the actual percentage. Percentages for the entire chart total 100.

**pilot operation** Type of installation whereby the entire new system is tried in just a small part of the organization.

**pixel** Picture element that is one component of an array, or matrix, of dots that makes up a visual image.

**pixel graphics** Pattern of pixels making up a graphic image; also known as bit mapping.

**Playback Control** Multimedia feature allowing the user to change the volume and other special effects measure-by-measure for audio data.

**plotter** An output device that produces line drawings by moving a pen across paper.

**plug-n-play** Capability to connect I/O hardware with minimum user involvement.

**point**   Unit of measure for type size. One point equals ¹/₇₂ inch.

**point-of-sale (POS) system**   Type of terminal by which sales data is read from price tags by a scanner and entered directly into the computer/cash register.

**portable document software**   Software that produces documents that can be read and printed by any user regardless of fonts or special effects.

**portable language**   Programming language that can be used without modification on a variety of computer hardware.

**portrait**   Vertical layout of a document page.

**POS**   *See* point-of-sale system.

**power management software**   Software that aids in reducing power use of a computer system, including starting sleep mode when screen is idle.

**presentation graphics**   Information technology application wherein computers are used to create two- or three-dimensional drawings.

**preventative maintenance procedure**   Running diagnostic checks and cleaning computer hardware before a crash occurs.

**print chart**   Document that shows how output will appear on paper.

**Print command**   Outputs hard copy of a file.

**printer**   Output hardware producing printed information on paper.

**Print Manager**   Windows program that allows the user to control the actions of individual printers and what files are being printed.

**print title**   Row or column of a worksheet that is output to every page.

**Privacy Act (1974)**   Federal agencies must show how they intend to use information kept in government files, and permission must be obtained from individuals before information is used for other purposes.

**PRN**   (DOS) Reserved word that references printer.

**procedure**   Systematic course of action.

**process control**   Situation wherein a computer constantly monitors and adjusts an activity.

**processing**   The action of a computer on data as it performs calculations and comparisons.

**processor**   Circuitry inside a computer that performs arithmetic and logical operations.

**product support**   Training and help with operational computer systems.

**production/sales data**   Facts and figures about products sold or services provided. Organizations that manufacture products would keep inventory levels and sales figures, whereas service-oriented organizations maintain data about the number of people served and how they were helped.

**program**   *See* computer program.

**programmable read-only memory (PROM)**   Type of nonvolatile memory that allows computer to update stored data.

**Program Manager**   Windows program displaying the opening screen with group icons and program icons that may be opened.

**programmer**   Person who translates program specifications into computer programs and tests new programs for errors.

**program revision**   Change made to existing software to improve operations or comply with changes in laws or company policy.

**program specifications**   Part of the system specifications dealing with the design of software.

**Project command**   (database) Allows users to create an abbreviated version of an existing database table.

**project dictionary**   A resident database used by CASE software that contains information about the IPOS cycle and other features of a new system.

**projection plate**   Hardware, fitting on an overhead projector, to display computer output on a wall screen.

**project management software**   Software package that helps people plan, track, and schedule projects through time management, job scheduling, and other features.

**PROM**   *See* programmable read-only memory.

**promotional software**   Software that shows the capabilities of an application package but which restricts the amount of data or the number of available program options. Software companies provide promotional software so potential users can try out the package before buying it.

**Prompt**   Internal DOS command that customizes the DOS prompt.

**Protect command**   (database) Controls access to data by requiring a password to access data or establishing data as read-only.

**Protect command**   (spreadsheet) Designates a worksheet or selected cells as read-only.

**protected file**   Can be used and copied, but the operating system prevents it from being deleted or changed; also known as a read-only file.

**protocol**   Predefined set of procedures for establishing, maintaining, and terminating data communication among remote hardware.

**prototyping**   Modeling user interfaces (screens and reports) as part of the initial system design.

**pseudocode**   Method of representing program logic by using English phrases in an outline form.

**public domain software**   Programs that are distributed free of charge.

**puck**   Small handheld device, moved across a board annotated with CAD commands and options. When desired feature is within the crosshairs of the puck, a button is pushed on the puck to indicate input.

**punched card**   A paper card on which data is represented by rows and columns of holes. Each card has 12 rows and 80 columns.

**punched-card reader**   Device that reads and translates the holes on a punched card for use in processing data.

**QBE**   *See* query by example.

**QIC**   *See* quarter-inch cartridge.

**quality control**   Routine checking of a product or process to make sure it meets a predefined standard.

**quarter-inch cartridge (QIC)**   Popular type of tape cartridge.

**query**   User-initiated request that retrieves data answering specific what-if questions.

**query by example (QBE)**   Graphical user interface that allows a user to structure a query by using a mouse to select desired fields and using the keyboard to identify examples.

**RAID drive**   *See* redundant array of inexpensive disks drive.

**RAM**   *See* random access memory.

**RAM drive**   *See* random access memory drive.

**random access memory (RAM)**   Temporary storage for data and programs.

**random access memory (RAM) drive**   Volatile memory set aside to temporarily substitute for disk storage. RAM drives have faster access speeds than disk drives, but data must be copied to some type of permanent storage media before the power is turned off.

**range**   Group of contiguous cells within a worksheet that are identified by the addresses of the first and last cells; also known as a block.

**range format**   Change the default display options for a group of worksheet cells.

**range name**   Label given to a cell or group of cells.

**raster scanning**   Constant refreshing of each pixel on-screen to maintain a clear image.

**RD**   *See* RMDIR.

**read**   Input data from storage media.

**readers' log**   Groupware feature that tracks who has accessed shared documents.

**readme file**   File found on the directory of newly installed software, containing operating instructions and helpful hints to users.

**read-only file**   Can be used and copied, but the operating system prevents it from being deleted or changed; also known as a protected file.

**read-only memory (ROM)**   Permanent memory which holds system programs and language translators.

**read/write head**   The mechanism in a tape drive or at the end of a disk drive access arm that picks up or records data.

**real-time processing**   Computer system processes a user request as soon as it is input.

**record**   Group of related fields.

**record view**   Displays data one record at a time.

**redlining**   Feature of some word processing software to allow editors to leave notes and correct errors in a document without changing the original words.

**reduce button**   (Windows 95) Icon with a horizontal line found as the left button of three in the top-right corner of the title bar next to the enlarge/restore button. Clicking on this button closes a window and places the program name on the taskbar.

**reduced instruction set computing (RISC)**   Processing steps through limiting the number of complex operations.

**redundant array of inexpensive disks (RAID) drive**   Collection of fixed hard disks working with a single controller to support fault-tolerant computers or high-speed access to data.

**relational database**   Data is organized into tables and integrated by joining the tables using fields that are common to both tables.

**relative cell reference**   (spreadsheet) Reference to a cell address within a formula that changes when it is moved or copied in order to maintain the cell relationships in the original formula.

**remote mouse**   Mouse without a cable connecting it to the computer that uses infrared or radio waves to communicate movements.

**removable disk**   Disk that is designed to be taken out of the disk drive when not in use.

**REN**   *See* RENAME.

**RENAME (REN)**   Internal DOS command that changes the spelling of a filename stored on a specific disk.

**repetitive strain injury (RSI)**   Any of a group of injuries—usually to neck, back, arms, and hands—that result from repeated movement (as in keyboard typing or mouse use).

**Replace command**   (spreadsheet) Locates and changes designated worksheet data or formula.

**Replace operation**   (word processing) User enters a word or phrase to be found in the document. In a global replace, all occurrences of the phrase are found and automatically replaced. In a discretionary replace, replacement of each occurrence of the phrase is decided by the user.

**report generator**   User interface that works with a data management system to support user design and modification of printed documents.

**request for proposal (RFP)**   Description of system specifications accompanying a request for bids by vendors.

**research data**   Facts and figures about past performance and plans for future projects, such as last year's sales figures, grant applications, and new product designs.

**reserved word**   Combination of characters DOS uses as a reference to designated hardware or system attributes. Reserved words include *CON, PRN, LPT1*, and *COM1*.

**resolution**   A measure of graphic-image sharpness in bits per inch or bits per line. The higher the resolution, the sharper the graphic image.

**response time**   The time it takes a computer to process and output user input.

**restore button**   (Windows) Icon with double arrows found in the top-right corner of the title bar next to the minimize button. Clicking on the restore button returns a maximized window to its original dimensions.

**retirement**   Point in time when computer program or an entire computer system is no longer used.

**reverse video**   Putting text into the opposite colors expected on a screen; done for emphasis.

**RFP**   *See* request for proposal.

**RGB monitor**   Monitor using red, green, and blue pixels to form a variety of colors.

**right alignment**   Feature of a document where all lines of text are flush to the right margin.

**Right to Financial Privacy Act (1978)**   Sets strict guidelines for federal agencies wishing to review bank accounts, but has no control over state agencies or bank employees.

**ring topology**   A network wherein each computer is connected to two other nodes, forming a circle.

**RISC**   *See* reduced instruction set computing.

**RJ45 jack**   Standard telephone wall jack that connects twisted-pair wires from computer to telephone network.

**RMDIR (RD)**   Internal DOS command that removes a sub-directory name from a designated disk directory. All program and data files must be deleted from the subdirectory before it can be removed.

**robotics**   A computer-controlled mechanical arm or device that can be programmed to do repetitive movements.

**ROM**   *See* read-only memory.

**root directory**   Primary disk directory that is created when the disk is formatted.

**RPG (Report Program Generator)**   High-level programming language used in business report-generating applications.

**RSI**   *See* repetitive strain injury.

**ruler bar**   Area above document in a word processing program that is marked like a ruler to allow setting of margins and tabs.

**run**   *See* execute.

**sans serif**   Lacking tails on printed characters. This results in a simple, block style of text.

**Save As command**   Stores file on disk after giving user a chance to change filename or disk location.

**Save command**   Stores file on disk, using designated filename.

**scanner**   Input peripheral used to sense patterns of bars, dots, images, or characters and convert them into digital data.

**Scissors tool**   Graphics tool that allows the user to indicate a part of the graphic that could be copied, moved, or altered.

**screen generation**   Feature of application generation software that creates example displays for users that look like proposed data entry or informational screens.

**screen pointer**   Icon, usually an arrow, that moves on-screen when the mouse or some other pointer device is moved. Program options are activated by using a mouse to move the screen pointer over the desired icon and clicking the mouse button.

**screen prompt**   Symbols and/or characters indicating that the computer is ready to accept a new command.

**screen saver**   Software that produces a moving screen display on an idle screen to prevent burning a single design onto the monitor.

**scroll**   The rolling of data up, down, and sideways on-screen.

**scroll arrow**   Arrow found at either end of a scroll bar. Users change the view of a window or list box by clicking on one of the scroll arrows.

**scroll bar**   Area that appears on the right or bottom edges of a window or list box when only a partial view is available. A scroll bar contains a scroll box and scroll arrows.

**scroll box**   Square within a scroll bar that identifies which portion of the window or list box is currently being viewed. Users can change the view by dragging the scroll box.

**search path**   Description of subdirectory or file location on disk with respect to the disk's root directory.

**second-generation computer**   Computer developed in the mid-to-late 1950s that used transistors as part of the processing hardware. It contained core memory, used an operating system, and was programmed in high-level programming languages.

**sector**   A subdivision of a disk track used to organize data.

**security**   Procedures designed to protect computer and information resources against unauthorized activities.

**selection**   Basic structure of a computer program whereby one or two alternate sequences of instructions are used, based upon a tested condition.

**self-directed work team**   Group of people empowered to make management decisions to solve a specific problem.

**seminar**   Also known as workshop; a professional educational meeting, concentrating on a single subject.

**sensor**   Input peripheral that detects physical data such as heat, light, or pressure.

**sequence**   Basic structure of a computer program whereby instructions are executed in the order in which they appear.

**sequential access**   Finding an individual record by looking at one record after another until required record is found.

**serial port**   I/O port that can send or receive data 1 bit at a time.

**serif**   Short line segment added to a type style to help the reader's eye flow across the page.

**server**   Node within a network that handles particular tasks.

**server-based network operating system**   Operating system that relies on system software running on a centralized database or file server which handles all network communications.

**service bureau**   Outside agency an organization hires to handle data processing needs.

**service technician**   Person who performs repairs and preventative maintenance on computer hardware.

**Shape tools**   Graphic tools that allow drawing of preset shapes such as circles and squares.

**shareware**   Type of public domain software that is shared by users who are asked to pay a nominal fee to the author.

**shell**   User interface that uses menus to identify program options and operations.

**Shockley, William (1910–1989)**   Coinventor, with John Bardeen and Walter Brattain, of the transistor and cowinner of the 1956 Nobel Prize for Physics.

**shortcut menu**   List of location-specific options that are activated by clicking the right mouse button.

**simulation**   A computer-generated environment that mimics a real-life or imaginary situation.

**site license**   Legal copyright agreement accompanying some software that restricts the number of users as well as the location at which the program can be accessed.

**sleep mode**   Lower-energy setting of computer system, started after predetermined idle time.

**smart card**   Credit card that contains processor and memory chip that stores and updates owner's credit information.

**soft copy**   Data displayed on a monitor.

**soft return**   A carriage return entered into the document by the word wrap function.

**soft-sectored diskette**   Floppy disk with one alignment hole.

**soft space**   Spaces added between words to fully justify text flush to the left and right margins.

**software**   Programs or instructions for the input, processing, output, and storage of data.

**software guide**   Software that asks leading questions and makes requests of users to facilitate easy completion of hardware installation or other tasks.

**Sort command**   Physically reorganizes records in a database file based on a key value designated by the user.

**sound synthesizer**   Output peripheral that generates recognizable sounds, such as warnings, voice, and music.

**source**   Specific filename and drive of a file to be copied.

**SPC**   *See* statistical process control.

**special-effects filter**   Free-drawing graphics program feature that changes the graphic by selectively shading or texturing areas for special effect.

**Speed Control**   Multimedia feature that controls the presentation speed, in frames per second, for film or video.

**spelling checker**   Online word processing feature that compares words in a document to a dictionary and flags words not found.

**SPOOLer (Simultaneous Peripheral Operation OnLine)**   Utility program that coordinates the transfer of data between the computer and peripheral hardware.

**Spraycan tool**   Graphics tool that sprays a spattering of a chosen color as the tool is moved around the screen. The speed of movement dictates the density of the spray.

**SQL**   *See* structured query language.

**stack**   Group of related hypermedia cards, similar to a data file.

**stacked-bar graph**   A bar graph in which each bar is broken down to show its components.

**Start button**   (Windows 95) Icon that provides a menu of programs that can be run.

**star topology**   A network with a central computer, the host, which has all other computers attached to it. The host coordinates data communication between the other nodes.

**statistical process control (SPC)**   Procedures used to eliminate quality control problems by statistically selecting certain parts or activities for detailed inspection.

**status line**   Part of a spreadsheet that displays the active mode of operation.

**stereolithography**   Using computer-controlled infrared beams to solidify a chemical mixture into plastic models.

**storage media**   Material on which data is recorded.

**strategic decision**   A long-term decision made by top management.

**Stretch option**   Graphics tool that lets the user manipulate figures drawn with a Shape tool.

**structure chart**   A graphic representation of the relationship between modules or objects in a program; also called a hierarchy chart.

**structured program**   A program organized to contain only three logical structures: sequence, selection, and iteration.

**structured query language (SQL)**   Popular command-driven interface that allows users to access data from a database by using designated keywords and attribute names.

**structured walkthrough**   A group review of a program design and/or code done by programmers and supervisors.

**stub testing**   Testing modules that will make up a computer program by combining them with temporary or incomplete modules.

**style sheet**   Document containing the margin settings, tab locations, justification instructions, line spacing, as well as other formatting specifications a user wants for an application.

**subdirectory**   Additional directory, subordinate to the root directory, that is added to a disk by a user.

**Subtract command**   Compares two database tables and creates a new table containing data the other tables do not have in common.

**suite**   Collection of separate application programs sold together and able to easily share data and objects.

**summary report**   A report that condenses day-to-day operational data into totals and averages.

**supercomputer**   Powerful, high-speed parallel processing computer capable of handling enormous amounts of data.

**superconductor**   Material that loses all electrical resistance at a set temperature.

**super VGA (super video graphics array)**   Color monitor standard that displays 1,024 by 768 pixels in 265 colors.

**supervisor**   Systems program that is loaded into a computer's memory from the start to coordinate all processing activities within a computer system.

**surf**   Explore network offerings.

**switch**   Optional DOS parameter designated by using a slash and letter added to the end of an instruction that identifies special activities the user wishes to accomplish.

**symbol chart**   Chart using colors and symbols to represent and highlight data in a presentation graphic.

**symmetrical multiprocessing**   A program is subdivided and executed on different processors in a parallel processing environment.

**synchronization**   Coordination of the timing for several audio channels.

**synchronous transmission**   Communication protocol whereby data is grouped into blocks for transmission.

**syntax**   Grammar, spacing, abbreviations, and symbols used by a command-driven interface or programming language.

**syntax error**   Program error that is not translatable.

**sysop**   *See* system operator.

**system operator (sysop)**   Person responsible for the operation, maintenance, and protection of data and programs found on an electronic bulletin board system.

**systems analyst**   Computer professional who works with users in developing computer systems that satisfy specific needs.

**systems development project**   Steps taken to define and create new system solutions to existing problems.

**system software**   Computer programs that control internal computer activities and external resources.

**system specifications**   Document detailing requirements and procedures to be incorporated into a new computer system.

**system test**   Part of the software development cycle that includes testing program modules, complete programs, and the entire system under realistic operating conditions.

**table**   Independent file within a relational database.

**table view**   Displays database data in a row-and-column format similar to a worksheet.

**tablet**   Sensitized surface on which the position of a special pen is used as data.

**tactical decision**   A short-term decision made by middle management.

**tape**   A machine-readable medium in which data is stored as magnetic patterns on strips of plastic coated with a metal oxide.

**tape cartridge**   Tape within a hard plastic shell.

**tape drive**   Storage hardware that reads and writes data using magnetic tape.

**tape streaming**   Backing up data from disk to tape by a continuous high-speed data transfer.

**tape track**   Channel on a tape for storing a single bit of data. Data from several tracks is combined to form the binary code for a specific byte of data.

**target**   Directory or disk to where a file is being copied.

**task**   Any operation performed by a computer system.

**taskbar**   (Windows 95) Area of screen which displays names of active programs.

**Task List**   (Windows) Feature that lists open programs and allows them to be arranged and closed.

**telecommunication**   Long-distance communication.

**telecommuting**   Working at home using a computer network for communication.

**teleconferencing**   Online meetings of people using network technology.

**teleprocessing**   Central computer system that exchanges data with physically remote I/O components.

**template**   A worksheet with labels and formulas but no values.

**terabyte**   1 trillion bytes of memory.

**terminal**   A combination of keyboard with screen or printer, providing input and output to a computer system.

**terminate stay resident (TSR)**   Program that resides in the computer's memory but stays inactive until a certain combination of keys is pressed.

**test data**   Sets of data that represent all extremes and normal conditions the program would experience.

**text**   *See* textual data.

**text box**   Accepts keyboard entries from user to identify new filenames and disk locations. Text boxes are often used within a dialog box.

**Text tool**   Graphics feature allowing a user to type text anywhere on a graphic image. Font and typeface may be changed.

**textual data**   Any combination of letters, numbers, or special characters such as #, $, %, @, etc.; also known as text or alphanumeric data.

**thermal printer**   Dot-matrix printer that uses heated wires to brand the character on paper.

**thesaurus**   Word processing software feature that will display synonyms for an indicated word.

**third-generation computer**   Computer developed during the 1960s that uses integrated circuits as the basis of processing. It normally has multitasking and online processing capabilities.

**three-dimensional worksheet**   Series of worksheets visually stacked on top of one another.

**tile**   (Windows) Arranging open windows by reducing them so that all windows may be seen concurrently.

**tile horizontally**   Reduces all active windows so they are all displayed top-to-bottom on-screen simultaneously.

**tile vertically**   Reduces all active windows so they are all displayed side-by-side on-screen simultaneously.

**time bomb**   Time-dependent computer program that invades a computer system to erase program and data files at a designated day and time. This type of troublemaking program is time activated, hides inside another program, and cannot self-replicate.

**timed backup**   Automatic saving of a file to disk after a designated amount of time has passed.

**timesharing**   Many users equally sharing the processing power of a single computer by having the operating system alternate executing each program.

**title bar**   Horizontal area across the top of a window, displaying the window's name.

**title locking**   Freezing selected worksheet columns and/or rows on-screen.

**toggle**   The press of a key turns a software feature on; another press of the same key turns the feature off.

**token passing**   Communication protocol to avoid data collisions on a network by passing an electronic signal (token) from node to node. A network node can transmit data only when it has the token.

**toolbox**   Graphics software feature that displays available drawing-tool options, such as brush size and shape.

**top management**   People who make long-term strategic decisions.

**total quality management**   Philosophy that focuses on customer satisfaction through quality control of every service and product.

**touch-sensitive screen**   Monitor whose surface, when touched, becomes an input device.

**tower configuration**   Arrangement of personal computer hardware in which the computer is tipped on its side (vertical) and stands on the floor, usually underneath a desk or table.

**trackball**   Input device with a ball in a housing. When the user moves the ball, a similar motion is reflected by the cursor on-screen.

**tracking**   Controlling the spacing between characters and lines in text. By using tight tracking, more type can be fit into a given space than with loose tracking.

**transaction**   Exchange of value, resulting in usable data.

**transaction cycle**   The input, processing, output, and storage of a single transaction.

**transaction processing system**   System that oversees the input, processing, output, and storage of an organization's transaction data.

**transfer rate**   The speed at which data can be input to or output from the computer's memory and storage media.

**transistor**   Small electronic component that is the basis of the second-generation computer.

**Trojan horse**   Program that invades a computer system to erase program and data files. This type of troublemaking program is usually introduced by an outside source, hides inside another program, and cannot self-replicate.

**troubleshooting procedure**   Action people take to detect and eliminate computer system problems.

**TSR**   *See* terminate stay resident.

**tuple**   One record or row in a database table. For example, all the data about one customer (first name, last name, address, telephone number) would be a database tuple.

**twisted-pair wire**   Communication channel that can handle a single transmission at speeds up to 10 million bps.

**TYPE**   Internal DOS command that displays file contents on-screen.

**typeface**   The design of characters in a font.

**Undelete**   Internal DOS command that adds a previously deleted filename back to the disk directory. Deleted files are identified by replacing the first character in the filename with a ?. When undeleting a file, the user is asked to reenter the filename's first character.

**Undo command**   Reverses the previous action taken by the software package under the user's direction.

**Unicode**   16-bit binary code used to identify a wide variety of data.

**uninterruptable power supply (UPS)**   Equipment that contains power-surge protection circuitry and a battery that can maintain computer system resources long enough for an orderly system shutdown.

**unstructured program**   Program using GOTO statements that are not organized according to structured techniques.

**update**   Add, change, or delete data in a file.

**Update command**   (database) Allows user to add records, delete records, or change data fields in records.

**upload**   Sending data or programs directly to another computer.

**UPS**   *See* uninterruptable power supply.

**user-developer**   End user who designs and tests his or her own computer applications.

**user-friendly**   An attribute of computers meaning "easy to use."

**user interface**   Combination of menu options, icons, and commands people use when working with a computer program.

**user's manual**   Printed information about a software package.

**utility program**   System program stored on DOS disk.

**utility software**   System software that performs processing tasks not under the control of the operating system.

**vaccine**   Computer program that identifies disk files that have been infected with a virus, worm, or other destructive program.

**vacuum tube**   Glass tube containing circuitry, which was the processing basis for first-generation computers.

**value**   Numeric data within a worksheet.

**value-added network (VAN)**   Wide area network with additional services available to users.

**VAN**   *See* value-added network.

**vaporware**   Computer programs that have been promised but do not exist.

**VDT**   *See* video display terminal.

**vector graphics**   Type of graphics whose images are based on solid lines and curves, rather than the points of bit-mapped graphics.

**VER**   Internal DOS command that displays the DOS version number currently running in the computer.

**verification**   Data being input is checked for errors by person entering it before processing is done.

**version**   Each new edition of software and documentation.

**VGA (video graphics array)**   Color monitor standard that displays 320 by 200 pixels in 256 colors.

**video display terminal (VDT)**   A screen that provides temporary output of information; also known as CRT or monitor.

**Video Privacy Protection Act (1988)**   Bars retailers from selling or disclosing video-rental data without a court order or the consumer's consent.

**virtual corporation**   A collection of independent companies legally forming a temporary corporation to produce specific goods or services.

**virtual memory**   Using secondary disk storage as an extension of a computer's main memory unit.

**virtual reality**   Computer-generated images displayed as a three-dimensional output in a set of goggles and controlled by the physical movements of the user.

**virus**   Destructive program that invades a computer system by attaching itself to other commonly used programs.

**Visual BASIC**   Object-oriented high-level programming language based on BASIC language. It is used for writing applications as well as application generators.

**voice mail**   Computer system that answers telephone calls with a prerecorded message and saves callers' message on disk for later playback.

**voice-recognition device**   A machine that accepts spoken commands.

**volatile memory**   Type of computer memory that is cleared out when the power to the memory is shut off.

**volume label**   11-character disk directory label.

**WAN**   *See* wide area network.

**Watson, Thomas John Sr. (1874–1956)**   President of IBM from 1924 to 1956. Under his leadership, IBM became the largest computer manufacturer in the world.

**white area**   Area of a document containing no text, graphics, or images.

**wide area information server**   Used to search through database indexes maintained by Internet host for topics of interest.

**wide area network (WAN)**   Public or private network covering a large geographic area.

**widow**   The last line of a paragraph appearing at the top of a document page when the rest of the paragraph is at the bottom of the preceding page.

**window**   Subdivision of a screen display to allow the user to look at several menus, dialog boxes, or status reports from more than one program.

**window frame**   Border around a window.

**Windows 3.1**   Graphical user interface designed and sold by Microsoft to work with the Microsoft disk operating system (MS-DOS).

**Windows 95**   Graphical operating system developed by the Microsoft Corporation.

**Windows Explorer** (Windows 95) System program that lets user perform basic housekeeping functions like creating file folders and copying, deleting, and renaming files.

**word** A collection of bits representing the instruction or data the CPU can process at one time.

**WordPad** Word processing program that comes with Windows 95.

**word processing program** Program that helps users write reports and letters.

**word wrap** When a document is entered without carriage returns, the word processor senses the margins and moves words to the next line as needed.

**workgroup computing** People using a network and groupware to share ideas and solve problems.

**worksheet** Related data organized into a row-and-column format.

**workshop** Educational meeting concentrating on a single topic.

**workstation** Personal computer connected to a mainframe or network.

**worm** Program that invades a computer system from an outside source, is self-contained, and self-replicates until it fills every available memory address.

**WORM disk** *See* write once read many disk.

**Wozniak, Steve (b. 1950)** Built the Apple I microcomputer in 1976 with Steve Jobs and later formed Apple Computer Corporation.

**write** Record data on storage media.

**write once read many (WORM) disk** Optical disk that can accept data for permanent storage. Once the data is recorded on the disk, it cannot be erased but can be read as many times as needed.

**write-protect notch** Section cut out of the side of a 5.25-inch floppy disk.

**write-protect window** Sliding tab on a 3.5-inch diskette.

**writing analyzer** Software that analyzes writing style, reading level, use of passive voice, and sentence complexity; highlights jargon; and provides other data about the quality of writing in a document.

**WYSIWYG (what you see is what you get)** The feature of a word processing or desktop publishing package to show on-screen exactly how a document will look when printed.

**xy graph** A line graph in which both vertical and horizontal scales represent continuous measurements like time or weight.

**XGA (extended graphics array)** Color monitor standard that displays 1,024 by 768 pixels in 65,536 colors.

# Index